The Cambridge Handbook of Endangered Languages

It is generally agreed that about 7,000 languages are spoken across the world today and at least half may no longer be spoken by the end of this century. This state-of-the-art *Handbook* examines the reasons behind this dramatic loss of linguistic diversity, why it matters, and what can be done to document and support endangered languages.

The volume is relevant not only to researchers in language endangerment, language shift and language death, but to anyone interested in the languages and cultures of the world. It is accessible to both specialists and non-specialists: researchers will find cutting-edge contributions from acknowledged experts in their fields, while students, activists and other interested readers will find a wealth of readable, yet thorough and up-to-date, information.

The *Handbook* covers the essentials of language documentation and archiving, and also includes hands-on chapters on advocacy and support for endangered languages, development of writing systems for previously unwritten languages, education, training the next generation of researchers and activists, dictionary making, the ecology of languages, language and culture, language and society, language policy, and harnessing technology and new media in support of endangered languages.

PETER K. AUSTIN is Märit Rausing Chair in Field Linguistics and Director of the Endangered Languages Academic Programme at the School of Oriental and African Studies, University of London.

JULIA SALLABANK is Lecturer in Language Support and Revitalisation in the Endangered Languages Academic Programme at the School of Oriental and African Studies, University of London.

CAMBRIDGE HANDBOOKS IN LANGUAGE AND LINGUISTICS

Genuinely broad in scope, each handbook in this series provides a complete state-of-the-field overview of a major sub-discipline within language study and research. Grouped into broad thematic areas, the chapters in each volume encompass the most important issues and topics within each subject, offering a coherent picture of the latest theories and findings. Together, the volumes will build into an integrated overview of the discipline in its entirety.

Published titles

The Cambridge Handbook of Phonology, edited by Paul de Lacy
The Cambridge Handbook of Linguistic Code-switching, edited by
    Barbara E. Bullock and Almeida Jacqueline Toribio
The Cambridge Handbook of Child Language, edited by Edith L. Bavin
The Cambridge Handbook of Endangered Languages, edited by Peter K. Austin
    and Julia Sallabank

Further titles planned for the series

The Cambridge Handbook of Sociolinguistics, edited by Rajend Mesthrie
The Cambridge Handbook of Pragmatics, edited by Keith Allan and
    Kasia M. Jaszczolt
The Cambridge Handbook of Language Policy, edited by Bernard Spolsky
The Cambridge Handbook of Biolinguistics, edited by Cedric Boeckx and
    Kleanthes K. Grohmann

The Cambridge Handbook of Endangered Languages

Edited by
Peter K. Austin
and
Julia Sallabank

CAMBRIDGE
UNIVERSITY PRESS

University Printing House, Cambridge CB2 8BS, United Kingdom

Cambridge University Press is part of the University of Cambridge.

It furthers the University's mission by disseminating knowledge in the pursuit of education, learning and research at the highest international levels of excellence.

www.cambridge.org
Information on this title: www.cambridge.org/9781107552449

© Cambridge University Press 2011

First published 2011
Reprinted 2012
First paperback edition 2015

A catalogue record for this publication is available from the British Library

Library of Congress Cataloguing in Publication data
The Cambridge handbook of endangered languages / [edited by] Peter K. Austin,
   Julia Sallabank.
     p. cm. – (Cambridge handbooks in language and linguistics)
   ISBN 978-0-521-88215-6 (hardback)
   1. Language obsolescence–Handbooks, manuals, etc.   2. Language and
   languages–Handbooks, manuals, etc.   I. Austin, Peter.   II. Sallabank, Julia.
   III. Title.   IV. Series.
   P40.5.L33C36   2011
   409–dc22
   2010051874

ISBN 978-0-521-88215-6 Hardback
ISBN 978-1-107-55244-9 Paperback

Contents

Figures

Tables

Contributors

Peter K. Austin, Department of Linguistics, School of Oriental and African Studies

Josh Berson, Max Planck Institute for the History of Science, Berlin

Michel Bert, Laboratoire DDL, Université Lumière Lyon 2

Claire Bowern, Department of Linguistics, Yale University

David Bradley, Department of Linguistics, La Trobe University

Lyle Campbell, Department of Linguistics, University of Utah

Lisa Conathan, Beinecke Rare Book and Manuscript Library, Yale University

Serafín M. Coronel-Molina, Department of Education, Indiana University, Bloomington

Lise M. Dobrin, Department of Anthropology, University of Virginia

Jeff Good, Department of Linguistics, University of Buffalo

Lenore A. Grenoble, Department of Slavic Languages and Literatures, University of Chicago

Colette Grinevald, Laboratoire DDL, Université Lumière Lyon 2

Wayne Harbert, Department of Linguistics, Cornell University

Leanne Hinton, Department of Linguistics, University of California, Berkeley

Gary Holton, Department of Linguistics, University of Fairbanks

Anthony Jukes, Department of Linguistics, La Trobe University

Friederike Lüpke, Department of Linguistics, School of Oriental and African Studies

Teresa L. McCarty, Division of Educational Leadership and Policy Studies, Arizona State University

Lev Michael, Department of Linguistics, University of California, Berkeley

Máiréad Moriarty, Department of Languages and Cultural Studies, University of Limerick

Ulrike Mosel, Department of Linguistics, University of Kiel

David Nathan, Department of Linguistics, School of Oriental and African Studies

Carmel O'Shannessy, Department of Linguistics, University of Michigan

Naomi Palosaari, Department of Linguistics, University of Utah

Julia Sallabank, Department of Linguistics, School of Oriental and African Studies

Bernard Spolsky, Department of English, Bar-Ilan University

Anthony C. Woodbury, Department of Linguistics, University of Texas at Austin

Acknowledgements

The idea for a *Handbook of Endangered Languages* was first proposed to Peter Austin by Andrew Winnard of Cambridge University Press back in 2006. Peter prepared a book outline, contacted potential authors, and submitted a detailed proposal describing the overall conception of the book and the scope of the individual chapters to CUP, which was duly refereed and accepted with some minor changes. The project stumbled along for a year and a half until Julia Sallabank joined SOAS in 2008 and agreed to co-edit the *Handbook*, bringing with her seventeen years of editorial experience at Oxford University Press, and a different and complementary perspective on language endangerment (as well as a different network of colleagues). The individual authors were then contracted to write their chapters, and the serious business of reading, editing and correcting drafts, cajoling and encouraging authors, and knocking the book into shape began in earnest.

Preparing a handbook with twenty-three chapters by authors located around the world has been a major undertaking and its completion has only been possible as a result of generous contributions from a number of sources. We would like to thank the following:

- the authors, who willingly took on the task of preparing their chapters and patiently responded to our suggestions for changes;
- Stuart McGill, who joined us during 2009 as a research assistant, reading all of the chapters and making numerous detailed and insightful comments on them;
- Jennifer Marshall, who worked tirelessly for many months checking and correcting bibliographical references;
- Andrew Winnard, for originally sponsoring the project, and for cajoling and nagging us at appropriate times to ensure that we were on track for completion.

- SOAS Department of Linguistics (and especially the Head of Department, Peter Sells), for ongoing support throughout the project, and for granting Peter Austin sabbatical leave, during which the final compilation and editing on the volume was done. Thanks are due to the Research Centre for Linguistic Typology, La Trobe University (and its Director, Randy La Polla), for hosting Peter during these final and vital stages.

1

Introduction

Peter K. Austin and Julia Sallabank

1.1 Language endangerment

It is generally agreed by linguists that today there are about 7,000 languages spoken across the world; and that at least half of these may no longer continue to exist after a few more generations as they are not being learnt by children as first languages. Such languages are said to be ENDANGERED LANGUAGES.[1]

Current language and population distributions across the world are heavily skewed: there is a small number of very large languages (the top twenty languages, like Chinese, English, Hindi/Urdu, Spanish have over 50 million speakers each and are together spoken by 50 per cent of the world's population), and a very large number of small languages with speaker communities in their thousands or hundreds. Economic, political, social and cultural power tends to be held by speakers of the majority languages, while the many thousands of minority languages are marginalized and their speakers are under pressure to shift to the dominant tongues. In the past sixty years, since around the end of World War II, there have been radical reductions in speaker numbers of minority AUTOCHTHONOUS languages, especially in Australia, Siberia, Asia and the Americas. In addition, the languages under pressure show shifting age profiles where it is only older people who continue to speak the threatened languages and younger people typically show LANGUAGE SHIFT, meaning they move to using more powerful regional, national or global languages. Language shift can take place rapidly, over a generation or two, or it can take place gradually, but continuously, over several generations. Language shift often takes place through a period of UNSTABLE BILINGUALISM or MULTILINGUALISM, that is, speakers use two or more languages but one (or more) of them is more dominant and used increasingly widely until finally it (or they) take over the roles previously carried by the endangered language(s).

Linguists are becoming increasingly alarmed at the rate at which languages are going out of use. A special issue of the journal *Language* (Hale *et al.* 1992), based on a colloquium held at the 1991 annual meeting of the Linguistic Society of America, drew the attention of the linguistics profession to the scale of language endangerment, and called for a concerted effort by linguists to record the remaining speakers, and to create linguistic archives for future reference. In this issue of *Language*, Krauss (1992) estimated that 90 per cent of the world's languages would be severely endangered or gone by 2100. According to more optimistic estimates such as Nettle and Romaine (2000) and Crystal (2000), 'only' 50 per cent will be lost.

This 'call to action' reinvigorated fieldwork and documentation of languages, which had characterized an earlier era of linguistics (associated with the work of Franz Boas and his students). In the past ten years a number of initiatives responding to the call of Hale, Krauss, Grinevald and Yamamoto (and others) have been launched, including:

- the Hans Rausing Endangered Languages Project,[2] funded by Arcadia, which gives research grants for language documentation projects, maintains a digital archive of recordings, transcriptions and metadata, and runs an academic programme with newly introduced MA and PhD degrees to train linguists and researchers;
- the Volkswagen Foundation's sponsorship of the DoBeS (Dokumentation Bedrohter Sprachen)[3] project;
- the US National Science Foundation (NSF) and National Endowment for the Humanities (NEH) Documenting Endangered Languages initiative (DEL), 'a new, multi-year effort to preserve records of key languages before they become extinct';[4]
- the European Science Foundation Better Analyses Based on Endangered Languages programme (EuroBABEL) whose main purpose is 'to promote empirical research on under-described endangered languages, both spoken and signed';[5]
- The Chirac Foundation for Sustainable Development and Cultural Dialogue Sorosoro programme 'so the languages of the world may prosper';[6]
- The World Oral Literature Project based at Cambridge University, 'to record the voices of vanishing worlds';[7]
- smaller non-profit initiatives, notably the Foundation for Endangered Languages,[8] the Endangered Language Fund,[9] and the Gesellschaft für bedrohte Sprachen.[10]

Intergovernmental agencies have taken on board the problem of the loss of linguistic diversity. The United Nations has a number of policy papers and guidelines for governmental action plans on the UNESCO website under the heading of safeguarding 'intangible cultural heritage' (UNESCO 2003a; 2003b; see Section 1.5.4 below for further discussion).

Table 1.1. *UNESCO's Language Vitality and Endangerment framework*

Degree of endangerment	Intergenerational language transmission
Safe	language is spoken by all generations; intergenerational transmission is uninterrupted
Vulnerable	most children speak the language, but it may be restricted to certain domains (e.g., home)
Definitely endangered	children no longer learn the language as mother tongue in the home
Severely endangered	language is spoken by grandparents and older generations; while the parent generation may understand it, they do not speak it to children or among themselves
Critically endangered	the youngest speakers are grandparents and older, and they speak the language partially and infrequently
Extinct	there are no speakers left

One of the tasks that UNESCO has tried to tackle is how to categorize levels of endangerment. Assessing levels of language knowledge and use is an important element of language documentation and planning because 'a language spoken by several thousand people on a daily basis presents a much different set of options for revitalization than a language that has a dozen native speakers who rarely use it' (Grenoble and Whaley 2006: 3). Although numerous schemes have been proposed, the most comprehensive is UNESCO's Language Vitality and Endangerment framework,[11] which is shown in Table 1.1. It establishes six degrees of vitality/endangerment based on nine factors. Of these factors, the most salient is that of intergenerational transmission: whether or not a language is used in the family and passed from an older generation to children. This factor is generally accepted as the 'gold standard' of language vitality (Fishman 1991). (For more on measuring language vitality, see Grenoble, Chapter 2, and Grinevald and Bert, Chapter 3.)

1.2 Counting languages

Overviews of the study of language endangerment usually start with a list of statistics about the number of languages in the world, the proportion considered endangered, and so on. The usual source of statistics concerning the number of languages and their users is *Ethnologue* (Lewis 2009), which listed 6,909 living languages at the time of going to press.

However, this headline figure masks inherent problems in the counting of languages, as the Introduction to *Ethnologue* itself recognizes. Many linguists use the criterion of MUTUAL INTELLIGIBILITY to distinguish languages: if users of two language varieties cannot understand each other, the varieties are considered to be different languages. If they can

understand each other, the varieties are considered mutually comprehensible dialects of the same language. However, mutual intelligibility
is to a certain extent a function of attitudes and politics; that is, whether
or not people want to understand each other. Such attitudes are, in part,
linked to whether a community considers itself to have a distinct ethnolinguistic identity, but members of a community may not agree about
this. Because of such issues, some linguists (especially sociolinguists and
anthropological linguists influenced by postmodern theories) now question whether language boundaries can be identified at all.

Politics also plays an important part in language differentiation.
Following nineteenth-century philosophers such as Herder, language
has been considered a crucial element of national identity, with 'one
state, one people, one language' being seen as the ideal. But languages
do not necessarily follow political boundaries. For example, Quechua is
often thought of as one language, but in fact this is an overarching name
which denotes a group of related language varieties (Coronel-Molina
and McCarty, Chapter 18). Linguists distinguish between twenty-seven
Quechuan indigenous languages in Peru, but the Peruvian government
only recognizes six of these as languages (the official national language
is the colonial language, Spanish). Minority groups may claim full 'language' status for their variety, especially if it has been disregarded as
a 'substandard' dialect in the past (e.g. Aragonese in Spain). Separatist
groups may highlight linguistic differences to support their cause,
while national governments may play these down. Paradoxes such as the
mutual incomprehensibility of Chinese 'dialects' compared to the mutual
comprehensibility of mainland Scandinavian languages are clearly motivated by political and nationalistic considerations rather than linguistic
ones. (See Bradley, Chapter 4, on the many complex issues connected to
delineating languages, with other examples from South-East Asia.)

In addition, complete information on all of the world's languages is not
available: the majority have not been recorded or analysed by linguists,
have no dictionaries or even written form, and are not recognized officially in the countries in which they are spoken. What information there
is available, is often out of date: for example, for Guernesiais (Channel
Islands, Europe) the information in *Ethnologue* is based on a 1976 estimate
and ignores more recent data such as the 2001 census.

The Introduction to *Ethnologue* admits that: 'Because languages are
dynamic and variable and undergo constant change, the total number of
living languages in the world cannot be known precisely.' Nevertheless,
the traditional approach to counting languages is still followed by
most researchers, and also by the UNESCO *Atlas of Languages in Danger of
Disappearing* (Moseley 2009). Despite their shortcomings however, at the
very least these compendia provide a useful guide to relative levels of
linguistic diversity around the world. Figure 1.1 shows the proportion of
languages in each continent. It can be seen that Europe is by far the least

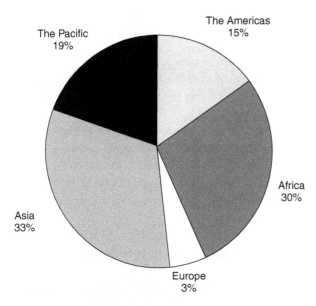

Figure 1.1. *The proportion of languages in each continent of the world*

linguistically diverse continent, which is worrying if other parts of the world continue to follow European trends.

1.3   Causes of language endangerment

The causes of language endangerment can be divided into four main categories (synthesized from Nettle and Romaine 2000; Crystal 2000; see also Grenoble, Chapter 2):

- natural catastrophes, famine, disease: for example, Malol, Papua New Guinea (earthquake); Andaman Islands (tsunami)
- war and genocide, for example, Tasmania (genocide by colonists); Brazilian indigenous peoples (disputes over land and resources); El Salvador (civil war)
- overt repression, often in the name of 'national unity' or ASSIMILATION (including forcible resettlement): for example, Kurdish, Welsh, Native American languages
- cultural/political/economic dominance, for example, Ainu, Manx, Sorbian, Quechua and many others.

Factors often overlap or occur together. The dividing lines can be difficult to distinguish. For example, in the Americas and Australia disease and suppression of indigenous cultures spread after colonization, and in Ireland many Irish speakers died or emigrated due to colonial government inaction which compounded the effects of the potato blight famine in the nineteenth century.

The fourth category, which is the most common, can be further sub-divided into five common factors (see also Grenoble, Chapter 2; Harbert, Chapter 20):

- **economic**: for example, rural poverty leads to migration to cities and further afield. If the local economy improves, tourism may bring speakers of majority languages
- **cultural dominance** by the majority community, for example, education and literature through the majority or state language only; indigenous language and culture may become 'folklorized'
- **political**: for example, education policies which ignore or exclude local languages, lack of recognition or political representation, bans on the use of minority languages in public life
- **historical**: for example, colonization, boundary disputes, the rise of one group and their language variety to political and cultural dominance
- **attitudinal**: for example, minority languages become associated with poverty, illiteracy and hardship, while the dominant language is associated with progress/escape.

More recently, there have been many community initiatives for LANGUAGE REVIVAL or LANGUAGE REVITALIZATION of endangered languages to expand the contexts in which they are used and to ensure they continue to be passed on to new generations (for examples see Grenoble and Whaley 2006; Hinton and Hale 2001; Hinton, Chapter 15; Moriarty, Chapter 22).

1.4 Why worry about language endangerment?

1.4.1 Value to linguistic science

Throughout history languages have died out and been replaced by others through LANGUAGE CONTACT; that is, contact between groups of people speaking different languages, or through DIVERGENCE due to lack of communication over distances (Dalby 2002). Until recently this was seen as a natural cycle of change. But the growing number of linguistic varieties no longer being learnt by children, coupled with a tendency for language shift, where speakers move to languages of wider communication (especially major languages like English or Spanish), means that unless the myriad inventive ways in which humans express themselves are documented now, future generations may have no knowledge of them. For example, Ubykh, a Caucasian language whose last fully competent speaker (Tevfik Esenç) died in 1992, has eighty-four distinct consonants and, according to some analyses, only two phonologically distinct vowels. This is the smallest proportion of vowels to consonants known, and the possibility that such languages could exist would have been unknown if linguists such as Georges Dumézil, Hans Vogt and George Hewitt had not recorded the last fluent speaker before he died and analysed the language (Palosaari and Campbell, Chapter 6, discuss and exemplify several other examples). Krauss (1992: 10) called for 'some rethinking of our priorities, lest linguistics go down in history as the only science that has presided obliviously over the disappearance of 90% of the very field to which it is dedicated'.

Several of the languages currently being documented by researchers are ENDANGERED SIGN LANGUAGES, which have been shown to reveal important insights into how humans communicate in non-oral modalities. Some of these endangered sign languages are still in the process of development and can thus also shed valuable light on linguistic evolution. Ahmad (2008) points out that most overviews of language endangerment omit mention of sign languages (an exception is Harrison 2007). As well as facing similar problems to other minority languages, users of sign languages have to counter prejudice from those who do not recognize them as full languages.

1.4.2 Cultural heritage

UNESCO's website states: 'Cultural diversity is a driving force of development, not only in respect of economic growth, but also as a means of leading a more fulfilling intellectual, emotional, moral and spiritual life.'[12] Linguistic diversity is cited as a 'pillar of cultural diversity' and:

> Languages, with their complex implications for identity, communication, social integration, education and development, are of strategic importance for people and the planet ... When languages fade, so does the world's rich tapestry of cultural diversity. Opportunities, traditions, memory, unique modes of thinking and expression – valuable resources for ensuring a better future are also lost.[13]

This is also the theme of David Harrison's (2007) book *When Languages Die* in which he demonstrates the many and varied ways in which aspects of human cultures and societies and aspects of human languages are intertwined and mutually affecting.[14] All societies throughout the planet have ORAL LITERATURE; that is, cultural traditions expressed through language in the form of stories, legends, historical narratives, poetry and songs. Harrison and others have argued that the loss of endangered languages means the loss of such knowledge and cultural richness, both to the communities who speak them and to human beings in general (what UNESCO has described as 'intangible cultural heritage').

1.4.3 Language and ecology

A number of authors identify parallels, and even correlations, between cultural and linguistic diversity and biological diversity. Biological scientists, especially Sutherland (2003), have found that places such as Indonesia and Papua New Guinea which have a high number of different biological species also have a large number of different languages, especially compared to Europe, which has the fewest of both. This theme has been taken up enthusiastically by the organization Terralingua[15] and some researchers and campaigners (e.g. Skutnabb-Kangas 2002). It has also received considerable public attention, e.g. in the UK, through a series of programmes on BBC Radio entitled *Lost for Words* and the TV chat show *Richard and Judy*.

Does this mean, however, that there is a causal link? Are the causes of language death and species decline the same? Sutherland (2003) concludes that although there is a clear correlation between cultural and biological diversity, the reasons for decline are likely to be different. However, a number of 'ecolinguists' employ the tools of critical discourse analysis to claim that the endangerment of the natural environment is in part caused by language, pointing out linguistic practices which reveal an exploitative attitude towards the natural environment (e.g. papers in Fill and Mühlhäusler, 2001). A more political interpretation might argue that the decline in both linguistic and biological diversity are by-products of globalization and/or international capitalism.

'Ecolinguistics' has a tendency to treat language as a living organism which, as Mackey (2001) reminds us, is a fallacy: languages are human artefacts not species, and do not have a life of their own outside human communities (see Michael, Chapter 7). Human communities therefore need to be sustainable in order to maintain their languages.

1.4.4 Language and identity

Languages are often seen as symbols of ethnic and national identity. Many endangered language campaigners claim that when a language dies out, a unique way of looking at the world also disappears (for example, Dalby 2002, Fishman 1989, Nettle and Romaine 2000). This can be seen as a weak version of the Sapir-Whorf hypothesis, which claims that our way of thinking, and thus our cultural identity, are determined by the lexicon and syntax of our language (Carroll 1956, Mandelbaum 1949). Discourse on endangered languages has therefore been criticized for being 'essentialist' and 'deterministic', especially by Duchêne and Heller (2007).

Many recent writers, influenced by postmodernism, see identities not as fixed, formal realities, but rather as fluid, constructed while people position themselves within and between the various social settings of their everyday lives (for example, Castells 2004, Omoniyi and White 2006), e.g. we may think of ourselves primarily as students at one point in the day, and as members of a sports team at another. This may help to account for the paradox whereby many endangered language speakers claim a strong identification with their language, yet do not transmit it to their children. As Le Page and Tabouret-Keller (1985: 239–40) note, feelings of ethnic identity can survive total language loss. Dorian (1999: 31) comments: 'Because it is only one of an almost infinite variety of potential identity markers, [a language] is easily replaced by others that are just as effective. In this respect the ancestral language is functionally expendable.'

Nevertheless, maintaining regional identity is seen as increasingly important in the era of globalization. Language is one of the ways in which people construct their identities, and thus may be highlighted when it seems salient. As Lanza and Svendsen (2007: 293) suggest: 'language might become important for identity when a group feels it is losing its identity due to political or social reasons' (see Grinevald and Bert, Chapter 3). Language planners and activists may promote symbolic ethnicity and 'localness' as means to encourage language revitalization.

1.4.5 Linguistic human rights

The right to use one's own language, in public or even in private, is not universally accepted. For example, in Turkey until recently, the existence of Kurdish was officially denied: Kurds were known as 'Mountain Turks', Kurdish names were not allowed, and there were no media or other services in the Kurdish language. In the last few years there have been some improvements in minority rights due to Turkey's application to join the European Union. The EU has declared overt support for linguistic diversity and minority rights, which has led to significant improvements in prospective member states (Commission of the European Communities 2004).

People who are not fluent in national or official languages need access to services such as education, the media and the justice system, and inadequate translation might deny them access to justice. In many countries (e.g. Uganda, Haiti, the Seychelles) the vast majority of the population do not speak or read/write the official (usually ex-colonial) languages, and are thus denied the opportunity to participate in public life.

Romaine (2008: 19) combines several of the above points by arguing that preserving linguistic ecology will ultimately benefit both human social justice and the natural world:

> The preservation of a language in its fullest sense ultimately entails the maintenance of the community who speaks it, and therefore the arguments in favour of doing something to reverse language shift are ultimately about sustaining cultures and habitats … Maintaining cultural and linguistic diversity is a matter of social justice because distinctiveness in culture and language has formed the basis for defining human identities.

However, it could be argued that many current linguistic ecologies are not healthy for endangered languages and need to be improved rather than preserved. (For more on linguistic ecologies, see Grenoble, Chapter 2.)

1.4.6   Education policy

Research has consistently found that education through the 'mother tongue' provides the best start for children (e.g. Baker 2006, Cummins 1979, 1991, Cummins and Swain 1986). ADDITIVE BILINGUALISM correlates with higher general educational achievement, including in other languages. However, the full advantages are only reaped if both linguistic varieties are afforded equal (or at least respected) status, and full BILITERACY is developed (Hornberger 2003, Kenner 2003), that is, people are able to read/write in both languages that they use (see Lüpke, Chapter 16, for critical discussion of literacy in minority and endangered languages). Children from minority-language backgrounds face disadvantages in 'submersion' situations in mainstream, majority-language classes where little linguistic support is provided (Edelsky *et al.* 1983; Coronel-Molina and McCarty, Chapter 18). SUBTRACTIVE BILINGUALISM, where one language is replaced by another, can lead to loss of self-confidence and lower achievement. If we really want children from minority backgrounds to fulfil their full educational and economic potential, their home languages should be supported; the majority population would also benefit from multilingual and cross-cultural education.

It is often assumed that shifting language will bring economic benefits. But linguistic intolerance can mask other discrimination, especially racism. Blommaert (2001), Sealey and Carter (2004) and Williams (1992) see language MINORITIZATION as a symptom of wider hegemonic ideologies and social and political inequalities. This point is echoed by Nettle and Romaine (2000), who note that linguistic minorities do not always benefit from shifting to a new language (see also Harbert, Chapter 20).

1.4.7   Wouldn't it be better if we all spoke one language?

Another common assumption, especially among non-linguists, is that using a single language would bring peace, either in a particular country or worldwide. Linguistic diversity is assumed to contribute to interethnic conflict (Brewer 2001) and is seen as a problem rather than a resource (Ruíz 1984). But as noted above, language conflicts are very rarely about language alone. Some of the worst violence in human history has occurred where language was not a factor at the start of the conflict, e.g. Rwanda or former Yugoslavia, or, further away in time, the Korean War, the American Civil War and the War of the Roses. In the case of former Yugoslavia, linguistic divergence was a consequence rather than a cause of conflict (Greenberg 2004): what was formerly known as Serbo-Croat is now split into Croatian, Serbian, Bosnian and Montenegrin, with different writing systems and different loan words which emphasize desired ethnic and religious affiliations. On the other hand, an increasing number of studies see recognition of linguistic rights and ethnic identity factors as necessary for conflict resolution (e.g. Ashmore *et al.* 2001; Daftary 2000).

1.4.8 Language usefulness

Speakers of minority languages often suggest that it would be 'more useful' to teach a major national or international language to their children than a 'useless' endangered language. For example, the following opinions were expressed by interviewees in Guernsey during research carried out by Sallabank when asked about teaching the local language Guernesiais:

> I think it would be more useful to teach a modern European language such as French or German. (Dentist, 40s)

> If children are going to learn another language at school they should learn proper French or German or Spanish, or even an Eastern language – a language that's widely used. (Retired teacher, 70s)

It is, however, a fallacy to assume that speakers have to give up one language in order to learn another. In fact, people who are bilingual find it easier to learn other languages. Moreover, it is not only major foreign languages (even if less commonly taught) which may prove useful. Even indigenous languages with no apparent relevance to the outside or modern world can prove useful, for example during World War II a number of Native American languages were used for military communications by 'code talkers', including Cherokee, Comanche, Meskwaki and Navajo. Moreover, a major international language does not necessarily fulfil the desire of many people in endangered language communities to get back to their perceived roots, as (Pooley 1998: 48) observes for Picardy in France:

> Chaque village a son propre parler picard; en apprenant le patois d'un autre village, on ne retrouvera pas ses racines.
> [Each village has its own variety of Picard; if you learn the dialect of another village, you won't find your roots.]

It can also be useful sometimes to have the option of saying things in a language that not everyone understands. Some teenagers interviewed in Guernsey have expressed interest in having 'a secret language of your own – cool'. This kind of identification, and the incorporation of endangered languages into popular youth culture, is not uncommon among minority young people, as Moriarty, Chapter 22, describes and illustrates. This indicates the possibility of a different type of identity expression to the traditional ESSENTIALIST type.

1.5   Responses and relevance[16]

With the loss of such a large percentage of the world's languages seemingly imminent, the global community has responded in several key ways: linguists have responded by increasing documentation efforts; funders have responded to support, primarily, language documentation and, to a lesser extent, revitalization efforts; and international organizations are paying increasing attention to indigenous rights and cultural heritage. These interconnected efforts have in turn affected other areas of research, funding, ethics and activism.

1.5.1   Documentation as key response

The single most notable response by linguists has been a push to document endangered languages while still possible. In those cases where only a few fluent speakers remain, this work is seen as very pressing. The documentation effort has, in turn, led to a number of developments in the field of linguistics, language technology, and elsewhere. Documentary linguistics has emerged as a relatively new field within linguistics; the documentary effort is driven by concern for endangered languages and enabled by advances in technology which have facilitated the recording, analysis and archiving of audio and video data in ways which were unimaginable not long ago. (For a detailed discussion of the theory and practice of language documentation, see Woodbury, Chapter 9, and Good, Chapter 11; Dobrin and Berson, Chapter 10, discuss the roles of speakers in documentation; and Bowern, Chapter 23, offers a nuts-and-bolts guide to planning a documentation project.)

1.5.2   Response by linguists

The push to document languages has in turn led to a shift in contemporary linguistics. There has been renewed interest in descriptive linguistics and fieldwork (see Woodbury, Chapter 9), areas which had received less attention in the latter half of the twentieth century in a move toward more theoretically driven formal linguistics. The shift to description, although by no means universal, has meant more varied linguistic data is available for theoretical linguists and typologists as well as for those interested in data for a specific language or a specific language family.

As Bowern, Chapter 23, points out, language documentation involves a long-term commitment on the part of linguists to work in and with communities. The ever-growing concern on the part of community members about what work is done, how it is done, and what happens to the results, has in turn had a major impact on ethical and practical considerations for linguists in the field. There has been invigorated examination of ethical practices, and new standards for community research have been set. Intellectual property rights and access to data have become major issues which linguists must take into account at all stages of a documentation project: in the beginning to assure that they have secured agreement from community members; in the process of documenting itself, as the project develops in the field; and in the final archiving stages of documentation. Most (if not all) funding agencies require evidence of, minimally, community support before they will fund documentation work. Many linguists have set deeper goals of establishing true collaborations, bona fide partnerships, with community members. We can only anticipate that such bona fide partnerships will in turn change the nature of the research itself, and not just have an impact on how it is conducted and what happens to the results (see also Grinevald and Bert, Chapter 3; Dobrin and Berson, Chapter 10).

1.5.3 Archiving projects

Archiving is not a new initiative, but the increased activity in language documentation, coupled with technological changes in the ways materials can be archived, accessed and disseminated, and increased sensitivity to the rights of speakers and communities to control access and use of these materials, have required significant changes in the ways we think about archives and maintain and develop them (Conathan, Chapter 12). Ongoing changes in technology have meant that archivists need to pay particular attention to new aspects of digital archiving to ensure preservation of the documentary materials, and conversion into future formats, as well as new ways of accessing and mobilizing the materials in ways that can best support the endangered languages they document. Specialist archiving initiatives have emerged at least in part as a response to the threats to endangered languages. Nathan, Chapter 13, discusses digital archiving in some detail.

In addition to institutionally established archives, language activists, teachers and linguists have created web-based resources which make data, analyses and the end products of their analyses (dictionaries, grammatical descriptions, textbooks) available to the wider community (if, of course, they have internet access). Some of these websites are anchored at universities, some at community organizations (such as through tribal councils in North America), and some are quite independent. In the extreme they represent a grassroots initiative aimed at collecting and disseminating language data and information about the language and culture, to make them more accessible to interested parties. Such sites often bring together archiving, documentation, research and educational goals; the best of them synthesize these into a coherent set of interconnected resources. The ways that information technologies and documentation materials can be used to support endangered languages are covered by Holton, Chapter 19, and the preparation of dictionaries is discussed by Mosel, Chapter 17.)

1.5.4   International responses and international organizations

International responses fall into two basic categories. In one are the groups which are largely driven by scientific or academic concerns and have focused on promoting language documentation. These are, by and large, funding agencies, and although some of them are governmental agencies, others (such as the Hans Rausing Endangered Languages Project sponsored by Arcadia, or the DoBeS Project sponsored by the Volkswagen Foundation) are private. Other organizations have made efforts to promote language tolerance for indigenous and minority languages, to increase the awareness of their importance and to create greater understanding of and support for multilingualism. As mentioned above, UNESCO has been active in promoting the safeguarding of endangered languages as part of its initiative for safeguarding intangible cultural heritage. The Permanent Forum of Indigenous Peoples of the United Nations is a group of indigenous representatives from around the world dedicated to preparing and disseminating expert advice on indigenous issues to the UN Council and other bodies and agencies of the UN. In September 2007 the UN adopted the Declaration on the Rights of Indigenous Peoples as the culmination of work which had begun prior to the creation of the Permanent Forum. The Declaration is not the direct result of the increased attention to endangered languages as such but, rather, the two efforts have taken place in tandem. Another example was the European Bureau for Lesser-Used Languages,[17] an umbrella organization funded by the European Union, which from 1985 to 2010 brought together many of its member countries to promote linguistic diversity in Europe. Part of its mission included support of Eurolang, an agency dedicated to disseminating information about the state of Europe's regional, stateless and minority language communities, some of which are endangered. The Chirac Foundation is one of the more recent private institutions to join this effort; it was officially launched in June 2008 by former President of France Jacques Chirac. The Chirac Foundation has focused its initial programmes on several key areas, one of these being threatened languages and cultures, as promoted by the Sorosoro programme.

1.5.5   Funder response

Work on endangered languages requires funding. Governmental and private agencies and institutions have responded by granting funds for language documentation and revitalization alike, although it seems safe to say that more of the funds are oriented toward documentation and description than they are toward revitalization. Some governmental funding agencies have responded by dedicating funds specifically to the documentation of endangered languages; a prime example is the Documenting Endangered Languages (DEL) Program, a joint initiative by the United States National Science Foundation, the National Endowment for the Humanities, and the Smithsonian Institution. This particular programme focuses primarily on documentation, which it views as a scientific endeavour and therefore worthy of funding to support research, as opposed to revitalization, which is considered to be part of education.

A number of non-profit and charitable organizations have also emerged to meet the funding needs of work in endangered languages. Many of these are funded through private donations, such as the Endangered Language Fund and the Foundation for Endangered Languages. Such organizations provide funds for revitalization and community-based education programmes as well as documentation.

1.5.6 Education

The last twenty years or so have seen the rise of a number of educational programmes which are aimed at teaching teachers how to teach minority and endangered languages. Many of these programmes are aimed at teaching the minority language as a second language, due to the effects of language shift over recent decades. To be effective, educational programmes must be supported by development of language policy and planning that clarifies the many issues associated with managing language in the family, the school, and elsewhere (see Sallabank, Chapter 14, and Spolsky, Chapter 8).

Beyond teacher training, one important emphasis in many programmes is the creation of pedagogical materials for the target language. Such materials include not only dictionaries, grammars and language workbooks but, for programmes which aim at language immersion, there is often a need to create textbooks for other subjects (e.g. mathematics, science, history) in the local language. This often requires not just writing and publishing the textbooks, but developing the technological terms to convey these concepts; many such textbook programmes also try to incorporate local learning paradigms with the Western one. In regions where internet access and computers are available, the use of such materials in the classroom is a key focus (see Coronel-Molina and McCarty, Chapter 18, for details).

Training is also a fundamental issue for community members and language activists. Here we distinguish programmes which are aimed at language education (and thus tied to revitalization or maintenance) and programmes which are more explicitly training for language documentation. Language education programmes which are based in communities must deal with the particulars of each community situation, particulars which include regional and/or national education laws and requirements, such as standardized tests in the national (non-local) language. (Jukes, Chapter 21, discusses training of researchers of various types, while Hinton, Chapter 15, discusses training in relation to language revitalization.)

1.6   Issues

The increased interest in endangered languages over the last two decades has resulted in gains on a number of fronts. Not only has there been heightened awareness of the issues of language endangerment, but this awareness has brought about increased research activity, not only in the area of documentary linguistics, but also in descriptive linguistics and fieldwork, and the incorporation of data from endangered languages into theoretical linguistics. There has also been significant growth in revitalization programmes. Important steps have been taken by the linguistics community to ensure that research conducted with any group of speakers is both ethical and collaborative, with the establishment of professional codes of practice being but one reflection of this change. There has been international recognition of the importance of languages to one's identity and the value of all languages for our cultural heritage. Yet despite these changes, and despite widespread coverage of these issues of endangered languages in the press, on television and on the internet, it is less clear that this awareness has had any kind of profound impact on the ways of thinking of the speakers of the handful of the world's majority languages (e.g. English, Mandarin, Spanish, Russian), either in terms of shifting their own attitudes to be more positive about multilingualism, or in terms of changing language policies to be more accommodating to speakers of other languages. Instead, if anything, the pressure for the use of a global language of wider communication (currently English) appears to be on the rise. There is broad consensus that the number of second-language speakers of English continues to grow, with more people speaking it as a second language than as a first language (Crystal 2003: 69). Beyond these large issues, there are some very specific issues which have emerged as a result of this increased interest in endangered languages.

1.6.1   The interests of linguists versus those of speakers and community members

One unresolved issue is a fundamental mismatch, in many places around the world, between the goals of linguists and the goals of language speakers and community members. Few, if any, linguists working in endangered language communities today can ignore the interests of the community (Dobrin and Berson, Chapter 10). Although the objectives and hopes of both sides vary, and vary among individuals in the speaker community and in the linguistic research community, by and large many linguists are most interested in their research, in documentation, description, analysis and archiving, and many community members are most interested in revitalization and education. This is obviously a simplification, but one that holds much truth. The differences in priorities can lead to conflicts and resentment on both sides. For example, when there are just a handful of speakers, how is their knowledge and time best put to use? Language activists may prefer them to serve as teachers, while linguists might want to work with them as consultants, sources for linguistic data. Obviously the two need not necessarily be in conflict, but when a speaker community is reduced to just a few fluent members, they are almost always elderly and may have health issues. They often cannot sustain prolonged work with either group. Who has priority? Another key issue is in the writing of descriptive materials. Linguists aim for complete, detailed descriptions that add to general knowledge of linguistic structures and advance linguistic theory. Community language teachers and learners prefer clear, jargon-free, simpler descriptions. These are just two of multiple possible examples, but they serve to illustrate some of the difficulties. One of the challenges is to consider how the two kinds of work can mutually reinforce one another, rather than competing for limited resources. Working to build honest, true collaborations is time-consuming, and people on all sides feel time pressure, pressure to achieve the work while it is still possible, pressure to complete dissertations or job or tenure applications within established time frames, and so on.

1.6.2 Commodification of languages

One of the more thought-provoking and challenging issues in tensions between linguists and language activists is that the approach taken by the academic endangered languages movement has resulted in a commodification or objectification of languages. The sense of commodification stems from a number of sources. One is the tendency for many linguists to view languages as static objects for descriptive study, objects which one can abstract out of their cultural or human setting, label their different parts, and shelve as a descriptive grammar and dictionary, and archive as a set of recordings and data. The initial development of documentary linguistics did much to promote this view, especially driven as it was by concerns with data formats, standards and so-called 'best practices' (see Good, Chapter 11). Subsequent, more critical, analysis and reflection has led to better understandings of the issues, though many questions remain unresolved (see Woodbury, Chapter 9).

There is also the question for each individual language documentation project of who is served by the documentary corpus, and what materials it should contain. Does the corpus exist to be used for linguistic research, as a 'permanent record' of sorts which 'preserves' the language? How does it relate to already existing materials, and to materials that some-one might want to add to it in the future? Could the corpus serve as a surrogate for native-speaker teachers who pass on the language through face-to-face channels of language learning? Although a corpus is admit-tedly a poor substitute for actual speakers, a well-designed corpus can be used not only to generate pedagogical materials (as is often argued, see Holton, Chapter 19 for examples) but also to provide speakers and potential speakers access to instances of bona fide language usage. These goals are not necessarily at odds, but the fact is that most documentation projects have not yet achieved the kinds of collections that would be use-ful to communities, to create, say, conversational textbooks or podcasts for learners to listen to. (See Woodbury, Chapter 9, in this regard: the sorts of projects he advocates would produce the kinds of materials com-munities often want to see: natural, culturally situated and contextual-ized discourse.)

The sense of objectification is further fueled by the rhetoric of the endangered languages movement. On the one hand linguists count, label and classify languages according to endangerment status (see above), while on the other they put forward arguments for documenting lan-guages that centre around the knowledge they contain, or claims that they are windows to the human mind. The enumeration of languages objectifies them and implies that they are discrete, independent units, a notion which goes against ample linguistic research in language/ dialect continua and linguistic variation. It is also at odds with the notion that languages are 'repositories of human knowledge'. Moreover, this kind of rhetoric brings about a commodification of the speakers as well (see Dobrin *et al.* 2009, Errington 2003, J. Hill 2002, for compelling arguments).

Another potential cause of commodification is what has been called 'hyperbolic valorization' of endangered languages (J. Hill 2002). In attempting to convince the general public of the value of these lan-guages, linguists often refer to them as 'priceless treasures' or 'invalu-able treasure troves'. The problem with this kind of rhetoric is that it turns languages into objects which seem to be better suited for museum showcases than for everyday usage by everyday people, especially by those wishing to live their lives in a modern world. Although it stems from honest attempts to give endangered languages prestige and value which dominant societies have taken from them, this kind of rhetoric has the net effect of turning endangered languages into a special kind of symbolic capital that can be seen as accessible or available only to the elite, i.e. the privileged (and dominant) culture (J. Hill 2002). Thus the result can be the opposite of what is intended: attempts to valorize endangered languages as 'treasures' can transform them into objects which are inaccessible to the speaker community.

A perhaps unexpected source of commodification of endangered languages is language revitalization. In order to counteract the disruption in intergenerational transmission, some language communities turn to school programmes to teach the languages which are being forgotten. The result is a radical shift in the means of language transmission, away from the 'caregiver's knee' to institutionalized programmes which are often ultimately overseen by the very authorities who were a factor in causing language shift in the first place. The institutionalized nature of language instruction can transform the language into an artificial object, to be learned and used only within the schools, while the living, organic form of the language used in society is no longer existent. There are programmes which have overcome this problem by actively recruiting parents and other caregivers to use the language in the home and in domains outside the school; the Mohawk revitalization programme at Kahnawà:ke provides one such example (see Jacobs 1998). But other language programmes have had difficulties crossing this barrier. Extending the domain of language use beyond the schools has been a problem for the Hawaiian revitalization programme *Kula Kaiapuni* (Warner 2001).

1.6.3   The nature of the research

As we have seen, endangered languages have fostered a new subdiscipline in linguistics, namely documentary linguistics. One unresolved issue, as of the present, is exactly how linguists should focus their documentation efforts (see Woodbury, Chapter 9). Given that even the most benign predictions estimate that some 3,500 or so languages will be lost over the course of this century, there are simply not enough resources (not enough linguists, not enough time and money) to thoroughly study and document all these languages. Adopting a strategy of recording as much and as quickly as possible is neither wise nor particularly feasible. The linguistic community as a whole has yet to engage in serious discussion of how to prioritize conflicting interests. One solution is to give top priority to languages which are nearly extinct, working with the last speakers while still possible. Yet another is to prioritize languages where revitalization is still possible. Alternatively, one could place top priority on languages which are LINGUISTIC ISOLATES, which have no known living relatives, or on languages which have not been studied by outsiders.

It is also unclear how to determine our goals with regard to documentation. The large number of undocumented languages means that we will not be able to document and describe them all in depth. Is it more important to document many languages but more superficially, or fewer languages but aiming for broad documentation and accompanying in-depth description? Is it possible to document in such a way that future linguists could return to a documentation corpus and carry out an in-depth linguistic analysis even if there were no remaining speakers? What counts as sufficient or even minimal documentation? These issues relate to what Woodbury, Chapter 9, calls CORPUS THEORIZATION, the development of theoretical perspectives on the construction and use of language documentation corpora and their associated apparatus.

The answers to how we prioritize are in large part determined by the goals of documentation. If the ultimate goal is scientific knowledge, then the argument to document and describe language isolates and 'exotic' languages has considerable merit. If, however, the overriding goal is maintaining as great a linguistic diversity as possible for as long as possible, then the possibility of revitalization becomes a primary concern. These goals need not necessarily be at odds with one another, but often are. To date, the scientific community has put greater emphasis on documentation than revitalization, and more funding is available for the former than the latter. To what extent this represents a larger political agenda is unclear. We do not know to what extent it represents the overall attraction of monolingualism to many nation states, or whether it just represents a bias in Western thinking and research paradigms, paradigms which value the discovery (and tallying) of new knowledge over (language) education.

Finally, we need to consider how the theoretical paradigms of today are influencing the kind and amount of data we collect and to question whether today's results will serve tomorrow's needs. What are we not doing now which, with future hindsight, we will wish we had done?

1.6.4 Training

There are ongoing issues regarding the inadequacy, and often lack, of appropriate training for linguists and community members for work in endangered language communities. Although new programmes have emerged (see Jukes, Chapter 21, for an overview listing), they do not appear to meet current demand, as they are oversubscribed and cannot accommodate all interested parties. Moreover, these programmes stand outside the regular curriculum and have limited availability, not just because demand exceeds space but also for a host of other reasons. They tend to be held in the summer, not during the regular academic year, which is the prime time for most linguists to be doing fieldwork, and/or for many communities the best time to live out their social and ceremonial lives. They are held primarily in North America and Europe, in places which are advantageous for North American and European scholars, but less so for minority scholars in other parts of the world. That said, the recent birth of such programmes represents a strong commitment on the part of linguists to improve training for language documentation. For more discussion of issues in training and capacity building, see Hinton, Chapter 15, and Jukes, Chapter 21.

1.6.5   The overall impact of globalization

Although globalization has been singled out here as one of the factors involved in language endangerment, there is in fact very little research on the impact of globalization on endangered languages. (Notable exceptions include Maurais and Morris 2003, Mufwene 2004, and Skutnabb-Kangas 2000.) Although we know with a fair amount of certainty that language shift and attrition is happening at unprecedented rates, we have little concrete evidence of the role of globalization in this shift, as opposed to the role of particular language policies and attitudes in individual nation states, for example. That said, there is broad consensus that language shift is frequently driven by socioeconomic factors; in this respect, a shift to English can provide speakers with employment and access to international networks. That is, shift to English has more to do with global economic integration and cultural shifts, in terms of lifestyle, than it does with language *per se* (Tonkin 2003; see also Harbert, Chapter 20). This in turn fosters the view of language as more of a marketable commodity than as a marker of ethnicity, furthering the commodification of languages (Heller 2003). More data on the interactions of economic globalization (and marginalization), sociocultural factors and language are needed.

Another global factor which has been largely overlooked in this equation is the role of climate change. Its impact is visible in the circumpolar North, where melting ice and shore erosion have already radically affected the lives of the indigenous peoples living there. Changes to the ice pack and the shorelines have already affected the traditional lifestyles of certain groups, and thus the local language ecologies. People have been dislocated and moved further inland, or have been forced to abandon traditional hunting and fishing patterns because of thinning sea ice, changes in animal migration, and so on. The maintenance of endangered languages is often linked to traditional lifestyles, because the domains of language use are linked to these lifestyles. (Examples include indigenous farming, herding, fishing and hunting practices.) It does not appear that climate change has forced the abandonment of indigenous languages but rather has accelerated shift processes that are already in place (see Harbert, Chapter 20, for a discussion of sustainable development).

1.7 Conclusions

Over the past twenty years it has become clear that the world's linguistic diversity is under threat and that languages everywhere are contracting in use and numbers of speakers. Among linguists, we can observe, with Romaine (2008), that there have been three categories of response since Hale *et al.*'s 'wake-up' call in 1992:

1. Do nothing – 'benign neglect'
   From our point of view as endangered languages researchers this is the least satisfactory, as it will lead to the continued loss of linguistic diversity. Inaction is in effect collusion in language endangerment and loss. Linguists should at least familiarize themselves with the fundamental issues, as laid out in the contributions of Grenoble, Grinevald and Bert, Bradley, O'Shannessy, Palosaari and Campbell, Michael, and Spolsky (Chapters 2 to 8).
2. Document languages before they disappear
   This has been criticized as a museum-oriented approach (e.g. by Maffi 2003), and indeed focusing on collecting as much material as possible as quickly as possible also runs the risk of commodifying languages and of letting the creation of archives of language data drive the priorities, methods, tools and outcomes of linguistic research (a tendency which has been called ARCHIVISM, see Nathan, Chapter 13, and Dobrin *et al.* 2009). Over the last ten years however, critical examination of the goals, methods, and theoretical underpinnings of language documentation have meant that we are now in a better position to engage with and understand it as a possible response to language endangerment. The contributions by Woodbury, Dobrin and Berson, Good, Conathan, and Nathan (Chapters 9 to 13), as well as those by Holton, Jukes and Bowern (Chapters 19, 21 and 23) contribute to this engagement and understanding.
3. Promote language revitalization
   This approach has the goal of maintaining living languages in their sociocultural contexts (i.e. in linguistic ecologies), and giving speakers the possibility to continue their use as well as passing them on to their descendants. It additionally extends the time frame for language documentation and description. But, perhaps most importantly, it is what many endangered language communities want (Grenoble 2009a). Language revitalization is still under-researched and under-theorized, and we must be careful to keep in mind Dorian's warnings in 1993 that focusing on language decline can obscure a longer term dynamic by overlooking revitalization efforts. Although the outlook for global linguistic diversity is still not good overall, an increasing number of communities are embarking on revitalization and other

language support programmes. The contributions of Sallabank, Hinton, Lüpke, Mosel, and Coronel-Molina and McCarty (Chapters 14 to 18) deal with issues in this area.

A fourth response, which has only recently started to be addressed by the linguistics community and others, is to relate language shift to wider socioeconomic policies, politics, environmental pressures and so on (as outlined in Sections 1.1 and 1.5.5 above), in order to examine and address the causes of language endangerment. Moving beyond the maintenance of current linguistic ecologies (which have so far failed to prevent language shift), such an approach would aim to alter linguistic ecologies to provide healthier sustainable environments for endangered languages. There is some rhetoric promoting such a view (e.g. Mühlhäusler, 2000, 2002, Romaine 2008), but to date there is little empirical research describing successful programmes. The chapters by Holton (19), Harbert (20), and Moriarty (22) are contributions that explore and exemplify the feasibility of maintaining local languages within sustainable communities, now and into the future, and confronting in a new way the challenges that face endangered languages across the world.

Notes

1 Throughout this handbook important terminology is shown in SMALL CAPITALS when it is first introduced.
2 www.hrelp.org (10 October 2009).
3 = 'Documentation of endangered languages', www.mpi.nl/DOBES/ (10 October 2009).
4 www.neh.gov/manage/fellowshipsgi_DEL_09_10.html (10 October 2009).
5 www.esf.org/activities/eurocores/programmes/eurobabel.html (10 October 2009).
6 www.fondationchirac.eu/en/sorosoro-program/ (10 October 2009).
7 www.oralliterature.org/ (10 October 2009).
8 www.ogmios.org (10 October 2009).
9 www.endangeredlanguagefund.org/ (10 October 2009).
10 www.uni-koeln.de/gbs// (4 March 2010).
11 www.unesco.org/culture/ich/index.php?pg=00139 (1 October 2009).
12 portal.unesco.org/culture/en/ev.php-URL_ID=34321andURL_DO=DO_TOPICandURL_SECTION=201.html (1 October 2009).
13 portal.unesco.org/culture/en/ev.php-URL_ID=35097andURL_DO=DO_TOPICandURL_SECTION=201.html (1 October 2009).
14 See also the *Living Tongues Institute for Endangered Languages* www.livingtongues.org (3 March 2010) founded by David Harrison and Gregory Anderson.

15 www.terralingua.org (9 October 2009).
16 The material in Sections 1.5 and 1.6 began life as sections within Lenore Grenoble's first draft of Chapter 2. Lenore agreed to excise this material and make it available to us (since we felt that it was tangential to the topic of her chapter but ideal for this introduction). We are extremely grateful to her for her generosity, and hereby absolve her of any errors arising from the way we have reshaped what she originally wrote.
17 www.eblul.org (4 March 2010).

Part 1

Endangered languages

2

Language ecology and endangerment

Lenore A. Grenoble

2.1 Overview of language endangerment

There are between 6,000 and 7,000 known languages in the world, and linguists estimate that 50–90 per cent of them will disappear during this century. In only a very few cases is LANGUAGE LOSS due to the loss of the speaker population itself. Instead, the primary cause for language loss is language shift, when speakers cease to speak their own native tongue in favour of the language of what is usually a politically and/or economically dominant neighbouring culture.

LANGUAGE CHANGE and language loss are inherent to all language situations. Although the rate of change varies greatly, each and every language constantly changes over time (unless it stops being spoken), and languages can change to such an extent that they evolve into what are considered to be completely different languages. The modern Romance languages, for example, are related to Latin, which is no longer spoken outside of certain religious settings. This represents a natural process stemming from sustained language change. A different kind of loss occurs when speakers cease speaking their heritage language in favour of another.

2.1.1 Distribution of languages and speakers
There is a very uneven distribution of languages around the world, both in terms of geographic distribution and in terms of number of speakers. A handful of languages are spoken by a very large percentage of the global population. A commonly used source for these statistics is the *Ethnologue* (Lewis 2009), although there is broad agreement that much of the data there is out-of-date and not entirely reliable. For example, Rerep, an Austronesian language of Vanuatu, is reported to have had 380 speakers in 1983 (no later information is given); or Weri, a trans-New

Guinea language of Papua New Guinea, is listed as having 4,160 speakers in 1978. In addition, there are a number of problems in counting numbers of languages and speakers. First of all, it is not always clear what constitutes a 'language' as opposed to a 'dialect' of another language. The factors involved in such determinations can be linguistic (such as the percentage of shared basic vocabulary), but are frequently political as well (e.g. separate statehood often demanding the recognition of linguistic separateness). Second, it is equally unclear just what is meant by being a 'speaker'. (See Grinevald and Bert, Chapter 3; Spolsky, Chapter 8; and Dobrin and Berson, Chapter 10, for further discussion of the terms 'language' and 'speaker'.) In addition, the data for speaker counts is generally based not on language proficiency tests and actual head counts but rather on self-reporting (see Bradley, Chapter 4), and it is well known that some groups overreport proficiency while others may under-report, depending on attitudes, ideologies, and the status of the language. Nearly a third of all languages are spoken in Asia, and 30% are spoken in Africa. Only 3.5% are spoken in Europe, and under 15% are spoken in North and South America combined. Although these figures are at best approximate, they provide a reasonable overall picture of worldwide language distribution.

Languages are also unevenly distributed according to the number of speakers. An estimated 5% of all languages (roughly 350) have over one million speakers each and account for 94% of the global population. This means that the remaining 95% of languages are spoken by just 6% of all people. Approximately half the world's population speaks one of just twenty languages, and just eight languages (Mandarin, Spanish, English, Bengali, Hindi, Portuguese, Russian and Japanese) are spoken by over 100 million people each. Although not all varieties of Arabic are mutually intelligible and the differences between them are more language-like than dialect-like, if all varieties of Arabic are combined, the total number of Arabic speakers exceeds some others (such as Russian and Japanese) on this list. By far the language with the greatest number of speakers is Mandarin; some estimates place it at over one billion speakers. Over 6,500 languages have fewer than one million speakers, and an estimated 5,625 languages have less than 100,000 speakers (Lewis 2009). This means in effect that a large number of the world's languages are spoken by relatively small groups of people.

These numbers provide a general picture of the map of the world's languages and speakers, although they should be used with caution (see also Bradley, Chapter 4, and Spolsky, Chapter 8, for more discussion). There are a number of difficulties in counting the numbers of languages. Determining the boundaries between languages and dialects is extremely complex. When are two varieties so different that they should be considered separate languages, and when should they be considered two dialects of the same language? Although linguists often cite mutual intelligibility as a key diagnostic, even this concept is fraught with problems. Some speakers are better at understanding another variety, and motivation and willingness to understand the speech of others plays a key role in mutual intelligibility. Language identification can be manipulated for political reasons, so that similar, dialect-like varieties may be labelled distinct languages so that their geographic domains correspond with the boundaries of nation states. This is true in mainland Scandinavian where, for example, the differences between Swedish and Norwegian are more dialect-like than language-like, but the identification of them as separate languages serves political purposes. This can cut both ways, and political parties may claim distinct languages to be 'mere' dialects of the national language. This is particularly true in territorial disputes, where one side claims (historical and perhaps moral) rights to territory because its inhabitants speak the 'same' language, while the opposing side claims the contrary. A further complication is that a number of regions around the world are still under-studied, large numbers of languages are under-described and even undescribed, and the actual number of languages spoken there is unknown. Researchers continue to identify or 'discover' new languages, either varieties that were previously misclassified as dialects of very different languages, or varieties which were unknown outside of the communities where they are spoken (see Bradley, Chapter 4, for examples from South-East Asia). Thus, paradoxically, the actual count of languages has risen over the last decade: the 14th edition of *Ethnologue* (Grimes and Grimes 2000) cited 6,809 different languages, while the 16th edition (Lewis 2009) brought the total up to 6,909. This apparent paradox does not mean, however, that language loss has slowed or stopped but rather that the numbers are hiding the reality of language attrition.

A second problem arises in counting speakers. Figures for speaker counts almost always try to give the number of first-language speakers, and yet these numbers reflect self-reporting, not actual assessment. Because language is an integral part of identity, people who identify with a particular ethnolinguistic (or heritage) culture may claim knowledge of the language even when they are far from fluent. Alternatively, when people are repressed for their ethnicity, they may claim not to know that particular language for fear of retribution. For example, the Basque people, along with all other minority cultures in Spain, suffered serious repression under the Franco regime. There was particularly brutal linguistic repression until the early 1950s, with complete prohibition of the use of Basque, even for interpersonal conversations, in church, in the schools (public or private), in all public gatherings and all publications. This repression effectively resulted in the loss of a generation of speakers. But the repression also spurred a strong nationalist movement which already in the early 1950s argued strongly that language was a significant indicator of Basque identity, considerably more so than racial or biological definitions. The group's initial mission was to promote traditional Basque culture and language, a goal which it managed to achieve, at least in part. Article 6 of the 1978 Spanish Constitution grants all citizens the right to know the Basque language (Urla 1988).

2.1.2   Language ecologies and linguistic diversity

The term LANGUAGE ECOLOGY refers to the relationship between languages and the people who speak them; it dates back to Voegelin *et al.* (1967) and is generally associated with Haugen (1972). The field of language ecology studies the interrelationships between speakers and their languages as situated in their full (contemporary and historical) context. An implicit and critical part of language ecology is the fact that language is not isolated from other social, cultural and ecological factors but interacts with them. Such factors include those which are traditionally considered to be within the realm of linguistics, such as the presence and use of other languages, as well as those which are not, such as economics, politics and the physical or natural environment. A broader sense of the term 'language ecology' is proposed by Mufwene (2001) who argues for language evolution in a way analogous but not identical to species evolution. In its strong version, a theory of language ecology likens competition between languages to the competition between species and provides mechanisms for accounting for the survival of the fittest (languages). Although this model of language survival is not without controversy (see Harbert, Chapter 20), one of its values is that it takes into account both language-internal factors for change and language-external factors, including how the target language is restructured in contact situations (see Palosaari and Campbell, Chapter 6; O'Shannessy, Chapter 5). Differing language ecologies can explain the differing experiences of language shift in Africa and Europe, for example. In Africa, it is largely the case that local languages are giving way to other African languages, not the languages of the colonizers (e.g. English, French, German, Portuguese). Thus we see the spread of national and even transnational lingua francas at the expense of local languages, such as Hausa or Fula in West Africa, or Kiswahili in East Africa. Local ecologies come into play: in Botswana it is Setswana traditional chiefs who hold power over other groups, determining land distribution and administrating local law. This power imbalance has supported the spread of Setswana at the expense of a host of local languages, such as Shiyeyi, Chikuhane, Sebirwa, Setswapong, Shua, Tswa, and Kua, as well as others (Batibo 2005: 93–4). In Europe, in contrast, there is a strong ideology that a nation state should have a single language, that a nation's borders should coincide with that language, and a strong tradition of standardizing and promoting that one language, at the expense of all others (Dorian 1998; Grinevald and Bert, Chapter 3).

Language planning should take into account the overall language ecology of any group, which can be seen as a framework or model for analysing the relationship between linguistic practices on the context, or milieu, in which they are situated, i.e. their ecolinguistic niche (Calvet 2006). For many proponents of this approach, the primary aim of an ecological approach to language planning is sustaining linguistic diversity. Ecolinguistics, a branch of language ecology, discounts the notion of competition and focuses more on the interconnections between languages and their environments (Mühlhäusler 1996, 2000). Drawing on the ecological metaphor, ecolinguistic language planning aims to support structured linguistic diversity, advocating equitable status for as many diverse languages as possible by strengthening the 'habitat' of differing languages in a language ecology and by creating links between them. (See also Spolsky, Chapter 8, and Sallabank, Chapter 14).

The goals and methods of ecolinguistics are in stark contrast to traditional language planning, whose chief objective is to reduce linguistic diversity and to promote single, standardized forms of (the planned) languages. Traditional language planning is top-down, driven and overseen by external language authorities, while ecolinguistic planning is envisioned as a bottom-up effort, formulated and supported by speakers and communities. In this regard, there is much that is attractive about ecolinguistic language planning to support the revitalization of endangered languages and their ongoing usage. At the same time, the tension between the desire to promote diversity and the perceived need for standardization holds in endangered language communities as it does for majority languages. Many endangered language communities grapple with issues surrounding standardization (of dialectal variation, of orthographies and spelling), arguably under the influence of the majority language policy makers and planners, who aim to eliminate it. Many language revitalization programmes have been hindered by the inability of community members to come to agreement on just what variety should be adapted as the norm, because such decisions involve privileging one over all others. For this reason alone, an ecolinguistic approach to language planning in minority communities may be attractive, but just how structured linguistic diversity is to be implemented and maintained is unclear. That said, proponents of an ecolinguistic approach, perhaps most notably Mühlhäusler (2003), argue that in order for linguists to have an impact on reversing diminishing linguistic diversity, they must refocus their efforts on preserving language ecologies, not languages. In this view, it is wrongheaded to see the languages themselves as disappearing; rather, the domains of language use and the more complex language ecologies in which language use is situated are themselves changing, which in turn is linked to language shift. Therefore, in order to arrest language shift, one must address issues in the impoverishment of these ecologies.

2.1.3 Kinds and rates of language shift

Language shift and language loss are not new phenomena. In some instances, language loss occurs when an entire population of speakers is lost through disease, natural disaster, or warfare. Such cases are more infrequent than one might think and relatively few instances of such sudden attrition have been documented historically. That said, in colonial times the spread of certain diseases which destroyed local populations certainly caused the loss of languages without any written documentation. More recently, ethnic and religious clashes, civil warfare, and the spread of certain diseases (such as HIV-AIDS) in certain parts of the world have contributed to language loss.

Such SUDDEN LANGUAGE LOSS (also called ABRUPT LANGUAGE LOSS) is relatively uncommon (Mühlhäusler 2003). By and large language loss comes about through LANGUAGE SHIFT and LANGUAGE ATTRITION, a more gradual kind of loss, where speakers of a language make a decision to stop speaking their ancestral tongue or not to speak it to their children and to use another language instead. In such cases of more gradual shift and attrition, speakers abandon their language in favour of a more dominant or 'useful' language over the course of one or more generations. This other language is almost always the language of a majority culture, usually in terms of population but, more importantly, is dominant, in the sense of having political, economic or social power over the minority language speakers. The language of the dominant population may thus have more social prestige, and be associated with socioeconomic development, a factor which often favours language shift (see Harbert, Chapter 20). In some cases, language shift may be facilitated or even created by language laws and policies which require speakers to give up their mother tongue. Examples of such policies include the US government's policies toward Native American languages and the Soviet government's policies toward indigenous minority (or 'small-numbered') languages in regions such as Siberia, policies which promoted the use of the majority language (English or Russian) and punished speakers of indigenous languages. One well-known example in each country is the boarding school system, which forced children into institutional schools and punished them for speaking their languages (Adams 1995). Similarly, from 1770, the Spanish colonial authorities in the Andean nations of South America implemented a forced policy of Spanish language use; the failed rebellion of 1780–1 resulted in even greater political and linguistic repression of the indigenous peoples (Adelaar 2007). More extreme examples of political repression have ended in genocide, such as with the Ona (or Selk'nam, a Chon language) peoples of Tierra del Fuego or the |Xam (a Khoisan language) in South Africa (Brenzinger 2007b: 184–5).

Global languages put even more pressure on indigenous languages. In regions of heavy multilingualism, social and political advancement may be linked to knowledge of English or French, for example, as well as local or national lingua francas. A prime example is the Autonomous Republic of Sakha (Yakutia) in the Russian Federation where speakers of minority indigenous languages may feel pressure to speak the regional language (Sakha/Yakut), the national language (Russian), and the global language (English). All three of these languages put pressure on local indigenous languages spoken by small groups of people in Sakha, such as Yukaghir, with only 243 speakers (comprising 16 per cent of the total ethnic population of 1,509), according to the 2002 All-Russian Census. Gradual attrition often involves TRANSITIONAL BILINGUALISM: as the speaker population is in the process of shift, certain groups primarily speak the local language and others the language of wider communication. Because this type of attrition is gradual, speaker communities may be unaware that it is in progress until it is quite advanced and the local language is seriously endangered. This is exacerbated in regions where multilingualism has traditionally been the norm, so that the older generations are not troubled to hear the children speaking a more dominant language, and sometimes miss the fact that they are not speaking their parents' (or grandparents') first language.

It is important to bear in mind that although language loss is not a new occurrence, the accelerated rate at which it is presently happening is. The dynamics of language shift are dependent on a complex set of factors stemming from local language ecologies and factors at regional, national and global levels. These vary considerably from group to group. Some speakers and communities are quicker to give up their languages than others. Some robustly maintain their languages despite apparent pressures not to. It is therefore difficult, if not impossible, to predict the exact rate of language shift globally. The most conservative estimates predict that 50 per cent of the world's languages will be lost over the course of this century, while the most dire prediction is that as many as 90 per cent will disappear (Krauss 1992). Even the conservative figure represents a radical reconfiguration of the world's linguistic landscape. None of the present accounts can fully foresee the effects of globalization, which is an unprecedented phenomenon in world history, nor can they determine whether current efforts at maintenance and revitalization will be able to offset this massive shift in any significant way.

2.1.4   Causes of language shift

There are a number of factors which are known to motivate language shift. They often centre around imbalances in prestige and power between the minority (or threatened) language and culture on the one hand, and the language(s) of wider communication and more dominant culture(s) on the other. While the specifics vary with each individual situation, several overarching factors are usually found: URBANIZATION, GLOBALIZATION and what have been called SOCIAL DISLOCATION and

CULTURAL DISLOCATION. Unequal levels of power often result in members of the minority community (or better, perhaps, LOCAL COMMUNITY, as the relevant factor is not population size but rather sociopolitical status) being socially disadvantaged in a number of ways with respect to the majority population. In concrete terms, this frequently means that compared to the majority/dominant population, local community members are relatively powerless politically, and are less educated, less wealthy (even living in poverty in many cases), with less access to modern conveniences and technologies (Harbert, Chapter 20). One common result is that this socially disadvantaged position becomes associated with, or even equated to, the local language and culture, and so knowledge of the local language is seen as an impediment to social and economic development. Socioeconomic improvement thus comes to be perceived as tied to knowledge of the language of wider communication, coupled with renunciation of the local language and culture; for this reason, the situation has been called SOCIAL DISLOCATION. Social dislocation stemming from lack of prestige and power is one of the most powerful motivating factors in language shift.

Related to social dislocation is CULTURAL DISLOCATION, which results from modernization and globalization. These two related forces bring together people from different cultures, speaking different languages, in a variety of settings, from informal to official, including religious and educational settings. Often this results in the culture of the minority giving way to that of the majority. At an extreme, globalization is feared to lead to cultural homogenization. The loss of cultural distinctions supports a loss of linguistic distinctions, since the culture is seen as embedded in the language. Globalization puts even greater pressure on local languages and can be a major factor in language shift. One of the results of globalization is the emergence of at least one global language of wider communication. The global nature of trade and commerce has in recent decades put increasing pressure on the need for an international lingua franca; English currently holds that position. Whereas historically it was important for key figures in world politics to be able to communicate, it is now critical that a much larger number of people in all walks of manufacturing and business life communicate with one another, increasing the need for a global language. Some local communities thus see the knowledge of a global language as necessary for socioeconomic advancement. In cases where knowledge of a national or regional language is also important, and in fact may be the only language of education, the need to know the global language can supplant the need or desire to know the local language. Such perceptions are further reinforced in the schools, where the national language is taught and one or more global or 'foreign' languages may be offered, but instruction is rarely given in the local, endangered language, which is presupposed to be not useful. Alternatively, in some areas the concept of trilingual education is taking hold. In Greenland, for example, since 1979 and the introduction of Home Rule, education is in West Greenlandic (the local language) and Danish (technically the national language). Since the inception of Self Government in 2009, there has been a concerted effort to make education in English accessible to all Greenlanders. Similar movements are seen in many parts of the European Union, due to increasing recognition of the importance of learning the regional language, the national language, and an international or global language. Trilingual primary education programmes can be found in a large number of countries, such as Finland, Germany, Luxembourg, northern Italy, both in regions where three languages are spoken and in regions where two languages are spoken and the third language is introduced as a foreign language, used primarily or exclusively within the school in these communities.

Urbanization is another key cause of language shift and is itself related to cultural and social dislocation. Urbanization brings people from different regions and cultures into the same living and working spaces. They are necessarily required to communicate with one another and so turn to an established lingua franca or language of wider communication. It is not surprising that we find the highest levels of language retention in rural areas; in general, the more isolated a community, the more likely it is to maintain use of the local language. Urbanization has the opposite effect: by bringing people into contact, it facilitates language shift, despite, in some cases, the existence of urban ghettos of minority groups.

In the modern world, multilingualism generally involves knowledge of one or more national languages and, increasingly, of the global language. This represents a change in traditional patterns, when speakers knew a number of local languages. The shift stems from a combination of factors including education, social prestige and socioeconomics. One factor which has led to diminished local-level multilingualism is the current importance of the national language in terms of access to education, higher paying jobs, the media and social advancement. The national language provides a language of wider communication which makes knowledge of multiple local languages less necessary or even superfluous, as the national language serves as a common lingua franca. A key characteristic of language endangerment is that use of the local language is limited, not only regionally but also functionally. In some cases, it is used only in the home, while in others it is used outside the home in the village but not for communication with people living outside of the immediate community, and so on. Broadcast media (and increasingly, the internet) bring languages of wider communication into the home, further diminishing the last sanctuary for the local language. Thus the uses of the local language become increasingly limited, with the net result that it is increasingly important, and usual, for people to learn only a national language of wider communication.

2.1.5 Broader implications

At first it might appear that there is a tremendous advantage to be gained from speaking a limited number of languages worldwide. Presumably this would facilitate communication, decrease translation, interpreting and publication costs, and enhance cross-cultural understanding. Yet in fact it is not clear that these benefits would actually be achieved; monolingualism has historically done little to help cross-cultural understanding, for example. There are at least three sets of compelling reasons for caring about language loss. First is their value to the heritage communities themselves; second their value to the scientific community; and third is the value of languages as part of world cultural heritage. Let us consider each of these separately.

For many, the most compelling reason to document, preserve and revitalize languages is their value to the heritage community. For many groups, language is an integral part of identity, and people who lose their language often speak of a deep sense of loss of self, of loss of identity. The situation is different for immigrant communities, who frequently assimilate to the more dominant culture. For these groups, there is still a 'homeland' where the heritage language is robustly spoken and their heritage culture is maintained (though often in a changed form). With endangered language communities, the loss is more dramatic and more profound. The right to use and develop one's native language is a basic human right, ratified by such leading international groups as the United Nations and UNESCO.[1] The United Nations' *Declaration on the Rights of Indigenous Peoples*, adopted 13 September 2007, gives specific rights to indigenous groups to promote their languages, as specified in Article 13, section 1:

Article 13

1. Indigenous peoples have the right to revitalize, use, develop and transmit to future generations their histories, languages, oral traditions, philosophies, writing systems and literatures, and to designate and retain their own names for communities, places and persons.

Such resolutions reflect broadly held opinions among indigenous communities that they have the right to use their languages, and the right to have the means to develop them. In this line of reasoning, the inherent right of all peoples to speak their languages and protect their usage is justification in and of itself for maintaining linguistic diversity.

The scientific community is another set of stakeholders in endangered language situations. Linguists require knowledge of the variety of possible language structures. With over half of the world's languages undescribed, we are still lacking key information about how the human mind packages and organizes basic information. Certain linguistic features found only in some endangered languages are relatively rare, such as the voiceless dental bilabially trilled affricate in Oro Win, a

Chapacura-Wanham language spoken in Brazil with at most five speakers (out of an ethnic population of approximately 55), or ENDOCLISIS (where CLITIC morphemes are located within a word, not at the periphery) in Udi, an East Caucasian language spoken primarily in just two villages (one in Azerbaijan and one in Georgia). If such languages were to disappear without a trace, we would never know the full range of human linguistic capability (see Palosaari and Campbell, Chapter 6, for further discussion and examples).

Another kind of scientific argument for maintaining linguistic diversity comes from the kinds of world knowledge which languages encode. Because language is used by people to process, organize and store information about local environments, biological systems, climate conditions and other parts of the physical aspects of a language ecology, they may contain important information about specific ecologies which is unknown to outsiders. Equally important to the knowledge itself is the way in which it is classified or organized, which may provide new insights into how the world is structured (Harrison 2007 and Nettle and Romaine 2000 both provide extensive examples). Recent research on climate change has tried to incorporate more TRADITIONAL ECOLOGICAL KNOWLEDGE into Western scientific paradigms, with the hope of better understanding not only the causes of global warming, but also its potential impact and ways to offset it. In a similar vein, linguistic systems encode alternative views of time, space and philosophy. Note that this argument centres on the premise that such knowledge will be lost not only because it has not been captured in any way (not recorded, or not translated into another language) but also, and critically, on the assumption that the knowledge itself is not directly translatable. It is also important to note that this view sets up an opposition between scientific knowledge held by Western specialists on the one hand, and knowledge in the minds of non-Western outsiders on the other, thus implicitly framing the Western approach as the base from which others (traditional, indigenous or local) deviate.

The lines between this argument and the CULTURAL HERITAGE argument are blurred. A prime example of the cultural heritage argument is UNESCO's Safeguarding Endangered Languages project, which maintains that safeguarding linguistic diversity is critical to maintaining cultural diversity because languages are the primary means of expressing culture and intangible cultural heritage. This, in turn, further relates to community members' sense that identity is linked to language, and thus a loss of language is coupled with a loss of identity.

One of the primary challenges going forward is to identify ways not only to document and describe, but also to revitalize and maintain small languages. This requires finding ways in which communities can be sustainable over the long term, not only linguistically, but culturally, economically and ecologically. There are no ready solutions at this time, but clearly they rest in part on adapting to changing environments and on embracing multilingualism as the norm (see Harbert, Chapter 20, for more discussion).

2.2   Assessing language endangerment

Up to this point we have addressed the issue of language endangerment as if there were two distinct and measurable states: endangered and not endangered. In fact most linguists would argue that it is possible to place language vitality along a continuum, with languages which are vital and in no way endangered (e.g. English, Mandarin, Spanish) on one end, and extinct languages which have no speakers and have vanished without descendent or daughter languages on the other end.[2]

2.2.1   Factors involved in determining levels of endangerment

There are a number of factors involved in determining the level of language endangerment. These are deeply interconnected with the causes of language shift and so assessing them and their roots can in fact be more useful than determining the exact level of endangerment itself. These can be organized into three broad categories: (1) the nature of the speaker base; (2) domains of use; and (3) both internal and external support for or pressures against using the language.

In 2003 an ad hoc expert group on endangered languages established by UNESCO determined a core set of nine criteria to be used in determining language endangerment: (1) intergenerational transmission; (2) absolute number of speakers; (3) proportion of speakers within the total population; (4) trends in existing language domains; (5) response to new domains and media; (6) materials for language education and literacy; (7) governmental and institutional attitudes and policies, including official status and use; (8) community members' attitudes toward their own language; and (9) amount and quality of documentation. These nine factors are key in assessing language vitality.

The nature of the speaker base is the single most important factor here. This base includes not only the number of speakers, but more importantly, the generational distribution of these speakers, and the proportion of speakers of the target language within the total population. A clear indicator of language shift is when children cease learning the language. In order for a language to survive, it needs to have future speakers. The number of speakers is relevant in that a smaller speaker base may be more susceptible to sudden shift, but in fact some languages with relatively small numbers of speakers can be quite stable, especially if the group remains in relative isolation, without sustained contact with other languages that involves an asymmetrical dominance relationship. The total number of speakers is further relevant in terms of the importance of the percentage of the population which speaks the language; with a large speaker base, if some of the speakers shift to another language, it is not a signal that the language is in danger. Krauss (2007: 2) argues that no language with fewer than 10,000 speakers could be seen as truly 'safe'. At issue here is not whether such a language is stable, but rather that the small number of speakers means an even smaller number of children speakers, and so rapid attrition (over the course of a single generation) could happen if the social or political situation changed to destabilize the community in some way.

Catalan provides an interesting example in this regard. The most recent data show that there are 9,118,882 speakers of Catalan, based on survey data from 2003–4 from the Generalitat de Catalunya.[3] Although the survey data do not distinguish monolingual speakers from those who also speak other languages, and do not distinguish level of proficiency in Catalan, it is still reasonably certain that Catalan is well above the threshold of 'endangered' in terms of number of speakers and should be considered 'safe' since it is the official language of Catalonia (and Andorra). But survey data from 2008 show that only 56% of the people born in Catalonia report using Catalan as their normal, day-to-day language, down from 66% in 2003. In addition, from the years 2000–2008, approximately one million people immigrated to Catalonia, primarily from Morocco and other Arabic-speaking countries. Only 4% of this population reports using Catalan as their habitual language. The 2008 survey shows that 36% of the total population of Catalonia uses Catalan as their habitual language, versus 46% using Spanish. Both figures are down from 2003 (46% using Catalan, 47% using Spanish), while Arabic speakers are on the rise (at 2% in 2008). (For more discussion and full survey data, see Comajoan 2009.) These trends, along with its long-standing status as a minority language as opposed to Spanish, have led some to argue that Catalan is in fact endangered (Junyent 1999).

Catalan does, however, have the advantage of official status, and this is an important indicator of long-term vitality. As a general rule, a language which has official status is the language of government, education and administration; in such cases the language is relatively safe and stable. This is because there is a strong link between language vitality and the domains in which it is used, and one sign of a healthy language is that it is used in all domains. The 1979 decision of the Home Rule government in Greenland to make West Greenlandic the official language there is seen as having been a critical measure in arresting language shift; today West Greenlandic is the only Arctic indigenous language with increasing numbers of speakers.

An additional consideration is the attitude of the community toward the language. As a general rule of thumb, a more positive attitude promotes language vitality, while a more negative attitude favours shift. Again, this is overly simplistic, but the correlation between language attitudes and vitality is clear. Finally, with regard to documentation, it should be noted that the act of documenting a language does not directly affect its vitality. But an existing large body of documentation may indicate that it is used robustly, in many domains; such is the case with English or any of the world's major languages. It may indicate that it was once robustly used, such as Manchu, which was once the main language of government and lingua franca in China during the first centuries of the Qing Dynasty, but is now highly endangered. More indirectly, the act of documentation may stimulate discussion in the community about language shift and may motivate community members to think about language vitality.

2.2.2 Different scales evaluating language endangerment

A number of different scales are in use to express the actual level of endangerment. In general these centre around speaker vitality, as determined by the percentage/proportion of speakers across generations, and language use, in terms of which domains the language is used in and which not. Grenoble and Whaley (2006: 18) propose a six-way distinction, arguing that at least this number of levels is required to capture different stages of endangerment: SAFE, AT RISK, DISAPPEARING, MORIBUND, NEARLY EXTINCT and EXTINCT.

SAFE: all generations use the language in all or nearly all domains, and the language has a large speaker base relative to others spoken in the same region. A safe language usually has official status, and typically functions as the language of government, education, and commerce. Safe languages generally enjoy high prestige.

AT RISK: there is no observable pattern of a shrinking speaker base, but the language lacks some of the properties of a safe language: it may be used in limited domains, or have a smaller number of speakers than other languages in the same region. Language attitudes may be key at this stage: positive attitudes toward the language may reinforce vitality, while negative attitudes may contribute to shift.

DISAPPEARING: a language is disappearing when there is an observable shift towards another language in the communities where it is spoken. With an overall decreasing proportion of intergenerational transfer, the speaker base shrinks because it is not being replenished. Disappearing languages are consequently used in a more restricted set of domains, and languages of wider communication begin to replace them in a greater percentage of homes.

MORIBUND: the language is no longer transmitted to children, and so the speaker base is consistently shrinking.

NEARLY EXTINCT: only a handful of speakers of the oldest generation remain.

EXTINCT: no remaining speakers.

Table 2.1. *Language endangerment scale proposed by Krauss (1997)*

a	the language is spoken by all generations, including all, or nearly all, children
a-	the language is learned by all or most children
b	the language is spoken by all adults, parental age and up, but learned by few or no children
b-	the language is spoken by adults aged 30 and older, but not by younger parents
c	the language is spoken only by adults aged 40 and older
c-	all speakers aged 50 and older
-d	all speakers aged 60 and older
d	all speakers aged 70 and older
d-	all speakers aged 70 and older, with fewer than 10 speakers
e	extinct, no speakers

Lack of transmission of the language to children marks a significant change in language vitality. This scale relies heavily on the overall patterns of speakers within the larger group of potential speakers. (The body of potential speakers is often understood to be the ethnic population, although this is not strictly accurate, as exemplified in language shift, when people from one 'group' switch to the language of another group.) One fundamental problem with any system for evaluating vitality is determining the number of speakers. At first it might appear that it is at least easy to establish when a language is extinct, when there are no speakers left, but this is not always the case. It is not just that there may be speakers who are hidden from or unknown to external researchers (Grinevald and Bert, Chapter 3, discuss 'ghost speakers' as one hidden category), but that the very notion of 'speaker' shifts as overall vitality shifts. Moreover, this scale does not take into account new speakers who emerge through language revitalization programmes (what Grinevald and Bert, Chapter 3, call 'neo-speakers'). Wampanoag (north-eastern USA) is a case of a language with no known speakers which has been resuscitated due to the efforts of a single individual, Jessie Little Doe Fermino; Manx Gaelic (spoken on the Isle of Man) has been reported to be extinct but actually has a growing speaker base thanks to active revitalization. (See Grinevald and Bert, Chapter 3, for more discussion of the issue of identifying different categories of speakers, including the so-called 'last speaker' of a language.)

One particularly fine-grained categorization comes from Krauss (1997) who uses a ten-way distinction, which distinguishes multiple levels according to the age and distribution of speakers and levels of usage. An advantage to this scale is that it avoids alarmist rhetoric such as 'dying' or 'moribund', terms which are themselves distressing to speaker groups (see J. Hill 2002). Krauss's scale is given in Table 2.1.

Krauss's scale is particularly informative because it breaks down the number of speakers by generation and by age within the older generations. This has possible advantages both for researchers who want to study the language and for activists who want to revitalize it. Researchers can study the language from the angle of fully fluent speakers or can look at it to study contact-induced change and attrition (O'Shannessy, Chapter 5, Palosaari and Campbell Chapter 6). Activists interested in revitalization need to assess, first and foremost, the kinds of resources they have available for such programmes. Knowing specific information about language usage across generations is a prerequisite for establishing any such programme (see Hinton, Chapter 15).

Thus, such scales are potentially useful for a number of reasons. They can be useful to funding agencies in determining where money is most needed for language documentation or revitalization programmes. They can be useful to researchers to help determine research priorities; all things being equal, linguists may prioritize language documentation efforts for seriously endangered languages, especially if little is known about such languages, or they have no close or obvious relatives. And they are potentially useful to language communities. A community embarking on language revitalization needs as accurate information as possible about the kinds of resources it has available (age and number of speakers, levels of fluency of community members, etc.) in order to determine what kind of programme is appropriate. Vitality scales do provide an overall template for helping to assess the resources which a community that is contemplating language revitalization or maintenance may have, with speaker resources being the single most important (Grenoble and Whaley 2006: 160–6).

That being said, assessments of vitality represent general trends, not hard-and-fast rules, and there are exceptions. From the standpoint of rapid language shift, it can be dangerous to overestimate vitality and not take preventative measures for language maintenance. Alternatively, a very negative assessment can be demoralizing and result in an overly pessimistic attitude toward revitalization, with speakers abandoning efforts which they have deemed to be hopeless. Perhaps not surprisingly, the overall usefulness of these scales seems to be limited. Although information about the level of endangerment could be used by communities to determine what kind of revitalization programme is needed and what is feasible, there is little evidence that such scales can be correlated with the rate of loss in any strictly quantifiable way, so that at best they give vague information about when action is needed to offset shift. They cannot help communities understand what specific steps to take at any given level. Additionally, although the assessment of endangerment is used by researchers in setting priorities for documentation, more research is needed to determine what factors can be linked to rate of shift. Finally, there is the disadvantage that such scales give the mistaken impression that it is possible to identify and count speakers. They present a black-and-white picture of language vitality which does not acknowledge different fluency levels for speakers (see Grinevald and Bert, Chapter 3) or cases where a language has been revived, with the creation of a new cadre of speakers.

Despite these misgivings, some assessment of language vitality is often to be recommended. Some of the hazards and benefits can be illustrated with the case of Navajo, an Athabascan language spoken in North America. The 1990 US census stated that 107,665 (of a total of 130,520) Navajo households reported using an 'American Indian' language in the home (Lee and McLaughlin 2001). The 2000 US census, ten years later, reports that 178,000 people speak Navajo, of a population of 298,197 (which includes people who are fully or partly of Navajo descent).[4] These figures mask the fact that the number of monolingual English-speaking Navajo is rising dramatically, in particular among children. The US census reports that in the age group 5–17, 12% of (self-identified) ethnic Navajo spoke English only as a first language in 1980, while that figure had risen to 49% in 2000. One problem with both sets of data is that they rely on self-reporting, and it is unclear how those reporting their own proficiency evaluated the 'language of the home'. A survey conducted by pre-school teachers (Platero 2001), however, suggests that language shift may be further advanced than even the 2000 Census reports: 54% of 682 children observed were monolingual speakers of English, while only 18% were monolingual speakers of Navajo. Bilingual speakers accounted for 28% of the children, although there is no indication of which of the two languages was primary for the children. Because these figures are based on direct observation, they are more reliable than the Census data.

2.3　Conclusion

The reasons for language loss are complex and varied, but we see unprecedented shift taking place throughout the modern world. If it continues unarrested, the result will be a significant restructuring of the linguistic landscape and a tremendous loss of linguistic diversity. Responses to language endangerment fall into two basic categories: efforts to document languages while still possible, and efforts to rejuvenate and invigorate language usage. Recent decades have seen an enormous surge in research on endangered languages. First and foremost, considerable effort and resources have gone into language documentation (Woodbury, Chapter 9). This interest, coupled with technological advances, has had a major impact on shaping documentary linguistics as a field, as well as increasing the corpus of language material that has been collected. Both of these trends have, in turn, had an impact on the field of linguistics, in terms of research, methods and training. In conjunction with these efforts, there has been a surge of interest in language revitalization, mainly as grassroots movements and often as parts of larger political agendas. Many communities have been galvanized to act to preserve their languages (Hinton, Chapter 15).

These efforts are reinforced by a growing awareness of and attention to language rights as basic human rights.

Language is often likened to the proverbial canary in the coal mine of culture. This is perhaps simply a different way of articulating the relationship between language and other elements of the human environment: language usage, and thus vitality, are deeply embedded in the complex nexus of components which make up a linguistic ecology. Viewed this way, it is clear that efforts to change the course of language shift cannot be successful until they also address those elements of the linguistic ecology which are themselves factors in language loss. Some of these, such as global influences, may be beyond the control of the speakers, but they need to be taken into account for successful revitalization. Others, even national policies in some (but not all) cases, can be changed by speaker communities. At a more local level, it is important to assess the language ecology and determine the underlying causes for shift and how to address them. Rarely does this mean returning to a past or static ecology, as this itself entails a return to the very situation which caused shift. The larger contexts in which the local ecology is embedded are themselves dynamic and changing; key to successfully reversing language shift is creating local language ecologies which retain those elements of historical structure and usage which are central to the culture, while at the same time being flexible and adaptable to a changing world.

Notes

1 The Charter of the United Nations is available online at www.un.org/en/documents/charter/index.shtml. The full text of the United Nations Declaration on the Rights of Indigenous Peoples is available online at www.un.org/esa/socdev/unpfii/en/declaration.html. For more information on UNESCO's programme, see www.unesco.org/culture/ich/index.php?pg=00136

2 Here I make a distinction between languages like Latin or Classical Greek, which are no longer spoken but have descendants (the modern Romance languages and modern Greek, respectively) and languages which have been lost because their natural development has ended due to one or more of the circumstances cited in 2.1.4.

3 www.gencat.cat (3 March 2010).

4 www.america.gov/st/educ-english/2008/August/200808051601491CJsamohT0.7349359.html (3 March 2010).

3

Speakers and communities

Colette Grinevald and Michel Bert

3.1   Introduction

We take it as a given that all fieldwork on an endangered language starts and develops thanks to some of its speakers. In the midst of a relative explosion of publications both on (linguistic) fieldwork and on endangered languages, it is therefore worth reminding ourselves that speakers are indeed the source, not to say the heart and soul of it all (see also Dobrin and Berson, Chapter 10).

   Speakers are mentioned in the literature on fieldwork, e.g. in university textbooks used for linguistic fieldwork methodology courses (see the classic Samarin 1967, or the more recent Crowley 2007, and Bowern 2008). One can also find in Newman and Ratliff (2001a) a rich collection of portraits of speakers who have worked with linguists around the world. The topic has also been considered in discussions of FIELDWORK FRAMEWORKS, in terms of the power relations that hold between the researcher and the researched, taken as individuals or as communities (Cameron *et al.* 1993a, Craig 1993, Grinevald 1997).

   But for all their centrality to the enterprise of language description, documentation and revitalization of endangered languages, relatively little research has been done so far on the great variety of speakers encountered in situations of language endangerment, and even less on what this variety means in terms of how to carry out fieldwork in such contexts. Yet, whenever specialists of fieldwork on endangered languages have paid attention to it, they have all recognized, on one hand, this great variety of speakers, and on the other, major profiles of speakers typical of such situations for particular endangered languages. The first to address the issue was Nancy Dorian, on the basis of her work on a dialect of Scottish Gaelic (Dorian 1977, 1981). Similar profiles of speakers

Colette Grinevald was formerly known as Colette G. Craig, of the University of Oregon until 1996.

were identified later in various other very different field situations, such as in the Rama language in Nicaragua (Craig 1992a, Grinevald 2007) in Central America, and in the Francoprovençal-speaking area in France (Bert 2001; 2009). The typology of speakers of endangered languages presented below is partly based on a comparison of these three field experiences, and on extensive discussions among these three linguists and with many colleagues.

Another essential feature of situations of endangered languages, beyond the great variety of types of speakers, is the fact that the total number of individual speakers does not comprise a linguistic community in the traditional sense of the term. Common features in situations of language endangerment include the fact that speakers are often neither readily identifiable nor easily accounted for, and also that last speakers (see below) might be very isolated and not even be known to be speakers. In the end, establishing where the boundaries of the community might lie depends in large part on awareness of the level of vitality of the language, combined with the level of mobilization of speakers and non-speakers on its behalf.

3.2   Towards a typology of speakers of endangered languages

There is typically a great variety of speakers in any linguistic community, but this section addresses the issue of what makes endangered language speakers different, and why it should matter to be aware of this great diversity when working on the description, documentation or revitalization of endangered languages. After considering the specificities of this issue (3.2.1), and the multiple variables needed to analyse the variety (3.2.2), a preliminary typology of speakers will be presented (3.2.3). This typology will then be projected into a dynamic dimension in order to highlight how speakers can be recategorized over time (3.2.4). By way of conclusion, the last section considers which types of speakers are best suited for which particular tasks in relation to projects on endangered languages (3.2.5).

3.2.1   The great variety of speakers of endangered languages

In all societies, including those using major literate dominant languages, as well as those using minority languages (which may have literacy and/ or oral traditions), there are always some people who are really good with language and others who are less so. People can be more or less aware of their language, curious about it, playful with it, or indifferent to it. There are many types of speakers with particular relations to any language, such as second-language learners and foreign-language speakers, but also speakers displaying signs of language attrition (for instance, because of emigration and exile, or for medical reasons; see Palosaari and Campbell, Chapter 6). So one could ask what is special about the claimed great variety of speakers of endangered languages.

There are two basic differences between the range of speakers of endangered and non-endangered languages. One is that, as the level of vitality of a language decreases, the proportion of supposedly marginal types of speakers will become more prevalent, perhaps rising eventually to become the bulk of the population of speakers. In this case, there may also be many varieties of second-language learners or speakers, as well as many speakers at different stages of language attrition. A second characteristic is that the phenomenon of language loss gives rise to some types of speakers that are specific to those circumstances, not so much in terms of their levels of knowledge of the language, but more in terms of sociopsychological traits that sometimes create unexpected interactions.

3.2.2   Elements of a typology of speakers of endangered languages

It will be argued below that beyond the range of speakers of endangered languages with their unique individual linguistic characteristics, some distinct PROFILES of speakers can be identified. The pioneering work of Dorian (1977, 1981) offered an initial typology that introduced the notion of SEMI-SPEAKER, now considered emblematic of language endangerment situations. The model was extended by Dressler (1981) and Campbell and Muntzel (1989), who added sociolinguistic variables in order to introduce another type of speaker typical of endangered language situations, the REMEMBERER. Reviews of early proposals for typologies of endangered language speakers can be found in Grinevald (1997) and Tsunoda (2005). What follows is a proposal for a more complex multidimensional and dynamic model that integrates a number of new parameters, and cross-tabulates them to identify with more precision a number of prototypes of speakers of endangered languages, some previously established in the literature and others not. The precision of the parameters and their various combinations allows also the identification of an infinite variation of more or less marginal exemplars that can be associated with those major categories.

The parameters form four distinct clusters:

1.   The language competence cluster
     This first cluster is anchored in the major parameter of LANGUAGE COMPETENCE of the individual speaker, considered to be more or less proficient, with all degrees observed between the extremes of mastery of the endangered language to those with very little knowledge

of it.[1] The proposal here is to link this level of competence to what accounts for it, by considering in addition both the LEVEL OF ACQUISITION ATTAINED and the possible DEGREE OF INDIVIDUAL LOSS of the language. The association of the knowledge parameter with these two parameters yields three major types of speakers: FLUENT SPEAKERS (full acquisition and no loss), SEMI-SPEAKERS (partial acquisition and possible loss), and so-called TERMINAL SPEAKERS (either limited acquisition or acquisition but advanced loss).

2. The sociolinguistic cluster: exposure to language versus vitality of language at time of acquisition

    A second cluster of parameters deals with factors that situate the individual speakers within particular endangered language communities at a particular time and at a particular phase in the process of decline of the language. This is important to take into account since different types of speakers, in varying proportions, will be found at different societal stages of language endangerment. The sociolinguistic factor of the LEVEL OF VITALITY OF THE ENDANGERED LANGUAGE (see Grenoble, chapter 2) must therefore be cross-tabulated with the DATE OF BIRTH OF THE INDIVIDUAL SPEAKER. Whether the language was endangered, very endangered or extremely endangered when the speaker was born certainly determines how much exposure to the language was possible, and what opportunities were available to learn and use it, particularly at the crucial early period of language acquisition. This accounts for the large spectrum of semi-speakers, particularly numerous at advanced stages of language shift.

3. Performance cluster: use and attitude

    The third cluster of parameters takes into account the relation of the individual speaker to the endangered language community. It requires assessing the LEVEL OF USE of the language (constrained of course if the process of endangerment is very advanced, as just considered) and the ATTITUDES of the individual speaker toward the language, which is influenced of course by general attitudes toward the language (see Spolsky, Chapter 8). It is obvious that both use and attitude will have an impact on the level of competence considered in the first cluster of parameters, while competence of course will also constrain usage and influence attitude. Those parameters will distinguish between latent and active speakers, and different types of more or less RUSTY speakers.

4. Self-evaluation of speakers and linguistic insecurity

    The final major parameter has a psycholinguistic nature, linked to the complex process of self-evaluation by speakers. One of the essential traits of many speakers of endangered languages is a profound sense of LINGUISTIC INSECURITY that can colour interactions in unexpected ways. This insecurity can extend to total denial of any knowledge of the language, in spite of proof to the contrary. A particular type of speaker has been identified around this extreme phenomenon of self-denial, that of the GHOST speaker. While this situation of under-evaluation is more common, one also needs to be aware of over-evaluation of competence in the case of certain speakers, because this self-confidence can easily be deflated in the course of interaction with a linguist and become a source of great discomfort.

It is therefore proposed that, in order to establish common profiles of speakers of endangered languages, one would need to handle a number of parameters of different natures and consider their interrelations.

3.2.3 A basic typology of speakers of endangered languages[2]

In this section seven types of speakers considered to be typical of situations of language endangerment will be identified. We note in passing that the terminology found so far in the literature and reported here is still rather controversial, as will be discussed in Section 3.4.1. The first three major types, namely FLUENT SPEAKERS, SEMI-SPEAKERS and TERMINAL SPEAKERS, are well known. The category of REMEMBERERS is less well defined but widely acknowledged, even if still subject to discussion. Less recognized are the categories of GHOST SPEAKERS, found in situations of advanced language loss, and of NEO-SPEAKERS emerging through language revitalization programmes. Finally, some remarks will be made about the partly mythological category of LAST SPEAKERS.

3.2.3.1 Fluent speakers

This first category constitutes the type of speakers most sought after by linguists wishing to carry out research on the language. They have sometimes been referred to as TRADITIONAL SPEAKERS due to their typically being the most conservative speakers in relation to others, who may have lower proficiency. But this does not necessarily mean that theirs is the most traditional type of speech, if it can be compared to older records of the language. A trait of these fluent speakers is that they have usually had and may still have conversation partners in the language. As the degree of language loss advances, there may in fact be very few of those fluent speakers left, until there are no more.

Dorian (1981) introduced a distinction between two subcategories, of OLD FLUENT SPEAKERS versus YOUNG FLUENT SPEAKERS. Young fluent speakers would be those fluent in the endangered language, but speaking it in a somewhat modified form compared to old fluent speakers, as the result of the process of LANGUAGE OBSOLESCENCE (see Palosaari and Campbell, Chapter 6). Typically, but not always, these new forms of language spoken by the young fluent speakers are not rejected by the old fluent speakers as being deviant; however, different individuals and communities show differing ideologies in this regard (with some individuals and groups showing an ideology of LINGUISTIC PURISM while others have an ideology that is more accepting of difference and change).

In the situation originally described by Dorian in Gaelic-speaking Scotland, the labels YOUNG and OLD corresponded to real age differences, between two generations of speakers. Although the link between age and level of proficiency generally holds in situations of more advanced language loss than the one she described, it will happen at some point that the so-called young fluent type become older, and will then represent the most fluent remaining speakers.

3.2.3.2 Semi-speakers

The category of semi-speakers, introduced by Dorian, is the most emblematic of situations of language endangerment. It is a large category which includes all members of the community with appropriate receptive skills in the language, but varying levels of productive skills. It can include speakers with relatively high fluency, especially in routine contexts such as casual conversations. This category also includes speakers with limited language knowledge but who are socially integrated into the endangered language community and can interact competently in most situations, possibly using minimal language forms but deploying them in socioculturally appropriate ways. In our experience, it is generally the case that, unlike speakers in the previous category, the semi-speakers have not had and do not have regular conversation partners in the endangered language, and operate most of their sociolinguistic lives in the dominant language rather than the endangered language.

It is characteristic of the speech of semi-speakers that it contains more modified forms than the speech of young fluent speakers, and that some of those modified forms are considered as mistakes by fluent speakers. It is worth noting that it is from this generally larger semi-speaker group that some of the most involved activists for language revitalization emerge (see Hinton, Chapter 15).

3.2.3.3 Terminal speakers

This is a term that is found in the literature, although its negative connotations make it controversial. Some have suggested the term PARTIAL is preferable, although this would not distinguish them qualitatively from semi-speakers. Terminal speakers are those with some passive knowledge of the language and very limited productive skills, sometimes reduced to frozen fixed expressions. This very limited knowledge can be the result of either very partial acquisition of the endangered language (say, overhearing it spoken irregularly by grandparents to each other), or of an advanced level of attrition in someone who might have been a more fluent speaker in childhood.

These first three types, identified primarily on the basis of level of competence, need to be considered from two perspectives. One is that of the level of vitality of the language, according to which the proportion of speakers of each type will vary. For instance, at the time a linguist encounters the situation, the language may be so endangered that there are no more old fluent speakers and the oldest speakers left are in fact young fluent or even semi-speakers. The second is that, according to the types of speakers available, discussions of standardization and revitalization will often involve choosing between different forms of speech to be taught to learners: perhaps those of older fluent or younger fluent speakers, but sometimes even those used by semi-speakers. The identification of the next categories relies on parameters of a sociolinguistic nature, although there is overlap at competence level with the types presented above.

3.2.3.4   Rememberers

In order to describe this type of speaker, we introduce the parameters of acquisition and loss. Speakers with limited knowledge of the endangered language due to attrition can be associated with the categories of semi-speaker or terminal speaker. Their language attrition is sometimes due to traumatic circumstances (such as ethnic massacres of the kind still retold in parts of the Americas) that have forced them to hide their knowledge of the language. The term 'rememberer' evokes the possibility that such speakers may regain or reacquire some partial active use of the language. They could be inhibited at first, or unwilling to participate, but they might join a documentation and/or revitalization project at a later point. They should not be overlooked in fieldwork since they can always help reconstitute or even reinvent a sense of community at organized gatherings and contribute to efforts at language revitalization.

3.2.3.5   Ghost speakers

Ghost speakers are those who conspicuously deny any knowledge of the endangered language in spite of evidence that they do have some level of competence. This denial is the manifestation of a strong negative attitude toward the language and a deep rejection of any identification with it, in particular in the eyes of outsiders. This type of (non-)speaker would seem to be characteristic of certain contexts of language endangerment, in particular where a much denigrated regional language is overpowered by a highly standardized and valued national language, as happens with regional languages of France.[3] To the extent that one cannot evaluate their language proficiency, it seems difficult to assign them to any of the fluent speaker, semi-speaker or terminal-speaker categories.

3.2.3.6   Neo-speakers

This type of speaker has not been referenced in the literature yet, but they are becoming central to language revitalization, whose aim is partly to produce this kind of speaker.

Neo-speakers are learners of endangered languages in the context of revitalization programmes and activities. The level of language competence achieved by these new speakers depends of course on the abilities of the individuals, and can correspond broadly to the different levels within the semi-speaker category, from low to higher fluency. Some exceptionally gifted new speakers could perhaps even reach the level of a young fluent speaker. These neo-speakers can be distinguished from other types in that the category may include outsiders to the language community. Also, their positive attitudes towards the endangered language and their particular vision of the endangered language community, precisely as a community, propels them into conscious efforts to learn it. It is also important to note the kinds of language forms they are being taught. The language could be at an advanced level of language endangerment already, with its use limited to somewhat artificial settings and the forms taught showing definite signs of language obsolescence (see Hinton, Chapter 15, and Hinton and Hale 2001).

3.2.3.7 Last speakers

Finally, we should consider one category widely reported in the press, and probably best known to the general public: the category of so-called last speaker. We believe that, interestingly, this type does not belong to a typology of speakers of endangered languages, but rather to another realm, one of social and political status, with a touch of myth. It nevertheless catches the imagination of non-specialists and has become a point of entry into the phenomenon of language endangerment.[4] It is a category which seems to be assigned by a community to a specific individual, although it can also be self-attributed. In any case, being the last speaker may be an important public and social role.[5] They are often strong personalities, who might denigrate the speech of others identified by outsiders or linguists as speakers (of one type or another), or even conceal the existence of other speakers (see Evans 2001 for discussion). And while the person fulfilling the role of last speaker is generally considered to be a traditional old fluent speaker, especially by the community, linguists may consider him or her to be a young fluent speaker, or a semi-speaker, or a rememberer, or even, at the end of the process of language loss, as a very partial terminal speaker.

3.2.4 Dynamics of the typology of speakers

An important aspect of situations of language endangerment is their dynamics, as much at the level of the individual speakers as at community level. We identify three types of dynamic going on simultaneously:

1. **steady loss of vitality of the language.** This manifests itself through the death of the speakers themselves, but also through

attrition of the competence of remaining speakers, due to increasing lack of use over time, and of course due to the natural aging process producing language limitations.

2. **increasing proficiency of speakers.** For instance, rememberers can sometimes demonstrate partial recovery of their fluency in an endangered language through renewed contact with more fluent speakers and/or participation in language-related activities. Semi-speakers can also display low fluency at first, and then become more fluent through activities in language programmes and/or contact with more proficient speakers. Sometimes their progress in handling the language is quite dramatic, to the point that some may become leaders in revitalization programmes. This obviously also includes non-speakers who become neo-speakers, reaching varying levels of fluency.[6]

3. **recategorization of speakers.** The categorization of certain speakers may need to be readjusted over time as their level of proficiency is reassessed. This can be the case of individuals originally considered non-speakers who turn out to have more knowledge than estimated, either because they hid their competence or because the opportunity never arose for them to claim they had any proficiency. Another possible surprise may occur with speakers who are claimed to be (good) speakers but who are found in the course of fieldwork not to know as much as they or others claimed, or perhaps believed they knew.

3.2.5 Speakers of and projects on endangered languages

By way of conclusion of our discussion about the diversity of endangered language speakers, we will consider how the different types of projects carried out on endangered languages can tap into this great variety of speakers, to make the best of the knowledge and goodwill available. Where resources are scarce, particularly in situations of advanced language demise, it becomes essential to look for all possible ways to work with all types of speakers, by adapting methodologies and goals to suit the contexts best.

Linguists working on undescribed or under-described languages have to work with speakers in order to gather documentation of all types of speech events (see Woodbury, Chapter 9), establish the grammatical structure of the language, produce dictionaries (see Mosel, Chapter 17), and so on. Some linguists dream of and search for native speakers who are so-called NATURAL LINGUISTS, that is, speakers who are meta-linguistically aware and interested in the form and function of their language. Although there are usually a few such people in any given speech community, there might be fewer for an endangered language simply because there are fewer speakers of any type. Interestingly, many linguists have observed that among last speakers there are often such natural linguists, possibly because they have consciously kept their language alive in their own minds or through using it with themselves[7], who are very attached to and intimate with it. It is often the case that such people welcome linguists wishing to carry out research on their language, and find great satisfaction in sharing their knowledge.[8]

Linguists also often look for good storytellers but again this is a talent that is not as widespread as might be thought; experts with extensive knowledge of vocabulary and an encyclopaedic approach to lexical studies are also quite rare. Speakers with such talents may be few in advanced stages of language loss. But one should not overlook semi-speakers, or even rememberers, because some may preserve memories of aspects of the language (and the culture) forgotten or abandoned by more fluent speakers.

Projects on endangered languages, particularly documentation projects, also rely on individuals who may be limited speakers themselves but who take on a key role as go-between and facilitator. They are very important as brokers between linguists and insecure or hidden speakers, or older native speakers who might be afraid of strangers. They can organize gatherings and explain the work to be done. And one should never forget interested young people from the community, who are most likely to be better learners of new technologies and who could become field assistants, even if they are only partial speakers or learners.

For projects oriented toward revitalization, the participation of language activists becomes essential. Language activists from within the community are often semi-speakers, aware of and concerned about the demise of the language (Hinton, Chapter 15). They are likely to have more formal education than others, maybe because they were not raised in traditional environments. Thus they might be able to handle new technologies or be prepared to be trained in them (see Holton, Chapter 19, on this point).

3.3 On endangered language communities

The nature of endangered language communities will be addressed first by considering them through the lens of their geographic locations and configurations (3.3.1). It will also be considered from the perspective of different concepts of LANGUAGE and SPEECH COMMUNITIES, in order to show how both concepts are intricately intertwined in endangered language communities (3.3.2). Finally, the issue of language endangerment in communities will be approached from the perspective of the evolution of their level of consciousness and their evolving attitudes, in the context of recently developed discourse about the preservation of worldwide biocultural diversity (3.3.3).

3.3.1 Geographical/field perspectives on endangered language communities

Here we consider the practical fieldwork issue of where a particular ENDANGERED LANGUAGE COMMUNITY can be located. Possibilities range from nomadic groups situated in deserts or tropical forests, some of whom may also live in sedentary settlements, to identifiable communities in old settlements on ancestral lands or on reservations they have been moved to. It is becoming increasingly frequent also to find more diffuse communities in urban centres as a result of emigration from traditional locations (Harbert, Chapter 20).

Endangered language communities can be located in well-defined territories, in a particular village, or in a number of settlements. One type of such a territory is the reservation system (of the type found in the USA), where different communities have generally been gathered through forced movement and settlement. In this case, the origin of the settlements and the nature of their current administrative organization often constrain the types of relations outsiders may have with speakers (see below). In many parts of the world today endangered language communities are pressing legal demands for the recognition of their ancestral territories.[9]

Endangered language communities are sometimes located in small isolated villages. These communities are almost always multilingual, and the speaker population is more or less identifiable, depending on the level of endangerment and of consciousness of this endangerment (see below). In the case of village communities, the level of endangerment needs to be assessed for each and every one of the settlements, since local history may result in very different situations.

Importantly, from a geographic point of view, endangered language communities are often found in transnational territories, for two major reasons. One is that they often have survived better away from urban centres of colonization, often near borders, and, second, because political borders were often drawn arbitrarily, cutting through ancestral territories. This is a common feature for Amazonian indigenous language communities, for instance (Queixalos and Renault-Lescure 2000), who may be split across several countries.

Another major trait of endangered language communities is their mobility, through migration and urbanization within a country as well as through transnational migrations, both as a result of economic hardship and persecution and wars (Harbert, Chapter 20). The phenomenon of rural exodus toward urban centres generally involves regrouping of the newly urbanized population, with some contact maintained with the home base and speakers left at home. This is a common situation for African and Native American communities. Sometimes the majority of an endangered language population can actually have become urbanized. Some home villages are practically drained of their workforce and a large proportion of the population (re)forms a new community in some faraway country. There are even cases where the language survives better in such diaspora communities than back home (as a result of increased wealth, changed attitudes and/or ideologies, and the influence of the attitudes and ideologies of the surrounding communities). Today new technologies, which permit rapid communication with the home base, also change the conditions of use of the language while facilitating language maintenance at a distance (see Holton, Chapter 19, and Moriarty, Chapter 22).

Endangered language communities thus take many shapes and can be found in many different configurations. They are not always small communities isolated in the jungle as much media coverage tends to project. When not in well-defined territories, they can be hard to locate and hard to reach. In the case of urbanization, they may be hard to identify.

3.3.2   Endangered language(s) and 'communities' of speakers

The two concepts of LANGUAGE COMMUNITIES and SPEECH COMMUNITIES will be reviewed first in order to show how endangered language communities are found at their intersection.

3.3.2.1   Language communities

These consist of communities of speakers of the 'same' language (leaving aside the complexities of the concept of 'language' itself; see Spolsky, Chapter 8). The language communities of the largest languages of the world (see the list of major languages in Austin 2008a), are languages with a high level of recognition, through extensive processes of standardization, with written norms that serve as common reference. These languages are usually taught and reinforced through formal education. At the opposite end of the continuum, endangered languages are, in essence, minority languages, many of which are not yet identified as languages, may have no name, no written tradition, and no standardization.

3.3.2.2   Speech communities

In contrast, speech communities are sociolinguistic entities rather than purely linguistic ones (see also Michael, Chapter 7). It is not necessary that all the members of a speech community speak the same way, or even have the same language. As a matter of fact, monolingual communities are more the exception than the rule around the world. Speech communities are communities of speakers in regular contact, who follow more or less established rules of communication dictating which language to speak to whom, when and where. Speech communities are commonly multilingual communities with complex language-contact situations, with well-established diglossic dynamics, and extensive practices of code switching (see O'Shannessy, Chapter 5). This contradicts the dominant ideology in many nation states of the righteousness, validity and normality of single-language speech communities.

Speech communities can be found at all levels of social organization. Nuclear as well as extended families constitute speech communities. Immigrant families that have settled in Europe participate in multilingual speech communities. Market-places in multilingual towns are speech communities too, and can be the setting for elaborate multilingual transactions. A nation, with its official language(s), and its laws on language(s) of education and public affairs is, at another level, a speech community.

3.3.2.3 'Communities' in the context of endangered languages

Both the above notions are challenged in endangered language situations so that endangered language communities must be envisaged as a combination of both. On the one hand, if the notion of 'language' is a matter of controversy, even for larger languages, it is a particularly complex issue with endangered languages in terms of language as an autonomous entity, clearly bounded and defined. Linguists may often have difficulties establishing the boundaries of an endangered language, due to lack of description of these languages and the absence of the kind of social consensus that writing traditions and accompanying standardization processes provide. Speakers themselves may have even more difficulty in identifying such languages as 'languages' for any number of reasons. In the first place, they might not even see them as 'real' languages, but think of them rather as 'jargon', 'lenguas', 'patois', 'slang' without grammar; and, even if they think of it as 'their' language, they are in general more conscious of local differences than of commonalities they share with neighbouring dialects of the same language (which accordingly may be considered unintelligible or completely separate from the local tongue). This means that, if there is a sense of community, it is more likely to remain at a local level of dialect community, rather than encompass a larger and more abstract level of language community.

The great variety of types of speakers (see section 3.2) also makes it more difficult to establish what endangered language communities are. The issue here lies in where to draw the boundaries of the community, in the sense of which types of speakers are included or not, and whether there is a consensus about who belongs and who does not belong to the language community (Dorian 1982). This consensus can be based on linguistic competence, or on ethnic and cultural identity without much trace of actual linguistic competence. Sometimes there is no such consensus; for example, when (older) fluent speakers do not consider partially competent speakers (semi-speakers, terminal speakers, rememberers) as real speakers, and may or may not consider them full members of the language community, while the latter may include themselves and their peers.

Another reason for difficulty in establishing the boundaries of an endangered language community is linked to processes of self-categorization. As we have seen, some speakers may hide their competence and refuse to be considered members of the community of speakers. Others, on the other hand, might think of themselves as speakers in spite of having limited competence: either in good faith or in order to enjoy the advantages which might be attached to speaker status, especially among 'last speakers'. Large and vital language communities might also have problems of defining boundaries, but this issue of boundary assignment constitutes one of the major challenges in identifying endangered language communities. The difficulty increases of course as the level of endangerment rises.

Endangered language communities are, by definition, multilingual speech communities, since language endangerment happens mostly through shift to a language of wider communication. In the speech community within which an endangered language is embedded, the use of the endangered language is constantly diminishing to the point of not being heard anymore, and may be hard to detect.

Beyond the reduction of numbers of speakers, even those speakers who might use the endangered language may not do so any more, either in public or in private, for any number of reasons. Social networks of endangered language users inexorably dissolve into micro-networks, creating an atomized community, to the point of losing a sense of community, with last speakers not uncommonly finding themselves in total isolation.

Communities identifying with endangered languages share an ancestral or heritage language and include marginal or non-speakers. An endangered language community thus includes all the different kinds of speakers who identify with that language, from last speakers to their family members, to supporters of revitalization projects who are not necessarily learners of the language but participate in cultural activities. The notion of ANCESTRAL LANGUAGE COMMUNITY is particularly important in the case of revitalization efforts for very endangered languages, as is the case with many North American communities of native peoples reclaiming their cultures and languages today (Hinton and Hale 2001, Hinton, Chapter 15).

3.3.3 Consciousness of endangerment and attitudes toward endangerment

The sense of the existence of an endangered language community depends crucially on the local level of consciousness of language endangerment, and of local attitudes toward this situation. Consciousness and attitudes may vary greatly from one community to another, and may also change drastically over time, so that both factors must be assessed independently for each community and at each step of a project.

The general level of consciousness within endangered language communities has been rising in the last two decades in most regions of the world. It has come in some cases from communities themselves demanding recognition of their identity and rights, while in other cases it can be a response to external events that confront a community with loss of an ancestral language.[10]

Discussions about safeguarding the world's biocultural diversity, international declarations of human linguistic rights, and worldwide declarations by the UN and UNESCO on INTANGIBLE CULTURAL HERITAGE have all increased the general awareness of the phenomenon of language endangerment. Today, endangered language communities can be found at all points on a continuum from lack of awareness or interest and indifference to linguists, to emerging awareness and corresponding openness to outside linguists, to the extreme of a militant stand with respect to the situation of endangerment and demands to linguists and politicians.

Today, one should expect constant change within endangered language communities. This requires fieldworkers to be flexible, and attentive to what the changes mean in terms of possibilities and conditions for any project on the language. In case of initially uninterested communities, it is not uncommon that the mere presence of the linguist might raise the level of consciousness and influence attitudes. In the case of hostile or reluctant communities, one may be well advised to wait and opt to work with a more welcoming community (sometimes simply a matter of going from one village to another) and anticipate that a certain domino effect may affect attitudes. Watching what happens in other communities, and observing the effect of the presence of a linguist working on the endangered language, may in time melt reluctance.

This raises the important issue that time is of the essence in work on endangered languages. But time pressure is not so much born of urgency from outside, as much as the time needed for endangered language communities to become aware of what losing their language may mean to them, and arrive at the point of wanting to do something about it themselves, which is perhaps best measured in terms of decades in most situations.[11]

3.4   Discussion

This section raises a number of issues about the proposed speaker typology (3.4.1), and about the impact of such a typology on the task of assessing the level of vitality of a language (3.4.2). Another line of unavoidable discussion considers the kind of terminology linguists have been using when talking about endangered languages and their speakers (3.4.3). This, in turn, raises the question of a new approach to work on endangered languages, as a NEW LINGUISTICS paradigm acknowledges the role of endangered language activists (3.4.4). In such an undertaking, the human factor is to be taken as seriously as technological and linguistic aspects. In the field, everything rests on relations between endangered language speakers, members of communities (whether speakers or not), and linguists, who are still mostly outsiders, but will hopefully in the future come more and more from the communities themselves (3.4.5).

3.4.1   The proposed typology of speakers

The proposed typology is a WORKING TYPOLOGY, in the sense that one should not pigeonhole speakers simply for the sake of it. In the first place, this would not make much sense; also, one might suspect that it could never be done considering the infinite variety of situations and their fluidity. This typology is a means to an end, that of helping sensitize anyone intending to work on endangered languages to the great diversity of speakers, by proposing ways to observe, analyse and talk about it.

The typological model espoused has several characteristics. First of all, it is multidimensional (see 3.2.2–3.2.4)[12]. It was argued earlier that such a typology is useful for assessing which speakers are likely to engage, or not, in work on the language, be it for documentation, description or revitalization. It clearly takes time to identify endangered language speakers, although having the typology in mind should help researchers to recognize more readily the kinds of speakers. Finally, it was emphasized how important it is to take into consideration the fact that endangered language field situations are in constant flux, and that any assessment of the number and types of speakers will need regular updating.

Lastly, we should warn that one of the reasons the typology will remain somewhat fluid is that views of what makes 'good speakers' are not the same on the part of linguists (who rely on linguistic traits such as ability to provide complete paradigms of data) and of speakers who pay more attention to sociolinguistic traits such as loyalty towards the language (and so might reject loanwords from contact languages).[13]

3.4.2   Evaluating language vitality

One of the points of the typology of endangered language speakers presented here is to demonstrate how it is practically impossible to count endangered language speakers. The difficulties include locating and identifying speakers in the first place, then evaluating their competence, which is also not so readily done, and then deciding, according to the final objective of the census, on the threshold of language competence to be considered in order to decide who to count in.

One context in which the issue of counting speakers arises is in the exercise of evaluating the level of vitality of a given language, such as through the UNESCO questionnaire (UNESCO 2010; see Grenoble,

Chapter 2). It should be clear from the present discussion that, in most cases, the best figures will be only estimates, and that better estimates can only be reached after much time in the field, through long-standing working relations with members of the community.

Clearly, the only way to improve reporting on endangered languages will be to confront head-on the issues of the great variety of speakers and the complexity of the notion of endangered language communities.

3.4.3 A pervasive terminological issue

One striking feature of all the discussions on endangered languages is the nature of the terminology used. The terms first established in the literature are all oriented toward a clinical diagnosis of loss, limitation and deviance, with a touch of doom. For instance one reads about 'language death' (e.g. Crystal 2000), and about 'dying' or 'moribund' languages.

The same terminology issue features prominently in existing proposals for typologies of endangered language speakers. Some speakers have been labelled 'weak' or 'imperfect', for instance, and the category of so-called 'terminal' speakers has even been subdivided into 'pre-terminal', 'better terminal' and 'worse terminal'. As for the emblematic 'semi-speakers' category, it is often taken so literally by non-specialists that it seems to evoke incompetent speakers, in spite of the fact that the category explicitly includes fluent speakers of a certain type.

Another terminological issue involves the traditional term 'informant', which was used in fieldwork textbooks until recently to describe speakers with whom linguists work to document and/or describe an endangered language. This term has also been subject to discussion in recent times, although no agreed-upon term has emerged: one finds in the literature alternative terms such as CONSULTANT or LANGUAGE TEACHER, for instance (Newman and Ratliff 2001a).

Some might be tempted to dismiss this terminology issue as one of political correctness, pertaining to the ivory tower of academia. But the issue needs to be dealt with in the real world. What is at stake is the nature of the relationship of outsiders, such as academic linguists, with language activists inside endangered-language communities (see section 3.4.4).

As suggested by members of many indigenous communities from the Americas, there is another way to look at the issue of language endangerment: to consider the miracle of the survival of so many languages, in spite of fierce adversity over the centuries and active attempts to destroy the peoples, their cultures and their languages.[14] So rather than focus on loss, the exercise might be to focus on survival and resistance, and acknowledge those that have safeguarded the languages, in whatever form, up until today. But whatever change in terminology might achieve this recognition, it might be advisable to hear what the people involved have to say, as increasingly members of endangered language communities are becoming engaged in efforts to document and revitalize their languages.

3.4.4 Endangered language communities and the 'new linguistics' paradigm

The relationship between linguists and speakers and communities has been considered in terms of power relations between the researcher and the researched, as individuals or as communities (Cameron *et al.* 1993a, Craig 1993, Grinevald 1997). Cameron originally suggested that over the second half of the twentieth century the way fieldwork was conducted followed an evolution through various stages. The traditional method of fieldwork ON the language had evolved by the 1970s to a more activist stand on fieldwork FOR the speakers and their communities, then developed into a collaborative framework of fieldwork WITH speakers, typical of the empowerment and action-research approach of the 1990s. This concept of an evolving fieldwork framework was applied to fieldwork on endangered languages by Craig (1993) and Grinevald (1997), and a final step in the empowerment process was added, at the request of interested parties, with the notion of work BY the speakers themselves (Grinevald 2002, 2007; echoed in Rice 2006).

Fieldwork frameworks have evolved yet further, so that in the twenty-first century, the dominant paradigm for work on endangered languages is conceived in terms of discourse about CAPACITY BUILDING, matching discourse on international policy developed by the United Nations or UNESCO, which is centred around the notion of GOOD PRACTICE. Florey (2008) suggests the term NEW LINGUISTICS for this more participatory and politicized approach to work on endangered languages. Its main characteristic is to put language activism in a central position, and to consider how external language activists (generally academic linguists) will support internal language activists (members of the endangered language community, of any type). As expected, this approach (whether termed empowerment or new linguistics) has a profound impact on how to conceive ethics, methods and practices in the field (Craig 1992a; Grinevald 2002, 2007; Dobrin and Berson, Chapter 10).

More and more often, fieldwork on endangered languages can no longer be conceived of as the enterprise of lone academics working with individual speakers.[15] This means that whether or not one wants to think of 'the community', and whether or not one feels inclined to deal with it, 'the community' is likely to feel that it has a stake in whatever the linguists do, whatever its link to the endangered language actually is. Indigenous communities all over the world are becoming aware of their internationally recognized rights over intellectual property, their control over strategies, and project planning in accordance with their aspirations and needs (see Bowern, Chapter 23). The extent of this pressure varies across regions of the world, but fieldworkers in Australia and North and South America have certainly had to embrace it.[16]

3.4.5 The human factor

Whether talking about individual speakers or the communities to which they feel they belong, this chapter has sought to emphasize human factors in the enterprise of work on endangered languages.

Regarding speakers, the most important issue is to work with the positive energies that exist, to be careful about undercurrents of linguistic insecurity, and not to overlook speakers who may at first not seem to have much to offer. As far as communities are concerned, one has to bear in mind that, by definition, they have often been traumatized into abandoning their language. They are all, to some extent, marginalized, and are often, as well expressed by Bowern (2008: 165), 'exhausted communities'. This means that it is wise not to plan overambitious projects that would put more stress on their limited resources and capacities, and prevent them from becoming empowered as full participants in the projects. Capacity building is of the essence, but it is a slow process that must be appropriately paced.

Linguists working on endangered languages often find themselves in challenging field situations that their academic training has done little to prepare them for. These situations require stamina, commitment bordering on stubbornness, and infinite inventiveness and flexibility. But they are also, for sure, a unique opportunity to participate in safeguarding the threatened biocultural and linguistic diversity of this world, and to find a real purpose for our hard-earned linguistic competences that make us valuable partners in describing, documenting and revitalizing the endangered languages of the world.

Notes

1 This evaluation of competence in endangered languages is problematic because of a lack of description and standards, and can only be determined following ample time in the field and by developing long-standing relationships with speakers.

2 This section has benefitted from extensive exchanges with Nancy Dorian. A much more detailed and updated discussion of the complex issue of accurately distinguishing between speakers, and of the differences between linguists' assessments of endangered language speakers and the speakers' own assessments is found in Dorian 2009.

3 This type of speaker was first identified through fieldwork on Francoprovençal in France (Bert 2001). They were the wives of self-proclaimed speakers who would stand in the back of kitchens watching their husbands being interviewed and would occasionally correct or complete the answers of their husband, while insisting that they did not know the language.

4 A particular instance of a last speaker was Ishi, the last survivor of the Yahi of Northern California described by Kroeber (1961). At the time he was encountered by white settlers, he was not particularly old, spoke Yana fluently, and had no living kin who also spoke the language. He is a striking example of how a language can die with its last perfectly fluent speaker (and, in his case, highly cultured individual).

5 The process of identifying last speakers of languages has probably been exacerbated in recent years under pressure from the media, looking for stories to attract public attention to the phenomenon of language death.

6 There is another special case of positive dynamics worth mentioning: that of research linguists becoming (very) good speakers of the language they are working on, and possibly becoming a so-called 'last speaker'. The late Ken Hale, who famously learned to speak the languages he worked on as a linguist with remarkable and rapidly acquired fluency, may have been considered such for a number of the Australian Aboriginal languages he carried out research on, such as Lardil from northern Queensland.

7 There are striking cases such as the late Harry Buchanan who is reported by Eades 1979 to have continued to speak the Gumbay-nggir language to his dog, in the absence of any other human interlocutors.

8 Although some very good speakers may refuse to work with linguists, or to teach their language to anyone else.

9 It is common in land claims that the use of a particular language is one of the parameters for the recognition of the boundaries of a territory and traditional associations of the claimants with it. There are numerous instances in Australia, North America and Latin America in which the help of linguists in studying TOPONYMS has been welcomed as a useful contribution in such legal disputes.

10 This was the case with the Rama community in Nicaragua that realized the significance of the loss of its otherwise quite despised ancestral language in the context of new autonomy laws giving linguistic rights to all ethnic communities (Craig 1992a, Grinevald 2007).

11 See for instance the case of the Rama language project in Grinevald (2007).

12 Increasingly important in works on language revitalization is the issue of ideology (Kroskrity 2009; Spolsky, Chapter 8).

13 Thanks to Dorian (p.c. and 2009) for pointing out the irreducibility of the typology to simple categories of speakers because of this situation.

14 See e.g. Hinton (2004) on Californian Indian demands, and England (1998) and Grinevald (2002) on the demands of the Mayas of Guatemala.

15 This evolution has been clear during the careers of both co-authors, who carried out traditional fieldwork on a language at the time of their thesis work (the 1970s in Guatemala for Craig, the 1990s in France for Bert), but who are both now involved in projects focused on revitalization within the 'new linguistics' paradigm (see Grinevald 2007, Bert *et al.* 2009) in response to local demands.

16 See Grinevald 2007 on differences between doing fieldwork on endangered languages in America (or Australia) versus Africa (or India).

4

A survey of language endangerment

David Bradley

4.1 Overview

This chapter outlines the state of endangerment across the world's languages, based on two recent comprehensive surveys (Brenzinger 2007a, Moseley 2007). It also draws on material from Moseley 2009, and selectively from three editions of the *Ethnologue* (Gordon 2005, Grimes 1992, Lewis 2009) to illustrate the pitfalls of such broad surveys.

Some widely used scales for endangerment are briefly discussed, including the current UNESCO standard, based on Wurm (1996, 2001) but using new terms. The UNESCO standard is used in all following discussion. Tables showing proportions of languages endangered to various degrees are presented, worldwide and in more detail by country for one area of the world where available data is more reliable, namely mainland South-East Asia.

Various widespread issues are outlined using examples from the situation in China, Burma/Myanmar and Thailand, based on original language survey data, to show the limitations of wide-scale surveys and the need for more finely grained survey work using a consistent methodology. These are drawn from my own field experience, showing in more detail the endangerment situation in those three areas and the complexity which a single classification of the level of endangerment for each language may hide. In Thailand, detailed surveys have been undertaken and most endangered languages have already been documented to some extent. In China, national policy and political and practical constraints have held back the recognition of the real linguistic diversity and the degree of language endangerment, and there are many areas in which the true situation is not yet fully known, let alone documented. In

I am pleased to acknowledge the funding support of the Australian Research Council (DP0772046) and of UNESCO.

Burma/Myanmar, non-linguistic issues have made fieldwork extremely problematic. China and Burma/Myanmar are not unique; there are other parts of the world where the full range of human linguistic diversity is not yet documented.

In conclusion, general strategies and procedures for surveying language endangerment are discussed.

4.2   Scales of endangerment

The terminology on degrees of endangerment is extremely diverse, and often inconsistent, even within the usage of one author (see Grenoble, Chapter 2). Furthermore, judgements about level of endangerment differ widely between authors, even in collective studies such as Brenzinger (2007a) where a specific scale was mandated. The maximum system is Fishman (1991: 87–109) which refers to eight numbered stages on his Graded Intergenerational Disruption Scale (GIDS). The most widely used scale is outlined in Wurm (1996), and has five degrees of endangerment: potentially endangered, endangered, severely endangered, moribund and extinct. Krauss (2007) provides a schema with seven points: A+ (safe), A (stable), A– (unstable/eroded), B (definitively endangered), C (severely endangered), D (critically endangered), and E (extinct). The UNESCO standard implemented in Moseley (2009) is the Wurm five-point scale with a new term Unsafe referring to languages which have some child speakers (equivalent to A– or unstable/eroded in the Krauss model and to potentially endangered in the Wurm model), followed by: definitively endangered, mostly used by the parental generation and up; severely endangered, mostly used by the grandparental generation and up; critically endangered (equivalent to D or critically endangered in the Krauss model and moribund in the Wurm model), mostly used by very few speakers of the great-grandparent generation; and extinct. For more discussion, see Chapter 2 by Grenoble in this volume.

A similar well-known problem is the definition of language and dialect. This issue is becoming acute, with the greatly increased number of languages recognized in the international codes for languages (ISO 639–3) as implemented in Lewis (2009), and the development of community interest in language status and language endangerment worldwide.

4.3   Language endangerment around the world

Table 4.1 summarizes data from Brenzinger (2007a) and Moseley (2007). Unfortunately, the nature of the *Ethnologue*, with its extremely numerous anonymous entry authors and lack of consistency of content and terminology, makes it impossible to extract comparable data from that source.

Table 4.1. *Degrees of endangerment by continent*

	Unsafe	Definitively endangered	Severely endangered	Critically endangered	Extinct
North America	14/55	5/47	11/44	32/40	10/124
Latin America	82/171	11/164	46/140	130/53	36/67
Eurasia	45/-	56/93	63/43	13/28	-/10
Middle East	15/-	0/3	0/3	0/2	1/0
S Asia	-/53	-/150	-/82	-/28	-/1
E/SE Asia	23/36	63/82	40/30	19/13	-/10
Africa	43/1	131/88	14/23	40/29	41/23
Australia	-/16	-/26	-/30	-/48	-/166
Oceania	128/121	110/106	44/40	43/44	1/55
Total	**350/453**	**376/758**	**218/435**	**277/285**	**89/456**

The numbers to the left of the slash are from chapters in Brenzinger (2007a), and those to the right of the slash are from chapters in Moseley (2007). Dashes indicate absence of data, not zero. Eurasia includes Europe plus the nations of the former USSR. Oceania includes insular South-East Asia, Papua New Guinea and the islands of the Pacific. These totals do not include pidgins which became endangered rather than becoming creolized; they are listed for some areas, but not all.

As can be seen, the overall total in Moseley (2007) is 1,931 languages endangered to some degree and 456 extinct languages. Clearly, different authors have followed different strategies; two authors in Brenzinger (2007a) have not listed endangered languages at all, and extinct languages are much more extensively listed in Moseley (2007) than in Brenzinger (2007a). Conversely, some contributors to Moseley (2007) chose not to include potentially endangered or unsafe languages; e.g. the Mvanip entry by Dimmendaal and Voeltz (2007: 622) states that it is one example of a potentially endangered language, but that others are not listed; Moseley's (2007) Middle East and Eurasia chapters have a similar lacuna. As can be seen, these figures are so inconsistent as to be almost meaningless, especially given the gaps of coverage in Brenzinger (2007). This is despite the fact that in some cases the same scholar contributed all or part of both sets of data. Moseley (2009) has a larger list with similar problems of consistency.

What these figures do show is that language endangerment is a major issue in every part of the world, and that it is not too late to do something about it. It is also important to recognize that diaspora or migrant communities also have language rights, even if their language is not endangered in the country of origin. Languages displaced by long-distance migration as an outcome of colonialism or more recent events are not usually listed as endangered if they are not endangered in some community location. This is not always the traditional territory; e.g. there are some languages of Eastern Indonesia which have more speakers in the Netherlands than in Indonesia.

Table 4.2. *Degrees of endangerment by countries, mainland South-East Asia*

	Unsafe	Definitively endangered	Severely endangered	Critically endangered	Extinct
Burma/Myanmar	1/2	4/8	4/5	5/0	0/4
Thailand	0/0	10/8	9/7	3/5	0/1
Laos	4/3	21/25	5/2	0/1	0/0
Vietnam	6/6	10/17	7/3	0/3	0/0
Cambodia	1/1	1/3	4/4	1/0	0/0
West Malaysia	0/1	4/7	10/4	0/1	0/1

As in Table 1, the numbers separated by slashes are from Bradley 2007a and 2009. Bradley (2007b) is essentially the same as Bradley (2007a); both were compiled in 2000. In some cases, dialects and languages are not treated exactly the same in both sources; for example, in Bradley (2007a: 289, 296) Bisu in Thailand, Hpyin in Burma/Myanmar and Laopin in China are separately listed, but work since 2000 has shown that these are in fact varieties of one language, Bisu. For a more detailed summary and discussion, see Bradley (2007d).

4.3.1 Language endangerment in mainland South-East Asia

In some areas, available overview data is both more comprehensive and has been collected using a more consistent methodology. Table 4.2 summarizes information in Bradley (2007a, 2009) on language endangerment in the nations of mainland South-East Asia. Where a language is endangered in more than one country, it will of course appear listed in every country where it is endangered, even if there is some location where it is not endangered; thus the totals in Table 4.2 are not directly comparable to those in Table 4.1. Also, the same language may be shown as endangered to a different degree in different countries in Table 4.2, whereas in Table 4.1 each language is listed only once according to the minimum degree of endangerment anywhere it is spoken. In such a survey, one may also be much more confident that the scale of degrees of endangerment has been applied consistently to all languages within the area.

The material in Table 4.2 shows the accumulation of knowledge possible if one researcher maintains an overview in an area. It also indicates that many languages are proceeding from one stage of endangerment to the next; five languages formerly listed as critically endangered have become extinct in this area fairly recently, and some other languages have moved from a lower to a higher endangerment category. Conversely, for a few languages, the level of endangerment has decreased due to community revitalization efforts, or evaluations based on new information.

All quantitative information presented in this section is extremely preliminary. Overall, Moseley (2009) is comparable to Brenzinger (2007a) and Moseley (2007) in its coverage, but more representative of the current state of our knowledge, as it was completed in December 2008. It can be consulted for an overview of current language endangerment in any area of the world.

4.4   Case studies in surveying endangerment

4.4.1   China

The listing of languages of China in the *Ethnologue* has increased gradually over its several editions, from 169 languages including 8 Chinese languages in Grimes (1992) to 236 including 13 Chinese spoken languages plus Chinese sign language in Gordon (2005) and 292 in Lewis (2009), including the same 13 Chinese languages within the Chinese macrolanguage. Two additions are due to the return of Hong Kong to China in 1997, but all the rest are the outcome of field surveys by various linguists, mainly SIL International members. This compares with recent work by Chinese linguists suggesting over 120 distinct languages among China's 55 national minorities (Shearer and Sun 2002) and of course only one Chinese majority language. Part of the difference is due to a terminological and attitudinal fact: Chinese linguists follow Chinese categories, which are broader than conventional linguistic ones and allow for very large internal differences within a *yuyan* (conventionally but inaccurately translated as 'language'; perhaps 'macro-language' as used in the *Ethnologue* would be a better translation), with no requirement for mutual intelligibility and a strong preference for historically established ethnic categories. The varieties of Chinese are termed *fangyan* (conventionally but inaccurately translated as 'dialect'), and a similar grid is applied to the languages of the national minorities by Chinese linguists. Much of the additional material in the *Ethnologue* comprises languages newly separated from previously recognized languages into additional distinct languages. Of course, not all of these added languages are endangered, and many will disagree about some of the decisions on language or dialect status. The revision work for Lewis (2009) was mainly completed during 2007. This process included the preparation of the new ISO 639–3 list of languages of the world (the full list is available on the SIL website), and the content of Lewis (2009) dates from mid-2009.

My research team has been surveying endangered and other languages in Yunnan Province in south-western China since 1984, initially for mapping purposes (see Wurm *et al.* 1987) as well as for documentation and sociolinguistic research.

In 1998, our survey (Bradley *et al.* 1999) of the Yi nationality in the region around Kunming, the capital of the province, located eight languages within this one nationality alone, four of them previously undescribed and endangered. This survey was conducted with approval from the Yunnan Province government, and carried out in cooperation with the Yunnan Academy of Social Sciences, with full participation by

Li Yongxiang, a local Yi scholar, and assistance from several other local scholars. We surveyed all the villages of the Yi nationality in five counties or districts around Kunming city, collecting demographic, historical, sociolinguistic and lexical material. Li Yongxiang later extended this survey to several surrounding counties, and one of the other local scholars has also continued to carry out similar surveys within the Hani nationality. It is also important to report back to the community in a way that is useful to them, as we have done in Bradley (2005).

Another recent survey within the Yi nationality in south-eastern Yunnan (Pelkey 2008) found 24 languages, many of them endangered, spoken by groups officially classified as Phula. In China, all Phula are officially linguistically classified as part of one *tuyu* or 'local subdialect' of the South-eastern Yi *fangyan* or 'dialect' of Yi. Four other related but quite distinct languages, Sani, Axi, Azhe and Azha, are also classified as *tuyu* of the South-eastern Yi *fangyan*. In Vietnam, the Phula are recognized as a separate ethnic group with a distinct language; only three of the languages within Phula are spoken in Vietnam. Another survey (Yang forthcoming a) among the Nisu in southern Yunnan, who are officially classified as speaking the Southern *fangyan* or 'dialect' of Yi, found four distinct languages, with a fifth endangered one recently located in western Yunnan. An ongoing survey in western Yunnan (Yang forthcoming b) has also found very substantial diversity within Lalo, which is officially classified as the Western *fangyan* or 'dialect' of Yi. Similar internal diversity is known to exist elsewhere within the Yi nationality in Yunnan Province, but has not yet been documented. All these examples are drawn from just one of China's 55 recognized national minorities – admittedly an unusually complex and diverse one (Bradley 2001a, 2001b).

Based on our various field surveys, I provided eighteen new language entries for Yunnan Province which appear in Lewis (2009); many additional new entries were provided by Pelkey and Yang who are following a similar methodology. In the main, contributions to the *Ethnologue* are restricted to SIL International members, though I am not a member. This unfortunately means that it is not fully representative of current worldwide linguistic knowledge, and will be subject to criticism for this and for its errors and inconsistencies. However, its coverage of the languages of Yunnan Province is a very substantial improvement on all previous versions.

As part of such surveys, one finds very interesting examples of the possible outcomes of contact during language shift. For example, the northern dialect of Lisu has now almost completely replaced Anung in China (for more discussion of Anung, see 4.4.2 below). However, in the meantime, the Anung system of nine male and nine female birth order names[1] has been borrowed into northern Lisu (Bradley 2008), replacing the original Lisu birth-order name system found in other dialects. It is also striking that northern Lisu female clothing is identical to that of the Anung, and quite different from Lisu female clothing elsewhere. The word for the main traditional priest in northern Lisu is also borrowed from Anung, and many other aspects of northern Lisu life resemble that of the Anung, whose language is in a different branch of the Tibeto-Burman family and thus not very closely related. According to oral history, Lisu arrived in the area about 250 years ago; perhaps these incoming Lisu were mainly men who married local Anung women, and so northern Lisu acquired various culturally important parts of Anung lexicon, including some entire semantic fields, while Anung was in the process of being replaced by Lisu.

4.4.2 Burma/Myanmar

In Burma/Myanmar, the official ethnic classification into 135 groups compares with a listing of 105 indigenous languages in Grimes (1992), 108 in Gordon (2005) and 113 in Lewis (2009); this can also be compared to the 66 languages mapped in Harlow and Bradley (1994) and 69 in Bradley (2007c). In many cases, the official classification is inaccurate and contains repeated entries for the same group under different names, or even the same group listed separately under the same name in different administrative areas. Conversely, the official government ethnic classification of some groups lumps distinct languages together; for example, it puts the Karen peoples into four ethnic groups (Karen, Kayah or Kayinni, Kayan and Pa'O), versus a classification into seventeen languages in the *Ethnologue* based on more solid linguistic criteria. This is not to say that the *Ethnologue* information is perfect; far from it. There are languages from nearby countries not spoken in Burma/Myanmar which have been carried through from edition to edition, like Nor(r)a (an extinct Tai language formerly spoken in north-eastern India and related to Khamyang there), Laopang (a variety of Phunoi spoken only in Laos) and Sansu (another name for Hlersu, a language spoken only in China). There are many gaps, such as Bisu and Laomian (listed for China and Thailand, but also spoken in Burma/Myanmar), Ganan and Sak (included incorrectly as part of Kadu) and so on. As in other parts of the world, the *Ethnologue* for Burma/Myanmar often recognizes as separate languages speech varieties more usually viewed as dialects, notably among the Chin groups. Much more work is needed in Burma/Myanmar to clarify the actual linguistic situation.

One interesting example of social reality overcoming linguistic difference and likely to lead to endangerment in the future is the Rawang ethnic group, which has about 145,000 members in Burma/Myanmar as well as 14,000 speakers who are members of the Dulong or Nu national minorities nearby in China. This is classified as one language in most sources, though in fact it comprises a cluster of three groups of languages: (1) Dulong, Zørwang[2] and Dvru; (2) Rawang proper including

Mvtwang and Dvngsar, and (3) Longmi with numerous local subvarieties. Most of these names are derived from river names, as are many of the designations for dialects within them. For further details and a map, see Bradley (2007c).

Rawang is the autonym of one cluster of languages, and of a large clan who speak the Mvtwang variety and formerly lived along the Mvt River. Since the 1950s, the name Rawang is also used in a wider sense for all six languages in the three clusters, and has now replaced the former exonym Nung in Burma/Myanmar. The Mvtwang variety of Rawang is used as a lingua franca and is the vehicle for literacy which has developed along with conversion to Christianity. Many Rawang now live mingled together around Putao town in far northern Burma/Myanmar, and many younger Rawang people there, from whichever group, speak only Mvtwang. As yet, none of the five other main languages within the Rawang ethnic group is endangered, but all apart from the Mvtwang variety of Rawang are likely to become endangered in the future.

Sometimes, the separate Anung group, with a further 4,000-odd speakers, is also included as part of Rawang. However, this is a further distinct but closely related language with its own written form which is now severely endangered in Burma/Myanmar and critically endangered in China, where it is known as Anong. Anung is being replaced by distantly related Lisu; there are only about 40 Anung speakers (few of whom are monolingual) left in China among about 7,300 Anung who are members of the Nu national minority[3]. There are also about 6,000 of 10,000 ethnic Anung in Burma/Myanmar who speak only Lisu; thus, overall, fewer than a quarter of the ethnic Anung can speak their traditional language.

At present, large-scale linguistic surveys inside Burma/Myanmar can only be conducted by local researchers. Various surveys have been undertaken, but the results are not widely disseminated so that these researchers can continue this work within the restrictions of the current political situation. In addition, such work can be carried out in neighbouring countries with individual members of groups from Burma/Myanmar, as we have been doing.

4.4.3 Thailand

Thailand provides a model of the outcome of relatively comprehensive and successful linguistic surveying, starting with Gainey and Thongkum (1977a, 1977b) and more recently Premsrirat *et al.* (2000). Thai linguists have also been extremely active in the documentation process, and in language-maintenance efforts in many communities.

The *Ethnologue* listing for Thailand in Grimes (1992) gives 82 languages including three sign languages, four foreign languages and two languages (Mang and Phunoi) spoken in nearby countries but not in Thailand.

Gordon (2005) lists 74 languages including three sign languages, one foreign language, and one language (Phunoi) spoken in Laos but not in Thailand. Quite a few of these languages are spoken by small populations of recent arrivals from Burma/Myanmar. Some others are the outcome of the former Thai practice of bringing entire villages of captured populations from what are now neighbouring countries, including Cambodia, Laos, Burma/Myanmar and even some from Vietnam and China, while many others are long-standing indigenous groups.

Some endangered languages in Thailand were initially located as a result of non-linguistic surveys. For example, the Gong[4] were first identified by a British surveyor in the 1920s who was looking for a railroad route between Thailand and Burma/Myanmar, and reported in Kerr 1927. This language shows a typical pattern of endangerment, in which the language is at different stages in different places, and has undergone extensive and apparently very rapid dialect diversification. The most accessible Gong village, Ban Lawa near Sangkhlaburi along the main branch of the Kwai River in Kanchanaburi Province of western Thailand, had many fluent speakers when the anthropologist Ted Stern passed through in the early 1960s on his way to surrounding Karen villages, but the speakers were already shifting to Karen then. At the time of my first survey in 1977, there were only a few old speakers (who had all died by the late 1980s), and ten years later, the village was displaced by a dam. Other former villages closer to Kanchanaburi town reported by Kerr in the 1920s were already completely assimilated, speaking and identifying themselves as Thai, by 1978. A few old rememberers were found along the other branch of the Kwai River in Na Suan village; this village has also since been displaced by another dam, and the rememberers have died. In another village further up this branch of the river, one old lady was found in 1982 who could remember one sentence. The Gong people across a watershed at Kok Chiang village in nearby Suphanburi Province claim to have come from there. The last Gong headman of Kok Chiang, who died in 1976, is reported to have said that his father was headman in the village of that old lady. The one other village where Gong is still spoken, Khok Khwaay just to the north of Kok Chiang in Uthai Thani Province, has a distinctive dialect which shows some similarities to the now-extinct Na Suan Gong dialect. Thus the two surviving dialects of Gong are both spoken outside traditional Gong territory in fairly remote locations where the arrival of the Gong is rather recent (for further details see Bradley 1989). Since then, language revitalization has been undertaken in Kok Chiang in cooperation with Mahidol University, but unfortunately the language continues to be severely endangered, perhaps partly because the community has made such remarkable social progress, with an excellent road, electricity, an irrigation system, its own primary school and Buddhist temple, and large numbers of Thai people moving in. During the time it has been under survey, there have been major changes in the phonology of Kok Chiang Gong, such as the loss of medial *l* clusters. The data on Gong also shows the need to survey repeatedly to trace the processes involved in language endangerment, and to work with any available speakers, semi-speakers or rememberers in every location, in order to document not just one speech variety, but as much as possible of the range of speech forms within a group and the remarkably rapid processes of variation and change in an endangered language (see Palosaari and Campbell, Chapter 6). It also gives an example in which the same language is simultaneously extinct, critically endangered and severely endangered in different places.

4.5   Conclusion: surveying endangerment

We are not yet in a position to know the full degree of language endangerment around the world, as in some areas much more work remains to be done. As we have seen, nearly all current statistics and lists must be viewed with extreme scepticism.

Another major issue is the categorization of dialects and languages. Some prefer to recognize more languages, others prefer to view some of these as dialects of another language, and thus would not consider a language to be endangered as long as one of its dialects is not endangered. We also need to respect the views of communities about their status, which may be based in part on linguistic factors and in part on other social factors. This may require the recognition of a larger or smaller number of distinct linguistic entities than some linguists might feel appropriate.

A survey should ideally be done by a small team including local scholars who can gain expertise through participation, and should cover an area comprehensively, with information on every location where each language is spoken. Surveys should be conducted in cooperation with local authorities, who may be a valuable source of many kinds of essential historical, demographic, geographical, sociolinguistic or other information, and with the local communities. A survey requires a consistent design, collecting locally appropriate lexicon based on sound phonological analysis, text material for morphosyntactic analysis and a well-designed sociolinguistic questionnaire. Ideally, each team should concentrate on all the related languages in an area, and have solid background knowledge about them, or there should be subteams with expertise on each group of related languages.

There are several standard survey questionnaires available, but none of them in sufficient sociolinguistic detail, and all are likely to yield highly inconsistent data when used by different kinds of survey collectors: community leaders, local authorities, local or outsider linguists of various persuasions, anthropologists, development workers and so on. One is the two-page survey questionnaire on which the *Ethnologue* and ISO 639–3 listing are based (Lewis 2009). Others include UNESCO questionnaires such as the nine-page UNESCO Etxea World Languages Report survey of 1997 (reprinted in Marti *et al.* 2005: 284–8) and the UNESCO Linguistic Vitality and Diversity survey (UNESCO 2008). For an example of the extreme degree of inconsistency within the raw data derived from a survey using the UNESCO Etxea questionnaire, see Toba *et al.* (2002), with an overall summary published later (Toba *et al.* 2005) reprocessing the raw data.

The sociolinguistic side of surveying needs to investigate many kinds of information sometimes neglected in documentary studies. These can be divided into four main subcategories:

1. **background** – personal and family history including surnames or clan names, genealogies and other family records, local history and migrations, current and past demographic information, geographical distribution, individual mobility, marriage patterns and related sociohistorical information;
2. **names** – all possible autonyms and names for other nearby groups, as well as exonyms used by others to refer to the group and any names for parts of the group, as well as any available information on the meanings and sources of these names, including folk etymologies;
3. **vitality** – attitudes about languages, domains of language use, age distribution of speakers and proportion of children who are speakers, degree of fluency within the community and attitudes to semi-speaker speech, degree of contact and multilingualism, and other factors;
4. **perceptual dialectology** – folk categories, perceptions about who elsewhere speaks the same, nearly the same, or a recognizably similar speech variety, speaker perceptions about vitality factors such as fluency among different age groups or in different locations, and folk dialect maps.

Researchers need to collect information both from local leaders and from other group members in a local setting. Leaders may be political, religious or other traditional experts, or members of a group of knowledgeable elders. Political leaders include village headmen, village-cluster leaders and so on; it is desirable and often necessary to start a survey through these authority figures and to carry out the rest of the survey with their consent and assistance. In a more in-depth survey, various kinds of traditional experts can be consulted to draw on other relevant kinds of special expertise, such as those with knowledge of traditional religion, medicine, agricultural skills, craft skills such as blacksmithing, silversmithing, basket making and so on. It is also important to find and record those who have knowledge of traditional texts of various types: rituals, stories, proverbs, historical narratives and so on.

Surveys should ideally take into account models for investigating the degree of linguistic differences, such as intelligibility testing, quantitative and other techniques for investigating the degree of genetic linguistic relationships, such as cladistics (Huson 1998) applied to lexical, phonological and morphosyntactic differences, measures of difference within cognate lexicon following Levenshtein (1966) or other models, and so on. It is also most important to be aware of and document the contact effects which are likely during the process of language shift, as further discussed by O'Shannessy (Chapter 5).

We may expect that most if not all currently unreported languages are endangered, and so the overall proportion of endangered languages among the languages of the world may be substantially higher than contemporary statistics would suggest. Of course, even the nearly 30 per cent implied by the figures in Section 1.3 above is already distressingly high.

Notes

1 Each person has a name based on their gender and order of birth; e.g. the first-born male in every family is named *Aphung* in Anung and closely related languages, and *Aphu* in northern Lisu. The first-born female is named *Anang* in Anung and *Ana* in northern Lisu, and so on. The traditional Lisu birth order names are better preserved in some other dialects; for example, the first-born male is named *Abe* in southern Lisu.

2 In the Rawang orthography, 'v' represents schwa and 'ø' represents the vowel symbolized in IPA by barred ɨ.

3 The Nu national minority is linguistically diverse; it includes some speakers of Dulong, all ethnic Anung, and speakers of two other languages related more closely to Lisu, Nusu and Rauruo.

4 The alternative name Ugong as found in the *Ethnologue* and elsewhere includes a first syllable meaning 'person', *'lu* or *u*; the language is called *Gong so*, with *so* meaning 'language'.

5

Language contact and change in endangered languages

Carmel O'Shannessy

5.1 Language contact and its outcomes

Languages and language varieties usually become endangered because their speakers are in contact with a group whose language or variety has, or is gaining, greater social, political and economic prestige in the local or wider arena. When speakers of a language begin to interact with speakers of one or more other languages, changes in the LANGUAGE ECOL- OGY of the speech community can take place. Social functions that were previously conducted in one language may now be conducted, at least partially, in another. Consequently, some degree of change in how one or more of the languages is spoken is a likely outcome. Changes may be observable in speakers' lexical choices, use of structure (phonology, phonotactics, morphology, syntax, semantics, discourse), or pragmatic conventions (the conventional ways that linguistic acts are performed). Some changes might not be observable in the speech of the first gen- eration of speakers in contact, but may be seen in that of subsequent generations.

When we consider LANGUAGE CONTACT phenomena, both social and structural factors must always be taken into account (Weinreich 1953). The underlying cause of language contact is social, in that speakers of different languages come into contact with each other, for a variety of reasons, including migration (which occurs for many reasons), trade, colonization or military occupation, and increased mobility of speakers (see Harbert, Chapter 20). Different social settings and attitudes lead to different outcomes. Some linguistic behaviours are both an outcome and a mechanism of change, depending on the social dynamics of the situation. For instance, code-switching, the use of two or more languages in one conversation, may be an outcome when it occurs often in a situ- ation of stable bilingualism, and is a mechanism when it is the means through which elements of one language come to be incorporated into another.

Social factors influencing mechanisms and outcomes include the reason for the contact, the differences in size and social prestige or dominance of the groups of speakers, the amount of social and cultural pressure groups exert on each other, and the relative INSTRUMENTAL VALUE of the languages. Instrumental value is a measure of how useful the language is for the economic and social advancement of the speaker (see also Harbert, Chapter 20). Each group's willingness to learn another language, and the level of proficiency to which they want to learn it, are important, which in turn depends at least partly on the afore-mentioned factors. Social–psychological factors include strategies of second and subsequent language learning, individual language dominance, attitudes to each language, linguistic ideology, and the extent to which speakers alter their own speech styles to align more or less with those of their interlocutors (a process called ACCOMMODATION). The notion of LANGUAGE DOMINANCE refers to two kinds of phenomena. One is the sociolinguistic situation in which a language is socially and politically dominant, and the other pertains to an individual's differential use of two or more languages. A bilingual or multilingual speaker will often use one language more frequently than another, so that language can be said to be dominant (Grosjean 2008).

I first present some outcomes of language contact, then linguistic and social–psychological mechanisms operating in contact situations. Following these, I discuss notions of how contact-induced change is perceived by speaker communities and others, and the question of whether contact-induced change is inevitable. In the final section I explain that new languages arising from contact might also be endangered and should be documented as valuable records of sociolinguistic processes.

5.1.1 Language maintenance

At a very broad level of categorization, the outcomes of language contact can be LANGUAGE MAINTENANCE, LANGUAGE SHIFT or LANGUAGE CREATION. The outcomes are all results of mechanisms commonly found in situations of language contact, but do not always lead to the extreme results of language shift or creation. Each language can potentially exert an effect on the other in patterns of structure and use.

In language maintenance situations the language continues to be spoken, but there is often some influence of one language on the other, in both structures and words. This does not necessarily lead to the loss of a language; it can still be maintained, but with some changes. Speakers of a maintained language typically borrow features from another language, and many languages contain some material which is originally from others. BORROWING is the incorporation of lexical or structural features of another language into the speakers' first language (Thomason and Kaufman 1988: 37), known also as 'recipient language agentivity' (Van Coetsem 2000). The agents of change through borrowing are either fluent bilinguals, or speakers with higher levels of proficiency in the recipient (borrowing) language than in the source language. Usually, when contact is not intense, lexical items are borrowed first and most often, and through them structural features can be borrowed, although this happens much less frequently. For example, a suffix can be borrowed along with a word on which it occurs and then be extended as a suffix on other words.

When contact is more intense, typically the case in contexts of language endangerment, structural features can spread from one language to another, so that the languages involved become more structurally similar, known as STRUCTURAL CONVERGENCE (see also Palosaari and Campbell, Chapter 6). The agents of the change are most likely bilingual or multilingual speakers dominant in the source language (Van Coetsem's (2000) 'source language agentivity'). They bring phonological and morphosyntactic features of their dominant language to their weaker language and these are then incorporated by other speakers of the recipient language. When several languages are in close contact, are in geographically neighbouring areas and structural features are transferred between languages, the resulting zone of structural convergence is known as a SPRACHBUND (Trubetskoy 1928, cited in Thomason 2001) or LINGUISTIC AREA. The languages involved might or might not be endangered. In a linguistic area, structural and lexical material can be transferred in both directions, by bilingual or multilingual speakers dominant in one language or the other, so that all languages involved are both recipient and source languages of different features (Gumperz and Wilson 1971), or material can be transferred from only some languages to the others.

Thomason and Kaufman (1988: 64–7) developed a robust hierarchy of types of borrowing as a result of different degrees of contact intensity, summarized in Table 5.1. Thomason and Kaufman (1988: 65) emphasize that social and attitudinal factors and typological distance between the languages involved can override the correlations on the scale. If the languages involved are more typologically similar, then more material can be transferred with less intense contact.

Stable bilingualism or multilingualism occurs most often when all of the languages involved have relatively large numbers of speakers and high social status in their local and wider communities. Sometimes two languages coexist in a DIGLOSSIC relationship in which the social functions of each are complementary (Blom and Gumperz 1972, Ferguson 1959). One language is used for official, governmental and church functions (so-called 'high' prestige functions, labelled H) and the other is used for personal, intimate functions (so-called 'low' prestige functions, labelled L).

Table 5.1. *Thomason and Kaufman's (1988) borrowing scale, as in Winford*
(2003: 30)

Stage	Features
1. Casual contact	Lexical borrowing only
2. Slightly more intense contact	Slight structural borrowing; conjunctions and adverbial particles
3. More intense contact	Slightly more structural borrowing; adpositions, derivations, affixes
4. Strong cultural pressure	Moderate structural borrowing (major structural features that cause relatively little typological change)
5. Very strong cultural pressure	Heavy structural borrowing (major structural features that cause significant typological disruption)

The low functions may include public but unofficial uses, such as in public meetings (Blom and Gumperz 1972). If there was previously only one language used for all functions, and then another came to be used in some of them, this situation can also be viewed as a case of partial language shift (Dimmendaal 1989, Weinreich 1953). There is an analogue for domains within a language; the incoming language might be used in some registers or genres before others, e.g. numerals are often replaced early by those of the dominant language. Documentation efforts could focus on vulnerable areas first. The functional separation of languages in a diglossic situation is an advantage for an endangered language because there will be specific functions for each of the languages in contact (Fishman 1967, 2001, 2002). When two or more languages can be used interchangeably for the same purpose, only one of them is needed. Provided that each language is used for a different set of functions, a minority language can be maintained within particular domains of use. It is common for an endangered language to be used for familial and home interactions, and a dominant language to be used for education, government, economic exchanges and administration. In many situations, the home domain is the last in which an endangered language is maintained, but in some situations of language shift traditional ceremonial purposes are the last domain in which a language is used (e.g. Mithun 1989: 244).

Bilingual and multilingual speakers often use two or more languages in one conversation, a practice called CODE-SWITCHING. A great deal of research has shown that bilinguals competent in both languages may frequently code-switch, and that code-switching is rule-governed, and is socially meaningful (e.g. Auer 1998, 2000, Bentahila and Davies 1995, Clyne 1980, 2003, Gal 1988, Grosjean 2008, Gumperz 1982; Jake and Myers-Scotton 1997, Muysken 1995, 1997, 2000, Myers-Scotton 1988, 2002a, 2002b, 2006, Myers-Scotton and Jake 2000, Pfaff 1982, Poplack 1980, Poplack and Meechan 1995). Several hypotheses have been put forward as to what triggers or facilitates a switch, and the ways in which the use of the two or more languages is grammatically constrained. Code-switching between languages can occur between sentences or clauses, called INTER-SENTENTIAL CODE-SWITCHING, or within a sentence or clause, called INTRA-SENTENTIAL CODE-SWITCHING (or CODE-MIXING by Muysken 2000). When the switching is intra-sentential it can be difficult to distinguish from borrowing, because both involve material from two or more languages in the same sentence. When individual words or morphemes from one language appear in a sentence which is otherwise in the other language, is the process borrowing or code-switching? Some researchers consider the distinction between borrowing and code-switching essential to theories of language contact (e.g. Poplack and Meechan 1995), others see the types of combination of material from each language as very closely related (e.g. Backus 2005, Myers-Scotton 1993). Single lexical items which are transferred by recipient language speakers become phonologically integrated into the recipient language, and after some time are accepted by all speakers as part of that language, and hence are generally accepted as borrowings. In contrast, a switch from lexicon and grammar of one language to that of another is widely accepted as code-switching (e.g. Muysken 2000).

Some of the reasons speakers may be motivated to code-switch include:

- indexing an element of their identity that is expressed by one language;
- expressing a nuance of meaning which is more accurately encapsulated by a word or phrase in one language;
- accommodating to an interlocutor's choice of code;
- packaging information for the listener in a certain way; or
- indicating a change in the contextualization of the interaction.

Code-switching can be the mechanism for material from one language to be transferred to another (e.g. Backus 2004, 2005). Code-switching can also be a mechanism for speakers to gradually use one language more often than the other, altering the previous balance of language complementarity, which could be a threat to the domains of use of a minority language. For this reason, sometimes speakers of an endangered language establish domains in which code-switching is discouraged (Collins 2005: 262). In contexts of heavy pressure to shift to another language (outlined below), code-switching can lead to the formation of a new language, but in situations of stable bilingualism or multilingualism usually does not. For theories of how code-switching leads to different structural outcomes see e.g. Backus (2005), Jake and Myers-Scotton (2003), McConvell (2008) and Myers-Scotton (2003).

5.1.2 Language shift

Clearly the most detrimental outcome for an endangered language is when a whole community shifts to another language; that is, members of the community stop speaking the pre-contact language habitually and mostly speak the post-contact language, which comes to be the language of the next generation. The shift may take place in only one or two generations. Thus, it is estimated that the number of people speaking Breton in France reduced by 80 per cent between 1950 and 1990, as it was no longer transmitted to children as their first language (Hornsby 2008: 129–130). But a shift may also take place over several generations.

When a group is shifting to another language, its members might not become first-language-like speakers of the language they are learning, but transfer features of their own first language to it. This situation is called SHIFT-INDUCED INTERFERENCE or SUBSTRATUM INFLUENCE (Thomason 2001, Thomason and Kaufman 1988), and differs from borrowing because the speakers performing the transfer are dominant in the source language which contains the features being transferred. This is another instance of source language agentivity (Van Coestem 2000). If the two groups integrate socially, both groups can eventually come to speak a version of the incoming language that includes differences brought about by the shifting group, as happened in the formation of Irish English (Odlin 1991, 1997). If the groups do not integrate socially, the shifting group may develop an additional variety of the incoming language (Thomason 2001, Thomason and Kaufman 1988), which may be spoken alongside an endangered language, or may gradually replace it. Examples are some varieties of English and other wide-currency languages spoken around the world which developed through migration and colonization (e.g. Aboriginal English, Indian English). Each variety is differentiated by features of the speakers' pre-existing language(s) appearing in the language to which they have shifted or which is now part of their linguistic repertoire.

When a group is shifting to another language, changes can take place in the pre-contact language through processes of LANGUAGE ATTRITION (also called LANGUAGE OBSOLESCENCE). Speakers may lose phonological distinctions in the pre-contact language that are not present in the incoming language, phonological contrasts with a low functional load may be lost (Andersen 1982: 95, Campbell and Muntzel 1989: 186), marked features (those which are less common, and less regular) may be replaced with unmarked features or else used more often than they once were, once-obligatory rules may occur optionally, or morphological and syntactic patterns may be reduced (Campbell and Muntzel 1989). The same kinds of changes take place in other language-contact situations, and also in language internal change in other contexts, but in the context of language attrition they often take place very rapidly. Not all of the changes reflect patterns in the incoming language (see Campbell and Muntzel 1989 and Palosaari and Campbell, Chapter 6, for more discussion and examples).

5.1.3 Language creation

Dramatic change in a contact situation can lead to the formation of new languages. The three main types are PIDGINS, CREOLES and BILINGUAL MIXED LANGUAGES. There are many views as to the development of each type, reflecting the diversity of social situations in which they can arise, the difficulty of interpreting sociohistorical mechanisms years after the situation occurred, the diversity of outcomes, and the many types of mechanisms involved. If the situation causing the creation of a new language occurs in the home territory of the source languages, and there are relatively few speakers of each, the source languages involved immediately become endangered and might subsequently be lost. For instance, the creation of a creole can mean that the creole is spoken in preference to the contributing languages, which are then under threat.

When speakers of several languages who do not speak each other's languages are suddenly thrust together and need to communicate (each speaker may be multilingual in several of the languages but not all speakers are multilingual in all of the languages); for example, in situations of colonial expansion, military invasion, slavery, or trade, a pidgin may develop. Researchers often posit a prototypical example of a language type, with which to compare the variety of attested cases. A PROTOTYPICAL PIDGIN (Thomason 1997: 76; Winford 2003) is autonomous, that is, not a variety of one of its source languages, and is conventionalized, that is, speakers know the rules and how to apply them, and is not a first language for any of its speakers. It is a contact language which is only used for purposes of communicating with speakers of the other languages, with whom one cannot use one's own language. Speakers might have limited desire or opportunity to learn the other languages fully. In these types of situation one of the languages (the socially dominant one, if the languages are in an unequal social relationship) becomes the source of much of the lexicon of the pidgin, although often with altered pronunciation and semantics, and is known as the LEXIFIER, or SUPERSTRATE LANGUAGE. The less socially dominant languages, often called the SUBSTRATE LANGUAGES, typically contribute grammatical rules, much of the phonology, and some of the semantics. A pidgin typically has simpler morphology than its sources, is used in fewer social domains, and does not have many of the functions of other languages. It is only used to talk about certain things in certain contexts, the topics that are the focus of the groups' immediate joint concerns. But pidgins are not only a combination of elements of their sources. They typically have some innovative grammatical features created by reanalysing and reinterpreting features of the sources. When a pidgin develops, the original languages are still being spoken, and maintain their distinctive in-group purposes, but the need for another communication code for intergroup use is a threat to them. A pidgin may cease to be used once the situation in which it developed no longer applies, or it may be learned by the next generation, expand in complexity, and be used to talk about anything. The expanded way of speaking is then the first language of its speakers, and by this point it has become a CREOLE.

Creole is the term for a contact language which develops under conditions of an immediate need for communication by speakers of many languages, in situations of extreme social disruption such as colonization, slavery or rapid migration, and becomes the first language of its speakers, displacing their prior languages. Creoles also usually have a structure in which most of the lexicon is from the socially dominant language, the lexifier, and much of the phonology, morphosyntax and semantics are from the other contributing languages, the substrates. There is debate about the extent to which creoles arise from the expansion of pidgins during transmission to the next generation (Bickerton 1984), or from second-language learning mechanisms, possibly over several generations (Chaudenson 2001; Mufwene 2001). Although creoles are most often categorized as a distinct type of language due to the sociohistorical factors in their development, their individual structural details vary greatly. Structurally creoles have less morphology than their sources (Arends *et al.* 1994, McWhorter 1998, 2005; Spears and Winford 1997). For discussions of the different situations in which pidgins and creoles arise and the mechanisms involved, see Arends and Bruyn (1994), Arends *et al.* (1995), Bickerton (1984), Holm (1988, 1989), Mühlhäusler (1986), Muysken and Smith (1986), Siegel (2000, 2003) and Spears and Winford (1997). Once a new language has become the first language of a group, the roles of the source languages change. Since a creole is developed by speakers in two or more language groups, and becomes a primary language, the languages which contributed to the creole cease to be the first languages of the creole-speaking generation. In cases of rapid creolization in which the new language develops in one generation, as happened in northern Australia (Harris 1991, 1993; Sandefur 1979), members of the generation older than those who developed the new language still speak their traditional languages, so the traditional languages can be learned from them as a second or subsequent language. Once formed, a creole language can be learned just as any language can, and can also be threatened by the rise of other languages in the area. Several creoles spoken today are endangered.

Another kind of language creation is that of BILINGUAL MIXED LANGUAGES (also called 'mixed codes' (Muysken 2007), 'split languages' (Myers-Scotton 2003, Myers-Scotton and Jake, 2000) or 'fused lects' (Auer 1999)), where bilingual speakers combine elements of two (or more) languages to create a third language. These languages are not created to enable communication with speakers of other languages, but for communication within the group that developed them. The ways in which the sources of mixed languages are combined, and the social reasons for the formation of the new languages vary (Bakker 1994, 2003, Bakker and Muysken 1994, Matras and Bakker 2003, Matras *et al.* 2007, Mous 2003, Muysken 1994, 2006). In situations of intense cultural pressure to shift, and where code-switching between languages is a typical way of speaking, a new bilingual mixed language may result from convention-alization of code-switching practices. Light Warlpiri (O'Shannessy 2005) and Gurindji-Kriol (McConvell and Meakins 2005) are bilingual mixed languages which have recently formed in this way in Australia.[1] The two new bilingual mixed languages represent partial maintenance of the endangered languages, Warlpiri and Gurindji respectively, in the face of great pressure to shift to the dominant languages, Kriol (an English-lexifier creole) and varieties of English. Structurally the verbal system in each is mostly from Kriol, and the nominal system is mostly from Warlpiri and Gurindji respectively. In addition to combining elements of the source languages, a new language can also show reinterpretations and reanalysis of elements from the source languages, leading to gram-matical elements in the new language that do not exist in either of the sources. In Light Warlpiri elements of the auxiliary systems of the source languages have been reanalysed to form a new auxiliary subparadigm (O'Shannessy 2005), as shown in example (1).[2]

(1) an   *nyuntu-wiyi*   **yu-m**   grow up   *ngula*   *ngana*
     and   2SG-before   2SG-NFUT   grow up   ANAPH   reportedly

     shop-*rla*   *mayi*   *nyamp*   nu-wan-*rla*   or   old-wan-*jangka-juku*
     shop-LOC   INTERR   DEM   new-one-LOC   or   old.one-ABL-still

     'And you, before, you grew up there they say, at the shop, did you? At the new one, or still at the old one?'

Although the endangered language is not maintained in its entirety in the mixed language, much of its lexicon and structure is retained. The newly created languages are viewed by the speakers and their com-munities as types of the traditional languages. Light Warlpiri appears to be the result of multiple motivations. It represents resistance to shift away from Warlpiri, and also establishment of a local identity within the wider Warlpiri speech community, that of young Warlpiri in one particu-lar community.

The point at which the way of speaking becomes a new language and is no longer code-switching can be difficult to determine. In terms of struc-ture, questions should be asked about the extent to which:

1. use of elements from one language or the other is obligatory in the newly emerging grammar, as opposed to code-switching in which, although there is considerable systematicity, speakers are free to choose each code when they wish;

2. structural sedimentation is occurring; that is, relationships between forms and functions are stabilizing and there is less variation in which functions are signalled by particular forms (Auer 1999);

3. the new code differs in structure from the previously spoken codes (Weinreich 1953); and
4. the new code contains elements not found in the source languages (O'Shannessy 2005).

In terms of language use, questions should be asked about the extent to which:

1. the breadth of function of the new code is increasing, for example, within the family, in administration and education, and in written forms; and
2. the speakers see the language as separate from the pre-contact language (Weinreich 1953).

A third question about language use is whether the code is learned by children from birth as one of their primary languages (O'Shannessy 2005). There are no absolute parameters for the social evaluations of the use issues in (1) and (2) immediately above, and they are subject to per-spectives of speakers and others, as discussed below. It should be noted that code-switching practices do not necessarily, or often, lead to the for-mation of a new language. Code-switching is often the expected way of speaking in stable bilingual and multilingual situations.

5.2   Mechanisms of contact-induced change

When we examine how and why contact-induced changes take place, we must always consider psychological, social and linguistic factors in interaction (Weinreich 1953: 3). Nevertheless, some kinds of linguistic transference are more common than others. I first outline some com-mon linguistic tendencies, then social and psychological factors that interact with them.

5.2.1   Linguistic factors in contact-induced change

What kinds of linguistic processes and results occur, and to what extent are they constrained by other linguistic factors? For some researchers one counterexample to a so-called rule means the rule does not hold; others interpret patterns and tendencies as constraints, acknowledging that they are influenced by social and psychological factors. The linguis-tic processes outlined in this section can occur in situations of language maintenance, shift or creation. The weighting given to each type of factor varies with each situation; many researchers agree that social-psychological factors can override linguistic tendencies or constraints (Johanson 2002: 5, Thomason 2001: 11, Thomason and Kaufman 1988: 14, Weinreich 1953, Winford 2003: 53), yet strong linguistic tendencies are seen to operate in particular sociolinguistic situations (Silva-Corvalan

2008: 221). In some situations it is difficult to disentangle three pos-sible paths of change: TRANSFERENCE of abstract or overt elements of one language's grammar to the other, INTERNAL CHANGE within a lan-guage due to processes of attrition, which in turn were caused by contact (e.g. Grenoble 2000: 119), or INTERNAL PROCESSES of change independent of contact. In the first two cases the change is contact-induced, but the extent to which contact between grammars is directly responsible in the second case is not clear.

There are some typological factors which perform a constraining role over many phenomena of change: TYPOLOGICAL SIMILARITY, TRANSPAR-ENCY and MARKEDNESS (Heath 1984, Thomason 2001, Thomason and Kaufman 1988, Weinreich 1953, Winford 2003). When languages have similar typological patterns, grammatical elements are more likely to be transferred from one to another (but see e.g. Campbell (1993) for examples of transference between dissimilar language types). In Eastern Anatolia, Turkish has influenced the structure of clause subordination in structurally similar Laz, but not in structurally dissimilar Iranian lan-guages, even though all are spoken in the same area (Haig 2001: 212). Markedness concerns how frequently elements occur across languages and whether they are part of a regular paradigm. Marked features occur less often, and make a paradigm less regular, and are therefore less easily learned when acquiring a second language. Evaluations of markedness should be relative to the language pairs under study, as well as to other languages. Markedness is most important in shift-induced interference, when a group is learning another language, as marked features might not be learned well, and might not be part of the shifting group's produc-tion of the dominant language. But marked features in an endangered language might be lost in favour of less-marked ones from the dominant language (Andersen 1982); examples from Pipil are given by Palosaari and Campbell, Chapter 6. Transparency, or the degree of integration of features, concerns how structurally integrated a morpheme is into its environment. A highly complex, bound, multifunctional, phonologic-ally reduced morpheme is less likely to be transferred than a simple, unbound, syllabic, unifunctional morpheme (Heath 1984, Thomason 2001: 77, Weinreich 1953, Winford 2003). Recall, for example, that whole words transfer easily by borrowing with minimally intense contact.

I now turn to some specific processes and patterns of occurrence of types of borrowing which are attested in endangered languages (and in other contexts). To begin with lexical borrowing, there is a hierarchy of which kinds of lexical items are more and less easily borrowed (Haugen 1950: 224). Open-class content words such as nouns and adjectives are more easily borrowed, while closed-class functional items such as pro-nouns and conjunctions are generally less easily borrowed (Haugen 1950, Winford 2003: 51), although sometimes conjunctions are borrowed early (Campbell 1993: 102, Matras 1998: 293, Sakel 2007: 26). Vocabulary for non-basic concepts (e.g. introduced religious or cultural concepts, names of foods, or implements, not previously needed) is borrowed first. Words can be transferred without direct contact with the source language, once one language group uses a word, others can borrow the word from that language (Bakker and Papen 2008: 265). When words are borrowed, their phonology is often altered to fit that of the recipient language, but under intense contact the words may be borrowed with their original phonology, and new sounds may spread beyond the words in which they were originally borrowed (Heath 1978, Thomason and Kaufman 1988: 84). Elements or patterns in the receding language that do not also occur in the dominant language may be lost, for instance phonological contrasts (Bullock and Gerfen 2004), or marked elements (Andersen 1982). (See Palosaari and Campbell, Chapter 6, for further discussion and examples.)

The grammatical subcategorizations and meanings from the source language of borrowed words are not always borrowed with them. In the process of RELEXIFICATION (Muysken 1994, 2000), or 'relabelling' (Lefebvre 1998, 2008), only the phonological shape of a word from the source language is transferred, and is combined with the meaning and grammatical specifications of a word in the recipient language. The process is common in creole formation and also occurs in other contact contexts. An example is from Haitian creole. The Fongbe word *hú* means 'to murder, to mutilate', while the French word *assassiner* means only 'to murder'. The Haitian Creole word *ansasinen*, though French in word shape, has the Fongbe meaning of *hú* 'to murder, to mutilate' (Lefebvre 2008: 92). Relexification can occur extensively in a language, as in the formation of Media Lengua, a mixed language in which Spanish word shapes have Quechua meanings (Muysken 1981, 2000). Another method of borrowing alters the meaning of the word because of its context of use, e.g. the English word 'sister' has been borrowed into Warlpiri as *jija*, 'nurse', from the context of 'sister' used to refer to a nursing sister in a health clinic.

The structure from one language can be translated word-for-word into another, called a LOAN TRANSLATION or CALQUE. Hill and Hill (1986: 140) report a Mexicano speaker using the phrase *nicpia apiztli*, 'I have hunger', based on the Spanish phrase *tengo hambre* 'I have hunger', instead of the earlier Mexicano *nimayana* 'I am hungry'. Sometimes only the structural specifications of a word or grammatical morpheme are transferred. In Evenki, a Tungusic language spoken in Siberia and under pressure from Russian, some case assignments have been reanalysed to become more like Russian. Agents in the passive voice are marked with instrumental case, as in Russian, rather than Evenki dative case; speech verbs are marked with dative case, as in Russian, instead of Evenki allative or accusative case (Grenoble 2000: 109).

Lexical items can be borrowed and then reanalysed as grammatical elements, altering the morphosyntactic properties of the recipient language, but not necessarily directly reflecting a pattern in the source language. In Laz, a South Caucasian language spoken in Turkey, the Turkish word for place, *yer*, has become a locative adposition, a function it does not perform in Turkish (Kutscher 2008: 95).[3]

(2)   didi   livadi   *yeri*   *beraberi*   mtxorumt
      big   garden   place   together   dig:1PL:PAST.PFV
      'We both dig in the big garden.' (Kutscher and Genc 1998: 56, cited in
      Kutscher 2008: 95)

In Upper Sorbian, a Slavic language spoken in East Germany, the proximal demonstrative ('this') has been grammaticalized to become a definite article under pressure from German (Heine and Kuteva 2008: 60). Heine and Kuteva (2008) show that some grammaticalization processes appear to operate only in one direction: from demonstrative to definite article, or from numeral 'one' to indefinite article. In addition, only particular forms are grammaticalized in a particular way: the verbs 'to go' or 'to want' grammaticalize into future tense markers, but other verbs do not. The consistent unidirectional changes, and selective matches of source and grammaticalized element, suggest grammatical constraints operate cross-linguistically. The constraints appear in internal language change also, so they are not restricted to language-contact contexts (Heine and Kuteva 2008: 81). Many grammaticalization processes have taken place slowly, over hundreds of years, as in the Upper Sorbian example, but they can also take place very quickly. The creation of new auxiliary forms in Light Warlpiri has occurred in one generation (O'Shannessy 2005).

In most situations of stable bilingualism, structural borrowing follows lexical borrowing (Haugen 1950, Thomason 2001, Weinreich 1953), but not always. A language may take on new grammatical categories and terms from another language without borrowing lexicon (Aikhenvald 1999). Speakers of Tariana, an Arawakan language spoken in Brazil, do not borrow lexical items from East-Tucanoan languages with which they are in close contact and which exert cultural pressure on Tariana. But they have transferred abstract grammatical properties from East-Tucanoan languages to Tariana, seen in the tense, aspect, case and evidentiality systems, through processes of reanalysis, reinterpretation and grammaticalization. Transfer of structural features with little or no lexical transfer is most likely in situations of language shift (Thomason 2001, Thomason and Kaufman 1988) and high degrees of bilingualism (Winford 2003).

Changes can take place that ultimately alter the core structural patterns of a language. For instance, Dyirbal, an endangered language of north-east Australia, indicates core grammatical relations through case-marking on nouns, and has free word order. Young speakers of Dyirbal (Schmidt 1985b: 49–52) use fewer allomorphs of the ergative case-marker, which indicates nominal subjects of transitive verbs. Individuals used them to differing extents, until ultimately the case-markers were not used at all by some speakers. When case-marking was no longer being used to indicate agents, fixed word order was used in an English-like pattern, so that for some speakers the syntax of Dyirbal became more like that of English, and the case-marking function was being lost. Individual speakers differed from each other in how often they use case-marking versus fixed word order to indicate agents. In this situation the case-marking and word-order patterns are in competition to indicate the same core grammatical functions. Competition can develop between phonetic forms, word forms, grammatical items or grammatical patterns. Such competition can be resolved by one pattern winning out, or by a complementary distribution of elements, e.g. case-marking might co-occur most often with non-English-like (non-SVO) word-order patterns.

One language may have a functional category that is not present in another. If the less dominant language lacks the category it might gain it from the other language, as in the case of Tariana mentioned above (Aikhenvald 1999), or if the less dominant language has the category, it might lose it (Winford 2003: 96). For instance, young speakers of Warlpiri use dual person forms less often than older speakers do, probably because of contact with English (Bavin 1989: 285). But it is not always clear that contact is the trigger: a category might have been lost through internal processes of change.

5.2.2 Social and psychological mechanisms in contact-induced change

Major social influences on the type of contact-induced changes that will occur include the relative size and sociopolitical status of the groups involved, the history and length of the contact, the types of social interactions in which speakers engage, their level of proficiency in each language, and the speakers' attitudes and ideologies (Thomason and Kaufman 1988; Winford 2003).

Although languages come into contact with each other for many reasons (see Grenoble, Chapter 2), languages become endangered when there is pressure on speakers of a language to speak a more dominant language or a LINGUA FRANCA of the area. A lingua franca may itself be a contact language, and may in turn exert pressure on (other) minority languages. A language can become dominant because it is seen to bring a reward to its speakers, and/or it fulfils a specific communicative function, as outlined by Fishman (2001c). Rewards that come from speaking a particular language are interrelated and include instrumental rewards, through needing to use the language for trade, education or to gain employment, and increased status, when the language is seen to be prestigious in increasing numbers of domains. Increased status may include young people seeing the language as a symbol of youth and modernity. When the speakers of a language become the dominant social, political and economic group, their language is often expected to be used in public functions, further increasing its prestige and expanding its role.

Layers of dominance may be observed in a geographical area, interacting with other social forces, so that layers of pressure are exerted on one or more minority languages from one or more others. For example, in northern Australia, the dominant language in terms of government administration and education is Standard Australian English (SAE), which is taught in schools and used in the majority of broadcast media. But for many Aboriginal people the usefulness of SAE beyond those domains is limited. Rather, Aboriginal English, which has arisen from contact between varieties of English, Kriol and indigenous Australian languages (Kaldor and Malcolm 1991), and/or Kriol are dominant as common languages among indigenous people, and the social pressure and need to use them when speaking to other indigenous people is high. Aboriginal English and Kriol are used in broadcast media but rarely in written media. All three languages, SAE, Aboriginal English and Kriol, exert pressure on the local languages, by narrowing or removing the communicative space in which the local languages have prestige. Use of the more dominant languages in private and public functions increases, and the reward for using them is participation in a larger social group. In small remote indigenous communities, there may be more pressure on the local traditional languages from Aboriginal English and Kriol than from SAE, because the speakers interact more with speakers of these and of other traditional languages, using the common language, than with speakers of SAE. Part of the appeal of Kriol may be that it is not the colonial language, and is a clear marker of indigeneity since very few non-indigenous people use the language. These factors, and the relatively large number of speakers, make Kriol a threat to the minority indigenous languages. Also, by speaking Kriol, individuals can maintain linguistic and cultural distinctiveness from the majority Australian community. Additionally, Kriol shows variation along geographical lines, and elements of traditional languages are typically brought into it. So speakers have access to a pan-indigenous language which shows local variation and distinction.

A psycholinguistic motivation for changes in one or both of a speaker's languages is that bilinguals need to respond rapidly to many different situations and interlocutors in different languages, a complex cognitive task. To reduce the cognitive load, they may regularize patterns, use infrequent constructions even less often, and use patterns which are similar in both languages more often, resulting in convergence of the two languages (Silva-Corvalan 2008: 215). Reducing cognitive load may be the motivation for bringing some elements, for instance, discourse markers, from the dominant language into utterances in the other language(s), reducing the number of competing options from which the bilingual speaker has to choose by using the discourse system of only one language, rather than two or more (Matras 2000a; Sakel 2007). The patterns of borrowing or switching may then become entrenched in the minority language.

In any verbal interaction speakers may highlight similarities to, or differences from, their partner's speech. CONVERGENCE, accentuating similarities with an interlocutor's speech style, and DIVERGENCE, emphasizing the differences, are concepts that have been developed in Communication Accommodation Theory (Giles and Coupland 1991; Giles *et al.* 1977, 1991). Convergence and divergence may be achieved through consciously or subconsciously manipulating a range of communication features, including language choice, accent, speech rate, vocal intensity, pause frequencies and gestures (Giles *et al.* 1991: 7). Convergence shows identification with an individual interlocutor's speech, while divergence shows identification with the patterns of a group external to the immediate interaction, namely the speaker's social group, as opposed to the interlocutor's. A speaker might accentuate differences from an interlocutor's style to show membership of another group or to maintain an identity (Giles *et al.* 1991: 37). Intergroup mechanisms of convergence and divergence may be part of long-term language and dialect shifts (Trudgill 1986) and language maintenance and survival (Giles *et al.* 1991). Introducing a new way of speaking requires an element of divergence. But once a change is underway, convergence might be a mechanism of continuing language shift. Converging with one's speech partner can lead to reinforcement of new, incoming ways of speaking, for example code-switching. In unstable bilingual situations, where language shift is a strong possibility, speakers often say that they want to maintain the traditional language, yet in their own interactions often use the incoming language. Accommodation theory helps to explain why this might occur, through the need to converge to one's interlocutor and conform to the conventions of one's speech community. Where an incoming language is used increasingly, convergence involves using it in a similar way. Divergence from the community interactional style by a speaker could be a mechanism for language shift reversal, through greater use of the endangered language, if that speaker's interlocutors in turn converged to his or her language choice. But the social cost and effectiveness of diverging from the conventional style of the community in language endangerment situations have not been fully explored.

5.3 How is change evaluated?

Just as categorization of a way of speaking as 'language X' or 'a variety of language X' is very much influenced by social and political factors, judgements about when a language has changed 'too much' to be considered the same language as before involve subjective social and political judgements. No linguistic community is homogeneous (Weinreich 1953), but if radical contact-induced changes take place, how are they viewed by speakers and others? Changes that occur over an extended time can result in great differences within a language, but it may still be perceived by speakers and others as being 'the same language'. Changes due to contact often occur much more quickly than internally motivated changes and may be viewed more negatively by speakers and others, such that there is controversy over the identity of the new code: is the emerging way of speaking still 'Language X'? A new way of speaking may be a threat to the traditional languages, but can also be seen as a form of language maintenance. For example, the new bilingual mixed languages in northern Australia are local, spoken only by members of the small communities in which they originated, and are considered by the speakers and others in the communities to be types of the traditional languages, yet they differ structurally and lexically from them. Community members accept the changes, perhaps because the new codes still remain distinct from varieties of English and Kriol, and contain many elements from the traditional languages. An example is New Tiwi, northern Australia, which has considerable material from English, but is still considered by the community to be Tiwi, yet it has a different status from traditional Tiwi in that the community does not consider it an appropriate variety of the language to be taught in school (Lee 1987). Speakers' views of a language that has undergone change may take into account the sources of the changes. In some circumstances speakers may be tolerant of receiving material from a fellow minority language, and prefer this to receiving material from a colonizing language. In linguistic areas speakers accept considerable structural material from other languages in the area, perhaps partly because they view those languages positively, in addition to the influence of the intense contact situation.

Within a particular speech community there may be different degrees of tolerance of change: some people tolerate borrowing words and structures, others resist. Resistance often focuses on lexical elements because they are the most salient (Dorian 1994). While it seems intuitive that the less foreign material that is brought into a language the stronger it will be, this is not necessarily true (Dorian 1994: 479). Allowing lexical and structural material into a language has been shown to be successful for maintenance in some situations, since the new material fulfils a communicative need, such as for coining new terms. If younger speakers' incorporation of material from other languages is frowned upon, they may be deterred from using the minority language (e.g. Sallabank 2005: 46). Strict oversight of use of language structures can discourage speakers from using the language; Poedjosoedarmo (2006: 117) reports a Javanese-speaking teenager telling her brother to speak Bahasa Indonesia to his elders to avoid committing an error in using the complex politeness system of Javanese. If there is extensive change which is not approved of by older speakers, opportunities to revitalize the language in its new form can be missed, so that the outlook for both the older and newer forms is less positive (Dorian 1994).

5.4   Is contact-induced change inevitable? Can it be halted or reversed?

When languages come into contact and speakers of one language are learning another, a change in language use has already taken place. Some lexical or structural change in one or both of the languages will often, but not always, occur. Some Native American languages have very little linguistic material from English, even though they are under intense pressure (Thomason 2008: 8). Yet these languages are severely endangered, so a change in language use has occurred, even if not in language structure or lexicon. How much and what type of change happens is a product of the interaction of socio-psychological and linguistic factors (see Backus 2004, 2005, Johanson 2002, Thomason 2003, Thomason and Kaufman 1988, Weinreich 1953, Winford 2003). How difficult is it for a relatively under-resourced group to implement social change through resistance to change in progress? Can this be achieved so that the minority language also has a role and dispenses rewards to its speakers (Fishman 1991, 2001a, 2001c)? These questions are bound up in issues of access to resources, awareness of speech styles and choices, mechanisms of conventionalization of language use, and complex interactions of intergenerational socioeconomic and political factors.

The prestige of a language may be viewed differently by different groups within the community; for example, younger versus older speakers, so use of a language or linguistic form may be evaluated differently among within-community groups. Speakers may be aware that their language is endangered but not aware of or confident about their own role in its maintenance. Young people often see a traditional language as somehow old-fashioned, representing past traditions rather than contemporary concerns (Moriarty, Chapter 22). To them, use of a language associated with technology, global communication media and modern music, for example, is more appealing and reflects their identity as contemporary youth in the modern world. In an attempt to present cultural knowledge and the traditional language as contemporary and currently relevant, one Warlpiri community in northern Australia created a biennial community music and dance event, in which traditional stories and cultural concepts are interpreted through both traditional and modern dance and music. Young people are integral to the performance and as a result their interest in traditional cultural knowledge has been stimulated (Pawu-Kurlpurlurnu *et al.* 2008: 36).

Speakers often see an economic and social advantage for their children speaking the dominant language of an area, in terms of access to higher education, advanced technologies, and national and international information, and sometimes reluctantly choose the dominant language over their own minority language for some institutional functions, for example, education, or even for personal use in the home (Ladefoged 1992: 810, Harbert, Chapter 20).

Another factor relates not to speaker attitudes but to speaker resources. Use of the dominant language(s) is often required for employment and administrative purposes. Governments are under pressure to show that they provide the resources for children to have the same educational participation and achievement levels in the national language(s) as children in other environments. This need not be at the expense of minority languages, because considerable research shows that participating in the early years of education in one's first language leads to greater achievement in education in the second language later (Baker 2006, Collier and Thomas 2004, Krashen 1997, Krashen and McField 2005). But sustaining formal education in minority languages takes considerable financial and human resources and commitment from both the local and wider communities (see Coronel-Molina and McCarty, Chapter 18). Although a community might prefer to promote several languages, speakers sometimes cannot see how that could be done with the limited resources they have. Where it can be done, the positive outcomes are many, although sometimes difficult to measure precisely. They include increased status of the language through its institutional role, and increased opportunities for exposure and use through school texts and in broadcast media. It is hypothesized that one of the reasons Warlpiri children in one community still learn traditional Warlpiri as well as the new contact language is their participation in a bilingual education programme (Meakins and O'Shannessy 2010). Additionally, bilingual education provides a purpose for minority language speakers to obtain higher education qualifications as there is a clear role for the combination of tertiary education and minority language use. Many teachers in bilingual education programmes in the Northern Territory of Australia have later moved on to other leadership roles in their local and wider communities because they have high levels of education and highly developed intercultural communication skills.

The question of degree of inevitability of change is linked to that of how conscious we are of our speech styles and of strategies of convergence and divergence. The extent to which speakers are aware of their moment-by-moment speech production is currently unresolved. If convergence is relatively automatic and not achieved self-consciously, then diverging will require overcoming one's automatic response through greater attention to both one's own speech and the interlocutor's. Speakers would need to alter their own language use patterns to halt a change in progress. This requires an initial divergence from the incoming code, then convergence by others to the once-divergent code. Are unconscious social pressures to converge to one's interlocutor too strong to allow speakers to implement conscious decisions about language use? Sociolinguistic work on language and identity suggests that conscious decisions about how we speak play a strong role. Speakers are often aware of the identity they want to project and how to do so (Bucholtz 2001; Eckert 2000, Irvine 2001, Labov 1966) including in multilingual interactions (Giles *et al.* 1977). Speakers' consciousness of their speech and their decisions about whether to accept material from other languages play a role in some contact situations (Aikhenvald 2003, Kroskrity 1978). People deliberately manipulate language patterns to create registers for specific cultural purposes (Finlayson 1984, Hale 1971, 1992, Irvine and Gal 2000) and create secret communication codes (Matras 2000b: 80). So there could be a role for conscious decision making at least in terms of resistance to change, or of apportioning distinct roles to each language. But it is also possible that the sociocultural pressure to speak the incoming language overrides all other considerations (see also Hinton, Chapter 15).

Contact varieties which arise at least partly as a form of resistance to language shift, such as bilingual mixed languages in Australia, can be seen as halting or delaying a shift. If the new language eventually gives way to one of the pressuring languages then it will have been a mechanism for slowing language shift. The extent to which deliberateness or consciousness are involved in constructing these new languages is not known at this point, but an element of consciousness seems likely, since the languages serve a social function of indicating identity (McConvell and Meakins 2005, O'Shannessy 2005).

5.5　Contact languages as endangered languages

Endangered-language documentation efforts typically have not paid attention to new contact varieties, because of what is perceived as a more urgent need to document the older, disappearing traditional languages (see Woodbury, Chapter 9). Creoles and mixed languages tend to be marginalized in popular ideologies about language, for two reasons (Garrett 2006: 178). First, those that currently exist have relatively short histories, less than 400 years, and were often created by people without a long history of living in their current territory (although this is certainly not always the case). Second, they are seen to lack autonomy: many creoles are spoken alongside their lexifiers, and a variety of types of both the creole and the lexifier languages emerge, so that boundaries between the two are not very clear (Garrett 2006: 180). But contact languages are no less interesting or important than pre-existing languages. Processes that take place during the emergence of contact languages provide valuable information about the possibilities of linguistic, psycholinguistic and sociolinguistic systems (see also Woodbury, Chapter 9).

An emergent contact language may turn out to be part of a longer term process of language shift. At the time that a new language or variety emerges, it is not clear how stable it will be in the long term. When a contact language emerges as a consequence of resistance to intense pressure to shift to a more prestigious language, the pressure to shift continues to be exerted, and is extended to the contact language, so that it too becomes endangered. The contact language is likely to have low prestige in the wider social arena, and might be only a temporary form of resistance. If it does not survive for many years, the opportunity to document it may be lost, and with it valuable information about what kinds of combinations and influences are possible and observable in languages in contact, the kinds of social situations that brought them about, and the role they played in the formation of the next linguistic situation. Often the outcomes of contact-induced change are studied well after the process of change is completed, yet many aspects of contact phenomena are difficult to analyse in the absence of detailed sociohistorical data, because crucial information such as the identity of the agents of change, the degree of bilingualism or multilingualism of the speakers, the relative dominance and use of the languages, and the types of interactions that took place are no longer known (Winford 2003: 65). But in many parts of the world dramatic changes are taking place right now where linguists can observe them as they unfold. In such cases there is an opportunity for more sociolinguistic information to be recorded, including speakers' own perceptions of their language use, and a more informative analysis of the social dynamics of the contexts can be developed. Documentation should include the processes applied to elements of the source languages as they appear in the new code, and relevant patterns of use in both the sources and in the new code. Our understandings of the interactions of particular sociopsychological and linguistic factors could be greatly enriched. Such information may assist in analysis of the tension between, for example, deliberate decision making and unconscious change, or linguistic versus social–psychological constraints.

The study of contact languages might also help to identify how language shift can be halted or reversed. If the socio-psychological factors in the emergence of a contact variety can be identified and conveyed to the community in focus and communities elsewhere, perhaps decisions could be made that would slow the rate, or alter the effect, of contact-induced change. Contact varieties can throw light on which elements of pre-existing languages are more likely to be maintained or lost in particular sociolinguistic circumstances.

5.6 Conclusions

When languages come into contact some change in structure and lexicon is common. It is possible for a minority language to coexist with other languages in a situation of stable multilingualism. There are differences in terms of how much change speakers of a language will accept as their language varies, with some groups accepting quite dramatic changes in the face of strong pressure to shift. Emergent contact languages, the results of dramatic change, can be accepted by a community of speakers as a form of maintenance, and should be documented because of the information they provide about language-contact situations, and because they themselves might have only short lives. An unresolved issue is how conscious speakers are of their speech patterns and how likely it is that they could alter them if they wanted to.

Notes

1 Light Warlpiri is spoken only by younger adults and children in one Warlpiri community; older adults speak traditional Warlpiri, and Light Warlpiri speakers speak traditional Warlpiri also.
2 In the examples, Warlpiri forms are in italics, Kriol and English are in plain text, and the innovated auxiliary is in bold. Abbreviations are: ABL ablative case; ANAPH anaphor; DEM demonstrative; INTERR interrogative; LOC locative case; NFUT non-future; 2SG second-person singular.
3 Elements from Laz are in plain font and those from Turkish in italics.

6

Structural aspects of language endangerment

Naomi Palosaari and Lyle Campbell

6.1 Introduction

This chapter addresses structural aspects of language endangerment from two perspectives: the contributions that the study of endangered languages make to typology and linguistic theory, and the structural consequences of language endangerment, including the kinds of changes that can take place in the phonology, morphology and syntax of endangered languages.

6.2 Contributions from endangered languages to typology and linguistic theory

A major goal of linguistics is to understand what is possible and what is impossible in human languages, and through this to understand the potentials and limitations of human cognition as reflected in language. It is important to obtain scientific information about endangered languages, for if they are lost without documentation, we stand to lose valuable information about the full range of human languages, about their parts and patterns, structures and uses, and how these things interact with one another. To illustrate this point, we present several examples of STRUCTURAL PHENOMENA (from both sound systems and morphosyntax) which have been uncovered from work on endangered languages and which could well have never been known if these languages had disappeared before they were documented and described. We illustrate how such findings contribute to language typology and linguistic theory. TYPOLOGY, broadly speaking, is the classification of languages according to linguistic traits and the comparison or classification of linguistic features and structures across languages.

More specifically, typology is understood in different ways; among them:

- the classification of structural types cross-linguistically;
- the investigation of cross-linguistic generalizations concerning patterns among linguistic traits; and
- as a general approach to linguistics which attempts to explain the patterns and classification through appeal to language function in cross-linguistic comparison; that is, the relation between linguistic form and function.

Typology is closely associated with the study of LINGUISTIC UNIVERSALS, which can be understood as the common characteristics of the world's languages, usually with the goal of providing insight into the fundamental nature of human language. Thus discoveries in typology and the identification of universals contribute to linguistic theory, which is aimed at understanding and explaining the nature of human language.[1] Section 6.2.1 discusses sounds and sound systems, and 6.2.2 explores morphosyntactic examples.

6.2.1　Sounds and sound systems

6.2.1.1　Unique speech sounds: a Nivaclé case study

Nivaclé (Chulupí), an endangered Matacoan language with c. 250 speakers in Argentina and c. 8,500 in Paraguay, has a speech sound not found in any other language.[2] It is a complex segment composed of a voiceless velar stop and a voiced alveolar lateral resonant, articulated and released simultaneously (that is, with both articulatory gestures formed at the same time and released as nearly simultaneously as possible), represented as /k͡l/ (Campbell and Grondona 2007, Campbell in preparation).[3] The discovery of a new speech sound is for linguists like the discovery of a new species is for biologists. We document and describe endangered languages precisely so information of this sort will not be lost to science. The discovery of this unique sound has considerable typological significance: we must add a new sound to the inventory of speech sounds in human languages, and its discovery has implications for general claims about languages.

The phonemic inventory of Nivaclé consonants is given in Table 6.1.

Nivaclé provides counterexamples to a number of proposed cross-linguistic generalizations about laterals and liquids, offering valuable evidence about the possible structure of sound systems. For example, Maddieson (1984: 88) proposed that:

(1)　a language with two or more liquids is expected to have a contrast between a lateral and a non-lateral. However, in Nivaclé both liquids are laterals and there are no non-lateral liquids (no 'r' sounds).

Table 6.1. *Nivaclé consonant inventory*

plain stops/affricates		p	t	ts	č	k	ʔ
glottalized stops/affricates[4]		p'	t'	ts'	č'	k'	
fricatives		φ		s	š	x	
lateral			ḷ̥				
velar + lateral			k͡l				
nasals		m	n				

(2) a language with one or more laterals typically has one voiced lateral approximant: for example, a marked lateral in a language implies the presence also of plain 'l', and voiceless 'l' also implies the presence of plain 'l'. This, however, is not true of Nivaclé; although it has two laterals, one is a voiceless approximant /ḷ̥/[5] and the other, /k͡l/, is not an approximant. Nivaclé has no plain (voiced) /l/.

(3) a language with two or more laterals is expected to contrast them either in point of articulation or in manner of articulation, but not in both. The Nivaclé laterals, however, differ both in point of articulation and manner of articulation.

Thus, the Nivaclé laterals illustrate well how the discovery of a new speech sound in the investigation of an endangered language can have an impact on general claims about language. Given the counterexamples just mentioned, all these proposed generalizations need to be reevaluated.

6.2.1.2 The Ubykh sound inventory

Ubykh is a now-extinct language of the North-West Caucasian family, formerly spoken in Turkey. Ubykh had perhaps the largest consonant inventory in the world – aside from some of the Khoisan click languages – with 81 documented native consonants, including glottalized, pharyngealized, labialized and palatalized series, and distinguishing at least 8 points of articulation, with some 27 distinct fricatives and 20 uvular consonants (Dumézil 1965, Vogt 1963). Ubykh was reasonably well described before becoming extinct, and so we know of its unusual inventory of consonants and of the fine-grained phonemic contrasts which it shows can exist in a single language. This is information that would be lost to science if it had become extinct without having been described. Still, it is almost certain that much more information of scientific value was irretrievably lost when Ubykh ceased to be spoken.

6.2.1.3 Other unique sounds

Other examples can easily be cited of previously unknown sounds that are now known to linguistic science through recent documentation and description of endangered languages. For example, Ladefoged and Everett (1996) made known the occurrence of a sound in the Chapakuran languages Wari' and Oro Win (Brazil) composed of a voiceless laminal dental plosive followed by a bilabial trill, [t͡ʙ], an allophone of /t/ before /o/ and /u/. Pirahã (Muran family, Brazil, with about 100 speakers) has two highly unusual sounds, a voiced bilabial trill [ʙ] (rare in other languages) and a lateral-apical double-flap [ɺ͡ɺ] (unique to Pirahã). The first is an allophone of /b/, the latter of /g/ (Everett 1984).

Again, such findings have implications for general claims about language. For example, some have claimed there is a connection between the size of a language's consonant inventory and the kinds of consonants expected to be in it. According to Lindblom and Maddieson's (1988) 'size principle', smaller inventories of consonants tend to contain only consonants which are simpler (to produce or to perceive) and more complex consonants are found in languages with larger consonant inventories.[6] This is certainly challenged by the examples cited here, since Pirahã has an extremely small phonemic inventory, with only eleven phonemes, and Wari' has only twelve. It is all too plausible that these languages of Amazonia could have become extinct without leaving any traces,[7] giving us no inkling that such sounds are possible in human languages and resulting in erroneous theorizing about constraints on possible sound systems in human languages.

Other examples of sounds discovered in endangered languages include the linguo-labial segments (tongue tip or blade against the upper lip, which is drawn downward to meet the tongue) in a group of languages in Vanuatu (on Espiritu Santo and Malekula) and in Umotina (extinct, Bororan family; Brazil) (Ladefoged and Maddieson 1996: 18–19, 43–4); and voiceless implosives, known now from, for example, Owerri Igbo, Uzere Isoko, and several languages of the K'ichean branch of Mayan (Campbell 1973, Ladefoged and Maddieson 1996: 87–9). Until the discovery of these sounds it was believed that implosives had to be voiced – as Maddieson (1984: 121) put it: 'an imploded segment is voiced' (see also Ladefoged and Maddieson 1996: 87–9).

6.2.1.4   Xinkan vowel harmony

Xinkan is a small family of four languages in Guatemala (not demonstrably related to any other languages or language families). Two of the languages recently became extinct and the other two each have only one or two semi-speakers (people who have learned the language imperfectly and are not fully fluent). Nevertheless, three of the four languages have been investigated rather intensively, resulting in reasonably extensive documentation and description (Rogers *et al.* in preparation).[8] Xinkan has a unique VOWEL HARMONY pattern (restrictions on which vowels can co-occur with one another in the same word). In most languages with vowel harmony, vowels within a word agree in frontness vs. backness or in roundness vs. non-roundness, or in having advanced tongue root (ATR) or lacking ATR. However, in Xinkan languages, the harmonic sets of vowels depend on vowel height, but with exceptional behaviour for

/ɨ/ (Rogers 2008). The harmonic sets of vowels (in which a member of a set can co-occur in a word with other members of that set, but not with vowels of the other sets) are: {i, u, a}, {e, o, a}, and {ɨ, a}. That is, within roots the high and mid vowels cannot co-occur, the low vowel /a/ is a neutral vowel which can occur with vowels of any height in any of the sets, and the high central vowel /ɨ/ can only co-occur with other instances of /ɨ/ or with neutral /a/.

(1) {i, u, a}
     hiiru   'monkey'
     ts'am'u   'close your eyes'
     pari   'day'
     ts'uułi   'non-Indian person'

(2) {o, e, a}
     k'oosek   'large'
     seema   'fish'
     goona   'hill'

(3) {ɨ, a}
     ts'ɨɨm'ał   'flea'
     ts'ɨɨrɨɨrɨ' 'hummingbird'
     waw'ɨya   'run' (of water)

This Xinkan vowel harmony pattern is interesting typologically for a number of reasons. Vowel harmony systems based on height of mid and high vowels (e.g. an /i, u/ set vs. an /e, o/ set) are very rare, though not unique. Of significance to general claims, however, is the fact that Xinkan harmonic sets of vowels are split based on vowel height, but with /a/ as neutral, occurring with both high vowels and mid vowels. This runs counter to the claim that vowel harmony is due to specific articulatory motivations – it is not possible to talk of a high vowel vs. mid vowel articulatory motivation when the low vowel /a/ occurs with both sets. In addition, the fact that the high central vowel /ɨ/ patterns differently from the other high vowels, and indeed from all other harmonizing vowels, does appear to be unique, and is not known from any other language which has vowel harmony. This has implications for theories of distinctive features, since prevailing views of distinctive features provide no adequate way of showing a natural class of /i, u/ (and /e, o/), while excluding /ɨ/. That is, [+high] does not exclude /ɨ/; [+high, αback, αround] is scarcely a satisfying natural class, since it must name three of the four major vowel features (and [−low] need not be mentioned only because of the universal convention that [+high] vowels cannot be [+low], rather than indicating anything revealing about this 'natural class'). If distinctive features recognized front, central, and back vowels instead of only [−back] (/i/) and [+back] (/ɨ/ and /u/), the problem of excluding /ɨ/ from the /i, u/ harmonic set would not be so difficult. (See Ladefoged and Maddieson (1996: 291–2) for arguments based on data from other languages.) Knowledge of this unique vowel harmony pattern, with its implications for distinctive feature theory, would never have come to light if all the Xinkan languages had become extinct without documentation.

6.2.1.5   Saami phonemic contrasts

The Saami languages (Uralic family) are spoken in northern parts of Finland, Norway, Russia, and Sweden. Eleven Saami languages are known; two (Kemi and Akkala Saami) are now extinct, and nine are at varying levels of endangerment, with numbers of speakers ranging from 1 to 25,000. Three Saami languages (Ume, Pite and Ter Saami) have fewer than 20 speakers each. The Saami languages have several unusual traits; for example, three different length contrasts for consonants and vowels (Aikio 2008).

The Saami examples presented here are from Aikio (2008), given in the accepted Saami orthography. The three degrees of contrast in consonant length are seen in examples (4–6) from North Saami (western Finnmark dialect):

(4) *short*   [l]   /palū/   'fear' (genitive)
(5) *geminate*   [l:]   /pollū/   'wooden bowl' (genitive)
(6) *long*   [l::]   /pol:lū/   'wooden bowl' (nominative)

Three degrees of vowel length are seen in examples (7–9) from North Saami (eastern Finnmark dialect):

(7) *short*   [æ]   /mähte/   (man's name) (nominative)
(8) *geminate*   [æ:]   / mä˙ähte/   (man's name) (genitive)
(9) *long*   [æ::]   /(in) mää˙hte/   '(I don't) know how to'

A two-way contrast between short and long vowels is common in languages of the world, but a contrast of three degrees of length is extremely rare and was unknown until fairly recently. Three degrees of vowel length have been reported also for Coatlán Mixe (Mixe-Zoquean, Mexico) and Yavapai (Yuman, Arizona), and a triple length contrast for both consonants and vowels occurs in Estonian, though conditioned by aspects of morphological structure (Ladefoged and Maddieson 1996: 320). The Saami case is the clearest and puts to rest the once common belief that languages could not contrast more than two degrees of length phonemically (for example, as encoded in the binary distinctive feature [±long] (or in some accounts of vowel length as [±tense] or [±ATR]).

6.2.2   Morphosyntactic structures

6.2.2.1   Word order

A telling example of the value of endangered-language documentation and description is the discovery of languages with OVS

(Object-Verb-Subject) and OSV (Object-Subject-Verb) BASIC WORD ORDER.[9] In his ground-breaking work on universals, Greenberg (1966[1963]) found only SVO, SOV and VSO basic word orders in the languages of his sample. His Universal 1 reflects this: 'In declarative sentences with nominal subject and object, the dominant order is almost always one in which the subject precedes the object' (Greenberg 1966[1963]: 177). Another version was stated as 'whenever the object precedes the verb the subject does likewise' (Greenberg 1978: 2, Derbyshire and Pullum (1986: 16–17)). Greenberg's sample contained no languages with OVS or OSV basic word order, and this universal as formulated suggests they cannot occur as basic word orders in human languages. However, these orders have now been found as the basic word orders in a few languages, first identified in languages of the Amazon (Derbyshire 1979).[10] An example that became well known is Hixkaryana (Cariban), with only 350 speakers, with OVS order as illustrated in:

(10) *toto   yonoye   Kamura*
     man   ate   jaguar
     'The jaguar ate the man.'

The discovery of these basic word orders as these languages came to be described forced the abandonment of the postulated universal, illustrating forcefully the value of describing and analysing little-known, endangered languages. It is all too plausible that the few languages which have these unusual basic word orders could have become extinct before they were documented, given, for example, the treatment of indigenous peoples of Brazil until recently (and still continuing at the hands of unscrupulous miners, ranchers and logging companies). The *World Atlas of Language Structures* (Haspelmath *et al.* 2005: 330–3) now reports nine cases of languages with OVS basic word order, including Asuriní (Tupían; Brazil), Cubeo (Tukanoan; Brazil, Venezuela, Colombia), Hixkaryana (Cariban; Brazil), Mangarrayi (Australian), Päri (Nilotic; Sudan), Selknam (Chonan; Argentina), Tiriyo (Cariban; Suriname, Brazil), Ngarinjin (Australian), and Urarina (isolate; Peru), and four instances of OSV order, found in Warao (isolate; Venezuela), Nadëb (Makúan; Brazil), Wik Ngathan (Pama-Nyungan; Australia), and Tobati (Austronesian; West Papua, Indonesia). Had all OVS and OSV languages become extinct without being documented or described, linguists would have forever believed in the postulated but erroneous universal about subject preceding object, and on its basis would have made hypotheses about Universal Grammar and about the potentials and limitations of human cognition. This possible but all too plausible case of potential loss of important linguistic information through language extinction illustrates the importance of documenting and describing endangered languages and shows the kinds of contributions they can make to the development of linguistic theory.

6.2.2.2   Nivaclé genitive classifiers

Nivaclé, mentioned above, has two GENITIVE CLASSIFIERS (also referred to as 'possessive classifiers') but no other classifiers. An expression such as 'my cow', for example, must use a classifier construction with the 'possessive domestic animal classifier'. Some examples are:[11]

(11) *y-ikla*   *waka*
        1SG.POSS-DOMESTIC.ANIMAL.CL   cow
        'my cow'

(12) *ḽ-ikla*   *kuwayu*
        3SG.POSS-DOMESTIC.ANIMAL.CL   horse
        'his horse'

Nivaclé also has a second possessive animal classifier, *-axeʔ* 'prey classifier' [hunted animal], for example:

(13) *y-axe*   *tašinša*
        1SG.POSS-GAME.CL   brocket.deer
        'my grey brocket deer (*Mazama gouazoubira*)'

We can contrast (13) with the similar form in (14), where *tašinštax* 'goat' (a domestic animal requiring the *-iklaʔ* genitive classifier when possessed) is derived from *tašinša* 'grey brocket deer' by the suffix *-tax* 'similar to', whereas *tašinša* 'grey brocket deer', because it is 'game' requires the *-axeʔ* classifer for game when possessed:

(14) *y-ikla*   *tašinštax*
        1SG.POSS-DOMESTIC.ANIMAL.CL   goat
        'my goat'

Genitive classifiers are rare in the languages of the world, occurring primarily in a few South American languages (for example Nadëb of the Makúan family, some languages from the Cariban, Tupí-Guaranían, Jêan, Guaicuruan families; Aikhenvald 2000: 147). However, in these languages, the genitive classifier is typically one in a system of noun classifiers, with several other classifiers found in the language. Nivaclé (together with some neighbouring languages of the Chaco area) is unusual in that it has no other classifiers, only the unusual genitive classifiers. Such unusual systems need to be studied in more detail to understand their role in classifier systems and in language typology generally. This information could be lost if these endangered languages are not documented; already younger speakers of Nivaclé do not know the 'game genitive classifier' (Campbell, in preparation).

6.2.2.3   Nivaclé demonstratives, tense and evidentiality

Nivaclé has an interesting deictic system shown in Table 6.2. (Similar systems are found in some other languages of South America's Gran Chaco region, also, though most are not well documented.)

Table 6.2. *Nivaclé demonstratives*

	Visible	Not visible (known from first-hand experience)	Not visible (hearsay, indirect knowledge)	Moving, deceased
Singular Masculine	na	xa	pa	ka
Plural Human	napi	xapi	papi	kapi
Plural Non-Human	nawa	xawa	pawa	kawa
Singular Feminine	l̥a	l̥xa	l̥pa	l̥ka

Though the deictic system itself is interesting, how this system interacts with tense–aspect and evidentiality is of special interest, since it is highly unusual. In spite of having verbs with long strings of affixes, Nivaclé verbs carry no grammatical markers of tense or aspect. Rather, tense and aspect are inferred from the demonstratives. For example:

(15) *yoy*   **na**   *siwanak*
      escape   DEM   dorado.fish
      'the dorado-fish is escaping' (visible)

(16) *yoy*   **xa**   *siwanak*
      escape   DEM   dorado.fish
      'the dorado-fish escaped' (not visible but known from personal experience)

Here, (15) and (16) are identical except for the demonstratives. There is no tense in the verb, but nevertheless tense is inferred from the pre-nominal demonstratives. In (15), **na** [visible] implies 'present'; in (16), **xa** [not visible but known] implies 'past' (seen previously but no longer present). Such a situation with tense signalled in the noun phrase is not unique (e.g. Nordlinger and Sadler 2004; Tonhauser 2007). Demonstratives in Movima (language isolate, Haude 2006) and Wichí (Matacoan family, Terraza 2008) also signal tense and are the only markers of tense in these languages; however, in these cases the demonstratives bear tense affixes and so the tense is not inferred from the semantics of the demonstratives as it is in Nivaclé, but is signalled directly by these affixes. Systems such as this are extremely rare and need to be studied more intensively.

The Nivaclé deictic system also interacts with evidentiality. Evidentiality markers indicate the source of knowledge for an utterance and the level of certainty assigned to it. As with tense, there are no verbal morphemes of evidentiality (present in many South American languages), rather the evidentiality is also inferred from the demonstratives. For example, sentences (17) and (18) are identical except for the demonstratives, and yet they are very different in meaning.

(17) *Boca*   *yuʔ-el̥*   **pa-pi**   *River*
      Boca   play-PL   DEM-PL.HUM   River
      'Boca play(ed) River' [two soccer teams in Argentina] (literally 'Boca played those River')

The plural demonstrative *pa-pi* [not visible, not known first-hand] shows that the speaker reports this not from first-hand experience, but rather as something reported (hearsay): 'they say that Boca play(ed) River, but I don't know this from personal experience and so I do not affirm whether it is true or not'.

(18) *Boca*   *yuʔ-el̥*   **na-pi**   *River*
      Boca   play-PL   DEM-PL.HUM   River
      'Boca is playing River'

The plural demonstrative **na-pi** [visible] shows that the speaker sees the event described and therefore affirms it is true: 'Boca is (truly) playing River'. The meaning of these demonstratives thus also involves evidentiality, accounting for the difference in evidentiality in the two sentences.

An interesting question arises here for linguistic typology: should Nivaclé be classified as a language with evidential markers, though evidentiality is only inferred from the demonstratives? In addition, what about cross-linguistic comparisons? Should we consider that these indicators of evidentiality in Nivaclé and the evidential systems marked on the verb in some other South American languages are equivalent and thus comparable in some way (see, for example, Epps 2005)?

6.2.2.4   Syntactic ergativity

In some languages subjects of intransitive verbs (bearing a grammatical function we can label as S), and objects of transitive verbs (functioning as O) are marked the same way, and differently from subjects of transitive verbs (functioning as A). This is referred to as MORPHOLOGICAL ERGATIVITY because the special A marking is called 'ergative' (and the S/O marking is termed 'absolutive'). Morphological ergativity is not especially uncommon among the world's languages. Ergativity is most often reflected only in morphology without major correlates in the syntactic organization of clauses. However, SYNTACTIC ERGATIVITY does exist, and was first reported for Dyirbal (Pama-Nyungan family; Australia), which has only a handful of speakers today (Dixon 1972). Syntactic ergativity refers to syntactic operations which treat the object of a transitive verb (O) and subject of an intransitive verb (S) as a single syntactic category (S/O). It is also sometimes called interclausal ergativity, since it is typically seen in how arguments are treated syntactically in two (or more) linked clauses, for example in relative clause constructions, subordination, and clausal coordination. In Dyirbal, the omission of coreferential noun phrases in relative clauses or coordinated clauses exhibits syntactic ergativity. In such clauses, the grammatical subject (S) of an intransitive verb can be elided only if it is coreferential with an intransitive subject S or a transitive object O in the (preceding) main clause, as in the following example of coordination:

(19)   *nguma*   *yabu-nggu*   *bura-n*   *banaga-nyu*
       father-ABS mother-ERG see-NONFUT return-NONFUT
       'Mother saw father and [father] returned.' (Dixon 1994: 162.)

In this sentence, with the literal gloss 'mother saw father and returned', the second clause is understood to mean 'father returned'. This is because the omitted subject of an intransitive verb like *banaga-nyu* 'returned' is understood as absolutive and is required to be coreferential with the absolutive object of the preceding transitive verb *bura-n* 'saw', i.e. *nguma* 'father'. It is not possible to understand the second clause in (19) with the meaning 'mother returned' (notice that in English omission in linked clauses requires coreference of intransitive subjects S or transitive subjects A, so in 'Mother saw father and returned' it is understood that 'mother returned'. English treats S/A as a single syntactic category).

Some aspects of syntactic ergativity have been reported in other languages, though it is uncommon. For instance, a few other Pama-Nyungan languages also have some degree of syntactic ergativity, e.g. Yidiny, Kalkatungu, Warrgamay and Bandjalang (Dixon 1994: 178). Of these, Kalkatungu recently became extinct and the others are critically endangered. Linguistic science would not know syntactic ergativity was possible if all these languages had been lost without being described.

In this section, we have given just a few additional examples of structural features found in endangered languages which have a significant impact on understanding what is possible in human languages. These examples illustrate compellingly the value of documenting and describing endangered languages.

6.3   What can happen to the structure of endangered languages?

Though there are various ways in which languages can become extinct, the most typical is through LANGUAGE SHIFT when a language gradually comes to have fewer and fewer speakers who use it in ever fewer domains until finally no one is able to speak it in any context (see Grenoble, Chapter 2). This process is sometimes called LANGUAGE OBSOLESCENCE, and a language which undergoes it is referred to as an OBSOLESCING LANGUAGE. There can be considerable impact on the structure of the endangered language in these situations (see Campbell and Muntzel 1989). This can have important implications for typological claims and for the study of language change in endangered languages. In this section we address these issues and the kinds of variation and change found in endangered languages. Specifically, we consider the impact that language endangerment can have on the structure of languages and the kinds of changes and structural differences they can exhibit in contrast to fully viable, non-endangered languages. In 6.3.1 we discuss variation and variability and in 6.3.2 we present types of changes found in endangered languages.

6.3.1 Variation and variability

6.3.1.1 Variation in endangered languages

Variation in obsolescing languages need not exhibit the negative or positive sociolinguistic evaluations usually correlated with social variables such as socioeconomic class, sex, ethnicity, etc. so often found in viable languages. That is, variability often does not bear the social meanings in speech communities undergoing severe language obsolescence that it may elsewhere.

Some changes which take place in endangered language situations are 'normal' or 'natural' changes which can take place in non-endangerment situations as well (see also O'Shannessy, Chapter 5). An example is the merger of uvular and velar consonants in endangered Mam of Tuxtla Chico (and indeed, also in several non-endangered branches of Mayan, as well). Although imperfect learning may be sufficient to explain many of these cases, the absence of the contrast from the dominant language (Spanish in this case) may also contribute to its loss in the endangered language.

Some changes in obsolescing languages are natural, but the rate of change can be accelerated, with a change occurring much more rapidly than it might in a healthy language situation. For example, in the Algonquian language Walpole Island Ottawa, the person prefix system exhibits variability and loss which was not known in the language as recently as twenty years ago, and which can be attributed to a natural process of vowel syncope (Fox 2005: 57).

6.3.1.2 Individual variability, the effect of semi-speakers

Most endangered language situations involve gradual decline in speaker numbers and speaker fluency. As more of the community shifts to the dominant language (cf. O'Shannessy, Chapter 5), fewer children learn the minority language, and often those who do so learn it imperfectly, resulting in SEMI-SPEAKERS – people who have learned the language to some degree and are not fully fluent (see Grenoble, Chapter 2). For example, Schmidt (1985a: 381) found that among Jambun Dyirbal (Australia) speakers, variability could be described on a continuum according to the degree of simplification of traditional Dyirbal, and this continuum correlated with the age of the speakers. This is typical of a gradual shift to a majority language: 'each individual had his own grammatical system for Dyirbal communication, involving simplification of the traditional grammatical norm to a greater or lesser degree.'

Languages can vary greatly in language endangerment situations, with potentially more kinds and greater frequency of variation than encountered in non-endangered languages. Things that are obligatory in a fully viable language may become optional or fail to apply and be lost in the language of semi-speakers. For example, semi-speakers of Tlahuica (a.k.a. Ocuilteco, Otomanguean family, Mexico) sometimes fail to voice stops after nasals (*nt* does not automatically become *nd*, a change which is obligatory in viable Ocuilteco), producing free variation. In Pipil (a.k.a. Nahuate or Nawat, a Uto-Aztecan language of El Salvador), /l/ is always voiceless in final position; in moribund Cuisnahuat Pipil, however, voiced 'l' was allowed also word-finally, with the result of seeming free variation between voiced 'l' and voiceless 'l' in this position. As Swadesh (1934, 1946) observed in his work with the last two speakers of Chitimacha (isolate, Louisiana), glottalized consonants could vary rather freely with their unglottalized counterparts (though original plain consonants did not vary with glottalized ones).

6.3.2   Types of change in endangered languages
6.3.2.1   Normal change (change typically encountered also in non-endangered languages)

As mentioned above, obsolescing languages can undergo ordinary changes that can also be observed to take place in languages which are not endangered. For example, in moribund Chiltiupan Pipil, *ts* changed to *s*. The change of an affricate to a fricative (*ts* > *s*) is not an uncommon sound change, and is found in the history of languages that are not endangered. In another example, Pipil speakers today, none of whom are fully fluent, have lost the original vowel length contrast and all long vowels have become short (V: > V); many have also lost the rule that devoices final *l* (for example /mi:l/ [mi:ɬ] > /mil/ [mil] 'cornfield').

Many changes of this sort may be attributable, at least in part, to influence from the locally dominant language. For example, the change of *ts* to *s* in Chiltiupan Pipil might also reflect influence from dominant Spanish, which has no segment *ts*; the loss of the vowel length contrast and of the voiceless 'l' in final position in varieties of Pipil, though both natural changes, may also reflect the absence of these sounds in Spanish. While influence from the dominant language (or languages) must always be taken seriously into consideration as possibly affecting the structure of endangered languages, we do not emphasize this in this section, concentrating rather on the kinds of structural changes languages can undergo regardless of whether these are abetted by influences from the dominant language (though see 6.3.2.6. below for discussion of 'acts of reception').

6.3.2.2   Overgeneralization of unmarked features (loss of marked features through replacement with unmarked counterparts)

MARKED FEATURES are traits of language which tend to be more unusual cross-linguistically, more difficult for children to learn, and more easily lost in language change. They tend to be replaced by less marked ones (more common cross-linguistically, more easily learned) in language change. That is, difficult contrasts may not be learned, or not learned well. For example, in endangered Mam of Tuxtla Chico (Mayan; Mexico), marked uvular stops were replaced by unmarked velars ($q > k$; $q' > k'$). Chipewyan (Athabaskan; Canada) semi-speakers change glottalized consonants to their plain counterparts ($C' > C$) (Cook 1989). These sorts of changes are also normal and can be found in the history of languages which are not threatened.

6.3.2.3   Overgeneralization of marked features

In several situations, things that seem 'exotic' from the point of view of speakers of the dominant language can come to be overused in unexpected contexts in an obsolescing language. For example, one Jumaytepeque Xinka (Xinkan family, Guatemala) semi-speaker pronounced nearly every consonant as glottalized ($C > C'$). This is not a natural change and would definitely not be expected to occur in fully viable languages. In moribund Teotepeque Pipil, some speakers over-generalized voiceless 'l', employing it everywhere at the expense of voiced 'l', though in fully viable Pipil, the voiceless 'l' is only an allophone of /l/ in final position. In instances such as this, it seems that the semi-speakers are aware of the unusual traits but have not learned where they correctly belong and so use them excessively but inappropriately, as a consequence of imperfect learning.

6.3.2.4   Loss or reduction in phonological contrasts (mergers)

Some instances of phonological merger have already been seen, as for example, Pipil $ts > s$, V: $> V$, (that is, ts, s $> s$; V:, V $> V$), and Mam of Tuxtla Chico $q > k$; $q' > k'$ ($q, k > k$; $q', k' > k'$). Documentation of both Chitimacha (isolate; Louisiana) (Swadesh 1934, 1946) and Tonkawa (isolate; Texas) (Hoijer 1933, 1946) (both now extinct) revealed that the last speakers often merged glottalized consonants with the non-glottalized counterparts.

6.3.2.5   Both overgeneralization and under-generalization

In some instances both overgeneralization and under-generalization can affect structural properties. For example, viable Pipil devoices non-nasal sonorants (*l*, *w*, *y*) word-finally; moribund Teotepeque Pipil, however, overgeneralized voiceless *l*, devoicing *l*'s in all environments, not just final ones, but undergeneralized in the case of *w* and *y* by not devoicing them finally (or anywhere else, for that matter). Through overgeneralization (of voiceless *l*) and under-generalization (of voiceless *w* and *y*) the sonorant final-devoicing process was eliminated. In some other Pipil dialects, as mentioned above, the final *l* also ceased to be devoiced, along with *w* and *y*, meaning that the rule of final devoicing of sonorants was also completely lost in these dialects, though in this case through under-generalization.

6.3.2.6 Acts of reception

ACTS OF RECEPTION in this context refer to instances in which the minority language 'receives', or takes on, traits from the dominant language judged by speakers of the dominant language to be highly valued and also avoiding native traits of the minority language which might be associated with traits of the dominant language which are judged undesirable. Some structural changes can be due to influence from the dominant language where the minority language takes on highly valued structural traits of the dominant language which are otherwise quite foreign to the minority language. For example, Teotepeque Pipil underwent the change *š* > *r* (where /š/ is a retroflex non-apical laminal fricative, equivalent to a [ʃ] that is retracted to the hard palate). This change is due to an act of reception in which attitudes about pronunciation of the local Spanish of the region are transferred to traits of the minority language, leading it to change. Spanish is the dominant language here, and where in standard Spanish the phoneme /r/ is a voiced alveolar trill, local Spanish has [š] as an additional non-standard variant of this phoneme. This variant in Spanish is stigmatized and considered undesirable by local Spanish speakers. This negative evaluation of the [š] variant in Spanish was taken over by Pipil speakers and the associated attitude caused moribund Teotepeque Pipil to shift the pronunciation of its native phoneme in order to match the [r] (trilled 'r') variant in standard Spanish of El Salvador, the prestigious variety. A change of a sibilant such as *š* to a trilled 'r' is highly unusual and unexpected (there are no 'r' sounds in viable Pipil).[12] In another example, some semi-speakers and non-native learners of Pipil often pronounce Pipil initial /y/ ([j] in IPA) as [ʒ], as in [ʒek] for /yek/ 'good', to make it match the [ʒ] prestige pronunciation of initial /y/ in Spanish, totally alien to viable Pipil, which has [j] as its only pronunciation. Acts of reception can also influence the lexicon. For example, native words in the endangered language whose meanings are neutral are sometimes avoided or replaced because they sound like words that are obscenities in the dominant language. An example of this is Nivaclé *puta* 'rabbit', which sounds like obscene *puta* 'whore' in dominant Spanish. Because this word sounds like an obscenity in the dominant language, it is replaced in the speech of most Nivaclé speakers by *nanxatetax* (derived from *nanxate* 'hare, jack rabbit' + *-tax* 'similar to'). Other examples of lexical avoidance of this sort are not difficult to find.

6.3.2.7 Morphological reduction

Two changes observed with some frequency across obsolescing languages are the decay of case systems and the tendency to change toward more rigid word order.[13] For example, semi-speakers of American Finnish fail to show adjectives agreeing with nouns in case and number, producing, for example, expressions like *vanha miehe-n* [old man-GENITIVE.SG] 'the old man's' and *vanha miehe-ltä* [old man-from] 'from the old man', where fully competent speakers have *vanha-n miehe-n* [old-GENITIVE.SG man-GENITIVE.SG] and *vanha-lta miehe-ltä* [old-from man-from], respectively, showing agreement. In another example, imperfect speakers of Tlahuica (mentioned above) often eliminate the dual and plural markers which fully fluent speakers do not leave out, as in the following examples where the material missing in the speech of semi-speakers is indicated in parentheses (Campbell and Muntzel 1989: 191–2):

(20) kiat-kwe-p-tyɨɨ(-nkwe(-βi))
      FUT-1PL-EXCL-sing(-DUAL(-EXCL))
      'We (two, but not you) will sing'

(21) kiat-kwe-p-tyɨɨ(-hñə(-βi))
      FUT-1PL-EXCL-sing(-PL(-EXCL))
      'We (all, but not you) will sing'

6.3.2.8 Preference for analytic constructions over synthetic ones

Sometimes obsolescing languages prefer analytic constructions over synthetic ones (see Campbell and Muntzel 1989: 192–4).[14] For example, Pipil used to have a synthetic morphological 'future':

(22) (a) ni-panu-s [I-pass-FUT] 'I will pass'
      (b) ti-panu-ske-t [we-pass-FUT-PL] 'we will pass'.

However, later in its more moribund stage, Pipil lost the synthetic morphological 'future' and had in its place the analytic syntactic 'future':

(23) (a) ni-yu ni-panu
           I-go I-pass
           'I will pass' (literally 'I'm going to pass')

      (b) ti-yawi-t ti-panu-t
           we-go-PL we-pass-PL
           'we will pass' ('we're going to pass').

In another example, Scottish Gaelic semi-speakers are reported by Dorian (1981: 15) to replace the synthetic conjugated prepositions (*riu-m* 'to-me', *bhu-atha* 'from-them') with analytic constructions of free-standing preposition and pronoun (*ri mis*' 'to me', *bho aid* 'from them').

6.3.2.9   Syntactic reduction

Loss of certain grammatical categories and syntactic options, particularly complex sentence constructions, is common in language obsolescence. (The loss of the morphological 'future' in Pipil is an example of this.) It is sometimes thought that complex linguistic structures learned later in childhood may be lost because it is at this age that children in many communities often stop using the endangered language. One example is the reduced use and loss of subordinate clauses in dying languages that can be explained in terms of two tendencies: (1) since speakers of moribund languages produce few complex sentences, a child exposed to such language input would have an inadequate model for acquiring them; (2) certain subordinate clauses tend to be used in higher (more formal) styles, but the strong solidarity function of the dying language in some communities emphasizes 'lower' (less formal) styles. This may strip away the complex constructions as the 'higher' styles cease to be used. When there are competing structures with the same function (meaning), they may tend to be reduced to a single structure in obsolescing language situations.

6.3.2.10   Stylistic shrinkage

Correlated with reduction in grammar is reduction in speech genres and stylistic alternatives (such as verbal art, oral literature, ritual language, formal registers and figurative language), called STYLISTIC SHRINKAGE. Stylistic shrinkage often begins at the formal end of the stylistic continuum, 'polystylism' moving to 'monostylism', where finally only casual speech remains (Dorian 1980, Hill 1978). However, shrinkage can also take place from the bottom-up, leaving the obsolescing language used only in formulaic ritual settings. Both situations involve stylistic shrinkage with severe reduction in the stylistic range available to speakers. Stylistic reduction correlates closely with syntactic reduction, since different styles are typically characterized by different syntactic options or different frequencies of usages for certain syntactic constructions over others. One example of this is the loss of the morphological future in Pipil (see 6.3.2.8 above), which was characteristic of elevated styles, leaving only the analytic future, more typical of less prestigious speech. Similarly, there may no longer be any Ocuilteco speakers competent in the formulaic ritual language employed in religious ceremonies and marriage petitions. This kind of speech relies heavily on paired couplets (repetition of the same content utilizing alternative semantic and syntactic forms). The last speaker competent in this style may well have been Martha Muntzel's ritual-language consultant, who died in the mid 1970s (Campbell and Muntzel 1989).

6.4   Conclusion

In this chapter we have presented a sample of the many unique or unusual structural phenomena which have been uncovered in research on endangered languages and which would have been lost to science if these languages had disappeared before they were documented and described. We presented examples of how these discoveries contribute to understanding more completely the full range of what is possible in human languages, challenging some general claims and helping to strengthen others, thus contributing to the development of linguistic theory. We also considered the kinds of variation and change found in endangered and obsolescing languages. We examined the considerable impact language endangerment can have on the structure of the languages involved. We pointed out implications for typological claims, for example that several putative universals and general claims about language must be modified or abandoned based on new findings encountered in various endangered languages. We also considered the kinds of changes encountered in endangered obsolescing languages and some consequences of these for general views about how languages change. All of these considerations show both jointly and individually the importance of documenting and describing endangered languages, and the contributions that findings from these languages can and do make to linguistic theory.

Notes

1 Examples are drawn from the literature and from our own fieldwork and first-hand experience with the languages mentioned. This explains why examples from the indigenous languages of the Americas figure so prominently here.

2 The Nivaclé findings reported here are from Campbell (in preparation), from research supported by the 2003–6 grant 'Description of Chorote, Nivaclé and Kadiwéu: three of the least known and most endangered languages of the Chaco' funded by the Endangered Languages Documentation Programme, School of Oriental and African Studies (co-principal investigators Lyle Campbell, Verónica Grondona, and Filomena Sandalo).

3 It should be noted that many speech sounds have more than one articulatory gesture; however, in cases where the multiple gestures are not articulated relatively simultaneously, it may not be possible to distinguish them phonetically from sequences of segments found in other languages which lack phonotactic evidence for interpreting them as single segments (Ladefoged and Maddieson 1996: 329). This is not the case with this Nivaclé sound. Also, the Nivaclé sound is different from a velar lateral, a sound which was also unknown until

relatively recently but now known to occur in Mid-Waghi, Melpa, Kanite, Yagaria (New Guinea), Kotoko (Chadic), and Comox (Salishan), where contact is in the velar region with air escaping around both sides of the contact in the region of the back molars (Ladefoged and Maddieson 1996: 190).

4 The glottalized stops and affricates are ejective consonants. In the Americanist phonetic tradition, glottalized consonants are represented by an apostrophe following the plain consonant symbol, thus *p', t', k'* ([p$^?$], [t$^?$], [k$^?$] in the International Phonetic Alphabet).

5 In Nivaclé the voiceless lateral is an approximant, not a fricative (see e.g. Ladefoged and Maddieson 1996: 198).

6 Lindblom and Maddieson (1988) are not specific about whether the inventories they have in mind refer only to phonemes or to all the speech sounds (phonemes and their allophones), and of course a more precise definition of what is intended by 'simpler' and 'complex' would be useful. Nevertheless, whether the intent is to refer only to the phonemic inventory or to the entire set of speech sounds (phones) in a language, instances such as Pirahã have both few phonemes and few phones, yet some of the sounds they do have are complex by any definition; for example, Pirahã's voiceless laminal dental plosive followed by a bilabial trill.

7 Indeed, many Amazonian languages have become extinct. If we take Loukotka's (1968) count of 1,491 languages once spoken in South America as relatively accurate and compare this with the roughly 420 languages still spoken, we would have to conclude that some 72% of South American languages have become extinct. Probably Loukotka's list includes some names that do not actually correspond to real languages and in some cases multiple names referring to the same language; however, even allowing for such problems, the number of languages which have become extinct, a great many with no documentation or description, is very large.

8 The investigation of Xinkan was supported in part by a grant from the National Science Foundation to the University of Utah, 'Xinkan, Pipil, and Mocho': Bringing Three Endangered Language Documentation Projects to Completion' (co-Principal Investigators: Lyle Campbell, Laura Martin, Terrence Kaufman.)

9 The term 'basic order' is identified with the order that occurs in stylistically neutral, independent, indicative clauses with full noun phrases for the S (Subject) and O (Object) arguments in transitive clauses. Basic order and dominant order are usually equated, though not always by all scholars (see Siewierska 1988: 8). To say a language has a basic word order of a particular kind does not mean that other orders are not possible within it.

10 VOS order was also not found in Greenberg's original sample of languages and was also excluded by his proposed universal, though a number of examples of VOS languages soon came to be identified.

11 Abbreviations used in the glosses are: ABS absolutive; CL classifier; DEM deictic; EXCL exclusive; ERG ergative; FUT future; HUM human; NONFUT non-future; PL plural; POSS possessive; SG singular.

12 Rhotacism might be mentioned, but this is not the form that rhotacism typically takes in languages where it is known, usually involving intervocalic /s/ and a non-trilled 'r'.

13 Similar changes, of course, can take place in non-obsolescing languages, but it is quite common to see such changes and for them to take place rapidly in obsolescing languages, generally more commonly and rapidly than in non-obsolescing languages. Naturally, the dominant language can influence decay of case and word-order change to reflect the character of the dominant language more, and the presence of case marking in the dominant language could retard decay of case in the obsolescing languages.

14 Changes towards analytic structures can also take place in non-obsolescing languages, but not typically as frequently nor as rapidly as in obsolescing languages.

7

Language and culture

Lev Michael

7.1 Introduction

LANGUAGE and CULTURE, having 'grown up together', to adapt Benjamin Whorf's (1956: 156) memorable phrase, are inextricably intermeshed. Despite programmatic efforts to define language in such a way as to sever its ties to culture, there is little indication that asocial and acultural theories of language are adequate to the task of providing valid scientific accounts of linguistic form and function (Evans and Levinson 2009). Scientific theories of language necessarily depend on accounts of the language–culture nexus.

While an understanding of the language–culture nexus is theoretically important in its own right, it is especially relevant in the case of endangered languages. In the first place, efforts to support or revitalize endangered languages must confront the fact that language shift takes place for complex social and cultural reasons (Grenoble, Chapter 2). Approaches to language that recognize it to be intimately enmeshed with culture and social practices offer purchase on the contexts of language shift, potentially giving those involved conceptual tools with which to understand the causes of language endangerment, and thereby develop locally apt strategies. In the second place, delimiting the goals of language documentation (Woodbury, Chapter 9) depends on models of the language–culture nexus. Given that the boundary between language and culture is an unclear one (see 7.2.2), and given that language documentation projects must contend with finite time and resources, the definition of what constitutes ADEQUATE DOCUMENTATION of a language depends in part on distinguishing language from the larger field of social practices in which it is embedded. This issue is relevant to all language documentation, but it is especially acute in the case of endangered languages, where opportunities to carry out documentation may be limited.

This chapter provides an overview of important strands of thought regarding the interrelation of language and culture, from the complementary perspectives of culture's influence on linguistic form and the role of linguistic form in social action and culture. We begin with a discussion of the conceptual relationship between the two elements of the dyad on which this chapter focuses.

7.2 Conceptual foundations

7.2.1 Culture

Although culture has been theorized in a variety of ways, most articulations of the concept share two features:

1. culture is a learned body of behaviours and/or knowledge transmitted by transgenerational learning; and
2. this body is predicated primarily of human groups and, only through membership in a group, of individuals.

The first feature serves to delimit culture by distinguishing it from human characteristics whose transmission can be attributed to genetic or other biological mechanisms (e.g. effects of nutrition), while the second feature seeks to distinguish individually idiosyncratic characteristics from those stemming from long-term group membership. These two features are both present as early as Tylor's 1958[1871] definition of culture:

> Culture ... is that complex whole which includes knowledge, belief, art, morals, law, custom and any other capabilities and habits acquired by man as a member of society. The condition of culture among the various societies of mankind ... is a subject apt for the study of laws of human thought and action.

Tylor's definition also exhibits in incipient form the distinction between THOUGHT and ACTION/BEHAVIOUR that subsequently developed into a tendency to conceptualize culture as either:

1. primarily related to human cognitive or interpretative activity; or
2. primarily related to behaviour and its material outcomes.

The following brief survey of culture theory reflects this dichotomy, concluding with a discussion of practice theory, an approach which seeks to transcend this IDEALIST/MATERIALIST DICHOTOMY.

7.2.1.1 Ideational accounts of culture

Ideational accounts of culture make concepts and meaning central to defining their object, and to explaining its properties and dynamics. The first clearly articulated ideational theories of culture, structuralist anthropology and ethnoscience/cognitive anthropology, have as their inspirations the versions of structuralist linguistics that developed on either side of the Atlantic. Structuralist anthropology took form with the work of Claude Lévi-Strauss (e.g. 1958), who married the notion of 'collective consciousness' inherited from Emile Durkheim (1912) to a model of cultural meaning inspired by Roman Jakobson's (1978[1942]) theory of phonological features. The result was a vision of culture as a kind of group mind in which sets of binary notional oppositions create collective representations of social life. As an ultimate aim, Lévi-Strauss sought to identify the sociocultural configurations of particular societies as combinations of the basic notional contrasts immanent in the human mind. Though influential in the postwar decades, this semantico-algebraic conception of culture came under increasing critique for its evacuation of action, agency and affect from social life (Bourdieu 1977a, Geertz 1973, Leach 1974).

Culture theory took a similarly ideational turn in North America in the 1950s, as the analysis of lexical meanings came to be seen as a powerful means to apprehend 'native' perspectives. Although the idea that lexical data offered a window onto culture was a central one in Boasian anthropology (see e.g. Sapir 1916: 432), the school of 'componential analysis' developed this idea further by adapting American structuralist notions of phonological contrast to the study of lexical meaning, and crafting feature-based analyses of lexical domains such as kinship terms (Goodenough 1956, Lounsbury 1956). This approach was seen by many as a powerful ethnographic methodology, inspiring the study of FOLK TAXONOMIES as a window onto cultural conceptual systems, and eventually leading to the definition of a society's culture as coextensive with the knowledge 'of whatever it is one has to know or believe in order to operate in a manner acceptable to its members' (Goodenough 1957: 167). Ultimately, debates over the feasibility of bridging the gap between 'native' conceptions and anthropologists' analytical frameworks, along with doubts about the psychological reality of cognitive analyses (Burling 1964, Schneider 1968, Wallace and Atkins 1960) indexed increasing dissatisfaction with cognitivist approaches,[1] and stimulated the development of symbolic, or interpretative, anthropology.

Whereas cognitive anthropologists saw their task as describing cultural knowledge, symbolic anthropologists saw their task as capturing the broader meaningfulness of social actions for the participants in those actions (Geertz 1973: 3–30). The task of the symbolic anthropologist was cast as a hermeneutic one, in which social action was theorized as constituting a form of interpretable 'text' (Turner 1967). Thus, for example, the central role of the white-sapped milk tree in Ndembu female initiation was interpreted as symbolizing the transition of the initiates into the role of child-bearing women. Significantly, cultural texts were understood as public representations, in contrast with the cognitivist focus on 'knowledge', which symbolic anthropologists argued misconstrued culture as private and individual.

Symbolic anthropology was the last influential ideational account of culture to develop in anthropology, where the culture concept has become increasingly contested. Two critiques have been leveled against the culture concept: one moral, and the other analytical. First, scholars such as Abu-Lughod (1991) have argued that the culture concept makes people into 'others', with a sense of hierarchy and distance invariably accompanying that of difference. In short, these scholars argue that one cannot speak of the culture of a given group without thereby marking that group as alien and inferior. Second, for scholars such as Appadurai (1996) and Rosaldo (1993), the culture concept ignores power relations and individual agency and exaggerates homogeneity by playing down the differences, inequalities, and processes of contestation within groups, thereby blinding analysts to important dimensions of the phenomena they are examining. Defenders of the culture concept, however, have pointed out that neither presuppositions of homogeneity nor entailments of inequality are inherent to the culture concept, and moreover, that no promising alternative exists to take its place (Bashkow 2004, Brumann 1999).

7.2.1.2 Behavioural accounts of culture

In the early twentieth century, the behavioural–ideational divide was frequently manifested in the competing notion of SOCIAL STRUCTURE versus CULTURE. For its advocates, social structure was conceived of as concrete, observable, social and material behaviour, to which the abstract culture concept was unfavourably compared (Radcliffe-Brown 1940). Social anthropologists focused on the types of social structures extant in human groups (e.g. exogamous clans and cross-cousin marriage), and their SOCIAL FUNCTION, which was theorized in a number of ways. One early conception of social function emerged from the work of Bronislaw Malinowski, who identified the FUNCTIONS of social structures as their roles in satisfying basic biophysical human needs. On this view, the family and marriage, for example, functioned to satisfy the biophysical need for reproduction (Malinowski 1939).

A second sense of social function, with roots in Durkheim's (1947[1893]) notion of 'social solidarity', was foregrounded in the work of Alfred Radcliffe-Brown (1935), which focused on the ways in which aspects of social structure contribute to the maintenance of the overarching social structure of which they are part. The British school of STRUCTURAL FUNCTIONALISM made this sense of function central to its analysis of human societies, leading to strong assumptions regarding the stasis of the societies examined, and to analyses of behaviour primarily in terms of their contributions to that stasis (Radcliffe-Brown 1935). Mounting ethnographic evidence, however, revealed that the presupposition of stasis and the concomitant neglect of history was untenable, significantly under-mining the structural–functionalist programme.

7.2.1.3   Practice theory

The conceptions of culture discussed so far are characterized by their tendency to either subordinate the behavioural and material aspects of social activity to their ideational ones, or to reverse this relationship. Under these dichotomized views, either ideational schemes are seen as guiding behaviour, which thereby becomes epiphenomenal and rela-tively uninteresting, or ideational schemes are seen as abstractions from behaviour, and hence considered vague theoretical constructs. PRACTICE THEORY emerged during the 1970s as an effort to transcend this dichotomy, and to address two related weaknesses in social and cul-tural theory:

1. the tendency to evacuate agency and strategy from analyses of human activity in favour of functional or structural explanations; and
2. the difficulty that both structuralist and functionalist theories had with accounting for and incorporating history and social change.

From the perspective of practice theory, these weaknesses had a com-mon root: inattention to PRACTICAL ACTION.

The key insight of practice theory is that individuals' behaviour displays a combination of strategic improvisation and routinization. Practice the-ory maintains that individuals are neither structuralist automatons work-ing out the logic of culture, not functionalist ants working to maintain the societies of which they are part, but are instead strategically savvy actors improvisationally attempting to realize projects of a variety of scales under pressing temporal, social and material constraints (Giddens 1979). At the same time, however, practice theory allows that practical action, while informed by actors' agency, tends to sediment into a body of dispositions, routines, and ready-at-hand schemas for action, which Bourdieu (1977a) calls HABITUS. Crucially, these resources for structuring action are understood to have a dual nature, in that they both inform practical action, and are reproduced and transformed by that action (Giddens 1984). The resulting DUALITY OF STRUCTURE effectively hybrid-izes the structuralist notion of culture with that of social function, while leaving space for individual agency and human creativity.

7.2.2   Distinguishing 'language' and 'culture'

Although the title of this chapter presupposes that the terms LANGUAGE and CULTURE are distinguishable, doing so precisely presents difficulties. Language, like culture, is an intergenerationally transmitted learned behaviour, and many early definitions of culture casually include lan-guage as a subcomponent. Indeed, the fact that lay definitions of language include much that overlaps with culture lies behind the efforts of scholars like Ferdinand de Saussure, Leonard Bloomfield and Noam Chomsky to delimit a restricted object of study for linguistics.

Bloomfield (1926: 154), for example, identified the object of linguistics as the residue that remains after communicative activity has been stripped of everything related to the social ends of communication. Chomsky evinced scepticism that LANGUAGE is a useful scientific concept (Chomsky, 1982: 107), and used the COMPETENCE/PERFORMANCE DISTINCTION to restrict linguistics to the study of those aspects of our communicative ability that are independent of speakers' social goals. As Hanks (1996: 36) points out, these delimitations serve to identify an aspect of communication that cannot be further analysed in terms of its social or interactional function, but must be analysed in terms of organizing principles internal to this domain: grammar (see also Silverstein 1987).

Viewed in this way, the understanding of language and culture that emerges is not one in which language and culture constitute distinct and bounded systems, but rather one in which it is possible to identify, within the larger systems of social practices of a society, a pole of linguistic form and grammatical organization that constitutes part of a broader set of motivating factors, resources and constraints that inform social action. Linguistics' disciplinary focus thus highlights those aspects of social practice located close to the pole of formal organization identified by Saussure and Bloomfield. From this perspective, the study of language and culture involves a focus on those aspects of social practices in which linguistic form and social action play important mutually constitutive roles, especially those that by virtue of their variability across human groups are seen as cultural in nature.

7.3 Approaches to the language–culture nexus

Whereas the study of linguistic form can be surveyed either from the perspective of organizational components (e.g. phonology, morphology, syntax and semantics) or in terms of identifiable theories (e.g. generativist, functionalist or cognitivist), the study of the language–culture nexus defies comprehensive exposition based on such rubrics. Rather, efforts to describe work on the language–culture nexus must confront a heterogeneous mixture of theoretical frameworks and relatively diffuse schools of thought, and perduring questions that cross-cut theories and intellectual traditions.

Among the schools of thought on the language–culture nexus, the UCLA, Chicago, and MPI Nijmegen schools are currently the most influential.[2] The UCLA school, exemplified by the work of Alessandro Duranti and Elinor Ochs, exhibits a strong ethnographic commitment that can be traced to its roots in the ethnography of communication tradition (see 7.3.1.1 below), which is reflected in a pervasive skepticism toward universalist accounts of linguo-cultural phenomena. As evident in Duranti's (1997) subdiscipline-defining textbook, this school draws on Vygotskyan psychology and continental philosophical thought (e.g. Wittgenstein, Husserl), and on the tradition stemming from Erving Goffman's ethnomethodological approaches to interaction, including its discourse-focused offshoot, conversational analysis (Goodwin and Heritage 1990).

The Chicago school's approach to the language–culture nexus, exemplified by the work of Michael Silverstein, is characterized by the prominent role of semiotic theory (see 7.3.1.4) in providing much of the tradition's ontological apparatus (Agha 2007a), which is combined with accounts of linguistic reflexivity (Lucy 1993) and language ideology (see 7.3.2.4) in order to couple basic semiotic elements and relations to larger scale social and cultural processes.

The MPI Nijmegen school,[3] exemplified by the work of Stephen Levinson and Nick Enfield, among others, contrasts with the previous two schools in a number of ways, including a strong theoretical focus on cognition, the use of experimental and stimuli-based methodologies, systematic cross-linguistic comparison and, despite a sensitivity to cultural variation, an underlying commitment to explanatory frameworks in which universal principles and mechanisms play a major role (e.g. Enfield and Stivers 2007, Levinson and Meira 2003).

7.3.1   Frameworks

7.3.1.1   Ethnography of communication

The ETHNOGRAPHY OF COMMUNICATION (EoC) was the earliest effort to develop a framework for the description of linguistic behaviour in wider social and cultural contexts. Hymes (1964) observed that linguistics' focus on linguistic form, and the general lack of sensitivity to language in cultural anthropology, led to inattention to the integration of language into social life in both disciplines. In response, EoC was aimed at developing culturally contextualized descriptions of language use that embraced holism at both the level of the community and at the level of recurrent communicative contexts, or SPEECH EVENTS.

At the community level, the goal of EoC was to characterize the VERBAL REPERTOIRE of communities and describe the circumstances under which the languages, registers and styles (Hymes, 1974b) comprising the repertoire were employed. In his study of interaction in the Indian community of Khalapur, for example, Gumperz (1964) characterizes the verbal repertoire of the former community as consisting of standard Hindi, the two major varieties of the Khalapur dialect, and three subdialects associated with the untouchable caste, and discusses how the distribution of the two major varieties depends on the formality of the speech context and social asymmetries between the participants.

At the level of the speech event, the goal was to holistically describe its social organization and the various WAYS OF SPEAKING involved in the event (see e.g. Sherzer 1983). To guide this task, Hymes (1972) developed the SPEAKING framework, which identified the following important descriptive dimensions: SITUATION (both the spatio-temporal setting and the socioculturally defined situation type), PARTICIPANTS (the actors and non-actors in the speech event), ENDS (goals and outcomes), ACT SEQUENCES, KEY (social valence: e.g. serious versus comic), INSTRUMENTALITIES (linguistic varieties and channels), NORMS (of interaction and interpretation), and GENRES. One of the most detailed descriptions resulting from this tradition is Duranti's (1981) work on the *fono*, a political gathering of Samoan chiefs and orators. This description ranges from an enumeration of eligible participants, their rank-based seating within the social space of the meeting house, the resulting division of the space into regions for formal and informal communication, and the sequential organization of the event into an opening *kava* drinking ceremony and a main speaking event. The description of the latter event is further decomposed into:

1. the specialized lexicon employed in the event, including 'respect vocabulary' (i.e. honorific) forms;
2. morphosyntactic characteristics of *fono* speech, which include a greater prevalence than in everyday conversation of grammatical elements such as overt NPs and tense–aspect markers; and
3. turn-taking organization, which varies from prototypical conversational organization (Sacks *et al.* 1974) during the informal stages of the *fono*, to a quasi-templatic structure which highly constrains the content, form and sequencing of turns at talk during the later formal stages.

The EoC came under criticism for its relatively atheoretical character (Levinson 1983: 375), which together with the vastness of the empirical task it set itself (Keating 2001: 294), and its relative isolation from mainstream anthropological concerns (Duranti 2003: 328), accounts for its decline as an active area of research in recent decades. Interestingly, EoC's descriptivist orientation (see e.g. Hymes, 1977: 53, Saville-Troike, 1982: 108) has led to a recent resurgence of interest in EoC among linguists as a holistic framework for comprehensive language documentation (Hill 2006, Himmelmann 1998, A. Woodbury 2003).

7.3.1.2 Language socialization

The field of LANGUAGE SOCIALIZATION (LS) arose in part as a developmental counterpart to the ethnography of communication and the pragmatics of the era (Ochs and Schieffelin 1979), but this 'socio-cultural framework for language acquisition' (Ochs 1988: 4) quickly outgrew its origins (Schieffelin and Ochs 1986), drawing inspiration from Piagetian and Vygotskyan psychology (Piaget 1952; Vygotsky 1962, 1978) and practice theory. The two central ideas of LS were (Ochs 1988: 14–17):

1. that knowledge of language and knowledge of culture are acquired simultaneously through social activity, so that linguistic knowledge is embedded in knowledge of appropriate language use in social context; and
2. that both linguistic and cultural skills are acquired via a process of 'internalization' in which novices first develop the ability to participate in joint activities with more expert individuals and then subsequently develop the ability to deploy these skills without this social scaffolding.

The vision of the language–culture nexus that emerges is thus one of integration of grammar, pragmatics and social action through their simultaneous and intermeshed childhood acquisition in joint activity.

An example of this process is provided by Schieffelin's (1986) discussion of the acquisition of rhetorical questions as a social control strategy among Kaluli children. Schieffelin describes how preverbal children experience the combination of rhetorical questions with direct interventions by caretakers to alter undesirable behaviours (e.g. 'Why are you climbing?', combined with the removal of the baby off of a woodpile). Later, verbally capable children are also included in triadic interactions in which caretakers model rhetorical questions for them to repeat to others as a way of modifying their undesirable behaviours (e.g. ' "Why are you crying?!" Say like that'). In this way, Kaluli children learn to interpret and use rhetorical questions as part of social control strategies, resulting in the holistic acquisition of intermeshed linguistic and social skills.

7.3.1.3   Pragmatics and ethnopragmatics

PRAGMATICS occupies an ambiguous position in the culturally informed study of language. Since pragmatics concerns linguistic meanings that arise in concrete contexts of language use, it can be seen as concerned with aspects of hybrid linguo-social phenomena lying closer to the pole of social action than to that of linguistic form. However, pragmatics is mainly concerned with universal aspects of context-dependent meaning, which arguably places this UNIVERSAL PRAGMATICS outside the realm of culture (Goddard 2006b).

ETHNOPRAGMATICS arose as a response to this acultural pragmatics, first emerging as a relativist critique of early Gricean pragmatics and Searlean speech act theory (e.g. Rosaldo 1982; Wierzbicka 1985), and subsequently developing into culturally informed accounts of pragmatics in different societies (e.g. Duranti 1993, Goddard 2006a; Wierzbicka

1991). Keenan (1976), an early example of the critical phase of this tradition, observed that vague and circumlocutory talk is common in conversational interactions among speakers of Malagasy, which appears to contradict the Gricean maxim that speakers 'be informative'. Keenan argues that the vagueness found in much Malagasy discourse stems from the desire of speakers to avoid epistemic commitments that entail social risks, and that the degree of informativeness that speakers exhibit depends on the sensitivity of the subject matter and their relation to the addressee. Keenan concludes that the norms governing communicative society must be calibrated to the society in question, and that serious thought needs to be given to the dependence of pragmatic reasoning on culture-specific situational parameters.

Although the term ethnopragmatics was first employed by Duranti (1993, 1994), it has come to be most closely associated with the tradition springing from Wierzbicka's (1991) CROSS-CULTURAL PRAGMATICS, rechristened ETHNOPRAGMATICS by Goddard (2002). This latter formulation of ethnopragmatics is clearly distinguished by its reliance on Wierzbicka's Natural Semantic Metalanguage (NSM), a set of approximately sixty supposedly cross-culturally valid conceptual primes, and the use of CULTURAL SCRIPTS, which are explicit schematized articulations of cultural values and reasoning in terms of NSM that speakers are said to employ in formulating and interpreting utterances.

Debate continues between ethnopragmaticists and proponents of a more universalizing vision of pragmatics, centring mainly on the issue of whether the principles of (neo-)Gricean and Searlean pragmatics are ethnocentric, and whether this entails the need for a distinct ethnopragmatics (Goddard 2006b). As the exchange between Enfield (2007) and Goddard (2007) illustrates, the core issue in this debate is whether a cross-culturally valid approach to pragmatic phenomena requires a set of universal inferencing strategies that combine with culture-specific pragmatic principles and schemas, or whether pragmatics is culture-specific 'all the way down'.

7.3.1.4   Semiotic approaches to language

One of the major challenges to studying the culture–language nexus is identifying and theorizing substantive linkages between communicative contexts and linguistic form and meaning. SEMIOTIC approaches to language address this challenge by focusing on INDEXICALITY, a type of meaning which is fixed by reference to variables that emerge from schematic parameterizations of utterance context, as exemplified by the canonical spatial indexical expressions 'here' and 'now'. Jakobson (1971) first brought indexicality to linguists' attention with his work on tense, and Silverstein (1976, 2003) subsequently developed a broadly gauged account of indexical contextual meanings that went beyond spatio-temporal ones to encompass social meaning.

The utility of indexicality for linking linguistic forms to social organization is nicely illustrated by deference indexicals, such as T/V PRONOUNS (labelled for the contrast found in many European languages in the second-person singular pronouns between familiar T (as in French *tu*) and formal V (French *vous*)) and HONORIFICS (Agha, 1994)). The Japanese honorific system, for example, exhibits a 'polite' verbal suffix -*mas* that is stereotypically used to address social superiors (Foley, 1997: 318–23). The presence or absence of this suffix thus produces a contrast reminiscent of European T/V systems, where the choice of linguistic form indexes (i.e. points to) the relative social positions of speech act participants in a local social hierarchy. In addition to addressee honorifics, the Japanese system exhibits reference honorifics, which stereotypically index the relative social status of a referent and the speaker, while other languages, such as Pohnepeian, also exhibit bystander honorifics (Keating 1998). While social indexicals can be seen as REFLECTING social facts by virtue of their context-presupposing properties, indexicals also play an important role in SHAPING social relations via the CREATIVE effects of presuppositional accommodation, which allow speakers to use deference indexicals to express social meanings that cannot be simply 'read off' of context.

Indexical approaches to language have yielded another important framework for understanding the social importance of language, that of INDEXICAL ORDERS (Silverstein 2003), which in essence provides an account of the diachronic development of social indexicality. The basic idea is straightforward: a first-order indexicality correlates particular linguistic characteristics (e.g. so-called Received Pronunciation (RP, see Agha 2007a) with a particular delimitable social group. A second-order indexicality can then develop, linking those linguistic characteristics with salient, ideologically mediated, characteristics of that group (e.g. a particular cultural sophistication). In this way, particular linguistic forms can become SOCIOLINGUISTIC MARKERS (Labov 1972) identifying individuals as members of particular social groups, with particular socially salient characteristics.

7.3.1.5 Communicative practice theory

PRACTICE-BASED approaches to communication take advantage of the integration of structure, agency and historicity achieved by practice theory to develop an approach to communication that moves beyond the static structuralism of most grammatical theories to embrace the strategic and temporal dimensions of language use, without abandoning notions of regularity and conventionalization. From the perspective of communicative practice theory, speakers' communicative activity is guided by their communicative habitus, i.e. their disposition to communicate in particular ways (in a manner consonant with Hymes' (1977) COMMUNICATIVE COMPETENCE), which is calibrated to particular social contexts via pervasive cultural ideologies and speakers' own interactional goals (Erickson 2004, Hanks 1987, 1996). On this view, grammar is one of a number of resources that speakers employ in their regularized (but not mechanically rule-governed) communicative actions, which form part of broader trajectories of goal-directed social action.

This approach to integrating grammar and social action is exemplified in Michael's (to appear) examination of how speakers of Nanti employ EVIDENTIALS in interaction. Grammaticalized evidentials (markers that indicate the sensory or cognitive modes of access that speakers have to the states of affairs expressed by their utterances, e.g. visual versus inference) are pervasive in Nanti discourse, but are not grammatically obligatory, so that Nantis' use of these grammatical resources is not predictable on structural grounds alone. However, Nantis' use of evidentials exhibits considerable regularity, which can be explained in terms of interactants' social goals and Nanti ideologies regarding moral responsibility. In particular, much of Nantis' deployment of evidentials stems from strategic efforts to distance themselves from particular events or individuals, by relying on implicatures of non-involvement generated by non-direct evidentials such as reportives and inferentials. Thus, while grammar alone significantly under-determines the distribution of evidentials in Nanti discourse, an account of Nanti communicative habitus, which incorporates relevant cultural ideologies and regularized social strategies, provides an understanding of their appearance in Nanti discourse.

An emerging area of research related to communicative practice theory involves the recognition that the basic insights of practice theory intersect significantly with those of grammaticalization theory (Bybee and Hopper 2001: 2, Evans 2003). Both theories are concerned with how structures both guide behaviour (without mechanically determining it) and emerge as the sedimentation of behaviour. Both frameworks are thus accounts of the regularization and conventionalization of behaviour that leave space for both agency and 'invisible hand' effects. This common ground between communicative practice theory and grammaticalization theory suggests a theory of cultural influence on linguistic form in which discourse plays a major mediating function. Specifically, cultural factors involved in the linguistic habitus influence the frequency of particular linguistic forms in discourse, which leads to increased grammaticalization of those forms.

An example of this process is given by the KINTAX (kinship syntax) constructions of numerous Australian Aboriginal languages: pieces of morphology or lexical alternations that indicate whether distinct human referents in a clause pertain to 'harmonic' generations (ego's generation $\pm$ 2n, n = 0, 1, 2, ...) or disharmonic ones (ego's generation $\pm$ (2n +1)) (Evans 2003: 23–7; Hale 1966). In his discussion of the Martuthunira harmonic verb suffix, for example, Dench (1987) argues that the kintactic sense developed from a collective/reciprocal suffix (still present in the language) was driven by the high-frequency use of reciprocals in descriptions of habitual cooperation among harmonic generation kin in community ceremonies. The Martuthunira example illustrates how cultural practices (cooperation among harmonic kin) can lead to increased frequency of particular linguistic forms (the use of reciprocals with reference to harmonic kin), yielding culturally driven grammaticalization.

7.3.2　Areas of inquiry

7.3.2.1　Culture-specific meaning and categorization: Ethnosemantics and Ethnosyntax

One of the principal ways in which CULTURE has been invoked in linguistics is in describing and accounting for meanings and semantic categorizations that vary considerably from language to language. The earliest culturally relativized approaches to meaning were the ethnosemantics and ethnoscience approaches of the 1960s and 1970s (see Section 7.2.1.1), which influenced the subsequent development of cognitive anthropology (D'Andrade 1995) and cognitive linguistics (Langacker 1987). These two fields have converged on a form of culturally informed semantics that has moved beyond the binary feature-based account of ethnosemantics, making use of notions of PROTOTYPICALITY and gradient membership (Rosch 1975) to address the vagueness and ambiguities characteristic of much natural language. Work on RADIAL CATEGORIES (categories defined by multiple criteria, none of which need be either logically necessary or sufficient for category membership by themselves), IMAGE SCHEMAS and the role of METAPHOR in categorial organization, have been especially influential (Lakoff 1987, Palmer 1996).

Lakoff's (1987: 92–102) discussion of Dyirbal noun classes (based on Dixon 1972) illustrates these cognitive approaches to categorization. Dyirbal exhibits four major noun classes: *bayi* (men, most animals, the moon), *balan* (women, fire, sun, most birds, stinging or dangerous animals), *balam* (edible plants, honey, cigarettes) and *bala* (a residual category). Membership in these categories illustrates the effects of:

1. GRADIENCE, e.g. tobacco is not as prototypical a 'food' as edible plants and honey, but it is a consumable, and hence falls in the *balam* radial category;
2. CHAINING, e.g. the hairy mary grub produces a sunburn-like sting, and thus falls in *balan*, with the sun; and
3. IDEALIZED MODELS, e.g. according to myths, the moon and sun are husband and wife, and so the moon falls with men in *bayi* and the sun with women in *balan*.

As Lakoff observes, although radial category effects are found across languages, the organization of categories in particular languages depends crucially on local understandings of similarity, and on culturally salient relationships between entities.

Another important approach to culturalized semantics focuses on lexical meanings as reflective of cultural concerns, especially with respect to the environment and culture-specific material practices (e.g. Sapir 1916). More recently, scholars such as Wierzbicka (1997) have argued that lexical items in a given society also reflect aspects of its ethos or regnant philosophies (see also Jocks 1998: 224–5). Wierzbicka goes further, arguing that languages exhibit KEY WORDS that give special insight into their associated cultures. She argues, for example, that the comparison of the roughly equivalent words for 'freedom' in English (*freedom*) and Russian (*svoboda*) reveals different understandings of an individual's option to act in the face of opposing pressures, and suggests that *svoboda* 'embodies a different perspective on human life' in its association with ease and well-being, a connotation absent from its English counterpart (Wierzbicka 1997: 139–40).

Attention to culturally grounded aspects of meaning have extended from the lexicon to morphosyntax. Work in the latter area has begun to crystallize under the rubric of ETHNOSYNTAX (Enfield 2002a, Wierzbicka 1979, 1992). Enfield (2002b) synthesizes several lines of thought regarding relationships between morphosyntax and culture, and lays out the empirical and analytical challenges inherent to this area of study (especially the dangers of circularity in relating linguistic form to cultural factors). Work in ethnosyntax draws on frameworks as diverse as ethnopragmatics (Goddard 2002), cognitive approaches to metaphor and metonymy (Langacker 2002) and grammaticalization theory.

An example of the latter is given by Burridge's (2002) examination of highly unusual degrammaticalization trajectories of modal verbs in the Pennsylvania German of Canadian Anabaptist communities. Burridge (2002: 221) notes, for example, that the common desiderative construction in this variety makes use of the main verb *wotte*, which has degrammaticalized from the former auxiliary verb *wollte*, the 'subjunctive of modest wish'. Burridge argues that this unusual trajectory can be understood as a consequence of Anabaptist cultural norms that prize humility and the subordination of self-will to God. She suggests that originally, 'wotte [as a subjunctive auxiliary] was used as a cautious and modest substitute for the indicative in utterances expressing a sense of "wishing"' (Burridge 2002: 221), but that due to its high frequency in desiderative contexts, it came to be 'stripped of its pragmatic component ... [becoming] reinterpreted as a lexical verb with the full sense of "wishing"' (Burridge 2002: 222).

7.3.2.2 Linguistic relativity

The question of culturally grounded meaning discussed in the previous section has strong ties with the topic of LINGUISTIC RELATIVITY. Since at least the nineteenth century (e.g. Humboldt 1988[1836]), scholars have speculated that language structure influences patterns of thought and perception. Modern work in this area stems from the Boasian emphasis on cultural diversity in the categorization of experience (Lucy 1992: 11–13), which was later coupled, in the work of Edward Sapir, to the notion that language plays a role in determining that experience (Sapir 1964[1931]). Benjamin Whorf extended Sapir's thinking in this area by going beyond Sapir's concern with overtly marked categories to include covert categories, including what are now called subcategorization classes. Whorf (1956: 221) further emphasized the unconscious nature of the linguistic influence on thought, and in turn, culture, concluding that:

> users of markedly different grammars are pointed by their grammars towards different types of observations and different evaluations of externally similar acts of observation, and hence are not equivalent as observers but must arrive at somewhat different views of the world.

As Lucy (1992: 41) observes, the SAPIR-WHORF HYPOTHESIS, as it came to be known, spawned considerable debate from the 1950s to the 1980s, but little substantive research. What little research was carried out either failed to properly distinguish linguistic structure and non-linguistic behaviour, leading to circularity (e.g. Lee 1944), or suffered from oversimplified analyses of the linguistic domain (e.g. Brown and Lenneberg 1954). Only in the 1980s did methodologically sophisticated work begin to be carried out. Lucy (1992), for example, examined the effect of grammaticalized classifier systems in languages on speakers' categorization practices. Lucy reasoned that in classifier languages like Yucatec, most referents are treated as 'measured' units of a substance (e.g. a sheet of paper may be morphologically expressed as a 'flexible 2-dimensional unit of paper-substance'), making 'substance' more ontologically salient than 'units' for Yucatec speakers. Lucy predicted that for this reason, Yucatec speakers would judge objects of the same substance, but different shapes, to be more alike than objects of the same shape but different substances, while predicting the exact opposite for English speakers, due to the lack of a grammaticalized classifier system in English. Experimental results confirmed Lucy's predictions.

In recent years, linguistic relativity has attracted the attention of psychologists as well (Gentner and Meadows 2003), who have shown that linguistic encoding serves to prime performance of certain cognitive tasks (Boroditsky 2001) and leads to increased similarity judgements for referents that share noun class features, such as gender (Boroditsky *et al.* 2003).

Another major strand of work in this area is animated by efforts to show that categorization in particular semantic domains shows systematic similarities despite cross-cultural variation. Although there has been significant work in this area with respect to kinship (e.g. Goodenough 1970) and ethnobiological terminology (e.g. Berlin 1992; cf. Hunn 1982), the greatest attention has been paid to colour terminology (Berlin and Kay, 1969). Although languages vary from having as few as two basic colour terms, as in the case of the Papuan language Dani, to as many as twelve, as in Russian, there is remarkably little variation among colour term systems of a given size in terms of the focal colours of each colour term, as determined by the use of a common set of stimuli. This fact appears to stem from the physiological characteristics of the retinal cells responsible for colour vision, which make particular colours especially perceptually salient (Kay and McDaniel 1978). A considerable critical literature has developed from this early work, challenging both its theoretical presuppositions, in particular, its ethnocentric definition of 'colour' (Lucy 1997), and aspects of its empirical validity (e.g. Levinson 2000). Recent work seeks to synthesize the strengths of both camps by showing that there is a combination of both universal tendencies and local linguistic convention in the emergence of language-specific colour categories (Regier *et al.* 2010).

7.3.2.3   Language ideologies

The frameworks and themes discussed to this point are not specifically concerned with aspects of the language–culture nexus of which speakers have conscious awareness. The study of LANGUAGE IDEOLOGY, in contrast, focuses on language as the conscious object of social action and culture. Although linguists have long noted (with varying degrees of seriousness and interest) speakers' explicit evaluative orientation to language in terms of LANGUAGE ATTITUDES or FOLK-THEORIES OF LANGUAGE (e.g. Bloomfield 1933: 22, cited in Woolard 1998: 11), substantial attention to this aspect of the language–culture nexus is a relatively recent phenomenon (Kroskrity 2000, Rumsey 1990, Schieffelin *et al.* 1998, Silverstein 1979). The use of IDEOLOGY in demarcating this area of study, instead of the more neutral term ATTITUDE, signals the premise within this framework that the evaluations and theories that form its objects of study are mainly thought to be contested ones implicated in webs of power relations, and are held by interested, socially situated groups.

One of the most studied language ideological complexes involves the association of 'nations' with human groups delimitable by their use of a (sufficiently) common language, a notion whose first clear articulation is attributed to Johann Gottfried Herder (Koepke 1990). Still very much relevant in present-day Europe, as evident in the role of language in the post-Soviet fragmentation of the former Warsaw block (Blommaert and Verschueren 1998), the Herderian equation of a single nation with a people speaking a single language was also exported around the world in the colonial period, as evident in the US English Only movement (González and Melis 2001), and the widespread suppression by nation states of minority languages around the world, a major factor, of course, in language endangerment (Dorian 1998).

7.4 Cultural consequences of language shift

The view that language loss has significant cultural consequences is a widely held one among both linguists (e.g. Dorian 1999: 31–3, Hale 1992: 6, Nettle and Romaine 2000) and speakers of endangered languages (e.g. Czaykowska-Higgins 2009: 32–3; Hinton 2002: 152–4). The cultural consequences of language loss have been theorized in a number of ways, and the empirical focus of work in this area varies from concerns with lexically expressed CULTURAL KNOWLEDGE, to the dependence of communicative functions on linguistic form, to critically oriented engagement with language ideologies.

Recent publications on language endangerment aimed at popular audiences implicate the shift from local languages to global ones in significant losses of cultural knowledge, especially detailed knowledge of local environments and resource use (e.g. Nettle and Romaine 2000: 50–77, *passim*). Harrison (2007: 24–7), for example, discusses the finely grained lexical distinctions drawn by speakers of Tofa in semantic domains such as types of reindeer, which are classified in terms of sex, age, and, if male, whether they are gelded. Harrison argues that the shift in Tofa communities to Russian has blocked the transmission of this kind of local knowledge, remarking 'we might even go a step further that the knowledge Marta [a speaker of Tofa] possesses *cannot* be expressed in an intact or efficient way in Russian' [emphasis in original] (Harrison 2007: 24). Under this view then, language shift *per se* plays a causal role in disrupting the transmission of cultural knowledge (Harrison 2007: 53).

Despite the centrality of claims like these to public discourses on language endangerment and shift, there is surprisingly little research that directly addresses them.[4] For example, while there is ample documentation of language loss being *associated* with the loss of specialized cultural knowledge, it is not entirely clear that the loss of such knowledge is a *consequence* of language loss, as opposed to being a simultaneous casualty of large-scale sociopolitical processes that devalue and erode entire life-spheres of indigenous and minority groups around the world (Rice 2007: 319). It remains an open question if loss of cultural knowledge, for example, the ability to identify plant and animal species, occurs even in contexts of language shift where the cultural knowledge in question retains its status, value and utility (however, see discussion of Hill 2001 below).

Whereas work linking cultural knowledge and the lexicon has strong resonances with ethnosemantics and ethnoscience, another strand of thinking regarding the cultural consequences of language shift has ties to construals of Whorfianism that see languages as embodying WORLD-VIEWS. Discussing the Hawaiian system of alienable and inalienable possession, for example, Nettle and Romaine (2000: 65) remark:

> One could argue that the distinctive system of Polynesian possessive marking is the backbone of the language. If this distinction disappears ... the language becomes but a shadow of its former self, and so does the traditional culture and worldview it encoded.

There are reasons to doubt that broad appeals to worldview in contexts of language shift are justified (Silverstein 1998a: 422), but as Harrison (2007: 185) points out, if subtler understandings of the relationship between language structure and habitual thought are essentially correct (see Section 7.3.2.2), then there should be empirically detectable cognitive consequences of language shift and loss.

A related line of research approaches the question of the impact of language shift on culture by considering what Woodbury (1998) calls FORM DEPENDENT EXPRESSION (aspects of language use and meaning that are particularly dependent on linguistic form as such). As Hale (1998: 204) observed, there are types of communicative activity that depend so crucially on linguistic form, metrical poetry, for example, that translation, though possible to some degree at the level of referential function, fails at other levels of communicative function.

Woodbury (1998) explores this issue by examining the expression of affect by Alaskan Cup'iks when they speak English. Woodbury allows that there are rough notional equivalences between Cup'ik affective suffixes and English affect words (e.g. 'poor Joe'), but argues that such equivalences do not support the use of English affect words in a way that parallels the use of affective suffixes in everyday Cup'ik discourse. Woodbury argues that because Cup'ik affective suffixes form part of morphological paradigms, they are less discursively salient than their English counterparts and, as such, afford considerably more frequent use. The fact that affective meanings are expressed by free words in English makes them objects of metalinguistic awareness in a way Cup'ik affective suffixes are not, rendering anomalous the pervasive expression of affect in English. Despite a certain notional equivalence between Cup'ik and English, therefore, the difference in the formal realization of these meanings entails the shift from Cup'ik to English resulted in the bleaching of affect from the discourse of ethnic Cup'iks.

Hill (2001) provides a complementary perspective on form dependence in a discussion of lexical contraction among speakers of Tohono O'odham (TO), suggesting that plant and animal names have not only denotative functions, but constitute crucial links in an embodied system of knowledge and affect, so that 'as words are lost, knowledge fades as well, *even when there is no concomitant cultural or environmental change*' [emphasis mine]. Hill notes, for example, that in interviews with TO speakers, uses of TO ethnobiological terms often evoked strong affective responses (e.g. disgust at rattlesnakes) and the recounting of associated cultural knowledge, while their English lexical counterparts rarely did (Hill 2001: 164), suggesting that although the TO and English terms may be denotationally equivalent, they play different cognitive roles for these speakers in relation to TO culture.

Regardless of how language shift affects culture-specific systems of knowledge, affect and expression, however, there can be no doubt that language and its relationship to culture and identity often become the objects of powerful language ideologies in contexts of language shift. The tendency for individuals to identify sociocultural groupings and their own identity by language use is sufficiently pervasive both cross-culturally (Fishman 1999: 449) and historically (Haarmann 1999: 63–6), that the contraction or cessation of use of a language often poses an ideological predicament for group identity (see e.g. McCarty and Zepeda 1999: 207–8, Dobrin and Berson, Chapter 10):

> If the Kaqchikel language is dying, it is the Kaqchikel people who are dying with its own Kaqchikel Maya identity. (COCADI, 1985: 12, cited in Fishman, 1997: 240)

The sense of crisis may be especially acute in cases where a given group associates its language with cherished cultural ideals, which is widespread among human groups (Fishman 1997). However, arguments are also made by members of affected groups for the resilience of sociocultural identity under circumstances of language shift. For example, Jocks (1998: 230), an ethnically Mohawk scholar, comments:

> In traditional circles one frequently hears the assertion that language and culture are inextricably linked, and that loss of an Indigenous language prefigures loss of distinct culture and identity. But one also hears the opposite assertion: that Native people can and do live traditional lives without speaking or understanding their traditional languages. I agree ... [I]n places where a sizable number of English-speaking people are nonetheless determined to forge some kind of traditional identity, a body of traditional discourse in English can arise that is related – though not identical – to discourse in the original, traditional language.

These apparently disparate views on the cultural consequences of language loss are reconcilable from the perspective on the language–culture nexus presented in Section 7.2.2, which holds that linguistic form is enmeshed with non-linguistic social practices to varying degrees in different areas of communicative practice. If in discussing language loss we restrict ourselves to a relatively circumscribed view of language centring on grammar, it is clear that there are significant aspects of culture and identity that are capable of surviving shifts in linguistic code, as Jocks suggests. At the same time, however, it is evident that some forms of cultural expression and cognition are tied to the use of specific linguistic resources, and that loss of these resources leaves a gap in social practices and knowledge. The more inclusive our delimitation of language becomes, encompassing communicative practices as well as linguistic code, however, the more closely culture loss becomes tied to language loss.

7.5 Conclusion

Language endangerment raises similar questions for both the communities whose histories are tied to the use of languages undergoing shift and for the linguists who work with these communities (these groups are increasingly overlapping): what can and should be done in the face of language shift? An understanding of the intertwined nature of language and culture has implications both for courses of action intended to affect processes of language shift and for the more narrowly linguistic tasks of language documentation, description and analysis. In the former case, it points to the importance of recognizing that language, narrowly construed, is intermeshed with broader sets of social practices, and that language maintenance or revitalization is not simply a question of revitalizing a linguistic code. It suggests, to the contrary, that for language revitalization or maintenance to be successful, it must engage with the factors leading to the erosion of whole cultural spheres.

 For linguistic work on endangered languages, the recognition that grammar is inextricably embedded in culture raises difficult issues regarding documentary and descriptive adequacy. As linguistic form and social practices are not neatly separable, delimiting the goals of language documentation, defined as concerned with 'observable linguistic behaviour' (Himmelmann 2008: 346), necessarily involves a theory of the language–culture nexus (however naive or sophisticated it may be). As described in Section 7.3.1.1, theorists of documentary linguistics have been attracted to the speech event framework of the ethnography of communication as a rubric for documenting the language–culture nexus, but many aspects of language use that are important areas of language documentation (e.g. pragmatics) do not clearly align with speech events as such. Despite issues of this sort, however, language documentation and scholarship on the language–culture nexus both stand to benefit from addressing the pressing question of what constitutes adequate documentation and description of communicative practices; the former field from the theoretical sophistication of the latter, and the latter from the resulting increased prominence of the social dimension of language within linguistics.

Notes

1 Although the appeal of cognitivist accounts of culture has waned in anthropology in recent decades, they have attracted considerable interest outside anthropology. Evolutionary psychology and related approaches in cognitive science and philosophy have advanced 'epidemiological' theories of culture which centre on the transmission and evolutionary selection of mental representations (Dennett 1991, Sperber 1996), in some cases articulating these accounts using Richard Dawkins' (1976) concept of the MEME, an isolable unit of socially learned knowledge (Durham 1991). Thus far such approaches have had relatively little positive impact in either anthropology or linguistics, although a critical literature has emerged in the former discipline (e.g. Harris 1999).

2 By choosing to name these 'schools of thought' after specific institutions I do not mean to suggest that practitioners in these schools are confined to these institutions (quite the opposite is true), or that these are the only institutions of importance insofar as scholarship on the language–culture nexus is concerned (far from it).

3 That is, the Max Planck Institute for Psycholinguistics, located in Nijmegen, the Netherlands.

4 As Himmelmann (2008: 343–4) and Errington (2003: 724) observe, linguists writing about the consequences of language shift face the challenge of writing to diverse audiences. One way to evaluate claims regarding the causal role of language shift in the loss of cultural knowledge may be as strategies, often linked to arguments about the universal utility of such knowledge (e.g. Nettle and Romaine 2000: 15–16, 69–77 *passim*; cf. J. Hill 2002, Muehlmann 2005), for recruiting public support for endangered-language maintenance, revitalization and documentation, and not as scientific or scholarly arguments.

8

Language and society

Bernard Spolsky

8.1 Introduction

Because language and society are always in flux, each influencing and influenced by the other, the study of endangered languages clearly requires a consideration of both. The goal of this chapter is to contextualize the notion of endangered languages in a model of language and society.

I start with the terms LANGUAGE and SOCIETY, the heading of this chapter. While linguists (at least since Saussure 1931) have recognized the social basis of language, they have commonly seen their task as to develop a full description (phonology, morphology, syntax, semantics and pragmatics) of named language varieties and then to propose a theory accounting for universal and dissimilar features of these varieties. The clarion warning of the loss of linguistic diversity (Hale 1992; Krauss 1992) drew attention to the impending diminution in the number of languages and the resulting impoverishment of ways of studying the assorted systems in which human beings have organized thought and communication, and added a sense of urgency to this work. But among linguists, the emphasis has been on language rather than on speakers. The contrast is highlighted in a recent paper by Labov (2008) who argues that a stigmatized dialect like Afro-American Vernacular English is in no danger of disappearing as long as the people who speak it continue to be socially isolated and discriminated against.

Linguists worry about the effects of language loss on their work, but it is sociolinguists (those who study language in society) who focus on the process, asking how varieties of language are redistributed demographically or functionally within a society or how speakers choose which variety to use in specific circumstances or how they shift from one variety to another. For sociolinguists, language loss, except as a result of extinction of speakers by natural disaster or mass murder, is an extreme case of a normal ongoing phenomenon, language shift. Perhaps the difference in the two approaches might be characterized in this way: appealing as they do to ecological rhetoric, many linguists see language loss as similar to the disappearance of animal or vegetable species; sociolinguists see rather the complex ecology in which language varieties are in constant flux, occupying and vacating available niches.

8.2   What are language varieties?

The simple answer, and one with which lay people will be comfortable, is that they are named languages like English, French, Navajo, Corsican or Eyak. Some lay people and most linguists will accept that they might be not just named languages but also dialects like American English, or Texan English, or Indian English, or Western Yiddish, or South Island Māori. Sociolinguists go much further: they deal with the differences within language varieties (such as written versus spoken or male versus female) and the different types of language variety.

The types of language that occur at the national level were defined and distinguished by Stewart (1968) as follows:

- CLASSICAL LANGUAGES – formal and no longer spoken but preserved in literary and religious texts[1];
- VERNACULAR LANGUAGES – spoken varieties believed by their speakers to be independent;
- STANDARD LANGUAGES – languages with published grammars and dictionaries and a popular belief that there is a correct version;
- DIALECTS – usually spoken varieties taken to be a regional or social modification of a standard language or vernacular;
- PIDGINS – hybrid varieties without native speakers;
- CREOLES – former pidgins that have acquired native speakers, and;
- ARTIFICIAL LANGUAGES – created languages like Esperanto.

Each type is understood to have a different social function and status. Only classical and standard languages are likely to be taught in schools and to be declared official languages; the other types are generally of lower status and often stigmatized. Each type also has a different method and likelihood of survival: classical languages, artificial languages, pidgins and some standard languages lack what Stewart calls VITALITY; namely the intergenerational transmission that comes from parents and care-givers speaking the language to their babies, so that their survival depends on continued reteaching or relearning. Standard languages, as well as classical and artificial, are taught and learned in educational settings; the others are learned or acquired at home or in the neighbourhood. One of the major forces speeding up language shift is that national governments use educational systems and other forms of management to encourage populations to switch from vernaculars and dialects to official standard languages.

Defining a language is a fundamental problem, exacerbated by a common practice of equating languages with language names (Blommaert 2001). This shows up in the uncertainty about the number of languages in the world. Take India for example. The first serious count of languages in India was by Grierson (1903–1928) who originally listed 179 languages and 554 dialects (Pandit 1975). In the 1961 Census of India, 1,652 language names were reported, classified into about 200 languages (Srivastava 1988). *Ethnologue* (Lewis 2009) listed 438 living languages for India, of which 22 are 'scheduled', listed as official in the eighth schedule of the Indian constitution. Counts of languages of the world show even more diversity. Crystal (2000: 3) cites estimates ranging from 1,000 in 1874 through 3,000 in the 1950s. The 1969 edition of *Ethnologue* listed 4,493 languages (Pittman 1969) and Voegelin and Voegelin (1977) about 4,500. The most commonly accepted number nowadays appears to be over 6,000; Austin (2008) quotes 6,912 from the 2005 *Ethnologue* (Gordon 2005). Gordon (2005) in his introduction presents the problem of counting languages:[2]

> Increasingly, scholars are recognizing that languages are not always easily treated as discrete isolatable units with clearly defined boundaries between them. Rather, languages are more often continua of features that extend across both geographic and social space. In addition, there is growing attention being given to the roles or functions that language varieties play within the linguistic ecology of a region or a speech community.
>
> The *Ethnologue* approach to listing and counting languages as though they were discrete, countable units does not preclude a more dynamic understanding of the linguistic makeup of the countries and regions in which clearly distinct varieties can be distinguished while at the same time recognizing that those languages and their 'dialects' exist in a complex set of relationships to each other.

This very fuzziness shows the complexity of our topic. For instance, many languages have more than one name. Even leaving out the fact that major world languages have different names (EXONYMS) in other languages (English, *Englisch, anglais, eigo*, etc), most of the languages listed in *Ethnologue* have multiple names: Crystal (2000: 7) notes that at that time the *Ethnologue* index listed 39,304 different names for its 6,703 language headings. Many of the modifications in the scope of named languages have resulted from political changes. Take Dutch for example. In 1932, *Flemish* in Belgium was officially renamed *Dutch*, but this disguised the fact that Belgian schoolchildren grow up speaking various Flemish or Walloon dialects and meet standard Dutch or French only at school. In South Africa on the other hand, the Dutch dialects spoken by the settlers were early renamed *Afrikaans*, although Afrikaans grammars and Bible translation appeared only in the later part of the nineteenth century. The various Scandinavian languages emerged as separate languages with political independence in the nineteenth century, just as the various nation states that succeeded Yugoslavia are now each claiming their own national language. On the other hand, the South American varieties of Spanish (each nation has its own language academy) are satisfied to call their language *Español*. Similarly, the Arabic-speaking nations list their language as *Arabic*, although the spoken variety in each country is different, and different from the classical sacred language and the standard written variety.

Generally, the national or official standard language is assumed to cover the various vernacular dialects actually spoken. English is thus taken to include not just the long-recognized British and American standard versions, but also British and American regional and social dialects, standardized and dialect versions of Canadian,[3] Australian, New Zealand and South African English, and the many languages or dialects now included under the term World Englishes. Norwegian, although it has long institutionalized two distinct written varieties, also includes its regional dialects under the rubric of its national language. Sweden, in signing the European Charter for Regional or Minority Languages in 2000, recognized three minority languages: Sámi (or Saami) (with over 5,000 speakers), Meänkali (otherwise known as Tornedalen, Meänkieli, Torne Valley Finnish, Tornedalsfinska or North Finnish, with about 80,000 speakers), and Finnish (with 200,000 speakers estimated in 1997), but determined that Scanian (or Skanian), listed in *Ethnologue* as having 80,000 speakers in 2002, was in fact a dialect and so exempt from the provisions of the Charter.

It is not simple to determine what is an endangered variety of language: for the linguist, it might be enough to focus on changes in the status and form of named languages; for the sociolinguist and for the speakers, it is likely to be changes in sociolinguistic ecology; that is, in the complex patterning of variations and their dynamic allocation to domains, functions and other ecological niches. Thus, Hebraists might be concerned that English seems to be spreading in Israel and that English words are invading Hebrew, and see this as endangerment; sociolinguists would look rather at the complex changes in Hebrew use and form associated with demographic and technological changes and see this as normal sociolinguistic dynamism. Thus, there are nations like Sweden where the success of English teaching and use means that Swedish is felt to need defence (Cabau 2009).

Generally, the status of national languages has depended on standardization, such as in France and Italy where dialects have been devalued as a result. There are a few cases where diversity is defended. The existence of POLYNOMIC languages was originally proposed to deal with the

Corsican situation by Jean-Baptiste Marcellesi (1984). Marcellesi argues that in Corsica there is no pressure for standardization, whether of the written or spoken variety, and a generalized belief in the acceptability of multilingualism and multidialectism. Marcellesi (1989: 170; cited and translated in Jaffe 2008) postulates the existence of:

> une langue à l'unité abstraite, à laquelle les utilisateurs reconnaissent plusieurs modalités d'existence, toutes également tolérées sans qu'il y ait entre elles hiérarchisation ou spécialisation de fonction. Elle s'accompagne de l'intertolérance entre utilisateurs de variétés différentes sur les plans phonologiques et morphologiques, de même que la multiplicité lexicale est conçue ailleurs comme un élément de richesse.

> [A language with an abstract unity, which users recognize in multiple modes of existence, all of which are equally tolerated and are not distinguished hierarchically or by functional specialization. It is accompanied by tolerance of phonological and morphological variation by users, who also view lexical diversity as a form of richness.] (page 227)

This notion provided an important argument for activists seeking to establish the place of Corsican in schools alongside the officially favoured French (Thiers 1999), although there remain questions as to how successful the polynomic school teaching has been in spreading the language outside the classroom (Blackwood 2008, Jaffe 2003, 2008).

The concept of polynomic language is useful in blunting the argument made by reluctant administrators that a multidialectal variety must be standardized before it can be used in schools or otherwise made official. While I have not seen the term used in describing the Norwegian situation, it would appear to fit: Norwegian language activists developed two standards for the written language but none for the spoken (Haugen 1966).

Dealing with dialect differences is relevant to efforts to reverse language shift. Cotter (2001) reported that Irish speakers prefer to listen to radio broadcasts in their own dialect and would switch off when another dialect was used. At the same time, it was hoped that radio would increase interdialectal intelligibility. Working in Canada, Johns and Mazurkewich (2001) suggest that lack of intelligibility between dialects is a cause of language endangerment. They cite Watson (1989) as saying that speakers of Scottish Gaelic switch to English rather than make the effort to understand speakers of other dialects. They therefore included training in Inuit dialect differences as a central part of a programme for native speakers. Dialect differences also play a role in Māori regeneration: Harlow (2007) points out that although the differences are not great (except in the case of South Island Māori), they are encouraged by

tribal leaders and the Maori Language Commission as a method of stress-
ing tribal differences even though it might serve to impede normalization. In the early days of bilingual education in New Zealand schools
(Spolsky 1989), I was told of a two-day debate in a school planning to
start Māori immersion teaching over the question of hiring a teacher
with a different tribal accent. Others argue that the maintenance of tribal dialects and accents is a strong motivation for language learning and
teaching: the two tribes with lowest Māori proficiency are reported to be
keenest on developing a strategy to re-establish their dialects.

All of this clearly reinforces and supports Blommaert's position when
he argues against ignoring the sociolinguistic complexity of language
varieties. Blommaert (2005: 10) says:

> [f]irst, as for *the nature of linguistic resources*, sociolinguistics has dem-
> onstrated that 'languages' as commonly understood (i.e. things that
> have names such as 'English', 'French', 'Hindi', 'Zulu') are sociolinguis-
> tically not the most relevant objects. These 'languages' are, in actual
> fact, complex and layered collections of *language varieties*, and the study
> of language in society should not be, for instance, a study of *English*
> in society but a study of all the different varieties that, when packed
> together, go under the label 'English'.

These varieties, he notes, may be distinguished for channel and mode of
communication (written or spoken, radio or newspaper), region, social
class, domain or style. But even more complexity is introduced when we
recognize the effect of multilingualism on the nature of actual language
use in live discourse. Blommaert (2005: 225ff) analyses a short passage
from a programme broadcast on the University of Capetown radio station
that includes Standard South African English, Black English, Township
English and Rasta Slang. Analysing data collected in San Francisco by
Whiteside (2006), Kramsch and Whiteside (2008: 667) report that they
found a complex linguistic ecology in which individuals are using varieties of Maya, Spanish, English and Chinese as they negotiate their elaborate changing identities and roles, forming 'complex, dynamic systems
where the usual axes of space and time are reordered along the lines of
various histories and subjectivities among the participants'. It is these
complex dynamic systems that we need to take into account when we
are investigating the relation of language and society rather than neatly
labelled 'languages'.

8.3   What is society?

Defining LANGUAGE then is a first problem. SOCIETY is not any simpler,
as we seek a definition of the social unit within which a language operates (Michael, Chapter 7). Before sociolinguistics, linguists referred to a

LANGUAGE COMMUNITY which meant all speakers of a given language in the world (e.g. the English speaking world, Francophonie, the surviving speakers of Yuchi).[4] Sociolinguists preferred the term SPEECH COMMUNITY, proposed by Gumperz (1962) and developed in Gumperz (1968), as the name of a local social unit characterized for any individual by locality and interaction. Hymes (1967, 1986) defined a speech community as one that shares rules for the use and interpretation of speech (by which he meant all forms of speech including writing and speech surrogates like whistling and drumming) and rules for the interpretation of at least one language variety. Developing this further, Labov (1966) argued that New York City was a speech community because its inhabitants shared values for certain linguistic variables[5] he studied, though their own practices differed. But there has been no attempt to define a size. Most recently, Patrick (2002) reviewed the many definitions that have been offered and wisely avoided any proposal other than 'a socially-based unit of linguistic analysis'. For more on communities of speakers of endangered languages, see Grinevald and Bert, Chapter 3.

The social units that sociolinguists choose for analysis vary in size from the smallest (perhaps a dyad, certainly a family or institution) to the largest (a city or a region or a nation state or a region). The distinguishing point is that it is studied as a sociolinguistic ECOLOGY, a term originally proposed by Haugen (1971, 1972), recognizing the many language varieties functioning in its various niches (Grenoble, Chapter 2). There are other ways to treat social units: Hymes suggested the notion of a SPEECH NETWORK, the linkages of a speaker through shared varieties and across communities. The concept has been fruitfully developed by Milroy (1980), who defines social networks as: 'informal social mechanisms supporting language varieties specific to particular social groups'. Milroy measured the density of her consultants' social networks and correlated them against the use of speech elements (especially phonological features), and found that the degree to which social networks were close-knit could be correlated with the use of particular linguistic features, and could hence be used to evaluate rates of language change. She established that people are more likely to use traditional and/or low-status ways of speaking with people from their close social circle, later extending this to the maintenance of endangered or minority language varieties in contact with more widespread or dominant varieties (Milroy 2002). Sallabank (forthcoming) notes that language ATTRITION can be exacerbated by the loss of social networks, as speakers of endangered languages become older, are less able to socialize, and lose their interlocutors. She suggests that revitalization efforts, especially master–apprentice-type programmes (see Hinton, Chapter 15) provide opportunities to bolster speakers' social networks and maintain language proficiency.

I find it useful to talk of DOMAINS (Fishman 1972), an empirically determined niche within a speech community with typical participants, location, topics and preference for language variety. In his study of a speech community in Jersey City, Fishman argued that the distribution of Spanish and English in different domains was a key factor in establishing stable bilingualism. Such distribution of language varieties by domain is often called DIGLOSSIA (see O'Shannessy, Chapter 5).

The home or family is a domain: participants include parents, children, siblings, grandparents and caretakers; the location is the apartment or home or igloo or hogan in which the family lives; an appropriate topic is daily life. Other domains of increasing size and complexity include the neighbourhood, religious institutions, schools, villages and towns and cities, health facilities, legal and security agencies, the military, the media, local, regional and national government, supranational and international organizations. Within each community or domain, one may distinguish the distribution and use of various languages or more precisely of language varieties or clusters of variants: in the family, for example, it is not unusual to find variants specific to that family (idiosyncratic names for people or pets or foods, for instance) as well as different participants using different varieties to each other, such as children addressing grandparents in the heritage language and each other in the dominant external language or regional language of wider communication.

Individual speakers of course participate in more than one domain as well as in more than one speech community. For the sociolinguist, then, society is not a single closed community covering a defined geographical or political unit, but rather a complex ecology comprising multiple communities and networks. The social or political boundaries do not necessarily coincide with linguistic boundaries: commonly speech communities include several languages and varieties. The boundaries are not static, but dynamic as social, demographic, religious and political conditions vary. It is this dynamism that determines loss or survival of a language variety.

8.4   Language policy and practice in society

Against this background, I want to explore briefly how LANGUAGE POLICY helps us to understand endangered languages and the possibilities of helping to maintain or revive them (see Sallabank, Chapter 14).

Language policy as I define it (Spolsky 2004), has three independent but related components:

- the LANGUAGE PRACTICES of a speech community or domain;
- LANGUAGE BELIEFS or IDEOLOGY of a speech community; and
- any LANGUAGE MANAGEMENT activities of an individual or institution claiming authority over the community and wishing to modify their language practices or language beliefs.

The LANGUAGE PRACTICES constitute the commonly accepted rules of language choice and variety within a speech community or a domain. Within this model, an ENDANGERED LANGUAGE is a variety with an observable ongoing reduction in the domains and functions of use and in the number of speakers, such that it is possible to envision a stage where both will approach zero. The typical process of language loss involves some members of the language community starting to use another language in certain domains for certain functions; the end point is when there are neither functions nor speakers left.

Language practices in the home or family domain constitute one of the most significant sites for evidence of the endangerment of a variety: the current state of the language is often expressed by referring to the age of the youngest speaker, and the absence of children speaking the language: evidence that intergenerational transmission of the language has ceased and that a variety may soon disappear (see Grinevald and Bert, Chapter 3). We may look at this from the point of view of practice, noting for example that older members of the family speak one variety and younger members speak another which is different from it (see Palosaari and Campbell, Chapter 6), or concentrate specifically on what variety is spoken to babies and young children. We may also look at specific cases of family-internal language management, such as parents attempting to persuade their children to speak either a heritage language or the standard variety valued by the wider society. In any case, we will also want to pay attention to ideology or beliefs as expressed in the values assigned to available language varieties.

Each domain can produce its own pressure towards language maintenance or shift. The language practices of the neighbourhood or the community or the region or the nation (or the world for that matter) reflect the stable or changing status of varieties. Demographic changes (movement of population from village to city or from one country to another, changing birth rates, changing age profiles as a result of better health care) all affect the future by altering both opportunities for use and learning of varieties and the values assigned to them (see Harbert, Chapter 20). For example, nineteenth-century famine and emigration are often cited as a major cause of Irish language loss. The move from Māori villages to the city changed the sociolinguistic situation in which Māori children grew up. Even without active language management, forced population movement as Stalin practised it had major effects on linguistic profiles, making Russian important not just as a state language but also as a needed lingua franca. Population movement in Europe is continuing to produce a new kind of multilingualism. It goes without saying that genocide is an effective method of destroying a language as well as its speakers and that 'ethnic cleansing' changes the status of varieties.

Essentially, as de Swaan (1998) claims, the number and distribution of speakers of a variety, as well as their social status, is in fact interpretable and interpreted as its usefulness. In other words, wider use of a language, whether by more people or by more important people or in more domains, raises its value and so increases the likelihood that other people will be willing to learn it. De Swaan (1998) notes in particular the value of use of a language as a SECOND LANGUAGE or LINGUA FRANCA.[6] In explaining the preference of continental Europeans for English, he points out that while there are more first-language speakers of German in mainland Europe, there are more second-language speakers of English. Similarly, the huge number of speakers of Chinese varieties is not as important as the fact that English is the language of wider communication preferred when speakers of Chinese, Russian, Korean and Japanese converse with members of one of the other groups. Put another way, the number of people who speak a variety in the home in the village is important, but there is strong pressure to learn the language that will be most useful when one goes to a town or to the city. Notice here that we are translating practices into beliefs: the more a language is used in practice, the more valuable it seems.

These LANGUAGE BELIEFS, derived from individual speakers' perceptions of the value of the competing varieties, become a central component of the language policy of a community, difficult to study though they turn out to be. The management component is more obvious because it is external. LANGUAGE MANAGEMENT[7] (Spolsky 2009a) has three major areas of activity:

- attempts to modify the status and the uses of a language variety or variant;
- attempts to change the corpus or actual form of a language variety; and
- efforts to modify the number and nature of speakers of a variety, especially by enabling or encouraging new speakers to learn it.[8]

The term was used by Jernudd and Neustupný (1987) and the concept has been further developed (Nekvapil 2006, Neustupný and Nekvapil 2003) to include:

- SIMPLE MANAGEMENT – defined as an individual solving his or her own communication problems by correcting, asking for help, or looking for a way to learn a variety better; and
- COMPLEX MANAGEMENT – where an authority attempts to solve communication problems in a specific community.

It ranges thus from the parent correcting a child's language or choosing what language to speak to them, to a national state passing laws or setting constitutional provisions in order to enforce a desired policy. In each domain and in each community one can find individuals or groups who take on this task.

Let me review some examples, leaving the more detailed study of language management to Sallabank, Chapter 14. At the family level, the choice of which language to speak to children is a critical issue, the final determination often of the survival or loss of a variety. The first decision is with the parents, but they may well be influenced by other participants in the family domain (grandparents or servants, for instance), and their decisions will be governed by their own language proficiency, by perceptions of the values of each variety they know, and by management efforts at other levels. Once a child is exposed to other choices (for instance, the influence of peers in the neighbourhood, or of older siblings who are already at school, or of education), a conflict may well arise. Harris (1998) argued for the greater influence of peers; Calvet (1987, 1998) saw the family as the first battlefield in language wars; Caldas (2006, 2008, Caldas and Caron-Caldas 2000) has recently reported a case study where home, school, and neighbourhood have battled for the language loyalty of growing children.

Once one looks beyond the family, it is clear that the number of domains in which a variety is used is highly significant. A language restricted to the home or the school or the church has less chance of survival than one used also at work or in business. Requiring Bahasa Melayu in school and government while allowing business and commerce to use English pressured the Malaysian government to propose using English to teach science and mathematics (Gill 2005, Rappa and Wee 2006). Similarly, the VALUE of a variety (translated normally into a belief that one should learn it oneself and teach it to one's children) is a function of significance of the domains in which it is used. Fishman's (1991) Graded Intergenerational Disruption Scale (GIDS, see Grenoble, Chapter 2) moves from the individual ('socially isolated old folks') to the intergenerational family, then to the 'home, school and community' and the lower work sphere (outside the neighbourhood), then to 'lower governmental services and mass media' and finally to 'higher level educational, occupational, governmental and media' levels. The fact or belief that the language is appropriately used at a higher level may encourage the belief that it should be used at a lower level.[9]

Fishman's scale does not specifically name religion as a critical domain, but he gives cases in which religious institutions provide significant support for language maintenance or apply pressure for shift. For Navajo, the effect of religion was mixed, but overall did little if anything to impede language shift. Traditional Navajo medicine, which involves hiring a singer to perform all-night ceremonies for two or three days for an individual who is ill, are still conducted in Navajo, the core being performance of a song like *Beautyway* (Wyman 1957) in Navajo. But even here, a Navajo-speaking relative might occasionally be asked to replace the patient when Navajo responses are needed, or to translate directions; rarely, a singer is reported to give directions in English. Originally, ceremonies of the Native American Church[10] consisted of songs in languages other than Navajo, with English the lingua franca, but there seems to be growing use of Navajo songs and of Navajo for interaction. Most Christian ceremonies were conducted only in English, but the Catholic Church now permits the Mass in Navajo. Some fundamentalist churches have services in Navajo, and some of them use written Navajo. The existence of a Navajo Bible encourages Navajo literacy, but the association of the Navajo language with traditional ceremonies led some Christian communities to oppose teaching Navajo in school (Blanchard *et al.* 2003: 204). Among the Māori, the Ringatu Church (an Old-Testament-based religion developed on the east coast of the North Island during the New Zealand Wars in the later years of the nineteenth century) still provides strong support for the language in the region.

Churches are often associated with management efforts to maintain otherwise endangered or classical languages. Islam is responsible for the spread of Classical Arabic, not just to conquered Middle Eastern and North African states, but also to Asia and Africa. The Roman Catholic Church established an educational system which long maintained Latin. Jewish religious schools kept Hebrew alive (read and written if not spoken) for nearly 2,000 years. Polynesian churches in Australia and New Zealand are reported to play an important role in maintaining Samoan, Tongan and other languages. The Greek Orthodox Church is an important force in teaching Greek in the United States.

Religion has a major influence on language shift and maintenance both because of the values it assigns to a variety and also as a result of the active management involved in the establishment of an educational system. In many societies, the first schools were established by religious institutions, and while the recent secularization of much of Europe has reduced this pressure there, the spread of religion has commonly involved setting up schools to teach a sacred language. The spread of Islam established Arabic in the Levant and across North Africa, where it became the standard language and dominates local varieties; further east and south, it became a sacred language required to be learnt by observant Muslims. Christian missionaries established their favoured languages as they spread the faith; Spanish and Portuguese became the languages of any education and all official use in different countries in Latin America; and while Eastern Orthodox Christianity accepted local languages, the normal practice was to encourage a single variety such as Old Church Slavonic. Protestant missionaries in Africa and the Pacific also initially chose to encourage literacy and Bible translation in one selected variety, but as they collaborated with colonial powers, worked towards the acceptance of metropolitan languages like English and French.

Education, particularly under the control of national states, has become one of the main forces for language shift and one of the main causes of endangerment of minority-language varieties. The school is usually the first social institution outside the family that has a major influence on the practices and values of a child. There is an obvious structure of authority, with adult teachers placed in charge of their pupils, and required by the next level of authority (principals, school boards, departments and ministers of education) to implement a specified central curriculum regularly requiring the use of a standard school language. Only in comparatively rare cases will school allow for transitional use of home languages; children in much of the world are forced to shift languages when they start school (Walter 2008). Thus, schooling becomes a major force in language shift, as children switch from their home language to the language of their teachers and peers. Lee (2007: 7) describes the major influence of school on even those Navajo teenagers who had learned Navajo at home:

> When I was a middle school student in the interior region of the Navajo Nation in the early 1980s, all my peers' first language was Navajo. Their choice in school at that time was to speak Navajo among themselves and with Navajo teachers. When I became a high school teacher on the reservation some fifteen years later, my students mostly spoke English with one another. Even if they spoke Navajo well, their language of choice in school was English.

Commonly, school children proceed to introduce the school language into the home, using it with their siblings and even with their parents. Parents also introduce the school language at home to ease their children's integration into school.

There are pragmatic reasons why schools reflect national policy in favouring a single standard language: in multilingual cities and areas, it is a major challenge to schools to recognize the many languages that their beginning pupils might speak. Brock-Utne (2005: 175) says the 'myth of many languages in Africa' is regularly offered as an excuse for using ex-colonial languages like French, Portuguese or English as media of instruction, although closer analysis will show that much of the diversity results from inaccurate identification and that a three-language model (the local language in elementary school, a regional African language in high school and an international language for higher education) would be more effective. Provision of education in each community language is obviously a complex task, requiring a serious sociolinguistic study to establish how many languages are involved and the degree of mutual intelligibility, the existence of lingua francas, and the numbers of second-language speakers. In Mexico, *El Instituto Nacional de Lenguas Indígenas* (National Institute of Indian Languages) recognizes sixty-eight languages, most with several distinct varieties (as many as eighty one in the case of Mixteco and sixty two in the case of Zapoteco (INALI 2008). To prepare teachers and materials for these languages is a major task, and requires strong activist pressure (for more on endangered language curriculum planning, see Coronel-Molina and McCarty, Chapter 18).

8.5   Language beliefs and ideologies

We have been talking about language practices and management, but have regularly drawn attention to the second component of language policy, language beliefs or ideologies. There is some overlap in the use of the terms 'beliefs', 'attitudes' and 'ideologies', which are interrelated (Baker 1992: 13). Ideologies are perceptions shared by a speech community, which tend to be seen as 'common sense'; sociolinguists see them as underlying individual beliefs and attitudes. Blommaert (1999: 1) defines language ideologies as 'socioculturally motivated ideas, perceptions and expectations of language, manifested in all sorts of language use'. Bednar *et al.* (2007) are developing a model which shows how 'cultural signatures' such as ideologies can develop within a culture (or a political party or other organization) while individual members continue to differ in behaviour and beliefs. This, they suggest, is the interaction of two forces, an internal pressure to be consistent and an external pressure to conform.

There are fundamental differences in tolerance for the existence of variability. The two extremes are:

1.   the reputed Anglo-Saxon assumption that one language is enough, a monoglot ideology (Silverstein 1996) which shows up in opposition to bilingual education (Crawford 2000) or foreign languages, as against;
2.   the Indian comfort with multilingualism and positive value assigned to plurilinguals (Annamalai 2003).

Language beliefs include these ideologies, but at a more fundamental level they include the way in which the diverse members of a speech community assign value to the language and varieties that make up the sociolinguistic ecology. Deeply committed parents can in fact band together, and establish their own schools. One of the best-known examples is the Māori language regeneration movement in New Zealand starting in the 1980s, by which time it was clear to the Māori community that their children were no longer speaking the language of their elders (Spolsky 2003, 2005b; see also Hinton, Chapter 15). For another case, see the example of Manx medium schools discussed by Sallabank, Chapter 14.

The pattern shown here, reported in many other cases including the late-nineteenth-century Hebrew revival in Ottoman Palestine, involved parents who found that the home domain was insufficiently powerful to effect the language management they wanted and who therefore joined together to set up community schools. A further step may come when minority groups seize political control of public schools in order to manage the school language goals. Of course, where a previously weak minority language group (minority referring to lack of power rather than numbers (Paulston 1994)) gains political power, it can use the power to change language policy. Among recent examples, autonomy in Spanish regions (especially Catalonia and the Basque Country), in Quebec, and in the Celtic periphery in the United Kingdom, and independence in former Soviet states, have led to efforts to establish or re-establish the power of territorial languages (Fishman 2001a). This political dimension, moving from the home to the community to the ethnic group to the autonomous region to the nation, reflects one strong recent trend. It should have also been the case with the newly independent African states in the 1960s, but was largely prevented by the fact that new state borders, following nineteenth-century colonial borders, did not divide the continent ethnically and linguistically or allow for the major tribal population movements that were in progress. As a result, most African states continue to be committed to using their colonial languages as official for government and education (Alexandre 1968, Bamgbose 2000, Breton 2003, Mesthrie 2002, Phillipson and Skutnabb-Kangas 1995a).

8.6 Conclusion

Looking at language policy and language management in a social context provides a useful framework for analysing the nature of language endangerment, looking at the forces involved, and considering the possible ways that the speakers of these languages can be supported in their efforts to preserve and maintain their strength. As Grenoble mentions in Chapter 2, it is crucial to treat this as an issue in sociolinguistic ecology rather than only one of language salvage. It is essential to see the complexity of the way in which language varieties are distributed in the many domains and niches of a speech community's practices, the diversity of values that members of the community and their institutions assign to the varieties, and the multiplicity of management efforts that are brought to bear on the phenomenon.

Notes

1 Popularly referred to as 'dead languages', which misses the fact that while lacking native speakers they are often learned in school and widely used.
2 This wording has been altered in the 2009 edition of *Ethnologue*: see www.ethnologue.com (2 March 2010).

3 A recent newspaper story complained about the loss of the Newfoundland dialect.

4 Silverstein (1998b: 130) also proposed the term LINGUISTIC COMMUNITY for a group marked by 'an ideology of speaking the same language'. Silverstein (1996) characterized this as a MONOGLOT IDEOLOGY, a belief that the community is in fact monolingual.

5 Such as the social value assigned to pronouncing an 'r' after a vowel in their variety of English.

6 Volume 29 of the *Annual Review of Applied Linguistics* is a recent survey of lingua franca languages.

7 I prefer the term 'management' to 'planning': for details, see Nekvapil (2006) and Spolsky (2009b).

8 These three interrelated phenomena are often called STATUS PLANNING, CORPUS PLANNING and LANGUAGE ACQUISITION PLANNING; see Sallabank, Chapter 14.

9 There is a reverse solidarity effect when one chooses to use a 'lower' variety to claim identity with one's peers: for example, officers in an army unit may use a lower class variety when speaking to their soldiers.

10 Formally established at the beginning of the twentieth century, there are estimated to be about 80,000 Navajos among the 250,000 members of the Native American Church, whose use of Peyote has been controversial.

Part II

Language documentation

9

Language documentation

Anthony C. Woodbury

9.1   What is language documentation?

LANGUAGE DOCUMENTATION is the creation, annotation, preservation
and dissemination of transparent records of a language. While simple in
concept, it is complex and multifaceted in practice because:

- its object, LANGUAGE, encompasses conscious and unconscious knowledge, ideation and cognitive ability, as well as overt social behaviour;
- RECORDS of these things must draw on concepts and techniques from
  linguistics, ethnography, psychology, computer science, recording
  arts and more;
- the CREATION, ANNOTATION, PRESERVATION and DISSEMINATION of
  such records pose new challenges in all the above fields, as well as
  information and archival sciences and;
- above all, humans experience their own and other people's languages
  viscerally and have differing stakes, purposes, goals and aspirations
  for language records and language documentation.

Language documentation, by this definition, is at least as old as writing. Attestations of the Homeric poems, for example, are records of what
were for a long time verbal performances that reflect a once-held competence for a language and its use. Their inscription was a feat of linguistic analysis, and their passage to us through nearly three millennia a
triumph of preservation and dissemination. For philologists, they have
served as the basis for editions, retellings, translations, concordances,
dictionaries and grammars. And these in turn have been valued by many
as poetry, rhetoric, narrative and logic; and as history, politics, psychology, religion and ethnic ideology.

I am grateful to Christine Beier, Stuart McGill, Keren Rice and Julia Sallabank for their extensive
comments on earlier drafts of this paper; and I acknowledge a debt to colleagues too numerous to
name for discussion of the general issues of this chapter over many years.

Likewise, the spread of writing to vernacular languages, along with ideologies of language standardization and practices of manuscript curation, constituted language documentation on an enormous scale over a millennial time frame.

In this chapter my concern is language documentation as it applies to endangered languages. I take LANGUAGE ENDANGERMENT to be the en masse, often radical shift away from unique, local languages and language practices, even as they may still be perceived as key emblems of community identity. As applied to endangered languages, language documentation is accelerated, enlarged, popularized and transformed. More and more communities have sought documentation of their languages just as they slip away; the languages for which documentation is sought show ever more genetic and typological diversity from one to the next; and the communities themselves are usually small in terms of population. Thus, what once might have been accomplished as a national project by many people with specialized training over many years, is instead forced to happen in only a few years, village by village, at the hands of a few people, often with little or no technical training. For their part, many linguists and scholars in related fields have been inspired by the human and scientific dimensions of the issue, have called for renewed attention to language documentation, and along with it a substantial reordering of their own disciplinary priorities and practices (Dobrin and Berson, Chapter 10).

Before evaluating critically the scholarly and popular contexts of endangered language documentation, let us first draw some basic corollaries and concomitants of the idea, in order to be clear what is at issue. We begin with RECORDS of a language, the products of language documentation. Minimally, such records are any kind of preservable representation of lexico-grammatical form, typically WRITING; or any kind of preservable, real-time replica of speech, typically (nowadays) a VIDEO-RECORDING or AUDIO-RECORDING. To be TRANSPARENT, interpretable by its future perceivers, a record requires what philologists call an APPARATUS: systematic information about the creation and provenance of the record and of the event it represents (technically termed METADATA; see Conathan, Chapter 12, and Good, Chapter 11); and TRANSLATION(s) into other languages, including at least one language of wider communication. To this, nearly all linguist practitioners would add TRANSCRIPTION (or retranscription, if the original is written) in the terms of a scientific analysis of the lexico-grammar, so that the identities of sounds and lexical elements are systematically elicited from contemporary speakers and thence transmitted to future perceivers. Nevertheless, users interested in the records for reasons other than the analysis of the lexico-grammatical code may consider transcription expendable (as is standard, for example, in films with audio in one language and subtitles in another). Beyond the bare minimum (such as the metadata set specified by the Open Language

Archives Consortium (OLAC), see Good, Chapter 11), metadata can be enriched with primary and secondary commentaries and links to other records (Nathan and Austin 2004), and translations can be multiplied at different compositional levels, passage-by-passage, clause-by-clause, word-by-word, or bit-by-bit of meaning, and supplemented with commentaries and with commentaries on commentaries from different perspectives (Evans and Sasse 2007, Woodbury 2007).

Language documentation is still language documentation whether or not the records that are produced 'add up' in some way; nevertheless, we do well to explore the many different ways that sets of records could cohere. For example, a set of records resulting from an endangered-language documentation project could:

- be tailored to certain interests of community members, or of scholars of different kinds, or of publics variously conceived;
- be assembled so as to tell a specific story, like the images in a photographic essay;
- comprise samples of talk in a specific community regardless of the language, or follow just one lexico-grammatical code across several communities;
- comprise samples of different speakers, or speakers of different social categories, or sample different genres;
- comprise samples of purely naturalistic, fly-on-the-wall records, or records of talk that is staged in different ways, or both; and
- comprise samples of speech from one moment in time, or (with the right resources) a sample across time.

The sets of records, coherent or not, are often called LANGUAGE DOCU-MENTATIONS; but since that is what we are calling the activity as a whole, I will call such sets LANGUAGE DOCUMENTARY CORPORA (or just CORPORA); and I will call the ideas according to which a corpus is said to cohere or 'add up' its (CORPUS) THEORIZATION. Corpus theorizations, and even principles for corpus theorization, can both offer a space for invention and become a matter of contention and debate; we will return to these in Sections 9.4.3 and 9.4.4.

Endangered-language documentation, the activity, can be an isolated occurrence, as when a person creates and keeps a few scraps or tapes, or when word lists are scribbled down during brief encounters, or when records emerge as by-products of other activities. But of special interest is the range of concerted, programmed documentary activities motivated by impending language loss and aimed at creating a final record. These activities raise issues of corpus theorization; but in addition, they raise questions about the participants, their purposes and the various stakeholders in the activity or programme of activity or project: we may refer to this set of questions as the PROJECT DESIGN (see Bowern, Chapter 23) of a language-documentation activity.

Regarding PARTICIPANTS (see Grinevald and Bert, Chapter 3, and Dobrin and Berson, Chapter 10), a language-documentation activity can be carried out by one or many people and raises questions of competence, capacity and entitlement: must a documenter be a native speaker (Ameka 2006), or at least a second-language speaker, of the language being documented? A community member or traditional political ally? A person making a common purpose or cause with some, many or all community members? Must a documenter be a linguist? An ethnographer? An oral historian, or specialist in verbal art, or ethnomusicologist, or educator? An audio- and video-recording artist and technician? An archivist? All of these, or at least one or several of them? (See further discussion in Section 9.4.2.)

Regarding PURPOSES, documentation can mean different things to different people. A project may be aimed at preservation, or revitalization, or the scientific study of language use or acquisition or grammar or lexical knowledge, or the reconstruction of linguistic or social history. It can be ideologically keyed to the establishment and maintenance of identity, or as a symbol of progress or global participation, or as art, reality, nostalgia or a general quest for knowledge; and this just scratches the surface.

Finally, regarding STAKEHOLDERS (see Austin 2003: 8–9, and Dobrin and Berson, Chapter 10), that is, who a project is for, and who takes part in shaping its design: can a project be conceived narrowly as just for the community being documented, or some sector of it, or just for science, or just for a generic wider public? Is there a compact among stakeholders that mediates among their different purposes, and how might those purposes intersect, or fail to intersect? And does being a 'stakeholder' of one sort or another give people equal say over how documentation is to proceed (or not proceed)?

9.2   How is documentation related to traditional academic projects and orientations?

As noted above, language documentation as defined here is as old as writing. But it has evolved considerably in the context of the massive, world-scale language contact of the past 500 years, leading to a scholarly discipline or framework now increasingly termed DOCUMENTARY LINGUISTICS, for which carrying out endangered language documentation has been the defining project or DISCIPLINARY CHARTER.[1] Much insight could be gained from a detailed study of the early origins and antecedents of documentary linguistics; but we will begin with Franz Boas, whose charter for ethnography encompassed a prototype of the modern notion of language documentation, and whose influence has been especially significant.[2]

Boas (1911: 59–73) saw the study of languages, including especially the collection of texts, as both a practical and a theoretical component in the study of aboriginal ethnography in the Americas: practically, as a way to obtain information about complex topics in contexts where neither investigators nor the most knowledgeable tribal members knew each others' languages well or at all; and theoretically because, in his view, much of the content of culture, e.g. rituals, oratory, narrative, verbal art and onomastics, was linguistic in nature. Furthermore, he considered linguistics itself a domain of ethnology, which he defined as 'the science dealing with the mental phenomena of the life of the peoples of the world' (Boas 1911: 63).

From a modern point of view, Boas's conception of language was both broad and interestingly free of dichotomization: there is no strong theoretical division between language use versus linguistic knowledge. There is an acknowledgement of a universal core of grammatical concepts, structures and categories, alongside an openness to areas where these may vary, and in the areas where they vary, an openness to both genetic inheritance and contact-based diffusion. In turn, his focus on particulars within this broadly conceived whole allowed for inferences about the histories of individual traits in preference to long-range, essentialist, all-or-nothing reckonings of the 'origins' of whole peoples, 'races', nations or cultures.

Despite this aversion to line-drawing in a theoretical sense, he advocated the creation of texts, grammars, and dictionaries (the so-called Boasian trilogy or triumvirate) as his theorization of language documentary corpora, as in Boas (1917: 1):

> We have vocabularies; but, excepting the old missionary grammars, there is very little systematic work. Even where we have grammars, we have no bodies of aboriginal texts … it has become more and more evident that large masses of texts are needed in order to elucidate the structure of the languages.

All three were interrelated parts of a documentary whole, treating, in different ways, overlapping empirical domains; and it would be a mistake to project from any one of these a specific theoretical domain or level of analysis.

The *International Journal of American Linguistics* (IJAL), together with university and museum monograph series, were to be the archiving mechanism for such corpora. For example, in IJAL's second year Speck (1918) published a 58-page collection of Penobscot texts with interlinear and free translations, the first of many text publications in IJAL's early years. Lexicons and sketch grammars were likewise published. Moreover, field notes were frequently archived for posterity (for example, in the extensive collection of original field notes on Native American languages at the Library of the American Philosophical Society, Philadelphia, which includes many of Boas' own notes).

Boas' corpus theorization included a broad view of so-called texts. He chafed at the limitations imposed by dictation (Boas 1917: 1):

> The slowness of dictation that is necessary for recording texts makes it difficult for the narrator to employ that freedom of diction that belongs to the well-told tale, and consequently an unnatural simplicity of syntax prevails in most of the dictated texts.

He was somewhat happier with texts written directly by native speakers. But still he complained:

> On the whole, however, the available material gives a one-sided presentation of linguistic data, because we have hardly any records of daily occurrences, every-day conversation, descriptions of industries, customs, and the like. For these reasons the vocabularies yielded by texts are one-sided and incomplete. (Boas 1917: 2)

He later elaborates:

> The problems treated in a linguistic journal must include also the literary forms of native production. Indian oratory has long been famous, but the number of recorded speeches from which we can judge their oratorical devices is exceedingly small. There is no doubt whatever that definite stylistic forms exist that are utilized to impress the hearer; but we do not know what they are. As yet, nobody has attempted a careful analysis of the style of narrative art as practiced by the various tribes. The crudeness of most records presents a serious obstacle for this study, which, however, should be taken up seriously. We can study the general structure of the narrative, the style of composition, of motives, their character and sequence; but the formal stylistic devices for obtaining effects are not so easily determined. (Boas 1917: 7)

He also advocated the study of other kinds of speech, including song words, speech distortion and play, and ritual language. Clearly the lack of practical recording techniques impeded this programme, but not for any want of basic conception; indeed his conception prefigures the current mainstream as will be described below.

For Boas, linguistics was one of four anthropological fields (alongside archaeology and physical and cultural anthropology) for which students were to receive training; and at least as carried out by Boas, this represented a robust, if ultimately temporary, disciplinary establishment of linguistic documentation. A further important feature, again prefiguring contemporary practice, was Boas's personal commitment to the training of native speakers as documenters: George Hunt produced volumes of written text material in Kwakwaka'wakw (discussed critically in Briggs and Bauman 1999); Ella Deloria co-authored with him a grammar of Dakota (Boas and Deloria 1941); and Zora Neale Hurston (1935) collected texts in African-American communities in Florida and elsewhere which were published as folklore and literature.

As structuralism (including eventually generative structuralism) took hold, linguists increasingly distinguished lexico-grammatical systems from language use and a subtle but important retheorization (or indeed detheorization) of documentary corpora and of the traditional text–dictionary–grammar trilogy took hold. The relationship, originally mutually reinforcing, becomes hierarchical: texts, elicited data, judgements and other exemplifications of use are the 'raw data' which allow for the extraction of lexical information for the dictionary and grammar. The dictionary generalizes over the lexical knowledge presupposed in the texts, and the grammar generalizes over the categories and relations instantiated in the texts and presupposed in the presentation of the dictionary: the sound system, general morphophonemics, word structure, parts of speech, the system of regular inflection, phrase and sentence formation and the like. This left texts and other 'raw data' corpora untheorized, except as they might inform the dictionary and grammar; for example, Samarin (1967: 46) pithily calls only for the publication with a grammar of 'enough texts to permit a verification of the analysis'. With text and other 'raw data' documentation theorized so narrowly, the grammar and dictionary themselves remain as documentation of internalized speaker knowledge or of a shared system, which in turn serves ends even higher on the hierarchy, including genetic classification, typology, or the testing of cross-linguistic theories. Alternatively, grammars and dictionaries might be recognized themselves as a level of analysis, in which case there is nearly nothing at all that is theorized as a documentary corpus, rendering texts or other data as epiphenomenal.

This made it possible to pursue grammar in a more or less non-documentary framework (see Himmelmann 2002: 3–4 for an analysis of how this approach came to be known as DESCRIPTIVE). Grammars were often published without texts, and the data in grammars were not always sourced or even drawn from texts at all. But even more significantly, grammars themselves became less highly valued within the disciplinary economy, so that by the 1980s there were debates as to whether the 'compilation' of a grammar could even serve as a doctoral dissertation in many major linguistics departments, while the work of grammar writing was, in significant measure, abandoned by secular academic linguists to their missionary colleagues, especially members of SIL International. More commonly, grammatical analysis was pursued in the context of typology and theory, presented in article-length works, and was often not even founded on systematic lexicographic analysis, let alone documentary records curated for long-term preservation or easy access.

Nevertheless, even as theoretical perspectives changed, there was a remarkable degree of persistence of the Boasian theorization, or at least of its main procedures, among Americanists. Both Edward Sapir, a student of Boas, and Leonard Bloomfield produced voluminous Boasian-style documentation despite their vanguard roles in the theoretical shifts. At mid century, Murray Emeneau and Mary Haas, both students of Sapir, presided at the University of California at Berkeley over a veritable factory of graduate students who produced Boasian grammar–dictionary–text trilogies published by the *University of California Publications in Linguistics*. These texts were linked to audio-recordings which, along with field notes and slip-files, were archived with the Survey of California Indian Languages. Michael Krauss established in the 1970s, as part of the Alaska Native Language Center at the University of Alaska, Fairbanks, 'an archival library whose holdings include almost every printed document, and much of the unpublished material, that has been written in or on an Alaska Native language' (Krauss 1980: 31–2), and which also included a significant sound archive.

Many scholars' life work touched every corner of Boasian practice. Consider, for example, Knut Bergsland's documentation of Aleut, a language spoken mainly by small pockets of elders on the Alaska Peninsula, the Aleutian chain, and some nearby islands. His documentary *oeuvre* begins with a dense philological presentation of Atkan and Attuan Aleut materials, including a catalogue of documentary sources, an exegesis of proper names, and interlinear texts from century-old sources written by Aleut church men, and from people whom he and others audio-recorded directly (Bergsland 1959). He continues, after a series of analytic, theory-oriented articles in the 1960s and 1970s, with:

- a pedagogical dictionary and grammar co-authored with Moses Dirks, a native speaker of Atkan Aleut (Bergsland and Dirks, 1978, 1981);
- a 715-page edition (with free translation only) of the texts written or wire-recorded by Waldemar Jochelson's expedition in 1909–10 (Bergsland and Dirks 1990);
- a 739-page dictionary covering all Aleut varieties, with extensive text-keyed exemplification and coverage of stems, productive derivation and special lexical areas including place names keyed to maps of the entire Aleut territory, technical terminologies and loans (Bergsland 1994);
- a 360-page grammar also covering all varieties and with copious text-keyed exemplification, often long and complicated (Bergsland 1997); and
- a monograph analysing and interpreting personal name data gathered by the Billings Expedition in 1790–2 (Bergsland 1998).

Although informed by post-Boasian structural linguistics, the philology, the breadth of focus, the interleaving of text, dictionary and grammar, and the concern for speaker training, represent a magnificent (and exceedingly brilliant) rendering of Boasian documentary theorization, decades after it stopped being forcefully articulated within the international linguistic mainstream. Moreover, to the extent that endangered-language research was pursued, Bergsland's Boasian orientation was hardly atypical.

Despite the generally counterdocumentary trend in the mainstream of linguistics from the 1950s onwards, there nevertheless were contexts in which something like the Boasian theorization of texts was taken up and elaborated. The ETHNOGRAPHY OF SPEAKING had as its charter the creation of comprehensive, grammar-like descriptions of language use in speech communities, notably defined by Gumperz (1962) as 'a social group which may be either monolingual or multilingual, held together by frequency of social interaction patterns and set off from the surrounding areas by weaknesses in the lines of communication' (see also Michael, Chapter 7, Dobrin and Berson, Chapter 10, and Spolsky, Chapter 8). Within this framework, descriptions were to be made in terms of parametric categories such as WAYS OF SPEAKING, FLUENT SPEAKERS, SPEECH COMMUNITY, SPEECH SITUATION, EVENT and ACT, and such components of speech itself as MESSAGE FORM (including language or code) and CONTENT, SETTING, SCENE, GOAL, CHANNEL, and PARTICIPANTS (Hymes 1974a: 45–58). This theorization at least implied balanced, selective documentary corpora. But it also would be fair to question whether documentation itself was its goal: writings on the ethnography of speaking were not explicit about methods for record creation, annotation, archiving or dissemination, nor was systematic grammatical investigation a part of the programme, especially given the focus on community rather than code per se. Thus work done within the framework approached these issues in a range of ways, and in this respect, many practitioners notwithstanding, the ethnography of speaking mirrored the structural linguistics of the same period.[3]

By the 1970s, with language documentation receded from the limelight and its parts parochialized, redefined or repurposed, several trends began emerging, most noticeably among students of endangered indigenous languages of the Americas and Australia. First and foremost, their work was conducted in a context of heightened concern, awareness and activism by both communities themselves, and outside linguists (Alvarez and Hale 1970, Hale *et al.* 1992, Krauss 1980, Wilkins 1992). Second, attention was increasingly drawn to the role of FIELD LINGUISTICS in exploring new structures relevant to theoretical concerns (e.g. Dixon 1972, 1976, Hale 1975, 1983), and from there to the methods of field linguistics, including the role of texts in language documentation (Heath 1985). Third, a reconceptualization of language documentation as a unified field of endeavour in its own right was under way (notably Sherzer 1987), challenging its subservience to more specialized kinds of inquiry in both ethnography and linguistics:

Both linguists and anthropologists have traditionally treated discourse as an invisible glass through which the researcher perceives the reality of grammar, social relations, ecological practices, and belief systems. But the glass itself, discourse and its structure, the actual medium through which knowledge (linguistic and cultural) is produced, conceived, transmitted, and acquired, by members of societies and by researchers, is given little attention. My stance here is quite different from the traditional one, and reflects a growing interest in discourse in many disciplines. I view language, culture, society, and the individual as all providing resources in a creative process which is actualized in discourse. In my discourse-centered approach, discourse is the broadest and most comprehensive level of linguistic form, content, and use. This is what I mean by saying that discourse and especially the process of discourse structuring is the locus of the language–culture relationship. Furthermore, it is in certain kinds of discourse, in which speech play and verbal art are heightened, as central moments in poetry, magic, politics, religion, respect, insult, and bargaining, that the language–culture–discourse relationship comes into sharpest focus and the organizing role of discourse in this relationship is highlighted. (Sherzer 1987: 305–6)

In this view documentation itself becomes the goal, and yet is theorized well beyond sampling or surveying by proposing a special status for verbal art and speech play. It is also essentially open as to whether documentation is community-based or lexico-grammatical code-based, leaving that to depend on participants' goals. Sherzer furthermore makes proposals for text transcription, annotation, and analysis that build on ideas of Jakobson (1968) and others for seeing linguistic constructs as primes in discourse artistry. This raises representation from an ad hoc matter to a theoretical issue.

All these trends among scholars of endangered languages were ingredients in a wholesale revival of interest in documentation; and they did not arise in a vacuum. There was a continuing increase of interest in language preservation by communities undergoing shift, a growing intellectual focus on diversity and diversity issues in linguistics more widely (Nichols 1992) and on neo-Whorfian approaches in linguistic anthropology (Lucy 1992), and rapid advances in computational archiving and analysis of linguistic mega-corpora, exemplified by the work of the Linguistic Data Consortium at the University of Pennsylvania, among others.

By the mid 1990s an explicit disciplinary ideology and set of practices for endangered-language documentation had emerged, from which point it underwent rapid, global institutionalization as an academic discipline or framework, termed DOCUMENTARY LINGUISTICS (or DOCUMENTARY AND DESCRIPTIVE LINGUISTICS). An important workshop organized by David Wilkins at the Max Planck Institute for Psycholinguistics in Nijmegen, The Netherlands, in October 1995 asked what the 'best record' of a language would look like. This is a question that can only be raised when documentation itself, rather than specific lines of linguistic or social inquiry, is the goal of study. The responses received included a number of disciplinary manifestos (Himmelmann 1998, Lehmann 2001, A. Woodbury 2003), all of which in one form or another pointed to the relative neglect of documentation and proposed documentation-centred approaches. Himmelmann in particular argued for a stronger division between documentation and description. He considered the creation and preservation of multipurpose records to be an endeavour distinct from dictionary-making and grammar-writing, although interrelated, and he argued that the contents of a documentation must be theorized beyond the immediate needs of description. In particular, dictionaries, grammars and perhaps ethnographies of speaking were to evolve as part of the documentary apparatus, much as in Boasian times or in the philological practice of even earlier, and even the conduct of paradigm elicitation or of a psycholinguistic experiment was to become amenable to treatment as a raw event recordable in the same ways as more traditional narrative or conversational texts.

Himmelmann (1998, elaborated somewhat differently in Himmelmann 2006a) also offers a quite specific format for a 'documentation', a comprehensive documentary corpus that focuses on a speech community (and thus not necessarily a single code) and includes a corpus of recorded events, lexical or other databases, and notes. It also includes metadata, commentary and annotation for these records, as well as general metadata about the community and, optionally, a descriptive grammar, ethnography and dictionary. This basic idea served as a charter for what was to be the first of a major series of funding efforts for endangered-language documentation, Dokumentation Bedrohter Sprachen, funded by the Volkswagen Foundation, the results of which are archived at the DoBeS Archive in Nijmegen.[4]

This was followed by other efforts in Canada (the Community-University Research Alliance and the Aboriginal Research Programme, both sponsored by the Social Sciences and Humanities Research Council of Canada), Japan (Vanishing Languages of the Pacific Rim, funded by the Japanese Ministry of Education), the UK (the Hans Rausing Endangered Languages Project (HRELP), funded by Arcadia Trust, which includes new granting, archiving, and academic programmes), and the US (the Documenting Endangered Languages (DEL) programme of the National Science Foundation and the National Endowment for the Humanities); and two smaller private charitable endeavours, the Foundation for Endangered Languages (FEL) in the UK, and the Endangered Language Fund (ELF) in the US. Each of these has led to projects animated by different conceptions of documentation: Pacific Rim and DEL with more allowance for grammars and dictionaries as documentation, HRELP with a strong recorded-text emphasis but allowing a more heterodox range of theorizations and project designs, and FEL and ELF with an emphasis on documentation in the context of community-driven language-preservation efforts.

Alongside these initiatives, archiving projects were developed. Some, as already noted, arose in conjunction with documentation projects, and some were continuations of older archives, including the archives of the Smithsonian, the Survey of California Indian Languages, Alaska Native Language Center, and SIL International. Yet others were new, regional initiatives such as the Archive of the Indigenous Languages of Latin America (AILLA) and the Pacific and Regional Archive for Digital Sources in Endangered Cultures (PARADISEC). All arose as part of an effort to organize and coordinate the archiving and cataloguing of endangered language documentation, including (see Nathan, Chapter 13 for the abbreviations): OLAC, IMDI, E-MELD and DELAMAN. Not surprisingly, the professional practices of archivists were unfamiliar to field linguists, especially given the wider, anti-documentarian trends mentioned; and even more so because of uncertainties about the nature and vulnerabilities of electronic documentation. Bird and Simons (2003) is an important general statement of the problems of making documentation last (see also Nathan, Chapter 13, and Good, Chapter 11).

Finally, documentary linguistics developed a general literature dealing with a wide range of issues, including a comprehensive handbook with thoughtful treatments of a set of issues and practices (Gippert *et al.* 2006), and important collections on field work (Newman and Ratliff 2001a) and grammar writing (Ameka *et al.* 2006, Payne and Weber 2007). Beginning in 2003, the yearly series *Language Documentation and Description*, edited by Peter K. Austin and published by SOAS, covered conceptual and technical questions, with special focus on community capacity building, multidisciplinary cooperation, archiving, documenting language variation and contact, meaning and translation, and literacy issues. The *Language Archives Newsletter* edited by David Nathan (SOAS), Peter Wittenburg and Paul Trilsbeek (MPI Nijmegen) and Marcus Uneson (Lund) published ten online issues between 2004 and 2007, covering technological and related issues. The year 2007 saw the founding of the online journal *Language Documentation and Conservation*[5] which publishes papers and reviews on a wide range of topics.

In summary, an influential academic charter for language documentation was articulated by Boas a century ago, leading in several important intellectual directions even as academic and popular attention to language loss waned. Documentary linguistics in its modern academic sense is an ambitious rewelding of the splintered pieces of the Boasian framework for language study. It arose as speaker communities and linguists drew more attention to language endangerment, as scientific interest in linguistic diversity renewed, as information management technologies burgeoned, and as linguists began to engage with the social and ethical dimensions of their work (see Dobrin and Berson, Chapter 10).

Documentary linguistics is new enough, however, that its scope, its scientific and humanistic goals, its stakeholders, participants, and practices are still being explored and debated both inside and outside academic contexts. After examining endangered language documentation in community contexts in Section 9.3, we will consider how a broad, inclusive idea of endangered-language documentation might be framed in order best to realize its potential, avoid pitfalls, and meet its challenges.

9.3 How is documentation related to community and other non-academic endangered language projects and perspectives?

We have considered the context and development of endangered-language documentation in academic research. But the stakeholders in documentation include the communities in which endangered languages are spoken. They may also include a wider array of publics with interests of different kinds, including friendship, literature, music, science, tourism, entertainment, nationalism, education policy, literacy, economic relations, development, subsistence, land acquisition, law enforcement, military conscription and religious conversion; and that only scratches the surface. In what follows I will focus mainly on documentation and community stakeholders and will have little to say of wider publics except as they may form part of the community context of endangered-language documentation.

In principle, the documentation of any language might be interesting or useful to anyone. If it is one's own or ancestral language, there may be special dimensions of identity, territory, spirituality, aesthetics, utility or nostalgia. And if one's own language is endangered, these may all be amplified and bring to the fore further personal, political, scientific and humanistic questions. Documentation, so far as it exists, is almost always a matter of interest in endangered-language communities, and sometimes a matter of controversy.

Certainly the form of language documentation longest at issue in endangered language communities has been writing, and through it the creation of indigenous language literatures, while audio- and video-documentation is of a more recent vintage. It is often the case that the development, support and teaching of writing is central in community-based language preservation programmes and a powerful emblem for language loyalty (see Lüpke, Chapter 16), whereas electronic documentation is often less debated or even accessible (see Bennett (2003) and Hinton (2001a) for some perspective, and Holton, Chapter 19).

Nevertheless, it is important to recognize that, within the wider realm of language activism, language planning and language revitalization and maintenance, documentation (written or otherwise) need not play a central role or even any role at all (Grounds 2007). And, when it does play a role, it will not necessarily be created, preserved or disseminated in ways that are professionalized. Rather, we find individuals in communities, insiders or outsiders, needing to make a case for documentation in relation to wider ideologies and aspirations for language and community, and doing so on the basis of their own conceptions of what documentation is, and how different forms of it are created, preserved and valued. For example, Hinton (1994a) (see also Conathan, Chapter 12) tells vividly the story of John Peabody Harrington, a dogged, skilled, but imperious language documenter of the early and mid twentieth-century American west who left almost a million pages and many recordings of material on over ninety languages; and how his work was later appreciated as it became central in community projects in California to reawaken languages falling out of use (see Hinton, Chapter 15, on the *Breath of Life Workshops* that trained community members on how to access and use such archival materials).

An excellent handbook by linguists for language maintenance and preservation work, with surveys of such efforts around the world, is Hinton and Hale (2001) (see also Grenoble and Whaley (2006) with partly similar goals). Its major section headings include language policy, language planning, immersion in schools and in private settings, and training, none of which centrally involve documentation; documentation comes up directly in a section on media and technology and, implicitly, literacy. The intellectual diversity of community-based (and often school-based) language revival and preservation work is evident in the edited proceedings of a continuing series of language revitalization conferences at Northern Arizona University, organized by Jon Reyhner (Burnaby and Reyhner 2002, Cantoni 1996, Reyhner 1997, Reyhner and Lockard 2009, Reyhner *et al.* 1999, 2000, 2003). Here too, documentation is but one among many tools, with a different range of uses in different conceptions and approaches to language revitalization.

Wilkins (1992), Hill (2006), Rice (2009) and Grenoble (2009b) describe and discuss differences in worldviews and agendas among speakers and non-speaker linguists. The differences can be described at times as irreducible; and seem the more so when individuals talk past each other. They argue for ethnographic awareness and openness to different goals and purposes on the parts of linguists, and for flexibility in designing projects that meet participants' goals (Grenoble, Chapter 2, Hinton, Chapter 15). This is a stance which I will pursue in Section 9.4.1 below.

J. Hill (2002), Dobrin (2008), and Dobrin *et al.* (2009) further turn the spotlight on presuppositions, assumptions, attitudes and discourses held by outside researchers, often in the deep background, that can affect their interactions in communities even with the best of intentions. J. Hill (2002) assesses metaphors of languages as riches that are enumerated, pointing out uncomfortable connections of this rhetoric with colonial extirpation. Dobrin *et al.* (2009) pursue the question of enumeration and its reductionistic extension, in academic discourses, to the valuation of documentary corpora. Dobrin (2008) discusses the high valuation of autonomy and self-determination in outsiders' assessments of the common good in their interactions, at times failing to parse their relationships in more locally familiar value systems, including especially systems where exchange is highly valued.

Finally, a key factor in any documentation, including endangered-language documentation, is the danger it may present, particularly in communities that feel marginalized and vulnerable at many levels (Conathan, Section 12.5). If data is collected and preserved for wide use and is genuinely multipurposed, then who is to stop it from getting into the wrong hands? Whereas from a utilitarian viewpoint this can be framed simply as leading to 'limitations' on documentation (Himmelmann 2006a: 16–17) and can be responded to within an ethical framework of INFORMED CONSENT, it must be seen in connection with the growing ubiquity of electronic record-making and surveillance in the contemporary world, and the kinds of trade-offs they present between having your voice heard or forging wider connections on the one hand, and a loss of control or fear of 'digging your own grave' on the other. Responses to this dilemma may differ from person to person, community to community, and time to time; but as technology continues to change no one ever fully imagines, let alone becomes 'informed,' of all the possible long-term effects of electronic record-making.

9.4 Toward a broad and inclusive view of endangered language documentation

The formulation of endangered-language documentation that I have presented is intentionally broad. At its core is the impulse people may have to make and keep records of languages that are falling into disuse through rapid language shift. That motivation serves many different goals and constituencies, and gives rise to many different disciplinary charters and programmatic approaches, as noted in the previous two sections. I defend a broad formulation because, even amidst such evident heterogeneity, there is a danger and even a tendency for individuals to establish and stipulate more specific practices aimed at just the situations they are most accustomed to, losing track of the greater whole.

In view of this, I think one of the principal functions of DOCUMENTARY LINGUISTICS, or better, of the whole patchwork of enterprises chartered in some way to see to or use endangered-language documentation, is to try to know, understand, acknowledge, analyse, and coordinate the enterprise in all its various, multifaceted forms. In some respects, this draws on particular bodies of expertise; for example, linguists have expertise in areas like transcription and lexical documentation, and archivists in record organization and preservation that are likely to be broadly applicable, whatever brand of documentation is to be undertaken. But it also requires an imagination for difference of purpose and aspiration, a flexibility in understanding data structuring and management and using expert tools (Good, Chapter 11), an awareness of quite different ideologies of language and speaking among academics and non-academics alike, and an openness to the social complexities of what often are radically multicultural projects (Dobrin and Berson, Chapter 10). My sense of the current state of affairs is reflected well by Dobrin *et al.* (2009: 45) when they write, in a somewhat more specific context:

> Even despite systematizing conceptual efforts within linguistics, such as Himmelmann's [1998] careful distinguishing of description from documentation, a set of agreed upon principles of language documentation with associated methods does not exist. The resulting questions that this leaves open are fundamental: are our goals activist or scientific? Is documentation a research activity, or is it more closely aligned with art and practice of creative media? Does our data consist of symbols or of audio and video? How should archives prioritise dissemination across the potential constituencies they serve (academics of various persuasions, speaker communities)? On what basis could we decide?

And I am very much in sympathy with their conclusion:

> Resolving the tensions we have been describing will require an approach to documentation that is more closely tied to the guiding vision that continues to attract linguists to the language endangerment problem. However, this goal is not well served by a totalising theory that distinguishes documentary work from the rest of linguistics as a distinct and separate entity (Himmelmann 1998, cf. Austin and Grenoble 2007). Linguistics already has theoretically-informed ways of comparing languages for a host of reasons that are orthogonal to their moral value, and it is by distancing themselves from these that documentary linguists have been led to ask confused and unproductive questions such as 'how do we know when to stop documenting?' or 'how many recording hours should I put in the archive?' (page 45)

Dobrin *et al.* (2009: 46–7) continue:

> What is needed instead is an explicit recognition that the singularity of languages is irreducible, and that the methods used to study them must be singular as well. Each research situation is unique, and documentary work derives its quality from its appropriateness to the particularities of that situation. Rather than approaching endangered languages with preformulated standards deriving from their own

culture, documentary linguists must strive to be singularly responsive – both to what is distinctive about each language as an object
of research, and to the particular culture, needs, and dispositions of
the speaker communities with whom their work brings them into
contact.

In this spirit, I wish to consider some ways documentary linguistics, in
the broadest, most inclusive sense, might best realize its potential and
address its challenges and pitfalls. To be more concrete, I will frame my
discussion always with an eye to different PROJECT DESIGNS, and their
accommodation and coordination within the larger whole.

9.4.1 Coordinating academic, community, and popular agendas for the design of documentation projects

As is clear from Sections 9.2 and 9.3 above, it is usually linguists who
initiate systematic language-documentation projects, and as linguists,
whether community members or not, we design and propose projects
organized around our disciplinary agendas. But, as noted, various linguists have argued for ethnographic awareness and openness to different goals and purposes and for flexibility in designing projects that meet
participants' goals. Wilkins (1992: 186) sums up as follows his PhD fieldwork 'under aboriginal control' after setting aside his linguist's agenda:

> It would be misleading, indeed it would be a boldfaced lie, to claim
> that my approach to learning, documenting, and building up a picture
> of Mparntwe Arrernte grammar was very systematic (especially from
> the point of view of an idealized, and generally antiseptic, field methods
> course) … [T]he development and directions of my research have not
> been independent of the changing developments and demands of my
> research for the Yipirinya School. I have just pointed out that much
> of the research for the school was joint research done by a team of
> people. The data-gathering techniques used for any individual project
> were established through conferencing among members of the group
> and through consultation with the Yipirinya Council … In these cases,
> then, I had input to, but did not determine, the research methods
> which would yield the information which I was to work with.

Among the advantages Wilkins cites for his approach were the opportunity to put linguistic skills to practical use, to gain a deeper knowledge of the language and its context, to have better access to community
members, and to benefit from collaboration and teamwork (see Bowern,
Chapter 23).

I see this approach as both a blueprint for the design of projects in an
inclusive documentary linguistics, but also an institutional challenge to
linguistics. It operates not only in practical terms but intellectual terms

too (see Woodbury 2010 for more discussion). On a practical level, agendas and activities are guided by goals, enthusiasms and capacities of all those involved. Linguists must be flexible and inventive (and their institutions more tolerant) about how and when to accomplish traditional linguistic agendas, and training takes centre stage as projects involve many people, with different expertise, roles and levels of training (Jukes, Chapter 21). On an intellectual level, documentation and related linguistic discovery require serious attention to language ideology (how people conceive of language and speaking, and relate them to territory, identity, aesthetics, spirituality and other domains), and to the relationship of language and context; and a focus on speaking in given communities problematizes a disciplinary focus on specific lexico-grammatical codes.

To the extent I am able, I try to keep sight of these issues in all of what follows.

9.4.2   Participants and training

Modern endangered-language documentation projects depart notably from earlier efforts, in involving interdisciplinary teams rather than a lone linguist. DoBeS made it a requirement to compose teams not only of linguists of various expertise, but other specialists such as ethnographers, musicologists, videographers and the like, and Himmelmann (2006a: 15) points out the need for such expertise and the unlikelihood that just one linguist can adequately handle it all (see also Austin 2007; Jukes, Chapter 21). Meanwhile, team participation has become a feature of documentary training in many university contexts (e.g. Woodbury and England 2004), and teams increasingly train community members as researchers or as trainers for other community members. For example, Kaufman *et al.* (2001) undertook a survey in 2007–9 of Zapotecan languages under the sponsorship of the Mexican Instituto Nacional de las Lenguas Indígenas that trained about twenty young speakers of Zapotec and Chatino languages to conduct surveys and transcribe and translate the interview. Our Chatino project, based at University of Texas at Austin and funded by ELDP, recruited the Chatino trainees from among people already working with us, making possible a 'ladder' of academic experiences.

This is clearly a way in which documentary linguistics has in its sights its potential for broadness and inclusivity. Yet it still raises significant challenges. Austin and Grenoble (2007: 22–3) suggest that interdisciplinary cooperation can be difficult to achieve. For example, with a language that is difficult for non-speakers to hear and transcribe, must non-linguist team members become fully proficient? Or, as in our Chatino project, where linguists are spread thinly over many significantly different varieties, must the team in fact be a family of 'lone linguists'? Moreover, how does participation in documentation projects fit into people's lives and future career goals? Are community members volunteers? Employees?

Entrepreneurs? Are academics professors, or postgraduate students? Are there coherent rewards for biologists, psychologists, musicologists, video-graphers, audio-recording specialists, and so on, who might enhance a project? To take one example, are there valued genres of filmmaking that fit with the documentarian's (perhaps futile) goal of creating records in which the depiction of context is stabilized by keeping the camera or cameras in one place for long periods of time and avoiding highly inter-pretive pans, sweeps and zooms? [6]

Moreover, what does documentary training look like for children and adults without a full secondary educational background? And at univer-sity and postgraduate levels, how, in two or three years, is it possible to train a good lexico-grammarian who can also find, handle, and thrive in a field situation, in their own community or somebody else's, and then record and archive properly? It may be too much to ask (but see Jukes, Chapter 21 for some discussion).

Somehow, all of these questions must be approached and addressed if endangered-language documentation is to reach its full potential.

9.4.3 Lexicogrammatical code, language use, nostalgia and contemporary realism

We now turn to a set of conceptual issues. Relatively unheeded in Himmelmann's (1998) programme for linguistic documentation is his idea that 'a language documentation ... aims at the record of the lin-guistic practices and traditions of a speech community' (Himmelmann 1998: 166), wherein, as he points out in a footnote, a speech community may share more than one language.

In fact though, endangered language projects are almost always focused on one specific (endangered) language. As such they are instances of what I have called DOCUMENTATIONS OF THE ANCESTRAL CODE (Woodbury 2005: 257). We may make several observations about such projects in order better to see their relationship to what Himmelmann proposed, as well as several other possibilities. In turn, this allows us to see certain controversies as misplaced, given the broader conception of documen-tary linguistics I am exploring here.

Documentation of the ancestral code requires that the language be 'put through its paces', studied in various contexts of use, and supple-mented with elicitation in order to fill lexical fields, paradigms and the like. Dictionaries and grammars can follow efficiently from such docu-mentation. And at a community level, it supports orthography creation, the preparation of pedagogical dictionaries, grammars and readers, and efforts to get the language taught in schools or recognized politically: in general, it performs well in contexts where communities wish to assert that their language, despite disparagement, is a language in the same sense that Spanish or English or Russian are languages.

Despite falling short of Himmelmann's call for documentation irre-spective of code, I think it is important to defend the status of such work as documentary, as long as the documentation is curated (Conathan, Chapter 12). Likewise, to push the limit still further, a project that archives its data properly may count as documentary even if it is mainly or solely focused on making dictionaries, and uses elicitation rather than text collection as its main method, such as the *Project for the Documentation of the Languages of Meso-America* (Kaufman et al. 2001).

Debates also arise as to whether grammar-writing and dictionary-making should be avoided in favour of more text collection or elicitation. In a review of Gippert *et al.* (2006), Evans (2008:348) defends the role of these activities:

> Something about the definitive appearance of these products brings out a higher level of scrutiny and a leap to new levels of accuracy in transcription and translation. Both times that I have been involved in producing dictionaries of Australian Aboriginal languages, there was a sudden upsurge in interest and in the supplying of new or extended lexical entries at the point where speakers of the language held in their hands a properly-produced book in their language.

He concludes:

> For these reasons I think it is a mistake for documentarist linguists to argue that they should consecrate all their time and effort to pure documentary activities at the expense of preparing descriptive gram-mars or other reference materials. A much more apt strategy is Colette Grinevald's (2001) vision of an eternal spiralling upwards through the elements of the classic Boasian trilogy – grammar, texts (now = docu-mentary corpus), and dictionary – with each step forward producing advances and refinements in how the other steps proceed. (page 348)

Indeed, to dichotomize 'description' versus 'documentation' to such an extent as to exclude or restrict code-focused documentation amounts to a kind of back-door structuralist recidivism, reenergizing the very dis-tinction that detheorized primary linguistic records in the first place.

Finally, documentation of the ancestral code, like the endangerment construct itself, can be termed, without any intention to disparage (see Williams 1973), as NOSTALGIC, in the sense that it selects as important from among all the speech in a community that speech which gives evidence of a feature of the past which may not persist long into the future, namely the ancestral code (see also Dobrin and Berson, Section 10.2). On the academic side, we may see linguistic reconstruction, or a focus on the most traditional variant forms, as nostalgic tendencies, while purism and assertions of the linguistic code as intrinsic to eth-nic or spiritual identity or to traditionalism are forms of nostalgia in a popular sense.

Himmelmann's speech-community perspective, mentioned earlier, is in keeping with the ethnography of speaking and its successors, which offer useful precedents. However, we might identify (at least) two possible models of this kind, one nostalgic, the other not (the discussion here draws on a typology presented in Woodbury 2005). One, a DOCUMENTATION OF ANCESTRAL COMMUNICATIVE PRACTICES, would focus on ENDANGERED WAYS OF SPEAKING, in any code, and in that sense would also count as nostalgic. This may include formal genres or speech situations falling out of use, but it may also involve informal conversation among people perceived as traditional, or speech in connection with traditional activities, and it may involve traditional forms of multilingualism, such as remnant uses of Russian in Alaska. Although basic documentation would involve translation and presumably transcription and some annotation, grammar-writing and dictionary-making would then not be an intrinsic part of the project, in keeping with Himmelmann; although it certainly could be.

Such an approach is consonant with any ideology that locates language mainly in its verbal products, and may more directly address a community's feelings of language loss than would a focus on lexico-grammatical code. As a scholarly approach, it fits well with Boas's broader 'ethnological' framework, but at the same times is susceptible to critiques of a more contemporary kind, voiced by Garrett (2004):

> A paradox lies near the heart of documentary linguistics. As an enterprise it relates to language ecology; it is founded on the same commitment to the sociocultural embeddedness of language. But a discipline of 'documentary sociocultural analysis' or 'documentary anthropology' could hardly exist without buying into the myth that cultures are static and there is some endangered moment that merits documentation: the discredited Boasian ethnographic present. What justifies the documentary enterprise in the case of language? The only clear rationale is the distinctness of language, its systematic character and structural integrity: Documentary linguistics presupposes the same assumption of linguistic autonomy that it purports to eschew.

While agreeing with this line of commentary, I think nostalgia plays a key role, for while it fits well with the essentializing tendency of structural analysis, in sociocultural realms nostalgic selectivity leads directly to the problems mentioned. Moreover, the issue can be placed in a different light by considering a second construction of Himmelmann's position, alluded to above, namely a rational attempt to produce a DOCUMENTATION OF CONTEMPORARY COMMUNICATIVE ECOLOGY. Such an approach would aim in some sense at the 'real' or immanent as opposed to the nostalgic, even if plagued with the problem of having to select just what, from among everything, to document. It might serve in a scholarly sense as a form of sociolinguistic survey of a community, irrespective of endangerment issues, or as a way of putting them in context, and it might fit with community ideologies where contemporary modes of speaking are a source of interest (for example, the popular interest in the United States in Spanish–English code switching). And although it would restrict itself to 'now', nothing in principle confines such a project to operating only in a single moment in time.

Finally, to round out the typology, there is the case where lexico-grammatical code is again the focus, but with a contemporary rather than nostalgic orientation: DOCUMENTATION OF AN EMERGENT CODE, that is, a focus on lexico-grammatical systems with an emphasis on their contemporary state, including the emergence of new forms, neologisms, coinage, syntactic innovation, contact convergence, borrowing and even indigenized versions of the language of wider communication (e.g., so-called 'Aboriginal English' or 'Indian English', see Woodbury 1993, 1998 for extended discussion; see also O'Shannessy, Chapter 5, on 'light Warlpiri'). While seemingly most appropriate to studies of creolization or sign language formation (Meir *et al.* in press) rather than language endangerment, it can be relevant and even essential to the study of so-called semi-speakers, and of the variation in communities undergoing rapid language shift. And it can support community efforts to grapple with linguistic purism and to accomplish such aspects of language planning as coinage and translation of foreign texts into the endangered vernacular. On the other hand, it may go against the grain of anyone, academic or not, with a strong sense of nostalgia. It also raises profound theoretical issues (Le Page and Tabouret-Keller 1985) about the focus, or degree of conventionalization, that a linguistic code may have; and the line between emergent code documentation as opposed to documentation of a contemporary communicative ecology may be blurry indeed.

In summary, a broad, inclusive documentary linguistics can stand a few paces back from the ideological fray in order to coordinate, in a rational way, different kinds of endeavours that contribute to endangered-language documentation.

9.4.4 Corpus theorization: adequacy, comprehensiveness, complementarity, quality and quantity in documentary corpora

There is considerable focus in the literature (Himmelmann 1998, 2006a, Lehmann 2001, Rhodes *et al.* 2006, A. Woodbury 2003) and in the design of specific projects on assembling corpora that are adequate and comprehensive overviews, much as grammars, dictionaries or ethnographies of speaking may be said to be. Assuming we make allowance for differences on such basic parameters as code versus community focus, nostalgic versus contemporary, and probably others too, there is nothing wrong with this in principle, nor is it wrong for there to be some amount of contention or variety in how corpora are to be theorized. Perhaps most comprehensively, Hymes (1974a) proposes an 'etic grid' of essentially orthogonal parameters, implying a scheme for sampling all values with all values. Or sampling can be boiled down to different kinds of speech (Himmelmann 1998), or certain kinds of speech can be privileged on principle such as verbal art (Sherzer 1987), or conversation (Levinson 1983: 284–5); or collection can be monitored in part by the dictates of dictionary and grammar making (Rhodes *et al.* 2006).

If there is one and only one chance ever to document a language, it makes especially good sense to strive for a result that is as complete as may be possible. All things being equal, a corpus should be DIVERSE, and any of the proposed theorizations would offer that. But for many (perhaps most) languages, some documentation already exists, and more may be done in the future. It is therefore worthwhile for project designs to take complementarity into account and recognize that corpus building should be ONGOING, DISTRIBUTED and OPPORTUNISTIC. For example, the documentation project of Taff (2004) for Aleut takes note of the fact that Bergsland's corpus, albeit exemplary, is long on narrative and lexicon but very short on conversation. Accordingly her project focuses almost exclusively on conversation, nearly the only Aleut genre now available, and thereby adds enormously to the overall documentation of Aleut. Likewise, within Bergsland's own corpus is his philological monograph analysing and interpreting personal name data gathered by the Billings Expedition in 1790–2 (Bergsland 1998). And in my own documentation of Central Alaskan Yupik, I spent an intensive three-year period assembling a large corpus of experimental productions designed to elucidate the intonational system, yielding, I think, a reasonable adjunct to the narratives, conversations, and music I had documented earlier. There is no reason not to engage in specific, narrow-cast documentation projects of this kind, especially as complements to a larger corpus.

Moreover, corpus theorization, and indeed the very design and conduct of documentation projects, is also driven by social, aesthetic and humanistic values in the speech community itself, as well as those that develop within the emergent communities of practice conducting the documentation (see Hill 2006). My own documentation of Central Alaskan Yupik began with a focus on recording elders' retellings of traditional myth and folk tales, a strong community interest at the time, and part of a tacitly agreed-upon function for documentation. It was only once a traditional men's house had been built that I was invited to record the conversation that took place there, licensed, so it seemed, by the setting the men's house offered.

By contrast, community interests and values have led to quite a different corpus theorization in the documentation project I am currently engaged in (Woodbury 2010). This project is focused on Chatino, a shallow family of languages spoken in Oaxaca, Mexico, and besides me it involves a group of six University of Texas graduate students, two of whom are native speakers. Writing Chatino emerges as a core goal throughout the region and a rejoinder to colonial claims that Chatino is just a dialect incapable of being written. Accordingly, our documentation has aimed at least to sample each substantially distinct variety through text recording and lexical elicitation in order to adapt an orthography to its segments, phonotactics, tones and tone sandhi well enough that we can teach it in communities.

At the same time, Chatino speakers hold in extremely high esteem the rapid-fire, classically Mesoamerican parallelistic oratory of traditional community political authorities, and our awareness of those linguistic practices and their 'leakage' into ritual, prayer and everyday speech has led Hilaria Cruz to seek out such instances and compile them into a coherently focused body of documentation (Cruz 2009).

Likewise, Emiliana Cruz, working from a sense that Chatino linguistic knowledge is significantly organized and ordered by its connection to territory, created an extensive corpus of audio- and video-recorded Chatino-language narratives, interviews, and atlas and dictionary research gained during long mountain forays with traditional land users to document flora, fauna, land forms, population distributions, land claims, trade routes, and ethnohistory in one sprawling municipality. She hopes to present the text and lexical materials linked to maps, along with exegeses, translations and interpretations as a LINGUISTIC ECOLOGY that draws on ethnographic discourses developed in Basso (1996), complements them with an emerging documentary genre, and addresses her community's understandings of language as it links to territory.

At the same time, alongside these fairly structured goals, we often find ourselves looking, in more or less abstract or general terms, for ways to diversify our corpus.

In the end, our corpus theorization involves a combination of considerations of various kinds represented here. Moreover, the fact that corpora are strongly shaped by the goals of their creators does not prevent them from becoming general, multiuse resources.

Finally, we consider the question of QUANTITY. All things being equal, more is better than less, although we hardly have good generic measures of what counts as adequate quantity. Liberman (2006) shows that documentary text and speech corpora are typically at least an order of magnitude smaller than corpora for major world languages or even than text corpora for major dead languages like Latin. He proposes technological approaches for rapid corpus acquisition in large quantities, some of which involve such shortcuts as the use of small, cheap (but widely distributed) hand-held digital recorders; oral interpretation on-the-fly into a language of wider communication; and recording slow, careful, (hopefully) philologically accessible 'respeakings' of recorded texts in place of written transcriptions made by, or in the presence of, native speakers (e.g. a project called *Basic Oral Language Documentation* that is being carried out by Stephen Bird in Papua New Guinea on various local languages has adopted this methodology)[7]. There is a tendency to dismiss such 'substandard' record-making and annotation; Liberman's point is that such records, in quantity, would appreciably augment the total documentary corpus and supplement the records made to standard specifications. His point, from a philological perspective, hardly seems controversial, and it contributes to the broadening of our notion of language documentation.

9.4.5 Annotation

Currently the typical annotated record is an audio- or video-recorded text that is described by metadata and annotated with transcription that is time-aligned to the transcription by chunks delimited by pause-, clause- or sentence-breaks. On the model of Bickel *et al.* (2004), there is a free-translation into a language of wider communication, as well as a morphological segmentation and a morphological gloss or parse line somehow aligned to it; and these analytic elements may be connected, via a look-up system such as Toolbox, to an independent lexicon. Schultze-Berndt (2006) gives an excellent discussion of these and other attributes of annotation (see also Good, Chapter 11).

On the one hand, representation and annotation are rich, complex topics and presuppose general theorizations of almost every area of grammar. A fully broad and inclusive framework for language documentation could undertake to build into its annotation practices more of what is commonly studied in typological and theoretical linguistics (e.g. Lieb and Drude 2000). For example, most syntacticians agree that phrasal constituency or dependency is a major feature of syntax and basis for semantic interpretation; and the stock examples of constituent ambiguity (like Groucho Marx's line, *I shot an elephant in my pajamas; what it was doing in my pajamas I'll never know!*) show that constituency is sometimes covert and verifiable only by test when context or translation fails to disambiguate it. Yet in their practice, documentary linguists rarely include constituency mark-up in their annotations (as is common, e.g. in corpus-based and computational linguistics) or perform the tests needed to complete it. Nor is the lack of this information perceived as a loss in the same way as a failure in transcription to note tone or test for a quiescent vowel would. There is a perception around that theoretical linguists are engaged in some debates that are irrelevant to the serious business of documentation. Theoreticians themselves may even agree, but they may also agree that they could play a key role in the framing of more general approaches to annotation, as well as the training of documenters interested in annotation.

On the other hand, it is worth assessing soberly to what extent annotation is required to meet minimal standards of record transparency.

Liberman (2006) raises this issue in connection with documentation in quantity. Austin and Grenoble (2007) raise questions about the choice of the language of wider communication. Within a broad view of endangered language documentation might fit projects whose leading actors are not professional linguists and whose primary aims are not code-focused, or even text-focused in the usual sense. A minimal documentation (as noted in section 9.1) might consist of just a recorded text and a free translation into a language of wider communication. It might be very hard to use for linguistic purposes, or for literacy-based language learning, but with respect to some aims, as discussed in Section 9.4.3 above, it may not be entirely useless. Particularly in an enlarged framework that is academically multidisciplinary as well as popular, one may ask whether 'useful for linguistic analysis' is a non-negotiable component of a multipurpose corpus, however non-negotiable it may be within linguistics and among linguists.

9.4.6   In what forms should documentation be stored and disseminated?

A related question is that of the forms in which documentation is to be stored and disseminated. An important distinction may be drawn between an archival form intended for preservation, and a presentational form, intended for engagement with a range of possible publics (Bird and Simon 2003; Good, Chapter 11). Books, monographs, and journal articles are the long-time default, some examples of which have already been cited. They can range from general collections to more specific projects. Among digital resources, the DoBeS presentation of its material via its IMDI tree structure offers a browsable collection of holistic documentations (viewable through the IMDI browser software). Other digital archives, such as AILLA, offer corpora that are not uniformly thematic, but are browsable and searchable (see also Nathan, Chapter 13). Meanwhile many projects make their materials accessible in ways that are locally appropriate, via the web or in print. Accessibility is one very important area for innovation and may best be accomplished with an eye toward specific themes and tailored to specific audiences.

9.5   Conclusion: toward a broad and inclusive view of endangered-language documentation

In this chapter we have explored several different dimensions along which our conceptions and practices of endangered-language documentation could acknowledge and extend its own potential for breadth and inclusivity. This must start with a recognition by linguists, whether native speakers or not of the language of study, of the interests of the people with whom they work and of the ways in which they might share projects and agendas (see Dobrin and Berson, Chapter 10; Bowern, Chapter 23).

Community context also bears on deeper intellectual and ideological questions underlying the design of projects focused variously on the speech of a specific community and the use of a specific lexico-grammatical code, and animated by varying humanistic stances. I try to emphasize that these intellectual and ideological questions face anyone considering language documentation, whether scholar, community member, both, or neither; and that different framings of these issues lead in many different, and I believe productive, directions.

Inasmuch as endangered language documentation is propelled by a sense of urgency, one may wish to construct the ultimate linguistic 'Noah's Ark', a final corpus theorization according to which any language can be encapsulated. But while it is possible to list desirable attributes for a corpus, all other things being equal, such a theorization is unlikely to fairy span the diversity of agendas and the intellectual and ideological stances we know to exist, and, correspondingly, unlikely uniformly to engage all those who might contribute.

Likewise, overly categorical stipulations of so-called 'best practice' in corpus creation may overlook tradeoffs between quality and quantity in documentation; and when applied to annotation and interpretation, may channel efforts unequally toward some uses of corpora over others, or even understate how ultimately difficult it is ever to fully translate or interpret a record of human behaviour in context.

Notes

1 The term DOCUMENTARY LINGUISTICS could reasonably be applied to any linguistic work that creates or uses documentation, including most work on major world languages in lexicography, corpus linguistics, language acquisition studies or sociolinguistics; nevertheless the term is ordinarily used in the context of research on endangered languages or other languages where linguistic field methods are involved. I will follow the ordinary usage.
2 Special thanks to Victor Golla for an illuminating exchange on shifting perspectives toward documentation in early and mid twentieth-century Americanist linguistics.
3 In striking contrast, Malinowski (1935) decades earlier offered a text-based approach to ethnography that was linguistics-free on principle, taking the view that meaning only exists in context (thus making dictionaries and grammars futile). Following that view (or perhaps in spite of it!) he presents a copious, explicitly theorized, varied documentary corpus of narratives, descriptions, technological discussions,

prayers, and magical incantations as part of an integrated treatment of agricultural practice and ritual in the Trobriand Islands that can still stand as a model for the ethnographic use of a documentary corpus.

4 See www.mpi.nl/DOBES (24 January 2009).

5 nflrc.hawaii.edu/ldc.

6 An interesting example of mutually rewarding collaboration is that between sound artist John Wynne, linguist Tyler Peterson and artist/ photographer Denise Hawrysio to make documentary recordings of speakers of Gitxsanimaax, an endangered indigenous language in northern British Columbia, Canada (in a project funded by ELDP). The materials from this research are incorporated into Wynne and Hawrysio's installation *Anspayaxw* (www.sensitivebrigade.com/ Anspayaxw.htm) which is part of the *Border Zones: New Art Across Cultures* exhibition showing at the Museum of Anthropology, Vancouver, from 23 January to 12 September 2010. When the exhibition travels to the 'Ksan Gallery in Gitxsan territory in 2011, Wynne and Peterson will also deposit at 'Ksan an archive of their materials for community use.

7 See www.boldpng.info (17 November 2010).

10

Speakers and language documentation

Lise M. Dobrin and Josh Berson

10.1 Introduction

The observation that guides this chapter is that the place of speakers in language documentation is being transformed by linguists' understanding of language endangerment not just as a problem of diminishing data for the science of language, but as a problem of social justice and human flourishing that calls upon linguistic expertise for its amelioration. As a result, work in language documentation has become increasingly applied, cognizant of its context, and committed to the social good. Indeed, contemporary documentary linguistics can usefully be thought of as a kind of social movement, one that has brought academic linguists out of their offices and libraries and into a shared space with communities of speakers, researchers working in other disciplines and non-academic institutions, and the public at large. No longer fully covered by the cloak of scholarship, linguists have found themselves revisiting some of the most fundamental political and ethical assumptions that underlie linguistic research. How should the study of language be conceived? What are its aims, who does it benefit, and what is the linguist's proper role in carrying it out?

Grappling with these and related questions has been eye-opening and even liberating for many linguists steeped in the structural linguistic tradition, where it is the explanatory constraints afforded by abstract linguistic patterns that have generally been accorded value, rather than their creative use by speaker–hearers as a means for social action. But because the endangered language movement was initially driven by

We extend our gratitude to Peter K. Austin, Ira Bashkow, Jan Blommaert, Jeff Good, Jeff Hantman, Elaine Kuffel, Karenne Wood, and Wende Marshall for comments and references that greatly improved this chapter. Berson also wishes to thank the staff and fellows of the Institut für die Wissenschaften vom Menschen, Vienna.

scholars trained and professionalized in this same disciplinary tradition, the intellectual resources documentary linguists have relied upon
in conceptualizing what they are trying to do have been unfortunately
limited (at times amounting to little more than their own culture-bound
intuitions) and disconnected from the substantial literatures that exist
on language as a sociocultural phenomenon, on the complex dynamics
of fieldwork, and on the moral issues raised by the prospect of representing cultural others.

In what follows we critically address some of the main issues surrounding the role of speakers that we see emerging in documentary linguistics,
bringing to bear examples both from linguistics and from neighbouring
disciplines. The perspective we take falls within the broad rubric of science
studies: treating linguistic research not as a value-neutral apprehension
of intrinsic facts about human symbolic life, but rather as a historically
contingent social activity through which linguistics constitutes itself as
a discipline (Latour 2005). From this perspective, as a number of critics
have recently pointed out, the focus in documentary linguistics on the
collection of specific genres of data and the generation of certain categories of products reflects a disciplinary consensus as to the nature of
language as an object of study (Makoni and Pennycook 2006, Moore *et al.*
2010, Silverstein 1998b). And it does seem clear that documentary linguists have been on relatively comfortable ground in thinking about the
PRODUCTS of their research: conceptually distinguishing an annotated
corpus or documentation of a language from a higher order description
of its patterning (Himmelmann 1998, Woodbury, Chapter 9), reasserting
the intellectual value of vocabulary (through the production of dictionaries, see Mosel, Chapter 17) and oral discourse (as represented in texts)
alongside grammar, extending the range of documentary outputs to
include items like primers and orthographies that are targeted directly
at non-academic audiences (Lüpke, Chapter 16). They have also enriched
the inventory of digital data models, formats and software tools to facilitate documentary research and enable the preservation and dissemination of its results (see Bender *et al.* 2004, Bird and Simons 2003, Boynton
et al. 2006, Good, Chapter 11, Nathan, Chapter 13).

This is not to say that there is full agreement about any of these products, how our investments in them should be prioritized, or even what
they properly consist of (see Woodbury, Chapter 9). Doubts have been
voiced, for example, about such fundamental issues as the role of elicited data in language documentation, the marginal value of transcribed
texts, and the practical viability of maintaining a documentation/
description boundary (on which see Dixon 2007, Newman 2009a, and
Austin and Grenoble 2007, respectively). Nevertheless, given the OBJECT-
ORIENTATION (see Agha 2007b) that linguists have historically brought
to bear in their dominant epistemological project – the notion, tracing
back to Saussure, that the languages we study (and that now stand to be

lost) are internally structured, autonomous symbol systems and hence in principle distinguishable, nameable, countable codes (Silverstein 1996, Lewis 2009) – these moves toward expanding the range of documentary linguistic products have been experienced more as stimulating challenges and advances than as serious disruptions.

But linguists have also begun devoting attention to the SOCIAL PROCESSES set in motion by their research, from the conceptualization of fieldwork to the dissemination of its products. This is a new development, so new, in fact, that even as recently as the late 1990s the editors of a volume exploring the practical and methodological issues raised by linguistic fieldwork (Newman and Ratliff 2001a) found themselves hard pressed to find a publisher (Newman 2009a). It is here that the discussions about language documentation taking place today are most exploratory and driven by tension. There is little doubt that this new awareness of social process has grown out of the revival of fieldwork as a core disciplinary activity for linguistics (Ahlers and Wertheim 2009, Himmelmann 2008). Many of the issues that documentary linguists now seem to be thinking about most actively follow from the recognition that there is a power imbalance in the documentary encounter that is at odds with the motivations for conducting the research in the first place.

These motivations, which involve fundamental (and often remarkably explicit) assumptions about the nature of the past, the significance of place and the way these are linked through present-day speakers, are discussed below in Section 10.2. Linguists' recognition of endangered language speakers as persons, as opposed to mere sources of data, has also created tensions in the conduct of documentary research. Some of the ways linguists are attempting to resolve these, both in their discourse and in practical implementation, are discussed in Section 10.3. Here we note the increasing attention being devoted to research ethics and quasilegal matters such as the negotiation of intellectual property, copyrights, and moral rights. Finally, in Section 10.4, we briefly consider some of the ways the field of documentary linguistics stands to mature as we move into the disciplinary space created by the endangered languages movement: recognizing the culturally and historically contingent nature of the values that shape our interlocutors' aims, and constructing for ourselves a professional genealogy that can help guide our thinking beyond the product-oriented mode of Boasian salvage.

10.2   Preserving a more perfect past

Stripped down to its essentials, preservation involves something that is accessed in the present and represented in a way that we anticipate will be useful in the future, but valued above all for its association with the past. To that extent, the documentary practices that are called upon to preserve endangered languages are motivated and constrained by linguists' understandings of what it is that the past holds and how its traces are carried through the vehicle of present-day speakers (Errington 2003, Moore 2006). Much has been written about the keying of small languages to inhabitants of specific locales that are similarly under threat. Language loss is sometimes characterized as being like the 'coal miner's canary' (see, e.g. Nettle and Romaine (2000: 14, 79); Grenoble and Whaley (2005: 974)), an index of the deterioration of local environments and cultures under the pressures of globalization (Cameron 2007, Edwards 2007a). The flip side of this linkage between language, people, and place is that documenting (especially the lexical repertoires of) endangered languages should give us a way of accessing what is (or was) inside the mines: it gives us a privileged glimpse into a segment of the world's past biodiversity and how local people's knowledge of it has been elaborated culturally (Harrison 2005, Maffi 2001). Capitalizing on a theme already well developed in public discourse by biodiversity conservationists, appealing to the localness of endangered and minority languages has done much to make the problem of language shift comprehensible to first-world audiences.

This view that endangered and indigenous languages are quintessentially local also has practical implications for language documentation, leading to the conclusion that research on such languages should be carried out in particular ways that are similarly keyed to place.[1] This is not only important for documenting ethnobiological knowledge (see, e.g., Haviland (2006: 137); also Diamond (1991), who offers a fascinating discussion of the problems associated with different techniques for eliciting local terms for species of birds in New Guinea). As Harrison (2005) nicely illustrates with the examples of directional verbs and mimetic hunting vocabulary in Tuvan, there can be aspects of a language, even down to its phonology, as Harrison shows, that are themselves so locally specific that they can only be profitably documented in situ. The pragmatics of deixis also call for an extended physical presence in the speaker community if they are to be adequately understood. As Hanks (2009: 19) points out, the use of deictic elements is exquisitely sensitive to so many contextual factors that it is nearly impossible to get an adequate picture of language use without simultaneous access to the speaker's own placement in the physical and social world: '[a]fter audio recording more than one hundred hours of talk over a year's fieldwork, I only made sense of usage around the home by setting the tape recorder aside, mapping the homestead into its kin and gender based spheres, and tracking speakers' and addressees' social relations to the objects they talked about'. Haviland (2005) shows how the use of verbal and proxemic-gestural shifters by a speaker of Zinacantec is structured by reference to a locally specific mental map that is couched in absolute geographic terms. So from this perspective, text collection and elicitation of grammatical patterns in town, in the office, or on the verandah, are at best only partial research methods, even if they are also in many ways expedient and revealing. Unfortunately, given the frequent dislocation of speakers from their homelands, the transformation of traditional lifeways, and the limitations of elderly speakers with reduced mobility, fieldwork under truly local field conditions is often unachievable (though see Dobrin *et al.* (2009: 46) for examples of how technology can be used creatively in some such cases as a work-around).

But there are also ways in which this view of minority and endangered languages as profoundly local may compromise our ability to apprehend the messy 'dynamics of language contact and change that we know to have been central to virtually every documented case of language shift and replacement' (see Moore *et al.* (2010: 2), from which we draw liberally here; see also Silverstein 1998b). The association of primordial natural settings with logically discrete communities of fully fluent (even monolingual) speakers is evident in the idiom of counting that is ubiquitous in endangered language discourse: 'n languages are spoken in Village X', or 'Language Y has n speakers', when it is often the case that the better one knows a given region, the more qualifications one feels compelled to append to such formulations (see, e.g., Hymes (2004 [1981]: 80 fn.3) for but one especially fitting illustration; Rigsby and Sutton 1980 is a classic study of this problem). What is at issue is not simply the fact that we are trafficking in idealizations (as scientists always are), but rather that the idealizations in question lead to a hierarchization of speakers measured with respect to a 'pre-contact' form of linguistic competence: complete mastery of a pure ANCESTRAL CODE (see Woodbury 2005 for sensitive discussion). Not only are individuals with such competence vanishingly rare in the present day, but in many cases there is no basis for assuming that they must have been typical at some point in the past.

Certainly, there are challenges here for documentary linguists seeking to assess linguistic vitality and identify promising language consultants. As Evans (2001) has pointed out, people's assertions about their own speakerhood may respond to a host of political and interactional factors that complicate the notion that 'knowing the language' involves a native ability to produce a delimited range of sounds and structures, revealing how 'being a speaker' can be as much about performance as it is about knowledge (see also Hill 1983, Moore 1988). Even when speakers are willing and able to speak a particular language, they may not always monitor the boundary between it and other languages in their repertoire, meaning that decisions must be made about how and to what extent the documentary products linguists create will distill the embedded code (see Vaux *et al.* 2007; O'Shannessy, Chapter 5). These issues can be illustrated by opening just about any of the notebooks from Dobrin's fieldwork on Arapesh languages (spoken in the Sepik coastal region of Papua New Guinea) at random and looking at the ratio of Arapesh to

Tok Pisin (the national lingua franca) found there. The following is an excerpt from a friendly discussion among a small group of uniformly fluent, knowledgeable speakers of Cemaun Arapesh. It is taken from an oral survey of village clan landholdings that one of the participants asked Dobrin to help him coordinate and record. It was not a contentious meeting: the structural authority and superior local knowledge of the main speaker was fully accepted by everyone present; one or two of the participants were taking notes. There was nothing about either the setting or substance of the conversation that directed speakers away from using the vernacular. Use of Tok Pisin was not directed at the researcher, who was construed less as a listener or even an overhearer in the situation than as a service provider; she was also absent much of the time, moving in and out of the room trying to monitor and manage the background noise. Bold in the text indicates Tok Pisin. Unmarked elements are Cemaun Arapesh.

[r2.50–53: CH 24–29]

CH: *Numioduokəm-Kərapehem   ecec-i-g.*
clan.name   cl8pl.pro-poss-cl3.sg
That land belongs to Numioduokəm-Kərapehem clan.

AW: **Em   long**   *Bərəgom.*
3sg   prep   place.name
You mean at Bərəgom.

CH: *Bərəgom.*
place.name
Yes, at Bərəgom.

Orait,   narapela   sait   long   *Kocimanit,*
alright,   other   side   prep   named.section.of.river

c-a-wɔr   *ənən   n-ə-nak-i,*
cl8pl-realis-cross.against.grain   cl7sg.pro   cl7sg-realis-go-
toward.speaker
And then on the other side of Kocimanit, where theirs meets his [the owner of previously identified lands],

orait   *ətidə   coku-t-i*   **barit**
alright   this:cl11sg   small-cl11sg-attrib   ditch

t-a-wɔr   *omom   h-ə-nak,*
cl11sg-realis-cross.against.grain   cl7pl.pro   cl7pl-realis-go
theirs goes until this little ditch that crosses

opudə   yərɨkitep   [inaudible]...
this:cl9sg   small.area.of.forest   [inaudible]...
it's this small area of forest [??]...

Kocimanit, *Wɔrikanip* *munop* *əno-p*
place.name, place.name named.section.of.land some-cl9sg

nopudək.
that.near.hearer:cl9sg
Kocimanit, Wɔrikanip is that piece of land.

Na, *dou, gandə yowiɲə-b=əm,*
and now there place.below-cl1.sg=relative
And then the place downriver from there,

Mɔruwɔgetehɨr **bai** **ihat** **long** **bai** *p-ɨ-su*
place.name future be-hard prep future 2pl-irr-hold

munop **inogat**,
named.section.of.land not,
Mɔruwɔgetehɨr, it would be hard to say who owns what particular pieces,

c-a-rib *məhiməhima,*
cl8pl-realis-clear.land.for.garden in.little.bits
they cut it up so much,

na **i-hat** **long** **bai** *p-ɨ-ni*
and be-hard prep future 2pl-irrealis-be.together.with

Numioduwokum-Kərapwehem [inaudible] **wantaim**
clan.name [inaudible] together
and it's hard because your clan and Numioduwokum-Kərapwehem
[hold it?] jointly

AW: *Munəs.*
named.section.of.land:pl
You mean the sections.

JG: *Yep.*
yes
Yep.

CH: *Omiə* *c-o-hʷar,* əh, **wanem** – [inaudible] **bihain**
which cl8pl-realis-call, əh, what [inaudible] later

urukum m-u-r, **gutpela.**
heart cl5sg-irrealis-be.inside, good
What do they call, um – [??] if I remember later then OK.

And so it continues. The speech recorded at this meeting is about as pure a form of the vernacular as Cemaun Arapesh speakers ever spontaneously produce, but it is ubiquitously multilingual, with constant switching to Tok Pisin from the matrix vernacular, as is 'the rule rather than the exception in the case of endangered languages' (Schultze-Berndt

2006: 231). In developing a markup schema for the set of Arapesh texts from which this was drawn for purposes of archiving, glossing, and association with a lexicon (Dobrin and Pitti 2009), it became clear that there was no way to create a coherent, self-standing documentary product without acknowledging this fact. The schema now embeds what is essentially a basic Tok Pisin lexicon within it, an inefficiency that cannot be avoided if the real complexity of this community's speech practices is to be accurately expressed. In other words, there can be something of a methodological gap between the desiderata of creating 'a lasting, multipurpose record of a language' construed as an ancestral code and collecting 'specimens of observable linguistic behaviour, i.e. examples of how the people actually communicate with each other' (Himmelmann 2006a: 1, 7).

There can also be a moral gap. Taking the lodestar of documentation to be '[f]luent monolingual speech, preferably employing 'classical' grammatical features and talking about 'traditional' topics (Moore *et al.* 2010: 16) can pose challenges for speakers, whose own partial abilities may be cast into sharp relief by understandings of exemplary speech, even under the presumably supportive conditions of language documentation work. Once again, Dobrin's fieldwork provides a concrete illustration. In returning to her field recordings now for purposes of analysis, one feature of the recorded interactions with speakers stands out painfully clearly: the researcher's regular urging to narrators who had reflexively switched to Tok Pisin to revert to the vernacular (see, e.g. www.arapesh.org/sample_texts_bethlehem.php). In a sense, of course, this was only natural: the ancestral code was, after all, what she was in the community to study. Speakers were always cheerful in accommodating these requests; they even came to anticipate them, at times catching themselves (or one another) and self-correcting as they shifted into Tok Pisin. But in fostering this kind of metalinguistic consciousness, the linguist was asking speakers to adjust their approach to deploying linguistic resources to culturally foreign ideas about the proper use of languages-as-codes (see Foley 2005: 168 on the 'valorisation of foreign elements in effective language' for a sense of what is informing these Melanesian speakers' behaviour). This is the same relationship of moral encompassment that has characterized Arapesh relations with Europeans in one form or another since the days of first contact, a pattern which current development activities often replicate, if in subtler and less intentional ways (see Dobrin 2008). Samuels (2006: 12) provides a poignant example of the way would-be speakers' ideas about the nature of linguistic competence can be affected by formal interventions with the local-language-as-code in his reflections on San Carlos Apache speaker Phillip Goode, who had worked first as a Bible translator with SIL and later with Samuels as his language teacher. Through his engagement in these activities Goode came to be seen as so capable and authoritative a speaker of Apache that when he passed away, many members of the reservation community had to be convinced (by Samuels, of all people) that the language itself had not died with him.

The complex forms of social agency implicated in speakerhood are also apparent when we contemplate the relationship between fluency and age under conditions of language shift. In many cases it is older speakers who are the obvious candidates for language consultants in documentary fieldwork because, unlike their children and grandchildren, they acquired the language in their youth and so speak it fluently. An aging population of speakers is often used as an index of decreased language vitality (see Krauss 2007, Ostler 1998: 12). Indeed, the experience of personal loss as one's elderly consultants and friends pass away over the course of one's career is a common tragic theme in conversations among linguists who do research on endangered languages.[2] But as fieldworkers also well know, there are many different kinds of knowledge holders. Individual speakers differ in their special linguistic abilities, some being engaging storytellers, others being insightful analysts, still others having expertise in particular cultural practices and hence lexical domains, and so on (see, e.g., Newman and Ratliff 2001b: 3). Needless to say, this differentiation also cuts across age. Maddieson (2001: 217–18) offers some of the physiological reasons why linguists should be wary of taking older people's speech as canonical in situations of phonetic fieldwork. Less obvious, perhaps, is the importance of grasping speakers' own ideas about the significance of generational difference for understanding linguistic competence. This topic is thoughtfully explored by Suslak (2009: 206; see also Reynolds 2009), who shows how indigenous Mixe youth in Oaxaca are reconciling their indigenous and modern identities by becoming 'some of the fiercest Mixe language purists', strategically reenregistering old forms in their code-switched speech. In this case, recognizing that age plays a role as not just an independent sociolinguistic variable (to be used as a reference point in assessing a language's 'degree of endangerment' or to be worked around in fieldwork), but as an identity category in its own right, is critical to understanding how the retained ancestral code is actually being used by speakers today. The Mixe youth Suslak studied may be using their traditional language, but they are doing so in decidedly non-traditional ways, employing it as a marker of sophistication and modern self-control.

As the previous example shows, a view of speakerhood that emphasizes a strain of speech that has been handed down 'naturally' (reflexively, locally and without interruption over time) runs the risk of under-theorizing the important role of mobility, diffusion and mixing in shaping endangered vernaculars, and in some cases sustaining their speakers (Dorian 1994, Pietikäinen 2008). Taking for granted that the motor of normal language formation is divergence both springs from and lends support to an intuition that the mixing of linguistically distinct groups of people is aberrant and linguistically unstable. But this intuition is not necessarily grounded in the observable facts of how people acquire and deploy the structural and pragmatic resources at their disposal (Matras and Bakker 2003, Mufwene 2001, 2008,). For linguistic communities today, the most highly valued variety may in fact be a mixed, diasporic, or otherwise non-local register that is intentionally developed to serve as an emblem of authentic difference (Errington 2003: 730–1, Grinevald 2005, LePage and Tabouret-Keller 1985). Consider, for example, the case of Monacan, an indigenous language of the Virginia Piedmont, USA, that has not been spoken for several generations and no record of which remains. Many members of the current Monacan community experience their linguistic heritage as a painful absence, a 'language ghost' which prevents them from fully realizing their spiritual connection to their ancestral lands (Wood 2009). Yet although they express deep feelings about their language and lands, there is also a movement in the Monacan community to revive the use of a genetically related Siouan language, Tutelo, even though it has not been spoken in Virginia for over a century (the descendent community now resides in Canada). Other Monacans identify with still more distant Plains Siouan cultural traditions, some even studying Lakota and offering prayers in that language at Monacan tribal gatherings. In short, even a point of linguistic contact that is many miles distant and thousands of years old can provide people with meaningful forms of social practice that they consider authentically their own. Bespeaking a similar conclusion is the fact that popular claims celebrating a twentieth-century Hebrew 'revival' still abound, although careful cultural and philological studies show that tracing Modern Israeli Hebrew's genealogical origin to the Biblical language is linguistically unjustified (see Harshav 1993, Zuckermann 2006).

As we have tried to illustrate, endangered language documentation requires sensitivity to speakers' understandings, conscious or otherwise, of what their languages are and what using them implies about themselves. The extent to which these correspond to those of western linguistic science is an empirical matter that is best approached ethnographically (see also Eira and Stebbins 2008). Because situated language use will both reflect and reconfirm these understandings, they must be taken into account as documentary products are conceived and the process of fieldwork unfolds (i.e. in determining who to record, whether a particular utterance counts as data, and so on). At the same time, linguists' conceptions of an endangered language's status, constituent elements and position in a family tree become part of the wider context that shapes the way speakers respond to its decline. This is especially true where the documentation linguists produce feeds directly back into the community, as is now so often the case (see England 2003 for one example). The following pair of case studies, both drawn from fieldwork in western North America, illustrates how dramatically incommensurate understandings of the processes involved in language shift and language documentation can be.

Moore (1988) discusses the use and loss of Wasco-Wishram, a Chinookan language spoken on the Warm Springs Reservation in the Columbia River basin of central Oregon, USA. During elicitation sessions, elder Wasco speakers were able to use the language's rich morphosyntactic resources to produce a number of structurally complex verbs that younger semi-speakers treated as lexicalized formations and hence either subjected them to further, historically unnecessary inflection, or else incorporated them innovatively into periphrastic constructions. But even as the changes Moore documented in Wasco could be analysed linguistically as following from younger speakers' lack of facility with the language's morphological resources, elder Wasco speakers understood language loss rather differently. For them, loss consisted in the lamentably shrinking repertoire (a 'forgetting') of lexical verb stems as evident in the 'broken' speech of younger generations. Taking up the notion of diminishing linguistic wealth implicit in this interpretation of language loss, younger speakers ascribed value to Wasco words as cultural property of an almost sacred kind, on the model of compositionally opaque personal names, which were traditionally bestowed ceremonially and uttered only under highly specified social circumstances in formal acts of display. As a result of this logic, speakers understood linguistic elicitation sessions as an occasion for the display of cultural wealth, and so as a potential source of moral hazard: Moore found that speakers were hesitant to produce noun and verb forms in elicitation interviews. When they did produce them, they would do so by 'citing' them, embedding them in the direct speech of an appropriate (deceased) relative, rather than speaking them under their own authority. For one younger speaker, producing any Wasco utterance longer than an isolated word was tantamount to myth recitation, a highly valued category of cultural display that was restricted to take place only during the winter season lest it bring about bad weather or even snow. But, as do many linguists, Moore was conducting fieldwork during his summers. So here the process of language documentation *as a social activity* was itself putting speakers in a cultural bind.

Muehlmann (2008) describes how a project originally intended to document the ecological terminology of Cucapá, a language traditionally spoken in the settlement of El Mayor, along the Mexico–California border, turned into an ethically complicated study of swearwords when she found that it was only the latter category of vocabulary that remained in active use in the community. In diverse areas of their lives, people in El Mayor find themselves under pressure to provide linguistic evidence of their indigeneity to the outsiders with whom they have contact. For development consultants, missionaries, and soldiers patrolling the border, the ability to speak Cucapá, a language which no outsider expects to be able to understand, is the signal indicator of Indian status. But because of this, the advanced state of language shift from Cucapá to Spanish leaves the community's younger people in a difficult position. As one young woman put it: '[i]t's embarrassing not to be able to speak Cucapá because everyone who comes to El Mayor says: "tell me how to say this in Cucapá" or "tell me how to say that". They think that we *have* to speak Cucapá because we are Indians' (Muehlmann 2008: 40). Resenting this humiliating linkage of their political and cultural identity to a language they cannot speak, younger members of the El Mayor community defy outsiders' demands to perform their indigeneity by responding to them with Cucapá obscenities, a move which never fails to satisfy their unwitting interrogators (see also Graham 2002). In fact, throughout the community, it is not fluent use of Cucapá but rather command of the language's vulgar lexicon that has become an emblem of political defiance and cultural resilience. Muehlmann's ability to achieve rapport with El Mayor residents followed from her learning how to curse in Cucapá. But understanding the community's ideas about their linguistic identity has also limited Muehlmann's ability to disseminate what she has learned. When the researcher began presenting her findings to her professional colleagues, she found them resistant to the notion that the language's vulgar register was truly indigenous in origin, revealing a professional ideology of local vernaculars as solemn vehicles of prestige. Even more seriously, Muehlmann determined that it would be unethical to publish vernacular forms and glosses for Cucapá swearwords (precisely that aspect of the language that remains most vital in the community) because to do so would betray the trust of speakers and compromise their ability to define themselves on their own terms, as opposed to the terms set by others.

As these cases suggest, linguists and speakers may bring dramatically different assumptions to the documentary encounter. In light of this, we must think carefully before deciding to 'help' speakers 'recognize' language endangerment as a problem and work to arouse their concern when we find that they do not (Bird 2009; Kroskrity 2009; Wurm 1998; see Cameron 1998 for a sobering lesson on how efforts to empower speakers by reforming their attitudes about language use can backfire). Such well-intended consciousness-raising does not represent something unambiguously beneficial for speakers. The motives for language shift cannot be reduced to a colonization of consciousness in which socially marginalized communities come to see their own speech practices as inferior. This much is clear from cases where avoidance registers play a role in accelerating lexical change. And where shift *is experienced by speakers* as voluntary, regardless of whether we analyse it that way social-structurally (see Bobaljik 1998, Nettle and

Romaine 2000), speaker agency is always implicated. Sometimes people express a desire to give up their language in order to better integrate into dominant economic and social spheres, and in such cases it can be less than obvious whether or how linguists should intervene. Ladefoged (1992) has been taken as the classic statement of this problem, but the stark, neo-liberal quality of his formulation makes it too easy to either embrace or dismiss, whereas speakers' attitudes are most often ambivalent and culturally inflected. García (2004, 2005) provides a fascinating discussion of indigenous Peruvian highlanders' attraction to, but ultimate rejection of, the Quechua vernacular education being promoted both as a matter of state policy and by linguistic and cultural activists (including indigenous intellectuals) working in the provincial capital, Cuzco. One Quechua parent explained his preference for monolingual Spanish schooling this way: '[y]ou [anthropologists] care about our culture. We too care. We [may] never be able to be [deindigenized] mestizos ... but by learning how to read and write [in Spanish], our children can defend themselves in the mestizo's world' (García 2005: 94).

Finally, and most importantly for any critical discussion of language documentation, the very imperative to preserve cultural form must be recognized as a culturally particular phenomenon, one that is manifest in a community in particular domains to varying degrees, or perhaps not at all. Linguists, anthropologists, and archaeologists bring to the work of preservation their own values regarding the disposition of cultural form, and these too are neither universal nor natural. One way that scholars have talked about the values implicated in the western 'will to preserve' is in terms of a particular HERITAGE IDEOLOGY (Kirshenblatt-Gimblett 2006). This heritage ideology is most explicit in initiatives like the 2003 UNESCO Convention for the Safeguarding of Intangible Heritage,[3] or the World Intellectual Property Organization's Creative Heritage Project,[4] which extends UNESCO's World Heritage scheme to the realm of non-material artefacts. Central to these projects is an idea of TRADITIONAL KNOWLEDGE of just the sort that we have seen used in the construction of endangered languages: an intellectual repertoire handed down from generation to generation in more or less inviolate form, the preservation of which is deemed crucial both for humanity and for the continuing existence of the originating community. UNESCO's designation of specific individuals as human vessels for the transmission of traditional knowledge instantiates the same kind of heritage ideology that underlies the publicly mourned 'last speakers' of endangered languages (Heller-Roazen 2005: 57ff., Grinevald and Bert, Chapter 3). But as legal scholar Sunder (2007) has observed, many efforts to protect traditional knowledge founder precisely on the incompatibility of this ideology, according to which it is sensible to create registries of intellectual artefacts (e.g. to issue listings of endangered languages such as the *Atlas of the World's Languages in Danger of Disappearing*[5]), or to establish individual practitioners of communally held, authorless oral traditions as 'living archives' (Kirshenblatt-Gimblett 2006), with the need to maintain traditions of knowledge-*making*, the preservation of which demands ongoing innovation. The great challenge for scholars concerned about the consequences of cultural change for speakers is not just to find better ways to isolate and capture the past, but to find ways to preserve ongoing innovation (Amery 2009). This is what makes language documentation such a stimulating potential field for collaborative methods in which linguists and speakers are co-engaged.

There are even situations in which the preservation of cultural form is alien (or inimical!) to the ideological complex by which the cultural life of a community is constituted. An example from archaeology will help make this point clear. Karlström (2002) discusses the tensions involved in preserving Theravada Buddhist temple architecture in Laos. In keeping with the Buddhist ideal of non-attachment to material wealth, that embodied above all in temple compounds, Laotian Theravada communities subscribe to a tradition of periodically destroying and rebuilding their local temples. This tradition flies in the face of UNESCO's determination to designate certain built environments, including local temple sites, exemplars of World Heritage since this presupposes a desire to make them permanent. Heritage ideology provides the political, academic and social motives for cultural preservation wherever it occurs. Yet, ironically, it also threatens to undermine the integrity and continuity of the very social practices which make the temples culturally significant in the first place. In this case, western observers were able come to terms with the contradiction between their own heritage ideology and local ideas about the nature of change only by documenting Lao cultural processes at work, incorporating video artefacts of temple destruction into the archival record.

To bring the discussion back to language and conclude this section, as Makoni and Pennycook (2006: 32) remind us, the creation of any linguistic product 'implies an intervention into people's lives', where the terms governing the interaction may be multiple and sometimes contradictory. This is not to say that we should not encourage speakers to participate in activities that reflect scientific understandings of language and cultural preservation. But we also must be careful not to dismiss the sometimes surprising patterns and theories of language use we encounter as irrational, unscientific, or self-defeating, lest the interventions that flow from western ideas about language and the will-to-preserve have 'unexpected adverse effects on exactly those same people whose interests we think we are promoting or safeguarding' (Makoni and Pennycook 2006: 32).

10.3   Indigenous rights and the crisis of documentation

The inspiration documentary linguistics derived from the endangered languages movement of the early 1990s has been discussed in detail elsewhere (Craig 1992a; Himmelmann 2008; Grinevald and Bert, Chapter 3). However, the place of speakers in language documentation cannot be understood without reference to the political wave which carried the problem of language endangerment to the forefront of the disciplinary conscience. Over the past several decades, the 'three hundred million original peoples worldwide who maintain attachments to "timeless" original traditions' (Niezen 2003: 120) have created a new political reality, an international indigenist movement 'originating in the terminology of international law' which found new venues for effectively asserting 'rights aimed at preserving cultural, religious, and linguistic identity' (Niezen (2003: 129); see also Muehlbach 2001). In the late 1980s and early 1990s, intense public attention was drawn to the issue of minority and indigenous rights by a number of international and grassroots organizations protesting the 500th anniversary of Columbus's arrival in the Americas. The high profile of indigenous issues during this period was reflected in important political achievements such as the passing of the Native American Languages Act of 1990, the awarding of the Nobel Peace Prize to Mayan rights activist Rigoberta Menchu Tum in 1992, and the establishment of the first International Year of Indigenous Peoples in 1993.[6] In this climate, speakers of minority languages became increasingly visible, to those linguists who were bothering to look (and some were looking quite intently), as something more than sources of data. They were now also members of 'endangered language communities' engaged in an urgent political struggle to achieve 'a position of strength and dignity for their linguistic and cultural wealth' (Hale *et al.* 1992: 2). This recognition of speakers not only as repositories of information but also as members of political groups asserting their rights to self-determination in relation to existing powers brought new meaning to the process of language documentation. By valuing the speakers of endangered languages for what their encompassing states so often did not, linguists began to see the work of language documentation and preservation as contributing to a political cause, a way of supporting the struggles of indigenous people through activities carried out within their own professional sphere.[7]

In Australia, ethnographers had been predicting the imminent extinction of its indigenous peoples since the 1830s, yet the remoteness of so much of the continent inhibited the development of documentary salvage projects along the lines of those fostered in the early twentieth century by Franz Boas, Alfred Kroeber, and Edward Sapir in western North America. When descriptive linguistics finally did gain momentum in the study of Australian Aboriginal languages around 1960, it was driven by a sense of pressing need to solve the longstanding problem of the genetic status of the continent's languages. But here, too, this took place against a political background: indigenous people's demands for citizenship, land return and recognition of their cultural, linguistic and territorial sovereignty (on language sovereignty in Australia, see Simpson 2006). Indigenous Australians' struggles for political rights have met with equivocal success (Ginsburg and Myers 2006). In 2007, the then Federal government marked the fortieth anniversary of the constitutional referendum that granted citizenship to the country's indigenous inhabitants by disparaging the educational role of local languages in indigenous communities (Gibson 2007, O'Shannessy 2007). But this is not for lack of critical engagement on the part of Australian linguists. On the contrary; in the current atmosphere of both professional linguistic and public fascination with language endangerment, Australia has emerged as an emblematic case, a place where all but a handful of the local languages will go out of use in the next generation, yet where linguists have risen to confront the impending loss by documenting and archiving material on the indigenous languages, participating in land claims cases (Morphy 2006, Sansom 2007, Sutton 2003), and facilitating linguistically oriented social programmes (McKay 2007). It is no accident that two figures at the centre of the early documentary revolution in Australia, Stephen Wurm and Ken Hale, both went on to play central roles in mobilizing the endangered languages agenda on the international linguistics scene (or that so many Australian linguists, or others who have carried out fieldwork there, are involved in contemporary research and discussions about endangered languages and their documentation and support).

It is useful to review such elements of political history here because they are at the root of a paradox that profoundly influences the place of speakers in current documentary linguistic discourse and practice: to the extent that the problem of preserving threatened linguistic diversity is tied, morally and politically, to the rights of speakers to determine their own futures and maintain control over their cultural heritage, linguists' scientific authority to document that heritage has become ethically problematic. This is because it takes for granted one group's power, derived from its association with the high-status western institution of the academy, to cast its gaze upon cultural others through the research process, and to represent them according to its own, externally imposed analytic categories in the resulting scholarly products. In other words, the act of creating documentary and descriptive linguistic objects as traditionally understood (grammar, lexicon and corpus of texts) reproduces the suspect power hierarchy that linguistics-in-recognition-of-indigenous-rights is intended to dismantle. This CRISIS OF DOCUMENTATION (to adapt the now widely used term for anthropology's great movement of self-reflection, the 'crisis of representation'[8]) is a problem which other disciplines that study human cultural production by means of fieldwork, such as anthropology, archaeology, and folklore, have been grappling with for decades as they have sought to eschew their historical relationship with colonialism and resituate themselves on a more morally justifiable epistemological footing. But it is really only now, with the development of a disciplinary conversation about the nature of linguistic fieldwork following from the endangered languages movement, that linguistics is confronting the politics of research and representation in its own domain.

This new political awareness is being played out in language documentation in a number of significant ways. One is through discussion about, and openness to, establishing more equitable social arrangements in the conduct of linguistic research. This is by no means the first time linguists have made overtures toward non-canonical research relations as a mode of scientific possibility and social responsibility. One early example is Ken Hale's argument for the cultivation of 'native speaker linguists' in his contribution to *Reinventing Anthropology* (Hymes 1972; see also Hale 1965), Dell Hymes's historic call for the humanistic field sciences to make themselves relevant to the people being studied. Another example is Cameron *et al.'s* (1992, 1993a) influential 'prepositional' model of the kinds of relationships obtaining between language researchers and the people they study. This model arranges research ON, FOR and WITH speakers according to a hierarchy of value, with collaborative research, research WITH, prominently at the apex (Grinevald and Bert, Chapter 3). But the thematicization of collaboration that we find emerging as a central methodological issue in documentary research today knows no precedent in the discipline.[9] Language documentation is now conceived by many in the field to be an activity that not only can but *should* be equally responsive to both the technical questions posed by linguists and the more immediate practical interests of speakers. Issues of rights and power are no longer mere afterthoughts, or even cause for hand-wringing. They are taken to be fundamental matters for negotiation between researchers and speakers, mandatorily addressed in research agreements and funding proposals, and threaded through documentation projects from their very conception (as Bowern, Chapter 23 emphasizes).

The new collaborative ideal is articulated clearly by Czaykowska-Higgins (2009).[10] Rejecting a LINGUIST-FOCUSED approach to documentary research on the grounds that 'there is no inherent reason why all the priorities and assumptions of linguists should always be privileged over those of the language-users' (Czaykowska-Higgins (2009: 25)), she elaborates a COMMUNITY-BASED model (where research is carried out BY the language-users) in which research is broadened to encompass not only traditional intellectual production, but also the improvement of local social conditions and the achievement of social justice through the redistribution of power. In this model, researchers train community members to conduct research on their own languages with 'the aim of making redundant the presence in the community of [outsider] academic linguists' (Czaykowska-Higgins 2009: 25). At the same time, community members train researchers about 'issues related to language, linguistics, and culture, as well as about how to conduct research and themselves appropriately within the community' (Czaykowska-Higgins 2009: 25). In this way, all parties involved in the research process can be engaged on equal footing in a mutual exchange of knowledge. We will offer some further thoughts on this approach in the concluding section below.

Also taking place is an unprecedented disciplinary conversation about the ethics of linguistic research. In addition to calling for more equitable relationships with speaker communities as just noted, linguists have begun avidly discussing a whole range of issues regarding rights and obligations that arise out of the documentary endeavour (see Rice 2006 for an overview).[11] Scholars have proposed guiding principles for ethical fieldwork (Austin 2010b, Dwyer 2006) and made efforts to identify ethical problem areas (Musgrave and Thieberger 2006, O'Meara and Good 2010). Whose consent is required to proceed with a project? Who owns the resulting materials? Who is to curate and distribute those materials, and in what form? How can we anticipate the harms that may follow when legacy materials are later accessed? How can we simultaneously respect the multiple cultural protocols that different stakeholders bring to a given project when they fail to converge?[12] Linguists continue to be stunned when, just as a dictionary or other project representing years of linguist-community engagement is reaching some long-awaited level of completion, new groups suddenly materialize and challenge the linguist's right to proceed. Often these disputes play out in an idiom of intellectual property (K. Hill 2002, Hinton and Weigel 2002: 168ff.), an area where those engaged in documentation of language and culture have found themselves having to exercise new levels of creativity. In the grammar of one Pacific language that is often held up as a model, the copyrights for the linguistic examples are explicitly assigned to the individual speakers who contributed them (Thieberger 2006). In the cultural archive developed for an Aboriginal Australian community, access to archived material is regulated by digitally encoded traditional cultural protocols (Christen 2008, 2009). A Pueblo community of the American Southwest has managed to develop and maintain a dictionary despite the potential threat such a written document poses for the control of their linguistic knowledge, which they hold to be sacred and proprietary, communally monitoring the dictionary's example sentences to make sure they are not inappropriately revealing (Debenport 2010). In the case of one Native American linguistic salvage project, community leaders have 'archived' their digitized materials in a salt mine to prevent them from becoming the object of unwelcome scrutiny (Lindstrom 2009: 103).

The aesthetic packaging of documentary products is yet another arena where the crisis of documentation has had visible effects. While linguists often acknowledge the need for documentation to serve different constituencies, creating a truly multifunctional record of a language requires an enormous amount of forethought, especially when members of the language community are among the intended users (see Rehg 2009, Rice and Saxon 2002). Moreover, documentary products may end up being used by speaker communities not only as resources for local language development as linguists imagine, but in other ways that have less foreseeable (and less obviously positive) outcomes: as legal evidence (Henderson and Nash 2002), as indicators of relative social standing vis à vis surrounding communities (Terrill 2002), or as moves in local power politics (Errington 2001), among other things. But regardless of how they end up being used by members of the source community, it is all but certain nowadays that they will be *seen* by them. Following from this, and from the collaborative ideal discussed above, Lindstrom (2009: 100) has observed a trend toward what he calls the 'personalization of grammar', a 'celebration of co-authorship' through the prominent inclusion of photographs of individuals closely tied to the research[13], and through the presentation of local narratives that directly reflect the community's interests. One recent grammar (Aikhenvald 2008) goes so far as to place a colourful group photograph of the language's speakers on the cover.

Finally, we can note a new willingness to ask hard questions about the wider disciplinary configuration within which language documentation is taking place. The endangered languages movement originated with a call for linguistics to revalue language description and community engagement as central professional endeavours (Krauss 1992: 10–11; see also Linguistic Society of America 1994):

> Universities and professional societies have crucial influence in determining research and educational priorities. To what extent are endangered languages a priority in modern linguistics? Which languages of the world receive the most attention? Are graduate students encouraged to document moribund or endangered languages for their dissertations? How much encouragement is there to compile a dictionary of one? How many academic departments encourage applied linguistics in communities for the support of endangered languages? How many departments provide appropriate training for speakers of these languages who are most ideally suited to do the most needed work?

Heeding this call has had ripple effects. If academic researchers are to be able to invest the time and effort necessary for primary documentation, this has to be acknowledged and rewarded as a form of intellectual work. One such development is the Linguistic Society of America's resolution supporting the recognition of electronic databases as academic publications (Linguistic Society of America 2005). We also find new institutions like the Ken Hale Chair, an endowed professorship to support the teaching of field methods at Linguistic Society of America Summer Institutes, and the development of a range of postgraduate programmes, training courses and summer schools (see also Jukes, Chapter 21). If they are to work directly with speakers, linguists obviously need training in how to do this, raising questions about whether and how field methods courses can be more thoroughly integrated into linguistics curricula (Newman 2009b). But in order to make lasting shifts in postgraduate linguistics curricula, departmental hiring and employment priorities must change.

Linguists have also begun calling for dialogue about the discipline's close collaboration with the well-funded missionary organization SIL International, the other major institution with which it shares the language documentation terrain (Dobrin and Good 2009). For decades academic linguists have enjoyed the technical infrastructure and 'mountains of data' SIL provides as a by-product of its work translating the Christian Bible into vernacular languages (Svelmoe 2009: 635). Not least of these helpful resources is an authoritative listing of the world's languages, the *Ethnologue*; due to recent developments in international standards, SIL now maintains the registry of international language codes (ISO-639) in an official capacity. The placement of academic linguistics in a passive 'consumer role' in relation to so many SIL resources raises questions about why this is so and whether the arrangement is ideal. In many areas of the world it is SIL that has been the primary outside agent assisting with language development in under-resourced communities, raising further questions about the social responsibilities of the academy. In the near term, SIL's support for minority and indigenous languages through the production of written materials and the cultivation of vernacular literacy skills seems consistent with the aims of secular endangered language activism. However, these activities are necessarily shaped by SIL's millenarian worldview, which has led the organization to focus its efforts on languages with greater rather than smaller speaker populations and selectively promote certain kinds of cultural change (Epps and Ladley 2009: 644). Linguistics has come a long way in renouncing the treatment of speakers as means to scientific ends. It remains to be seen where the discipline will come to stand on the treatment of speakers as means to metaphysical ends.

10.4   Recontextualizing the documentary encounter, rehumanizing linguistics

Joseph (2004: 226) points to the danger of abstracting away from speakers in the study of language:

If people's use of language is reduced analytically to how meaning is formed and represented in sound, or communicated from one person to another, or even the conjunction of the two, something vital has been abstracted away: the people themselves, who, prior to such abstraction, are always present in what they say ... A full account of linguistic communication would have to start with, not a message, but again the speakers themselves, and their interpretation of each other that determines, interactively, their interpretation of what is said.

Because the languages prioritized for documentation are often deeply significant for their speakers as emblems of identity, the movement to study endangered languages has had the salutary effect of rehumanizing linguistics, making it all but impossible to abstract the speakers away regardless of what science might seem to require. In attempting to navigate this newly enlivened disciplinary terrain whose character is so thoroughly shaped by human striving and interpretations of social difference, documentary linguists have gone to great lengths to establish more equitable power relations with speakers through use of participatory, community-based research protocols. But overcoming differences of power is only part of the challenge of ethical documentation. '[B]reaking down the boundaries between researchers and language-users' (Czaykowska-Higgins 2009: 25) is hard because those boundaries are real, embodying in microcosm speakers' understandings of themselves as bearers of culture in relation to others (Bashkow 2004). They are the very understandings that are the driving force behind language shift. The particular ideas and feelings that inform speakers' attitudes toward the use, transmission, and development of their languages are not always consciously communicable or negotiable; as with grammar, much of culture is implicit. Respecting the interests of speakers therefore demands a willingness not only to build relationships across difference, but to approach those relationships analytically.

All research has its social context. For documentary linguistics, that context is especially complex: linguistic insight emerges slowly over time through open-ended interactions with people in uncontrolled conditions (i.e. wherever or whatever 'the field' is). Researchers and speakers cannot take for granted that they are operating on the basis of a shared set of cultural assumptions.[14] Documentation frequently takes place against the backdrop of evolving community leadership structures and rapidly shifting (and therefore significantly heterogenous) linguistic and cultural norms. Learning to analyse how the research encounter itself is shaped by historical, cultural, and personal factors has not generally been treated as a proper part of linguistic field methods. But we are convinced that it must be if linguists are to 'put their money where their mouth is' and take language endangerment seriously as the crucial context for current documentary work. In short, we suggest, linguists need to work toward an ethnographic understanding of their research encounters. Ethnography 'remains our best tool for capturing rapid and confusing social change and its correlates: phenomena that do not fit clear-cut patterns or categories but represent moments of change, conflict, and movement in social systems' (Blommaert 2009: 438). It is hard to imagine a more apt description of the setting for most language documentation projects today.

The motives animating the other main party to the language documentation process also warrant critical reflection. Documentary linguists rightly celebrate the continuities that exist between their present goals and those pursued by the Boasian anthropologists of the early twentieth century: the moral imperative 'to save what can yet be saved' of native cultures (Cole 1983: 50), the collection of texts as a valuable form of data, and the cultivation of native-speaker researchers (see Woodbury, Chapter 9). Yet while these parallels have served as useful rallying points for the documentary movement, there are certain limits to such PRESENTIST uses of history, which look to the past to justify disciplinary practices we wish to promote today (Stocking 1968). The context of linguistic research has changed radically since Boas's time. We are no longer trying to discredit the notion that languages are ranked along an evolutionary scale of complexity, or to disentangle language from culture and race, as were our Boasian predecessors. Most importantly, the role of native speakers in the documentary enterprise is rather different now than it was in the early Americanist period. To be sure, Boas treated highly motivated, culturally astute speakers as collaborators in the documentation process. But this was more a practical than an ethical move; training them to produce texts in their languages was an efficient means for getting at the native point of view (Berman 1996). Rarely were trained speakers accorded status as equals worthy of authorship or ownership of their scholarly output (Darnell 2001: 18–19). There was certainly nothing corresponding to the present push to empower native speakers to address their own concerns. Moreover, as Briggs (2002) argues, language was of special interest to Boas because of its automatic and unconscious nature, which he believed provided a vehicle for studying human social life that would be free from 'secondary explanations' (people's post hoc rationalizations for why they do what they do) that 'so plague the study of culture' (Briggs 2002: 484). The tidied-up view of language this engendered, 'neatly separated from that which is nonlinguistic, supposedly including culture and society', lives on in the artefactual ideology that continues to dissuade us from viewing languages 'as loci of heterogeneity, agency, and creativity', as media for human action and self-expression (Briggs 2002: 493).

Taking a cue from our speaker-collaborators we should draw upon all the intellectual resources at our disposal, past and present. There are many models that may be profitable to learn from if we are willing to look farther afield, including beyond the boundaries of linguistics to neighbouring disciplines. Consider, for example, the decade-long Fox project undertaken in the Meskwaki community by anthropologist Sol Tax and his students in the 1940s and 1950s under the rubric of ACTION ANTHROPOLOGY (Daubenmier 2008, Gearing *et al.* 1960, Tax 1952). Action anthropology was conceived as a way of making anthropology useful at the same time that it produces new knowledge. Action anthropologists would assist community members and provide them with information to help inform their decision making, but refrain from exercising any power over them. Ethnobotany offers another example. Ethnobotanists were among the first ethnographic field scientists to adopt a code of ethics that recognized the intellectual property issues at stake in their work with politically marginalized communities. This was the Declaration of Belém, orchestrated by American ethnobotanist Darrell Posey in 1988, four years before the Convention on Biological Diversity made 'access and benefits sharing' a metonym for ethical research practice (Posey 2004; Hayden 2003). Or, consider the approach to conservation taken by many current NGOs that have been analysed as exercises in CONSERVATION-AS-DEVELOPMENT (e.g. West 2006). Conservation-as-development schemes assume that the means for local people to take control of their lives will flow naturally from projects aimed at protecting their natural resources (see also Harbert, Chapter 20). Such examples could be multiplied; this is just a sample with which to begin. The point is not to try to advance any one of these as a new historical precedent to be followed uncritically; all have their ambiguities and limitations as well as their strengths. But by looking at the trajectories and outcomes of other intercultural collaborations meant to further the ideals of self-determination, conservation, and the protection of property rights, documentary linguists may be able to think in fresh ways about the challenge presented by the well-known inadequacy of good intentions to produce good outcomes. As we move forward in developing documentary linguistics as an ethical field, we need to take the broadest possible view of the past of our endeavour. We should remember that we ourselves, like the speakers of the languages we study, need not seek in the past a model to simply reproduce, but resources with which to creatively improvise the future.

Notes

1 As opposed to 'taking the main informants out of the noisy environment of their homes and villages and working with them in a guest house, trailer, or hotel nearby' (Himmelmann 2008: 341).
2 Although exploring the researchers' sense of loss has been recognized as epistemologically productive in some genres of anthropological writing (Behar 1996, Rosaldo 1993), this pervasive feature of the contemporary salvage linguist's experience has unfortunately

not yet found much expression in linguists' writing on endangered languages. One exception is Bowern's (2008) fieldwork manual. As Bowern writes (2008: 166): '[i]t's depressing to build up strong and extremely close relationships with elderly people who then pass away. You have complicated links to your consultants, who will become your friends as well as your collaborators and teachers. You may feel guilty that you might have done a better job or recorded more of the language, and it's too late now. This is a commonly reported feeling amongst linguists who work on highly endangered languages.'

3   portal.unesco.org/culture/en/ev.php-URL_ID=34325andURL_DO=DO_TOPICandURL_SECTION=201.html (accessed 28 February, 2010).

4   www.wipo.int/tk/en/folklore/culturalheritage (accessed 28 February, 2010).

5   www.unesco.org/culture/ich/index.php?pg=00139 (accessed 28 February 2010).

6   Thanks are due to Guy Lopez for helpful discussion of these events.

7   Charity (2008) surveys some of the other ways linguists have brought their professional skills to bear in supporting progressive social causes.

8   Beginning in the 1960s, anthropologists began asking themselves how they could avoid perpetuating the injustices of colonialism that had constructed certain kinds of people as fit objects of study in the first place. Was it structurally possible to conduct fieldwork without subordinating one's interlocutors? Was documenting cultural difference ineluctably defined by a nostalgic longing to see our own complement in the primitive other (Fabian 2002)? How is the hierarchy of authoritative subject and disempowered object reproduced through the conventions of ethnographic writing, premised as they are on the anthropologist's right to portray cultural others in their texts (Clifford and Marcus 1986, Marcus and Fischer 1986)? Concepts which had been taken for granted ('culture', 'the field') became the objects of intense questioning (Clifford 1988, Gupta and Ferguson 1997). In recent years, anthropologists seem to be making their peace with the basic parameters of their project, learning about others through the experience of 'being there' with them (Borneman and Hammoudi 2009). Yet the outcome of this generation-long *crise de coeur* has been a new sensitivity to how field researchers inevitably become implicated in the events they have gone to the field to describe, along with a willingness to take seriously the problem of 'research[ing] research itself' (Elyachar 2006).

9   In line with this, the theme of the splendidly received First International Conference on Language Documentation and Conservation that took place at the University of Hawai'i in March, 2009 was 'supporting small languages together'.

10 It is no coincidence that Czaykowska-Higgins is a scholar of Native American languages working in Canada. While a live issue elsewhere (especially Australia, another powerful Anglo settler nation), the new emphasis on the politics of fieldwork has been driven predominantly by Americanist concerns. Hence, those few scholars who have approached the politicization of linguistic research more critically base their arguments on experience in other parts of the world (Childs and Koroma 2008, Dobrin 2008, Ladefoged 1992, Newman 2003).

11 Ethical awareness has been integral to the endangered languages movement from its inception; see Craig (1992a: 33).

12 This concern with research ethics has spilled over into the discipline of linguistics at large. In 2006, at the urging of the Committee on Endangered Languages and their Preservation, the Linguistic Society of America (LSA) formed an ad hoc Ethics Committee with the goal of drafting an ethics statement on the Society's behalf. The committee membership consisted of linguists working in a number of subfields, not only documentary linguistics, but also sociolinguistics, experimental speech research and anthropological linguistics. In 2009 the Ethics Committee was made a standing committee of the LSA, and the Society adopted its first ever Statement of Ethics (www.lsadc.org/info/lsa-res.cfm). While other linguistic associations have issued formal ethical guidelines, codes, or statements (see Wilkins 1992 for reflections on the early efforts to codify ethics in the Australian linguistics community), the LSA's recent embrace of ethics as a matter for systematic professional development illustrates the great strides the endangered language movement has made in demanding that linguistics make itself responsive to human needs.

13 Actual co-authorship is of course known from Australia, dating back to the 1980s when publications of texts and dictionaries appeared under the names of the speakers who supplied the materials and the linguist(s) who codified them (see also Woodbury, Chapter 9, on native speaker linguist authorship dating back to the time of Boas in North America).

14 The effects of this problem can be seen in even more controlled research settings, such as interviews; see Briggs 1986 for a thoughtful analysis.

11

Data and language documentation

Jeff Good

11.1 Introduction

The topic of this chapter is the relationship between data and language documentation. Unlike many fields of study within linguistics, concerns regarding data collection and manipulation play a central role in our understanding of, and theorizing about, language documentation. The field to a large extent, in fact, owes its existence to a shift in focus away from the goals of linguistic description which are concerned with outputs derived from primary data, like grammars and dictionaries, to the collection and analysis of the primary data itself (see Woodbury, Chapter 9).

When trying to understand the role of data in language documentation, the first question we must consider is what precisely do we mean by DATA? Beginning with the work of Himmelmann (1998), it has become customary in language documentation to distinguish between PRIMARY DATA (constituting recordings, notes on recordings and transcriptions) and ANALYTICAL RESOURCES (like descriptive grammars and dictionaries) constructed on the basis of, and via generalization over, primary data. While making this conceptual distinction is essential to the practice and theorizing of language documentation, most individuals or teams working on language documentation projects are ultimately interested in both collecting and analysing primary data, as well as producing the kinds of analytical resources associated with traditional language description, most prominently grammars, dictionaries, and texts (whether oriented for community or academic use). Therefore, each will be considered here. That is, the discussion will cover topics related to the collection, storage and manipulation of primary data as well as the mobilization of that data to create analytical resources (see Holton, Chapter 19). While it is also important to keep in mind that documentation DATA is not synonymous with DIGITAL DATA, for the most part, in this chapter, only digital data will be discussed. Generally, digital, rather than analogue, data has been the focus of work in language documentation, both because new data is typically recorded in digital form at present and because analogue materials are increasingly being digitized so that they can be manipulated and disseminated with digital tools. Discussion of important aspects of digitization, i.e. the process through which a digital representation of a non-digital object is created, can be found in the E-MELD School of Best Practices in Digital Language Documentation[1] (Boynton *et al.* 2006), and an exemplary case study of the digitization process can be found in Simons *et al.* (2007).

This chapter will focus on conceptual issues rather than specific technical recommendations, though such recommendations may be discussed to provide illustrative examples. This is because our understanding of the conceptual issues evolves at a much slower rate than the technical recommendations, which change as the technologies we use for recording and analysing data themselves change and, therefore, largely outpace the speed through which books like this make their way into publication. At least for the time being, the best way to find answers to questions like *What audio-recording device should I use?* or *What software should I use for text annotation?* will be to use online resources like the E-MELD School just mentioned above, electronic publications like *Language Documentation and Conservation*[2] or the *Transient Languages and Cultures* blog,[3] and email lists like the Resource Network for Linguistic Diversity.[4] The role of a chapter like this one is, therefore, not so much to tell language documenters what to do but, rather, to put issues surrounding data in a broader context, to allow them to understand why recommendations take a particular shape, and to better equip them to evaluate new technologies as they become available. Readers looking to augment the discussion here with more specific recommendations will find Austin (2006) helpful, as it covers similar subject matter to this chapter but on a more concrete level. More advanced conceptual discussion can be found in Bird and Simons (2003) which overlaps partially with the discussion here, but also goes beyond it in many respects.

This chapter divides the discussion into the following topics: data types in Section 11.2, data structures in Section 11.3, data formats in Section 11.4, metadata in Section 11.5, a brief discussion of needs assessment in Section 11.6, and a concluding section on the linguist's responsibilities for navigating the relationship between their data and new technologies in Section 11.7.

11.2   Data types

The discussion in this section is subdivided into the topics of recordings, transcriptions and traditional descriptive resources, each of which is treated in turn, followed by discussion of community-oriented versus academic-oriented data. I do not cover written language, as opposed to transcription, specifically here both because of the general emphasis in language documentation on collecting instances of spoken language (though, see Woodbury, Chapter 9) and because, from a data management perspective, written representations do not generally differ significantly from transcription. I also do not discuss scanned images, though these can play a role in language documentation, as well, particularly for projects making use of paper-based materials (see Simons *et al.* 2007 for a relevant case study using scanned images to create high-quality documentary resources).

11.2.1 Recordings

In the present context, following Himmelmann (1998: 162), PRIMARY DATA will be used to refer to two very distinct classes of resources: direct recordings of events on the one hand, and written representations of those events on the other. Direct recordings include, most prominently, audio-recordings and, increasingly, video-recordings as well as photographs, though they can also include more 'exotic' resources like laryngographs or palatograms. These kinds of resources are sometimes referred to as RAW DATA (see, for example, Schultze-Berndt 2006: 215), to highlight the fact that they can be created without extensive linguistic analysis, unlike transcriptions, for example.

However, one should not be complacent and assume that the 'rawness' of this data implies that it represents a purely objective rendering of a given communicative event. All recording involves selection: what to record, when to record, how to record, etc. And these selections, made by a person, not a machine, can shape the recording tremendously, not only influencing the perceived quality of the recording but also emphasizing and deemphasizing features of the recorded event and the language in possibly significant ways. For example, use of a unidirectional microphone in making an audio-recording will result in a resource where one speaker is framed as more central to a speech event than any others, while use of an omnidirectional microphone will produce a resource where different participants' voices may be recorded more equally. Analytical linguistic factors may influence which kind of microphone is chosen for a given recording. In a grammatical elicitation session with a single speaker, for example, a lavalier microphone is more likely be chosen, while for a recording made of a story a stereo microphone may be used even though only one participant has the special role of storyteller, if the story is being told in a society where audience participation is the norm. Similar issues arise in choosing to make video-recordings in addition to audio ones. For certain kinds of events – or even languages, in the case of sign languages – use of video may be essential, but the question of what visual aspects of a scene to frame and record is a particularly clear kind of selection.

Therefore, while the production of raw recordings involves less intensive linguistic analysis than creating, say, a transcription, it should not be forgotten that it involves a series of choices, some of which may be mostly pragmatic in nature (e.g. not to use a video-recorder for a given session to conserve scarce battery power) while others (e.g. not to use a video-recorder because a session is deemed to be visually 'uninteresting') may actually be informed by an underlying, if only implicit, theory of recording. This point carries special importance for researchers choosing to adopt collaborative modes of fieldwork with their communities (see, e.g. Dwyer 2006, Grinevald 2003, Mithun 2001 for relevant discussion) or who intend their work to assist in community language maintenance and revitalization projects (see, e.g. Mosel 2006, Nathan 2006b and Chapters 15 and 18 in this volume), since community input may be required to ensure that the form of the recordings is not unduly skewed towards research needs.

11.2.2 Transcriptions

Transcriptions (which are often annotated – see Schultze-Berndt (2006) for detailed discussion of annotation) have generally been treated under the heading of primary data due to the fact that they are intended to be a representation of a particular speech event rather than serving as generalizations over distinct speech events. Unlike recordings, however, the creation of transcriptions implies extensive linguistic analysis (see, e.g. Himmelmann 2006b), and they therefore occupy a territory between documentation and description. (The same could be said for written representations of language in general, though in some cases written examples of language serve as primary data not merely by convention but because they constitute the only available sources of a given use of language.)

A crucial difference between transcriptions and recordings, however, is that recording techniques and technologies tend to be general in nature while transcription is a specifically linguistic task. The devices used by linguists to make audio-recordings are more or less the same as those used by musicians, oral historians, journalists, etc. However, many of the transcription conventions used by linguists, e.g. the International Phonetic Alphabet or aligned glossing, are discipline-specific and largely under the control of the linguistic community.

An important consequence of this is that while language documenters will generally be reactive in the domain of recording techniques, they will often need to be proactive in the domain of transcription techniques. Thus, language documentation work is at the forefront of the current generation of transcription and annotation tools, as evidenced, for example, by the ELAN annotation tool[5] (see Berez 2007 for a review) produced specifically in the context of the Dokumentation Bedrohter Sprachen (DoBeS) programme and widely used by other documentation researchers.

11.2.3 Descriptive resources

Three kinds of resources have long been given a special place in descriptive linguistics: texts, dictionaries and grammars. If the most important feature distinguishing descriptive resources from documentary resources is the fact that they attempt to arrive at generalizations about a language based on raw data, it is clear that texts are less prototypically descriptive than dictionaries and grammars. However, to the extent that they are normalized and edited for internal consistency, they shift from being records of a specific speech event, as with a transcription, to being representations of an idealized speech event and, therefore, begin to show characteristics of description.

By contrast, dictionaries and grammars are unambiguously instances of description. A dictionary is an attempt to generalize over the known lexical items of a language to create a concise summary of their uses and meanings, while a grammar generalizes over textual and elicited data to create a summary of the phonological, morphological and syntactic constructions of a language. Formal work making use of extensive language data is not generally construed as an essential part of the creation of an adequate description of a language. However, in the present context it could, in principle, also be included under the broad heading of language description. In practice, however, the field of linguistics tends to reserve the term for INFORMAL DESCRIPTION rather than FORMAL DESCRIPTION (see Dryer (2006) for discussion of relevant issues).

11.2.4 Community data versus academic data

It has become standard practice for linguists documenting under-resourced languages to consider ways in which their work can result in outputs not only for use in academic spheres, but also community ones (see Dobrin and Berson, Chapter 10). Accordingly, brief discussion of this issue is in order here.

It is important to be clear that trying to serve multiple communities of users will always require more work than serving only one community. At the same time, modern technology can significantly reduce the extra burden placed on language documenters who opt to do this. This is because digital data, unlike data on paper, can be copied and transformed relatively easily. To take an example outside of the domain of language documentation, it has now become commonplace for individuals to transform text documents from whatever format they were originally composed in (e.g. in the native format of their word-processing programme) to Portable Document Format (PDF), which was specifically designed to create documents which are readable across a wide range of computer platforms. This transformation process has been largely automated, requiring only a trivial investment of time on the part of the user.

The kinds of data transformations required to allow a single language resource to serve speaker and researcher communities, of course, will never be as straightforwardly automated as conversion to PDF if for no other reason than the fact that groups interested in such functionality do not have the economic power to attract the interest of large software companies. However, as will be discussed in the following sections, if the data collected by a project is encoded in certain ways, having it serve multiple audiences becomes more manageable. Furthermore, if non-proprietary, open formats are used and the way the data is encoded is well documented (see Section 11.4); anyone with sufficient technical expertise will be able to transform the original material into new formats, substantially increasing the potential impact of a project and perhaps also decreasing the workload of language documenters who would not, then, be required to perform such data transformations themselves.[6]

11.3   Data structure versus implementation

Often, when researchers talk about their data, they conflate the abstract structure of the various datatypes they collect with the ways those datatypes happen to be encoded in a particular VIEW, that is, a way of representing the data in a human-readable form. Thus, for example linguists often speak of INTERLINEAR GLOSSED TEXT as a basic data type when, in reality, it is probably better understood as a specific way of expressing a data type we might refer to MORPHOLOGICALLY ANALYSED TEXT, i.e. text on which an exhaustive morphological analysis has been performed. Interlinear glossing has become widely adopted as an effective way of presenting such a morphological analysis, in particular on the printed page, but it is just one of many imaginable ways of doing this. For example, in early twentieth-century published texts one sometimes finds a convention where individual words are associated with endnotes giving analytical details well beyond what is possible with a short gloss (see, for example, the texts in Boas 1911). And, of course, using modern hypertext methods, interactive forms of glossing have become possible as well.

Linguists tend to think of interlinear glossed text as a basic data type in and of itself because it represents a primary way that they interact with texts, and, this is, of course, a perfectly natural conflation. However, when it comes to encoding data on a computer, it is important not to let one particular view unduly influence the way the data itself is coded. Each view is optimized for a particular use, and encoding data too closely to one particular view on a computer will make it hard for it to be reused to create other views. Instead, one should attempt an analysis of the underlying logical structure of the data being represented, encode it using that logical structure, and then allow software tools to create views of the data tailored for use by the various interested communities and individuals.

Section 11.4 will cover specific issues relating to the encoding of language data on a computer. In the remainder of this section, the notion of an underlying data structure will be explored in more detail (Section 11.3.1) and general aspects of the problem of encoding that structure in machine-readable format will be introduced (Section 11.3.2). For purposes of illustration, the discussion will focus on the structure of a simple entry in a word list.

11.3.1   Underlying data structures

In trying to determine what the basic underlying structure is for a given kind of data, the first point one must keep in mind is that this is a complex analytical task and developing a universal mechanistic algorithm to determine the underlying structure of language data is no easier than, say, developing such an algorithm for discovering the phoneme inventory of a language based on phonetic transcriptions. Each kind of data from each language will present its own conceptual difficulties, though just as with grammatical analysis, these will often be variations on a theme rather than completely unexplored problems.

To make the discussion more concrete, consider the very simple lexical entry in (1), associating a French word with a part of speech and an English translation. (See Austin (2006: 97–8) for comparable discussion of the structure of a lexical entry.)

(1)   *chat* **n.** cat

The example in (1) gives a particular view of a bilingual lexical entry consisting of a headword from the language being described in italics, an indication of its part of speech in bold face, and a basic translation in plain text. The underlying structure of the data is largely implicit, though the view does at least make clear that the data can be analysed into three core pieces. We can give a first approximation of the underlying structure of the data in (1) as in (2), where the typological conventions of (1) are repeated in the interests of clarity.

(2)   *headword* **pos** gloss

While (2), at first, may seem to be a reasonable representation of the logical structure of (1), it, in fact, still leaves many characteristics of the data itself implicit. This is because it only analyses those features of the data explicitly represented in the view seen in (1), leaving out many important other features, which, while easily reconstructible from context by a human, will be unknown to a computer without explicit coding. Perhaps the most important of these implicit features is the most easily overlooked: the three logical pieces in (2) are part of a larger unit we might refer to as an ENTRY, and represent as in:

(3) [[*headword*] [**pos**] [gloss]]$_{entry}$

There is at least one set of important additional characteristics associated with the entry in (1) not yet described by the analysis in (3), namely that each of the parts of the entry is associated with a particular language. The headword is in French, the part-of-speech label is an abbreviation from English (though an abbreviation like **n** is, of course, potentially ambiguous as to what language it is drawn from), and the gloss is in English. We might, therefore, want to expand our analysis of the underlying structure of the word list entry in (1) as in:

(4) [[*headword*]$_{lang:french}$ [**pos**]$_{lang:english}$ [gloss]$_{lang:english}$]$_{entry}$

While (4) is significantly more complex than (2), it is still just a beginning. Nowhere is it explicitly indicated yet, for example, that the part-of-speech label applies to the headword and not to the gloss. Nor is there any indication of the nature of the representation of the headword; that is, we do not know (without using outside knowledge) whether the sequence *chat* is a phonetic, phonemic or orthographic representation.

Should we further refine the analysis given in (4), then? How one answers this depends on the details of the data being collected and analysed as well as what the data will be used for. For example, if one was working with a dataset where some of the headwords were given in an orthographic representation while others were given in phonetic transcription, then it would be important to include the possibility for specifying the nature of the headword's representation in an analysis of the entry's underlying structure. However, if all the headwords used an orthographic representation, this would be relatively less important.

11.3.2 Implementing a data structure

Analysing some data in order to arrive at an understanding of its underlying structure could, in principle, be a purely theoretical enterprise. However, in language documentation, it is mostly a means to an end: what one wants to be able to do is store data on a computer in a form which will facilitate its being used to produce human-usable language resources. Therefore, there will generally be a point when some analysis of this structure, even one that may be known to be imperfect, must be chosen for IMPLEMENTATION on a computer; that is, a method must be devised for it to be expressed in a machine-readable form which can be straightforwardly manipulated by the user.

Deciding on an implementation for a given data structure, ultimately, is largely dependent on practical considerations relating to the intended uses for the data and the range of data manipulation tools available to the language documenter. Nevertheless, it is still essential to devote some time to abstract data modelling of the sort described in Section 11.3.1. Simply put, the better one understands the underlying structure of one's data, the easier it will be to arrive at an implementation which will be sustainable over the lifespan of a given project.

An implementation of a data structure will, by definition, need to be done using some computational tool. From the present perspective, one of the most crucial factors in choosing a tool is that it will be able to straightforwardly create a reasonable implementation of the under-lying data structure one chooses to work with. In that sense, one of the most ubiquitous kinds of application, the word processor, is usually insufficient since word processors are optimized to work with a par-ticular kind of data, namely unannotated text documents, that plays a relatively minor role in language documentation. Thus, while one may be able to create reasonable presentations of data (see Section 11.4.3), like what is seen in (1) using a word processor, the resulting resource will not actually code the structure of the data but, rather, aspects of formatting (e.g. bold and italics) that are only indirectly related to the structure. Another common office application, spreadsheet software, by contrast, can be used profitably to implement data structures which are well expressed in a table. The crucial issue here is not the fact that each of these products was designed for use in an office environ-ment. Rather, it is that one kind of application (spreadsheet software) incorporates a basic kind of data structure (the table) directly into its design.

Software specifically designed for language documentation will be opti-mized to work with a particular linguistic data type (or set of datatypes), e.g. time-aligned annotated texts in the case of ELAN. But, such software will not be available for every kind of data and, depending on the needs of a project, may not always be the ideal choice, particularly when a documentary team consists of not only linguists but also non-linguists, who might not be familiar with the ways that linguists think about their data which inform the design of the linguistics-specific tools.

Returning to the example of a lexical entry discussed in Section 11.3.1, how might we implement the data structure associated with it? In this case, the structure is relatively simple, and we could straightforwardly implement it in a spreadsheet where each row corresponds to an entry, and where each part of the entry occupies a single cell of the row, along the lines of what is depicted in Table 11.1 (see section 11.4.2 for an alter-native way of encoding the data).

Table 11.1. *Tabular implementation of word list entries*

Headword	Part of speech	Gloss
chat	n.	cat
chien	n.	dog

The implementation in Table 11.1 does not contain all the information found in the underlying data analysis presented in Section 11.3.1. For example, there is no specific indication that the headword is French and the glossing language is English. Some of the structure is explicitly indicated, however, in the header line which labels the data types of each column. In this case, the missing language information does not pose particular problems since it could be straightforwardly rectified with accompanying information documenting the nature of the data in the file, which could be as easy as giving the spreadsheet a title like 'French word list with English glosses'. In this case, we are dealing with data that has a relatively simple structure and which, therefore, can be given a fairly simple implementation using a widely available kind of software.

Of course, this is just an illustrative example. In many, perhaps most, cases the data collected while documenting a language will be more complex than the example given in (1). Bell and Bird's (2000) survey, for example, of the structure of lexical entries across a wide range of published work gives a good indication of the level of complexity involved when one looks at real lexical data (see also Mosel, Chapter 17). A full dictionary entry, as opposed to word list entry, which might contain multiple senses of a given word, example sentences for each sense, and comparative notes, among other things, will require a tool allowing the definition of data structures with hierarchical relationships within an entry, for example linguistics-specific software like SIL International's Toolbox or LexiquePro, or commercial general-purpose database software like FileMaker Pro. Similarly, in a language-documentation project, one will often want to create machine-readable representations of the relationship between textual data and audio- or video-recordings (e.g. in the form of time-aligned transcription). Doing this requires software which allows one to make direct associations between portions of distinct computer files, something beyond the power of a spreadsheet programme but which is made easy with a tool like ELAN.

While the use of linguistics-specific software will generally facilitate the creation of implementations that are faithful to the underlying structure of the data, simply using such software does not guarantee that the data will come out 'right'. For instance, a lexicon tool may make it straightforward to specify morphosyntactic information like part of speech, but in a language where it is deemed valuable to list multiple paradigmatic forms of a word within a lexical entry, one may want to indicate not only a part of speech at the level of the lexeme but also associate each word form with additional grammatical categories (e.g. a case label). This requires a two-tiered model of grammatical specification, at the lexeme level. A given lexicon creation programme may support this, but it cannot 'know' to make use of such a feature unless the documenter is aware that it is needed in the first place. A 'perfect' implementation of a flawed analysis of the structure of some data will be of little long-term value and, at least for now, arriving at good structural analyses of linguistic data is a task well beyond the skills of any machine.

It would be ideal of course, if, in a chapter like this one, it would be possible to give explicit recommendations about what software is 'best' for language data of a particular type. Unfortunately, the needs of every project are too particular for this to be possible, and there is always a tradeoff between being able to implement a data model as faithfully as possible to its underlying logical structure, employing a tool that everyone on a project team can use comfortably, and ensuring that the tool that is used can produce resources which can be put to use by the audiences to be served by a project. The main advice one can give is to outline the overall goals of a project and data types to be collected in advance (see Section 11.6) and then to solicit advice from experienced researchers when making choices of software. One important factor to consider when choosing software will be the kinds of formats it is able to work with (see Section 11.4).

11.3.3 Audio and video resources and publications

It may seem like a gap in the discussion in this section that it has focused on 'traditional' text-oriented resources rather than recordings. There is a reason for this: many of the important components of the documentary record of a language employ data types which are of interest to communities well outside of the arena of language documentation and which, therefore, will be well-supported independent of language documentation efforts. Audio- and video-recordings are a prime example of this: technologies for capturing, storing and manipulating audio and video data have a large, stable market of which language documentation work is only a minute part. Therefore, efforts will be made to model the structure of audiovisual information and implement those models regardless of the activities of language documenters.

Publication technologies are similar in this regard. The audience for old (e.g. print publication) and new (e.g. multimedia) modes of information dissemination is vast, and new models and technologies for producing publications, in a broad sense of the term, will emerge with or without language-documentation work. Therefore, given limited resources, language documenters will need to devote more energy to issues relating to the modelling and implementation of data types specific to documenting languages, like annotated texts, lexicons and grammars. Nordhoff's (2008) discussion of a possible set of design principles and implementation decisions for the creation of 'ideal' electronic grammars is a good recent example of the kind of work which is needed.

11.4 Data formats

Closely related to the notion of data model implementation is the notion of data FORMAT, that is, the way that information is encoded in a digital resource. When using this term, we must first recognize that it is potentially quite vague and is better understood as a multidimensional concept referring to a number of distinct 'layers' of data encoding rather than a single monolithic notion. In particular, in the present context it is useful to distinguish between FILE FORMAT and MARKUP FORMAT. The former concept is likely the more familiar since it refers to the different file types associated with software applications. These include, for example, the DOC format created by Microsoft Word, PDF format or WAV audio format. The details of the structure and digital composition of these formats are largely irrelevant to language documenters, though, as will be discussed in Section 11.4.1, some are more suitable for language documentation than others. By contrast, markup format, in the present context, refers to the way the substantive content of a resource (at least from the documenter's perspective) is encoded on top of a particular file format. As such, it is directly relevant to language documenters and will be discussed in more detail in Section 11.4.2. In Section 11.4.3, a third way of categorizing formats, by their intended function, will be discussed.

This section will focus primarily on conceptual issues relating to data formats. For specific recommendations regarding appropriate formats to use for different kinds of data (e.g. text, audio or video) and for different kinds of functions (e.g. archiving versus presentation), it is best to refer to up-to-date online resources (e.g. the E-MELD School of Best Practice) or to contact a digital archivist or other individual with the relevant expertise. Recommendations and standards for digital formats tend to evolve rapidly, and periodic review of the state-of-the-art is required for successful language documentation. Video formats, in particular, have yet to see the same degree of stabilization as text and audio formats.

11.4.1 File formats: open versus proprietary
The most important way in which file formats can differ from the perspective of language documentation is whether or not they are OPEN or PROPRIETARY. Devising satisfactory definitions of these terms is not

completely straightforward, but, practically speaking, the distinction centres around whether a given format is designed to be used in any application which may find that format a useful way to store data, or whether it is intended to be used only by the format's owner or via licensing agreements with that owner.

Among the most widely used open file formats is the 'raw' text file (sometimes referred to as a TXT file, or by the file extension .txt), consisting of a sequence of unformatted characters, these days, ideally Unicode characters (see Anderson 2003 and Gippert (2006: 337–61) for an overview of Unicode). Such files can be created and read by a wide array of programmes on all commonly used operating systems, and no single organization has any kind of ownership over the format. By contrast, a well-known proprietary format is the Microsoft DOC format. While this format is creatable and readable by programmes not produced and sold by Microsoft (such as by OpenOffice, for example), it was not designed specifically for this, and the format has been subject to change under Microsoft's discretion regardless of how this may have impacted the ability for other software to create and read files in that format.[7]

For work on language documentation, one of the most important recommendations is to prefer the use of open formats whenever possible, and always for resources that will be deposited in an archive (see Section 11.4.3). There are two major reasons for this. First, open formats, by their nature, are more likely to be created and read by different computer programmes, which means that resources encoded in open formats will generally be available to a wider audience than proprietary formats. Furthermore, open formats are much more likely to be supported by cost-free programmes since, very often, the reason why a format is proprietary in the first place is so a company can profit from selling software which can work with files in that format. While the issue of cost may not be particularly relevant to linguists working at well-funded universities, one must keep in mind that the larger audience for a documentary resource will often include individuals or groups which are not particularly privileged financially.

The second reason to disprefer proprietary formats is that, by virtue of being largely under the control of a particular company, they are more likely to become obsolete. That is, resources encoded using them are more likely to become unreadable or uneditable, because the company controlling them may decide to change the format that its software supports over time, while discontinuing support for its earlier formats, or because the company itself may disappear, meaning that its formats will no longer be supported by any programme. With open formats, even if one organization making software supporting that format should cease to exist, the nature of the format itself makes it relatively easy for a new group to create tools supporting use of that format.[8]

11.4.2 Markup formats

MARKUP, in a digital context, refers to the means by which all or part of the content of a document is explicitly 'marked' as representing some type of information. Continuing the example of a word list entry discussed in Section 11.3.1, markup could be used to indicate, among other things, that: (i) the data in question is a lexical entry; (ii) the first element of the lexical entry is the headword; (iii) the second element is the part of speech; and (iv) the third element is a gloss.

An example of the data in (1) presented in a possible markup format is given in (5), where a markup language known as Extensible Markup Language (XML) is used. XML is a widely used open standard for marking up data using a system of start and end tags which surround data whose type is specified by the tag. The distinction between a start and an end tag is maintained by prefixing a forward slash before the name of an end tag. Start tags can have complex structure wherein they include not only the tag but also specification of attributes of the data using feature-value pairs indicated with equal signs (with the value included in double quotation marks). In (5) these are used to specify the language of the content surrounded by the tags. Readers familiar with HyperText Markup Language (HTML), the dominant markup format for web pages, should find the overall syntax of XML to be familiar since the two use the same basic conventions (see Gippert (2006: 352–61) for additional relevant discussion).[9]

(5)   \<lexicalEntry\>
              \<headword lang="French"\>
              chat
              \</headword\>
              \<pos\>
              n.
              \</pos\>
              \<gloss lang="English"\>
              cat
              \</gloss\>
       \</lexicalEntry\>

The XML in (5) is well formed but somewhat less complex than most real-world specifications (see Austin 2006 for more complex examples of lexical entries and interlinear text). Nevertheless, it gives a basic idea of data markup in general and XML specifically. While numerous markup languages have been developed, XML has been chosen here for illustration since, at present, it enjoys widespread popularity within the software development world as a markup format facilitating the exchange of data between users and computer programmes, and is considered an appropriate markup format for language data where markup is relevant.

XML has at least four attributes which make it especially well suited for language documentation. First, it can be expressed in plain text, i.e. the markup tags do not use any special characters or formatting not found in plain text files. This means that XML files can make use of a widely adopted open format and that facilitates archiving. Second, while XML is primarily designed to be a machine-readable markup format, the fact that the tags can make use of mnemonic text strings (e.g. "lexicalEntry" in (5)) means that it can be, secondarily, human-readable. Thus, even in the absence of materials documenting the specific markup conventions used in a given file, it will still often be possible to discern the content of a document marked up with XML by inspecting it with a plain text editor. This self-documenting feature of XML markup is a desirable characteristic for the long-term preservation of the data in the document since it helps ensure its interpretability even if a document becomes separated from its metadata (see Section 11.5). Third, XML is flexible enough to mark up a wide range of data types for diverse kinds of content; one simply needs to define a new kind of tag to mark up a new kind of data. Finally, XML has been widely adopted in both commercial and non-commercial contexts. As a result, there is extensive tool support for processing and manipulating XML documents, going well beyond what would be possible to create with the resources solely devoted to language documentation.

While the XML example in (5) may make it appear to be a markup format of use only for describing data which would traditionally be printed (e.g. as dictionaries or texts), it can also be used to annotate other kinds of resources, like audio- and video-recordings or images using so-called STAND-OFF markup, wherein the markup itself is stored in a separate file from the resource it describes. Such stand-off markup can then specify which part of an external resource it refers to using some kind of 'pointer', for example the specification of horizontal and vertical coordinates in a scanned image. A common use of such stand-off markup in language documentation is to create a time-aligned transcription of a recorded text where the text transcription is encoded in an XML file containing pointers to times in an audio file, as is done in the EAF files produced by the ELAN annotation tool. (Although these files end in the extension .eaf rather than .xml, the data contained within them is expressed in XML. Note also that .trs files produced by the Transcriber annotation tool are similarly encoded in XML.)

While use of a markup language like XML solves many problems associated with describing the content of a language resource, it is important to understand that, on its own, it is merely a scheme for marking data with different kinds of tags, not, for example, a standardized way of encoding lexical data or annotated text. Rather, one must, beforehand, develop an abstract model of a lexicon or a text, and then implement it in XML (see Section 11.3 for discussion of modelling and implementation).

XML, or any other generalized markup language, serves merely as a kind of 'skeleton' on which domain-specific markup schemes can be constructed. In the long run, the creation of long-lasting, repurposable language documentation will be greatly facilitated by the use of common markup conventions for basic linguistic data types, which will allow for the development of tools which can work with the data from diverse documentation projects that are encoded making use of these conventions. At present, however, general consensus has yet to emerge for most aspects of the markup of linguistic data.[10] In the absence of such consensus, the best strategy is to employ markup conventions using mnemonic labels and to document how those labels are to be interpreted in the context of a given resource.

Finally, in general, users will not manipulate markup directly, for example by editing an XML document in a text editor. Rather, they will typically use software providing a graphical interface to the markup (as ELAN does with its XML format, for example) or software which allows for the files it creates to be exported to an appropriate markup format, as is the case with, for example, Toolbox's XML export. However, while users do not need to learn how to create or edit a suitable markup format directly, it is important to be able to determine whether a markup format is sufficiently open and transparent to be appropriate for a project's documentary needs, which requires some knowledge of the relevant issues.

11.4.3   Archival, working and presentation formats

In addition to classifying formats by their various technical features, one can also classify a format by virtue of its possible or optimal functions. In the context of language documentation, three particular functions stand out: ARCHIVAL, WORKING and PRESENTATION. An archival format is one designed for longevity. In the ideal case, a resource stored in an archival format today would be readable in a hundred years or more (assuming it has not been lost on unreadable media). A working format is one manipulated by a given software programme as the user creates or edits a resource; this is the format language documenters will spend most of their time with. A presentation format is one that is optimized for use by a specific community. Presentation formats can range from a print dictionary to a multimedia presentation, and are typically the formats that those not involved in the language documentation process itself would generally consider to be the 'normal' kind of language materials. For discussion of archival, working and presentation formats for different data types referencing specific formats, consult the E-MELD School of Best Practice.

In an ideal world, a single format could function simultaneously as an archival, working and presentation format for a given kind of resource.

However, this is a practical impossibility. This is most clearly the case for presentation formats which are, by definition, audience-specific (e.g. an ideal linguist's dictionary has a very different form from a language learner's dictionary, even if they can be based on the same underlying lexical database) and also may require optimization for certain modes of dissemination (e.g. an audio file may need to be reduced in size, and possibly also quality, in order to become suitable for distribution via the internet). Though such problems are not as acute when comparing archival formats and working formats, they do not disappear entirely. For example, archival formats often tend to be large and 'verbose'; that is, they may express their content with lots of redundancy since this helps ensure their long-term readability. Working formats, by contrast, are often more useful if expressed in ways that are concise, since this allows them to be manipulated more efficiently by a computer.

A language documentation project, therefore, needs to anticipate the use of formats with distinct functions over its lifespan, working formats for performing day-to-day tasks, archival formats for long-term storage, and a variety of presentation formats depending on the communities it wishes to serve and the ways it wishes to serve them. The need for such a variety will inevitably complicate the management of a documentation project, though such complications can be alleviated by forward planning (see Section 11.6) and the use of tools either natively using open formats as working formats or allowing easy and reliable export of their working format to an open format, since such formats tend to be more straightforwardly transformable to appropriate archival and presentation formats than proprietary formats.

11.5   Metadata

In order for the data collected and analysed by a project to be usable in the long term, it not only needs to be well-structured internally but also must be associated with appropriate METADATA; that is, information describing the constituent resources of a documentary corpus, including, for example, their content, creators and any access restrictions (see Good (2002) for introductory discussion in a linguistic context). Metadata is an essential part of any documentary corpus, and a metadata plan forms an integral part of a general data plan.

Since materials deposited in an archive will need to be associated with their metadata in order for them to be accessioned (see Conathan, Chapter 12), the best place to turn to for advice in terms of what metadata to include with one's materials is the archive where the data will be deposited. This may involve some research to determine what archive is best placed to accept the resources created by a project. While the metadata policies for language archives are all broadly similar, each archive will have its own specific expectations and, in some cases, an existing set of forms which can be used for metadata entry and which the archive has designed to facilitate its own accessioning process.

In devising a metadata plan for a language documentation project, it is useful to think about metadata needs across two broad parameters: the different kinds of items that will require metadata, and the different users of the metadata. I will not consider here in detail the specific metadata 'fields' one may want to record, since there are a number of complicated considerations relating to specific project requirements and resources (though see Conathan, Section 12.3.2) for relevant suggestions). At a minimum, it is necessary to record basic 'bibliographic' information like the identity of the creators (a cover term encompassing anyone involved in a resource's creation), date of creation, place of creation, language being documented, access restrictions and a brief descriptive title or keyword (see Johnson 2004: 250). At a maximum, one can consider the extensive IMDI[11] metadata set; most projects will fall somewhere in between. When starting a new project, it may be useful to look at the latest version of the IMDI set to get an idea for the range of information that, in principle, might be worth keeping track of.

11.5.1   What requires metadata?

Most of the documentary objects requiring metadata can be arranged in a hierarchy from more general to more specific using the categories PROJECT, CORPUS, SESSION and RESOURCE.[12] An additional set of 'objects' requiring metadata, but which do not fit directly into this hierarchy, are the various PEOPLE involved, including most prominently the speakers and documenters.

A RESOURCE, in this context, is a unique object, either a physical item or a computer file, comprising part of the documentation of a language. Often multiple resources are created as part of the record of a single event (e.g. an audio-recording, a transcription, a photograph). These would then be grouped into a SESSION (following the terminology adopted by IMDI, as discussed in Brugman *et al.* (2003), though the term BUNDLE is also used for this concept).[13] Sessions may then belong to some user-defined higher level grouping which can be referred to as a CORPUS, which might, for example, consist of all the sessions documenting a specific language in a multilingual documentation project. Finally, a set of corpora may be joined together into a larger PROJECT, for example all the materials collected by a given documentary team. While it is generally possible to apply the notions RESOURCE and SESSION (or BUNDLE) fairly consistently, CORPUS and PROJECT are somewhat more subjective and are more likely to be employed using conventions specific to a given documentary team.

Conceiving of the items produced by a language-documentation project as belonging to a hierarchy is useful insofar as it allows one to avoid repeating the same information in multiple places. For example, if documentary work is externally funded, it will often be necessary to acknowledge the funder(s) somewhere in the metadata. This is most conveniently done at a high level, like that of PROJECT, as opposed to specifying it for each individual resource. Similarly, resources documenting a single speech event will share information like CREATORS and DATE, thus making it useful to employ the notion of SESSION. Finally, since most information about people is independent of the actual resources they contributed to, person metadata constitutes a level on its own. Each person can be associated with a unique identifier (e.g. their name, if appropriate), which can then be referred to in session metadata.

11.5.2   Metadata users

When creating metadata, one should consider the range of users who are likely to make use of it, with the most important division being those directly involved in a project versus those outside of it. On the one hand, those involved in a project are unlikely to be, for example, interested in project-level metadata since they will already be aware of such information. By contrast, they are likely to be very interested in session-level metadata as a means of keeping track of a project's progress. On the other hand, those outside of a project may want to refer to project-level metadata (such as which languages are being documented), as a first 'entry point' into a set of documentary materials and will only be interested in session-level metadata for projects which they have decided are relevant to their interests.

A documentary team will presumably keep track of the metadata it needs for its own purposes without special considerations, but may forget to record information that is shared among the team but will be unknown to outsiders. For example, the fact that a given speaker is an elder will be obvious to those working directly with that speaker, but could be very difficult to determine from an audio-recording. Therefore, the language documenter must try to keep in mind that the users of metadata are not privy to the same level or kinds of information that a documentary team will be. In fact, the concerns of one particular group of 'outside' users should resonate particularly strongly with experienced documenters: future versions of themselves who are likely to have forgotten quite a bit about the context of their old recordings, but who will still be interested in using them.

This two-way distinction between project members and those outside of a project is, of course, quite simplistic and masks many internal subdivisions within those categories. With respect to outsiders, a further important division involves researchers versus community members.

Existing metadata schemes for language resources, like IMDI (see above) and the Open Language Archives Community metadata set (OLAC; Simons and Bird 2008) are oriented towards the research community, and speaker communities are likely to have different interests in terms of the information they find valuable. For example, linguists are typically more concerned with the languages a given speaker's parents may have spoken at home than they are with who that person's parents actually are, while speaker communities are quite likely to be interested in the genealogical relations of those who participated in the creation of a set of documentary resources, especially if they are close relatives.

11.5.3   Practical considerations

While it is not possible here to go into detail regarding metadata management techniques, two practical considerations are especially crucial. First, every resource created by a documentation project should be associated with a unique identifier. For computer files, this identifier should be the name of the file itself, which, therefore, needs to be created with uniqueness in mind. For physical resources, this identifier should be marked on the resource itself directly or with an adhesive label (see Johnson 2004: 149–51 for examples of possible schemes for creating unique identifiers in a language documentation context). In an ideal world, a given resource would be indelibly associated with its metadata so that its content would always be completely clear. However, in practice, metadata tends to be stored separately from the resource itself. Therefore, it is also useful for a resource's identifier to give some minimal information about its content. Then, even if the resource cannot be straightforwardly associated with its metadata at a given time, some information about it can be gleaned from its label. For example, a recording of Angela Merkel in German made on 1 May 2009 might have a label like *deu-AM-20090501.wav*. This identifier contains a three-letter language code, followed by the initials of the speaker, a date (in an internationally recognizable format), and, finally, a file extension indicating this is a WAV audio-recording. Obviously, such an identifier does not substitute for a full metadata record, but at least it gives some information about a resource which will be quite valuable in case its metadata becomes lost.[14]

A second practical consideration regarding metadata is that, especially in field settings, it is essential that metadata entry be made as straightforward as possible. Ideally, metadata will be recorded for a resource on the same day it is created, while one's memory is still fresh. But, language documentation can often be a tiring task, leaving little energy at the end of the day to work with a complex metadata management system. Since metadata usually has a fairly simple structure, almost any program one might use to create a table or a database, e.g. Microsoft Excel, FileMaker or Toolbox, can be used for metadata entry and storage. Since one of these is already likely be used for other aspects of documentation, the most straightforward route is to co-opt it for use as a metadata entry and storage tool as well, at least when in the field.[15]

11.6   Needs assessment

Implicit in the discussion to this point has been the assumption that, either formally or informally, a given project has undertaken a technical needs assessment. That is, the overall goals of a project have been outlined, an enumeration of the different resources required to reach those goals has been formulated, and a workplan has been devised to ensure that those resources can be acquired or developed over the course of the project. Bowern (Chapter 23) contains a general overview of issues relating to project planning, including some discussion of how to integrate a project's data needs into its overall design.

A useful notion to keep in mind while considering the data management aspects of a needs assessment is the WORKFLOW of the individuals involved in the project; that is, what will be the series of day-to-day tasks each project participant will work on at each phase of the project. Modelling a project's workflow will help to ensure that the optimal solutions are chosen to accomplish its goals since it will clarify the specific technological needs of each member of the project team. So-called 'lone wolf' research carried out entirely by a single individual may only require an informal understanding of a project's workflow, but projects involving large and diverse teams will usually benefit from a more formalised depiction of workflow breaking down project work into a set of interconnected tasks. A very large project may even require a member of the documentary team to invest substantial (paid) time in managing its overall workflow.

11.7   The documenter's responsibility

This chapter can only give a brief outline of the relationship between data and language documentation. Furthermore, because the technologies for recording and storing data are continually evolving, our understanding of data in the context of language documentation will also continually evolve, and language documenters will have to periodically reconsider their technological practices and keep abreast of new developments by consulting up-to-date sources.

Unlike, say, learning how to transcribe using the International Phonetic Alphabet, working with the data produced during language documentation is not something that can simply be 'learnt once'. Rather, it will be an ongoing, career-long process. Furthermore, since in many cases the access that many language documenters have to new technologies greatly exceeds that of the communities they work with, it is, to some extent, the researchers' responsibility to serve as the conduit through which information about these technologies and their application reaches these communities (see Jukes, Chapter 21, for relevant discussion).

The most succinct way to summarize these points is: understanding how data collection and management fits into a documentation project is a kind of RESEARCH. It, therefore, is amenable to all the requirements of research: keeping up with the field, knowing the limits of one's expertise, tracking down outside sources, constantly evaluating and reevaluating one's conceptual understanding and methodological practices, and instructing collaborators on appropriate practices. Just as analysing data requires research, so does working with the data itself.

Notes

1 e-meld.org/school
2 nflrc.hawaii.edu/ldc
3 blogs.usyd.edu.au/elac
4 rnld.org
5 www.lat-mpi.eu/tools/elan
6 We should clearly distinguish here between encoding data in non-proprietary, open formats which, in principle, allow it to be straightforwardly repurposed and actually making the data available to other parties for repurposing, e.g. by posting it on a website. Open access and open formats are distinct concepts, and neither implies the other.
7 In recent years, the DOC format has been replaced by the DOCX format which, in principle, is an open-file format, although, in practice, it has not yet been widely adopted outside of Microsoft.
8 It is important to distinguish between open source and open format. Open source refers to whether or not the computer code that forms the basis of a programme is made freely available for inspection and modification. In practice, open source programmes are more likely to use open formats for various reasons, some practical and some social. However, many closed-source programmes also allow one to produce files in open formats (e.g. Microsoft Word allows documents to be saved in the open HTML format).
9 The example in (5) is formatted for easy reading and comprehension by humans; often an XML file would not have carriage returns and indentation within it, i.e. the information would appear as a string:
`<lexicalEntry><headword lang="French">chat</headword><pos>n.`
`</pos><gloss lang="English">cat</gloss></lexicalEntry>.`

10 To take one example, despite being fairly well studied, consensus has yet to emerge on a standard markup format for interlinear glossed text (see Palmer and Erk (2007) for recent discussion).

11 www.mpi.nl/imdi.

12 The conceptual metadata scheme discussed here is derived from work done in the context of IMDI. See Brugman *et al.* (2003).

13 Note that 'session' is a logical and not a processural notion, i.e. it does not necessarily refer to a 'recording session' with one or more speakers since this might contain several logically distinct 'sessions' (or 'bundles') such as folk-story telling, language elicitation, paradigm checking, and so on. Similarly, a single session may incorporate materials split over two or more files, e.g. if a recording flash card fills up in the middle of a narration and is replaced by another when the recording continues.

14 For similar reasons, it is helpful to record some brief metadata at the beginning of an audio- or video-recording.

15 The Archive of Indigenous Languages of Latin America (AILLA) has examples of Excel spreadsheets and Toolbox templates which can be used for metadata management.

12

Archiving and language documentation

Lisa Conathan

12.1 Introduction

This chapter describes how archives appraise, acquire, arrange, describe, preserve and provide access to archival material, and the relevance of these activities to the documentation of endangered languages.[1] Each section includes suggested practices for creating durable and accessible documentary records that can be effectively preserved and used in archives. The principles and practices discussed apply to archival record of all formats. The bulk of existing documentation is in analogue formats (such as notebooks, slip files and analogue audiovisual recordings) but most newly created documentation is in digital formats. Even contemporary projects, however, usually generate analogue records such as notebooks, journals, scrapbooks and research files. A comprehensive approach to archiving language documentation must address the challenges of a wide variety of media. David Nathan addresses issues related to digital archives in detail in Chapter 13.

The preservation of unique records of endangered languages is an essential part of language documentation. All documentation projects should have an archiving plan, and consider the long-term preservation of their records from the outset. Even research outside the context of a comprehensive documentation project can result in valuable records that can be archived. One can argue that professional ethics compel any field worker who records data about an endangered language to deposit the records in an archive, provided that this is possible while respecting privacy and cultural sensitivity.

Archival practices vary significantly and show national, cultural, and institutional differences; it is not possible to provide a single checklist of criteria for an ideal archival documentary corpus. Readers can consult resources such as Johnson (2004), Trilsbeek and Wittenburg (2006), and the publication series *Language Documentation and Description* (edited

by Peter K. Austin) for specific recommendations and practical considerations when creating an archival corpus of language documentation.
The overview in this chapter provides sufficient context to archival
functions to help researchers and documenters create, deposit and use
archival records.

Effective archival management of endangered language documentation is dependent not only on the actions that archives take to acquire,
preserve and provide access to records, but also on the foresight and
contributions of the creators and prior custodians of those records. It is
imperative for linguists to understand both the possibilities and the limitations of current archival practices so they can prepare for and advocate for the best possible management of the records they create, and of
legacy archival collections.

The chapter is organized around core archival functions: appraisal,
accession, arrangement, description, preservation, access and use.
Section 12.2 covers appraisal and accession, the processes by which
an archive assesses the value of a collection and determines whether
to acquire it, sometimes choosing only a subset of records. Section 12.3
covers arrangement and description, whereby an archive determines a
meaningful arrangement for material in a collection and identifies or
creates METADATA (the data about data that makes the archived materials
understandable, findable and usable). Section 12.4 covers preservation,
the process of ensuring long-term usability by preventing destruction
of or damage to records. Section 12.5 covers access and use, identifying
the diverse uses for archival collections and mechanisms for restricting
access to personally or culturally sensitive material.

When carrying out each of the core functions, the steps taken by an
archive to preserve and provide access to documentation of endangered
languages depend on the actions of creators and collectors of the material. In order to ensure the best possible archival outcomes, participants
in a documentary project should operate under the assumption that they
are creating a lasting body of material that will be useful in the future
for a diverse set of researchers, taking appropriate steps to preserve and
provide access to the documentation they create.

12.1.1   Role of archives in language documentation

Archives maintain and provide access to records of enduring value. A
RECORD is 'data or information that has been fixed on some medium;
that has content, context and structure; and that is used as an extension of human memory or to demonstrate accountability' (Pearce-
Moses 2005). In the case of endangered-language documentation, such
records include material, regardless of medium (e.g. audiovisual recordings, notes or photographs), that documents some aspect of the target
language and, secondarily, any derivative or analytical material (e.g.

transcriptions, drafts of analysis, slip files, databases, dictionaries) that contextualizes and elucidates the primary documentation. The records of a defined project or activity, or the records created by a person or organization, form a COLLECTION or corpus. The term 'collection' has a specialized meaning in an archival context. It is often used to distinguish an artificial collection from archival FONDS. A collection is brought together from a variety of sources while an archival fonds is generated organically by a single person or organization. The term 'collection' is also used more generally to mean any group of material with some unifying characteristic.

Some collections of documentation are conceived of narrowly, including only primary data. Others have a broader scope and include, for example, correspondence, grant applications, analytical notes and curricula vitae. This broader approach documents not only the target language but also the academic, historic, or social context of the research project. Many linguists are concerned with archiving data exclusively, while archivists often want to preserve broader documentation of the context in which the data was created and used. A grant application, for example, succinctly lays out the goals of a research project and the roles of major participants, valuable context that could otherwise be obscure to future researchers.

Archival records, unlike published books or journals, are unique. The context in which they are created and kept reveals the history of a project or individual. The increasing ease of replicating digital records and the independence of data (e.g. a database) from its carrier (e.g. a disc), however, challenges this concept of the uniqueness of archival records. It is now possible, even encouraged, for linguists to deposit multiple copies of documentary collections with multiple archives in order to best serve different user groups.

Field notebooks are typical archival records generated by a documentation project. A notebook is unique. In addition to data gathered through elicitation or observation, it may contain names and biographical information about linguistic consultants, the locations, dates and times of work or incidental observations. Ideally, this material should be captured and organized as metadata when a collection is acquired by an archive (see also Good, Chapter 11, Nathan, Chapter 13). Often, however, the original record (here, a field notebook) includes more information about the context of gathering and recording data than can be expressed in a typical standard metadata record. The data recorded in a field notebook may be repurposed for a variety of projects. The same elicited verb paradigms may provide data for a phonological sketch, be excerpted in a syntactic analysis, form the basis for a textbook problem set or be compiled in a lexicon. The field notebook can be cited as a primary source in each case so that the data can be verified and the analysis tested or replicated. When used as a resource by future fieldworkers, the information in the notebook may prevent the duplication of research efforts or stimulate research in a particular area.

In some cases, material in archives may be the only accessible record of a language. Such is the case with Mutsun, a Costanoan language formerly spoken natively in northern California. The language was documented extensively by nineteenth-century mission priest Felipe Arroyo de la Cuesta (1862) and, later, linguist John Peabody Harrington (Papers, 1907–1959). The last native speaker of Mutsun, Ascencion Solorsano, died in 1930 but the accessibility of records from her work with Harrington has had remarkable results. Okrand (1977) used a small fraction of Harrington's notes to write a grammar. This grammar later inspired certain aspects of his construction of the Klingon language (a constructed language featured in the Star Trek television and movie series). Today, Mutsun people use Harrington's notes to relearn their language and have a successful revitalization programme (see Warner 2007). None of these projects would have been possible without the accessibility of documentary records at the National Anthropological Archives and the University of California.

Archives exist in order to preserve and provide access to the records in their custody for an indefinite period of time. Their time scale is longer than that of scholarly researchers, who must take into account grant applications, publications and tenure deadlines. Archives exist under the assumption that the value and usefulness of their collections will increase over time, extending far beyond the lifetimes of current project participants.

Archival records have usefulness that extends beyond the purpose for which they were originally created. It is for this reason that they can contribute to the goal of documentation to create a lasting, multipurpose record of a language (Himmelmann 2006a: 1). Over time, the importance of records may change and records may be put to unanticipated uses. A phonologist may record a series of plant and animal names to demonstrate a language's phonological inventory, but fifty years later an ethnobotanist may find archaic vocabulary and usage documented in this simple word list. Archivists conceive of the value of documentary records in the widest possible manner, attempting to anticipate the diverse ways in which researchers will retrieve and view the records. This long-term view of the archivist complements the typical perspective of a linguist, who may be caught up in a short-term research project or topic.

In recent decades, the size and complexity of documentary projects has increased, due in part to major international documentation initiatives and also to the wider availability of technology that enables the creation and preservation of audiovisual records. Recent initiatives reflect a growing worldwide interest in protecting and documenting endangered languages and cultures. Relative to earlier documentation, which consisted primarily of handwritten notes and, later, audio tapes, recent projects produce an enormous amount of material in diverse formats, including audiovisual recordings, time-aligned transcriptions, databases, and digital photographs and maps. The complexity of these records requires that their creators and collectors take deliberate steps to ensure the long-term usability of the material. Specific guidelines for creating and collecting well-organized durable data are described in several publications, such as Bowern (2008), Gippert *et al.* (2006), and Good (Chapter 11).

Only a small fraction of endangered-language documentation is accessible and discoverable in archives. While it is impossible to estimate how small this fraction is, any fieldworker can provide anecdotes about boxes of recordings and notebooks stored in attics, basements or on office shelves. Such documentation is effectively dormant until it is deposited in an archive and made publicly accessible. Even material in archives may not be fully accessible or discoverable because it is uncatalogued or insufficiently described. Because of the amount of work necessary to catalogue, describe and preserve archival material, it may take months or even years for an archive to fully process a collection and make it available for research. This time lag can be significantly shortened if researchers work with the archive in advance to prepare the records and metadata according to an appropriate standard.

In order to facilitate discoverability of existing resources, the Open Language Archives Community (OLAC) encourages individual researchers and institutions to submit basic metadata about records to a central portal.[2] The improved access to archival collections that results from this and other initiatives allows assessment of the quality, quantity and research importance of existing documentation. This assessment will in turn inform future documentation efforts.

Language documentation is open-ended. All projects, even well-funded multiyear projects, result in the documentation of only selected domains of language form and usage. Documentation is best done over a period of years by a variety of researchers with different skills, resources and interests. In order to assess the needs for future documentation efforts, archives must preserve and provide access to currently existing documentary records.

The benefits of archiving to language documentation are clear, but these benefits extend well beyond the domain of documentary linguistics. Archives increase the accountability of the field of linguistics as a whole by enabling scholars to cite and verify data and analysis. They stimulate further research by providing data to fuel analysis. They provide a resource for community revitalization efforts. They document the history of linguistics. If linguists fully recognize these benefits, they can effectively advocate on behalf of the archives at their home institutions and support the essential mission of collecting, preserving and providing access to documentation of endangered languages.

12.1.2   Types of archival repositories

An early part of any documentation project should be the determination of where the resulting records will be archived. This choice may be easy if an archive plan is specified as a condition of funding, or if the project is carried out by a government or organization with an institutional archive. Linguists may, however, need to consult with a variety of archives in order to determine the best fit for the records, considering the archives' location, scope, user population and available resources. Endangered-language documentation is found in all types of archives, including institutional archives, collecting repositories, community-based archives and subject-specific archives dedicated exclusively to language documentation.

The mission of a government, tribal, university or other institutional archive is to document the organization itself, providing a record of the activities of the organization. Records are appraised based on the organizational functions or activities they document. In the case of a university, this includes administration, teaching and research. University archives generally acquire only a small subset of faculty research records and rarely collect student research records. Usually the accession of records into institutional archives is subject to predetermined records schedules. University archives should not be confused with special collections or manuscript libraries that are affiliated with a university. While these two types of archives may be managed together at a small college or university, their functions are distinct.

The mission of a collecting archive (including special collections or manuscript libraries) will be defined by topics, geographic locations, genres or formats that often reflect the research and educational goals of a university or other affiliated institution. Unlike institutional archives, which are essentially inward looking and document their own organization, collecting archives are outward-looking and document a particular subject area (Early Modern History, Eugenics, Japanese Film).

In the past decade, several collecting repositories devoted primarily to language documentation have been founded.[3] These archives are able to treat language documentation with subject-specific expertise and fuel progress on standards for metadata, citation and access. All of these institutions are young by archival standards and they have yet to face many of the challenges that come with the management of legacy documentation.

12.2   Appraisal and accession

APPRAISAL is the process by which an archive identifies which records have sufficient value to be accessioned or retained. This process can occur at any of several stages and may be repeated over time if collection or retention policies change. In some cases, archives publicize their collection development policies, which specify the types of records they acquire. In the absence of formal collection development policies, short mission statements or other information about an archive may indicate whether the subject, scope and format of a particular collection would fit within an archive's collecting scope.

Appraisal often occurs in the absence of creators and collectors of the records (i.e. after their death). This situation is undesirable and is often the result of lack of planning on the part of creators and collectors. In such a case, it is essential that information about the collection be stored with the material in a way that is accessible both to specialists and non-specialists. In a researcher's absence, the records may be appraised by an archivist with no particular expertise in the subject area of linguistics or in the culture being documented. In the absence of good metadata, archivists will not be able to properly assess the contents and preservation needs of the records.

As with other areas of archival management, appraisal and accession relies on information provided by the creators of the records. In order to ensure effective appraisal, collectors should take care to create and retain essential metadata, with particular emphasis on the quality and format of audiovisual recordings and any electronic media (see Nathan, Chapter 13, for further detail on quality and format of digital audiovisual recordings). The metadata must communicate the importance of each group of records and their relationship to the overall collection.

Archival appraisal, like all archival functions, is informed by the PRINCIPLE OF PROVENANCE, which requires that records created by a single organization or person, or during the course of a single activity, be kept together and distinct from other records. In keeping with this principle, it is undesirable to split a collection with a single provenance among more than one archive unless there is a compelling reason to do so. Collectors often attempt to analyse the subject interest of material and distribute it accordingly ('The children's stories I recorded would be useful in the community school library, but the linguistic elicitation is better sent to my university archives'). This is rarely a satisfactory solution since it disrupts the provenance, context and original arrangement of a body of material. Fortunately, the ready availability of copies of digital media allows researchers to distribute multiple copies of parts of corpora. A researcher can deposit a copy of record of the whole collection with the university archives and send copies of the children's stories to the community school library.

An archive should always record a donation of records in a deed of gift, copies of which are retained by the donor and the archive. Elements

of a donor agreement, informed by the Society of American Archivists'
brochure *A Guide to Deeds of Gift*[4] and Vanni (2002), are:

(1)   *Elements of a donor agreement*
       Identify the donor and the recipient repository
       Title and description of the donated records
       Transfer of legal ownership and physical custody of the records
       Transfer or retention of intellectual property rights (including
          copyright)
       Length of and rationale for access restrictions
       Explanation (and preferably copies) of agreements with consultants
       Provisions for separated or discarded materials
       Explanation of the archive's rights under copyright law
       Explanation of the archive's rights to display the material in an
          exhibit or use it for publicity
       Any amendment to the agreement must be signed by both parties

The donor agreement is an opportunity for both the depositor and
the archive to articulate the implications and conditions of a gift. The
agreement identifies the donor, who is not necessarily the creator or col-
lector of the records (he or she could be an heir or co-participant in a
documentation project). A statement clarifying the donor's role is helpful ('researcher for the [XX] language documentation project'). The title
for the collection of records should be specific and should communicate
the nature of the entirety of the collection ('Records of the [XX] documentation project' or '[Collector] collection of audio recordings of [XX
language(s)]'). The description of the records may be a short paragraph or
may include extensive metadata as described in Section 12.3. Transfer of
physical ownership may or may not include transfer of intellectual property rights. Any conditions on this transfer (e.g. restrictions on access to
a subset of records) must be clearly articulated at the time of donation.
The donor may request that any records the archive does not retain be
returned to the donor or offered elsewhere. Vanni (2002) also suggests
that archives articulate rights that they have, but that donors may not be
aware of. In the United States, for example, such rights include certain
exemptions to copyright law under provisions 107 and 108, which allow
libraries and archives to copy material for patron use or preservation
purposes without violating copyright.

Both parties should pay particular attention to intellectual property
provisions in donor agreements. Physical ownership of the records does
not entail ownership of the intellectual property (including copyright) of
works documented in the records. In the absence of agreements between
researchers and language speakers, it may not be clear how many people
have a stake in the intellectual property associated with the records.
Archivists and linguists must assume, in the absence of contrary information, that language consultants or speakers retain intellectual property

rights to songs, poems, stories, or other creative works in the records. A donor cannot transfer these rights because he or she does not own them. Other parties such as transcribers and translators may also retain intellectual property rights in the absence of an explicit agreement to the contrary.

If the donor does not wish to transfer any intellectual property rights, the agreement can specify that these rights be retained, or specify a later date at which all the donor's rights will be transferred. Transfer of intellectual property rights to the repository may help ensure the widest possible use of the records at a later date and may save the time and resources necessary to track down future heirs in order to communicate requests to publish or otherwise distribute the records. Further discussion of legal and ethical considerations surrounding intellectual property is to be found in Section 12.5.2.

12.3   Arrangement and description

Arrangement and description are the processes by which archives gain physical and intellectual CONTROL over records (an understanding of the physical and intellectual nature of the records and an ability to communicate this nature to potential researchers). These processes rely heavily on metadata provided by the donors or creators of the records. The consistent recording and storage of metadata from the time the records are created is an essential contribution to archival control.

Archival arrangement and description are hierarchical, and therefore differ fundamentally from bibliographic description, such as is commonly used in a library's online public-access catalogue. Bibliographic description treats resources as items, for example providing an author, title, publisher (if published) and date as a catalogue record for an item. Item-level description works well for individual resources that are not part of a large aggregate of related records.

Archival description is applied to groups of records that are hierarchically organized, with metadata attached at any of several nodes in the hierarchy, as is commonly found in finding aids. Sometimes this hierarchy is very simple and consists of only a list of sister nodes. In other cases it may consist of several layers of groups, subgroups, series, subseries, headings, files or items. Within the hierarchy, daughter nodes inherit information from parent nodes, maximizing descriptive economy. Hierarchical description is best applied to groups of records consisting of a large number of individual items that have an inherent original order or organization. For example, a two-year documentation project may result in one hundred video-tapes created during four field trips and featuring ten linguistic consultants. Some information, such as the scope, length and principal investigator of the documentation project, is inherited by each recording. The location, date and participants for a recording session are inherited by subsets of recordings. The title or description of contents may be inherited by a single recording or part of a recording. Notes about an instance of vowel harmony may apply only to a small segment of a recording.

Hierarchical description ensures that a future user of the records will be able to put small excerpts of data into context. If a future researcher reads a journal article about vowel harmony and follows the author's reference to a specific segment of a video-recording, he or she will be able to discover other recordings created on the same date, in the same location or with the same speaker. The researcher will be able to identify the research project that resulted in the recording and discover basic information about the scope, length and purpose of the project.

The conceptual organization of metadata into a hierarchy is format-independent. Some researchers prefer to structure their metadata in XML documents which are valid according to a schema such as the Open Language Archive Consortium (OLAC) or Encoded Archival Description (EAD) (see Good, Chapter 11). Others may simply type out a text document with the relevant metadata, indicating hierarchical organization with labels, tabs or text formatting. The format of the metadata will determine the ease with which it can be extended, repurposed or displayed flexibly. The importance of producing well-structured metadata that conforms to an international standard increases as the size of a collection grows or as the level of description becomes more granular.

12.3.1 Arrangement

Archives typically arrange and organize collections according to the principles of provenance and ORIGINAL ORDER, reflecting the records' creation and use. The principle of original order requires that the records be arranged in a manner similar to that in which they were created or used, since this original arrangement often reveals important contextual information about the records.

In practice, original order is not always a useful concept for arranging collections of language documentation (or, for that matter, many types of collections). Some types of records, such as corpora or databases, fall outside of common rubrics and pose problems of presentation. (What is the original order of a corpus that can be sorted at will by the researcher?). In other cases, material is so disorganized upon accession that archivists impose an arrangement that is most suitable to the records.

12.3.2 Description

Description is the process by which archives make information about records (metadata) accessible to researchers. Description can take the form of catalogue records, finding aids, inventories or subject guides. Catalogue records have a defined set of fields that provide access to basic metadata about a record or group of records. Finding aids usually include a list (inventory) of material and a description of the contents and context of the records, history of their creation and biographical or historical information about the creator(s). A subject guide describes resources related to a particular topic, such as a language or geographic area.

Descriptive practices vary widely by institution and country. Though recent decades have seen increasing standardization, there is as yet no universal international archival descriptive standard. In the United States, *Describing Archives: A Content Standard* (2007) (DACS) has been approved by the Society of American Archivists and now informs archival description in many institutions. In Canada the standard is *Rules for Archival Description* (2008) (RAD). These standards were developed out of a recognition that wider descriptive standards in use by libraries, such as Anglo American Cataloging Rules (AACR), were not sufficient for archival records. AACR applies a bibliographic approach to description, which is inefficient and impractical for archives.

The broad applicability of standards such as DACS and RAD results in description that is flexible, extensible and widely accessible. Many linguists who collect and organize meticulous fine-grained metadata on their corpora, however, will find that descriptions created according to these standards are unsatisfactory. In finding aids and catalogue records, distinctions among several metadata fields may be collapsed and others omitted entirely. For example, most online public-access library catalogues (OPACs) do not distinguish an author from a researcher or linguistic consultant. In such catalogue records, any creator or contributor is collapsed into a single 'author' role or possibly excluded from the catalogue record.

Linguists have developed subject-specific metadata standards that fulfil the needs of linguistic documentation. The Open Language Archives Community (OLAC), for example, defined a set of roles to allow a nuanced description of the creators, collectors and speakers that contribute to a language documentation project:

(2) *OLAC roles*

annotator	illustrator	research_participant
author	interpreter	responder
compiler	interviewer	singer
consultant	participant	signer
data_inputter	performer	speaker
depositor	photographer	sponsor
developer	recorder	transcriber
editor	researcher	translator

OLAC metadata provides an accessible way for linguists to create flexible metadata at any level of granularity that can be added to a catalogue of language resources or repurposed in other ways by an archive. The ISLE metadata initiative (IMDI) is a more comprehensive metadata system that can be used to manage several archival functions, including not only description but also preservation and access. Both IMDI and OLAC allow hierarchical browsing and sophisticated search queries, depending on their presentation. Access to OLAC and IMDI metadata is currently largely limited to subject-specific browsers,[5] though both standards can be mapped onto widely used international standards such as Dublin Core, Machine Readable Cataloging (MARC) or Encoded Archival Description (EAD), allowing for access through traditional library catalogues and finding aids.

Individual archives vary greatly in the level of granularity and amount of information they provide in publicly available catalogues, browsers or web sites. OPACs usually do not include item-level or more granular metadata but at a minimum consist of an informative collection-level description. In order to facilitate the creation of an effective collection-level description, it is advisable for depositors to include collection-level metadata when they donate their records to an archive. Minimal collection-level metadata includes the following:

(3)   *Minimal collection-level metadata*
    Name, contact information and role of the primary collector or
       creator
    Identification of the provenance of the records
    Description of the scope and duration of the project that produced
       the records, if applicable
    Date range during which the records were created
    ISO-639 codes[6] for the language(s) documented in the records
    Names of language(s) or dialects documented in the records (include
       information necessary to distinguish close varieties)
    Description of the quantity, format(s) and media of the records
    Description of equipment used to create the records (e.g. audio-visual
       equipment or computer software)
    Abstract of the contents of the records and their importance
    Identification of any personally or culturally sensitive material

This collection-level metadata can take any form, as long as it is easily understood, accessed and repurposed by the archive. Some archives specify a preferred format for metadata or provide a form for depositors. Others will be happy just to find a handwritten note in a shoebox of audio tapes.

Where the resources are available, archivists describe collections at a more granular level, including descriptions of each box, file, folder, recording, text or item. These descriptions typically take the form of inventories, finding aids or item-level database entries. Many archives do not have the resources to create such fine-grained descriptions if they do not already exist or cannot easily be repurposed. If a depositor does not provide granular description, the archivist is unlikely to be able to develop the expertise and devote the time necessary to describe the collection as well as the depositor could have. If, however, the depositor creates well-structured metadata that adheres to a widely used standard, the archive will be able to repurpose that information and enhance publicly available descriptions. The consistent recording and maintenance of metadata is among the most important steps a linguist can take to ensure that documentation will be accessible and discoverable via archival description.

A minimal list of item-level metadata to create and keep with records is given in (4). Often such metadata is inherited from a parent node in the descriptive hierarchy and need not be repeated at the level of each item. This inheritance of descriptive metadata preserves the context of the records' creation.

(4) *Minimal item-level metadata*
     Title or short description
     Date the record was created
     Primary creator or author
     Co-creators, contributors or consultants
     ISO-639 codes for the language(s) documented in the item
     Names of the language(s) or dialects documented in the item
     Description of the contents of the item and its importance
     Format or medium of the item
     Physical extent of record, size of electronic file, or length of audio-
          visual recording

The list in (4) can be augmented, depending on the particular metadata schema in use or on the requirements of a particular archive. The definition of 'item' and the scope of item-level metadata depends on the nature of the project. An 'item' may be defined as, for example, an audiovisual tape, a notebook, a set of experiment stimuli, a text or a bundle of resources associated with an elicitation session.

Archives have robust descriptive standards that function well to provide access to metadata about diverse records. Archival standards fall short, however, when describing the people and organizations that create those records. Encoded Archival Context (EAC) is an emerging standard (yet to be widely implemented) that provides a document type definition to encode descriptions of people and organizations. This standard will minimize duplication of the work of writing historical and biographical information. There is also hope that standards such as EAC will provide a structure to use appropriate biographical information in public-access catalogues in a more consistent manner. (A search of any library catalogue for the contributions of a linguistic consultant by name will confirm that such information is routinely absent from library catalogues.)

Biographical information about language consultants and other participants is an essential part of language documentation. It can be crucial, for example, in understanding the relationship between closely related varieties or in studying the effects of social networks on language change. Minimal metadata to collect about each participant in a documentation project is:

(5) *Minimal biographical information*
   Full name
   Nicknames, if relevant
   Date of birth
   Place of birth
   Primary language(s)
   Secondary language(s)
   Role in creation of the collection

Biographical information must be collected and stored with sensitivity to cultural context and the list in (5) is not appropriate for all contexts. Considerations for the privacy or safety of project participants override the need to collect and keep such information. In one context, a person's place of birth may be considered highly politically sensitive, while in another it could be a source of pride. Biographical information can be flagged as sensitive or private if necessary, and can be restricted by the archive.

Archives are by nature conservative institutions that operate on a long time scale, and descriptive practices are slow to adapt to technological innovation. One area that could stand much improvement is the incorporation of researcher-generated description into publicly available catalogues. Currently, descriptions are largely static. An archive creates or edits metadata and presents it to the public. The avenues for editing, correcting or adding to these descriptions are cumbersome and ineffective. Some archives have begun to experiment with ways to add layers of user-generated comments or content to this static description (see Yakel *et al.* 2007), as is common in commercial applications such as Footnote, Flickr and Facebook (see Nathan, Chapter 13, on developments along these lines at the Endangered Languages Archive at SOAS).

Archives value the authority and authenticity of their description and are therefore reluctant to incorporate user-generated content. User-generated descriptions cannot replace quality metadata created by depositors and archivists, but it can supplement it in creative ways. For example, a field methods class could collaborate on the transcription of a text corpus and annotate the archival description with their transcripts, or a community member could supply biographical or historical information about a consultant or identify people in a photograph. Such user-generated content should always be additive, supplementing but not replacing other information, in order to preserve the authenticity and original context of the records.

12.4 Preservation

Archives have a long-term commitment to preserve the physical form and intellectual content of their collections. The ease and effectiveness of preservation depends on the condition and format of the records when they are created, used and stored. Preservation encompasses macro-level considerations such as disaster planning, security and accurate intellectual control over an archive's holdings, as well as physical treatments to material such as copying or reformatting, encapsulation in a protective cover, rehousing or deacidification. Creators of archival documentation should be aware of the basic principles of preservation so they can take steps from the very beginning of a project to ensure that their records can be easily preserved.

Most paper records are best preserved simply by maintaining intellectual control over collections and controlling the environment in which they are stored and used. The longevity of paper records is maximized if they are stored at a constant temperature and humidity that is relatively cool and dry, and secure from pests, leaks and theft. Acid-neutral paper may last indefinitely if kept in such a controlled environment. Highly acidic paper such as newsprint is best avoided, but if necessary it can be photocopied onto acid-neutral paper to preserve its contents. Fieldwork manuals recommend the use of acid-neutral paper in order to ensure the longevity of fieldnotes.

Film, video tape, audio tape and photographs pose challenges specific to their media and require more specialized storage, handling and preservation than paper records. Of particular concern to documentary linguists is the vast amount of audio tape that, never having been accessioned into an archive, is currently degrading in offices, basements and attics. Exposure to fluctuations in heat and humidity can cause irreversible damage to audio tape. Even if they are stored in ideal conditions, audio tapes deteriorate over time, and the quality of the documentation is degraded. Most audio-visual archives strive to reformat older magnetic media (such as audio tape) into a digital format that, while posing its own preservation challenges, allows increased access to the material without damaging the original tape, and preserves the recordings as long as the digital files are properly maintained. Reformatting, however, is costly and time-consuming and many archives face an enormous queue of material to be digitized. Linguists may wish to reformat the analogue recordings in their custody and should take particular care to produce high-quality digital copies, making use of the best audiovisual equipment available to them, or hiring a digitization service.[7]

Recent increases in the amount of digital material in archives, especially digital audiovisual material, pose preservation challenges that differ significantly from the challenges posed by paper or analogue audiovisual recordings. Preservation of digital records may include not only reformatting but also migration or extraction of data. The goal of preserving digital records is to maintain the content and context (the information, data and structure of the records) but not necessarily the original carrier (e.g. the disc or tape on which it was originally stored). The increasing complexity of digital documentation and digital preservation compels documentary linguists to consider the long-term preservation of their digital data when choosing media, equipment and tools. In order to ensure the best preservation outcome, digital files should be created and stored in a non-proprietary uncompressed format so that a variety of operating systems and software can be used to access them (see Good, Chapter 11). Unnecessary compression and format conversion of audiovisual files can result in unintended distortion of the file. The use of compressed files may also have unforeseen consequences for future preservation when the files must be migrated to a new format. Further details about digital preservation are discussed in Nathan (Chapter 13).

12.5   Access and use

The motivation for archival arrangement, description and preservation is that archives exist in order to be used: for research, for teaching, for language revitalization and for future purposes we cannot possibly anticipate. To facilitate effective use, archives must provide efficient and complete access to metadata and records. The interests and expectations of archivists, linguists, consultants and language community members are sometimes in conflict when it comes to access and use. Archivists generally promote the widest possible access to and use of material while respecting legal and ethical limits of intellectual property and personal and cultural sensitivity. Linguists may feel proprietary about a collection they invested years to create, transcribe and meticulously analyse. Community members may assume an inalienable right to all documentation of their heritage. Linguists must balance these interests from the beginning of a documentation project and clearly communicate about issues of access and use when donating material to an archive. Any restrictions on access to and use of material should be communicated at the time of accession to an archive and documented in a deed of gift or donor agreement.

12.5.1   Personally or culturally sensitive material

Depositors have the right to restrict access to material that is personally or culturally sensitive. Such restrictions should always be crafted in consultation with the depositing archives and should be clearly limited in scope and/or time. Such consultation can prevent the creation of restrictions that are difficult or impossible to enforce.

Linguists should document their agreements with project participants. The agreements should explain the purpose and scope of the research project, and make clear that the documentation will be deposited in an archive. Neither linguists nor language consultants can anticipate the nature, extent and future use of the records they create, but both parties should understand that one of the goals of language documentation is to create a lasting record that will be accessible in an archive.

Negotiating access restrictions involves balancing diverse expectations, rights and interests. It is common for a depositor to want to provide access only to community members. This type of restriction may be appropriate in some contexts (e.g. in a community-based institution) but puts an unacceptable burden on the staff of public or university archives. The enforcement of such a restriction forces the archive to determine an individual's membership in a community, usually an impossible or invasive task. Linguists may be hesitant to cede control to an archive and wish to retain an exclusive right to access the data for a fixed period of time in order to publish their research findings. Some archives allow these restrictions (for one, two, three or five years); others do not.

Restrictions for a fixed period of time are common in order to protect the privacy of individuals. Depending on the cultural context, it may be appropriate to restrict personally identifiable information, autobiographical material, personal stories or genealogical notes during the lifetime of the persons involved. Usually, the depositor and archivist agree on a fixed date (e.g. seventy years from the creation of the material) to end privacy-related restrictions.

If the sensitive material concerns the privacy of a group rather than an individual, the nature of any restrictions is a more delicate matter. Cultural privacy is a concept that is not currently protected by national or international laws or conventions, but researchers or archivists may consider the respect of group privacy rights to be an ethical imperative. Culturally private knowledge may include esoteric language such as prayers or ceremonies (though it is not true that all prayers and ceremonies fall into this category). These records may document particular features that a linguist wants to document, describe and analyse. In such cases, respectful handling of the material is best determined in consultation with the language community. Linguists and archivists are not necessarily experts on what constitutes culturally sensitive knowledge. In most cases, archives can restrict, control or contextualize access to and use of a discrete set of culturally sensitive material.

Linguists may decide that such sensitive documentation should not be archived. Such decisions must be made on a case-by-base basis, considering the quality of the documentation and level of endangerment of the language. The decision to discard or withhold documentation should be considered with seriousness since it is counter to the goals of language documentation. Toelken (1998) describes the author's difficult decision to discard a set of field recordings of the Navajo-language stories of Hugh Yellowman. One of Toelken's concerns about the recordings centred on the Navajo cultural context in which the stories are appropriate only during certain times of the year. Toelken could not reach a satisfactory agreement with an archive that would ensure that this restriction would apply in perpetuity. He weighed the potential cultural harm of inappropriate access against the research benefits of making the stories accessible and chose to destroy the material.

In most cases, material that is truly culturally private comprises only a very small part of language-documentation material. Linguists should consider at the outset whether the documentation of such domains is within the scope of their research project. Depositors should consider carefully the necessity of any restrictions, striving to create and preserve records that can be freely accessed, since restrictions may hamper research and revitalization to an unforeseen extent.

12.5.2 Intellectual and cultural property

In the absence of a documented transfer of intellectual property rights such as copyright, archivists will assume that these rights are retained by their original owners (including poets, singers, authors, photographers, translators and transcribers who participate in language-documentation projects). Intellectual property rights vary significantly from country to country, and linguists should familiarize themselves with the basics of relevant laws and customs in the context of their research and fieldwork. COPYRIGHT is a relatively narrow concept that applies to a creative work in a fixed medium and includes the right to reproduce the work, create derivative works (e.g. a translation), and distribute, display or perform the work (as well as to buy and sell works). INTELLECTUAL PROPERTY is a broader term that, in addition to copyright, includes trademarks, patents, publicity rights, performance rights, and MORAL RIGHTS (the right of creators to have their works attributed to them and to protect the integrity of their works).[8]

Cultural property interests are more difficult to define precisely than intellectual property interests, and are a matter of urgent ethical and professional responsibility. Small communities of endangered language speakers may identify their language as an essential and inalienable aspect of their culture, and wish to control access to or use of documentation of their language. Language is a cultural, political, religious and emotional focus in endangered language communities. Successful documentation projects should be able to navigate within and incorporate these tensions and emotions into the documentary records.

Two recently developed protocols for indigenous archival material advocate for a wider interpretation of community rights that includes greater control over documentation of indigenous cultures. The *Aboriginal and Torres Strait Islander Library and Information Resources Network Protocols* encourage archives to include Aboriginal people at all levels of archival management, and to recognize the moral rights of indigenous contributors to cultural documentation. The *Protocols for Native American Archival Materials* articulate a need for cultural privacy and express particular concern about legacy material that may have been collected or created in contravention of community rights. In both cases, indigenous groups are seeking to extend rights already commonly afforded to individuals to groups.

Legal and ethical rights and interests are a cause of anxiety among many field workers who donate their material to an archive. The status of language as an essential or even sacred aspect of a community's culture need not impede full and open documentation. Linguists, however, need to operate according to protocols that respect a community's interests in the documentation. Such agreements are best negotiated locally with the individuals, groups and institutions of the documented culture. As a matter of course, linguists should communicate openly with project participants and others about intellectual and cultural property, and document their agreements with individuals and community representatives.

12.5.3   Uses for archival records

Archival documentation of languages can be used in many ways: to provide data for dictionaries (e.g. Goddard 1994, H. Woodbury 2003), support linguistic description and analysis (e.g. Costa 2003), conduct historical and comparative research, provide input for language revitalization (e.g. Warner 2006, 2007), and contribute to journalistic reporting and artistic media. The nature of archival records is such that we cannot fully anticipate future use. It would have been inconceivable to seventeenth-century resident of the Jamestown Colony William Strachey that his 500-word list of Virginia Algonquian would be used by linguist Blair Rudes and filmmaker Terrence Malick to create dialogue for Malick's 2006 film *The New World* long after the language ceased to be natively spoken.

The current explosion in the amount and accessibility of documentary corpora will undoubtedly transform the way linguists find, use, refer to and verify data and analyses, perhaps even amounting to a 'revolution caused by an unprecedented level of access to the raw materials of our discipline' (Whalen 2003: 339). Data and analyses can be cited and sourced with increasing accuracy, bringing new accountability to linguistics as a field. To support this increased accountability, the editors and reviewers of student papers, articles and book manuscripts should critically assess the author's citation of data sources. Archival corpora can be cited with increasing accuracy as information about records becomes more available (in fact, the Digital Endangered Languages and Musics Archives Network (DELAMAN) has proposed a series of citation standards for archived corpus materials – see www.delaman.org).

This transformation is underway not only in the discipline of linguistics, but in other areas that rely on data collected in the field. Fabian (2008) describes the ready availability of ethnographic texts in digital archives. Increased accessibility of primary sources frees ethnographers from the constraints of using excerpts, summaries and interpretations as the sole representation of source material.

Linguists, members of small language groups, scholars in related disciplines and the general public interested in science and history will benefit from increased availability of records in archives. The benefits extend far beyond the realm of academic scholarship and linguistic theory, as demonstrated by the regular use of archives in language and cultural community activities and events, including language revitalization.

Notes

1 I would like to thank Jennifer Meehan for her valuable comments on an earlier draft of this paper.
2 The catalogue is accessible at www.language-archives.org.
3 These include the Archive of the Indigenous Languages of Latin America (AILLA), the Dokumentation Bedrohter Sprachen Archive (DoBeS), the Endangered Languages Archive (ELAR) of the Hans Rausing Endangered Languages Project, the Leipzig Endangered Language Archive (LELA), and the Pacific and Regional Archive for Digital Sources in Endangered Cultures (PARADISEC).
4 Accessible at www.archivists.org/publications/deed_of_gift.asp.
5 The OLAC catalog is accessible at linguistlist.org/olac and the IMDI browser is accessible at corpus1.mpi.nl/ds/imdi_browser.
6 ISO-639 codes can be found at www.loc.gov/standards/iso639-2.
7 The E-MELD School of Best Practice provides guidelines for digitizing audio and video. Also see the excellent chapter on 'Becoming digital' in Cohen and Rosenzweig (2006).
8 Definitions of intellectual property concepts are based on those in Pearce-Moses (2005). For a more detailed discussion of copyright and intellectual property in the context of language documentation, see Dwyer (2006) and Newman (2007).

13

Digital archiving

David Nathan

13.1　Introduction

This chapter is about digital archives and digital archiving of language
materials, especially materials from endangered languages. The term
DIGITAL ARCHIVE is used here to refer to a FACILITY that has been established with the primary goal of preserving digital data. In this sense,
digital archive does not refer to backup, original or compressed files, or
files that have been set aside and not subject to further change. From
the archives' point of view, activities include appraising and giving feedback on submitted materials, and then, for those materials which are
accepted, their curation, preservation and dissemination, all of which
involve processes and equipment unique to the digital domain (see
Conathan, Chapter 12). Some digital archives are involved in associated
activities such as training and software development.

　From the language documenter's point of view, digital archiving is a
diverse set of activities including creating, selecting, preparing and documenting materials for deposit with the digital archive. Many of these
activities should be understood as aspects of data management (Good,
Chapter 11), rather than required only for archiving.

13.2　Digital data

Strictly speaking, DIGITAL DATA is something that 'happens' rather than
actually 'exists'. Digital information is stored as physical (i.e. analogue)
changes on carriers, such as tiny holes in plastic disks or changes in
magnetic fields on metal disks. A computer can read the disks, interpret them as sequences of symbols, and then present that data in a form
that is comprehensible to an agent that understands the symbols (for
example, some software, or a human).

Many forms of data are not digital, such as an audio-recording on a cassette tape. One could digitize its audio information by playing the cassette and turning its analogue audio-signal into sequences of symbolic values. Equally, digital information does not have to be stored on computers. The digitized audio information could be printed on paper (or carved into stone) as zeros and ones, or as barcodes, which might be argued to be preferable from a purely preservation point of view, since magnetic and optical storage is quite fragile. Traditional written and printed content on paper can thus be regarded as in a sense 'digital'. In the case of our cassette example, however, each minute of digitized audio would occupy over 10,000 paper pages!

Of course, digital data usually refers to computer-readable files, not symbols written on paper (or stone), and the term will be used henceforth in that conventional way. Unlike physical information-bearing objects like books, digital data is inherently separated from its means of storage. Digital data cannot be directly experienced by human senses; it needs hardware, software and interfaces to render it accessible via screens, headphones, or touch. This separation, the abstraction of content from its physical form, is the fundamental property of digitization, and it is what enables the copying, transmission, modification, linking, networking, searching and combining of digital data. But it also introduces severe obstacles to preservation. Objects such as paper, or even gradually degrading tapes and film reels, do not suddenly fail in the way that every computer system will, given sufficient time. It is hard to envisage preserving our digital data for as long as the Rosetta Stone (over 2,000 years) or some Australian Aboriginal art (over 40,000 years) have endured, although that is the goal of digital archives.

13.3   The digital dividend

In the past, many people who made field recordings did not archive them, in the sense of depositing them in a digital archive facility. This was partly because they were focused on other things, such as writing up grammars and other linguistic descriptions. It has been estimated[1] that 90 per cent of the world's recorded cultural heritage materials, many of them unique and irreplaceable, lie stranded on researchers' shelves, unknown to their originating communities and to the wider world, and irretrievably decaying.

Recently, this unhappy situation has been improving. Following general recognition of the consequences of language endangerment and loss, the discipline of documentary linguistics has emerged, together with specialist archives to support it (Woodbury, Chapter 9). Both the discipline and its archives rely extensively on digital technologies, which are now central elements of every phase of language documentation, research, preservation and dissemination. Audio- and video-recording, data management, and many other activities including transcription and lexicography, are all performed using computers and other electronic devices. With the exception of hand-written fieldnotes, most researchers write nowadays using computers, thereby creating digital files. They do this because they welcome the ease with which computers allow the revision, searching, copying, sending and printing of those files compared to paper-based materials. More complex processes, such as restructuring or modification of information in files, or combining contents of different files, are now possible using databases, spreadsheets or other computer programmes. While it was always possible to manipulate data manually, computers enable processes such as reorganizing or sending large amounts of data that would have previously been so time consuming that they were rarely pursued. Software enables flexible integration of text with media, formerly only possible in highly specialized areas such as film production.[2] Thus, being digital makes data fluid and adaptable, so that resources such as audio, texts, lexica etc. can, often without too much work, be quickly repurposed for important and urgent tasks in language documentation and language revitalization and support (see Holton, Chapter 19, for examples). By using digital resources we can exploit rapidly expanding internet-based communications not only to make data available but also to collaborate with distant others in developing materials to support languages.

Despite all these capabilities representing a thorough transformation from the data management methodologies of twenty years ago, there is only one reason why it is *necessary* to use digital technology to archive endangered-language documentation; long-term preservation of audio and video is only possible if they are held in digital form. Until recently, audio and video were captured by recorders/cameras which turn their energy into electronic signals[3] and then use those signals to physically shape the properties of some carrier medium, e.g. the magnetic patterns on a cassette tape. There is an unbroken causal and physical chain between the original energy source and the media carrier, which is therefore an 'analogue' of the original event. Inevitably, recording and playback processes are mediated by the nature, quality and performance of the actual objects involved (the recorder and the tapes), so that no rendition can ever be said to be 'perfect'.

Since analogue media carriers cannot physically last forever (or even stay exactly the same from one usage to another), preservation of the content requires it eventually to be copied from one carrier to another, making long-term preservation in principle impossible, as the International Association of Sound and Audiovisual Archives (IASA 2005: 5) notes:

> In the analogue domain, the primary information suffers an increase in degradation each time it is copied. Only the digital domain offers

the possibility of lossless copying when refreshing or migrating recordings … For the long-term preservation of the primary information contained on an analogue carrier it is necessary, therefore, to first transfer it to the digital domain.

Without digital technologies, it would be possible neither to rescue the legacy materials already recorded, nor to preserve those that are presently being recorded. We are fortunate that the availability of digital technologies coincided with the growth of interest in language documentation and archiving. The long-term preservation of audio and video is *impossible* without digital technologies; only through them will future generations be able to hear the sounds of endangered languages that are spoken today.

13.4   Encoding digital data

As we saw above, the essence of digital processing is the creation, storage and manipulation of symbols. Computers thus provide a natural and efficient means of working with orthographic text. In fact, they could be said to be machines that 'renativize' text as a medium of popular communication following a century of the dominance of sound and image through the analogue technologies of radio, cinema, and television (Levinson 1999: chapter 4). Text data is so compact that storage costs are negligible; it is easily transmissible, searchable and able to be copied and manipulated. Texts of almost any kind provide few challenges to the digital archive, provided that its symbols are properly encoded.

In digital form, a text is stored as a linear sequence of binary symbols (usually thought of as 0 and 1). There are several layers of encoding that stand between this stored sequence of drab 0s and 1s ('bits') and the varied orthographic and typographic information found on the typical screen or printed page. Looking from the screen display inwards, what we see are, firstly, GLYPHS, which are character images drawn from fonts. Each glyph is specified by a number at the software level drawn from a CHARACTER SET that lists correspondences between a set of character concepts and a range of numbers. In turn those glyph numbers are packaged together into sequences of binary symbols that we call, appropriately enough, FILES. Table 13.1 shows examples: in the first row, the character concept 'Latin capital A' is allocated to number 65 in the ASCII character set, the next two rows show how the same underlying 'data' is understood as different characters depending on how it is packaged by association with a character set. The final row shows that the concept 'Latin small schwa' is allocated to number 601 in Unicode. For more on character encoding, see Gippert 2006, Wood nd, and Korpela nd.

Table 13.1. *Binary symbols in files are mapped onto orthographic characters through standardized character sets or encodings.*

Binary digits (in file)	Decimal equivalent	Character set	Character concept	Glyph, in font Arial Unicode
01000001	65	ASCII	Latin capital A	= A
11111110	254	ISO 8859-1 or Latin 1	Lowercase 'thorn'	= þ
11111110	254	ISO 8859-9 or Latin 5 (Turkish)	Lowercase 's' with cedilla	= ş
0000001001011001	601	Unicode	Latin small schwa	= ə

But not all text files are created equal. So-called PLAIN TEXT files work as just described, and a computer only has to know how the basic sequence is chunked into units (e.g. into groups of eight or sixteen bits[4]) and how to turn each of those units into numbers and consequently characters (which will, as the examples in Table 13.1 show, only be guaranteed to be as intended if the character encoding has been explicitly specified).

There are other kinds of files that are packaged differently, into formats typically called PROPRIETARY FORMATS, usually because they are used by commercial, or proprietary, software. These formats allow for more complex types of information than just sequences of characters, for example formatting in varying sizes and colours, spacing, tables, other layout options and even images. None of this formatting can be represented as a sequence of characters that transparently corresponds to the content. And in turn, specialized software is needed to create and view such files.

An example of a proprietary format is Microsoft Word. We tend to think little of the complexity Word adds because the world of print is so familiar, but such proprietary formats do present several challenges for digital archiving. First, they encourage documenters to rely on typographic conventions instead of writing down knowledge explicitly in its own terms. When knowledge is transparently and explicitly provided independent of format, layout and need for specific software, we have the best chance of ensuring that the content is accessible long after today's software (and its manufacturers) is forgotten.

Second, any user of the materials (as well as the archive managing the materials), may be required to use the same software that created the files in order to view them, which limits accessibility of the content. Finally, the software manufacturer may change its formats over time (i.e. change the way it packages and renders the content), so that in order to retain access to the data content, an archive either needs to preserve and make available the relevant software versions (which may not be feasible due to expense or copyright), or to be aware of formats that are becoming defunct and migrate all content to another format while still possible. All of these complexities create a resource burden for an archive and jeopardize long-term preservation, so archives strongly prefer to receive plain text in which any additional structural or formatting information is encoded in standard, explicit and open formats such as XML (see also Good, Chapter 11).

Most archives will request metadata to accompany deposited materials. Conathan, Chapter 12, discusses metadata in detail, describing how researchers' contextual knowledge and the assumptions and conventions they use in writing up data should be included together with the data. Since the role of metadata is to facilitate the preservation, understanding, administration and appropriate usages of data, it is even more crucial that metadata is provided in transparent formats that do not rely on specific software.

13.4.1   Non-text materials

The archival value of images is frequently underestimated. Photographs of fieldwork settings, of consultants, objects, environment, events and equipment setups, can all be very useful both for contextualizing linguistic data and in their own right as documentations of the language community's life. Images are easy to store and use; for many purposes, a few photographs could be equally, if not more effective than video, while consuming far fewer resources. Other sources of images include fieldnotes (especially useful if they contain drawings, diagrams or examples of consultants' handwriting) or written materials found in the community. Today's digital cameras, used under good lighting, have sufficient resolution to make good quality images if scanning is not possible. All images should be accompanied by captions and descriptions, and linked to the relevant texts and recordings.

Turning to time-based media, we have seen that digitization provides the only route to the future for audio and video. The format options for audio are now quite stable. Audio should be provided to archives in the form of WAV files (also known as linear PCM[5]) which involve no compression.[6] The trend in language documentation is towards capturing the full spatial 'image' of speakers' voices in their real-world acoustic contexts, so stereo is preferred. Currently, the most common parameters used in these files are a sampling rate of 44.1 kHz and a bit depth of 16 bits. Some archives are starting to recommend parameters of 48 kHz and 24 bits, and these are expected to become standards for audio over the next decade. Note that these figures apply to digital originals, i.e. what could be called BORN DIGITAL recordings. When analogue materials such as tapes are digitized then higher resolutions (sampling rates and bit depth) should be used to capture the 'undesirable artefacts' arising from the carrier due to its physical manufacture, storage or handling. Accurately capturing these artefacts increases the likelihood of being able to use software to successfully identify and remove them if restoration is attempted in the future (IASA 2005: 7).[7] However, the current standard of 44.1 kHz/16 bits is generally sufficient to represent the full acoustic detail of human speech, and all computers and software support it, so it is likely to remain a practical and acceptable choice for some time.[8] For further details, background and recommendations regarding sampling rate and bit depth parameters, see IASA (2005: 8).

There are, of course, other audio-formats such as the ubiquitous MP3. MP3 files are compressed but listenable versions which are useful as dissemination copies (see Holton, Chapter 19, for examples of their use), or for playing back in portable players, but should never be used for primary recording since there is no reason to strip out various frequencies from the original acoustic data in order to make the file size smaller. The main archiving requirement, however, is that audio should be delivered to the archive in its original form, with appropriate metadata; it should not be covertly converted to a different format. If, for example, audio is recorded originally as MP3, but then converted to WAV (perhaps in an ill-fated attempt to keep an archivist happy), the actual audio information remains compressed; what was originally lost cannot be restored by the format conversion. The archive receives no record of the initial compression, which may cause problems for preservation and for future attempts to create compressed listening copies (since compression of already compressed files can cause problems due to interactions between compression algorithms).

The situation for video is totally different from that of audio; the formats and parameters are far from stable. As of 2010, the technology is rampant with format variants from different manufacturers, and archives are forced to store highly compressed versions for purely practical reasons of size and the cost of storage. Discussion of video formats is beyond the scope of this chapter, and they are in any case undergoing rapid change at the time of writing. However, see Section 13.9.3 below for further reflections on archiving digital video.

Digital audio and video must be accompanied by text-based metadata (and transcription, annotation or other associated text information) that can be listed, sorted and searched so that users can identify media content. Without such text data, those searching for information are forced to play media files right through to get an indication of their content. The media resource is effectively hidden, unfindable and unusable, forever. The richness of the information that accompanies media files should be proportionate to their documentary value and the high costs of storing large media resources.

13.5 Archive strategies

Archives have traditionally made decisions about which materials they accept for deposit, based on their collection policy (see Conathan, Chapter 12). An archive might be devoted to preserving materials for a particular community, group or region, or its policies might be orientated to particular genres of materials. When an archive is established to hold digital materials, its procedures, equipment and management of the deposits will be tailored to the specific needs of the digital domain, including appraisal in order to select those materials that have both sufficient value and are feasible to ingest and preserve (see Conathan, Chapter 12, concerning appraisal).

New partnerships between granting bodies and archives hold great promise for the growth of digital data management in the documentation field and for the strength of resultant archived collections. A small number of archives are now affiliated with organizations that fund documentation of endangered languages, such as the DoBeS archive based at the Max Planck Institute for Psycholinguistics, Nijmegen, and associated with the Volkswagen Foundation, and the Endangered Languages Archive (ELAR) based at SOAS and associated with the Endangered Languages Documentation Programme (ELDP) funded by the Arcadia Fund. These archives are tasked with preserving the outcomes of funded projects. Their respective granting bodies (Volkswagen Foundation and ELDP) want to ensure that the outcomes of their funded research are securely and visibly preserved. In addition, these funder/archive partnerships provide training and technical support of various kinds throughout the lifespan of documentation projects (see Jukes, Chapter 21), so that there is potentially greater interaction and cooperation between researchers and archives than is generally found. While conventional archives typically receive materials 'in the absence of creators and collectors' (as Conathan, Chapter 12, points out), these new partnerships allow documenters and archives to inform each other and to engage in long-term relationships.

These partnerships also give new roles to archives. To the extent that archives inform their granting agency's policies and procedures, and their selection processes, they can influence the nature and quality of their collections by, for example, specifying the skills, methods, processes and equipment choices that should be evident in a successful grant application. On the other hand, the archive's responsibility to grantees may result in having to deal with problems that an independent archive would not face. For example, ELDP applications in some years saw an escalation in applicants' intended numbers of hours of audio- and video-recordings, presumably in the hope that this would make their applications look more attractive. But should these intentions come to fruition, the archive's planned capacity for curation and storage will be stretched or exceeded.

13.6   Standards and diversity

Standards are important for the effective operation of digital archives. Standards are promoted in pursuit of three goals: QUALITY, INTEROPER- ABILITY and the INTEGRITY of the archive's collections.

Some standards provide benchmarks for the quality of resources according to the expectations of a given field or for a particular task. These may be QUANTITATIVE, such as the requirement for audio to have an adequate sampling rate (at least 44.1 kHz). Or they may be CATEGORICAL, for example a requirement that text is encoded in Unicode (but mainly because Unicode increases interoperability; see below).

But most quality issues are QUALITATIVE and CONTEXT DEPENDENT, such as the accuracy and listenability of an audio-recording, the clarity and explicitness of the representation of data, or the accuracy of a transcrip- tion. It is these qualitative questions that have been patchily addressed in the theory and practice of language documentation (but see Nathan 2010a concerning audio-recording). It remains unclear to what extent they are desiderata to be addressed through linguistic curricula or other training (via the programmes, workshops and summer schools described by Jukes, Chapter 21, for example), or whether they should be addressed by archives. The limited attention paid to them in university Linguistics department curricula has led to digital archives frequently being iden- tified as the sources of standards, in turn leading to excessive focus on technical parameters, at the expense of qualitative evaluation.[9]

Metadata schemes such as that proposed by the Open Language Archives Community (OLAC, see Good, Chapter 11) use standard and conventional sets of categories, which archives use to populate their catalogues and to serve as 'finding aids' to make resources discoverable (Bird and Simons 2003, Conathan, Chapter 12). In this way, metadata functions in the same way as catalogue records for books in a library, which have categories including author, title, date, ISBN and publisher that users can expect to find. In addition to these standard categories, specialist libraries create additional metadata to serve the particular needs of their clients.

Despite the widespread use of compact library-like metadata schemas such as OLAC, the set of categories required for capturing the context and significance of endangered language documentation materials is not yet delineated. Because language documentation is a developing field, in contrast to the maturity of libraries and publishing, it is peremptory to constrain documenters to particular schemes. ELAR encourages docu- menters to design metadata to reflect their own research environments and needs. Following four years of operation, the metadata received by ELAR shows that categories vary according to the particularities of each project's goals, participants' skills and preferences, and the nature of language communities, cultures and settings:

- each documentation project can have its own unique 'recipe' for metadata, depending on factors such as the language's typology, consultant knowledge and community values
- each language documenter has their own skills and priorities that determine what metadata categories they use and how they encode them
- ELAR's goal of maximizing quality and quantity of metadata for each deposit requires the encouragement of diversity.[10]

It is thus necessary to distinguish between metadata schemes that are used across the board by an archive or group of archives, and the broader and varied sets of metadata that assiduous documenters provide (see also Nathan 2010b).

Returning to the analogy with libraries, archivists and depositors function as 'joint librarians' in the digital archiving of endangered-language materials. In fact, depositors play the major role, because they are the ones who know the details of the fieldwork situation, the research project and the data. The depositor, not the archivist, has access to the language content, consultants and the language community in order to provide metadata such as speaker details, access conditions, ethnographic context and captions for photographs.

13.7 Digital archives and their services

The policies and technologies of today's digital language archives have their origins in the earliest digital libraries. Later, the development of an Open Archives Information System architecture (OAIS 2002) highlighted the importance of identifying an archive's intended user groups (its DESIGNATED COMMUNITIES) in order to provide them with versions and formats appropriate to their needs. More recently, several archives have been established which are specifically dedicated to endangered language materials, including AILLA, DoBeS, ELAR, LACITO, Paradisec and others (see Appendix). The associated initiatives OLAC and E-MELD (Electronic Metastructure for Endangered Languages Documentation, a project funded by the US National Science Foundation) have vigorously promoted within the linguistic community the importance of creating digital data that is technically robust and flexibly reusable, accompanied by metadata that, suitably catalogued, enables users to discover and access materials (Bird and Simons 2003: 563).

There are alternative providers of digital preservation. There may be national, sector-based, or institutional facilities in individual countries that can offer preservation. In the UK, the trajectory of these has been uncertain, as funding is influenced by economic circumstances and the perceived value of competing disciplinary areas. Then there is the possibility of managed outsourcing. Companies such as Amazon provide mass data storage (through its Simple Storage Service, which allows for the customization of access), but current sentiments would rule against trusting commercial companies with collections of irreplaceable and culturally sensitive data. Note, though, that we are dependent on commercial businesses for the supply of storage appliances, networks, and communication services, and that we have gained from competition between them, especially in terms of the plummeting cost of mass storage, for example. In the future, it might be feasible to outsource data storage to companies with domain specializations. These companies could provide appropriate levels of service, commitment and trust, in the same way that, for example, we are generally satisfied to store our email with Google or Yahoo! and our money with banks.

Given the scale of language endangerment, within a few years digital language archives are likely to become the repositories of much of the world's linguistic and cultural heritage, and the major sources for research on and the revival of moribund or extinct languages. It is therefore important for archives to disseminate materials, functioning as specialist electronic libraries that are equipped to deal with the new genres of documentation that are characterized by an emphasis on media, few alternative channels for distribution, and nuanced restrictions on access.

13.8 Access

The large investment in the creation, management and preservation of digital resources demands appropriate resulting benefits. Access and distribution flow naturally from the existing digital infrastructure, since data can be copied cheaply and perfectly, and quickly transmitted to most parts of the world. However, access and usage have to be managed, and digital archives have to steer a narrow path between reasons for data to be freely accessible, on the one hand, and, on the other hand, for data to be protected or closed. There are several constituencies on the 'open' side, starting with the source language communities and those who wish to assist them in language maintenance and revitalization activities. Such groups should not be prevented from accessing data that they morally 'own' or which can facilitate their efforts. The second is the scientific community which champions openness and the neutrality of data. Third, it is frequently argued that the public should have access to the outcomes of publicly funded research.

Despite all these compelling arguments, factors at the core of language endangerment argue against across-the-board free access to data. First, there is the nature of the data itself. Since language documentation consists ideally of recordings of spontaneous language usage in everyday social contexts, such recordings can be expected to contain instances of private, embarrassing, secret, sacred or other restricted content that may cause harm to the speakers or others.

At the Endangered Languages Archive (ELAR), we use the term PROTO-COL as shorthand for the concepts and processes that apply to the formulation and implementation of language speakers' rights and sensitivities. Corpus linguistics has long taken note of protocol; for example, recorded subjects are asked whether their identity can be revealed and measures such as anonymization are taken where necessary. Protocol issues are heightened in endangered language situations, which typically involve minority communities under socioeconomic, political or military pressures. In such communities it is almost impossible to be anonymous; even the slightest bit of apparently harmless information can reveal someone's identity, whether to another community member or to some external, perhaps hostile, agency. At ELAR we are developing an innovative method for implementing flexible access control that builds on developments in social networking software; it is discussed further in Section 13.9.5 below.

Language documentation's often private or sensitive content means that some protection of intellectual property and/or copyright is required. Many archives have statements which those accessing materials must agree to, typically prohibiting commercial use or republishing without explicit written permission. The level of protection required depends on the nature of the resource and the goals of the information providers. Some language communities welcome the opportunity to showcase their language and culture to the wider world; others are more reluctant to do so. One way of specifying permitted usage and distribution is by means of Creative Commons licences. The Creative Commons initiative, with its catch cry 'some rights reserved', is more oriented to facilitating the sharing of resources for personal, non-profit and creative usages, and has various formulations that require acknowledgement only, or that restrict usage and distribution to non-profit purposes. The licences also formulate varying controls on the creation and onward distribution of materials that incorporate some or all of a given resource but with additional content, called DERIVATIVE WORKS, a category that could apply to analyses of linguistic materials, lexical material that is reorganized or combined with other data, and various types of multimedia (see Holton, Chapter 19, for examples).

What about technical solutions for controlling access and distribution? While there exist some technologies that can protect files from unauthorized copying and distribution, such as mechanisms for DIGITAL RIGHTS MANAGEMENT and audio watermarks, these are in general tailored for use by large companies to protect commercial music and similar products, and language archives running on limited budgets are unlikely to be able to implement them. In any case, such technologies are in themselves a threat to the robustness of short- and long-term archiving, since they involve encrypting the contents of files, often by secret and proprietary methods. A digital archivist's perspective is that long-term preservation is best facilitated by keeping resources in standard and transparent formats, and designing protection and distribution systems based around generally accepted behaviour. The risks of inappropriate access should be imposed at the point of managing access to resources, rather than through solutions that modify the resources themselves. An archive with sufficient technical and financial infrastructure could preserve originals as well as create protected versions for dissemination, but the costs of implementing such a system and keeping pace with changing technologies are unrealistic for most archives. Nevertheless, experience so far suggests that the actual level of unauthorized copying in the domain of indigenous cultural/intellectual property is actually very low.

13.9   Preservation issues

Digital archives have to take account of many factors to ensure long-term preservation, from the broader political, organizational and financial issues that guarantee their sustainable operations, to budget and equipment planning, to technical details of scheduling automated tape backups. Full discussion of all of these is outside the scope of this chapter, and many tend to be generic to digital preservation of all kinds. Below, some topics that intersect with language documentation are described briefly.

13.9.1   Prospects for hardware and storage

The history of digital technologies is a giddy progression of steady trends in hardware, punctuated by sudden changes in architectures (such as operating systems), and unforeseen revolutions in the ways that the technology is used (e.g. the arrival of the World Wide Web, and the current transition to mass participation in it via Web 2.0). The predictable trends tend to be in hardware capabilities, such as the rapid but predictable increases in processor speeds[11] and data density (holding capacity per drive unit). These are of immense relevance and benefit to archives, especially language archives that need to survive on low budgets, because the advances allow the transmission and storage of more data, more quickly, and at less cost.

The price of conventional hard disk space continues to tumble, with the cost per megabyte halving about every two years. This has introduced new possibilities for mass data storage, for example:

1.   expanded use of redundancy techniques, which ensure that data can survive hardware failures;

2. the use of disk rather than tape for backup;
3. greater storage within a single appliance (currently allowing up to about 100TB in a single unit), which greatly reduces costs by simplifying systems and avoiding costly enterprise-level solutions that were until recently necessary for storing large volumes of data; and
4. the feasibility of setting up project-local archives (note, however, that local data 'archiving' should not be confused with the services of committed institutional archives that guarantee behind-the-scenes backup, data migration, data dissemination and other services.).[12]

The years 2009–2010 also saw rapid reductions in the price of solid state drives (SSDs). Although they currently still cost ten times the price per megabyte compared to their corresponding conventional (magnetic) hard disk drives, their adoption in the laptop computer market is likely to result in further price reductions, so that at some point in the future, archiving storage will also transition to SSD technology. This in turn will have many positive implications for language archives' costs, robustness, and flexibility, due to SSD's inherent reliability, increased read/write speeds, reduced size, and a large reduction in energy costs (for both running and cooling).

13.9.2 Data migration

Earlier discussion in Section 13.4 on digital encoding showed that the retrieval and meaning of digital data is dependent on character and file encoding. While some encodings (e.g. plain text as Unicode) are widely supported by a range of software, including open-source software, and openly accessible as International Organization for Standardization Office (ISO) standards, it is inevitably impossible to guarantee that all files involved in language documentation will be stable or usable in the medium or long term. Vulnerable examples include media files, most particularly video (see further discussion in Section 13.9.3 below), and proprietary formats (e.g. MS Word, Excel, Filemaker Pro and others). Other files needing special care include specialist linguistic materials such as Toolbox and ELAN files. While their underlying file formats may be enduring (e.g. ELAN uses Unicode, XML plain text), they may not be usable in the expected way when the software itself no longer runs on new versions of operating systems.[13] A central function of digital archives, therefore (and complementary with their role in educating the documentation community to use the most stable formats possible) is to catalogue the file-preservation characteristics of all files in their collections, and, at the appropriate time, to MIGRATE vulnerable files to new and safer formats.

13.9.3 Video

The benefits of digitization are only fully realized when data and file formats have become stable. At the time of writing, digital video formats are volatile, varying with carrier type (e.g. hard disk, flash card, DV tape), camera manufacturer, and processing software. Video provides an interesting test case for the capabilities and limits of digital data management, storage and delivery.

Video has many merits for language documentation, offering a record integrating audio together with visual representation of language speakers, their gestures, body movements, locations and contexts. The breadth of this potential, however, invites many problems. Many documentation projects are not concerned with gestural or spatial information, so to shoot (and archive) video may not be a good use of resources. Even if projects do have aims that make video relevant, the filming methodology (or lack thereof) may not effectively capture the phenomena concerned. But, most importantly, there are substantial costs and inconveniences of using video: equipment purchase, electricity consumption, weight (including necessary accessories such as a tripod and, depending on conditions, lighting), need for training, intrusion and distraction to both researchers and researched, time and money needed for capture and processing, and storage. These all provide bottlenecks and constraints on good outcomes from the use of video in language documentation.

High-resolution video (such as that captured directly from miniDV tape) is very large in volume; at least three or four times its typical distribution size and ranging from ten to a hundred times the size of audio of comparable length. In addition, the high-resolution versions captured directly from cameras are often in proprietary formats specific to the particular brand of camera and/or software used for transfer. Thus, due to practical and theoretical limitations on language archives' data systems, the high-resolution video that comes directly from cameras (the most informative version that would normally be preferred for archiving) cannot in general be preserved. Only compressed files such as those in MPEG format are sufficiently tractable in size and standard in format for both archiving and practical usage, so most archives have, to date, accepted video only in the highly compressed MPEG2 format. But this proves to be merely a short-term or misleading strategy, perhaps with a blind ending. Almost any subsequent processing of the video, including editing, subtitling or re-rendering to other formats for migration or delivery, should be derived not from MPEG2 (archived) versions but from original high-resolution versions, because editing is normally followed by re-rendering involving another compression, causing great loss of video quality. This leads to two conundrums, if not contradictions, for digital archiving of video.

First, the fundamental reason for adopting digital archiving, namely its long-term support for preservation of media data through the ability to make perfect copies (see Section 13.3), is negated, due to the repeated re-encoding that will be needed for migration as video formats continue to change. The loss over each generation of re-encoding simply recapitulates the original problem with analogue carriers.

Second, consider the scenario where researchers want to create some products from their video, for example to support language revitalization. Editing should proceed from original high-resolution formats, which are unlikely to have been archived, and, if they have been retained at all, it is more likely that they have not been transmitted elsewhere but have been stored locally by the original researcher. So what we see is a reversal of normal archiving strategies; in this case only the researcher, not the archive, is in a position to preserve the 'best version'.[14]

13.9.4   Archive assessment

There are currently a small number of dedicated digital archives for endangered-language documentation (see Appendix). This chapter has discussed only a few of the strategic and operational complexities that these archives must face.

Documenters wanting to archive their data need to choose a suitable archive facility. In part, they will do this by matching their type of materials with the collection policy of a relevant archive. More generally, depositors (and others; see below) might want to evaluate the qualities of archives before they trust their precious data to the curation, care and custodianship of a particular archive facility.

Several initiatives have been set up to help such depositors, as well as to assist archives to assess their own digital preservation policies and practices. These include Drambora,[15] NINCH,[16] Data Seal of Approval[17] and the Digital Curation Centre's toolkit.[18] They provide participating archives with document requirements or templates (e.g. policy and planning documents for access control, backup, security, disaster recovery, staffing and funding) and various sets of operational criteria. While most digital endangered-language archives have not yet defined which initiative is the most suitable, nor uniformly subscribed to any of them, such assessment schemes are expected to play a greater role in the future, for example as funders require their grantees to archive with an approved archive, or archives form federations (Broeder *et al.* 2008) with those that share similar goals and strategies.

13.9.5   Redefining language-documentation archives

Section 13.8 on access above described how protocol issues are highlighted by the nature of language-documentation data. Many materials need to be subject to controlled access, and conditions of access can change over time and depend on who is seeking access.

Following the explosive growth of social networking, or Web 2.0, between 2005–2010, people worldwide have proved keen to conduct interactions, negotiations and relationships via the World Wide Web. The use of social networking sites such as Facebook and MySpace are now embedded in lifestyles in both wealthy and poorer nations.

The Endangered Languages Archive (ELAR) at SOAS is currently pioneering the application of these social networking models to providing controlled access to endangered-language documentation (Nathan 2010c). Via the archive's web-based catalogue system, depositors can manage access conditions, respond to access requests from individuals and monitor the usage of their materials. By devolving access management to depositors, the system neatly addresses the sensitive nature of many archived materials, whilst also solving the problem of managing complex access conditions for an ever-growing collection with a fixed and small staffing level.

This new approach highlights the transactional functions that are foregrounded for the depositors and users of a modern digital archive. Preservation functions are slowly receding into the background as essential but generic services that businesses, government and educational institutions all have to provide to carry out their work. The question for the future is not whether such an approach is likely to be widely adopted but how wide-reaching its effects will be; will, for example, blogs, wikis and media-sharing websites also take their place in the language preservation and dissemination landscape? Whatever the precise outcome, the 'public face' of a digital archive is no longer its data preservation function, but as a forum for conducting relationships between information providers (usually the depositors) and information users (language speakers, linguists and others).

13.10 Conclusion

In this chapter we have seen how the abstract nature of digital data enables long-term preservation of media resources as well as flexible usage and sharing of data of all kinds. On the other hand, storage and retrieval of digital data inevitably require complex processing and computing hardware, so that the feasibility of long-term preservation depends on reducing the complexity of the layers that stand between the underlying data carriers and the users of the data. The future usefulness of resources depends on careful documentation of data at all levels, from the methods by which characters and files are stored, to rich descriptions of the resources and their contexts that enable their content to be identified, retrieved and understood.

In an emerging field such as documentation of endangered languages, archives can draw on digital technologies and standards developed over the last forty years, but they still have to provide discipline-specific facilities to meet the needs of their users. Maturing web technologies and new understandings of the role of digital archives in preservation and dissemination are recasting archives as amplifiers of the value of language documentation by linking documenters, their documentation materials, and the diverse users of these materials, now and into the future.

Appendix: Select list of archives for endangered languages that host digital materials

Aboriginal Studies Electronic Data Archive, Australian Institute of Aboriginal and Torres Strait Islander Studies
  www1.aiatsis.gov.au/ASEDA
Alaskan Native Language Center Archives (ANLC) University of Alaska
  www.alaska.edu/uaf/anlc
Archive of the Indigenous Languages of Latin America (AILLA), University of Texas
  www.ailla.utexas.org/site/welcome.html
Digital Endangered Languages and Musics Archives Network (DELAMAN)
  www.delaman.org
Dokumentation Bedrohter Sprachen Archive (DoBeS), Max Planck Institute Nijmegen
  www.mpi.nl/DOBES
Endangered Languages Archive (ELAR), School of Oriental and African Studies
  www.hrelp.org
Langues et Civilisation et Traditions Orales (LACITO), Centre National de la Recherche Scientifique
  lacito.vjf.cnrs.fr/archivage/index.htm
Leipzig Endangered Languages Archive (LELA), Max Planck Institute Leipzig
  www.eva.mpg.de/lingua/resources/lela.php
Northeastern North American Indigenous Languages Archive, University of Buffalo
  nnaila.org
Pacific and Regional Archive for Digital Sources in Endangered Cultures (Paradisec), University of Melbourne and University of Sydney
  paradisec.org.au
Rosetta Project, Long Now Foundation
  www.rosettaproject.org

Notes

1 By Dietrich Schüller of the Vienna Phonogrammarchiv.
2 Although see Woodbury, Chapter 9, on the (hard-copy) publishing of texts time-aligned to cassette timestamps in the Boasian tradition.
3 Electronic signals as varying levels of energy, not as digital data.
4 A bit is a binary digit, i.e. 0 or 1. A group of eight bits is called a byte.
5 A variant of WAV that contains preservation-oriented and other metadata embedded within the file is called BWF (Broadcast WAV format).
6 Strictly speaking, digitization involves initial sampling of an audio-signal which could be regarded as a kind of compression; however, providing the sampling rate and accuracy are high enough, the full range of acoustic information that humans can hear is retained.
7 For example, 96 kHz, 24 bit. See IASA TC-03 (2005), page 6.
8 In any case, conversions between resolutions are relatively straight-forward.
9 Elsewhere I have called this 'archivism' (Nathan 2006a; see also Dobrin *et al.* 2009).
10 Of course this also imposes costs. Additional work is required to integrate eclectic sets of metadata into a catalogue.
11 This is more precisely known as 'Moore's Law', which predicts that the number of transistor (basic processor) units that can be physically fitted together into a computer's Central Processing Unit (CPU) doubles every two years.
12 See also the discussion about video below.
13 In the medium term, we cannot anticipate the fortunes of the organizations or companies that produce, maintain and/or sell software; in the longer term (hundreds of years and beyond) the likelihood of today's software remaining usable is close to zero.
14 There are two positives, however: video-editing and production is more likely to be appropriate in the context of the original project, or language community; and this situation provides a good incentive for the development of small-scale local or personal digital archives.
15 www.repositoryaudit.eu
16 www.ninch.org/programs/practice
17 www.datasealofapproval.org
18 www.dcc.ac.uk

Part III

Responses

14

Language policy for endangered languages

Julia Sallabank

14.1 Introduction

Language policy and planning were originally associated with language and literacy policy in post-colonial states, in particular the choice and standardization of a national language (e.g. Fishman 1974, Rubin and Jernudd 1971, Tauli 1968). Such policies became increasingly criticized for treating multilingualism as a problem: promoting national languages as tools of nation-building and unification, while ignoring, and even discouraging, linguistic diversity and minority languages (e.g. Mühlhäusler 2000, Tollefson 1991, Williams 1992, 1996). Since the 1990s there has been a growth in interest in language policies which view linguistic diversity as a 'good thing' (Wright 2004: 219) and aim to support minority and endangered languages (e.g. Annamalai 2003, Canagarajah 2005, Paulston 1994, Ramanathan 2005, Romaine 2002b).

14.2 Language policy, planning and management

There is considerable overlap in definitions of LANGUAGE POLICY and LANGUAGE PLANNING, and the two terms are often conflated (Hornberger 2006, Schiffman 1996). There is also a considerable lack of clarity in the literature in distinguishing policy from practice, and studies frequently go into considerable detail about particular practices when discussing policy (e.g. Coluzzi 2005, Edwards 1984, Ferrer 2004, Heinrich 2004). There is a lack of straightforward causal connections: outcomes depend on context, and the existence of a policy does not necessarily mean that it will be implemented effectively (Schiffman 1996, Spolsky 2004). There is also a lack of well-defined models for analysing and comparing different policy approaches, or ways to evaluate outcomes that can be applied across different settings (Ricento 2006: 18).

Table 14.1. *Definitions of language policy and planning*

	Scope	Direction
Policy	positions, principles, decisions, strategy	top-down, official policy towards languages
Planning	concrete measures, practices	bottom-up, grassroots measures to support languages

For the purposes of this chapter, language policy and language planning will be distinguished in terms of scope and direction, as shown in Table 14.1. Scope refers to the degree of strategy or practicality involved, while Direction refers to who is involved in the decision-making process.

Spolsky (2009a and Chapter 8) prefers the term language management (following Nekvapil 2006), because of the connotations of the term language planning described in the first paragraph above. However, 'management' itself has connotations in that it could imply a static approach to managing the status quo, whereas 'planning' has more forward-thinking, strategic connotations. In this chapter I therefore prefer to use the more traditional (yet forward-looking) term.

Policy typically indicates official, top-down decision-making processes, while planning is usually used with reference to grassroots efforts on behalf of languages.[1] However, as will be seen in this chapter, these distinctions are not hard and fast; for example, discussion of language planning includes 'bottom-up' versus 'top-down' planning, while Spolsky (2004) points out that language policies can be formulated and implemented at any level, from intergovernmental to families and individuals. There is rarely explicit policy formulation at family level (Spolsky 2004: 43), yet this sphere is crucial for language survival.

14.2.1 Frameworks of language planning

Language planning is better defined than policy, and has a more widely accepted framework. As noted by Kaplan and Baldauf (1997: 28, 2003), researchers differentiate two main kinds of language-planning activities: attempts to modify a language itself, and attempts to modify the environment in which a language is used. These were originally designated corpus planning and status planning by Kloss and Verdoodt (1969). The original definition of status planning has since been divided into three separate areas (Kaplan and Baldauf 1997, 2003), although it is acknowledged that in practice none of the categories can be implemented without overlap (e.g. Fishman 2006, Spolsky 2004).

14.2.1.1 Corpus planning

Corpus planning is the only category directly concerned with the language itself. It includes documentation (see Woodbury, Chapter 9), codification, graphization, standardization, modernization and orthography development (see Lüpke, Chapter 16), and the production of dictionaries (see Mosel, Chapter 17), grammars and language-learning materials (see Holton, Chapter 19), which are a prerequisite for LANGUAGE-IN-EDUCATION PLANNING (see below).

Corpus planning aims to address issues which are common among endangered languages (see Hornberger and López 1998: 234):

- they are frequently viewed as inferior and inelegant, and therefore incapable of expressing higher level thoughts;
- they lack a standardized orthography or grammar;
- they show lexical poverty with respect to technology and abstractions;
- a lack of teachers trained to teach the language;
- fragmentation into regional varieties with no unifying standard.

As noted by Grenoble and Whaley (2006: 116), 'people have been conditioned to think that only a language of wider communication is "worthy" of a written form, that it suffices for all purposes, and that the local language does not merit writing.' What is more, an unwritten language may not be considered a 'proper' language, so recognition may be withheld by governments and education authorities. The lack of an accepted standard orthography also makes it more difficult for a linguist to conduct documentation and analyse any written texts which might exist, as these are likely to display a wide variety of spellings.

Corpus planning may involve bitter disputes regarding choice of standard, writing system(s) and spelling. If speakers wish to expand the use of a language to new domains (such as education or technology), new vocabulary will undoubtedly be required, which may arouse further controversy: how will new terms be decided, and by whom? Should they be influenced by the majority language, or emphasize differences?

Corpus planning is not universally seen as a 'good thing'. Mühlhäusler (1990) claims that 'reduction to writing' is not always beneficial for an endangered language, especially one without a tradition of literacy, and challenges the view that revitalization must involve standardization, modernization and expanding domains of use. Standardization may promote one regional variety over others and thus entail loss of dialectal diversity; while promoting literacy may result in the loss of oracy and oral traditions (Grenoble and Whaley 2006: 119). Nevertheless, language ecologies are not static, and an endangered language which remains an unwritten oral vernacular will not survive if it is not being transmitted in the family (see Lüpke, Chapter 16 for more on orthography development).

Where minority languages have been standardized, it is not unusual for divergence to develop between younger speakers who have learnt a 'unified' version through education, and older native speakers of 'authentic' varieties (Bercero 2003, Grenoble and Whaley 2006). This divergence can pull in opposite directions in different contexts: in some, the school version converges towards the dominant language, especially if the children are non-native speakers of the endangered language, as in Occitan (Paulston 1987) or Basque (Urtéaga 2005); while in others, the school version is 'purified' of contact features and loan words which have become common in the usage of native speakers, as with Unified Quichua in Lagunas, Ecuador (Hornberger and King 1996).

Even if such issues can be resolved, there may well be little to read in a minority language. Lösch (2000: 56) notes that strong motivation is needed to write in a language where the circle of recipients is limited, and all literacy functions are covered by another language. The market for publications is typically small, and may require subsidization to be viable.

14.2.1.2   Status planning

Status planning refers to attempts to secure official/political recognition for a language (Wright 2004: 1). It also includes expansion of the domains in which a language is used (e.g. legal and governmental fields and new media; see Moriarty, Chapter 22), and, crucially, obtaining funding for other types of language planning. The status of a linguistic variety in terms of whether it is categorized as a 'language' or as a 'dialect' may also be an issue.

Only 4 per cent of the world's languages are official languages in the states in which they are used, and opinions are divided as to the value of official recognition for language revitalization. Spolsky (2004: 198 and p.c.), commenting on Māori revitalization (see also Moriarty, Chapter 22), sees eventual government recognition and support as essential for language survival; it undoubtedly provides more resources than private groups and individuals have at their disposal. Dorian (1987: 63–4) and Bourdieu (1991) suggest that an official reversal of attitudes can cause a shift in the 'linguistic market' and revaluation of a previously low-status language, a view which is supported by an empirical study in Ireland by Ó Riagáin (2004). Keskitalo (1981) argues that lack of official recognition can lead to resignation and passivity on the part of speakers, both in daily life and in the political field, and thus to language shift.

However, recognition of a minority language in public services is often symbolic rather than functional. Mougeon and Beniak (1989: 293) note that by the time it is thought to offer bureaucratic services (e.g. legal interpreting, health information) in minority languages, they are usually superfluous because most speakers have become bilingual. At the same time, there is a tendency for language revitalization movements to focus on areas such as official support and education, rather than on promoting speaking the language in the home; this will be discussed further below.

The distinction between a LANGUAGE and a DIALECT is slippery and ideological in nature, and can be addressed in both linguistic and socio-linguistic terms. Linguistically, it can be said that dialects are mutually comprehensible varieties of languages, while languages are mutually incomprehensible. But this neat distinction does not take into account dialect continua in border areas, nor paradoxical situations such as the mutual incomprehensibility of Chinese 'dialects', contrasted with dif-fering names for very similar language varieties in neighbouring states (e.g. Sesotho, Setswana and Sepedi in southern Africa (Batibo 2005: 2); Moldovan and Romanian in Europe).

Some of these paradoxes can be explained by political factors. Languages are commonly symbols of ethnic and national identity, while majority groups and centralizing governments may denigrate a minority variety by denying it the status of a language (and thus constitutional rights and privileges) and denoting it a 'mere' dialect (Grillo 1989, Trudgill 1992). The lack of linguistic status for a variety 'is certainly a significant factor in its decline, in so far as it made [speakers] less committed to the survival of the vernacular, and influenced the attitude of their children' (Spence 1993: 4). Thiers (1986) notes that linguists tend to take little account of popular opinions in assessing interlingual distance, although they are a determining factor in public debate.

More and more linguists are challenging the distinction between lan-guage and dialect and whether boundaries between languages can be established at all, especially those influenced by postmodernism such as Irvine and Gal (2000), Ricento (2006), Pennycook (2006), Mar-Molinero and Stevenson (2006), Makoni and Pennycook (2006). However, as noted by May (2004), Patrick (2004) and Brumfit (2006), distinguishing oneself by linguistic differentiation continues to be important for the identity construction of groups and individuals; for speakers of minoritized var-ieties linguistic status is a very relevant issue.

14.2.1.3 Language-in-education planning

Also known as ACQUISITION PLANNING, this refers to deliberate attempts to increase the number of speakers of a language. As Grenoble and Whaley (2006: 10) note: 'a crucial domain for language usage is edu-cation ... When mandatory schooling occurs exclusively in a national language, the use of local languages almost inevitably declines.' Many endangered-language researchers document how children who spoke minority languages have been stigmatized at school, often with a tan-gible symbol of shame such as a wooden shoe: e.g. Breton and Occitan in France (e.g. McDonald 1989, Paulston 1987), Gikuyu in Kenya (Skutnabb-Kangas *et al.* 1995: 21). Many of my own consultants in Guernsey stated that a major reason for stopping speaking Guernesiais in the home was that it was not approved of in school. Gaining acceptance in schools therefore plays a key symbolic role in many revitalization movements' aims, as it increases status, prestige and perceived utility.

Language-education policy is generally aimed at school-age children, but can involve any age group, from birth (and even before) to great-grandparents. An innovative programme in Wales and Scotland teaches childcare classes through Welsh and Gaelic to parents-to-be (Edwards and Newcombe 2005a), while the master–apprentice schemes described by Hinton (Chapter 15) assist older speakers to retain their fluency while passing on their languages to younger learners.

Language-in-education planning covers a wide range of provision, from very small amounts of extra-curricular teaching to bilingual, immersion and minority-language-medium education such as in Hawai'i and autonomous areas of Spain or Mexico (Artigal 1993, Baker 1999, Francis and Reyhner 2002, Kapono 1995). Grenoble and Whaley (2006) maintain that including the minority language as a secondary subject is not an adequate response to language endangerment, citing the statement by the UNESCO working group (2003b): 'education in the language is *essential* for language vitality' (emphasis in original). Researchers and activists agree that the most effective pattern of education for the maintenance of endangered languages and cultures is to have schools run through the medium of the language, with the curriculum decided by the community; however, it is rare for this ideal to be implemented in full (Hornberger 2008).

Nevertheless, there is debate worldwide about the role of schools in language revitalization (Benham and Cooper 2000, Dorian 1978, Edwards and Newcombe 2005b, Fishman 1996, Hornberger 2008, Jaffe 2008, Mahapatra 1989, McCarty 2002, Romaine 2006a). Although the received wisdom, and prevalent rhetoric, in revitalization movements is that of Fishman (1991): that promoting the speaking of a language in the home is the most effective way of saving it, most revitalization movements at some point focus on schools. However, in contexts such as Wales and New Zealand where a whole generation has now been educated through the medium of the indigenous language, it is by no means certain that children who only learn a language at school will speak it outside, and even less certain that they will raise children speaking it (Edwards and Newcombe 2005b). One reason for this is that the kind of language learnt at school is not necessarily the kind used in childcare: the traditional allocation of domains of language use has become almost reversed (Romaine 2006a). Nevertheless, Cooper (1989: 13) notes that in Israel (which in many ways is an exceptional case) 'what led to the use of Hebrew at home was its prior promotion as the language of instruction at school'. Education policy and curricula for endangered languages are discussed further by Coronel-Molina and McCarty (Chapter 18).

14.2.1.4 Prestige planning

The term PRESTIGE PLANNING was introduced by Haarmann (1984, 1990) to differentiate activities aimed at promoting a positive view of a language from those concerned with political status or functions: 'not only the content of planning activities is important but also the acceptance or rejection of planning efforts' (Haarmann 1990: 105). Prestige planning is thus crucial for the success of language revitalization measures (Dorian 1987: 63–4, Trudgill 1992). Prestige planning relates to language attitudes, which are discussed in 14.3 below.

Williamson (1991), Dauenhauer and Dauenhauer (1998) and Fennell (1981) warn that official support cannot save a language without community commitment. Cooper (1989: 161) contrasts the relative success of language planning for the revitalization of Māori and Irish, commenting that in New Zealand: 'the initiative for the revitalization program has come from the Maoris [sic.] themselves', whereas in Ireland: 'the government promoters of maintenance made no serious attempt to promote the enthusiasm of people of the Gaeltacht themselves. The initiative came from outside.'

Ager (2005) introduced a new distinction between prestige planning and IMAGE PLANNING, i.e. increasing confidence in and goodwill towards a language. Image planning thus covers many of the areas formerly subsumed under prestige planning.

14.2.2 Language policy

The field of language policy does not seem to have broadly accepted frameworks such as those described for language planning, and as mentioned, there is considerable overlap between 'policy', 'planning', 'management' and implementation. Schiffman (1996: 2–3) observes that language policy can itself be both cause and product. For example, multilingualism is a feature of many language-contact situations, and policy can seek either to reap the maximum benefits or to promote the use of particular language(s) over others.

Nation states may adopt enlightened language policies which promote the interests of minority languages (Baetens Beardsmore 1993–1994, Sallabank 2006), although these often come rather late, as with the UK's recognition of Cornish, 200 years after the death of the last monolingual speaker (BBC 2002, Duffy 2002). Thiers (1986) observes wryly that official recognition and status for Corsican have come just as the language is being used less and less; a cynic might argue that 'too late' is the most convenient time for a nation state to recognize linguistic minorities.

Supranational bodies such as UNESCO and the European Union now place overt value on linguistic diversity. The European Bureau for Lesser-used Languages disseminates information about EU policies and funding programmes, while the Council of Europe, a human rights organization, originated the European Charter for Regional or Minority Languages[2] and monitors the measures that signatories have taken to fulfil their commitments (see Grinevald and Bert, Chapter 3).

In many countries and localities, however, there is no overt official language policy. In such cases policy may be covert or naive (Shohamy 2006); however, as Wright (2004: 187) comments, '*Laissez-faire* policies mean that the languages of power and prestige will eventually take over in all situations of contact. Benign neglect … [is] always *de facto* support for the language of the group that is already dominant.'

Ruíz (1984) identified three 'orientations' towards language policy:

1. 'language as a problem': in this view, multilingualism can lead to lack of social cohesion and ethnic conflict. Minority languages are associated with poverty and disadvantage.
2. 'language as a right': to participate fully in society through one's own language, which may require the provision of educational resources, interpreters etc. As this may entail expense and confrontation, it can also be seen as a problem-oriented approach.
3. 'language as a resource': multilingualism increases the skills of society as a whole, enhances the status of subordinate groups, promotes local economies and cultures, encourages awareness of other points of view and mutual respect rather than dominance. Minority-language communities are seen as sources of expertise.

Spolsky (2004) notes that language policy is often an attempt to control the language usage of others, as noted also by Grillo (1989), Joseph (1987) and Milroy and Milroy (1999): an example of a 'language as problem' approach.

Language policy is not necessarily concerned with the whole of a language, but often with aspects such as pronunciation, dialect versus standard (or which dialect should be the standard), or eradicating 'poor' usage (see also Cameron 1995, Wee 2005).

14.2.3 Top-down and bottom-up

As noted by Ager (2005), top-down planners tend to focus on status and corpus planning, whereas bottom-up campaigners focus on image and prestige. Fishman (1991) stressed PRIOR IDEOLOGICAL CLARIFICATION, i.e. basic principles such as what exactly activists are trying to preserve, and why it is desirable. Ten years later, Fishman (2001a: 541) admitted that it is quite common for enthusiasts to embark on language planning and revitalization activities without such clarification, and without convincing arguments with which to counter critics. For example, a large proportion of the case studies in Bradley and Bradley (2002) demonstrate this. Prior to the appointment of a language officer in 2008, all language-planning efforts in Guernsey were bottom-up, by groups and individuals with little knowledge of linguistics, sociolinguistics or language planning theory, and virtually no support from official bodies (Sallabank 2005).

Baldauf (1993–1994) suggests that there is a need to take more account of 'unplanned' language planning in policy-making, for the reasons discussed in 14.2.1.4. Kaplan and Baldauf (1997) suggest a 'macro – meso – micro' framework, noting that traditionally most language planning has taken place at the macro (governmental) and the meso (regional implementation) levels. Baldauf (2004) elaborates the 'micro' level by providing examples such as language planning by businesses, individuals' discourse practices and families' deliberate attempts to maintain a HERITAGE LANGUAGE. Amery (2001) uses this term to describe efforts to revive Kaurna, the language of the Adelaide Plains in Australia, which had probably not been used on a daily basis for 130 years. Using descriptive evidence, efforts are now being made to piece the language together and to develop a written and spoken language that addresses contemporary needs. Micro-language planning in this context involves individual learners and users of the language, small groups and very small organizations. Amery concludes that language planning has as much to offer in these situations as it does for major world languages.

14.3 Language attitudes, beliefs and ideologies in language policy

Individuals' everyday language choices tend to be based on perceptions and received attitudes rather than on rational input and decision-making. Examples of such perceptions may be that a certain linguistic variety is 'only' a dialect rather than a 'proper' language; that languages need to be written to be considered 'full' languages; that people who speak a particular language are uneducated, illiterate, inferior. Such beliefs and ideologies are absorbed through upbringing and social stereotypes and held subconsciously, and may therefore influence behaviour more profoundly than overtly expressed opinions. Politicians and policy-makers are not immune to such influences, and may even exploit them through 'populist' policies. The study of language attitudes and ideologies is therefore relevant to policy-making (see Spolsky, Chapter 8).

Baker (1992) points out that language planning and revival movements depend on the assumption that attitudes can (or should) change. Garrett *et al.* (2003) also note that common sense and advertising commonly assume that attitudes can be influenced, and in turn alter behaviour.

Dorian (1993) observes that the youngest members of some endangered language groups have begun to berate their elders for choosing not to transmit the ancestral language and allowing it to die. Crystal (2000: 106) concurs that 'this kind of reaction [regret at not knowing the language] is common among the members of a community two generations after the one which failed to pass its language on'. Skeet (2000) notes that research into language attitudes tends to focus on language decline, with relatively little research into the attitudes and motivation of people involved in revitalization efforts. Dorian (1993) warns that research which only reports on the abandonment phase of a language, and which concentrates on negative attitudes, can obscure a longer term dynamic by overlooking revitalization efforts by later generations.

Language policy for endangered languages thus needs to take into account traditional ideologies, but also the possibility (and often necessity) of changing attitudes. This underlines the importance of prestige planning. But given that they are usually by definition a minority, the attitudes of endangered-language speakers do not necessarily carry weight with decision-makers. For language maintenance and revitalization measures to gain the support of gate-keeping and funding authorities, they need to be accepted by the majority community. Prestige planning, or public relations efforts to raise awareness and interest in endangered languages, therefore need to focus on majority populations too.

14.3.1   Factors in language attitudes and maintenance

Williamson (1991: 78–9) identifies four main factors in attitudes towards minority languages: age, social class, gender and rural versus urban. However, researchers have found widely varying responses in different contexts.

Economic necessity is often cited as a reason for abandoning a minority language: speakers are instrumentally motivated to learn a language with wider currency in order to increase their economic and social mobility (see Harbert, Chapter 20). Pierre Bourdieu, French sociologist and anthropologist, posited an analogy between unequal sociolinguistic relationships and economic relationships, which he termed the 'linguistic market' (Bourdieu 1977a, 1990, 1991). In this metaphorical model, ECONOMIC CAPITAL is associated with material wealth, while CULTURAL CAPITAL includes language. Where cultural and economic values come into conflict, it is generally economic ones which win out. Endangered languages are often described as 'useless' (e.g. Gal 1989: 317, Williamson 1991: 114). Lindgren (1984) notes that even a minority language which has high prestige as a LINGUA SACRA cannot usually compete with the even higher prestige of a language associated with modernism.

Gender issues are highly relevant to language vitality. Intergenerational transmission is carried out in the home, and usually falls to mothers. The language use and attitudes of women are thus crucial for language maintenance, yet are rarely taken into account by policy-makers (or, in many cases, researchers).

In sociolinguistic studies, women are generally seen as more likely to use higher status language varieties (or to aspire to use them) (Coates 1998, Philips *et al.* 1987). Lindgren (1984) suggests that women, either consciously or unconsciously, associate a more 'backward' language with their own lower status in traditional society, and associate the majority language with modernity and thus more liberal attitudes towards women's status. Men often favour a minority language for its 'macho' connotations and traditional, even anti-social, activities undertaken in it (e.g. in the case studied by Lindgren, reindeer theft). Williamson (1991: 79) notes that in Brittany: 'cultural changes were motivated in addition by a desire to change social status. Women, who were affected strongly by the drudgery of farm work, were the first to seek escape from a Breton identity' (see also Gal 1978). Williamson also notes that children often refuse to answer parents in the minority language, which forces women, as the main caregivers, to speak the majority language.

In many places there has been a shift in attitudes towards regional traditional languages in the last twenty years, and Pooley (2003) wonders whether, as attitudes become more positive, the traditional gender bias may begin to change. My own research in Guernsey has found women just as involved in language activism as men, possibly as a reflection of a change in women's status as well as linguistic attitudes. The status of women does seem to make a difference: Aikio (1992: 496) found that in contrast to many traditional societies, the status of women in Reindeer Sámi society was high, which led Sámi women to reject the majority language.

Emigration for economic advancement often leads to language shift (as Harbert, Chapter 20 points out); this also has a gender element, as it is men who are most likely to emigrate and to be socially mobile. Urbanization is also a common factor in language shift in Africa (Lüpke, p.c.). In the Tashelhit ('Berber') communities in south-western Morocco studied by Hoffman (2003), the majority of men emigrate to find work in cities, where they speak Arabic, while women remain in their villages to work the land and raise families; the traditional language is strongly linked to the rural locality. Hoffman concludes that language maintenance in this context depends on the continued seclusion and economic disadvantage of rural women.

Eckert (1980: 1055) notes that: 'the promise of socioeconomic mobility has led masses of labouring people to abandon their vernacular language'. Language maintenance policies thus need to address economic and gender disadvantages, and find ways of helping minority groups to develop economically while maintaining their communities. This is, of course, not easy: Grin (1989: 153) suggests that even pouring money into minority-language areas will yield disappointing results unless there is a firm commitment to improving the status of the language (see also Harbert, Chapter 20). However, Dorian (1987: 64) stresses that language revitalization efforts, especially if they have official support, invariably have beneficial effects on the community, both economic and in terms of its self-confidence.

14.4 Language and human rights

Language policy is intimately bound up with 'the right to speak one's own language' (Wright 2007). Ricento (2006) singles out linguistic human rights as a major contribution to the understanding of language policy, with the effects of power on language practices a key factor.

Of course language policy cannot exist in a vacuum, and very often languages are endangered because their speakers are marginalized. Language rights (or the lack thereof) are therefore linked to political and other human rights. A large number of studies testify to the wrongs done to linguistic minorities, often in the name of national unity (e.g. Argenter and McKenna Brown 2004, Benham and Cooper 1998, Benson *et al.* 1998, Berthet 1982, Hornberger 1987, Karetu 1994, Kontra *et al.* 1999, Phillipson and Skutnabb-Kangas 1995b, Skutnabb-Kangas 2000, Skutnabb-Kangas *et al.* 1995, Zwilling 2004).

According to Skutnabb-Kangas *et al.* (1994: 2), observing linguistic human rights implies at an *individual* level that everyone has the right to:

- identify positively with their mother tongue, and have that identification respected by others, whether minority or majority language;
- learn the mother tongue;
- use it in official contexts.

At a *collective* level it implies:

- the right of minority groups to exist (i.e. the right to be 'different');
- the right to develop and enjoy their language;
- the right for minorities to establish and maintain schools and other educational institutions, with control of curricula;
- autonomy in administrative matters internal to the group.

Although it is easy to deplore abuses, establishing a clear definition of linguistic human rights is not simple, let alone implementing them. Grin (1994: 38) suggests that: 'treating on a equal footing languages in unequal positions is tantamount to giving the stronger language an edge to increase its influence and spread ... minority language survival requires an asymmetric policy that will help reduce the power of the larger language group – or groups.'

The rhetoric of language rights has also been challenged, on the grounds that it may further exoticization of indigenous groups and 'localist' interpretations of language and ethnicity, essentialism and linguistic purism (Errington 2003, Freeland and Patrick 2004, Wright 2007). May (2003: 111) argues that: 'it is a *reductio ad absurdum* to argue ... that the presence of internal differences within minority groups over the question of minority language(s), or even active dissent, somehow negates the legitimacy of minority-language claims.' He also notes that educational and linguistic research over the last forty years which demonstrates unequivocally that bilingualism is a cognitive advantage rather than a deficit has been 'conveniently overlooked' (2003: 117).

14.5 Conclusions

14.5.1 Language policy and revitalization

Two main strands can be identified in language policy with regard to endangered language revitalization: I term these DOMAIN EXPANSION and the PHATIC ROUTE. Domain expansion is the prevalent model in Westernized countries such as Europe and North America. It usually relies heavily on schooling for language transmission, and necessarily involves standardization and modernization. However, as mentioned earlier, it rarely results in the reestablishment of intergenerational transmission in the family (Edwards and Newcombe 2005b, Romaine 2006a).

The phatic route involves promoting the use of the endangered language in the home and encouraging users to identify with it as their primary medium of socialization, and hence fostering a link between language and identity. This might be equated with traditional DIGLOSSIA, that is, the use of two codes in distinct and separate domains and functions, one set 'high' and the other 'low' (see also O'Shannessy, Chapter 5), but tries to avoid the stigma and lack of social mobility traditionally associated with diglossia.[3]

In several cases, language revitalization movements start at grassroots level, then eventually attain official recognition and funding (e.g. Hawai'i, Isle of Man). Although, as mentioned earlier, this provides more resources than voluntary efforts, there is the danger that communities will come to rely on state intervention and scale down or cease their own, bottom-up activities. For example, in the Isle of Man parents who decided to bring up their children through Manx successfully lobbied for state-funded Manx-medium educational provision; but although the school has grown, fewer families are now using Manx in the home. Language communities and activists may find it easier to focus on a campaign to get their language introduced into the school curriculum than on changing their own and their neighbours' behaviour (Dauenhauer and Dauenhauer 1998, King 2001).

14.5.2 The role of a linguist in language policy

It is increasingly recognized that researchers cannot remain detached and 'objective' (Cameron *et al.* 1993b, Grinevald 2003, Dobrin and Berson,

Chapter 10). The very act of visiting a language community to conduct linguistic research signifies external (academic, high-status) interest in the language, which can raise awareness among the community and increase the prestige of the language. A researcher with access to literature on measures undertaken in other contexts can provide valuable information and contacts to speaker groups, who may well not know about other endangered language communities in similar circumstances, and may feel isolated and powerless. Linguists who had not considered such matters before may be called on to advise on language policy, or to mediate between local groups and governments.

Not all linguists agree that we should concern ourselves with anything other than pure linguistic research. Newman (2003) stresses that the urgency of recording dying languages should have primacy above all other concerns: 'we are linguists not social workers'. But when a language has few speakers, their fluency is likely to deteriorate due to lack of practice. Judicious application of language policies, e.g. revitalization measures such as master–apprentice programmes (see Hinton, Chapter 15, and Coronel-Molina and McCarty, Chapter 18), can extend the time available for documentation by enabling a speaker base to be maintained for longer.

Kymlicka and Patten (2003: 32) comment that doing nothing about language endangerment in effect ensures the disappearance of languages. I would argue that the same is true for linguists: to remain 'neutral' in a situation of language endangerment is tantamount to condoning language loss. The need for linguists to engage with language policy is an essential element of social responsibility in research.

Notes

1 Although Fettes (1997) uses the terms in the opposite way.
2 conventions.coe.int/treaty/en/Treaties/Html/148.htm (2 September, 2006).
3 For discussion of this issue see the Special Issue of the *International Journal of the Sociology of Language* on Diglossia, 2002: vol. 157.

15

Revitalization of endangered languages

Leanne Hinton

15.1   Introduction

The terms LANGUAGE REVITALIZATION, LANGUAGE REVIVAL and LANGUAGE RECLAMATION, among others, are all applied to the phenomenon of attempting to bring endangered languages back to some level of use within their communities (and elsewhere) after a period of reduction in usage. By comparison, the term LANGUAGE MAINTENANCE is used to refer to efforts to support or strengthen a language which is still vital, i.e. which is still acquiring young speakers, but where incipient decline is starting to be apparent.

There are also rival terms for languages with no speakers. The common terms long used in academic scholarship have been 'extinct', or 'dead'. However, the descendants of the speakers of these languages can and do still make efforts toward language revitalization, so long as there has been at least some documentation of them. Terms with such depressing finality as 'extinct' or 'dead' are argued against by language activists working to bring their languages into use again: in the context of revitalization, languages with no speakers are often referred to as SLEEPING, or DORMANT (Hinton 2001a). The term language revival is sometimes used to refer to efforts to resume language use in communities which have no living native speakers (Dorian 1994, Ó Laoire 1995). Language reclamation carries the connotation that the language was taken away by outside forces, and implies that the agency to bring it back comes from

Many people were very helpful to me in writing this chapter, more even than I will be able to remember here! I would especially like to thank Wes Leonard, Natasha Warner, Janine Pease, Ryan Wilson, Finlay MacLeod, Darrell Kipp, William Wilson, Rebecca Blum-Martinez and Margaret Florey for checking facts in parts of the chapter, and giving me suggestions that have greatly improved both my knowledge and the resulting chapter. Thanks to Susan Penfield for assistance and commiseration as a fellow author, and to my husband Gary Scott, for his constant help and encouragement. Thanks too to our editors, Peter K. Austin and Julia Sallabank, for both their patience and their prodding.

within the community (Leonard 2007). Here language revitalization will be used as a general cover term that can include the connotations of the other terms as well.

The terms COMMUNITY or SPEECH COMMUNITY are used loosely in this chapter, but both terms are also fraught. For one thing, acts of language revitalization are sometimes undertaken by a few individuals on their own, rather than by some centralized organization representing a whole community. A speech community may include one or more languages, and its members usually have in common a set of ideas or beliefs about how communication works and how language(s) should be used. What we think of as a LANGUAGE COMMUNITY usually has a language in common among its members, but for endangered or dormant languages it may be only the remembered knowledge of a language, or a shared understanding that their ancestors once had this language, that binds the group into a speech community. Nor may it be a community in any geographic sense: the group that once shared the language may have no geographic centre or unification, and may be scattered by the forces of history (Warner 2009) (for more on communities, see Dobrin and Berson, Chapter 10, and Grinevald and Bert, Chapter 3).

The primary groups or individuals who show concern in language decline and loss are indigenous people or communities, whose way of life and stewardship of the land are being destroyed, along with their languages, by the forces of nationalism, colonialism, and economic globalization (see Harbert, Chapter 20). However, language revitalization also takes place in languages that are not considered indigenous, such as minority Romance and Germanic languages, Hebrew, and Yiddish. Endangered dialects (Wolfram 2000), endangered sign languages (Nonaka 2004), and endangered pidgins and creoles and mixed languages, such as Michif (Rosen and Souter 2009, see also O'Shannessy, Chapter 5), all have possibilities for undergoing processes of revitalization.

The effort to bring endangered or dormant languages back into use can take many forms and have varying degrees of intensity. It may involve:

- learning a few words such as greetings and introductions or short speeches for formulaic use;
- collecting linguistic publications, fieldnotes and sound recordings as part of the creation of a community-based resource and archive;
- development of a writing system and creation of community-based dictionaries (Mosel, Chapter 17), and pedagogical grammars (what Bowern, Chapter 23, calls 'learner's guides');
- making audio- or video-recordings of the remaining speakers with the goal of documenting and archiving instances of their language use by creating a corpus of materials of various types;
- having language classes, summer schools or language camps (see Section 15.3 below);

- running full immersion schools for children in communities with the resources to support them (see Section 15.2.5 below).

There may also be individual efforts to learn the endangered language, where a dedicated person may study the language on their own, working with a speaker or through study of existing documentation or language lessons. There are also cases where parents and care-givers have decided to employ their endangered heritage language in the home, even without the support of a community programme.

Communities and individuals throughout human history have made efforts to learn their endangered languages when regular transmission in the home has failed. There have been historic events such as the early twentieth-century revitalization of spoken Hebrew in Israel. But the background of the current impetus for language revitalization comes out of the history of human rights conceptualization in the twentieth century, growing especially strong in Europe after World War II, and finding its stride in the United States in the Civil Rights Movement of the 1960s. Nations and international organizations, most notably the United Nations, focused primarily on defining individual rights. But grassroots movements increasingly demanded group rights: the rights for minority groups to maintain their identity and culture (Casals 2006).

There are two major tasks for language revitalization:

1. to teach the language to those who do not know it;
2. to get both learners and those who already know the language to *use* the language in a broadening set of situations.

Only through the second task can the ultimate goal of achieving intergenerational transmission be reached (if indeed this is the ultimate goal; see Grenoble, Chapter 2 for critical discussion of this concept). Other related issues such as language documentation, literacy and new vocabulary development are tools toward these ends rather than primary goals of language revitalization, and may be viewed by some as unnecessary or even undesirable, depending on a group's language ideology. It is important for goals and means to be discussed by those involved in language revitalization (see Coronel-Molina and McCarty, Chapter 18, for discussion of the evaluation of language programmes). The great challenge has been to find ways for these two tasks to be successfully carried out. With communities at different levels of language loss, different remedies must take place. In his seminal book *Reversing Language Shift* (which gave rise to the acronym RLS), Joshua Fishman (1991: 113) writes that:

the landscape is littered with the relatively lifeless remains of societally marginalized and exhausted RLS movements that have engaged in the wrong front ... without real awareness of what they were doing or the problems that faced them.

Fishman's GRADED INTERGENERATIONAL DISRUPTION SCALE (GIDS, which is discussed in detail by Grenoble, Chapter 2), has great value for both theorists and practitioners of language revitalization. The development of the GIDS scale was informed by Fishman's long experience with languages like Yiddish, Gaelic and Catalan. But for minority indigenous non-literate societies, like many Native American, First Nations, Australian, African or Pacific languages, the GIDS scale is less applicable. Steps 1–3 are actually irrelevant to most minority indigenous languages. Stages 4–5 can and do get used for indigenous languages, but they are not part of the revitalization of traditional ways of using language, and instead are part of modernization (see Moriarty, Chapter 22). And revitalization from documentation when there are no speakers left at all is not even mentioned (though we can extrapolate that this must be stage 9; and of course 10 would be the case where there is not even any documentation of the language, analogous to the Richter earthquake intensity scale level 10 of total destruction).

Furthermore, successful language movements such as those which have been developed for Hawaiian and Māori have not necessarily followed the GIDS steps in order. In both these cases, and many others, revitalization in the school setting (Stages 4, 5) precedes revitalization in the home, for the most part (Stage 6), and may become the main inspiration for language use at home. For example, intergenerational transfer of the language at home is a developing movement now in Hawai'i in large part thanks to the existence of immersion schools (Wilson and Kamanā 2001).[1]

Finally, for minority indigenous communities, people simply do what they can, with the resources available to them. They may only have resources that allow for a summer camp, or the collection of materials on the language, or even just weekly language gatherings where they learn words from the elders. Though limited programmes such as these usually do not directly lead to new fluent speakers, they provide stepping stones and inspiration to people who might be in a position to do more in the future. (See Grenoble and Whaley 2006 for a discussion of models of language revitalization.)

15.2   School-based language revitalization

Since the 1970s at least, schools have been part of language-revitalization efforts. This is a major change from the previous hundred years of educational philosophy, which, under the control of the dominant society, aimed at the eradication of indigenous languages, with schools as the primary tool to do so. Now many of those same schools are being put to work for language revitalization.

School-based programmes include examples of the most successful cases of language revitalization. Contributing to that success is the fact that relatively large groups of potential language learners are obliged to be present in the schools for a large portion of the day, thus providing the opportunity to teach an entire generation of future speakers. Furthermore, at the school, children can be taught their heritage tongue while they are still at the stage of life where language learning takes place most quickly and easily; although as discussed below and by Coronel-Molina and McCarty (Chapter 18), the effectiveness of such programmes depends on the quality and quantity of exposure, levels of motivation, etc.

15.2.1 Language classes

A common form that the teaching of endangered languages takes is classes during the day, usually lasting an hour or so and taking place one to five times per week. These kinds of language classes can be found in schools ranging from preschool to university/college, or in adult evening classes, in locations around the world. There is enormous variation in objectives and methodologies, ranging from the teaching of single words to connected speech, from an orally based approach to a focus on literacy, from a grammar and translation methodology to more functional methods that emphasize conversation. While more intensive programmes show better results in the development of fluent speakers, for many groups this level of classroom teaching is felt to be better than not making any effort at all, given the lack of human and financial resources, and resistance from schoolteachers and administrators. Other options are after-school programmes and summer programmes, or approaches not based on formal education. The all-too-common assumption that school-based teaching is the only possible way of revitalizing a language needs to be looked at in the light of Fishman's (1991) advice on PRIOR IDEOLOGICAL CLARIFICATION, the setting of considered and achievable goals and means (see Kroskrity (2009) for a comparison of revitalization efforts in the light of this).

Some endangered languages, especially those in Europe, have had a presence in schools for many years. Celtic languages, for example, are taught widely in the British Isles, with Irish and Scots Gaelic and Welsh being required classes for schoolchildren in the traditional locales; yet these languages are still considered endangered.

In linguistically diverse parts of the world like the Americas, language teaching programmes are generally small and localized. But a very large number of schools now offer some kind of programme for the local languages, and courses can be taken in local colleges that have a sufficient indigenous population. One problem with the teaching of indigenous endangered languages in the school system is that most speakers of endangered languages do not have teaching credentials, and regulations and the law make it difficult for them to be involved in language instruction. In some places, special laws have been passed setting up mechanisms where speakers of endangered languages can be awarded special credentials allowing them to teach in classrooms. In Australia, native speakers may be employed as 'teacher's aides' to assist non-indigenous teachers in the classroom. A lack of teacher training, materials, orthographies and fluent speakers can also affect such programmes.

15.2.2 Bilingual education

BILINGUAL EDUCATION is a model where academic subjects are taught in both a child's native language and in the dominant language of the school system. The educational theory underlying bilingual education is that if children start out learning educational content in their first language at the same time that they are learning the dominant language of education in their community, they will not lag behind, and will be able to transfer their learning to the dominant language when they have mastered it (Baker 2006). Bilingual education is supported by governments in many countries, but governments do not generally see it as a tool for revitalization of the minority language, but rather as an educational support system for children who are learning a majority language. In fact, it is seen as a model for teaching the dominant language and transferring it to children (see Coronel-Molina and McCarty, Chapter 18, for more on this).

However, once the principles and funding of bilingual education became available, indigenous peoples and other minority populations saw it as an opportunity for language survival. Where mainstream and boarding/dormitory schools had punished children for speaking their languages, ridiculed the languages and caused internalized disrespect for their languages among generations of children, bringing the languages back into the school situation allowed languages to regain prestige, and younger generations to redevelop positive attitudes toward them. It also provided opportunities for development of new vocabulary, writing systems and reading materials, and new written genres. Even in communities where children still learned their language at home, parents could see that some realms of vocabulary were eroding and being replaced by borrowings from the dominant language; schooling then provided the opportunity for teaching children the missing material. However, not all elders welcome the language change and standardization that such developments bring (see also Moriarty, Chapter 22).

15.2.3 The Hualapai bilingual education programme

During the heyday of bilingual education in the United States, one of the model programmes was the Hualapai bilingual education programme, led by pioneering educator Lucille Watahomigie, one of the first people in the Hualapai tribe to be certified to teach (Watahomigie and McCarty 1994). At the time the bilingual education programme began, about half the children in the public school on the Hualapai reservation had Hualapai as their first language, and the rest were dominant in English. Watahomigie saw bilingual education as a way to help children do better in school, because it would help them see school as relevant to their lives. Furthermore, she hoped that it would help stop the erosion of the language (Stiles 1997).

As with many Native American languages, the Hualapai language did not have a writing system. The first several years of the programme saw intensive activity around literacy: developing the writing system and creating reading materials, learning materials, and reference books. Most of the reading materials were about daily Hualapai life, Hualapai history and culture, and the natural history of Hualapai land. Watahomigie knew that when the children went to high school (80 kilometres away in Kingman, Arizona), they tended to view themselves as a disadvantaged minority. She wanted them instead to go with pride in what they had that others lacked, namely important knowledge, values and language that only Hualapais know (Watahomigie, p.c.). This was one of the goals that shaped the Hualapai bilingual programme. Among the rewards were increased commitment and performance from students, staff and parents.

15.2.4 Problems for bilingual education

Almost from the inception of bilingual education in the United States, there has been political backlash by politicians concerned about its cost and by majority communities (Crawford 1992, McGroarty 1992). Funding of programmes was never certain, and training and other systems of support were never developed sufficiently.

But beyond the politics, it also became apparent over the years that even the best bilingual schools were failing to turn around language loss in most communities. Language shift in the home meant that fewer and fewer children were coming to school with speaking ability in their heritage language, and the bilingual education model was not sufficient to counter that. It became clear that the focus could no longer be on language maintenance, but must be on language revitalization. Many of the strong indigenous bilingual education programmes in the United States have gone on to an immersion model, which has been successful in bringing fluency in endangered languages to children who did not learn them at home.

15.2.5 Immersion schools and language nests

An IMMERSION SCHOOL for an endangered language, also called a LAN-GUAGE SURVIVAL SCHOOL, is a school where the language of instruction is the endangered language itself. For endangered languages, immersion schools started to develop in the United States in the 1980s. In its purest form, the dominant language of the society is not used at all in the school except as a FOREIGN LANGUAGE. All other subjects are taught in the endangered language; even playground activities should be structured so that the language will be used there. The classroom books are in the language, as are all written materials on the walls and around the classroom. (In reality, some schools may allow more use of the dominant language than others, by policy or by lack of training and resources.)

Immersion schools can also provide training and exposure to cultural practices, values, indigenous knowledge of the environment, and indigenous philosophy, religion and ceremonies. Traditional singing may be taught; some schools have gardens with indigenous plants that the students learn to husband and to prepare for use. Fieldtrips can be made to locations where the language or culture are in use.

The first immersion schools for endangered languages were actually pre-schools or LANGUAGE NESTS, based on the concept that the grandparent generation, who were the last generation of first-language native speakers, would care for and teach the young children using only the indigenous language. By 1980 the Māoris of New Zealand and the Native Hawaiians in the US state of Hawai'i had shifted almost entirely to the use of English as their daily language. Surveys showed that almost all speakers of Māori were over forty (King 2000) and almost all speakers of Hawaiian were over fifty (Warner 2001). The notion of the language nest (*Te Kōhanga Reo* in Māori and *Pūnana Leo* in Hawaiian) was first developed by the Māori in 1981, and the first Māori language nest officially opened in 1982. The Hawaiians opened their first language nest in 1984. The language nest has proved to be a simple but highly effective means of bringing children to fluency in their ancestral language and giving them early education in indigenous culture and values.

The Language Nest movement has spread around the world: to Polynesia, Australia, Europe, Canada, the mainland US, Latin America and elsewhere. For example, *Nidos de Lengua* have been established in Mexico, especially Oaxaca, beginning in 2008, with at least ten language nests in existence by late 2009, serving the Mixtec, Zapotec and Cuicatec languages (Meyer and Soberanes Bojórquez 2009). In Europe, language nests have been established for a variety of languages from Sámi to Manx.

One issue that immersion schools must address is concerns by community members that children will be educationally disadvantaged when they later enter schools and universities which use the majority language as medium of education. Children may therefore be removed from language nest programmes before their linguistic development is complete, with deleterious effects on both languages (May and Hill 2008). However, over the thirty years of this movement, it has been repeatedly shown that the children coming out of strong immersion models always match or surpass their cohorts from the majority-language programmes, in both classroom performance and standardized testing (Pease Pretty-On-Top n.d.).

Some schools run programmes that combine the immersion and bilingual education models. For example, the Navajo Immersion School in Fort Defiance, Arizona, USA follows a full immersion model for kindergarten and the first two years of schooling, then gradually introduces English as a medium of instruction for subsequent grades till grade 8, when English and Navajo are each used 50 per cent of the time (Christine Sims, p.c., 2009).

While language nests allow the children to acquire their endangered heritage languages at an age early enough to call it one of their first languages, that promising beginning can be quickly lost if the child goes on to a dominant-language-medium school without further input from the endangered language. From the beginning, people in New Zealand and Hawai'i knew that they would have to go further. As the lead groups of students grew older, teachers and their support organizations worked feverishly to develop primary-school and eventually high-school curriculum and materials, so that now a Māori or Hawaiian child may receive all primary and high-school education in their heritage tongue. Even most of a person's university education can take place in the Hawaiian or Māori languages. The movement has expanded downward in age as well as upward. For example, in 2008, at the school Nāwahīokalani'ōpu'u in Hilo, a daycare centre was established where working parents can bring children as young as six weeks of age.

Immersion schools often collide with laws and regulations of the school system. For example, Hawai'i's 1893 law that all education must take place in English was an obstacle that had to be surmounted before Hawaiian immersion education could get off the ground (Warner 2001). Through great effort by the Hawaiian people and sympathetic legislators, that law was changed in the 1980s to allow Hawaiian-medium education, and Hawaiian was made one of the official languages of the state, beside English.

The schools stress Hawaiian culture and values at the same time that they teach content that adheres to national or state standards. This highly successful and still-growing movement has resulted in a new generation of bilingual young people. Schools such as Nāwahīokalani'ōpu'u have also shown that the immersion school students graduate with the capacity to go on to successful university education and careers (Wilson and Kamanā 2001).

15.2.6 Small immersion schools

By necessity, the smaller language groups on the mainland of North America have immersion schools that are smaller in scope. An example of a successful small immersion school is Cuts Wood School, in Browning, Montana (Kipp 2000), with just twenty to twenty-five students enrolled in the school at any one time. Cuts Wood was founded in 1995 by the non-profit Piegan Institute, first as a pre-school, and then going on to elementary and junior high grades under pressure from the parents of the lead group. They started out with a pilot of three groups – English only, English/Blackfoot bilingual, and Blackfoot only. After two years it was clear that Blackfoot only was the most successful model, and the school has settled comfortably into Blackfoot immersion education. Today the school goes from 1st to 8th grade, with several grades combined into each of the classrooms. Like many other immersion schools, the TPR (Total Physical Response) method strongly informs the language teaching at Cuts Wood. TPR combines language use with physical activity, object manipulation, and gesture and mime (Asher 1982). The school also uses Plains Sign Language, an important part of Blackfoot cultural heritage, which brings a strong cultural component to the TPR approach.

While some teachers at Cuts Wood have been native speakers, most have by necessity been second language learners, who learn their language on the job using the master–apprentice method (see below). In 2010 for the first time, all teachers were second-language learners. Over the fifteen years of operation of this school, one constant project for the staff and linguistic consultants has been the development of recordings, books and online materials, so that increasingly rich offerings are available to the students.

After the 8th grade, children go into the English-medium public high school system in Browning. Cuts Wood has produced many children who speak their language well and are proud of it. They also do very well in high school, making the transition with ease. One challenge when children have to enter an English-medium school after an indigenous immersion education is the question of how their indigenous language can continue to be supported. Cuts Wood tries to bring back their graduates as tutors for the immersion school. Tribal ceremonials are also a venue where the children can use their language. As speakers of the Blackfoot language, the alumni also have the opportunity to play important roles in the ceremonies as they mature. Cuts Wood also provides university scholarships for former Cuts Wood students who plan to major in education with the ambition of returning to teach at the school (Hinton 2008a).

Both the bad news and the good news is that soon the number of young Blackfoot speakers coming out of Cuts Wood school will outnumber the native speakers of the older generations. The next challenge is whether this will lead to community and home use (see Moriarty, Chapter 22, for suggestions).

15.3 Community-based learning

Many communities, whether or not they have school-based language programmes, have language and culture camps in the summer time. They
often follow the same language-teaching methodologies found in immersion
schools. While summer programmes alone cannot provide the year-round
input necessary for someone to develop full fluency in a language, they can
still provide intensive input (if designed to do so) all day for weeks or months.
Language camps also have the advantage of being free from school culture
and can provide rich cultural input. As Leonard and Shoemaker (forthcoming) write about the Miami language of Indiana, Ohio and Oklahoma, USA:

> Since the [Miami language and culture] camps began in the early1990s,
> their role has grown and evolved in the two main Miami communities
> to the point where 'camp' has become not only a major annual program
> for youth, but also an underlying philosophy that reconnects multiple
> aspects of community as part of ongoing decolonization efforts.

Another example of a summer camp that has successfully raised awareness of traditional culture and produced improved language proficiency is
the Karaim Summer School in Vilnius, Lithuania (Csató and Nathan 2006)
which uses a drama-based teaching method (Fang and Nathan 2009).

The Cochitis of New Mexico, USA are one group who have put a great
deal of constructive energy into after-school programmes and especially
intensive summer-long language and culture programmes. The decline
of the vitality of the Cochiti language (Keres) began in the post-World
War II era, and accelerated drastically in the late 1960s, when a series of
events related to national and regional politics struck unforeseen serious
blows to the language and culture:

- a new education policy brought the English language and monolingual ideologies to preschool children;
- housing policy changed the social geography of the village; and
- the building of a dam on Cochiti land, which among other things
  accidentally flooded and destroyed almost all of the village's planting
  fields, forcing a shift to English-speaking wage economy.

A 1993 survey found that generally only people over thirty-five years old
were fluent speakers, so the community decided to take action. The community leaders developed mandatory language-learning programmes
for all tribal employees, and also developed language programmes for
the children. Pecos and Blum-Martinez (2001: 79) write:

> Their concern was to develop language-learning activities which were
> embedded in culturally appropriate settings. For this reason, they

focused more on language learning within the community and less on language learning in the public schools. Similarly, they decided that the basis for all language learning would be the traditional ceremonial calendar. Preparing learners to participate in these activities would insure their incorporation into the most significant events of the community. Moreover, learners would have the opportunity to participate in real, meaningful communication. During those times when nothing was occurring within this religious realm, learners could focus on traditional cultural activities such as pottery, cooking, or handicrafts.

As a result of the need to support revitalization of the home-based transmission of the language, the Cochitis focused on reviving traditional community practices where the language had previously flourished, such as visiting and community clean-up projects. Young people were paired with elders to assist them with chores and learn Keres in the process. But most rewarding was the development of a summer programme for children, with a focus on traditional activities. A Keres-only rule was established for the teachers, who receive two-weeks of training in immersion techniques before the camp. The children themselves were allowed to speak in English at first, but by the third week of the first year of the programme, many children were producing much of their speech in Keres. The cultural emphasis of the programme allowed the children to develop closer ties to Cochiti heritage and values. A profound result of the summer programme has been to reestablish the habits of speaking Keres among the native speakers.

Other examples of small-scale community initiatives include a walking club and football club which use the Manx language on the Isle of Man. In Scotland, advertisements go out for the formation of Gaelic-language interest groups in such activities as woodworking or cooking.

15.4   Adult language learning

Adult language learning is an essential part of language revitalization. Many endangered languages have been unused for so long that they are only remembered by elders. Thus in any second-language-learning programme for endangered languages, many of the teachers are by necessity second-language learners themselves. In Hawai'i, for example, most of the teachers in the immersion schools learned Hawaiian as a second language, usually at the campuses of the University of Hawai'i, which has excellent adult language programmes.

Education in endangered languages is often hampered by a critical shortage of teachers who can speak the language, given that most native speakers were not teachers, and are also beyond retirement age. In New Zealand, by 2000 there were some forty-five training centres to teach

Māori to younger adults who would then become teachers in the immersion schools (King 2000). In Hawai'i, the University of Hawai'i's Mānoa and Hilo campuses provide intensive training in Hawaiian language and culture for the same purpose, as well as overseeing the development of curriculum and materials for the immersion schools (Warner 2001).

But in most cases, adults who want to learn their heritage language have fewer venues available to them even than children. University classes are available for NATIONAL ENDANGERED LANGUAGES such as Māori, Hawaiian or Irish, but only a small minority of indigenous endangered languages are taught in universities; and those that are often lack the methodology and number of hours of exposure that are necessary for the development of conversational competence. Although communities often offer evening classes, these are usually informal and meet once a week or less.

However, adults possess capabilities of finding their own resources and forming strong commitments to manage their own learning. One programme that takes advantage of these capabilities is the Master–Apprentice Language Learning Program, founded in California by the Advocates for Indigenous California Language Survival. This popular method has spread around the world, with programmes all over the United States, and known applications in Canada, Brazil, Spain and Australia. The method pairs a speaker and a committed learner, and provides training in language immersion techniques. The basic principles are:

1. work together at least ten to twenty hours per week;
2. leave the majority language behind. All communication between master and apprentice should take place in the target language, even to the point of frustration;
3. make yourself understood by nonverbal communication such as gestures, facial expressions, props, actions and activities, which is the same way that children learn their first language;
4. focus on listening and speaking, rather than reading and writing;
5. use the language in the context of real activities and real communication. Choose activities that help make language use fun;
6. the apprentice should be a proactive learner. They should elicit words and phrases in the target language, suggest activities, bring props, learn to ask (without using any of the majority language) for repetition or other help, and learn to remind the master to stay in the language;
7. for the master, learn to correct without criticizing. For the apprentice, learn to take correction positively.

The rationale for and details of these principles are taught in an initial two- to five-day training session. Exercises to help the teams learn how to apply the principles are central to the training. All these principles and

methods are also detailed in the manual for the master–apprentice programme (Hinton *et al.* 2002). While it is theoretically possible for teams
to do the entire programme on their own, having a mentor for teams is
very helpful for problem-solving and encouragement. Subsequent training workshops provide added energy and assistance with overcoming
plateaus. The programme does not work for everyone, primarily because
many teams cannot manage Principle 1 (ten to twenty hours per week)
or do not take Principle 2 (leave the majority language behind) seriously
enough. However, the method has resulted in many adults who have
become conversationally proficient in their endangered languages.

15.5   Family-based language revitalization

The ultimate goal for language revitalization would be for it to regain
its place as a language of daily communication within the speech community. For this to happen, the language must go beyond being a school
language, or a camp language, or the language of an elder and apprentice. It must become a language of home. Richard Littlebear (1996: xii)
writes: 'to reverse this influence of English, families must retrieve their
rightful position as the first teachers of our languages'. Some apprentices
in the master–apprentice programmes have started using their language
at home; and a growing number of Māori and Hawaiian families also
use their language at home with their children. But the big gap in most
language revitalization programmes has been in providing support to
families to help them use their language at home.

   The Hawaiians have recognized the need for family support. The first
Aha Pūnana Leo preschools outside of Ni'ihau (the one island where children still learn Hawaiian at home) were established by second-language-
learner parents with an interest in expanding the Hawaiian-language
development of their children (Wilson 2001). As the programme developed, many parents who did not know the language themselves wanted
their children to attend the Hawaiian-medium preschools. A policy was
established where parents could avoid paying tuition fees if they volunteered to work in the classroom. With the no-English policy already
firmly in place, parents had to maintain silence or learn to speak in
Hawaiian, which they managed to do along with their children, through
night classes or through the university.

15.5.1   Scotland: Gaelic in the home
A very direct language teaching and support programme for parents who
want to use Gaelic at home has been developed by Scottish Pre-School
and Adult Educator Finlay M. Macleod. He claimed that the standard
teaching methods for Gaelic in Scotland used English as the medium of

instruction, did not teach conversational Gaelic, and in particular never taught people how to use the language for daily family life.

Macleod was instrumental in the establishment of *Comhairle nan Sgoiltean Araich* (CNSA the Gaelic Pre-school Council), in the 1980s, with the result that as of 2010 there are some 135 groups in Scotland, with over 2000 students currently enrolled. Yet he felt strongly that Gaelic should be learned earlier, and learned first at home. The big problem was that parents did not generally know Gaelic well enough to transmit it to their children. In response to these issues, he developed the TOTAL IMMERSION PLUS (TIP) methodology for adult Gaelic conversational language learning, as well as several family and parent programmes.[2]

His *Bumps and Babies* language learning programme and *Gaelic in the Home* course use TIP methods to train parents and future parents in using child-centred language at home, focusing especially on the first three years of life. Parents learn how to use Gaelic for all aspects of life with children, for waking up, going to bed, bathing, feeding, playing, going for a drive, calming a crying child and almost anything else a parent can imagine. He focuses especially on the language of affection, believing that when a parent and child interact lovingly, not only does the child bond with the parent, but also with the language that they are using to form and express that bond (Finlay Macleod, p.c.). His courses take them through various modules depending on the age of the child; for example, there is one whole set of modules for children age 0–9 months, and another from 9 months to 2 years, the age range when language production emerges. His *Gaelic in the Home* course also covers interactions with older children.

Local Development Officers and trained tutors work with the families to develop their language use, devise family language plans, find community-language resources (such as other families and groups using Gaelic), and to keep records of language choice in daily conversation, to increase their consciousness of how much Gaelic they are using as opposed to English. His programmes have increasing popularity in Scotland, and even more in Nova Scotia, Canada, where a large population of Scots Gaelic heritage are hungry for their language.[3]

15.6   Revitalization of sleeping languages

If a language has no speakers, second-language learning is much more difficult. There is no easy replacement for language learning through immersion-based interaction with native speakers. However, the situation is far from hopeless. It has already been shown that language revitalization can be successful even when starting only from documentation. For example, the last native speaker of Cornish, a Celtic language of the United Kingdom, probably died in the late 1700s (Ellis 1974). Yet due to a revival beginning in 1903, it is now spoken daily by hundreds of speakers, and the *Ethnologue* reports that there are now some native speakers among people under twenty (Lewis 2009). In the case of Kaurna in South Australia, a language with no native speakers, the community has made great strides in learning and using their language in the last fifteen years or so (Amery 1995, 2002).

In the cases of Miami (of Indiana, Ohio and Oklahoma, USA), and Wampanoag (Massachusetts, USA), both Algonquian languages, each movement was led by a talented individual tribal member who did the major step of learning the language fluently from documentation, and then leading their families and communities in language-learning efforts with more orally based approaches. Daryl Baldwin (Miami) was born sometime after the death of the last Miami speaker (Leonard 2007). He sought out graduate training in linguistics in order to learn how to find, read and analyse the 300 years' worth of documentation on the Miami language, by missionaries, anthropologists, linguists and the Miamis themselves, who went through a period of Miami literacy before beginning to use English as their language of writing. The Wampanoag language declined rapidly after the American Revolutionary War, so its period of dormancy has been much longer. Like Daryl Baldwin, Wampanoag language activist Jessie Little Doe Baird pursued a post-graduate degree in linguistics, and taught herself the Wampanoag language from documentation. She now teaches Wampanoag to an enthusiastic group of people, using full immersion methodology, and is raising a daughter who is bilingual in Wampanoag and English.

15.7   The role of linguistics in language revitalization

Baldwin (2003: 8–9) has acknowledged the linguist Dr David Costa for first inspiring Miami people to begin having an interest in language revitalization:

> What motivated our initial language efforts was the research of Dr. David Costa from the University of California. David reconstructed the phonology and morphology of Miami-Illinois, giving us an important piece from which to work and launch our reclamation efforts. I met David back in the 1980s and we began to communicate about the language. During that time, there was a general feeling among the Miami community that the spoken language was gone and that there was little documentation of it. David changed that perception, as he found a great deal of documentation on Miami-Illinois. He traveled throughout the Midwest and the East, including the Smithsonian Institute, Indiana, and Oklahoma. What he found was that the Miami-Illinois language was very heavily documented in written form for 300 years.

Linguists often play a very important role in inspiring communities to start the process of revitalizing their languages. The very act of linguistic documentation, or in Costa's case, of organizing and analysing older documentation, can give people in the speech community new views on their language, and show them opportunities they might not have been aware of before. Linguists working with endangered languages increasingly work closely with the communities to involve themselves in language teaching and learning programmes. Linguists have also become major developers of materials for language learning and reference, and many community-language activists have undergone linguistic training to help them in their efforts.

Linguistic documentation has been increasingly informed by community desires, expanding from its older base of a focus on vocabulary and grammar, to the recording of a range of speech genres and, especially useful for revitalization, everyday conversation (see Woodbury, Chapter 9). Linguists are also frequently called upon to help communities develop writing systems for their languages and develop learning materials.

Language revitalization has itself become an area of study. In Linguistics, Anthropology and Education programmes at universities there are an increasing number of dissertations coming out on language revitalization. As an example, ProQuest lists some fifty-six North American PhD dissertations since 1991 that have the term Language Revitalization in their titles or abstracts.[4]

The fit of linguistics and language revitalization is not perfect. The demands of academia are often in conflict with community needs and desires (Hinton 1994b, Kipp 2000, Rice 2009). Linguists and community-language workers may also have very different ideas about teaching methods and writing systems (Hinton 2008b). While linguists have often written about the importance of 'saving a language' through documentation (for example see Krauss 1992), the members of communities who are trying to save their languages have something different in mind. Most frequently, their goal is the creation of new speakers. Fishman (1996: 168–9) reports a statement from Ainu in Japan:

> We will not go into the museum. We will not be archivized. We can still become pregnant. We can still bear children. And they can still laugh with Ainu on their lips.

Some community language activists even fear that documentation of the last speakers of a language takes away vital time and energy from language revitalization. Grounds 2007 writes the following about Yuchi, which has only a handful of elderly fluent speakers:

> The climax came when the linguist offered the idea that the Yuchis would have a dictionary on their shelves 100 years from now. I countered

that 100 years from now I wanted the Yuchis to have the language on their own tongues.

On the other hand, those communities who have no speakers left can still work to revitalize their languages so far as the languages have been documented. As Krauss (1992: 8–9) writes:

> With such documentation, however, it remains always possible to maintain or establish a limited crucial role for the language institutionalized within the society, e.g. in schools or ceremonial life. From that position, even after the last native speaker has died, it is possible – as shown by the case of Hebrew and perhaps others, such as Cornish – for that limited role to expand back to first-language use, where the WILL of the people is strong enough. For this purpose, adequate documentation is most certainly feasible.

Language revitalization demands an understanding of many fields of expertise, including education, language acquisition, and language teaching and learning theory and methodology. Rarely are the linguists who document endangered languages well prepared in all these fields. Furthermore, there is much less funding available for revitalization than for documentation and linguistic studies. In rare cases, a linguist is hired full-time by the community and can treat language revitalization as their primary effort rather than as a part-time sideline.

Although linguistic approaches to language learning are valuable for some people and in some contexts, language learning in a revitalization context needs a different approach. Leonard and Shoemaker (forthcoming) put it well in a review of the history of a programme of language camps in the Miami Nation of Oklahoma:

> While many people did in fact learn parts of the language and the camps were an enjoyable time, among the early findings in Oklahoma language reclamation efforts was that these efforts were overly focused on language as a set of linguistic rules, and not on language as something that people would actively feel the desire to use within various social domains and everyday practice.

Nevertheless, there is increasing understanding by many linguists that learning about first- and second-language teaching and acquisition is an important part of their work with communities. There is also an increasing number of community members with training in linguistics, such that outside experts are not as essential. Furthermore, linguistic documentation, whether done from a view to revitalization or not, has played a dramatic role, especially in the revitalization of dormant languages. Linguists and language activists working together have produced excellent results in language revitalization (Rice 2009).

15.7.1 Linguistic training for language revitalization

People whose aim it is to become fluent in their heritage tongue often find that acquiring knowledge of linguistics is very useful to them. If an adult is learning an endangered language with little or no availability of effective (or any) classes or pedagogical materials, as is frequently the case, then it is crucial to learn how to read and understand the linguistic documentation on that language in order to learn from it or make pedagogical materials for oneself or others. Thus some of the most successful language revitalization activists within their communities have undergraduate or graduate degrees in linguistics. The training of indigenous language activists in linguistics is potentially of great benefit to community efforts in language revitalization. It is important to reiterate that part of the reason that Baldwin and Little Doe Baird were so successful in their language-learning efforts was that they went through advanced training in Linguistics programmes to acquire an understanding of phonetics and linguistic analysis, allowing them to develop needed expertise in handling the written documents that formed the corpus from which they could learn. Some universities (e.g. MIT (USA), University of Hawai'i (USA), Victoria University (Canada), and the University of Canterbury (New Zealand) have developed certification programmes or MA and PhD programmes specifically oriented toward indigenous students planning to work in their communities on language revitalization. (For more on Researcher Training and Capacity Development, see Jukes, Chapter 21.)

An effective language worker needs to know far more than linguistics. Among other things, they must also know the principles and methods of second-language teaching and learning. A venerable and much beloved summer programme for teaching linguistics and language-teaching to language workers is the American Indian Languages Development Institute (AILDI), which celebrated its thirtieth birthday in 2009. Participants can take courses in linguistics, curriculum development and teaching methods for language revitalization.

15.7.2 Language Centres

Language Centres in Australia are a creative and useful model of collaboration between linguists and community language workers. The first such centre established, the Kimberley Language Resource Centre in the northwest of Western Australia, was founded twenty-five years ago, following extensive consultation with numerous Aboriginal communities and organizations across hundreds of kilometres in the Kimberley region. Now some forty language centres exist throughout Australia, under the umbrella of the Federation of Aboriginal and Torres Strait Islander Languages (FATSIL). These centres provide on-site training of Aboriginal language workers, act as localized resource centres of linguistic data and materials, and provide support and training for community-language programmes as well as policy advocacy (Genetti and Florey, p.c.). In other countries, the Alaska Native Language Center in the USA and the Yukon Native Language Center and Yinka Dené Language Institute in Canada serve some of these same purposes (Florey and Himmelmann 2010).

15.7.3   Archives and language revitalization

Language revitalization has brought a new level of intensity to the use of language materials in university and museum archives (Conathan, Chapter 12). Linguistic fieldnotes and recordings are now much in demand by indigenous communities; fieldnotes and recordings have advantages for language revitalization that most published articles lack. Linguistic publications tend to be theoretical in nature, with much jargon, and focus more on a theoretical point than on full presentation of data. The notes themselves, and recordings, are the raw data most needed by communities with no fluent speakers. Communities order copies of the old materials and house them in local libraries or administrative centres. These materials can be used for the development of dictionaries, phrasebooks, reference grammars, the publication of texts and the development of learning materials of all sorts.

The importance of archival materials to language revitalization brings new demands and pressures on archives to make these materials more accessible. At the same time, the archives are subjected to new questions about access rights, intellectual property rights, and the handling of sensitive material (Conathan, Chapter 12). An example of the latter relates to the vast amounts of material in the National Anthropological Archives in Washington, DC on the Cherokee language, written in the Cherokee syllabary by medicine men in the nineteenth century. They wrote down formulas that present-day Cherokees consider to be dangerous to uninitiated laymen, and asked the archive to put a warning on those materials.

15.7.4   The Breath of Life Language Workshop

One summer programme centred around archives is the Breath of Life Language Workshop, held biennially since 1992 at the University of California at Berkeley. This workshop was developed primarily for Californian Indian languages without speakers, and gives training to the participants in searching archives to find the documentation that has been done on their languages, and teaches the fundamentals of linguistics so that they can read and analyse the materials they find. Emphasis is also placed on the use of these materials in the development of dictionaries and language lessons, and oral competency (Hinton 2001d). Each language group also has a postgraduate student or faculty mentor who works with them closely. The Breath of Life Language Workshop has generated energy in a number of California tribes whose languages have no speakers; they have gone on to develop dictionaries, grammars and teaching materials, and to develop various ways to use their language (Warner *et al.* 2009, Yamane 2000).

15.8 Conclusion

As Fishman (1996: 174) wrote:

> And what we have to ask ourselves, 'Is reversing language shift a lost cause?' Well, perhaps it is. But all of life is a lost cause. ... We all know the road leads only downward into the grave. There is no other way it will go. Those that have hope at least share the benefits of hope, and one of those benefits is community. Reversing language shift efforts on behalf of the intergenerational mother-tongue transmission is community building, that is what is essentially required, in and through the beloved language.

Language activists are pioneers in a new but long-term process with an unknown final outcome; but to most of them, the process itself has great rewards. Yet the future of language revitalization always lies with the next generation. What will the generations that learn the language in the immersion schools or from second-language speaking parents do next? Except for Hebrew in Israel, there is no endangered language where the community can sit back and say that their language 'has been revitalized'. For some communities, such as Māori and Hawaiian and Scots Gaelic, it is possible to foresee a future where the language will regain its status as a language that is widely used and transmitted in a bilingual society. For others, the goal is simply not to let it die. As language activist Julian Lang once said to me of the Karuk language: 'The last speakers will be dead in twenty years. But if each speaker would take on just one apprentice to live with him and learn the language, then that's another fifty years or more that the language will stay alive.' Or as another once said to a doubter: 'Yes, the language may die. But it won't die on my watch!'

Notes

1 For an opposing view see Romaine 2006a.
2 see www.ti-plus.com (22 February 2010).
3 See www.electricscotland.com/gaelic/finlay/finlay1.htm (22 February 2010).
4 ProQuest www.proquest.com (15 January 2010).

16

Orthography development

Friederike Lüpke

16.1   Introduction

> Vernacular literacy involves much more than merely devising the optimal orthography for a given language as many linguists would have us believe. (Mühlhäusler 1990: 205)

Many endangered languages are not written; therefore, researchers and speech communities often wish for their GRAPHIZATION (Fishman 1974). The existence of a written code is seen as an essential prerequisite for many activities in favour of their maintenance and revitalization, such as dictionary writing (see Mosel, Chapter 17), curriculum development and the design of language-teaching courses (see Coronel-Molina and McCarty, Chapter 18).

Graphization or orthography development is a complex task which requires a careful assessment of issues going beyond purely linguistic decisions. The successful creation of an orthography involves the consideration of historical, religious, cultural, identity-related and practical factors in addition to linguistic ones. Although writing in the mother tongue is recognized as an important linguistic right, literacy can only be successful if there are adequate and varied materials available for reading (and instruction). This means that the potential role and scope

Many people have contributed to shape my thoughts on this issue. First and foremost, I am indebted to the Jalonke speech community in Saare Kindia (Guinea) for sparking my initial interest in orthography development. The participants and audiences of the ELAP workshop on training and capacity building for endangered-language communities in February 2004, on endangered-languages and literacy in December 2005, and of the ESF exploratory workshop on contact between Mande and Atlantic languages in September 2008, all held at SOAS, London, got me further engaged with the subject. Finally, I would like to thank the following colleagues at SOAS for sharing their experiences with me: Peter Budd, Gerardo De Caro, Stuart McGill, Julia Sallabank and Lameen Souag. The responsibility for any misrepresentation of their views lies exclusively with me.

of literacy (as a social practice rather than a technical skill) in an endangered language needs to be evaluated prior to orthography development, and that graphization has to be embedded with care into the larger task of 'corpus planning' (Kloss 1968, Sallabank, Chapter 14).

Endangered languages are usually spoken in multilingual environments, and in most instances at least one contact language[1] already exists in a written form and is used for formal contexts of writing. It is therefore important to identify an ecological niche for writing in the endangered language, that is, registers and contexts which are predisposed for writing in it instead of in a contact language. If and when such a context has been found, a writing system and script need to be selected.

A writing system is the abstract underlying type (for instance LOGO-GRAPHIC, SYLLABIC, ALPHABETIC, etc.) of which scripts (i.e. Arabic, Latin, Devanagari, etc.) are instances. Scripts are not identical with orthographies/spellings, the standardized versions of scripts for specific languages or varieties thereof (e.g. American versus British spelling). Many twentieth-century REFERENCE ALPHABETS (e.g. the Bamako 1966 and Niamey 1978 alphabets for African languages), are based, in the colonial spirit, on the Latin script, and can ultimately be linked to missionary societies who commissioned the first unified reference alphabet (Lepsius 1863).

It is often assumed that the writing systems of modern orthographies will be of the alphabetic type, but other writing systems persist and need to be taken into account. In addition to preferring alphabetic writing systems, within this type many linguists may lean towards the Latin script because of its closeness to the Latin-based International Phonetic Alphabet (IPA) in which they often produce phonetic and phonological transcriptions. However, in many areas of the world, alternative scripts exist, and in these areas script choice requires conscious and informed decisions. Once this hurdle is overcome, a number of analytical and practical issues need to be addressed.

The written use of a language presupposes its standardization, which is often seen as concomitant with writing. Depending on the internal diversity of the endangered language and the attitudes of speakers to its different varieties, there are several possibilities: creating a KOINÉ variety, an underspecified orthography, or promoting one variety to standard by basing the orthography on it. These choices can have far-reaching consequences on linguistic diversity, the ecological equilibrium of varieties involved, the acceleration of cultural change and loss of the phatic values of the vernacular, as Bielenberg (1999), Mühlhäusler (1990) and Sallabank (2002) warn.

Since Pike (1947) it has become customary to regard orthographies as 'optimal' if they adhere to the often invoked 'phonemic principle' according to which a one-to-one relationship between phonemes and GRAPHEMES is ideal. Yet, scholars of writing do not cease to stress the differences between orthographies and phonetic or phonological transcriptions (Coulmas 2003, Venezky 2004), so thought must be given to the number and shape of graphemes and their relationship to the phonemes and phones of the language as well as to criteria determining word boundaries. Finally, reflections on how to facilitate the creation and sustainability of a written environment are in order if the orthography is meant to have a lasting impact.

Section 16.2 starts by exploring the ecology of writing in endangered-language communities discussing spoken and written repertoires (16.2.1), DIGRAPHIA (16.2.2), EXOGRAPHIA (16.2.3) and the significance of global narratives of writing and education in this context (16.2.4). Section 16.3 identifies the main issues at hand when choosing a writing system or script, touching on the relations of script with identity and religion (16.3.1), investigating whether there is a natural proclivity of certain scripts to be used for particular languages (16.3.2), and concludes with a discussion of practical matters associated with script choice (16.3.3). The non-linguistic, linguistic and practical questions surrounding orthography development are examined in Section 16.4. Just like scripts, orthographies reflect traditions and identities, and this function is discussed in Section 16.4.1. Section 16.4.2 offers general design considerations for non-logographic orthographies[2] stemming from psycholinguistic research on reading and writing. Section 16.4.3 is dedicated to the practical consequences of orthographic choices. The conclusion reflects to what extent universal discourses on the languages used for writing and education and their roles reflect the linguistic, cultural and socioeconomic realities of endangered-language communities in different endangerment situations and what realistic expectations for the role of writing and the scope of literacy in endangered languages might be.

16.2   The ecology of writing in multilingual endangered language communities

> The bilingual is *not* the sum of two complete or incomplete monolinguals; rather, he or she has a unique and specific configuration … The bilingual uses the two languages – separately or together – for different purposes, in different domains of life, with different people. (Grosjean 2008: 13–14)

This section first presents the different ways in which spoken and written modalities interact in, typically multilingual, endangered language communities by giving an overview of repertoires and functions often associated with endangered and contact languages in the two MODALITIES. Writing traditions using one script versus multiple scripts/orthographies are discussed and contrasted with situations characterized by the total absence of writing. The notion of DIGRAPHIA, often used to characterize multigraphic practices, is introduced, and its usefulness scrutinized in

16.2.2. EXOGRAPHIA, or the absence of vernacular writing, is discussed in 16.2.3. The concept of ECOLOGY OF WRITING, inspired by the concept of ecology of language (Mufwene 2001), which does not see contact languages globally in competition with each other but rather understands them as competing for functions, is then compared with global narratives of writing and education with more essentialist assumptions on (oral and written) language use in Section 16.2.4.

16.2.1 Spoken and written repertoires in multilingual speech communities

It is rarely the case in multilingual speech communities, even those using major languages, that their members have identical repertoires in all languages. This observation holds at the level of the oral modality and even more so for the written modality. In contrast to spoken language, writing is not acquired by exposure over a long period of time at a young age, but by more regulated apprenticeship, generally associated with some form of schooling, and requiring technology (stylus, pen, paper, parchment, slate, word processor, etc.). Since writing is more 'costly' than speaking, it is a safe assumption that there will be even less overlap in written repertoires than in spoken ones, i.e. it will be more improbable to find two written languages in a speech community being used for the same functions and contexts than to find overlap in spoken repertoires.

An example from my own experience, the endangered Mande language Jalonke, spoken in Guinea, West Africa (Lüpke 2004, 2005), may serve to illustrate this point. In the local speech community, Jalonke is confined to the oral sphere and has mainly the status of a home language. In all public contexts, the contact language Fula is spoken. Written communication regarding personal and religious matters, and book-keeping at the village level, takes place in Fula, in an Arabic-based script. Written interaction with the authorities and official documents is in French, the official language of Guinea. Each of the languages thus occupies its own ecological niche with very specific functions for the spoken and written modes. If one wished to develop a written code for Jalonke, a careful consideration of its purpose would be required.

Similarly, speakers of the endangered Austronesian language Touo, spoken in the Solomon Islands, employ a variety of Touo and Solomon Island Pijin (Terrill and Dunn 2003). The language learned at school used to be Roviana, another contact language, when it was taught in Methodist schools, until Roviana was replaced by English in this context. Depending on their Christian creed, Touo speakers now write different contact languages in informal contexts: community members who are Seventh Day Adventists are more exposed to writing in the contact language Ughele used by missionaries of this creed, whereas members of churches which descended from the Methodist mission are still exposed to written Roviana. Since the orthographies for the two languages follow different design principles, the delicate problem of avoiding religiously motivated digraphia for Touo poses itself to orthography developers (see 16.2.2 below).

16.2.2   Digraphia

DIGRAPHIA is a concept with two different interpretations. For some (DeFrancis 1984, Humery forthcoming, Zima 1974) it is used by analogy with the term DIGLOSSIA, which according to Ferguson (1959) describes a situation in which two or more language varieties which are used by the same community but are employed in separate contexts and functions, usually considered to be in a hierarchical relationship and hence labelled H (for 'high') and L (for 'low'). On this reading, digraphia only denotes MULTIGRAPHIC writing traditions in contexts where one of the traditions is the dominant one, either synchronically or diachronically. Others (e.g. Coulmas 2001, Grivelet 2003: 231) disregard this interpretation and understand digraphia to 'simply' mean 'the use of two different scripts, writing systems or orthographies for the same language'. I consider it useful to reserve the term DIGRAPHIA for hierarchical separated functional relationships between written codes, and use the more neutral terms BIGRAPHIA or MULTIGRAPHIA (henceforth used interchangeably), coined following the example of bilingualism and multilingualism, for the simple coexistence of two or more written codes for a language or variety (see Fishman, 1967 for an analogous proposal of multilingualism).

Both digraphia and multigraphia are common for languages which have, for a variety of reasons, come into contact with more than one written code, and there are many textbook examples available for larger languages (e.g. Hindi and Urdu, Serbian and Croatian, Chinese characters versus Pinyin[3], etc.). One would hope that digraphia and multigraphia would not be an issue for minority and endangered languages, since their existence increases the complexity of creating and maintaining a written ecology for these languages even more, but unfortunately this is not the case. Touo, mentioned above, is a case in point. Terrill and Dunn (2003) were facing the problem that, depending on their religious orientation, speakers of this language (which has only approximately 1,800 speakers), favoured either a 'Seventh Day Adventist' orthography based on the contact language Ughele, or one of Methodist provenance based on the contact language Roviana, and were not prepared to accept a compromise. For Touo, this unfortunate situation stems from non-coordinated orthography creation by missionaries with different affiliations.

An additional example of multigraphia from my own research concerns the endangered Atlantic language Baïnouk, spoken in Senegal

Table 16.1. *Differences between NTM alphabet and national alphabet for Baïnouk with IPA correspondences*

NTM grapheme	National alphabet grapheme	Corresponding IPA symbol
<a>	<a>	[a], [ɑ], [ɐ]
<e>	<e>	[ɛ]
<i>	<i>	[ɪ]
<o>	<o>	[ɔ]
<u>	<u>	[ʊ]
<á>	<ë>	[ə]
<é>	<é>	[e]
<í>		[i]
<ó>	<ó>	[o]
<ú>		[u]

(West Africa). Here, missionaries of the New Tribes Mission (NTM) created an alphabet for one variety of the language, without taking orthographical conventions existing at the national or regional level into account. When the Baïnouk speech community applied for 'codification' of the language – that is, its recognition as a national language with the right to be used in the public sphere – the existing NTM alphabet needed to be adapted to the standard (see Table 16.1 for correspondences). In the NTM alphabet, closed vowels have an acute accent above the vowel grapheme. However, <á>[4] is used by the NTM alphabet to write the schwa sound [ə][5], and hence a closed [ɐ] is not written <á>, breaking the logic of notating closed vowels with an acute accent for the other vowels. In the national alphabet, <ë> stands for schwa, and degree of aperture is only distinguished for the front mid vowel pair and the back mid vowel pair. In view of these inconsistencies, all existing literacy materials for Baïnouk became obsolete overnight.

Dominant personalities and/or cultural and religious institutions can have a huge impact on how an endangered language is written, and in many cases it will be difficult, if not impossible, to reverse resulting multigraphia once it is established. The continuation of this variability (rather than pressing for standardization) can be adopted by language activists, as in the case of the endangered language Guernesiais or Guernsey French, a Norman language spoken on Guernsey, one of the Channel Islands. Sallabank (2002: 241) reports the following note from the *Bulletin of L'Assembllaie d'Guernesiais*: 'Notaai s'y vous plait: L'Epellage des les articles du Bulletin a etaai lesi a la discretion des contribuables. [Please note: spelling in the articles of the Bulletin has been left to the discretion of the contributors.]' Another newspaper, the *Globe*, adopts a similar stance to variation, and Sallabank (2002: 231) lists some examples; for instance the Guernesiais form for 'young' written as <jeuaune>, <jeonne> and <jonne>.

Multigraphic practices can come into existence when endangered-language communities are dispersed over territories belonging to different countries with different national script traditions and standards. The speakers of the Indo-Iranian language Taleshi, for instance, are found in northern Iran and Azerbaijan, a former Soviet Republic. This endangered language has been written using Arabic, a modified Cyrillic alphabet, and a number of modified Latin alphabets: the Azeri alphabet introduced in 2001 (which replaced the Cyrillic alphabet in Azerbaijan), and modified IPA-based scripts (Gerardo De Caro, p.c.). Linguists and activists aiming at long-lasting usability of their orthographies and literacy materials are therefore advised to survey existing writing traditions in the endangered language and surrounding languages, existing conventions and recommendations at higher levels, and to consult members of the endangered-language speech communities in order to avoid digraphia or multigraphia or to minimize its divisive effects by, for instance, producing multigraphic materials or creating transliteration guidelines or computer programmes that will map between scripts.

16.2.3 Exographia

I use the term EXOGRAPHIA to designate writing which takes place exclusively in another language. Exographia is very widespread in endangered and minority languages for which no written variety is available at all. It is often the case that an official language (often an ex-colonial one) occupies formal writing contexts and a regional lingua franca is used for writing in semiformal and informal contexts such as adult literacy campaigns, the writing of personal letters, etc. Exographic writing traditions are often overlooked or marginalized (see 16.2.4 below), but it is always worthwhile to conduct a detailed study on functions and uses of writing in other languages prior to embarking on orthography development for an endangered language. If no ecological niche for writing can be found for the endangered language, exographia may be its fate, and it is disputable whether this is cause for concern or not. Endangered languages are often used in small-scale rural communities whose members see each other on a daily basis. If they already have another language at their disposal for writing and if this language is larger and consequently more able to offer a satisfactory written environment, then there may be no need for writing in the endangered language, unless the resources to support long-term DOMAIN EXPANSION are available, e.g. as part of a revitalization programme (see Hinton, Chapter 15).

Many fieldworkers report that finding appropriate contexts for writing is the biggest obstacle they encounter. Often, literacy materials produced in the endangered language are warmly welcomed because of the prestige they lend to the language, but they have little or no practical use because established exographic traditions pre-empt the introduction of

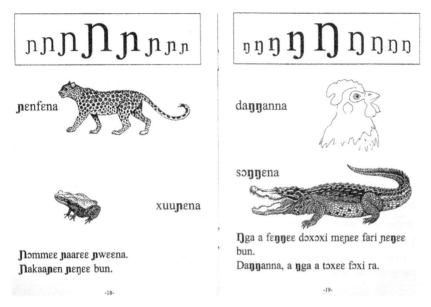

ɲɲɲ**Ɲ**ɲ ɲ ɲɲ   ŋŋŋ**Ŋ Ŋ** Ŋ ŋŋŋ

ɲenfena

daŋŋanna

soŋŋena

xuuɲena

Ɲommɛɛ ɲaarɛɛ ɲwɛɛna.
Ɲakaaɲen ɲeɲɛɛ bun.

-18-

Ŋga a feŋŋɛɛ dɔxɔxi meɲɛɛ fari ɲeɲɛɛ
bun.
Daŋŋanna, a ŋga a tɔxɛɛ fɔxi ra.

-19-

Figure 16.1. *Sample pages of the Jalonke primer using a Latin-based
orthography (Lüpke et al., 2000)*

ENDOGRAPHIC ones for the same functions.[6] I had this experience in my
own research on Jalonke, when I developed a primer using a Latin-based
orthography (see Figure 16.1). Although the primer was in high demand
and even speakers of the dominant contact language Fula queued for
their copy, nobody except my two main language consultants ever wrote
in this orthography. The established literacy practice in this endangered
language community is to write in Fula, using an Arabic-based script
commonly used in the area and carrying strong positive connotations
such as links to Qur'anic scholarship.

16.2.4   Writing endangered languages and global narratives of writing and education

The stance towards exographia taken in 16.2.3 above is in stark contrast with discourses of language rights that promote endographia or
writing in the 'mother tongue'. Advocates of linguistic human rights
(e.g. Skuttnab-Kangas and Phillipson 1995) stress the cognitive and psychological advantages of learning to read and write in and through the
mother tongue as opposed to a foreign language, and indigenous literacy
is seen as an important factor for language maintenance (Crystal 2000,
Fishman 1991). At the same time, numerous political, practical, financial and communicative obstacles to the implementation of mother-
tongue education have been identified, especially in endangered and
minority language communities (Fishman 1995, 2001b; Romaine 2006b;
Spolsky 2004).

Side-stepping feasibility issues, I would like to pause and consider the very notion of 'mother tongue' and 'writing in the mother tongue' and its universal applicability. There are instances where it is impossible to identify the mother tongue of a multilingual individual or the first language of an endangered language community unequivocally.[7] For the African context, for instance, current recommendations for language teaching, for instance from the UNESCO Institute of Education, avoid the term 'mother tongue' altogether and stress instead the advantages of using a familiar language, which in most cases will be an African contact language, as the medium of instruction. This development takes into account the difficulties of unequivocally identifying a mother tongue in contexts of extensive multilingualism (see Blench 1998 and McLaughlin and Sall 2001 for African cases, and Evans 2001 for similar observations on Australia).

Where exographic traditions exist, it may be useful to distinguish two radically different types:

1. a situation where a written majority language with close cultural and/or linguistic affiliations is already present in the multilingual repertoire;
2. exographic practices using an official (often ex-colonial) language that is not part of the everyday repertoire of the endangered language community (for instance the official languages in most countries of sub-Saharan Africa, which have to be acquired in spoken and written modes while at the same time serving as the medium of instruction).

Another widespread but problematic belief is the necessity for a language to be written in order to be a fully fledged language. The existence of a written form lends almost mythical qualities to a language. This language ideology, which Blommaert (2004) calls 'graphocentrism', means that revitalization and maintenance campaigns for minority and endangered languages often focus on the introduction of writing (see 16.2.3 above). While the cognitive and socioeconomic benefits of literacy are undisputed, it is an open question whether this literacy needs to be endographic in all cases, or whether certain exographic approaches may have equally positive effects.

The development of an orthography is often seen as an essential component of language documentation. Seifart (2006: 275) argues that:

> [m]uch of the success of a language documentation depends on casting these records in an orthography that appeals to the speech community. As a matter of fact, if it is accepted that the documentation has to be accessible to the speech community, the development and implementation of a practical orthography in the speech community is an absolutely necessary task in an early phase of a documentation project.

While I absolutely agree with the tenet of making documentation access-ible to the endangered language speakers, I would like to propose that developing an orthography is no longer necessarily the most suitable way to achieve this goal. In the past, when written documents were the only type of documentation produced by linguists, the accessibility of the lan-guage indeed depended on an accurate rendition of its pronunciation, although it is impossible for an orthography to entirely achieve this (see also Coulmas 2003: 26–35 on the differences between transcription and orthography). Even the most faithful transcriptions are limited in terms of what they represent (e.g. the segmental phonology of consonants and vowels, but ignoring prosodic features of spoken language), and so it is doubtful that spoken language can be rendered in all its facets by any transcription system in use today. Modern technology, however, has ena-bled language documentation to make audio- and video records access-ible to speakers of endangered languages without having to resort to a written representation. Fluent speakers rely much less on phonological information in reading than language learners (among them outside linguists). Semi-speakers and rememberers (see Grinevald and Bert, Chapter 3, for these terms) can learn the language based on audio- and video-records, their transcriptions and annotations. The presentation of oral genres in oral formats (annotations notwithstanding) also preserves their distinct nature in terms of genre, variation, phatic value, etc. and allows the delicate issue to be side-stepped of how to render communi-cative events of predominantly oral languages in written form, or what new written genres to create.

A written form for their languages features among the strongest wishes of many endangered language communities. However, these positive attitudes towards literacy are not necessarily matched by actual literacy practices. In my research on Baïnouk, 97% of the speech com-munity reported seeing literacy in their language as very positive; how-ever, only 22% attended the literacy classes offered by NTM missionaries, which have now stopped. There are numerous accounts of unsuccessful literacy programmes, especially in developing countries, signalling the huge challenges to be overcome, and these campaigns focus on majority languages for the most part (see Dumestre 1994, 1997 and Prah 2001 for some African observations, and Elwert 2001 and Triebel 2001 for general discussion).

Unless there is a real need and willingness to introduce endangered language literacy in the community, and unless this is backed up by adequate resources, I therefore consider a consistent and documented transcription sufficient and would recommend disseminating audio- and video-records as widely as possible by copying, distributing or broadcast-ing them, instead of trying to introduce endographia against all odds.

Transcriptions and dictionaries can supply evidence that the lan-guage can be written, contrary to popular beliefs, and make a number of emblematic documents available. A successful orthography, however, requires a much larger investment, including:

- selection of a writing system and set of graphemes
- establishment of rules specifying the relationship between sounds (PHONES and PHONEMES) and graphemes
- determination of rules specifying word boundaries and punctuation
- production of a dictionary listing spellings and materials for learning and later independent reading, etc.

16.3   Choosing a script

> The place of writing systems in the study of language planning and language policies is often seen as secondary. The various questions related to writing, such as the choice of writing systems, the type of orthography, etc., are often understood as being obvious, based on two main assumptions: first, that the Latin script is the most suitable to form the base of a new writing system; and second, that a writing system should be phonemic. However, these answers are mainly based on linguistic observations, without much concern for the place and role of a writing system in society. (Grivelet 2001: 1)

This section identifies the main factors in deciding on a script. It starts with investigating the relationship between script and religion and other aspects of historically grown identity that need to be taken into account. Section 16.3.2 discusses a myth circulating among linguists, educational practitioners and speech communities that some scripts are better suited for the writing of particular languages than others. This section illustrates how symbols can be adapted, their inventory extended and the type of writing system matched to the structure of a new language. Section 16.3.3 addresses a number of practical questions related to script choice, such as its consequences for the use of technology (and vice versa) and the production of written materials.

16.3.1   Script, religion and identity

The famous maxim 'alphabet follows religion' (Diringer and Regensburger 1968) stems from the observation that the spread of writing systems is largely coextensive with that of the world's major religions. Religion is a central part of identity, and by looking at a world map which shows the distribution of both scripts and religions, the powerful correlation between religion and script becomes obvious. Examples include the correlations between, for instance, Orthodox Christianity and the Cyrillic script, Roman-derived Christianity and use of the Latin script, Islam and the Arabic script, Confucian religion and Chinese script, Brāhmī-Buddhist religion and the use of one of the Indian scripts, Judaism and Hebrew script, to name but a few.

However, religion is only one facet of identity conveyed by the use of a particular script, and there are numerous exceptions to this observation. For instance, Fula-speaking people in Africa are among the proponents of AJAMI or Arabic-based writing in sub-Saharan Africa, because they were among the first to be in contact with Islam. Ajami writing traditions are still dominant in many varieties of Fula, for instance in Guinea and Cameroon. Speakers of the Pular variety in Senegal, however, have broken with the tradition of Ajami writing and prefer a recently introduced Latin-based orthography, although they are still Muslims (Humery-Dieng 2001, 2010). The reasons for this shift lie in the fact that in Senegal, Ajami writing was promoted by the Mourides, a Sufi brotherhood whose membership is mainly Wolof. In consequence, the Ajami tradition in Senegal became so strongly associated with its use for Wolof (called Wolofal) that speakers of Pular saw a Latin-based orthography as more appropriate for expressing their distinct identity.

Nevertheless, many endangered language communities come into contact with writing their own language for the first time through religious proselytizing, for instance by Christian missionaries aiming at Bible translation and consequently engaging in literacy work. Therefore, the correlation between script and religion can still be very strong, even though the rise of the Latin alphabet through the global impact of information technologies and English sometimes makes it seem a 'neutral' script. Religious and identity aspects which influence the preference for one script over another may be very fine grained and not always deducible from general trends, and therefore, the careful investigation of identity-related issues is necessary prior to addressing the more technical sides of orthography development.

Scripts may serve to mark identity far beyond practical purposes. The Tifinagh script is an example of the powerful symbolism scripts or even single emblematic graphemes of them can carry. Tifinagh is an ancient Berber script whose actual use is probably negligible, despite the existence of a modern variety, Neo-Tifinagh. Yet, anybody remotely interested in Berber culture will have come across the grapheme *yaz*, prominently featured on the Berber flag (Figure 16.2).

Even if an old indigenous script is not used as the basis for a newly developed orthography, it is recommended to determine transliteration principles, if possible, and highly symbolic graphemes may be graphically integrated, for instance by turning them into a logo. If at all feasible, the production of multigraphic documents should be considered, such as the bilingual and bigraphic Manding–English dictionary, which gives every LEMMA in the N'ko script used for the writing of a number of Manding varieties in Guinea, Côte d'Ivoire and Mali (Vydrine 1999); see Figure 16.3.[8]

Figure 16.2. *Berber flag adopted in 1998 by the Amazigh World Congress, featuring the Tifinagh grapheme yaz commons.wikimedia.org/wiki/File:Berber_flag.svg (29 January, 2009).*

16.3.2   Are some scripts better than others for particular languages?

Another widely held belief about writing proposes that there is a natural proclivity of certain languages to be written with certain scripts. It is common, for instance, even among linguists, to voice objections against the use of an Arabic-based script for the writing of languages other than Arabic on the grounds that it would be impossible to represent the vowels of that language. Arabic has only three short vowels, and the role of vowels in written Arabic is smaller than that of consonants, reflecting the importance of CONSONANTIC roots and NON-CONCATENATIVE morphology in this and other Semitic languages. However, since the inception of writing, existing scripts have been adapted to suit the structures of very different languages repeatedly, often changing the type of writing system in the process.

To illustrate how the Arabic script may be used for languages with very different phonological and morphological properties, I present some examples. Most languages written in the Arabic script have more than three vowels, and many have consonants not found in Arabic. Three solutions to the problem of missing graphemes are available:

1. creation of new graphemes;
2. neutralization of contrasts of the spoken language in writing; or
3. appropriation of existing graphemes.

Hausa, an Afro-Asiatic language with a long Ajami writing tradition (Philips 2000), has adopted all three solutions. In contrast to Arabic, Hausa has five vowels. Vowel length is distinctive, as in Arabic. The

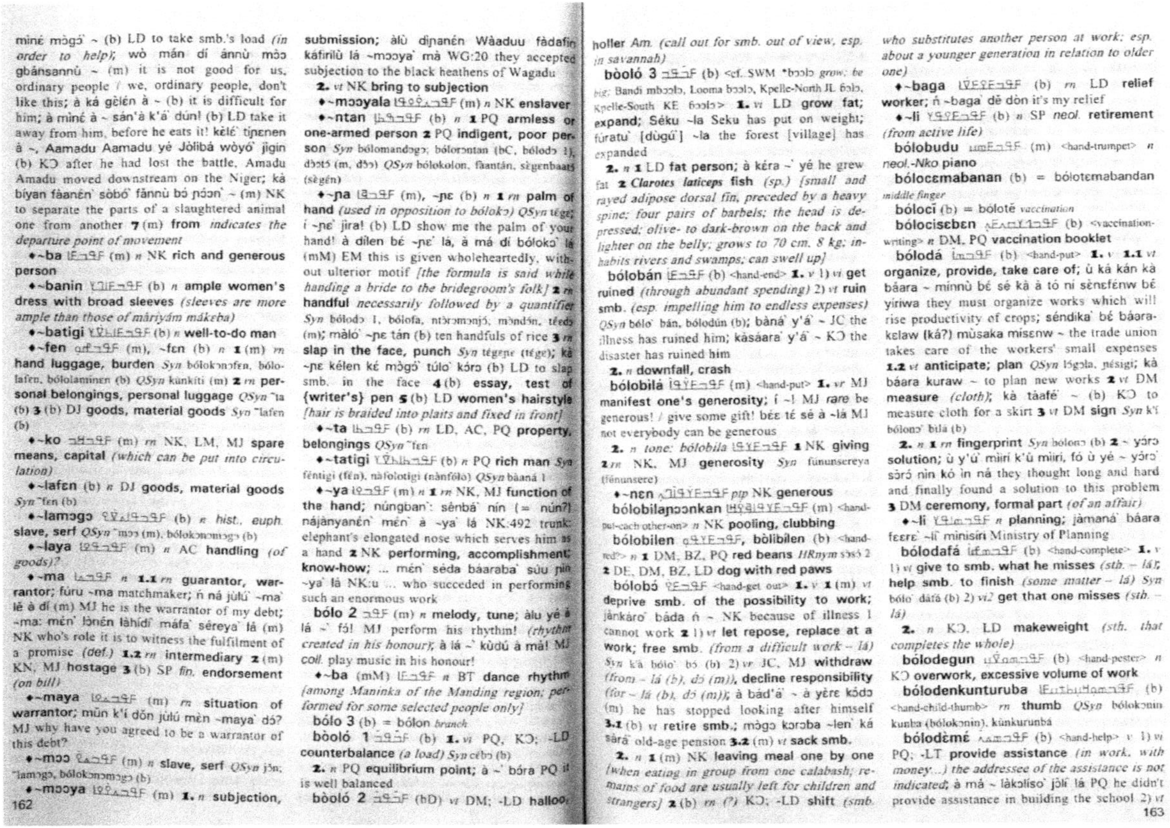

Figure 16.3. Sample pages from the Manding-English dictionary: bigraphic in Latin and Nk'o script (Vydrine 1999)

short vowels /a/ and /i/ are written with the same diacritics as in Arabic, the *fatha* < ´ > and *kasra* < ˌ > respectively. Their long counterparts use the *'alif* < ا > and *yā'* < ي >. The phoneme /e/, not in the grapheme inventory of Arabic, is represented by a diacritic used in the Warsh tradition of writing the Qur'an widespread in North and West Africa, a dot below or a vertical stroke above the letter. Its long counterpart is shown by an additional diacritic resembling a grave accent above the letter. Just like in Hausa, the Warsh grapheme indicates a phonetic [e] (see Table 16.2 for a chart of Hausa Ajami letters and their Romanized equivalents). The contrast between Hausa /u/ and /o/ and their long counterparts (signalled by a macron above the letter in Romanized Hausa) is neutralized, as both are represented by a symbol resembling the Arabic grapheme *damma* < ´ >.

The consonant inventory of many languages with Ajami writing is different from that of Arabic, and again, the same three different strategies can be observed. If the contrast is not neutralized, either a new symbol is created, such as < گ >, based on the letter *kāf* with an additional diacritic used to write /g/ in Persian. In Hausa, the *ghain* symbol < غ > is used to represent the same phoneme. Lameen Souag (p.c.) reports that the Arabic letter < ت > serves to write the affricates /dz/ as well as /ts/ in the endangered Songhay language Korandje of southwestern Algeria, an example of APPROPRIATION. Hausa, in contrast, represents /ts/ with a *ṭā* with three dots above (see Figure 16.4). A fourth adaptation strategy, also reported by Lameen Souag, is the use of a special diacritic that only specifies that a letter is to be pronounced like a similar, non-Arabic sound in the language being written, while leaving the exact pronunciation of that sound unspecified.

16.3.3 Practical matters

It is important to anticipate practical problems that might arise through the use of the chosen script. An important consideration concerns whether the script will be mainly read (often the case of endangered language literacies, as Trudell (2006) reports for three Cameroonian languages) or also actively written, and in which circumstances. The larger and less standardized the grapheme inventory, the less suitable is it for the use of new technologies in writing. Many manuscript cultures, for instance character-based writing systems such as the Chinese one, have a large inventory of characters that require complex input methods on a computer keyboard. The signs of these scripts can either represent a morpheme in Chinese or the language borrowing the script, or, through the phonetic form of the morpheme, a specific sound value (for instance the initial sound), and these differences will have a dramatic impact on the number of graphemes. Other scripts from manuscript cultures will typically contain graphemes that are not part of the

Table 16.2. *Hausa Ajami chart after Philips (2000: 21f.)*

ROMAN LETTER	SOUND (IPA)	INITIAL	MEDIAL	FINAL	ALONE
a	/ā/	ﺍ	ﺎ	ﺎ	ﺍ
b	/b/	ﺑ	ﺒ	ﺐ	ﺏ
ɓ	/ɓ/	ﺑ	ﺒ	ﺐ	ﺏ
t	/t/	ﺗ	ﺘ	ﺖ	ﺕ
c	/tʃ/ [in Kano]	ﺛ	ﺜ	ﺚ	ﺙ
j	/dʒ/	ﺟ	ﺠ	ﺞ	ﺝ
h	/h/	ﺧ	ﺨ	ﺦ	ﺥ
h	/h/	ﺣ	ﺤ	ﺢ	ﺡ
d	/d/	ﺩ	ﺪ	ﺪ	ﺩ
z	/z/	ﺫ	ﺬ	ﺬ	ﺫ
r	/r/	ﺭ	ﺮ	ﺮ	ﺭ
z	/z/	ﺯ	ﺰ	ﺰ	ﺯ
s	/s/	ﺳ	ﺴ	ﺲ	ﺱ
sh	/ʃ/	ﺷ	ﺸ	ﺶ	ﺵ
c	/tʃ/ [in Sokoto]	ﺑﺶ	ﺒﺶ	ﺒﺶ	ﺑﺶ
s	/s/	ﺻ	ﺼ	ﺺ	ﺹ
l	/l/	ﺿ	ﻀ	ﺾ	ﺽ
ɗ	/ɗ/	ﻃ	ﻄ	ﻂ	ﻁ
z	/z/	ﻇ	ﻈ	ﻆ	ﻅ
ts	/ts/	ﻇ	ﻈ	ﻆ	ﻅ
'	/ʔ/	ﻋ	ﻌ	ﻊ	ﻉ
g	/g/	ﻏ	ﻐ	ﻎ	ﻍ
f	/f/	ﻓ	ﻔ	ﻒ	ﻑ
ƙ	/ƙ/	ﻗ	ﻘ	ﻖ	ﻕ
k	/k/	ﻛ	ﻜ	ﻚ	ﻙ
l	/l/	ﻟ	ﻠ	ﻞ	ﻝ
m	/m/	ﻣ	ﻤ	ﻢ	ﻡ
n	/n/	ﻧ	ﻨ	ﻦ	ﻥ
h	/h/	ﻫ	ﻬ	ﻪ	ﻩ
'w' or 'u'	/w/ or /ū/	ﻭ	ﻮ	ﻮ	ﻭ
'y' or 'i'	/y/ or /ī/	ﻳ	ﻴ	ﻰ	ﻱ
'	/ʔ/	ء	ء	ء	ء
ky	/ky/	ﻛﻲ	ﻜﻲ	ﻜﻲ	ﻛﻲ
kw	/kw/	ﻛﻮ	ﻜﻮ	ﻜﻮ	ﻛﻮ
ƙy	/ƙy/	ﻗﻲ	ﻘﻲ	ﻘﻲ	ﻗﻲ
ƙw	/ƙw/	ﻗﻮ	ﻘﻮ	ﻘﻮ	ﻗﻮ
gy	/gy/	ﻏﻲ	ﻐﻲ	ﻐﻲ	ﻏﻲ
gw	/gw/	ﻏﻮ	ﻐﻮ	ﻐﻮ	ﻏﻮ
'y	/'y/	ﻳ	ﻴ	ﻲ	ﻱ
e	/e/	ـ	ـ	ـ	ـ
e	/ē/	ﻳ	ﻴ	ﻰ	ﻯ

(Right to left) Yesterday, today, tomorrow: women's rights are stifled by conservative Arab elites (January 1985)

Figure 16.4. *Palestinian cartoon by Naji al-Ali (2009: 32)*

Unicode standard (that determines the universal assignment of codes to characters for their use with computers). This is the case for many Ajami scripts.

It is not recommended to use characters on a computer keyboard that are not encoded in a Unicode standard on a computer, so there are two solutions if a transition from a manuscript culture of writing to word-processing (or text messaging on mobile phones) is desired: either the script is adapted so it uses only characters approved by the Unicode consortium,[9] or a proposal for a new script or character is submitted for approval. The latter is a time-consuming process only likely to be successful if the character or script is not an idiosyncrasy of one minority language, and it is therefore not a promising route for endangered languages. However, depending on the envisaged scope and function of literacy in the language, it may not be necessary to use computers to write it. Handwritten texts can be copied, scanned and disseminated, and local particularities of the manuscript culture can thus be preserved. This strategy may also be useful in contexts where computers are not widely available, or not equipped to handle complex scripts which are not contained in the regional Unicode sub-set of the area or which do not have the necessary fonts installed to display them. It is, however, generally advised to adhere to Unicode standards in order to cater for possible future developments that would make computers more accessible to the language community (see also Holton, Chapter 19).

In addition, a new and unexpected use of vernacular literacy sidesteps standardized and more formal literacies: text messaging. In many African situations, for instance, as observed by Stuart McGill (p.c.) and myself, text messages are the most common, if not the only, context in which local languages are used in writing. If it turns out that this register is going to be one of the predominant contexts for writing in an endangered language, this has a drastic impact on the inventory of graphemes available to be used for the orthography.

If the immediate use of the endangered language on computers is desired, some further considerations are in order. Most logographic scripts have complex interfaces for character input which will not be further discussed here. For alphabetic scripts, it is worth considering which keyboard(s) is/are standard in the areas in which the script is to be used. Although many linguists use keyboard mapping software to create tailored keyboards for specific languages or master other input methods, it should not be forgotten that in many areas of the world computers are only accessible in internet cafes and chat rooms where only standard keyboards will be available, and where users are not necessarily familiar with short cuts or the use of the character map etc. in order to insert characters into a document (e.g. it is not convenient to write diacritics using keyboards geared towards English). See Seifart (2006) for similar points.

Finally, the directionality of the selected script will dictate the flow of writing on the page. In addition, it will also influence conventions for picture reading: not just for the interpretation of sequences of pictures but also for expectations on their composition (for instance the location of an agent to the right versus the left of a picture: Dobel *et al.* 2007, Maass and Russo 2003). This factor should be taken into account when planning the creation or reuse of illustrations for publications in the endangered language, illustrated for Arabic in Figure 16.4.

16.4 Choosing an orthography

Philologists, linguists and educators have insisted for several centuries that the ideal orthography has a one-to-one correspondence between grapheme and phoneme. Others, however, have suggested deviations for such functions as distinguishing homophones, displaying popular alternative spellings, and retaining morpheme identity. If, indeed, the one-to-one ideal were accepted, the International Phonetic Alphabet should become the orthographic standard for all enlightened nations,

> yet the failure of even a single country to adopt it for practical writing
> suggests that other factors besides phonology are considered import-
> ant for a writing system. (Venezky 2004: 139)

This section is concerned with the non-linguistic, linguistic and practical questions surrounding the development of an orthography once
a script or writing system has been determined. The section begins by
examining how orthographies, like scripts, may reflect a community's
identity through the choice of particular graphemes, spellings, etc.
These choices can either express proximity to an existing orthography
by copying its conventions, or distance by using different graphemes and
spelling norms from surrounding orthography traditions. Section 16.4.2,
on design considerations, outlines some fundamental linguistic and psycholinguistic principles on the relationships between sounds and graphemes, shallow versus deep orthographies, etc. Section 16.4.3 discusses
the practical impacts of particular choices of, e.g. graphemes, diacritics,
digraphs, etc. on the production of written materials and scope of use of
the orthography.

16.4.1 Orthography and identity

It is not only scripts which signal proximity to or distance from surrounding religions and ethnic and/or linguistic groups; orthographies,
too, express similar aspects of identity. The retention of graphemes
already in use in the speech community or in nearby literacies will situ-
ate the orthography within their tradition. This may be acceptable to the
endangered language community, or it might be seen as intolerable. If
choices are not constrained by higher order decisions such as national or
regional conventions, it may be necessary for acceptance to take speakers' concerns regarding the choice of particular symbols seriously. For
instance, members of the Miraña speech community in South America
insisted on choosing graphemes that were visually different from those
of the neighbouring Bora group, as Seifart (2006) reports. The motivation to express a distinct identity through different graphemes is sociopolitical; the Mirañas are outnumbered by the closely related Bora and
strive to maintain their own ethnic identity. A contrasting driving force
underlies the use of <ʉ> to write a high central vowel in the different
alphabets for Cameroonian languages of the Bamileke group (Bird 2001).
The different Bamileke varieties do not have a unified orthography, yet
the barred ʉ has become a symbol of cultural unity. Other Grassfields
languages not belonging to the group write the high central vowel as
<ɨ>. A new would-be standard orthography for the entire group retains
<ʉ> although it does not conform to orthographic conventions.

Identity-related motivations may sometimes conflict with linguists'
attempts to create an orthography with transparent and predictable

grapheme inventories that are consistent with conventions for neighbouring languages, although (or maybe because) the latter would facilitate transfer of literacy skills. Similar issues hold for the spellings of individual words. While not all orthographies are committed to reflecting the etymology of words (see Section 16.4.2 below), specific items may be of particular cultural significance, and communities may insist on spelling these words according to different principles than others, or on spelling them to reflect folk etymologies. It is recommended to evaluate identity-related issues with members of the language community, bearing in mind orthographic systems in regional and national use, in order to avoid decisions that might result in the rejection of the orthography by the community or some members of it (which might lead to digraphia or multigraphia; see Section 16.2.2 above).

16.4.2 Design considerations for orthographies

It is widely assumed by linguists that the basis of the ideal orthography is phonemic. If this was the case, the main difference between a phonemic transcription and an orthography would be the inventory of symbols used; IPA symbols in the former, a different and potentially open-ended set of graphemes in the latter case. Writing and reading are, however, cognitive tasks that are very different from speaking and hearing, and rely to a much lesser extent on phonological recoding than orthography developers often believe. This being said, there are indeed orthographies that are very close to the phonology of the language written: so-called SHALLOW or SURFACE ORTHOGRAPHIES (of which a famous example is the Finnish orthography), but their existence owes as much to the number of phonological processes in the language as to orthography design.

At the opposite end of the spectrum are DEEP ORTHOGRAPHIES, of which English is a notorious example. These do not have a close correspondence to the phonological structure of isolated words, so that irregular phoneme–grapheme relationships are common. (The properties characterizing connected speech are generally not encoded by orthographies.) However, even shallow orthographies can deviate from the often invoked 'phonemic ideal' on principled grounds, specifically when faced with capturing phonological processes at the word level. It may be desirable not to represent their pronunciation exactly but to preserve the identity of morphemes in written form. In English, for instance, the plural morpheme is written <s> despite voicing contrasts in, for example, /kæts/ <cats> vs. /dɒgz/ <dogs>, so that the identity of the plural morpheme /-s/ is preserved even in contexts of neutralization. In Dutch, the preference is to match the pronunciation difference in writing, hence <reizen>, 'travel' vs. <reijst>, 'travels'. It may be useful to let speakers decide in these contexts: they may be more alert to the existence of certain phonological processes than others, for instance. Speakers of the endangered

Austronesian language Bierebo, spoken in Vanuatu, systematically failed to apply the phonemic principle underlying the newly created orthography in one specific case: the language has HOMORGANIC PRENASALIZED STOPS, but following the phonemic principle it was decided not to represent the prenasalization orthographically. Nonetheless, native speakers intuitively do represent it when speaking, particularly intervocalically, spelling 'butterfly' as <kulbembe> rather than as <kulbebe> (Peter Budd, p.c.). However, if an orthography is being developed primarily in order to provide language-learning materials for non-native speakers, knowledge of such principles may need to be encoded through the orthography.

While it is commonly assumed that it is better in an orthography to overspecify than to underspecify, UNDERSPECIFICATION (or the conflation of several phonemes into one grapheme) can be a powerful tool for the creation of a PANDIALECTAL orthography in the case of unstandardized and internally diverse speech varieties. Seifart (2006) reports the case of the Austronesian language Sasak, spoken in Indonesia. The practical orthography of Sasak as proposed by Peter K. Austin only contains five vowels, although some dialects have up to eight vowel contrasts other dialects have fewer. A unified orthography is here seen as outweighing the fact that the under-differentiation of vowels in some dialects leads to the existence of homographs. Since semantic and collocational cues are available in reading, this does not render the orthography less effective.

While it is important to decide at a SEGMENTAL level whether an orthography should systematically give preference to morpheme identity vs. representation of some phonological processes, it is a matter of debate whether it should encode SUPRASEGMENTAL properties of speech such as distinctive stress or tone. Many orthographies notate tone using diacritics, numbers or other graphemes, depending on regional convention. Yet studies of some recent orthographies of complex tone languages question the effectiveness of tone notation, for both writing and reading. In a survey of tone-marking conventions for African languages, Bird (1999) reports the result of an evaluation of tone writing in the Cameroonian Grassfields language Dschang. Tone in this language is written with diacritics; the low tone is not marked. The tonal conventions result in 56 per cent of written vowels bearing a tonal diacritic. However, most speakers of Dschang do not master the tone notation conventions at all, which may be due to the large number of tone SANDHI and to the additional presence of grammatical tone in the language. Similar problems in writing tone have been reported from other languages. It may be crucial to carry out a detailed investigation of tone initially, in order to understand its functional load in the language. It can then be decided what its functional load in an orthography might be (not the same), and a pilot orthography can be tested with community members for both reading and writing.

The issue of the functional load of graphemes is of more general relevance, and pertains to the representation of low-frequency phonemes in the orthography. In Jalonke for instance, the VELAR NASAL /ŋ/ is only contrastive in medial position. It is the only nasal to occur morpheme-finally. My choice was to allocate this sound its own grapheme (see Figure 16.1), but an alternative would have been to represent it with the same grapheme as was used for the ALVEOLAR NASAL /n/, (where the POINT OF ARTICULATION is the result of REGRESSIVE ASSIMILATION and hence not phonemic anyway). It would then have been written <nga>, while <daŋŋɛɛ>, where the velar nasal occurs at a morpheme boundary followed by the definite suffix, /-ɛɛ/, would be written <dannɛɛ>. Instead of leaving this sometimes difficult choice to the linguist, the speech community can be involved in the decision-making process. McGill and Wade (2008) not only present clear guidelines for their proposed orthography of the endangered Benue-Congo language Cicipu of Nigeria, but also explain their choices so that the speech community can accept or reject parts of it on informed grounds. For instance, they present two possibilities for writing [tʃ]: either <c>, as in the contact language Hausa, or <ch>, as in the official language English.

Other design considerations concern the representation of GEMINATION and vowel length. Guidelines on the official Māori orthography, for example,[10] determine not only that long vowels are written with a MACRON diacritic above the vowel (<āhua>), but also that they are not written when their appearance at morpheme boundaries would result in an extra-long vowel. Morpheme boundaries thus remain GRAPHOTACTICALLY intact by representing two vowel graphemes instead of vowel plus macron. In the case of <ā>, when it combines with a base ending in <a>, <aa> is written: e.g. <whaka> + <āhua> becomes <whakaahua>, not *<whakaāhua> or *<whakāhua>. As the Māori example also illustrates, conventions for determining word boundaries (often said to be an artefact of writing in the first place) and how to write complex words need to be established and explained.

Finally, a SORT ORDER must be established to specify in which order the graphemes will follow each other, e.g. in a dictionary. All these tasks are not isolated technical problems but relate to the issues laid out above, since they all serve the potential purpose of signalling through borrowing or preserving, abolishing or innovating features from existing orthographies to position social practices in a multidimensional network.

16.4.3 Practical matters

The practical issues mentioned in Section 16.3.3 do not only hold for script choice, but also for orthographies. In addition, some more specific reflections are in order when developing a script. Directly related to its usability is the question of how its graphemes can be typed on a computer keyboard. Regional differences such as the British and American QWERTY versus the French AZERTY versus the Latin American QWERTY have an impact on how ergonomically glyphs can be typed, depending on where on the keyboard they are located (if they have keys allocated at all). The use of computers, not just to type glyphs but also to manage databases etc., as well as the involvement of Unicode, also require some attention to grapheme–glyph correspondences, the use of digraphs, punctuation marks, etc. It is crucial to select the correct character (i.e. not just a form resembling the intended grapheme but with the correct properties and semantics, e.g. a letter not a punctuation mark or a numeral) to represent the intended grapheme out of the huge inventory of 96,000 Unicode characters, and to find the correct upper and lower case matches for it.

For instance, in the past, it has been a regional convention in Côte d'Ivoire to use punctuation marks to signal tone (Bird 2001). Punctuation marks are also frequently used to encode vowel length, e.g. <:> in IPA, and in some orthographies the glottal stop [?] becomes <?> for ease of typing (e.g. the use of <!> and <#> to encode click sounds in some Khoisan language orthographies). These practices do not conform to Unicode, and using them would mean that these marks are not considered part of a word by computers, but rather to signal a word boundary, as they do in major languages like English or French. This causes major problems for spelling checkers, concordancing software, internet search engines or sorting entries in a dictionary database, and so on. Unicode also has a fixed inventory of COMBINING DIACRITICS (i.e. diacritics that 'fuse' with the character they modify) and non-combining diacritics. It is not recommended to use characters that are not part of the Standard, such as characters in the Private Use Area.[11] In light of the growing importance of computers, mobile phones and other electronic devices, it is advisable to follow Unicode-dictated and other technical considerations even if the planned orthography is intended for a currently manuscript culture. While it is not necessary to write aided by a computer or a mobile phone, it is certainly short-sighted to exclude the future use of such devices through selecting non-standardized non-Unicode characters etc. (For more on the use of new technologies with endangered languages, see Holton, Chapter 19.)

16.5 Conclusion

The script of a language, usually considered an interchangeable exterior form, works as a potential factor in its development, because, like writing systems and spelling conventions, it is perceived by the speech community as important. Since language is a mental *and* a social fact, this in itself causes writing to have an impact on language (Coulmas 2003: 240; emphasis added).

This chapter has placed orthography development within a wider context of language ecology, where written language use is seen as one of the many registers available to communities and individuals, not just to convey and decode messages but to mark their social, religious, historical and/or linguistic identity. In the case of multilingual speech communities, these different features of identity can be associated with different spoken and written languages and/or writing systems or orthographies. It is therefore impossible to reduce the task of orthography development to a practical endeavour that requires clearly delimited linguistic or pedagogical expertise only. Rather, it has been argued that the parameters governing the selection of a writing system, script and orthography that constitutes the best fit for a community are multiple and multidimensional. Therefore, the different steps involved in the complex task of assessing the potential use of writing in and for an endangered language, and then devising an orthography, go beyond the capacity of one field linguist working single-handedly. Instead, they should be envisaged as a collaborative and multidisciplinary enterprise in close consultation with speakers of the endangered language throughout the process.

Graphization is impossible to achieve as an add-on to a linguistic documentation project unless sufficient time and resources are set aside for orthography development, to avoid short-lived and tokenistic outcomes. It can only be hoped that funding bodies which focus on the documentation of endangered languages and exclude measures such as orthography development from their scope will in the future become more sensitive to the pressing need to derive useful products from language documentation that can be of direct benefit for the communities themselves.

Notes

1 This chapter uses the term 'contact language' to mean any language of wider communication, a wider definition than that in Chapter 5.
2 Logographic scripts function very differently from syllabic and alphabetic ones, which create conventionalized (albeit very different) relationships between sounds and graphemes and rely on the category of word. Since logographic scripts for endangered languages are mainly confined to East Asia and are beyond the scope of my own research, they are not covered here. Syllabic scripts are similar to alphabets in that they have a varying degree of correspondence with the sounds of the language, but differ in the basic unit they assume, the syllable. Since my own experiences are with alphabetic orthographies I do not address syllabic orthographies in detail, although their design principles are close to those for alphabets.
3 As the different language names in two of the cited cases demonstrate, it is a delicate and controversial issue whether varieties with different

multigraphic, national, and/or religious affiliations are to be regarded as one language or two. This issue is not independent of the graphic traditions associated with them, since writing systems are markers of identity and languages are not purely linguistic entities but constructs relying on shared identity according to a number of social, political, historical, religious, etc. factors.

4 Throughout the chapter I write graphemes between < >, phonemes between / /, and phones between [ ].

5 Description of Baïnouk is currently under way, and only a preliminary phonological analysis is available. Specifically, the question of whether degree of aperture is distinctive for all vowel pairs, particularly [i] and [u] and their open counterparts, is still undecided. Therefore, only a phonetic notation is used here, although it does not represent a narrow phonetic transcription of the attested vowel values.

6 This problem of corpus planning preceding prestige planning and status planning is addressed by Sallabank, Chapter 14.

7 Skuttnab-Kangas and Phillipson (1995) concede that the notion of 'mother tongue' may be problematic and therefore suggest that an individual can have at least two mother tongues. This suggestion only reinforces the inadequacy of the term.

8 An even more inclusive but also tremendously time-consuming solution for this dictionary would have been to also include Ajami representation of the lemmata, as Ajami writing is also attested for Manding (Vydrine 1998).

9 see www.unicode.org/ (1 March, 2010).

10 www.tetaurawhiri.govt.nz/english/pub_e/conventions2.shtml (26 January, 2009).

11 A wealth of information and guidance is available at the homepage of the Unicode consortium (www.unicode.org).

17

Lexicography in endangered language communities

Ulrike Mosel

17.1 Trying to square the circle

This chapter discusses a number of problems which are characteristic of lexicographic work in language-documentation projects on endangered languages and addresses the following issues: cooperation with the speech community, the selection of which variety to document, and the challenge of producing a useful piece of work meeting the scientific standards of lexicography despite having limited resources of time, money and staff. Drawing on my experiences with dictionary projects in Samoa and Bougainville, Papua New Guinea, I outline the differences between lexical databases that typically result from language-documentation projects on the one hand and the kind of dictionaries minority speech communities want for educational and other purposes on the other, and then show how such lexical databases can be exploited for the design of dictionaries that both satisfy the needs of native speakers and the interests of linguists. Since it is impossible to create a truly comprehensive dictionary in a language-documentation project, I have applied the so-called THEMATIC APPROACH, in which lexicographers work on particular semantic domains such as trees, architecture or fishing that were selected by the speech community because of their cultural significance. The result of this approach is a series of small dictionaries, so-called MINI-DICTIONARIES, which not only contain linguistic but also encyclopaedic information.

The main differences between dictionary projects for major languages and those for endangered languages are that the latter are non-profit enterprises, and the linguist who is responsible for the project is in most cases not a native speaker of the language. Dictionaries of minority or endangered languages are often compiled by a single person, for instance a teacher or a missionary who lives in the community, or by linguists or anthropologists regularly visiting the speech community over many years, either as a part of or a by-product of their research projects. Lexicography of this kind only receives acknowledgement from a few specialists. However, thanks to the growing awareness of the endangerment of languages and cultures, language documentation projects are now being supported by research institutions and funding agencies in increasing numbers, and lexicographic work is being acknowledged as an important component of language documentation (Coward and Grimes 2000, Frawley *et al.* 2002, Haviland 2006).

The staff working on the dictionary team typically consists of a linguist and a few members of the endangered-language speech community. While the linguist may not have a thorough knowledge of the language under investigation, the native speakers may not be trained in linguistics; and to complicate matters, both parties may not be fluent in the lingua franca they share as a means of communication. This situation, however, has begun to change, as more speakers of minority languages gain access to university education, summer schools and specialized workshops (Jukes, Chapter 21, A. Woodbury 2003).

This chapter discusses the following issues: the planning of the lexical database and the dictionary (17.2), the compilation of word lists (17.3), the writing of entries (17.4), the transformation of the lexical database into a dictionary (17.5), and capacity building in the speech community (17.6). I suggest a variety of problem-solving strategies, but as my personal experience as a lexicographer is limited to only two Austronesian Oceanic languages in the South Pacific, the Polynesian language Samoan and the previously unresearched Western Melanesian language Teop[1], these strategies may not work equally well in other parts of the world.

17.2   Planning the lexical database and the dictionary

The central component of a language documentation project is the corpus of recordings with transcriptions and translations (Woodbury, Chapter 9) which is usually accompanied by a lexical database that is assembled during the process of transcribing and translating. Toolbox, the most widely used software for making dictionaries of previously unresearched languages (Coward and Grimes 2000) allows researchers to structure database entries like dictionary entries and export them into various formats, including Rich Text Format (RTF) which can be read into a word-processing programme such as Microsoft Word. Although a print-out of the exported lexicon has the look of an ordinary dictionary, it significantly differs from any kind of dictionary. But before we discuss these differences and the strategies of transforming the lexical database into dictionaries in Section 17.5 below, we will deal with those lexicographic issues that are relevant for both the lexical database and the dictionary. This section focuses on the planning of the dictionary project including setting the goals (Section 17.2.1), the time factor (Section 17.2.2), the selection of a language variety (Section 17.2.3), orthographical matters (Section 17.2.4), and the question of how much grammatical information is necessary or desirable (Section 17.2.5). The Sections 17.3 and 17.4 give an overview of how to compile word lists and to write entries.

17.2.1 Setting the goals

In contrast to bilingual dictionaries of major languages, a dictionary of an endangered language does not primarily serve as a tool for translation or foreign-language acquisition, but more typically as a resource for research and a repository of information that is valuable for language revitalization and teaching in the speech community. Before creating a dictionary on the basis of the lexical database one must, as in any kind of dictionary project, identify the prospective users and the purposes of the dictionary. Since it will be compiled in close cooperation with the speech community, the dictionary should serve the needs and interests of both the speech community and the academic community of linguists and anthropologists. Consequently, an electronic database, which seems to be the best medium for academic purposes, must be accompanied by a printed version for speech communities which do not have access to modern technology (e.g. Schwartz *et al.* 2007), and by a dictionary or a series of mini-dictionaries.

Only recently linguists have become aware of ethical issues surrounding language documentation: what does a fieldworker, or in our case the researcher in a language-documentation project, owe to the speech community as a proper acknowledgement of their contribution? What are their intellectual property rights? (see Bowern 2008: 148–69, Dwyer 2006, Hinton and Weigel 2002, Newman 2007, Newman and Ratliff 2001b: 9, Conathan, Chapter 12). From this perspective the individual local dictionary makers and the speech community have a right to receive copies of the lexicographic work in a form and with content they appreciate, and this means for most endangered language speech communities a printed version of the dictionary. The acknowledgement of intellectual property rights implies that all the conditions made by the community must be satisfied before the dictionary can be printed and published (e.g. K. Hill 2002).

Respecting the community's rights may also have implications for the orthography employed, the selection of words (e.g. no taboo words), the macro-structure (e.g. strict alphabetical order or nesting), the micro-structure (e.g. not too much linguistic information in the entries) and the layout (e.g. use of a large typeface). Conflicts between linguistic standards and scientific interests on the one hand, and user-friendliness as defined by the local dictionary makers on the other, can be solved by producing two editions of the dictionary, one for scientific purposes and one for the speech community. If there is not enough time or money for both, the community dictionary should have priority.

17.2.2   The selection of the variety of language

The language to be represented in the dictionary may be spoken in more than one variety. In general, one dialect has to be given preference over the others. Quite often it is simply the dialect of the people who invited the linguists to work with them; in other cases representatives of the speech community might make the decision. If linguists have the opportunity to select a dialect, they should consider the following criteria: which dialect is the most viable and is used in the greatest range of speech situations? Are there children or young people who still use the dialect? Which dialect is the most widespread? Where do the linguists find the most cooperative people? Where are the best native language experts? And where are the best living conditions? Careful consideration is necessary. The mere fact that one dialect or speech variety is chosen for the compilation of a dictionary can make it become the standard, a consequence that would certainly have some impact on the future development of the language.

Choosing the most viable dialect and giving it the prestige of being documented in a dictionary, or even becoming the standard language, may be a death sentence for other dialects. On the other hand, the choice of a less viable dialect means that the dictionary and the language documentation would not cover the greatest possible range of speech situations.

17.2.3   The time factor: small is useful

Since lexicographic projects are usually constrained by limited resources of money, staff and time, the project must be organized in such a way that even after a very short period of time the dictionary makers can produce a useful piece of work. Instead of planning a comprehensive dictionary which would take decades to complete, one should be less ambitious and search for alternatives. There are, as far as I can see, two alternatives, which can be combined: CORPUS-BASED DICTIONARIES and THEMATIC DICTIONARIES.

Similar to the dictionaries of Classical Latin or Biblical Hebrew, corpus-based dictionaries only contain those words which occur in a particular corpus of texts. The disadvantage of these dictionaries is that their content solely depends on the topics of the texts and the more or less accidental choice of words by the speakers or writers of the materials in the corpus. For example, as there are no cooking recipes in the Bible, the vocabulary of food preparation, which is surely essential in any community, is under-represented in the dictionaries of Biblical Hebrew.

Thematic dictionaries, on the other hand, only cover the words of the selected semantic domains such as gardening or house building, and may lack even the most common other words. The advantage of thematic dictionaries, however, is that within a very short period of time a short, but comprehensive dictionary can be produced which both meets scientific standards and is also interesting for people of the speech community, as well as for researchers in various fields.

The first dictionary project I was asked to organize was a monolingual Samoan dictionary for the Ministry of Youth, Sports and Culture in Western Samoa in 1994. The project was funded by the Australian South Pacific Cultural Fund with 10,000 Australian dollars. How could a staff member of the Ministry and I as his consultant produce a monolingual dictionary with these scarce resources? Necessity is the mother of invention, so our first project was a little booklet on Samoan architecture and furniture (Mosel and Fulu 1997), later to be followed by similar mini-dictionaries on food (Fulu 1997), and other culturally important practices (see Section 17.5 below).

17.2.4 Orthographical matters: working without a standard

Most endangered languages are not written or do not have a standardized orthography (see Lüpke, Chapter 16). If the native speakers who assist the linguist are literate in another language, they can cooperate in developing a standardized orthography. Decisions on orthographic matters should be made in close consultation with local dictionary makers, for example in workshops (see Section 17.6). As the standardization of the orthography is often a political matter, it can be difficult to resolve, but it should not delay the production or distribution of the dictionary by neverending debates (Aoki (2002: 295–7), Hinton and Weigel (2002: 156–60), Seifart 2006). While linguists should always keep in mind that there is no such thing as the perfect orthography and not insist on their suggestions when the local dictionary makers take a different view, the latter should understand that not having a standardized orthography will make the compilation of the dictionary cumbersome (Rice and Saxon 2002).

Sometimes, however, alternative spellings cannot be avoided. In Teop, for instance, vowel length is distinctive and in the orthography long vowels are distinguished from their short counterparts by repeating the vowel letter, e.g. *na* a tense marker and *naa* 'I'. Since the phonology of Teop has not yet been investigated in detail, we are often not sure how variation in vowel length is to be interpreted. In such cases we give the spelling variant just after the headword, whereas in example sentences we rely on the intuitions of the local dictionary makers and often have the vowel spelled in different ways.

From the point of view of many linguists it might appear unreasonable or even irresponsible not to do a thorough phonological analysis before starting work on the dictionary. However, it should not be forgotten that dictionary work on an endangered language and culture is frequently under severe time pressure as old people who can provide the most valuable information may die one after the other. In the context of the cultural aspects of our work, vowel length is a negligible problem (see also Hinton and Weigel 2002: 167–8).

17.2.5 Grammatical information

Unless it is accompanied by a grammar, the dictionary should contain in the front matter at least as much information on the grammatical structure of the language as is necessary to fully understand the abbreviations used in the dictionary entries, e.g. those used for the different parts of speech and their subclasses. A mere list of abbreviations, e.g. *v.* 'verb' and *v.t.* 'transitive verb' is not sufficient. Since 'verb' and 'transitive verb' can mean very different things in different languages, and in different grammars of the same language, the grammatical features of the word classes and subclasses should be briefly explained.

17.3   Word lists

17.3.1 Headwords and subheadwords

The HEADWORD is the first item in a lexical entry. It serves as the keyword for all the information given in the entry. Consequently, a headword like *horse* not only represents a single lexeme, e.g. *horse*, with its two senses of 'animal' and 'piece of sports equipment' but is also the key for multiword expressions such as *horse sense* or *straight from the horse's mouth*. A derived lexeme, e.g. *quickly*, can be treated either as a headword itself (e.g. LDOCE 2005, OALD 2000), or be subsumed as a SUBHEADWORD (also called SECONDARY HEADWORD or RUN-ON) under the headword of the root, e.g. *quick* (e.g. COBUILD 1987, Coward and Grimes (2000: 77–87)).

When the derivational morphemes are prefixes, as in the case of the Samoan causative morpheme *fa'a-*, a root-oriented approach may impede the search for derived lexemes because the causative will be listed out of alphabetical sequence under its root, e.g. *fa'a-mate* 'kill' will be found under the headword *mate* 'die' (Milner 1966: 138). For the Samoan monolingual school dictionary all causatives are listed as headwords with the result that entries for the letter F cover 20 per cent of the published dictionary (So'o and Mosel 2000). In contrast, the Teop preferred to follow the root-oriented approach and accommodated the causative as a subheadword in the entry of the root, e.g. *vaa-mate* 'kill', listed under *mate* 'die'. (Schwartz *et al.* 2007) Perhaps they are more aware of derivational processes than the Samoans, although their language is morphologically similar. Some Teop even write the causative prefix as a separate word. In other words, the question of whether the root-oriented or the lexeme-oriented approach is preferable for a particular dictionary cannot be answered by linguists on the basis of the morphological structure of the language, since the user-friendliness of one or the other approach depends on speaker preferences, and perhaps also on how much the speakers intuitively or consciously know about their language.

In principle, the headword can be any kind of lexical item that the lexicographers consider a useful keyword for users. Such keywords are not necessarily lexemes but can also be inflected wordforms whose stems are difficult to recognize like *bought* (the past tense of *buy*), suppletive wordforms like *went* (root *go*), or even bound morphemes like the Samoan and Teop causative prefixes.

17.3.2 Bad words: a note on purism

With regard to the selection of headwords, the local dictionary makers may be purists and wish to exclude borrowed words or expressions they consider obscene. For borrowed words, my policy is to try to convince them that those which are adapted to the structure of the language belong to the language and consequently should have their place in the dictionary. Otherwise the dictionary would not represent the living language as ordinary people use it. Obscene and other taboo words are a more difficult issue. Perhaps the speech community would agree to include them in a special scientific edition of the dictionary, or in a database with restricted access (Hinton and Weigel 2002: 166). What kind of words a community does not want to include in the dictionary can sometimes be unpredictable. Thus, the compilers of the Hopi dictionary had to exclude any information relating to ritual (K. Hill 2002: 303).

17.3.3 Writing word lists

There are three methods of compiling WORD LISTS:

- translating word lists in the lingua franca into the indigenous language, as suggested at least for basic vocabulary in many field manuals (see 17.3.3.1);
- eliciting words by techniques which encourage the dictionary helpers to produce word lists without translation (see 17.3.3.2);
- creating word lists by extracting items from a corpus (see 17.3.3.3);
- participant observation (see 17.3.3.4).

In the very first phase of a language documentation project, word lists are often compiled for a preliminary study of phonetics and phonology and the design of a practical orthography (Crowley 2007: 95–7). Later they are mainly extracted from the corpus, and elicitation is only used to check and supplement the data derived from the corpus.

17.3.3.1   The flaws of translating prefabricated word lists

In many fieldwork manuals (e.g. Abbi 2001: 244–7, Bowern 2008: 223–4, Kibrik 1977: 103–23, Samarin 1967: 220, Vaux et al. (2007: 89–96)) there are word lists in English which are intended to assist with collecting basic vocabulary by translating the English words into the target language being researched. Two computerized analogues of this exist: the Dictionary Development Process (DDP)[2] which is a Toolbox file with thousands of source language items organized by semantic fields that can be used to elicit translations.[3] A related program (Albright and Hatton 2007) that is intended to be used by trained native speakers is WeSay,[4] which exists in several versions with the source language being English or French.[5] For two reasons this method has to be used with caution: word lists based on a European or other contact language, even a closely related one, will not be representative of the lexicon of the target language and consequently may miss many culturally specific concepts (Bradley 2007e). On the other hand, the list may contain terms which do not have a translation equivalent in the target language. Even items that might be thought of as the most 'basic vocabulary' like 'eat', 'drink' and 'sit' may be missing in the target language (Goddard 2001). Asking local dictionary research assistants to translate an expression X of the contact language into their native language, can mean that 'X comes from a different linguistic system than the mother tongue of the person being asked' (Grimes 2002: 71). The meaning of the target-language expression may be broader or narrower than its counterpart in the contact language, and the items in either language may be polysemous in different ways, so that their meanings may only partly overlap.

When he started compiling a dictionary of Wayan, a Fijian language, beginning in the 1960s and using a dictionary of standard Fijian for his first elicitation sesssions, Pawley (2009: 18) found that: 'Eliciting from lists can certainly yield quick results but my experience is that unless it is combined with a good practical knowledge of the language and careful checking it will leave a lot of errors.' Words which have been elicited by translation always need to be cross-checked by back-translation into the contact language, and by asking for example sentences and explanations of their meaning. In relation to comprehensiveness, a useful tool is the extensive questionnaires on traditional technology, ethnobiology and anatomy in Bouquiaux and Thomas (1992: 401–687), which also contain numerous illustrations.

Even more dangerous than errors in semantic analysis are psychological aspects of the translation method. The local dictionary assistants might feel very embarrassed when they are asked to translate a word they do not understand, or even worse, a word which they cannot translate because they have forgotten the indigenous equivalent.

17.3.3.2 Active eliciting

The problems of the translation method can be avoided by a method I call ACTIVE ELICITING. Active eliciting means that the local assistants are asked to create their own set of data without translating words or sentences. After having discussed the aims of the session, e.g. the compilation of a list of words that are suitable for combining into phrases and clauses, and that in addition will be used for the study of sounds, the assistants may choose a narrowly defined semantic domain such as food and list, for example, the names of vegetables, colour terms and words that have something to do with the preparation of meals ('get some water', 'peel', 'cut', 'wash', 'make a fire', 'pot' etc.). In this way, each word of the list is associated with a particular context of the speech community's culture and thus naturally renders a concept expressed in their language. Another way of eliciting lexemes is to give a basic word of a particular semantic domain, for example the speech act verb 'say', and ask for similar words, e.g. 'whisper', 'murmur', 'shout', 'ask', answer'. For further information on lexical elicitation methods and a critical discussion see Haviland (2006: 148–59) and Grimes (2002).

17.3.3.3 Extracting word lists from a text corpus

The corpus-based compilation of word lists has the advantage that it provides the words in their actual contexts of use. However, as the sense of a word in a particular context is often not its only sense, this method has to be supplemented by asking native speakers for further examples that might reveal different senses, metaphorical uses, and so on. Furthermore, a text corpus compiled in a documentation project over three to five years is usually too small to cover a substantial part of the lexicon of the language so that the dictionary makers must also resort to active eliciting.

17.3.3.4 Participant observation

Another method of obtaining naturalistic data is listening to people speaking and noting down utterances that we encounter 'in circumstances that we do not control' (Grimes 2002: 76). As Mithun (2001: 38) observes: 'a substantial proportion of the most interesting vocabulary emerges only in spontaneous speech, in what speakers themselves choose to say in different contexts'. One should be careful with recording such overheard language however, as it may sometimes contain taboo items or expressions which the community considers obscene or inappropriate for inclusion in a published dictionary. Additionally, slips of the tongue and speech errors occasionally occur, so all overheard material should be cross-checked with native speakers to validate its authenticity and use. Note also that, as with extracting materials from texts (Section 17.3.3.3), alternative senses of overheard expressions may exist (and, in fact, these other senses may be more common than the particular sense of the item identified on the occasion that it was observed) and so supplementary checking of meaning range and uses is in order.

17.4   Writing entries

17.4.1   The structure of the entry

The lexical database should provide for each entry and subentry a number of fields that in the process of the corpus analysis and elicitation or translation can be filled with grammatical, semantic and pragmatic information, as well as with illustrative sentences. For a detailed description of entries in databases and dictionaries of European languages see Atkins and Rundell (2008: 100–1, 317–79) and Svensén (1993: 210–18). For how to build a Toolbox lexical database, see Coward and Grimes (2000).

The lexical entry should start with a field for the headword followed by fields for information on homonyms (items with the same form but different semantics), variants, pronunciation, part of speech and inflection. In the case of polysemous headwords like English *mouse*, the lexical database should provide:

- a field to identify each sense (e.g. a sense ID number);
- within each sense, fields for grammatical information, such as 1. Plural *mice*, 2. Plural *mouses*;
- the meaning of each sense, e.g. '1. animal …' and '2. computer pointing device …';
- citations from the corpus and examples created by native speakers, together with references indicating where the examples come from;
- whatever additional fields the lexicographer considers important for each sense.

The sequence of the senses of the headword can follow various organizing principles (Svensén 1993: 193–214). Ideally, the most general meaning should come first and then meanings that are restricted to certain contexts or are derived by metaphor or metonymy should come later. Thus, in the entry for *atovo* in the Teop lexical database the sense 'sago palm' precedes the sense 'thatch made from sago palm leaves'. However, note that sense discrimination and the distinction between polysemy and homonymy is very difficult from both a practical and a theoretical perspective. For further information on this topic see Atkins and Rundell (2008: 263–316), Cruse (1986: 49–83), and Cruse (2000: 104–42).

If a headword belongs to more than one part of speech category, like the English word *strike*, which functions as both a verb and a noun, the part-of-speech field should be clearly marked off 'to inform the user immediately that the entry contains more than one part of speech' (Svensén 1993: 210); compare the entry for *strike* in the OALD 2000 and in COBUILD 1987. Another possibility is to give each form that belongs to different parts of speech the status of a headword, e.g. to treat *strike* n. and *strike* v. as two separate headwords (LDOCE 2005).

17.4.2 Inflectional versus derivational morphology

When building a lexical database of a previously unresearched language, it may be impossible to decide whether a morphologically complex item, for example a word which contains reduplicated segments, is an inflected wordform or a derived lexeme, because we may not know to what extent the respective morphological processes are productive, and in certain contexts obligatory. In the Teop lexical database we therefore enter such items as subheadwords. Ideally, before the database is transformed into a dictionary, the grammatical analysis of the language should have resolved this problem in order to avoid unnecessarily complex entries.

17.4.3 The definition

The traditional division of dictionaries into monolingual and bilingual dictionaries does not need to be strictly observed in dictionaries of endangered languages because they are not primarily used for transla-tion. In fact, for many headwords a translation equivalent is not suffi-cient because it would not capture the full semantics of the term in the language being documented (Haviland 2006). In such cases the transla-tion can be accompanied by a definition, which ideally is given in the indigenous language first and then translated. Such bilingual definitions would:

- preserve the interpretation of the meaning by the native speakers, thereby reducing the danger of misunderstandings on the part of the linguist;
- show the semantics of the headword and its relations to other expres-sions in the language;
- make the dictionary a resource for further linguistic and anthropo-logical research;
- be able later to be used for the development of a monolingual diction-ary and teaching materials.

For each semantic domain the dictionary writing team needs to pre-pare a style guide that suggests what kind of information the definition should contain. For fishes this can be, for example, the habitat, size, col-our, age and whatever the local fishermen regard as important (Coward and Grimes 2000: 137–52). In contrast to translations, such plant and animal definitions could also show FOLK TAXONOMIES, that is, relation-ships between items that reveal classificatory hierarchical relationships. In Samoan, for instance, *atu* 'tuna', *malie* 'shark', *mumua* 'dolphin', and *laumei* 'turtle' are classified as the same kind of animal, and referred to as *i'a*. A bilingual dictionary entry for *laumei*, for example, would probably only give the translation 'turtle', and not explain that it belongs to the class of *i'a*, which is mostly translated as 'fish'. In the Samoan monolingual dictionary *i'a* is defined as *O le meaola e nofo i le sami ma le vai. O isi e tautu'ufua a o ni isi i'a e fanafanau* 'animal living in salt or sweet water, giving birth to living offspring or laying eggs' (So'o and Mosel 2000: 19).

As already mentioned, lexicography for endangered languages is often severely restricted by considerations of time and money so that lexicographers are forced to be selective regarding the number of headwords they translate or define and the amount of information they give. In the Teop lexical database we entered all lexemes we came across, but for various reasons we could not employ a biologist who would have been able to identify the scientific names of animals and plants. Very often we could not even translate the Teop plant and animal names into English, and had to resort to a definition that would provide the term for the superordinate class and a description of typical characteristics, e.g. 'a hardwood tree growing near the coast whose timber is used for carving canoes'. Wherever possible, this kind of definition should be illustrated by drawings and photographs.

17.4.4 Examples

Included in the database should be example phrases and sentences which are citations from the corpus giving evidence of the usage of the lexical units, i.e. instances of the lexeme or lexicalized multiword expressions in their particular senses; see Cruse (1986: 23ff), Atkins and Rundell (2008: 162f). Only for elicited lexical items should the native-speaker assistants create examples. Both types of examples can serve the grammatical and semantic analysis of lexical units. In contrast, the examples in the dictionary should reflect the results of this analysis and help the reader to better understand the salient grammatical and semantic features of the lexical unit. Since space does not matter in the lexical database, the lexicographic team can collect everything that seems useful for the analysis, but when they transform the database into a dictionary, they must be selective and choose only one or two examples for each type of usage. Furthermore, many citations will prove unsuitable as dictionary examples because they are too complex, only comprehensible in their wider context, or not representative. An example of this would be the following citation from a Teop legend: 'The old woman hid the moon in her saucepan.' Thus for practical reasons many citations may need to be abridged, adapted to the format of example sentences, or replaced by specially created representative examples.

Even if all lexical units of a headword seem to be well illustrated by citations from the corpus, it is advisable to ask native speakers to supply additional examples. Such created examples may illustrate more typical or different usages of the lexical unit, and reveal misinterpretations. In the Teop lexical database, for instance, *babanihi* and *matavus* were both translated by 'door' and hence regarded as synonyms, until one of our local lexicographers provided the example:

(1) O   babanihi no   matavus   paa taketau.
     'The   door   of.the   door   is loose.'

We then realized that the two senses of the polysemous English word 'door', namely 'door-panel' and 'door-way' (Cruse 1986: 65) are rendered in Teop by the two distinct lexemes *babanihi* 'door-panel' and *matavus* 'door-way'. A good summary of the functions that example sentences can play in a bilingual dictionary can be in found in Bartholomew and Schoenhals (1983: 59–69).

17.4.5 Idioms and proverbs

As far as the limited time and funds permit, lexicalized phrases and patterns of expression should be included in the dictionary, because the native speaker's linguistic competence not only encompasses the phonology, grammar and lexicon, but also the phraseology of their language (Pawley 1992, 1993). One might also wish to include idioms and proverbs, because they reflect the culture of a speech community more than any other kind of linguistic unit; however, the explanation of their meaning and use can be difficult. A classification of multiword expressions and description of how they are treated in various types of English dictionaries is given in Atkins and Rundell (2008: 166–76, 222–5).

17.4.6 Etymology

Although many people are interested in the history of languages, exploring and documenting the etymology of headwords should be postponed. The documentation of an endangered language as a living language should have priority, and the reconstruction of its history has to wait.

17.5 Turning the lexical database into mini-dictionaries

Since the entries of the dictionary are typically alphabetically ordered, many people think that the writing of a dictionary starts with the letter A. In fact, many dictionary projects used this alphabetical approach and some of them were never finished, but stopped somewhere in the middle of the alphabet. A dictionary covering only the letters A to K is not a very useful book. In the case of endangered languages, for most of which no previous dictionary exists, the alphabetical approach is disastrous if for whatever reasons the dictionary work comes to an end before the project is completed.

17.5.1   Advantages of the thematic approach

As already mentioned in Section 17.2.3, an alternative to the alphabetic approach is a thematic approach, because a mini-dictionary can be produced in a rather short time and serve as a resource for teachers, linguists and ethnographers (Mosel and Fulu 1997). Furthermore, the completion of such a mini-dictionary can raise the motivation of local lexicographers to continue the dictionary work by themselves once the outside consultant has left (Fulu 1997).

Whether researchers work over an extended period in a community, or only come to visit once a year for a short time, they can never be sure that they can always work with the same people. The thematic approach provides the opportunity to finish the lexicographic work on one domain or subdomain with a given team, which will result in a more consistent piece of work than working on multiple domains with different people.

Another advantage of the thematic approach is that local dictionary makers can work on their special field of interest and interview experts on certain subject areas (e.g. fishing, architecture, healing), which typically reinforces their motivation. Furthermore, this approach bears an important advantage for the training of local lexicographers: as a rule, specialized vocabulary is less frequently used than general vocabulary, and is less polysemous and consequently easier to describe (Atkins and Rundell 2008: 263). Because of its low frequency it also tends to be the most endangered vocabulary, so documenting it should have a higher priority.

The production of a non-commercial dictionary is expensive. It may not be possible to provide every teacher with a dictionary, but if every school receives a set of mini-dictionaries, the teachers can share this set. While one teacher is using the mini-dictionary on architecture, the others may prepare their lessons with the fishing, gardening, tree or shellfish mini-dictionaries. The animal and plant mini-dictionaries will also foster awareness of biodiversity and may eventually contribute to the protection of the environment.

17.5.2   The choice of themes

Since time and financial resources are limited, the project has to set priorities. Two criteria seem to be useful in guiding the selection of the first semantic domains: which domains do the elders and teachers consider as the most important for the transmission of their cultural knowledge to future generations? Which domains do you as a linguist or anthropologist regard as the most endangered?

Food preparation may be an excellent domain to start with because direct observation, photos and videos can help the lexicographic team to understand the terms denoting ingredients and activities, whereas documenting the concepts of traditional law and cosmology would presuppose a deep understanding of the history and culture of the people.

A drawback of the thematic approach, however, is that some lexemes are polysemous like Teop *atovo* 1. 'sago palm', 2. 'thatch of sago palm leaves' so that their various senses would belong to different mini-dictionaries, e.g. in this case the tree dictionary and the house dictionary. For the Teop mini-dictionaries we solved this problem by always giving the basic sense first, even if it belongs to a different semantic domain. Thus in the house dictionary the entry of *atovo* starts with the sense 'sago palm'.

17.5.3 Turning the lexical database into a mini-dictionary

After having selected the semantic domains, the lexical units of the lexical database (i.e. the sets of senses of a headword) are accordingly classified by entering the respective keywords into a special semantic domain field. If a lexical unit relates to more than one domain, the field can be filled with more than one keyword (for how to do this with Toolbox see Coward and Grimes (2000: 26, 191)). The semantic domain field can be hierarchically structured, e.g. in Teop *atovo* 'sago palm': plant, tree; *taruvana* 'giant pandanus': plant, pandanus (Atkins and Rundell 2008: 182–4).

If the lexical database is filtered, for each semantic domain, e.g. 'plant', or subdomain, e.g. 'tree', a separate mini-database can be created. The data in these specialized mini-databases can then be exported and printed in a format that looks like the planned mini-dictionaries so they can be discussed with experts and teachers of the speech community and accordingly be revised and supplemented. Eventually the project should produce a paper and an electronic version of the mini-dictionaries.

17.6 Capacity building: apprenticeship and workshops

The outcome of any kind of lexicographic project heavily relies on the cooperation between the outsiders and their local counterparts, which in the first place requires emotional intelligence and social competence on both sides. But it is the outside linguists who bear the full responsibility for a smooth effective workflow as it is they who introduce a new activity, dictionary making, into the community. It is also they who should know how much and what kind of work is involved, as set out in Svensén's (1993: 236–49) overview of the various stages of dictionary projects from the planning phase to the final proofreading.

17.6.1   Mutual apprenticeship

At the beginning of the project I recommend working with no more than three local people. Depending on their personal interests and skills, they can be trained on an individual basis on specific lexico-graphic tasks like compiling word lists, writing definitions and example sentences, and proofreading. These individuals are not, however, just apprentices of the craft of dictionary making, but are at the same time the linguists' mentors, teaching them the language and leading them to an understanding of their culture. Consequently, capacity building involves both providing local people with linguistic know-how as well as acquiring invaluable knowledge and experience through working with them.

17.6.2   Workshops

In developing countries, workshops are frequently conducted by foreign-aid agencies and non-governmental organizations in order to dissemin-ate information, knowledge and new technology. Since the organization of workshops is time consuming and expensive, the purpose and possible outcomes of a workshop need careful consideration. From my experience three kinds of workshops are useful:

- introductory workshops for community representatives, local lan-guage experts and teachers to inform them about the work processes involved in dictionary making, identify and correct wrong expect-ations, set realistic aims, justify the presence of the outside linguist in the speech community, and help to recruit local lexicographers;
- workshops that discuss the form and content of the dictionary or the choice of orthography, in order to facilitate the general acceptance of the dictionary;
- workshops for teachers on the use of the dictionary or other lexico-graphical materials resulting from the project.

From our experience with the Samoan monolingual school diction-ary it does not seem advisable to run workshops on compiling word lists or dictionary entries. Certainly, it is possible to accumulate hun-dreds of pages of material in a two-day workshop with twenty people, but it will take months of frustrating work to sort out and revise these materials.

When considering whether to conduct a workshop, it is important to form a small planning committee to become aware of the speech com-munity's expectations, discuss objectives and feasibility issues, and cal-culate the costs of transport, stationery, food and accommodation. The committee should also inform the outsiders about what kinds of rituals and traditions of public discourse have to be observed, and assist in designing a programme.

17.7 Concluding remarks

Compiling a dictionary of a poorly researched language means making compromises. The first dictionary of an endangered language is sure not to be a perfect dictionary. But as long as the dictionary makers are aware of their problems, and explicitly state in the front matter what kinds of problems they encountered and what kind of compromises or solutions they decided on, the dictionary can become a valuable resource for future research and language-maintenance measures.

It is important to recognize that it is not only the product, the dictionary, that can serve language maintenance. The whole process of making a dictionary, if carried out in a spirit of cooperation and mutual respect for each other's capacities, can raise awareness of the uniqueness and value of a language.

Notes

1 Samoan is not an endangered, unresearched language and the dictionary projects I was involved in were monolingual, but my experiences there helped me to develop strategies to deal with the time problem and to learn to work in a team with indigenous people. Special thanks go to my Samoan counterparts Mose Fulu and Ainslie So'o. The Teop team comprises so many people that they cannot be enumerated here; I am most grateful to all of them, especially to Ruth Saovana Spriggs who introduced me to her language and people and to Ruth Siimaa Rigamu my host, best friend and teacher in Hiovabon, Bougainville. The Samoan projects were funded by the Australian South Pacific Cultures Fund and AusAid, and the Teop Language Documentation Project by the Volkswagen Foundation (www.mpi.nl/DOBES/Teop).
2 See www.sil.org/computing/ddp.
3 DDP is available in English, Spanish, French, Swahili and Malay; files for Chinese, Nepali, Thai, Tamil, Amharic and Portuguese are being prepared.
4 See www.wesay.org/wiki/Main_Page.
5 Indonesian, Thai and Burmese are planned.

18

Language curriculum design and evaluation for endangered languages

Serafin M. Coronel-Molina and Teresa L. McCarty

18.1 Introduction

Consider the following commentary by Northern Cheyenne language educator Richard Littlebear (1996: xii–xiv):

> [S]ome of us said, 'Let's get our languages into written form' and we did and still our Native American languages kept on dying ... Then we said, 'Let's let the schools teach the languages' and we did, and still the languages kept on dying. Then we said, 'Let's develop culturally-relevant materials' and we did and still our languages kept on dying ... In this litany, we have viewed each item as the one that will save our languages – and they haven't.

These comments illuminate the problems with conventional definitions of CURRICULUM and EVALUATION when applied to endangered languages. We tend to think of curriculum in academic terms, as something written, official, standardized and prescriptive. Similarly, language evaluation typically connotes standardized assessments of predetermined proficiency levels, with success and failure defined by a score on a test. These perspectives are both limited and limiting, and, as Littlebear suggests, they have not served us well as tools for revitalizing endangered languages.

In this chapter we conceptualize curriculum and evaluation as both products and processes, situated within particular socio-cultural contexts and informed by local language planning and policy (LPP) goals (Sallabank, Chapter 14). We begin by defining key terms. We then discuss a range of examples of LPP-oriented curriculum and evaluation. Because the majority of the world's endangered languages are those spoken by Indigenous peoples, we focus on these languages, although the content is relevant to many endangered languages. In the final section, we offer a comparative perspective on these curricular approaches and their outcomes, drawing out larger implications for the sustainability of endangered languages and speech communities.

18.2 Curriculum and evaluation from an LPP perspective

CURRICULUM for endangered languages can be defined as any intentional learning experiences designed to promote spoken and/or written development in the endangered language. From this perspective, curriculum involves situated social and cultural practices rooted in locally meaningful knowledge, social networks and communicative activities. EVALUATION is any systematic method to assess a curriculum's effectiveness in accomplishing its long- and short-term goals. Evaluation does not refer solely to narrow assessments of language fluency or proficiency (as we will see, these ends may be more or less important depending on curricular goals). Rather, evaluation should be viewed in light of broader LPP goals, which may include strengthening the intergenerational ties through which language is transmitted, (re)building communal systems to support language learning, elevating the status of an endangered language vis-à-vis languages of wider communication, documenting the language in written or audio-visual form, increasing the numbers of speakers and contexts in which an endangered language is used, or some combination of outcomes. As we show, these processes take place both in and out of 'official' settings such as classrooms and schools.

To understand curriculum and evaluation from a language policy and planning perspective, we need to briefly discuss these terms. LANGUAGE PLANNING, that is, deliberate efforts to influence people's language choices and practices, is typically viewed as a foundation for official rules or laws which serve to monitor and enforce language planning goals (Kaplan and Baldauf 1997). Here, we take a broader view of planning and policy. LPP may be both implicit and explicit, unofficial and official, de facto and de jure (Hornberger 2006; McCarty *et al.* 2009, Schiffman 1996, Shohamy 2006). As social processes, planning and policy making are integrated, overlapping and recursive (see Sallabank, Chapter 14), and involve decisions about:

1. the relative statuses of languages within particular linguistic ecologies;
2. linguistic forms and norms for grammar, lexicon, orthography and so forth;
3. how languages will be acquired.

LPP-oriented curriculum and evaluation are one means through which these mutually constitutive LPP decisions are enacted, and usually encompass aspects of all three.

18.3   LPP curriculum and evaluation in practice

We turn now to consider LPP curriculum and evaluation in practice. What does curriculum for endangered languages look like in actual practice? How is language curriculum for endangered languages developed and evaluated? To address these questions we explore several illustrative cases that reflect a range of linguistic and cultural settings and goals, including curricula designed to revitalize languages with few remaining first-language speakers (often referred to as OBSOLESCING or MORIBUND languages), and efforts to restore intergenerational language transmission at the level of families and communities. This is what Fishman (1991, 2001a) calls 'reversing language shift'. For each case or example, we begin with some background on the sociohistorical context for language loss and contemporary LPP goals. As we will see, each case raises different questions about what constitutes effective or successful LPP curriculum and evaluation.

18.3.1   LPP curriculum design for languages with few remaining speakers: the master–apprentice approach

What curricular approaches have been employed for revitalizing languages with few remaining first-language speakers? One constellation of languages that fit this description are Native American languages in present-day California. Before the arrival of Europeans, the far western reaches of the North American continent were among the most linguistically and culturally diverse regions of the world. In California alone there were 300,000 to 400,000 Native American people who spoke some 100 languages (Hinton 1998: 85, 2001b: 217). Colonization by Spaniards, Mexicans and Anglo-Americans brought disease, indiscriminate slaughter and enslavement (Hinton 2001b: 217, Sims 1998: 97). As Acoma Pueblo language educator Christine Sims (1998: 99–100) notes, by the early twentieth century these disruptions had 'set the stage for an increasingly tenuous linguistic situation.' Recent estimates are that fifty California Native American languages are still spoken, none as a first language by children, and only four have more than a hundred speakers (Hinton 2001b). Clearly the languages are in a critical state.

California languages encompass some eighteen different language families. Thus, Native California tribes do not have a single identity or language into which human and financial resources can be invested; each language must be dealt with individually, which requires greater resources and makes their situations more challenging to address. And, unlike some SLEEPING languages such as Miami, there is not a large corpus of written materials (Hinton 1998: 86; 2001b: 218; Rinehart 2007). Instead, individuals interested in learning their heritage language have turned to elders and intertribal networks as essential curriculum resources.

The emphasis on elders as language teachers is the heart of the California MASTER–APPRENTICE language-learning approach. 'This is not a traditional classroom situation with a trained teacher who [decides] what the student is to learn' Hinton *et al.* (2002: xii–xiii) point out in their guidebook *How To Keep Your Language Alive*, an easy-to-follow guide which provides detailed suggestions for structured activities around which to organize master–apprentice sessions, from the beginners' level through to advanced language learning. Master speakers/teachers are paired with younger language learners in a one-on-one immersion setting. The teams work together for ten to twenty hours per week and one to three years at a time (sometimes longer, depending on the team).

In contrast to some school-based language-learning approaches that focus on formal study of linguistic structures (e.g. grammar exercises), the master–apprentice curriculum is communication between master and apprentice in the context of everyday activities and tasks. The ten principles which guide this approach are set out in Hinton (Chapter 15). Unlike grammar-based language learning and teaching, in TASK-BASED LANGUAGE LEARNING of the sort employed by the master–apprentice approach, 'the point of departure is not an ordered list of linguistic items, but a collection of tasks' that constitute the cornerstone of the curriculum (Nunan 1999: 24). Task-based language learning provides learners with meaningful opportunities to explore the peculiarities of the language through a set of tasks in order to be exposed to practical, authentic and functional language uses in a systematic way. Task-based language learning is based on the following principles:

1. an emphasis on learning to communicate through interaction in the target language;
2. opportunities for learners to focus not only on language per se, but also on the language learning process itself;
3. enhancement of learners' personal experiences as an important goal in the curriculum. (Nunan 1991: 279)[1]

In the context of master–apprentice tasks and activities, both learner and master teacher interact in the language ('What is this?' 'What am I doing?'), using gestured and spoken commands and visual cues to aid comprehension. This is followed by a 'post-mortem' debriefing about the immersion set ('There might have been things the apprentice couldn't understand ... You may also want to talk about improvements you could make' as Hinton *et al.* (2002: 26–7) advise), like planning for the next session, and farewells. The California master–apprentice curriculum includes a periodic two-part assessment, though not in the form of a strict written test. Instead, the master teacher first asks questions and observes how the apprentice responds, then gives the apprentice a picture and asks her or him to say anything she or he can about it. Are there lapses into English? How conversant has the apprentice become? The assessment is usually video-taped and used as a tool for planning and future learning (Hinton *et al.* 2002: 99–101).

As Hinton (2001b: 223) notes, the goal is for apprentices to be 'at least conversationally proficient in their language' and ready to teach it to others within three years – a goal that many apprentices have achieved. Conversational proficiency is thus one measure of curricular success. Another measure is the transferability of this approach to other settings. The master–apprentice programme has been adopted and adapted by other indigenous communities. The Comanche Nation in Oklahoma, for instance, has run a master–apprentice programme since the late 1990s that has produced fluent speakers (Hinton *et al.* 2002: 101). Other less quantifiable or observable yet significant indicators of success include strengthening intergenerational ties and 'bringing people back in touch with their roots' (Hinton 2001b: 225). 'The passion and dedication of those who are working with their languages is obvious and inspiring to others' Hinton (1998: 92) says and adds: 'It is a healthy movement ... toward recovery from the devastating social and cultural wounds inflicted by the European incursion into California.' This assessment suggests that cultural revitalization is another important measure of curricular success.

18.3.2   Heritage language schooling for 'moribund' languages and languages 'at risk'

While the approaches discussed thus far are largely community and home based, many language curricula for endangered languages have been developed in the more formal or official context of state-run and locally run schools. School-based approaches have been criticized because they transfer responsibility for heritage language transmission from its natural domain, the home and family, to a secondary or tertiary institution (Fishman 1991, Krauss 1998). Moreover, as historically assimilative institutions, schools have played a major role in linguistic and cultural oppression and the eradication of Indigenous and minority tongues. Yet, in recent years, grassroots ethnolinguistic revitalization movements have reclaimed local authority over the content and medium of instruction in many schools serving students from endangered language communities (see e.g. McCarty 1998). While still facing many challenges (discussed later in this chapter), these initiatives are having positive effects on the reclamation of endangered languages (Hornberger 2008). As May and Aikman (2003: 141) point out, schools have come to be seen as 'key arenas' for simultaneously revitalizing threatened languages and improving educational outcomes for minority language students. In this section we examine cases of these curricular innovations from New Zealand, the US and Norway.

Among the most promising school-based efforts are those undertaken by the Hawaiians in the US and the Māori in Aotearoa/New Zealand. Hawaiian and Māori are Eastern Polynesian languages belonging to the Austronesian family, and their language-revitalization initiatives have followed intertwined paths. Following the voyages of Captain James Cook in the late eighteenth century, Aotearoa/New Zealand and Hawai'i were increasingly drawn into an international trade and political system. In Hawai'i, an indigenous monarchy emerged, with Hawaiian as the language of government, business, trade, education, religion, print media and intercultural communication. The Hawaiian Kingdom persisted until 1893, when the US military staged an illegal coup, annexing Hawai'i as a US territory. At the time, the literacy rate in Hawaiian was higher than in any other language used in the Hawaiian islands (Wilson and Kamanā 2006). In 1959 Hawai'i became the fiftieth US state. In Aotearoa/New Zealand, although the Treaty of Waitangi, signed in 1840 between the British Crown and Māori chiefs, guaranteed the Māori possession of their lands, homes and treasured possessions, the treaty was quickly violated by white settlers in pursuit of Māori lands. In both cases, the Indigenous peoples experienced 'political disenfranchisement, misappropriation of land, population and health decline, educational disadvantage and socioeconomic marginalization' (May 2005: 366). By the mid twentieth century, language death was imminent (May 2005: 367, Wilson *et al.* 2006: 42).

These events were the impetus for parallel grassroots language and ethnic revitalization movements. In 1978, Hawaiian became co-official with English in the state of Hawai'i. In 1987, the Māori Language Act was passed, recognizing Māori as co-official with English (and more recently, also with New Zealand Sign Language). Full-immersion Māori LAN-GUAGE NEST preschools or *Te Kōhanga Reo* began in 1982. In 1983 the first Hawaiian immersion preschools were established (called '*Aha Pūnana Leo* and also meaning language nest) (May 2005, Warner, 1999, Wilson 1999). These largely family-run preschools facilitate the interaction of children with fluent speakers entirely in the Indigenous language. The goal is to cultivate fluency and knowledge of the Indigenous language and culture in 'much the same way that they were in the home in earlier generations' (Wilson and Kamanā 2001: 151). The preschools set the stage for establishing Indigenous-language tracks and whole-school immersion programmes within their respective public school systems, and, as we discuss later for Hawaiian, a comprehensive system of indigenous language support.

Hill and May (2011) examine factors that contribute to the educational effectiveness of Māori-medium schooling, looking specifically at the Te Wharekura o Rakaumangamanga (Rakaumanga) School on

New Zealand's North Island. One of the largest and oldest Māori-medium schools, having begun bilingual education in the 1970s, Rakaumanga provides Māori-medium schooling for students from year 1 (age 5) to year 13 (age 18). The school's philosophy builds on student strengths, embracing Māori culture as an essential factor in student achievement (Hill and May 2011). Following the 'seven year Māori immersion principle', entering students must have attended Kōhanga Reo for at least two years, laying the foundation for four years of full Māori immersion, after which English is introduced for three to four hours per week (Hill and May 2011, Spolsky 2003). To ensure integrity of the Māori language environment, Māori and English instruction are separated by time, place and teacher. The goal is for full bilingualism and biliteracy as a means of preparing students to be 'citizens of the world' (Hill and May 2010).

To assess reading in Māori, the school uses a Māori language framework called *Nga Kete Korero* (New Zealand Ministry of Education 1999). Each reading level is described as a *kete*, or traditional woven flax bag named for a Māori plant; within each *kete* are sublevels arranged according to difficulty (Hill and May 2011). Māori writing is also assessed using non-fiction Māori texts. According to Hill and May (2011: 178), these literacy assessments demonstrate that by year 8, students have reached or are approaching age-appropriate literacy development in both languages and are 'well on their way to achieving the goal of bilingualism and biliteracy—a key aim of Māori-medium education.' A recent study by Māori educator Cath Rau (2005) indicates that these evaluation findings extend to other Māori-medium schools; she reports a significant increase in student reading and writing scores from 1995 to 2002–3 as a result of increased support and resources for Māori curriculum development, reading materials, and teachers' professional development.

Wilson and Kamanā (2001) report on the Nāwahīokalani'ōpu'u (Nāwahī) Laboratory School in Hilo, Hawai'i, a full-immersion, early childhood through high school programme affiliated with the University of Hawai'i-Hilo's College of Hawaiian Language and the 'Aha Pūnana Leo. The school teaches all subjects through Hawaiian language and values, offering a college preparatory curriculum and 'an explicit understanding that use of the Hawaiian language has priority over ... English' (Wilson and Kamanā 2001: 158). Students also learn a 'useful' third language such as Japanese. Nāwahī students not only surpass their non-immersion peers on English standardized tests, they outperform the state average for all ethnic groups on high school graduation, college attendance and academic honours (Wilson *et al.* 2006: 42).

Of special interest in the Nāwahī case is its role as part of an integrated system of Hawaiian-medium structures 'that can develop, protect, nurture and enrich young adult and child fluency in Hawaiian along with the crucial disposition to use Hawaiian with Hawaiian speaking peers' (Wilson and Kawai'ae'a 2007: 38). These structures and systems are captured by the Hawaiian term *honua*, 'places, circumstances, [and] structures where use of Hawaiian is dominant' (Wilson and Kawai'ae'a 2007: 38). Like Rakaumanga, the curricular goal is for learners to achieve Hawaiian dominance alongside high levels of English fluency and literacy, but also to produce students who 'psychologically identify Hawaiian as their dominant language and the one that they will speak with peers and their own children when they have them' (Wilson and Kawai'ae'a 2007: 39).

A critical component in achieving these goals is Ka Haka 'Ula O Ke'elikōlani College. This fully Hawaiian self-governing unit provides curriculum support to pre-kindergarten through grade 12 laboratory schools (including Nāwahī) in partnership with the 'Aha Pūnana Leo. The college's 43-credit bachelor's degree programme includes an additional twenty-eight hours of language study, and is conducted entirely in Hawaiian after the first year. As Wilson and Kawai'ae'a (2007: 45) describe the curriculum:

> Students first experience sole use of Hawaiian when they enter the second year course. By the third year, they are expected to use only Hawaiian among themselves. By the fourth year, students are expected to take leadership roles in moving lower level students to full use of Hawaiian.

An extension of this curriculum is the college's Kahuawaiola Indigenous Teacher Education Programme, officially accredited in 2001. The teacher preparation curriculum is based on traditional Hawaiian beliefs that 'knowledge comes from direct experience' (Wilson and Kawai'ae'a 2007: 45). Entering students must have had eight semesters of Hawaiian language, a course on Hawaiian culture, and have volunteered for at least seventy-five hours in a Hawaiian-medium school; they must also pass a rigorous Hawaiian language fluency exam and are expected to be able to transcribe elders speaking on cultural topics and translate a contemporary newspaper article from English to Hawaiian 'from a Hawaiian cultural perspective … a skill important for teachers developing classroom curriculum … in a language with an educational materials resource base thousands of times smaller than that of English' (Wilson and Kawai'ae'e 2007: 46).

Kahuawaiola students begin with intensive immersion in a six-week summer residency at Nāwahī during which they 'live their lives entirely in Hawaiian' (Wilson and Kawai'ae'e 2007: 46). This is followed by a year of student teaching in which they work with master teachers in Hawaiian-medium schools and participate in weekly seminars and special workshops through distance education. As part of their coursework, pre-service teachers design lesson plans aligned with state standards and Hawaiian *Nā Honua Mauli Ola Hawai'i Guidelines for Culturally Healthy and Responsive Learning Environments* (Native Hawaiian Education Council 2002).

Additional supports to Hawaiian-medium schooling in which Ka Haka 'Ula O Ke'elikōlani College has been instrumental are three Hawaiian teacher content licenses, a Hawaiian Teacher Standards Board, a new PhD in Hawaiian and Indigenous Language and Culture Revitalization, and a new master's degree in Indigenous Language and Culture Education that provides 'the next layer of professional development' for teacher education candidates (Wilson and Kawai'ae'e 2007: 49).

Hawaiian-medium education now serves 2,000 students of Hawaiian ancestry and others in a coordinated set of schools, beginning with the preschools and moving through full Hawaiian-medium elementary and secondary education (Wilson *et al.* 2006). In Aotearoa/New Zealand, 25,000 primary-age children are enrolled in 430 Māori-medium schools designated as Level 1 (81–100 per cent Māori immersion), Level 2 (51–80 per cent immersion), Level 3 (30–50 per cent immersion) or Level 4 (less than 30 per cent immersion but at least three hours per week) (May and Hill 2005: 395, Rau 2005).

How can these curricula be evaluated? Several previously discussed criteria are relevant here: linguistic fluency and biliteracy among a new generation of speakers, an increase in the number of speakers of the heritage language, and cultural revitalization. As Spolsky (2003) describes the outcomes for Māori, while natural intergenerational transmission has not been fully restored, the combination of school and community efforts has stemmed language loss and is leading to language maintenance. In Hawai'i, as many as 15,000 Hawaiians use or understand Hawaiian, the vast majority of whom are the products of Hawaiian-medium schooling. Wilson and Kamanā (2001: 153) cite two other outcomes of these efforts in Hawai'i: the development of an interconnected group of young parents who are increasing their proficiency in Hawaiian, and the creation of a more general social climate of Native-language support.

But these cases add something new that is not necessarily a goal in other cases: academic success through the heritage tongue. Importantly, and consistent with research on second-language acquisition from around the world, the most significant achievement gains occur in whole-school settings that provide an overall additive language-learning environment designed to produce high levels of bilingualism and biliteracy. Thus, across a spectrum of evaluation outcomes, Māori and Hawaiian can rightfully be called heritage-language-medium 'success stories' that effectively respond to the concerns expressed by Richard Littlebear in Section 18.1 above. Similar outcomes have been reported for full-immersion Indigenous heritage-language schooling among the Navajo, Blackfeet and Ojibwe in the US (McCarty 2010), and in Canada, Latin America and Africa (Hornberger 1996, 2008).

Often, however, the results of Indigenous curricular reforms have been more mixed. The Sámi are the Indigenous people of the Nordic countries who live in what is now Norway, Sweden, Finland and western Russia. Of a total population of 100,000, nearly half (about 40,000) live in Norway (Magga and Skutnabb-Kangas 2003). Sámi is a Finno-Ugric language with three major branches, North Sámi, Lule Sámi, and South Sámi, and eleven subgroups. Until the mid-twentieth century, the Sámi language remained outside the school walls. As Hirvonen (2008: 17) describes it, beginning in the 1800s, 'there was a strongly-felt desire to create powerful nation states in Norway and the other Nordic countries' and 'one of the many effects of this was that the Sámi lost their language rights'. As in other colonizing situations, schools became a primary instrument for linguistic and cultural assimilation. This and similar campaigns in other parts of Sámiland led to the decline of all eleven Sámi languages. One is now extinct, four are considered moribund, and the remaining six are considered endangered or severely endangered (Magga and Skutnabb-Kangas 2003).

Following the Second World War, a Sámi ethnic revival took root, and in 1959, Sámi was permitted as a language of instruction. The biggest step in education, however, occurred in the 1990s with the approval of a Norwegian national curriculum initiative known as Reform 97. As Hirvonen (2008: 21) writes, this was 'the first time in the educational history of Norway and the Nordic countries [when] there was a separate Sámi curriculum' with equal status with the national curriculum. Importantly, this reform not only guarantees heritage language and culture instruction for Sámi children in high-density Sámi residential areas (the Sámi core), but provides for teaching in and of the Sámi language outside the Sámi core area as well (Hirvonen 2008: 22). The reform supports three curriculum options: (1) Sámi as a first language, (2) Sámi as a second language with the goal of functional bilingualism, and (3) Sámi language and culture instruction for children with limited background in these areas. The overarching goal is for every student to learn about Sámi culture and for as many as possible to become bilingual (Hirvonen 2008).

In the core Sámi area, where Sámi has high status, these goals are being achieved with a high level of success. However, outside the core area, in mixed Sámi–Norwegian speaking classrooms, Sámi children are typically instructed through Norwegian, with 'pull-out' instruction in Sámi language and culture. According to Hirvonen, these schools are not providing education that makes it possible for children to become bilingual in their heritage language (2008: 33). The ongoing challenges include limited Sámi teaching materials, limited numbers of Sámi-speaking teachers, a lack of Sámi language assessments, and the fact that there is no written language policy in all schools serving Sámi students.

In these cases we see another factor at work in the relative success of curricular reforms for endangered languages: the extent to which those reforms elevate the status of the heritage language vis-à-vis the language(s) of wider communication. As Romaine (2006a: 452) points out: 'imbalance of power is the key feature that distinguishes diglossia from societal bilingualism'. In the Māori, Hawaiian and Sámi cases, power imbalances have been contested, if not completely transformed, through formal status planning (officialization of the languages). For Māori, Hawaiian and Sámi in the Sámi core, this is reinforced by educational programming that provides an overall additive language-learning environment and embeds language acquisition in academic content. Precisely because they are threatened languages, these kinds of LPP reforms require additional support, what Hirvonen (2008: 38) calls 'positive discrimination', so that the Indigenous language and culture are integral rather than ancillary to the school curriculum and the larger social milieu and linguistic ecology.

18.3.3 Curriculum design for multidialectal/multinational languages: Quechua, crossing the digital divide[2]

The sociolinguistic makeup of the Quechua language is complex due to the mosaic of varieties scattered across South America, each of which has a different status as well as different socio-historical circumstances. Quechua is considered an endangered language because like many minority languages, it exists in a diglossic situation in which the high-status language is so powerful that it forces the low-status language slowly into extinction. In this case, Spanish is the prestige language, while Quechua (and nearly every other Indigenous language in Latin America) is, generally speaking, the devalued language. As the language of the colonizers, Spanish has exercised considerable influence over the fortunes of Quechua, and indeed, over all Indigenous languages on the continent. However, one significant difference distinguishing Quechua from other endangered languages is that it currently boasts an estimated 8 to 12 million speakers (Hornberger and King 2001: 166).

One might wonder how a language with so many speakers could be considered endangered. It is important to understand not only the historical situation of contact that Quechua has suffered for more than 500 years, but also the linguistic diversity within the language that is disguised by the use of one name to refer to multiple varieties. Most scholars agree that Quechua can be divided into two major braches, Hauainhuash (classified by linguists as Quechua I) and Huampuy (Quechua II) (Parker 1963, 1969–1971, Torero 1964, 1974). Varieties of both branches can be considered at risk or nearly extinct, while some southern varieties of Quechua II continue to be transmitted intergenerationally and can be considered enduring. Because different varieties are spoken in different communities and each community exists within its own cultural and national context, each variety faces unique challenges. So although there *may* be linguistic commonalities across regions, the great mosaic of sociocultural experiences makes it difficult to generalize regarding a single monolithic 'Quechua situation'.[3]

New technologies can play an essential role in education and the creation of teaching materials (see Holton, Chapter 19), and there are efforts in this direction for a number of varieties of Quechua. Indigenous rights have become increasingly important in Latin American politics since the 1970s. López and Sichra (online: 2), for instance, have noted that Indigenous organizations and leaders have become increasingly powerful, and a resurgence of ethnicity has 'pushed governments into reconsidering their positions with respect to indigenous populations'. Such reconsiderations have included, since the 1980s and 1990s, specific recognition of the multilingual, pluri-cultural, and multiethnic nature of numerous countries' populations in revisions of their national constitutions.

Educational reform has been central to the fight for Indigenous representation, rights, and self-determination in many of these countries. Again according to López and Sichra, very often educational reforms and intercultural bilingual approaches (for instance, in Bolivia and Ecuador) have resulted from the political mobilization of these Indigenous organizations. This has proved to be a self-perpetuating cycle: 'bilingual education has contributed to increased political awareness and organizational processes among Indigenous people'.

However, this is not to say that educational reform is something new within the last few decades. Bilingual education for Indigenous groups has been alternately proposed and contested since the early twentieth century. In fact, Mexico, Peru and Ecuador were all sites for experimental programmes in bilingual education. The Summer Institute of Linguistics (SIL) was a major player in these efforts, since they viewed it as a way of converting these groups to Christianity. Later, in the mid-twentieth century, the governments of several countries borrowed from these early programmes to develop their own bilingual education initiatives. Such initiatives were often called Intercultural Bilingual Education (IBE) as a means of emphasizing the inclusion of both language and culture in the curricula. Similarly to the SIL, these programmes had ulterior motives; at their inception, they were conceived of as tools for assimilation and easy transition to the dominant Spanish language. In other words, ultimately, the governments were not necessarily interested in the rights of the Indigenous peoples, linguistic or cultural. Although promoted as CULTURAL AWARENESS programmes, these were actually intended as transitional rather than maintenance bilingual programmes. Today, at least on paper, that orientation has for the most part changed to one of maintenance and development of the Indigenous languages.

When well planned and implemented, IBE has the potential to have a significant positive impact on a language's perceived status, not only among the language's users, but also among mainstream society as well. It makes sense, then, to incorporate new technologies into such programmes. One specific example is the creation and use of digital archives in audio and video to facilitate the students' use of language in its true cultural context. These audio-visual materials include a range of communicative situations, both formal and informal, in a variety of different contexts. They also include examples of communicative and pragmatic functions of the language, as well as some of its paralinguistic features (see also Nathan, Chapter 13).

Another example is the development of a wide range of educational multimedia resources for publication in DVD or on the internet, such as electronic workbooks in multimedia format, which are complementary resources for printed textbooks. Likewise, new technologies are being used in the production of interactive textbooks in Quechua for students who participate in IBE in Andean countries.

With regard to the production of dictionaries, grammars and glossaries, new technologies, particularly the internet, play a fundamental role in LPP curriculum design, so much so that a great number of publications in different varieties of Quechua already exist. A significant contribution in this direction is the online publication of several specialized dictionaries in Quechua. Four comprehensive sites that contain a wealth of resources for Quechua are Cultures of the Andes (*Culturas de los Andes*), Quechua Language and Linguistics, Runasimi-Kuchu.com (Cyberquechua) and Runasimipi Qespisqa Software (Project to Create Free Software for Quechua).

In addition, some academic audio-visual productions have been developed by a number of institutions in collaboration with anthropologists, literary scholars, musicologists, linguists and native speakers of Andean languages. One such is a series of audio and video materials on anthropology, history and art of the Andean region produced by the Pontificia Universidad Católica of Peru. Another significant contribution is an audio-visual archive of ethnographic materials produced by researchers affiliated with the French Institute of Andean Studies, which has maintained the archive since 2001.

Perhaps not surprisingly, the software firm Microsoft is working in close cooperation with native speakers and translators in numerous countries around the world to create a series of glossaries of common terms used in computer interfaces; for example: menu, start, print, save, edit, back, insert. These linguistic sets have already been overlaid on Windows XP and Office programmes called Windows® XP Qhishwa Rimaypa T'iqinta, thus providing Native-language interfaces for very popular and widely used computer programmes. Quechua is one of these language sets. In another effort, Google has already produced a search engine entirely in Quechua. While they are not educational efforts per se, these programmes are used often enough in educational pursuits that their existence in Quechua definitely benefits educational efforts. (For more information about revitalization of Quechua involving technology, see Coronel-Molina, 2005: 31–82.)

All of these examples demonstrate the curricular opportunities that communication technologies offer. One of the biggest obstacles in the use of these technologies, however, is connectivity. In previous years, these connections were blocked by the topography of the Andean countries. Thanks to developments in satellite and wireless technologies, it is now possible to overcome these difficulties with greater ease and cost efficiency (see also Holton, Chapter 19).

Similarly, taking advantage of any technological resource implies costs on a scale that the great majority of Indigenous communities cannot afford, given that they are often hard-pressed just to put together the resources for daily living. Even so, it is possible for even the most remote and isolated communities to have access to new technologies through solid planning at the technological, linguistic and financial levels, carried out between the federal government, language planners, political leaders, teachers and Indigenous organizations.

In this discussion of new ways to transmit Quechua and promote education in and about the language, it is difficult to talk of evaluation. Some of what has been discussed has already been attempted, and some has even been implemented. But there is no organized curriculum to speak of that incorporates technology, so there is nothing concrete to evaluate in any of the ways previously discussed. Given that in many instances we are speaking of new technologies, it seems fair to assume that we must consider new means to evaluate their efficacy.

One could say that the users of Indigenous languages are the only ones truly in charge of transmitting their languages from generation to generation, and that they should ultimately be in charge of the content and evaluation of their children's education. Nevertheless, the matter is much more complex than might be imagined due to innumerable political, social and economic barriers that confront Indigenous communities. To solidify the objectives of language revitalization and Indigenous language education, it is necessary to take strong measures at every level, and to consolidate, unite and multiply efforts. It is also critical to have robust linguistic, financial and technological planning, and genuine educational reform, to allow Indigenous languages to take their rightful place in the contemporary world. All of this needs to happen from top-down and bottom-up with the active participation of Indigenous peoples and all other sectors and vectors of the society as a whole.

Beyond technology-driven curriculum reform, there are many contributions to status, corpus and acquisition planning throughout the Andean region. Quechua as an international subject of study is very common; there are more than twenty American universities at which Quechua is taught, and several universities in Asia and Europe offer Quechua as well. In rural areas of the Andean countries, IBE in Quechua and Spanish is being implemented at the elementary level, and Quechua has official status at the governmental level as well. The challenge is how to evaluate these multiple efforts scattered across the vast Andean territory and the virtual world. As in the Sámi case discussed above, IBE in the Andean context has been insufficient to reverse language shift and, in fact, 'weak' forms of IBE (i.e. transitional bilingual education) can accelerate the shift toward the powerful language. The next step may be approaching these efforts from a system-wide perspective as has been done for the strong 'level 1' heritage-language revitalization initiatives for Māori and Hawaiian.

18.4 Summary and conclusions

In this chapter we have examined formal and informal curricula for endangered languages, including those seated primarily in the home and community (the California master–apprentice language–learning programme), schools (Māori, Hawaiian, Sámi), and the virtual world (Quechua). We have also shown how these approaches are situated in distinctive sociolinguistic ecologies aligned with varying degrees of language vitality and risk. Although we have focused on Indigenous languages, similar approaches are being used to strengthen threatened languages around the world. In Scotland and Nova Scotia, for instance, a method called Total Immersion Plus (TIP) is being implemented to teach Gaelic to adult language learners (Desveaux 2008). Through weekly courses, day-long workshops, and summer immersion camps, this community-based curriculum seeks to bring young adult and middle-aged speakers (the necessary 'plus' for intergenerational transmission) to fluency in their heritage mother tongue. Although TIP is in the early stages of implementation, it is already generating considerable local support, including that of elder speakers 'who feel vindicated in the enthusiasm that is now greeting the revival of the language that was repressed and stigmatized in their youth' (Desveaux 2008). In this case, as with those discussed above, success is measured not solely in terms of language fluency (although that is a long-term goal), but in the restoration of ethnolinguistic pride.

Can the same criteria of curricular success be used across all of these sociolinguistic situations, or does each require its own evaluative measures? The cases examined here suggest that there are no universal measures. Rather, LPP curriculum must be evaluated in light of locally meaningful goals, whether they are:

- language revitalization, biliteracy and academic success, as in the cases of Māori, Hawaiian and Sámi;
- conversational proficiency, as in the case of the master–apprentice language learning approach; or

- fostering utility for the heritage language, positive language attitudes and a renewed sense of community and cultural revitalization (goals shared by all of these approaches).

Some of these outcomes (e.g. biliteracy and academic achievement) are appropriately evaluated by quantifiable measures, while others, such as community building, require more subjective assessment. Further, not all of these efforts will restore intergenerational language transmission, nor should that be the *sine qua non* for determining LPP curricular success. It may well be, as Romaine (2006a: 465) argues, that in putting the onus 'on restoration of intergenerational transmission as the sole criterion of success, we run the risk of dismissing the value of the journey, which is at least as, if not more, important than the endpoint, as long as each step is regarded as valuable to the community concerned'.

Finally, while some LPP curriculum designs have been more effective in achieving their aims than others, all face ongoing challenges and constraints. As Slate (1993) wrote with reference to Navajo, an endangered Indigenous language of the US Southwest, clear goal-setting and eternal watchfulness are the price for language regeneration that succeeds in accomplishing its locally determined goals.

Notes

1 In classroom settings, task-based approaches also include the use of authentic texts (i.e., literature, periodicals, etc. in the usual form of the language, not adapted for learners), and linking classroom learning with language activation outside the classroom in the course of socially meaningful activity (Nunan 1991: 279).

2 For a comprehensive treatment of LPP in the Quechua context, see Hornberger and Coronel-Molina (2004).

3 Proto-Quechua developed into the two branches Huaihuash (QI) and Huampuy (QII). Huaihuash (QI) then developed into the Pacaraos variety and the complex of varieties known as Central Quechua. Central Quechua, in turn, has three sub-branches, known as Huailay, AP-AM-AH (abbreviations of the three dialects in this subbranch) and Huancay, which were named approximately for the geographic regions where they developed. Each of these subbranches gave rise to its respective varieties. Huampuy (QII), for its part, also comprises two subbranches, Yungay (QIIA) and Chinchay (QIIB-C), each of which is further subdivided into two regional groups, Yungay and Chinchay. Historically, QII has received the most attention from linguists and language planners, largely because its varieties are much more widely spoken than those of QI. Unfortunately, QI, found only in northern

and central Peru, in the departments of Ancash, Huánuco, Pasco and Junín, and those northeastern areas of the department of Lima where Quechua has traditionally been spoken, is also the branch with the varieties most in danger of dying out, given the small size of the populations speaking them (Cerrón-Palomino 1997: 62).

19

The role of information technology in supporting minority and endangered languages

Gary Holton

19.1 Introduction

In what may well be a seminal article on the subject, Buszard-Welcher (2001) posed the question: 'Can the web save my language?' While intended rhetorically, this question clearly reflects a growing enthusiasm for incorporating information technology (IT) into language-maintenance efforts. As the World Wide Web and associated internet technologies increasingly become a part of all information technology solutions, we can restate this question as: 'Can information technology save my language?' This too, of course, must be interpreted rhetorically, for clearly technology alone cannot save a language any more than it can, say, write a book or build a car. But just as desktop publishing software can assist with book production, and robotic technology can help to build an automobile, information technology has important roles to play in supporting minority and endangered languages.

The fundamental scalability of information technology can be thought of as a great equalizer which puts the powerful resources developed for major world languages into the hands of minority language communities. For example, technologies developed to digitally represent non-Latin writing systems such as those used in Chinese and Hindi – languages with hundreds of millions of speakers – can be employed effectively for minority languages, whose communities might not otherwise have the resources to develop such technologies independently. Further, information technology has the potential to create virtual language communities which bridge the gaps created by language shift in minority-language communities. In particular, information technology can bring together speakers and learners who are scattered over great distances.

19.1.1   The technology hurdle

In the interests of full disclosure, it should be mentioned that while IT has the potential to support language-maintenance efforts, it can also be a hindrance to those efforts if not considered carefully. One area where this is true is orthography. Text has played a crucial role in IT as the primary medium through which language is conveyed, and this has remained true in spite of the increasing prevalence of multimedia. While some IT products strive to avoid use of text, most multimedia products include a text component. Thus, while an online dictionary may include images and audio files, it will often require a user to click on textual links in the target language in order to navigate around it. Other IT products such as blogs and email listservs rely almost exclusively on text, both for display of language information and for language input. This is unproblematic provided the language employs a standard keyboard available for a language of wider communication (be it Latin-based, Cyrillic, etc.). However, if the language employs a specialized orthography, it may present difficulties for the development of language-learning software. In many cases even sending email messages may be difficult. The frustrations involved in using fonts and special characters are summed up nicely in the following statement from the Yukon Native Language Centre (2006).

> Anyone who does specialized language work can confirm that the issues of special characters, fonts, keystrokes, document exchange, websites, and others have cost much time and anxiety.

Admittedly, this situation has changed somewhat in recent years as the Unicode character encoding initiative has become more widely implemented in standard commercial operating systems and software (see Good, Chapter 11). However, the problem of data entry remains. Consider the case of Han Athabascan, a language spoken along the border of Alaska and Canada. Han has six vowels and seven diphthongs, each of which may be nasalized and may occur with one of four tones. The most commonly occurring vowel is a low-tone, nasalized, low back vowel. There is no single Unicode character representing this sound. Rather, it must be expressed as a combination of characters. Unfortunately, there is no unique combination to represent the vowel, but rather at least three different combinations of three Unicode characters.[1] None of these technological obstacles is insurmountable, but we do well to acknowledge them and to be aware of potential barriers as we begin language maintenance projects. Information technology is not a silver bullet but rather a powerful tool which must be carefully deployed.

19.1.2   Technology for whom? The IT access barrier

Assuming these technology hurdles can be overcome, there remains the additional danger that technology will become a barrier to the very language learners who are being targeted. Technology can become a barrier between generations and between rich and poor. Within an endangered language community, the generational barrier is especially poignant, for a break in intergenerational transmission already separates the older language speakers from the younger non-speakers and language learners. Many software developers have noted the importance of including elders in the development process in order to ensure that IT products remain faithful to the spirit of the indigenous language.

A much greater danger is that IT resources will not be equally available to all language learners, particularly those lacking access to computers, the internet and other technology platforms. It is true that endangered languages tend to be spoken by those with less access to IT. Indeed, it can be argued that economic irrelevance is one of the major factors underpinning the shift from minority to majority languages (Harbert, Chapter 20). Nevertheless, there are many exceptions to this correlation, and in particular, a global trend of urban migration has resulted in many potential heritage-language learners residing in urban environments with good access to IT. That is, while many endangered languages are spoken in locations which lack access to IT, language shift within these communities is most pronounced among emigrant communities living in urban environments, and these emigrant communities are often both the most keen to pursue language revitalization and the most versed in the use of IT. While access to information technology may not be uniform across a language community, technological solutions must be tailored to the needs and constraints of a particular audience. Often, the segment of the community with the greatest access to technology may also be the segment with the greatest potential to benefit from language technology solutions. Watering down technology to the lowest common denominator deprives those with better access from taking advantage of those solutions.

Finally, it must be recognized that access to technology is not static but can change dramatically within the period of development of a language technology project, especially in rural settings where many endangered languages are spoken. At the onset of a recent project to develop an electronic archive for the Alaskan language Dena'ina, we nearly abandoned a web-based model for the project due to lack of internet access in remoter regions of the language area. Yet, by the end of the project even smaller villages had sprouted wireless networks. When I began fieldwork on the eastern Indonesian island of Pantar in 2004, there was no mobile phone service in the entire regency, an area of nearly 300,000 hectares. Three years later mobile phone signals penetrated all but the most remote parts of the island. As barriers to IT access continue to erode, endangered language projects must look toward the future of technology, not the present.

19.1.3   Preservation versus presentation

It is important that endangered-language-technology projects recognize the distinction between ARCHIVAL (or PRESERVATION) and PRESENTATION formats (Good, Chapter 11) The motivation for many language technology projects is to 'mobilize' existing resources (Nathan 2006b). In such cases, the outputs of language documentation in the form of recordings, word lists, texts, etc. can be viewed as a distinct body of work from which the technology project can draw. This allows technology projects to make use of proprietary software development tools and convenient presentation formats such as compressed audio or embedded video in order to create cutting-edge products. The fact that such formats may not be accessible in the long term need not be of immediate concern, since presumably archival versions of the underlying media are stored elsewhere using preservation formats. So long as this is the case, endangered language technology projects need not be overly concerned with preservation formats.

However, in practice endangered language projects are often more holistic, engaging simultaneously in PRIMARY DOCUMENTATION while at the same time supporting LANGUAGE REVITALIZATION efforts. For most minority languages these two activities are rarely distinguished, except that they might be mentioned in different parts of a funding proposal. These projects are often undertaken by small teams of extremely dedicated individuals who naturally see the need to pursue both documentation and revitalization simultaneously. Kroskrity and Reynolds (2001) describe how the production of a multimedia CD-ROM for Western Mono was embedded within the context of a much larger project which included work on dictionaries, texts and other forms of primary documentation and description. In such cases it can be difficult to draw a clear line between documentation, which creates material that warrants archival preservation (see Conathan, Chapter 12), and supporting products which make use of that documentation. Even where an established body of documentation already exists, revitalization projects often end up adding to that documentation in the process. For example, although the Dena'ina electronic archive was originally conceived as a portal to provide access to existing documentation of Dena'ina, in working with the community the developers quickly identified a need to make new recordings of conversational language which did not exist in the archival materials. These recordings in turn become archival items themselves, so that care had to be taken to create recordings in appropriate formats for the archive (in this case .wav files) as well as presentation formats for use online (in this case .mp3 and .swf files).

In sum, while language technology products are in some sense free from the burdens of archival preservation, developers must nonetheless remain keenly aware of the distinction between preservation and presentation.

19.1.4   Types of technologies

In the following sections I distinguish two broad types of technologies which may support endangered languages. The first are PRODUCTS which are created by a group of developers or authors for a specific user community or audience. The second type consists of ONLINE TECHNOLOGIES such as email listservs which foster communities of language learners and language users.

19.2   Products

By the term PRODUCT I mean something produced by a developer or group of developers for an intended target audience. The use of this term is not meant to imply or connote commercialization of endangered language resources but only to indicate that something is produced by one party for use by another party. Indeed, most EL products are non-commercial, created by non-profit organizations and distributed at no or nominal cost. The crucial feature of products as opposed to other technologies is their essentially asynchronous nature. While EL products can (and should) be created with input from end users, there remains a fundamental distinction between the creation of the product on the one hand, and the use of the product on the other. As web technologies continue to evolve these distinctions begin to blur. Nevertheless, the notion of product serves as a useful rubric for this discussion. The following sections cover various types of products.

19.2.1   Multimedia

Almost all technologies for language revitalization make use of MULTI-MEDIA. Indeed, the word multimedia applies to such a broad range of revitalization products that it can be awkward to use the term multimedia to refer to just one type of product. Multimedia products combine text, images, audio and video into a single package, making liberal use of hyperlinks between materials. While many of these features are often included in computer-assisted language-learning products (discussed below), multimedia products are distinguished in that their focus need not be restricted to language learning per se. Often, multimedia products include significant non-linguistic or metalinguistic aspects, notably the inclusion of cultural information such as oral histories or songs or place name maps. Even in terms of strict linguistic content, the focus of a multimedia product need not be limited to language learning, but may more broadly include linguistic reference materials, such as interactive dictionaries and word lists. This is not to say that multimedia products do not strive toward language learning; rather, language learning may be only one aspect of the product.

Multimedia products may be stand-alone or web-based, or may combine elements of both. There are advantages and disadvantages to both approaches. The stand-alone approach allows the developer much more control over the final product and allows more functionality. Multimedia authoring tools such as Adobe Director provide access to scripting languages which enable the developer to implement customized features. One disadvantage of this approach is that it requires distribution of the multimedia via CD or DVD, and updates to the product require another round of distribution. Below, each type is discussed in turn.

19.2.1.1   Stand-alone multimedia

The archetypal endangered-language multimedia product is one delivered on a stand-alone CD-ROM. Such products predate the emergence of the internet and became well known in the education field beginning in the late 1980s. Straightforward software tools facilitated the development of interactive multimedia content linking text, graphics and audio.[2] The CD-ROM format provides a convenient method for distributing media-rich content without depending on high-bandwidth internet access, or indeed any internet access at all. The goal of an interactive multimedia product is often to serve as a single source package of language information, providing a broad view of language within the context of oral culture. Kroskrity and Reynolds (2001: 319) describe the goal of the Western Mono CD-ROM as:

> designed to be informative, useful, and entertaining to a wide range of users who have an interest in learning more about this California Indian people by seeing, hearing, and understanding four performances of traditional and contemporary verbal art in the native language.

Notice in particular the focus on 'people' and 'verbal art'. As Kroskrity and Reynolds (2001) point out, the significance of oral performance in orally based cultures has long been recognized within the academic community, but multimedia provides a way to convey that importance of orality without resorting to opaque symbolic ethnopoetic conventions commonly used in written materials. Rather than having to interpret typographic conventions such as spacing, indenting or font faces, users can listen directly to the oral performance.

The power of oral performance in the multimedia context has led many multimedia projects to choose to focus a CD-ROM project around the common thread of a story, song or other narrative. Other features can be included as well, such as pronunciation guides or grammatical information. But the story provides a way of guiding the user through the product. The story becomes a vehicle for incorporating culture.

There are many ways to present audio/video with text. The entire text may be presented as a separate document, either hyperlinked to the media or displayed alongside it. More usefully the text may be presented in a time-aligned fashion so that the user can readily see which text corresponds to which segment of media. This can be achieved by embedding subtitles within a media clip or by presenting the text on the same screen. There is some controversy about whether the accompanying text should include a translation or not. This will depend to a large extent on the pedagogical goals of the particular project. Often the best solution is to provide the user with the option to view accompanying text in the target language, a translation language, both languages or neither.

While recorded stories are often the central focus of a CD-ROM project, because of their stand-alone nature these projects often strive to include a variety of supporting resources, such as a short dictionary or concordance linked to the texts. Cultural information such as place name maps, music or even slideshows with kinship information may be included. The Spoken Karaim CD-ROM even includes morphosyntactic information, allowing users to drag and drop affixes onto stems in order to explore inflectional morphology (Nathan 2000).

Stand-alone multimedia products are software programmes which must be installed on a user's computer, and ideally, no other software is required in order to run the programme.[3] To create a stand-alone multimedia product, the developer uses software known as a (multimedia) AUTHORING TOOL. A full-featured authoring tool allows the development of rich multimedia content but requires a significant investment in training in order to be used effectively. However, by using such professional authoring software, language projects are able to recruit from an existing pool of skilled developers. A variety of inexpensive or free authoring tools are also available; however, potential developers of stand-alone multimedia should be cautioned that the cost of the software represents a small portion of the overall cost of a multimedia project; other costs may include salary for developers, graphic artists, and interface designers and costs of image licensing, etc. Moreover, depending on the complexity of the CD-ROM being produced the use of a professional authoring tool may actually save money, as developing a full-featured CD-ROM without such tools requires a significant investment of developer time (Nathan 2006b).

Once completed, stand-alone multimedia products are usually distributed on CD-ROM or DVD-ROM as a stand-alone software package which the user installs on their computer. Developers may choose to publish and distribute the product through an existing publisher. Multimedia products for endangered languages are often published by or at least distributed by university presses; this is particularly true when academic professionals are involved in the development process. For example, the Western Mono Ways of Speaking CD-ROM (Kroskrity *et al.* 2002) is published by the University of Oklahoma Press, and the Spoken Karaim CD-ROM (Nathan 2000) is distributed through the School of Oriental and African Studies. Distribution via an established press frees local language communities from the logistical burden associated with taking orders, maintaining inventory and shipping. In addition, the press may take on the responsibility of reprinting the CD-ROM should it go out of print.

Those wishing more control over the distribution process may choose to handle distribution locally through a regional language centre. Local distribution may be public, as with the *Dákeyi* CD-ROM, which may be purchased via the Yukon Native Language Centre website. Local distribution may also be private, restricted only to certain users identified and vetted by the language centre. Often, distribution of stand-alone multimedia for endangered languages falls somewhere between public and private, being made available to all users but not widely advertised. A potential disadvantage of this grey-market approach to distribution is that copies of the product may not end up in libraries and archives.

19.2.1.2 The web-based approach

The line between stand-alone and web-based products will become increasingly blurred as the multimedia capabilities of web browsers increase and multimedia authoring tools offer more web-based options. It is already possible to transfer a stand-alone project to a web-based one using existing authoring tools. An example of this is the *Dákeyi* Southern Tutchone Place Names CD-ROM (Yukon Native Language Centre 1996), which was originally created using a professional authoring tool and then converted for the web in 2008.[4] In this case the original CD-ROM had become outdated and no longer functioned properly on modern computers. Conversion to a web-based format was a convenient alternative to updating and redistributing the CD-ROM. Yukon Native Language Centre has since made the content of all of its CD-ROMs available online. However, developers should be cautioned that the process of transferring stand-alone products to web-based ones may involve a significant investment of time and effort, particularly if the original stand-alone product is highly customized. An alternative is to develop simultaneously for the web and CD-ROM formats from the outset. This approach was followed effectively for the Alutiiq *Sharing Words* CD-ROM, which is distributed both in stand-alone CD format as well as online (Counceller and Steffian 2003).[5] By developing simultaneously for CD and web formats conversion problems are averted.

The representation of complex orthographies continues to present a challenge for the development of web-based multimedia.[6] Stand-alone solutions offer much greater control over font display, whereas web-based approaches are more dependent on the configuration of the user's web browser, over which the developer has no control. Developers such as the Yukon Native Language Centre have circumvented this issue by representing complex orthographies as image files rather than text, as in Figure 19.1.

Kwädą ch'äw dän Mäťàtäna Mãn kay ts'àn łu

yè sambay ka nànadàl kwäch'e ttha'y. Ätľa

Łughą nátthe kàkwäni. Dazhän män kay shų

ń-ch'įyè krúda ätlą kųlįnà kwän. Äyet ts'än

tän à'àn Äzuch'än Dakwà'yù dhäl datü kwàdą

kwäche, Sí Mãn yè Tashäl Mãn kwäts'àn. Äyü

shų nena ka łänajèl nu.

Figure 19.1. *Southern Tutchone text image (www.ynlc.ca/culture/dakeyi)*

While the text in Figure 19.1 could in theory be represented in a web browser directly using a Unicode font, the use of an image ensures that all users will be able to see the text correctly, irrespective of the particular configuration or browser on their computer.

Another difference between stand-alone and web-based multimedia in practice is that web-based products tend to be less comprehensive in nature. Stand-alone products are usually viewed as one-off creations, often undertaken at great expense in order to 'preserve' a language. Thus, developers often choose to include as many aspects of language and culture as feasible, so that a CD-ROM may include time-aligned texts, an alphabet guide, a talking dictionary, place name maps and the like. In contrast, the extensible nature of material delivered on the internet favours the development of more focused products, which can then be linked to other complementary online language resources.

Such a distributed approach is seen in several web-based multimedia applications developed for the Dena'ina language by a number of different authors. These include a phrasebook (Balluta and Evanoff 2005), an alphabet guide (Williams 2005), a collection of texts with aligned audio (Kari and Berez 2005), field recordings (Kari and Holton 2005) and a more comprehensive site focused on the Kenai dialect of Dena'ina (Boraas and Christian 2005). Each of these projects was developed independently by different teams, and each focuses on different aspects of the Dena'ina language. Yet when combined by linking they become a much more powerful distributed resource. Moreover, this combined resource is organic in that it can grow in response to community needs. Each individual project site can be modified and adapted as necessary, and additional projects can be developed and linked in. Uniformity is sacrificed in favour of extensibility. The individual sites do not all have the same look and feel, and information may be repeated across more than one site, e.g. a Dena'ina alphabet guide can be found in both Boraas' and Williams' sites.

Figure 19.2. *Story excerpt from Dane Wajich (Doig River First Nation 2007)*

Such a decentralized approach is not necessarily obligatory for a web-based project. Web-based multimedia may be every bit as media rich and polished as stand-alone multimedia. A good example of this is the *Dane Wajich* project website hosted by the Virtual Museum of Canada (Doig River First Nation 2007) shown in Figure 19.2. This site is organized around the rediscovery of a drum which had been lost for some years. It includes links to place names, stories, songs, and biographies of Dreamers who make songs. The polished form of the site makes it almost indistinguishable from a well-made stand-alone product. As with many multimedia products, the core of the content focuses on time-aligned recordings, in this case video-recordings displayed with time-aligned Dane-Zaa transcriptions and English or French translations (depending on choice of interface language).

But even a polished, comprehensive product such as the Dane Wajich site takes advantage of the extensibility of the web to incorporate virtually embedded language information, including an alphabet pronunciation guide included within the site, with the same look and feel. It also includes a link to an interactive conversational phrasebook based on an earlier printed phrasebook (Holdstock and Holdstock 1992). The phrasebook site has a completely different look and feel from the Dane Wajich site, having been developed under the auspices of different institutions with a different project team.[7] There is some overlap between the sites; for example, both include a pronunciation guide. But in the end, users benefit from multiple points of view, and developers benefit by being able to split large tasks into manageable chunks. This virtual integration of essentially separate sites demonstrates the true power of the web for multimedia language development.

An additional advantage of the web-based approach is the possibility that the project can continue beyond a defined time-frame. Unlike stand-alone products, web-based products need not cease development once they achieve final publication and distribution. This may better suit the needs of language revitalization efforts, which must of necessity involve a long-term commitment rather than a product or project-based focus. Web-based products thus allow for a continued dialogue between developers and users, as users provide feedback and developers continue to build and refine the online product.

19.2.2 Computer-assisted language learning

COMPUTER-ASSISTED LANGUAGE LEARNING (CALL) is a particular type of multimedia product which focuses on language learning. While other multimedia products may also address aspects of language learning, CALL products differ in: (i) having a (typically) exclusive focus on language learning, and (ii) taking advantage of established pedagogical principles for language learning. In this respect it is important to distinguish between LEARNING LANGUAGE on the one hand, and LEARNING ABOUT LANGUAGE on the other. While CALL focuses on the former, many other multimedia products focus on learning about language. That is, the developer of a CALL product has as a goal helping the user to become a fluent speaker (and/or writer) of the language.

At face value, fluency may seem to be the goal of all language technology products. However, it has been widely acknowledged that the goals of language revitalization often do not coincide precisely with the goal of creating a community of fluent speakers (Golla 2001, Thieberger 2002, Hinton, Chapter 15). Fluency is often only one piece of what is often a more holistic approach to language and culture revitalization. A product focused strictly on language learning may thus fail to address some of the other goals of cultural fluency. Those goals may be better met through products which focus on stories, such as the Dane Wajich site discussed in Section 19.2.1. Still, the two approaches are not in conflict, and it may even be possible to include aspects of CALL in a larger multimedia product.

While CALL is relatively new for endangered languages, it is an established field for world languages, where CALL products are generally viewed as a type of 'courseware'. Compared with more standard multimedia products, developing CALL courseware typically requires a much

Figure 19.3. *Screenshot of RosettaStone Iñupiaq*

larger investment of time and financial resources. Endangered language communities with access to sufficient resources can avail themselves of commercial CALL developers such as RosettaStone.[8] Already established as a major developer of commercial CALL product for world languages, RosettaStone recently embarked on a programme to collaborate with indigenous communities to develop CALL products for endangered languages. One of the first such products to be developed is for the Iñupiaq language (NANA 2007; See Figure 19.3). This CD-ROM follows the standard template of other RosettaStone CALL products but makes use of locally sourced images, at least in part. Users hear a word or phrase pronounced, with or without an accompanying text transcription. They then select the image that best corresponds to the audio. As the frequency of correct responses increases, the user progresses further through the lessons.

Other vendors of commercial CALL software may not explicitly offer an endangered language development service, but some do offer language-teaching software for minority languages. EuroTalk markets a CALL product for Cornish.[9] Communities wishing to develop CALL projects without recourse to commercial software developers may be able to take advantage of freely available or low cost templates (see Ward and van Genabith 2003).[10]

One particularly popular type of CALL for minority languages is the so-called 'talking book', essentially a way of presenting literacy materials without requiring literacy as a prerequisite. Talking books teach literacy by providing story narration while also displaying written text and illustrative photos or graphics. Talking books can be created from scratch by composing the text as part of the project or by using a basic template which can be translated into the language. The Yukon Native Language Centre's audio storybooks make use of four basic story templates (At Home, Camping, Fish Camp and Moose Hunt), each of which has been translated into as many as eleven different languages using the same basic set of accompanying images.[11] Talking books are also a great way to bring new life to old primers which are not attractive to young language learners. For many endangered languages early efforts at literacy generated dozens of printed literacy primers which have found little use since the emergence of new media. These texts can be recorded and converted to a talking-book format with relatively little effort.

While CALL can be an effective tool, language-maintenance projects should be cautioned to carefully evaluate their goals before pursuing a CALL project. The RosettaStone Iñupiaq program described above does little if anything to promote cultural fluency. A few local images are incorporated, but many stock images from urban North American life are also included. And there are no texts or stories which allow users to contextualize the language. Talking books may better achieve the goal of cultural fluency, but their pedagogical effectiveness has yet to be fully explored. For many small language communities a more holistic application such as a CD-ROM or web portal, perhaps incorporating a CALL component, may better serve their desired goals.

19.2.3   Electronic dictionaries

The BILINGUAL DICTIONARY is a standard reference for learners of world languages. For minority and endangered languages a dictionary often serves as more than a mere reference tool: in many cases it may be a primary resource for language maintenance (see Mosel, Chapter 17). IT can help to overcome two major difficulties faced by learners trying to use dictionary resources. First, by incorporating linked audio- (and video-) recordings, an electronic dictionary can provide models of pronunciation which may not be available elsewhere. Users of bilingual dictionaries for world languages can generally rely on other sources, like recorded phrases, radio and television programmes, or immersion in the language situation, for assistance with pronunciation. Learners of minority and endangered languages may not have ready access to such models. Second, by incorporating a searchable interface an electronic dictionary can overcome complex issues of dictionary organization which result from particular language structures (e.g. Frawley *et al.* 2002). Consider Athabascan languages, which have presented a particular challenge to developers of dictionaries. Athabascan verbs are built from a sequence of one or more inflectional prefixes plus a (possibly discontinuous) stem, which itself varies in form. Listing entries in alphabetical order obscures important relationships between related words, particularly those which share the same stem. Traditional Athabascan dictionaries overcome this difficulty by organizing verbs according to an abstract form of the stem, which can be extremely difficult to identify for even the most advanced language learners (Hargus 2007). In contrast, an electronic dictionary allows multiple points of access into the lexicon, avoiding the artificially imposed limitations of the print interface.

There are many tools available for creating electronic dictionaries. While it is possible to build an electronic dictionary from scratch, most revitalization and maintenance projects make use of existing lexical databases as the source of the content in the dictionary. The degree of customization work necessary to create an electronic dictionary will largely depend on the structure of the underlying lexical database on which the electronic dictionary is built (see Mosel, Chapter 17). One of the most popular formats for lexical databases stores information as tagged text files, such as that employed by the Toolbox software (Coward and Grimes 2000). A database created in this way can be displayed using a dictionary presentation tool such as Lexique Pro. Provided the under-lying data are well structured, little or no customization will be required in order to display dictionary data. LexiquePro is sometimes misun-derstood as a tool for creating and managing lexicons (see Guérin and Lacrampe 2007), but while it may be possible to use it for that purpose, the real power of LexiquePro is as a tool for viewing and distributing lexicons. As stated clearly on the LexiquePro website, 'LexiquePro reads data from a Toolbox database and formats it in an interactive viewer, the aim being to make it as clear and user-friendly as possible'.[12]

LexiquePro installs as a Windows software programme. It can open a Toolbox-type standard format database file and related configuration file in order to automatically set up font choices and alphabetization. These features can be further customized from within the programme. A lim-ited amount of multimedia capability is built in. Image files are displayed right in the entry, and audio-files play in the programme itself, without reference to external audio-players. An example of an entry with these features is shown in Figure 19.4. A fairly powerful system of hyperlinks allows users to jump to related entries based on lexical functions such as synonyms or antonyms defined in the underlying Toolbox database. A search facility allows both structured and unstructured searches.

Multiple translation languages can be displayed, and the programme interface itself can be viewed in several world languages.[13] A webpage of introductory information about the language can be linked to the 'About' button. As noted above, Lexique Pro is not intended as a tool for creating dictionaries for scratch; however, the built-in editing facilities do permit users to easily modify or enrich the underlying lexicon; for example, by adding images or sound files.

Figure 19.4. *Screenshot of Lexique Pro viewing the Western Pantar lexicon*

Once a dictionary has been prepared using Lexique Pro, two distribution options are available. The first is to distribute the dictionary as
a Lexique Pro software package. This will require users to install the
dictionary as a stand-alone programme. The underlying database files
can be encrypted so that they cannot be modified by the end user, and
the software itself can be distributed via the internet or on a CD-ROM.
This option provides the greatest degree of functionality, as users have
access to all of the multimedia capabilities of the Lexique Pro interface.
A second option is to export the dictionary to a set of web pages. This
option actually creates a large number of HTML files which work together
to implement the functionality of the stand-alone Lexique Pro interface.
The advantage of this approach is that users do not need to install any
software on their computer; the dictionary is accessed via a standard
web browser. The disadvantage of this approach is that it does not allow
all Lexique Pro features to be implemented; in particular, the web version lacks any structured search capability.[14] Finally, note that Lexique
Pro also supports export to a text document so that a print version of the
dictionary can be produced, something that Mosel (Chapter 17) considers
to be a desideratum for any endangered language dictionary.

Another good dictionary presentation tool is Kirrkirr.[15] Like Lexique
Pro, Kirrkirr provides access to an existing lexical database with

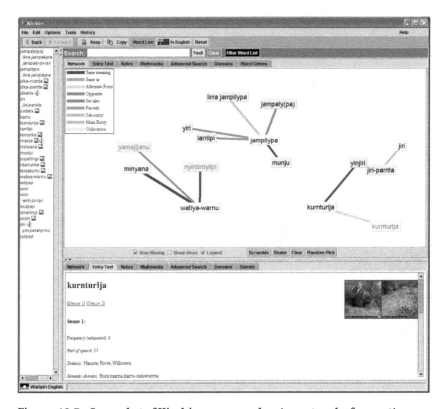

Figure 19.5. *Screenshot of* Kirrkirr *program showing network of semantic relationships*

embedded multimedia content. Kirrkirr has several distinct advantages over Lexique Pro, providing a much richer interface, in particular, the ability to view and navigate entries as a semantic network, as shown in Figure 19.5.

Kirrkirr also includes several language games based on the dictionary entries; these can be fun and motivating for the end user. While Kirrkirr does not support web page export, it is cross-platform and so can be used with both Windows and Macintosh operating systems. However, the richness of the Kirrkirr interface comes at a price. Kirrkirr requires that the underlying lexical data be in a well-structured XML format (see Good, Chapter 11) and that an XSLT style sheet be developed to describe how those data should be viewed. Unfortunately, many existing lexical databases for endangered languages (especially those using Toolbox) are not well-structured, so some work is usually required in order to bring them into an XML format and to develop the XSLT stylesheet.

An alternative to using existing dictionary presentation tools is to develop a custom, purpose-built, hypertext dictionary. Examples include the online Iñupiaq dictionary (Webster and Zibell 1970) and the Deg Xinag Learners' Dictionary (MacAlpine, *et al.* 2007). These dictionaries are exclusively web-based and have generally less functionality than dictionaries implemented with LexiquePro or Kirrkirr. Moreover, there are two distinct disadvantages to purpose-built dictionary interfaces. First, because they rely on server-based scripting languages, implementing a purpose-built dictionary requires that a web-server be maintained and that the dictionary scripts be updated and rewritten as the web-server itself is updated. Second, a significant investment of technical expertise is required in order to create, maintain and update a purpose-built dictionary. A dictionary generated using Lexique Pro can be updated and revised by someone with no programming skills. In contrast, with a purpose-built dictionary even simple edits such as fixing typographical errors or adding images and sound files may require programming skills. These programming and technical skills can be better employed in formatting a lexical database for use with a standard dictionary presentation tool such as Lexique Pro or Kirrkirr.

19.2.4 Web portals

A WEB PORTAL is a website which provides a single point of access to a wide range of related resources. For languages which already have an established body of documentary materials, a web portal is a useful technology for bringing these materials together in a unified way. While the range of functions supported by web portals is quite diverse, many are designed to provide access to archival documents. The Dena'ina Qenaga (Dena'ina Language) web portal was conceived in response to an expressed need for users to be able to access an existing corpus of documentary materials housed in an established language archive (Holton *et al.* 2007). A searchable digital archive serves as the core of the site, but it also functions as a more general point of access for information about Dena'ina. This additional content was mostly created as part of distinct, separate language projects but is brought together under one virtual roof within the concept of a portal. In this way a portal with extremely rich content may come to resemble a web-based multimedia product. The essential difference is that a portal draws largely on already existing content rather than creating significant new content. However, the line between portals and multimedia is fuzzy.

The Haida Language website *Xaat Kíl* serves as a portal to various kinds of information about the Haida language, but much of it was created specifically for the site, so in some sense it resembles a multimedia product.[16] The site contains links to a pronunciation guide, an audio phrasebook, a Haida story and several grammar lessons. The story is provided in Haida with interlinear English translation, and each Haida word is hyperlinked to a glossary entry. The grammar lessons include interactive quizzes which test learners' knowledge of Haida grammar. The various pieces of this site were created at different times, and they do not all have the same 'look and feel' as one might expect in a full-fledged multimedia product. Yet, *Xaat Kíl* functions as a web portal to bring all of these features within a single umbrella so that users have comprehensive access to Haida-language resources.

Ideally, a web portal should be bilingual, permitting access in the language itself in addition to a language of wider communication. Though not strictly a portal, the 'Aha Pūnana Leo, an organization supporting Hawaiian immersion schooling, has a website with an interface entirely in Hawaiian.[17] By using Hawaiian as the interface language, the site itself becomes a learning tool. As more language is used on the site the web portal itself becomes a potential community focal point, serving to foster language use.

19.2.5   Making use of commercial off-the-shelf tools

The preceding sections have focused on the development of specific IT products using specialized tools. Creating a product such as a standalone multimedia CD-ROM, an electronic dictionary or CALL software can involve a significant investment of time, personnel and/or money. Smaller and less well-off language communities may not have sufficient resources to create such products. Fortunately, there are many OFF-THE-SHELF TECHNOLOGIES which can be adapted for language-maintenance purposes. These include both: (i) commercial software applications intended for the wider public; and (ii) software tools which have been adopted by or designed to assist language-documentation efforts.

One of the most useful tools in the first category is Apple's iTunes, proprietary software which is freely distributed and available for both Windows and Macintosh platforms. iTunes is designed for organizing digital media downloaded from the internet or transferred from pre-recorded CDs, and for transferring those media to Apple's iPod music player. However, iTunes can be used more generally to store and organize any collection of digital audio and video. Its sophisticated search facilities and user-friendly interface make iTunes ideal for building a digital media jukebox for endangered languages.

One of the difficulties faced by many small and endangered-language situations lies in bridging the gap necessary to make archival documentary materials accessible and useful. Using iTunes can greatly facilitate this process. Once archival audio- and video-recordings are available in digital format, they can be readily edited into short segments using freely available digital audio editors. A recording of traditional stories or songs might be edited into short files so that each file corresponds to an individual story or song. These files can then be imported into iTunes as 'songs'. The iTunes metadata fields can be adapted to language-specific uses. For example, the 'Artist' field can be used to denote the speaker(s); the 'Album' field might be used to denote a collection of stories; and the 'Genre' field can be completely customized to categories recognized as culturally significant by the community. The 'Album Artwork' feature can be used to add still images of speakers or other contextual information. Once a body of digital recordings has been imported into iTunes and metadata has been added, the digital jukebox is ready; no additional packaging or preparation is necessary. The iTunes jukebox can be installed on a computer at a language centre or other publicly accessible venue, or the entire iTunes library can be distributed for use on individual computers or iPod players.

Interestingly, an iTunes jukebox is not merely a passive means for distributing digital media but rather has a built-in interactive component. iTunes includes the ability for users to create playlists which organize custom selections of songs from the library of media within the jukebox. This feature allows users to participate directly in structuring the content. Barwick *et al.* (2005) describe the important role of playlists in an iTunes jukebox of music recordings repatriated to an Aboriginal Australian community. Users actively engaged in the creation of playlists, building on the playlists created by other users, so that a large collection of playlists quickly and organically developed. iTunes also offers the potential for continued interaction between developers and users, as language projects can continue to add recordings to an existing jukebox over time.

Many tools developed for language documentation can also be effectively repurposed to support language revitalization and maintenance. Even a simple tool for audio transcription and time-alignment such as Transcriber or ELAN can be used as a player for listening to a time-aligned transcript of a recording. This approach becomes even more useful if multiple time-aligned recordings are combined into a single player with search capabilities, as is possible with the Audiamus corpus browser. Admittedly, these tools are burdened with what some users might view as unfriendly interfaces. Documentation tools lack the professional interfaces of commercial products such as iTunes, but documentation tools are also loaded with powerful editing features designed to create an annotated corpus rather than merely access an established collection of files. Still, many users will be willing to overlook such deficiencies in order to gain access to language resources which might otherwise be inaccessible. Moreover, efforts are currently underway to develop tools which can create user-friendly presentation formats from standard documentary formats for interlinear, time-aligned texts (e.g. Cox and Berez 2009, Schroeter and Thieberger 2006). As such tools become established and more widely available, the pathway from documentation to presentation will become much shorter and more direct.

9.3   Fostering language communities

For the most part, the technologies described in the preceding section foster individual language learning. But IT can also play a role in developing and fostering a language community. One important difference between major or world languages and minor or endangered languages is that the latter almost by definition lack thriving language communities. Information technology can assist by helping to foster what Golla (2001) has described as 'secondary language communities'.

19.3.1   Discussion groups

A DISCUSSION GROUP, also known as an electronic mailing list or listserv, is a way of distributing email messages to a large group of users. The sender need only send the email message to a single address and the message is then redistributed to all users who have subscribed to the discussion group. Message recipients can respond to the entire list, thus furthering a large group discussion. A discussion group can serve as a communicative domain for using an endangered language. In a community of language learners, message recipients will have differing levels of fluency. The asynchronous nature of email allows recipients to take extra time deciphering the message and composing a reply. Thus, the receipt of a message becomes a language-learning opportunity, and crafting the reply provides an opportunity for creativity in the language.

Many free tools are available to support electronic discussion groups. Commercial web portals such as Google and Yahoo! include mailing lists as part of free discussion groups.[18] Membership in these groups is managed by an administrator who oversees the group. Limited support is provided for multimedia content and reference materials.

19.3.2   Interactive websites

INTERACTIVE WEBSITES allow for the co-construction of online multimedia content by a community of users.[19] Examples include blogs (web logs), wikis and social networking services. The focus of these sites is on participation. Users may submit, retrieve, comment on and even alter content submitted by others. In this way interactive websites foster a virtual language community which is not constrained by physical borders and distance.

A blog (or web log) is very much like a listserv except that messages are posted permanently to a website in reverse chronological order rather than being distributed via email. Like a mailing list, access can be limited to a defined group of members if desired. The advantage of blogs over mailing lists is that messages to be viewed repeatedly in context, together with any responses, web links, and supporting materials. Support for multimedia content is generally much richer compared to mailing lists. Because a blog is accessed via a web page, many supporting features such as dictionaries or podcasts can be linked in directly. Hyperlinks and search facilities allow for easy navigation between blog entries. For some minority languages blogging is well developed. The BBC hosts a political blog written by Vaughan Roderick entirely in Welsh, with comments also in Welsh.[20] For most endangered languages blogging is less well developed. For example, blogs for indigenous American languages tend to provide information about indigenous languages through the medium of English.

A wiki is an interactive website which provides simple online tools for the creation of interlinked web pages. In contrast to blogs, which generally present timely information, wikis are useful for the co-construction of lasting reference materials. In the realm of minority languages this may consist of a set of reference materials for language documentation and language learning. However, wikis have the greatest potential to support minority languages when they are written in the language itself. This can be done relatively easily by creating an endangered language version of an existing wiki, such as Wikipedia.org. The Navajo version of Wikipedia contains 371 pages written in Navajo with contributions by 1,134 different authors.[21] The Navajo wiki even employs a nativized version of the word Wikipedia, namely Wikiibíídiiya. Most of the pages are not just translations into Navajo from English, but rather pages created in Navajo. Wikis constructed in this way not only foster a language community but also help to build a repository of indigenous knowledge written in the indigenous language.

A social networking service provides users with the means to share personal information (including photographs and media) and to connect with each other in a virtual world, usually via a website. The Gwich'in language group, a subcommunity of the Facebook social networking service, provides a forum for Gwich'in speakers and learners to share information about themselves. In particular, language learners can practise use of new phrases with an online community which is already larger than most Gwich'in villages. Because of their focus on social interaction, social networking services provide an ideal location to foster language use and hence may have the greatest potential to support minority language maintenance and revitalization.

19.3.3 Word-of-the-day

Another popular way of interacting with language learners is the so-called WORD-OF-THE-DAY concept. This involves communicating a new word or phrase to learners on a regular basis, via an email list, website or other means. The time cycle need not be daily. There can also be word-of-the-week or word-of-the-month services. The amount of content can vary as well. Some word-of-the-day approaches include only a written word and its translation into a dominant language. Others include audio- or even video-recordings. Some include a phrase which demonstrates the use of the word in context, and yet others include a short story or text which illustrates the significance of the word. What all of these approaches share in common is engaging in a short but regular interaction with users. There are many users who find they have little time for full-fledged language-learning programmes but who have become devotees of a word-of-the-day.

Word-of-the-day services often include cultural information as well. For example, the Alutiiq Word of the Week sponsored by the Alutiiq Museum includes not only words and example sentences, but also encyclopaedic cultural information which situates the word in its cultural context.[22] For example, the entry for the Alutiiq word *amaq* 'amber' includes not only the word and an example sentence with audio, but also: a scientific definition (e.g. 'this hard, yellowish-brown substance forms when a tree's gummy oils oxidize'); cultural information (e.g. 'these pieces of resin were more precious than even sea otter furs or the slender white dentalium shells used to decorate the garments of the wealthy'); and historical information (e.g. 'amber is also one of the materials Alutiiq people traded to communities on the Alaska Peninsula').

Word-of-the-day content has been delivered over radio and television for many years. Implementing a word-of-the-day using new media has the advantage of allowing the user to return to the word to hear it pronounced again and to easily browse an archive of past words. From a developer's point of view, an online word-of-the-day service can also be easier to manage, since daily or weekly offerings can be drawn automatically from a database. Word-of-the-day services can be delivered via an electronic mailing list, a blog, a podcast or a combination of these methods.

19.3.4 Podcasts

A PODCAST is a series of audio- or video recordings that are distributed over the internet via a subscription-based service. That is, once a user subscribes to the podcast, they are able to receive regular instalments of episodes of the podcast. A podcast has two primary advantages over other new media technologies. First, because they do not include text, podcasts do not require a focus on literacy but instead allow listeners to hear the language directly. Audio and video can of course be embedded in other multimedia products through hyperlinks, but a podcast removes the need for the user to click or navigate through an interface in order to hear the language. A second advantage of podcasts is their portability.

Users can download a podcast to a portable digital music player and listen to the language while engaged in other activities.

Podcasts are a popular way to deliver short language lessons and word-of-the-day instalments. For example, the Tlingit Time podcast[23] provides mini language lessons, and the Athabascan Word of the Week[24] podcast provides images, songs and cultural information. A recent episode of the Athabascan Word-of-the-Week even featured a discussion of climate change and Athabascan language.

19.3.5 Audio–video conferencing

One of the significant challenges to maintaining minority and endangered languages is that fluent speakers and language learners may be dispersed across large distances. Migration to urban centres has made it increasingly difficult for learners and fluent speakers to gather together to practise using the language. Taff (1997) has noted the importance of telephone audio-conferencing systems in language classes held in scattered remote Alaskan communities. The emergence of web-based technologies has the potential to bring audio–video conferencing within the reach of many more language communities. Gardner (2005) shows how web-based video conferencing can be used to connect elders and students across remote communities. Several free tools such as Skype are available for web-based video-conferencing.[25] Users need only have a web camera and headset, in addition to a computer with an internet connection.

19.3.6 Web-based language courses

The various electronic communication tools described above not only foster the growth of language communities; they also make possible more formal language instruction via distance delivery. Discussion groups, blogs, podcasts and audio–video conferencing can be combined into a WEB-BASED LANGUAGE COURSE which brings together students, fluent speakers and instructors to deliver language instruction. The University of Alaska Southeast began a web-based course in Haida language in 2008. This course makes use of a commercially available online learning system, which allows participants to collaborate visually and orally.[26] The 'Aha Pūnana Leo offers fee-based courses in Hawaiian language which are delivered via the internet, making use of web-based courseware (WebCT) and web-conferencing (Skype). Students are able to record their assignments to be evaluated by an instructor.

19.3.7 Text messaging

In areas of the world where internet penetration remains thin, mobile phone text messaging often fulfils the roles of many of the technologies discussed above. For example, in Indonesia, a country with more than 700 languages, many of them endangered, internet access remains limited in rural areas, but the number of mobile phone users has now reached fifty per cent of the population. Encouraging users to send and receive text messages in an endangered language can promote literacy development and, more importantly, help bring the language into new contexts. As text message users create an indigenous short-hand vocabulary they become active users of the language rather than just passive consumers of language-learning materials.

There has been some recent adaptation of multimedia dictionaries of endangered languages for so-called 'smart phones' using Java applets (see www.pfed.info/wksite/) and as the capabilities of these devices increase and they become cheaper and more widespread, opportunities will exist for mobile phones to serve as a major platform for language support and revitalization.

19.3.8   Software localization

SOFTWARE LOCALIZATION refers to the process of translating menu items, buttons, dialog boxes, and even help files into a particular language. Localization can provide support for minority and endangered languages by encouraging the use of the language in the electronic domain. For example, while it is certainly possible to compose an email in an endangered language using an interface written in a world language, a minority language interface may help to promote such activity. Composing an email message in Dena'ina may be more rewarding if the process is concluded by clicking 'niɬkits' rather than 'send'. Localization need not be restricted to personal computers but can be applied to many electronic devices, including mobile phones. Many common software tools offer instructions on the localization process; in general, it requires translation of a list of words and phrases. Complete localization of powerful programmes such as the OpenOffice suite may require translation of more than 20,000 text strings; however, it is not necessary to translate every piece of text. Localization projects can begin with commonly used text such as menu items and proceed into less commonly accessed areas of the programme. In this way a localization project itself may inspire a community of learners, as participants collaborate to provide the necessary translations.

19.4   Outlook

19.4.1   Whose technology?

While information technology has the potential to support language-maintenance efforts, realizing that potential depends ultimately on how that technology is brought into the language community. Technology for minority and endangered languages must be viewed not merely as an end but as a practice (Auld 2007). In other words, the choice of technology and its application must be undertaken as part of a collaborative process within the language community (Nathan 2004). This means including end-users (including language learners) in the design process and working in coordination with all aspects of community language efforts. This means also allowing interface designs to emerge organically rather than being imposed by an outside structure. Of course, it is not necessarily the case that all community members will be in agreement about the roles of technology in language maintenance. A website may be deemed useless by those without access or unaccustomed to using a website, while deemed extremely useful by others. And while technology has the ability to place large amounts of language into the public domain, in effect leveling the field for minority languages (Slimane 2008), not all language communities may see this as beneficial. What is crucial is that developers know their audience, both for content and technology. This is best achieved by recognizing that the dialogue about the roles of technology must take place within the community itself (Villa 2002).

Furthermore, it should be recognized that choice of technology will also depend to some extent on the resources of the individual developers. While many authoring tools have similar functionality in terms of what they can present for the end user, they differ in the particulars of how that functionality is implemented behind the scenes. Multimedia developers often have a significant investment in particular authoring platforms and may be reluctant to adopt new tools. A multimedia developer who has spent a decade working with Adobe (Macromedia) Director has a significant skill set which may not translate easily to another development environment such as Revolution. Choosing a suitable authoring tool requires balancing the needs of the community with the needs of the developers who will be using the tool.

19.4.2 Coping with technology evolution

EVOLUTION is a fact of technology, and endangered languages are not exempt. Evolution affects both the authoring tools used to develop endangered language products, and the use of the products themselves. Kroskrity and Reynolds (2001) describe difficulties experienced following the discontinuation of the Apple Media Tool authoring tool. But perhaps the prime example of the evolution of authoring tools is the somewhat earlier demise of Apple's HyperCard. Originally released in 1987, HyperCard was quickly adopted by the education community and by a number of early efforts to support endangered languages (Bradin and Howard 1998). The discontinuation of HyperCard in 2004 has left a legacy of HyperCard-based materials which cannot be easily accessed.[27]

A related problem concerns websites. The mere creation of content for a website does not ensure that the material will be accessible into the future. Already, the list of links to language-related websites which are broken continues to grow, so that endangered language websites may be just as endangered as the languages they are designed to support. In order for a website to persist, the domain name must be continually licensed. Websites often disappear simply because the developers have lost contact with the person responsible for paying the bill for the domain name. The domain name charges are not large, and often a concerned and altruistic individual will simply pay the charges out of their own pocket. But it is not clear that this strategy is viable in the long term. Hosting a site as part of an institutional domain such as a university domain may help to ensure that domain names do not disappear, but unless the site has official support within the relevant institution, there is no guarantee that it will persist. Many endangered language websites are hosted unofficially within faculty or departmental websites at universities. As personnel change and institutions are restructured, these unofficial sites may be lost.

An additional problem for the maintenance of websites concerns the web server which hosts the site. Even if the domain name can be maintained, the site itself must be physically hosted somewhere. There are three basic approaches to hosting: (i) run a web server independently; (ii) make use of an institutional web server; and (iii) rent space on a commercial web server. The first option requires continual maintenance and will in practice rely on the dedication and continued availability of the individual responsible for the web server. Moreover, funds must be allocated to maintain, upgrade, and replace equipment. The institutional option relieves the developers from the need to support and maintain a web server; however, as noted above, unless the site has official support within the institution there is no guarantee that it will continue to support the site once the individuals responsible for it move on to other positions. The third option replaces institutional difficulties with commercial ones. By choosing to host a site on a commercial web server, developers must make a long-term commitment to paying hosting fees. Often, these fees are tied to bandwidth usage, so that as a site increases in popularity, charges may increase as well.

Finally, a difficulty with all three of these hosting solutions is that the evolution of web technologies may render sites inaccessible (see Figure 19.6). Sites with rich media content and interactivity often make use of so-called SERVER-SIDE TECHNOLOGIES; that is, technologies which rely on special software which runs on the server itself. If the web server is migrated to make use of different server-side technologies, or if the site is moved to a different server which uses different server-side technologies, some or all of the functionality may be lost.

Figure 19.6. *An all-too-common response from an endangered language website*

All of these experiences speak to the fact that technology for language maintenance and revitalization cannot be viewed as a one-off activity. Rather, as discussed above, technology support must be integrated into the larger context of community language efforts. Technologies must be continually revisited and updated as standards and platforms evolve. If undertaken in a collaborative environment, technology evolution itself can actually contribute to language maintenance by requiring continual engagement with technology by a community of language activists.

19.4.3 Tempering expectations

Finally, in advocating the use of technology to support small languages there is always the danger of placing too great a burden on the technology. None of the technologies discussed in this chapter should be considered a silver bullet which will somehow revitalize an endangered language. It is all too easy to view the product, especially a professionally produced CD-ROM or website, as the end rather than the means. But there is no 'technical fix' (Dauenhauer and Dauenhauer 1998). Information technology, whether in the form of a CD-ROM, a multimedia website, a talking dictionary, a blog, a web portal or anything else, cannot in and of itself revitalize or maintain a language. We would do well to remember

Krauss' (1998) warning that specialists 'often become preoccupied with more and better technologies such as the computer and multimedia for teaching language in the school'. It has long been recognized that inter-generational transmission is the key to complete language revitalization. As Fishman (1991) notes:

> Although cyber-space can be put to use for [reversing language shift] purposes, neither computer programmes, e-mail, search engines, the web as a whole, chat boxes or anything directly related to any or all of them can substitute for face-to-face interaction with *real family imbedded in real community*. [emphasis in original]

That said, in the nearly two decades which have passed since Fishman's warning, information technologies have permeated our lives, becoming ubiquitous, leading us to rethink just what it means to be a 'real' community. For many minority languages, revitalization and maintenance means the construction of new communities which are geographically dispersed and discontinuous (Golla 2001). Information technologies have the potential to unite and foster such secondary linguistic communities. We cannot expect a multimedia programme or website to create new speakers of an endangered language. What we can expect from information technology resources is that they contribute to the development and appreciation of endangered languages in new terms.

For this to happen language communities must engage with information technology. This is especially true when language learners become not merely consumers of technology but also practising creators of technology.

Notes

1 For example, one such combination is a–umlaut (Unicode 00E4) with combining nasal hook (Unicode 0328) and combining grave accent (Unicode 0300).
2 The most well known of these early interactive multimedia development tools was Apple's Hypercard, released in 1987.
3 Some multimedia software may require that certain supporting programmes such as Java or Direct-X be pre-installed on the user's computer. This may present problems with older computers.
4 www.ynlc.ca/culture/dakeyi.
5 www.alutiiqmuseum.org/files/sharing_words_main.htm.
6 See Lüpke, Chapter 16, on the importance of designing orthographies with computers in mind
7 This site was actually originally developed as a stand-alone CD-ROM.
8 www.rosettastone.com/global/endangered.
9 www.eurotalk.com.

10 Hot Potatoes hotpot.uvic.ca.

11 www.ynlc.ca/materials/story_books.html.

12 www.lexiquepro.com/features.htm (28 August, 2009).

13 Interface languages include English, French, Spanish, Portuguese, Kinyarwanda and Chinese.

14 A web version of the Western Pantar dictionary in Figure 19.4 generated using Lexique Pro can be viewed at www.alor-pantar.org/wp/lexicon.

15 nlp.stanford.edu/kirrkirr.

16 www.haidalanguage.org.

17 www.ahapunanaleo.org.

18 groups.google.com; http://groups.yahoo.com.

19 Interactive web technologies were initially referred to as 'Web 2.0', though most commentators now view these technologies as part of the natural evolution of the World Wide Web.

20 www.bbc.co.uk/blogs/thereporters/vaughanroderick.

21 nv.wikipedia.org. Statistics from meta.wikimedia.org/wiki/List_of_Wikipedias (28 August, 2009).

22 www.alutiiqmuseum.org/index.php?option=com_alphacontentand Itemid=82.

23 www.khns.org/listen_tlingit_archive.php.

24 www.newsminer.com/podcasts/athabascan-word-week.

25 www.skype.com.

26 www.elluminate.com.

27 Limited support for products created with HyperCard continues in the form of other authoring tools which can import legacy products. These range from products such as HyperStudio, which are essentially modern extensions of HyperCard, to full-fledged authoring environments such as Revolution.

Part IV

Challenges

20

Endangered languages and economic development

Wayne Harbert

20.1   Introduction

The variables which can affect the status and trajectory of minority languages are numerous, internally complex and liable to intricate interactions. They include attitudes of speakers toward their languages, geographic/social/cultural cohesiveness and separateness of the linguistic community, demographic factors such as age of the fluent speakers, modes of transmission, domains of use, official status, governmental attitudes and policies, and attitudes of the speakers of the dominant language, to name just a few (see Grenoble, Chapter 2). This chapter focuses on one particular set of variables, those involving the economic circumstances of speakers and language communities, and explores their implications for the tasks of arresting and reversing language shift.

20.2   Economic aspects of language shift

ECONOMICS is to be understood here in the narrow sense of market economics, namely access to and allocation of material resources. The term has been deployed in a broader sense in some work in sociology, for example, which extends the model of economics to linguistic transactions and language competition, interpreting them as a kind of economic exchange taking place in symbolic markets, and involving the expenditure or accrual of symbolic capital and profits. An economic model of the LINGUISTIC MARKETPLACE is developed in a non-quantitative way in Bourdieu (1977b, 1991), and is given a quantitative basis in de Swaan (2001), and Grin (1992). De Swaan proposes that languages competing in a multilingual situation can be assigned a 'Q-Value', which determines the likelihood of language shift. The Q-value of a language is the product of its PREVALENCE, i.e. the proportion of individuals in the community who speak it, and its CENTRALITY, i.e. the proportion of multilingual speakers in whose repertoire it is included. Speakers are attracted to languages that allow them to communicate with the largest numbers of other speakers, hence to languages with high Q-values. Grin (1992), addressing the specific question of determining thresholds in language shift, also develops economic formulas which take into account the demographic variables of the percentage of speakers speaking each of the competing languages and the proportion of time spent by individuals carrying out activities in each (the latter being taken to indirectly reflect language preference.)

The basic thesis of this chapter is that, as proposed by Grenoble and Whaley (1998: 37, 52), the fundamental shapers of the fortunes of endangered languages are economic in the narrower sense: people change their linguistic behaviours, including shifting from one language to another, most typically because of real or perceived or desired changes in their material circumstances. The status and viability of endangered languages can thus be affected (positively or negatively) by measures that affect the material circumstances of speakers and the economies of their communities. As de Swaan himself notes (2001: 42), the preference for high Q-value languages is rooted in more than just an abstract desire to maximize communication; it involves the perceived role of more widely used languages as keys to material and cultural resources and choices. The CULTURAL CAPITAL assigned to one language relative to others is to a considerable degree determined by the need or desirability of employing it in the material marketplace. Speakers of dominant languages tend to have, or are perceived as having, greater access to material resources and the things that lead to them, such as education, jobs, information and 'networks' (Grin 2007: 275), and these languages thus tend to accrue symbolic value, often at the expense of minority languages. The connection between the perceived value of a language and its actual value in securing economic advancement is not rigid, though. This is exemplified by the fact that, while Spanish speakers in the US who speak English generally earn more than those who do not (Bloom and Grenier 1992: 449), Rodriguez (1991: 37) and others report that Puerto Ricans, with higher average levels of English proficiency than other Hispanic groups, lag behind these other groups economically.

Some qualifications are in order. First, as Grin's measure suggests, the perceived value of a language is not simply a function of the prestige of the domains in which it is used, but partly of the frequency of opportunities for its use (see also Evas 2000: 298). Second, languages also have intrinsic value to their speakers independent of their evaluation as instruments of economic advancement. Grin (1999: 180), asserts that, while minority languages may lack market value, 'it does not follow that they have no *economic* value. One should not forget that, ultimately, economics is not about financial or material performance, but about *utility*, or satisfaction.' This value, as 'symbolic capital' or 'collective cultural capital' (de Swaan 2001: 42), or 'non-market value' (Grin 2007: 281), can serve to maintain the linguistic loyalty of speakers even in the face of material–economic hardship. Members of Khwe communities in Namibia, as discussed in Brenzinger (2008), remain loyal to their language in spite of great poverty. Crystal (2000: 128) cites the example of the Tewa of Arizona. In the typical case, however, the two notions of value tend to align, as interaction between minority-language communities and the dominant-language community increases.

Language shift and language death normally follow specifically on economic disruptions, involving changes in the material economy of a language community or changes in the economic expectations and perceptions of the members of that community. These disruptions create the circumstances under which minority languages come into unequal competition with others in the linguistic marketplace (see Batibo 2008). Thus, language shift typically follows in the wake of such events as dislocation of populations, disruption of traditional modes of livelihood, depletion of resources, developments in the exploitation of previously unexploited resources, increases in (or increased awareness of) economic opportunities outside the linguistic community and the like. Given that these are significant causes of language shift and language death, it follows that remedies should address them; the establishment of successful language maintenance and revitalization programmes must take into account the economic setting of the language, the wealth or poverty of its speakers, and the linguistic demands associated with prospects for material survival and advancement. As Edwards (2007b: 245) notes: 'one cannot maintain a language by dealing with language alone'.

Typologies categorizing the situations of minority languages along a number of dimensions have been advanced, and have proved to be of value for understanding the dynamics of language shift. Economics is listed as a variable in many of these, but not typically accorded a prominent place, and to date there has been no systematic attempt to create a typology of the economic circumstances of endangered languages, along such lines as the nature of the local economy (whether it is wage-based, whether the population is sedentary or nomadic and so on), the nature of the disruptions to that economy and the demographic effects of those disruptions. This chapter can be viewed as an initial step toward the creation of such a typology. It will begin by discussing some of the more usual causes and forms of economic disruption which affect endangered language communities. It will conclude by considering prospects, strategies and challenges in addressing the economic dimensions of language endangerment.

20.3   Toward a typology of economic disruptions of language communities

Intergenerational language transmission happens as a matter of course in a stable, monolingual language community, and therefore language death is not an expected occurrence in such contexts. Whether multi-lingualism is inherently unstable even in the absence of socioeconomic inequalities among speakers is in part still an open question, though there are instances of bilingual communities which have persisted over centuries. Walker (1993: 75) asserts that in these contexts, too, 'where the traditional economy is still intact and perceived as adequate, bilin-gualism will be additive, rather than replacive'. Some series of disrup-tive events must therefore take place to interfere with the continuity of such communities, in order to set the stage for language shift. In an extreme but not unexampled situation, the disruption takes the form of the abrupt death of the members of the community, as a result of natural catastrophe, disease (Brenzinger 2007a: 188, Crystal 2000: 71) or genocide (Brenzinger 2007b: 185). More usually, it involves the dissolution (or at least diminution) of the community through the out-migration of all or some of the speakers.

20.3.1   Language shift resulting from population movement
Such population shifts sometimes result from non-economic factors, including natural disasters, wars and ethnic cleansing campaigns, as in the present case of southern Sudan (see Brenzinger 2008). The magnitude of the refugee population generated globally by such forces is indicated in the tables in Rassool (2007: 133ff.). In still other instances, they follow from political and economic decisions by governments or other author-ities. These cases include, for example, resettlement programmes (Tomei 1995: 181), relocation in the wake of dam building, a frequent occurrence globally (see e.g. Lastra 2001: 153, Nettle and Romaine 2000: 10, Pecos and Blum-Martinez 2001: 76, Tsunoda 2005: 58, and Bradley, Chapter 4), diversion of water resources to cities (Lastra 2001: 153) and the like. Such decisions may even be rooted in efforts to protect resources. Batibo (2008: 25f.) observes that in some cases in Africa, government efforts to establish game reserves have resulted in the displacement of groups of hunter-gatherers. Most often, though, out-migration is driven by eco-nomic factors within the community and anteceded by some disruption in the traditional ways of earning a living. At one extreme, the local economy of the language community is brought to the point at which the local modes of livelihood no longer allow for the continuation of the community in its original location, and survival depends on relocation. This case, labelled 'absolute poverty' by Brenzinger (2008: 37) or 'extreme

poverty' (Grenoble, Rice and Richards 2008: 187), can result from natural disaster, climate change, famine or the cumulative effects of human
activity, including the destruction of habitat, deforestation, over-hunting
or population growth. The World Bank estimates that 1.1 billion people
live in extreme poverty around the world.

In less extreme situations, characterized by Brenzinger (2008: 37) as
'relative poverty', scarcity of resources does not lead by itself to population movement. Communities can remain relatively stable even under
conditions of hardship so long as subsistence is possible. Relative poverty
of some minority-language communities arises historically from the fact
that they have been forced into (or allowed to continue to occupy) only
regions which are economically marginal, and therefore of relatively little interest to their more numerous and powerful neighbours (see, e.g.,
Brenzinger 2008, Vaillancourt 2008). The relative poverty and lack of
resources of their speakers may in fact serve to protect these languages
from potentially destabilizing influences from the outside precisely by
making the areas in which they are spoken undesirable for economic
exploitation (see, e.g. Brenzinger 2008; Grenoble *et al.* 2008). Brenzinger
(2008: 41) goes so far as to assert that relative poverty has '"saved" large
numbers of African languages' in this way. This phenomenon is responsible in part (though not entirely) for the rough correlation between
areas of the world with the highest language densities and those with
the highest incidence of poverty (see Romaine 2009).

In the most benign cases, the thing which destabilizes language communities may take the form of increased availability of information from
outside, leading to an awareness that a life of greater choice and pros-
perity is possible away from the community and consequently resulting in changes in the economic expectations of individuals. As pointed
out by Crystal (2000: 132), economic disruption can even take the form
of a sudden increase in wealth, occasioned by an oil boom, for example.
Crawford (1996: 63) cites the case of the Mississippi Choctaw community,
whose traditionally high level of language maintenance is being threatened
by the effects of sudden economic expansion. Walker (1993: 72) reports that
Tobati speakers in Indonesia sold their land to developers, increasing their
short-term wealth, but at the cost of their traditional economic base.

Economic motivations, arrayed on a scale from increased awareness
of outside opportunities at one pole to absolute poverty at the other,
underlie the phenomenon of URBANIZATION, the increased concentration of people in cities, where, as a rule, they have at least potentially a
greater range of economic prospects. Though urbanization has been in
operation throughout history, it seems to have accelerated markedly in
the twentieth century. Usually, it is speakers of minority languages who
move into urban centres in which nationally dominant languages pre-
vail, though the opposite case sometimes occurs; Pujolar (2003) reports
that large numbers of Castilian Spanish speakers moved into Barcelona

in the mid-twentieth century, taking lower paying jobs, and thus locally elevating the prestige of the Catalan language native to that region.

20.3.1.1   Consequences of urbanization

Urbanization puts small languages at risk in both their original contexts and the new ones into which they are transplanted. On the one hand, it leads to the depopulation of the language community remaining behind, and a corresponding loss of linguistic vitality *in situ*. On the other hand, it removes the displaced language from areas in which it was tradition-ally established, and from the local cultural institutions in which it had played a central role, and puts it into competition with other languages which its speakers may find to be more economically necessary or advan-tageous. In addition to the loss of its cultural anchors, its potential use in everyday communication can be diminished in the new context, depend-ing on patterns of resettlement, through the isolation of the displaced speakers from each other (although, as Holton, Chapter 19, points out, modern technologies and social networking software in particular can overcome some of this isolation and encourage minority language use). The pressure to shift languages in new urban surroundings may be greater than in the past, due to the increasing importance of linguistic skills in the marketplace. Rassool (2007: 127) speaks of a 'language-based economy placing high reliance on a range of sophisticated linguistic skills, discursive knowledges, and worker awarenesses'.

The effects of urbanization on minority languages are not necessarily wholly negative. A boom in the extractive industries in the nineteenth century led to migration to industrial cities in Wales, where numbers of Welsh speakers grew markedly. According to one view, this was a crucial step forward for the language, enabling Welsh to be recast as the lan-guage of a modern urban culture which, with increased political, eco-nomic and social status, was more able to compete with English for the cultural high-ground. For a review of the history and a critique of its interpretations, see Williams (1990). Urbanized languages can therefore benefit in some ways in terms of increased cultural capital, though not usually sufficiently to offset the negative effects.

Out-migration from a language community thus creates two groups of concern: those who remain in the (diminished) language community and those who are displaced. The needs and resources of the two groups with respect to the task of language maintenance and revitalization are different. The former have the advantage of continued connection with the traditional locus and supporting institutions of the language, and less direct pressure to shift to the dominant language. The latter, while under greater pressure toward language shift, may in the best case be better situated in terms of time and resources to cultivate their attach-ment to their native language and its associated arts (as Holton, Chapter 19, notes). Urbanized speakers are often economically better off than those who remain behind. Scottish Gaelic speakers who emigrated to the large urban centres of Scotland in the wake of economically motivated dislocations beginning in the middle of the eighteenth century, for example, prospered relatively, and continue to do so. Gaelic speakers are still proportionately better represented in higher managerial, professional and skilled labour categories in the traditionally English-speaking Lowland areas than in traditional Gaelic-speaking areas (MacKinnon 2000: 73ff.). Moreover, urbanized speakers are potentially better networked with others sharing their cultural and linguistic interests, given the greater concentration of population and the greater availability of transportation, and now, greater access to information and communication technologies such as computers and mobile phones. They may also sometimes possess a stronger attachment to the language arising from feelings of nostalgia. Though Gaelic was far less successful in surviving the transition to urban settings than Welsh, urbanized Gaels, regarding their former language with fondness, lobbied for changes in laws and encouraged the creation of institutions which supported the language in its original territories, thus boosting its prestige there. Walker (2000: 79) reports similarly that Waropen speakers who have migrated to towns in Indonesia maintain a higher degree of interest in their language and a higher level of advocacy for its maintenance than the population remaining in the area where it is traditionally spoken.

Feelings of loss and attachment frequently motivate the development of a new set of cultural institutions for the language, such as evening classes, language societies, singing societies, theatre troupes, films, nursery schools, cultural and literary competitions and the like. For example, Jansma (1993) notes the development of new cultural and social institutions among Frisian speakers who have moved out of their home regions for economic reasons. Such institutions, though, often involve only functionally restricted, occasional and primarily symbolic language use. Moreover, nostalgic attachment to the native language among displaced speakers is not universal. Batibo (2008: 26) reports that in Africa many children transplanted into urban areas have negative attitudes toward the ethnic languages of their parents, and associate rather with the local lingua francas. Even in favourable cases, the overall balance of effects of urbanization on immigrant languages works strongly in favour of language shift, especially in the third and subsequent generations.

20.3.1.2 In-migration
Small languages can also be weakened by economically motivated in-migration of non-speakers, following on the discovery or reevaluation by outside groups of local resources which had previously been unknown or deemed unworthy of economic exploitation. Much of the history of the era of colonialism and empire falls under this broad heading, but

such forces are still at work, and, if anything, operate even more efficiently as new technologies of resource exploitation arise. For example, in many areas of the world, previously sparsely populated forest areas have witnessed large influxes of new residents, as improvements in transportation and technology have made logging more profitable, and as growing scarcity of agricultural products elsewhere, or the development of new uses for them, such as biofuels, has increased the economic value of the soil on which the forests grow. In many cases, this influx is accompanied by the expropriation and displacement of the indigenous population (Hinton and Hale 2001: 4), but even when it is not, the effect of the resultant cultural and demographic changes can be equally harmful to small languages. For example, Cenoz (2008: 94) reports that in-migration into the Basque regions in connection with industrialization during the third quarter of the twentieth century amounted to one third of the current population of the Basque Autonomous Community, with the result that 'Basque is a minority within its own territory' (Cenoz 2008: 103). More contemporary instances can be seen in the development of so-called 'cultural tourism' in areas associated with minority, and especially indigenous, populations where outsiders move in to 'perform' as minority group members in cultural shows of singing, dancing and handicrafts for tourists; Taiwan and China have clear examples of this phenomenon.

The interplay of in-migration and out-migration may vary from situation to situation. The same nineteenth century boom that brought Welsh speakers into the industrial centre in Wales attracted English speakers in far greater numbers, for example, causing Welsh to decline in terms of the proportion of residents who spoke it, even as it increased in absolute numbers of speakers (Jones 1993: 546). In present-day Wales, the two directions of population movement complement each other. As Welsh speakers leave for employment outside, monoglot English speakers, often from English cities, move in to purchase the houses and businesses left behind, attracted by relatively bargain prices. In the frequently discussed case of Ireland (e.g. Carnie 1996), attempts to stem the economically driven exodus of minority-language speakers from the *Gaeltachtaí*, the traditionally Gaelic areas, by importing new industries, led to in-migration of majority-language speakers as an undesirable side-effect. Edwards (2007b) characterizes this phenomenon as the 'paradox of the *Gaeltacht*', but similar occurrences elsewhere, in Botswana, for example (Batibo 2008: 26), demonstrate it to be one of the general dilemmas of language planning. If nothing is done, marginalized language communities are likely to continue to suffer from population loss. If the usual sorts of economic revitalization efforts are implemented, they are likely to suffer from other forms of economic and demographic destabilization, including the influx of non-speakers.

20.3.2 Language shift without population movement

Language shift can also occur without movement of populations. Again, the motivations for such shift are typically economic. They may involve changes in the local economy which require (or confer advantage on) increased interactions in dominant regional languages. Brenzinger (2008) points out in the context of Africa that language shift sometimes accompanies the adoption of new modes of livelihood from neighbouring groups. The linkage is not rigid, though; Paciotto (1996: 176) notes that the adoption of new herding practices from their neighbours by speakers of Tarahumara in Mexico has in fact worked in favour of the mainten-ance of linguistic and cultural autonomy, at least temporarily, by allow-ing them to continue to be economically autonomous. A detailed analysis of one case of language shift accompanying shift in modes of livelihood was presented in a pioneering study by Gal (1979), which examined the history of language shift from Hungarian to German in eastern Austria in the twentieth century, accompanying the shift from an agricultural economy to a wage-labour and money-based economy.

20.4 Implications and applications: some considerations in addressing the economic causes of language endangerment

At the macroeconomic level, the connections between language and eco-nomics are not well understood. We are not in a position, for example, to answer definitively the question of whether maintenance of minority and endangered languages (or of multilingualism more generally) is in general a reasonable or desirable objective from a purely economic stand-point. While studies have demonstrated a possible correlation between high levels of linguistic diversity and low Gross National Product (Robinson 1996: 26ff.), no causal connection has been established, and it is difficult to disentangle language from other, apparently more predict-ive, variables. Grin (2007: 276) reports that 'By and large, no net correl-ation, positive or negative, has been found between linguistic diversity and macroeconomic indicators of economic performance.' This question is, in any case, only one component of the larger question of whether minority-language maintenance is a desirable social goal, the answer to which also depends in part on considerations of national unity and human rights.

20.4.1 The importance of minority languages in development

The interactions between language and economics are better under-stood on the micro level, and, as we have suggested, they operate in both directions. On the one hand we have seen that the fates of endangered languages are often determined by the material circumstances of their speakers, and the choices that speakers make in the face of those circumstances. Conversely, the material circumstances of individuals are determined in part by the languages which they speak, or do not speak. Speaking certain languages can give people access to roles, markets and information which can improve their well-being. Not speaking those languages can deny them access. In the preceding, we have emphasized language as a key to access to employment, and therefore to money, but this is by no means the only domain in question. Wealth and poverty can be assessed by various non-monetary measures. Vaillancourt (2008: 147) lists, among others, health poverty (the incidence of illness), nutritional poverty (caloric intake), and educational poverty. Indeed, since many, perhaps most, severely endangered languages are used in communities whose modes of employment and exchange are not based on money, such non-monetary measures are often of greater relevance than the monetary measures commonly employed in economic studies. The problem of linguistic access to education is discussed by Coronel-Molina and McCarty, Chapter 18. Besides the significant role of language in determining access to employment and education, the material well-being of speakers can be improved by removing linguistic impediments to access to information about health care, agricultural techniques and markets, as well as to the delivery of medical and other social services. A particularly interesting emerging category under this heading is that of LOCALIZATION in information and communication technology, the task of making information with potential economic value (such as agricultural techniques or market information) available over the internet or on mobile phones to speakers of minority languages (including those who may not be literate in any language); see Holton, Chapter 19 for discussion. The problem of access to information is particularly acute in the nations of Africa, for example, where, by one estimate (Mackey 1989: 5) as many as 90 per cent of the inhabitants have no knowledge of the official language of the nation in which they live. Batibo (2008) and Brenzinger (2008) cite, in particular, the choice of languages as an important factor in disseminating information about health care, with specific reference to the AIDS epidemic which is a major component of the problem of poverty in Africa.

The existence of such interconnections between language and economics raises a number of so-far largely unanswered questions of both principle and practical implementation for people and organizations working on a broad range of social problems. How do governments, linguists, language activists, health workers, development specialists and others take them into account in forming their policies, developing their projects and carrying out their activities? In spite of the importance of these questions, they have so far tended to be overlooked or underemphasized both by those who work toward preserving endangered languages and those concerned with alleviating poverty or developing economies. This is in part a result of differences in the ways in which different disciplines frame their questions, and in part of differences in the size of the geographic, political and social units on which they focus. Linguists and language documenters, on the one hand, tend to focus on linguistic, demographic and educational aspects of the problems of minority and endangered languages, to the exclusion of economic aspects. Many checklists for assessing the status of such languages including, for example, the one advanced in UNESCO (2003) for establishing the Language Vitality Index (see Grenoble, Chapter 2), do not include economic variables. Conversely, measures intended to alleviate poverty and to promote development are very typically developed without reference to language. The authors of the UNESCO report observe, for example, that 'national HIV/AIDS awareness or poverty-alleviation programmes often do not consider minority communities, even if they are illiterate' (UNESCO 2003: 6). Robinson (1996: 16), in a detailed case study of the role of language in rural development in Cameroon, states that 'language issues have rarely been addressed in the design of development projects, but have rather been on the agenda at the level of implementation'. He explains this as resulting in part from the fact that it is the nation state which has traditionally been the unit of economic analysis and development planning (Robinson 1996: 26). Policies and projects thus emerge from a perspective too coarse-grained to take into account concerns of minority languages, which become prominent only at more local levels. The rural setting of many minority and endangered languages also becomes a factor, as the result of prejudices which favour the perspective, needs and concerns of urban dwellers over those of rural groups (Robinson 1996: 40).

There is an emerging awareness, however, that development, poverty alleviation and health improvement efforts can be fully successful only if they take into account the linguistic situation of the locales in which they are implemented, build on an understanding of what languages are used by whom, and in what situations, and make use of local languages as a resource. That is, minority languages do have a role in successful economic development. Robinson (1996: 39ff.) notes, for example, a recent movement in the practice of rural development intervention in Africa toward aiming efforts at the micro-level, returning control of decision making to local people, and paying greater attention to local needs. This trend is rooted in the observation that top-down approaches in poverty-alleviation programmes, insufficiently informed by sociological information, tend to fail or fall short of their objectives (Robinson 1996: 45). These alternative, local, participatory, community-controlled models for development, in turn, cannot avoid taking into account in a central way local language use and language interactions. Thus, minority languages are important to development because people use them, and development plans can be made more effective and more targeted, and the delivery of services more efficient and more equitable, if linguistic access is extended to all local stakeholders. Along these lines, health workers, for example, are becoming increasingly aware of the important role that linguistic, sociolinguistic and cultural awareness can play in effective delivery of health-care services to minority groups (see, for example, Matharu 2009). Even in the case of minority-language groups which are overwhelmingly bilingual in the dominant language, as in the case of Welsh speakers, it is argued (Williams 1994) that when social services are available only in a language not native to the client, delivery of such services is less than ideally efficient, and potential clients may be discouraged from making use of them. This may be particularly true for older minority language speakers.

Aside from such matters of access, enfranchisement and participation, there is another respect in which indigenous languages can play a role in development. It has been proposed that such languages often embody systems of knowledge about local environments and traditional technologies which can serve as the basis for alternative modes of exploiting local resources, modes which are less ecologically and culturally disruptive and more sustainable than are industries and technologies imported from outside. Nettle and Romaine (2000: 166ff.) and Harrison (2007: 163–6) provide specific examples of such potentially exploitable systems of knowledge. Romaine (2009) challenges standard approaches to poverty alleviation and economic development based on importation of Western economic and technological concepts, and sets forth a general vision for an alternative model based on cultivation of local economic and technological traditions. The latter, in her view, unlike the former, addresses the three-fold objectives of stabilization of minority languages and cultures, equitable poverty reduction and minimization of disruption to local ecosystems.

20.4.2   Economic intervention on behalf of displaced languages

It would seem that if ECONOMIC DISRUPTION of communities is among the main factors leading to language shift and language death, then activities which contribute to the economic stability of such communities, by boosting the economy, with appropriate circumspection, should in turn strengthen threatened languages. That is, it should be possible to pursue the goal of stabilizing and revitalizing endangered languages by means of activities aimed more broadly at improving the local standard of living.

It is not unreasonable to suggest that even the first-line response to disasters of various sorts which result in large-scale population displacement (evacuations or refugee crises) should take into account goals of limiting social and linguistic disruption, and that professionals in the relevant disciplines should create general protocols and guidelines for the information of emergency workers involved in such enterprises.

In instances of gradual out-migration, both the remnant community and the population of displaced or urbanized speakers may endure poverty, but the causes and the remedies are different, as are the prospects that economic intervention can arrest language shift. As Vaillancourt (2008: 172) notes, the remnant community is likely to continue to suffer from lack of resources, while the urbanized portion of the population is likely to suffer from competition in the job market, compounded by linguistic and/or ethnic discrimination. Regional development is an appropriate policy response in the former case, while language laws are more appropriate in the latter.

The two situations also differ with respect to strategies and prospects for language maintenance. Among urbanized speakers, the displaced language is brought into direct competition with others from which it had originally been separated (and protected) by geographical distance. There are economic and sociological pressures on its speakers to adopt the dominant language, and to transmit that language to their children. The minority language may now be stigmatized by its association with a less prosperous way of life, and lacking the support formerly provided by its traditional cultural and social institutions. The task of maintaining a minority language over the long term once it has been cut adrift from its traditional moorings and placed in head-to-head competition with a more socio-economically privileged language, in an urban setting, for example, is highly challenging. There is a widespread view that strict DIGLOSSIA, i.e. functional, if not geographic, separation of the languages, is a requisite condition for stable bilingualism and the prevention of language shift. The theoretical model of Abrams and Strogatz (2003) (hampered by the unduly restrictive assumption of monolingual speakers) in fact predicts that without such separation: 'two languages cannot co-exist stably – one will eventually drive the other to extinction'. Exceptions, they claim: 'generally involve split populations that have lived without significant interaction, effectively in separate, monolingual societies'. Even these investigators conclude, however, that the equations can be made to yield a stable bilingual fixed point by incorporating a control through active feedback on the variable encoding PERCEIVED STATUS, defined as: 'a parameter that reflects the social or economic opportunities afforded its speakers'. This variable is the target of what has been labelled STATUS PLANNING, i.e. efforts directed at increasing the social and economic utility of the minority language (see Sallabank, Chapter 14). The status of speakers of minority and endangered languages can be raised by legislation prohibiting linguistic discrimination, and establishing rights of speakers to use their languages for public purposes and to expect delivery of public services in those languages ('linguistic normalization', in the terms of Thomas 1994). New cultural institutions, such as language societies, can be established, serving the dual purpose of generating positive attitudes toward the language and providing it with new exclusive domains (such as its sole use in meetings of such societies). Finally, linguistic engineering can be applied to the minority language itself, equipping it linguistically for extension into new socioeconomic domains. In addition to the development and standardization of a written form, such efforts can involve the development of terminology appropriate to new domains of use. Thus, for example, one quarter of the papers in a volume on language discrimination in Namibia (Pütz 1996) focus on the task of 'technicalizing' the lexicons of minority languages (see Sallabank, Chapter 14, for further discussion).

20.4.3 Economic intervention in remnant communities

Even with such measures, minority-language maintenance in urban settings remains an uphill struggle, in the face of linguistic competition, weakening of linguistic networks, reducing opportunities for language use, and loss of domains in which the minority language was formerly normalized. The bilingual fixed point of Abrams and Strogatz (2003), mentioned above is, at best, difficult to achieve. The remnant community would thus seem to be a more promising locus for language-maintenance efforts, boasting the advantages of geographical and functional isolation from the dominant language. Geographic isolation, of course, does not constitute the bastion that it once did, in an age in which even the most remote areas can receive television and radio broadcasts in the medium of the regionally dominant language. In recognition of this, many language-maintenance initiatives place a high priority on the development of alternative broadcast programmes and channels for minority languages (see Moriarty, Chapter 22).

The robustness of these advantages may be undercut, in some cases seriously, by population loss and the negative economic forces that led to it, though as noted, the remnant community may derive some benefit from the transplantation of some of its speakers into an urban setting. Blench (2007: 152) observes that 'if a language can be adapted to "modern" life it paradoxically gains more prestige in rural areas'. The population of the remnant community may dwindle to a point at which the language is no longer viable even if further diminution is arrested. Such factors as the age and reproduction rate of the remnant population, and whether out-migration of speakers is accompanied by in-migration of nonspeakers, play a role in determining this threshold, as does, potentially, the subjective assessment on the part of those in a position to intervene on behalf of the language about whether the population is still sufficiently large or viable to merit intervention.

20.4.4 Types of intervention

Efforts to support minority and endangered languages in such contexts by economic means can be divided for present purposes into three categories. In some cases, the attempt has taken the form of direct financial incentives paid to individual speakers who use the language. These have included subsidies paid to families in Ireland whose children demonstrate proficiency in Irish by examination. Broadly construed, they also include cases in which evidence of linguistic competence is taken as evidence of membership in a tribal or ethnic group eligible for a grant or subsidy (e.g. Crystal 2000: 125). I know of no general account of the efficacy of such measures, but the specific case of Ireland suggests that such payments may have a depressing effect on the prestige of the language, without stemming language-shift (Carnie 1996: 105). Economic subsidy for individuals is indeed the only means for economic intervention in instances in which the language no longer has a speaker community. The master–apprentice programme for Native Californian languages described by Hinton (2001b: 219) attempts to revive languages with very small remaining populations by pairing native speakers and learners, and paying each team member a stipend for participation in an extended teaching/learning relationship. The stipend in this instance differs from the Irish case in that it is not awarded merely on the basis of language competence, but for participation in a language-transmitting activity (see Hinton, Chapter 15).

I am not aware of instances in which subsidies based on language use are extended to communities or businesses, rather than individuals, but such measures, in the form of tax incentives (Evas 2000: 301) or restrictions on loans (McLeod 2002), have been suggested as means for promoting the normalization of bilingual policies in the workplace.

In other cases, the focus has been on stabilization of the linguistic community through addressing the material needs of its inhabitants more generally, without specific reference to language. In non-wage-based economies, measures which can serve that purpose include improvement of health care and sanitation, development of water supplies and transportation systems, and provision of technical support for sustainable utilization of natural and agricultural resources. On the bright side, as Crawford (1996: 65) points out, because of the marginal nature of typical communities and economies of the type in question, relatively small sums may suffice, the targets in some cases being in the reach of private foundations, non-governmental organizations, corporations and tribes, as well as governments. Measures of these sorts have been tried: Craig (1992a: 21) notes that the provision of access to food distribution and health services for community members formed an important part of the Nicaraguan government's strategic support for the Rama Language Project (which continues to pursue its objectives on fronts, including land claims, that go beyond strictly linguistic issues; see Grinevald 2007: 74).

England (1998) reports that the Academy of Mayan Languages, an autonomous state institution in Guatemala, invested considerable effort in a reforestation project. Such broad approaches may be controversial, if perceived by critics as being too far removed from the proper scope of language maintenance activities. England reports such criticism in the Mayan case (see also Crystal 2000: 125).

Offering services and information through local languages, which has been shown to improve the efficiency and effectiveness of their delivery, may help sustain those languages in ways more specific than simply helping to stem out-migration. Burnaby (1996: 32) reports that the highest levels of fluency in Australian Aboriginal languages exists in those communities with the most Aboriginal language services, including newspapers, radio, television, government publications and community meetings.

In the case of wage-based economies, the achievement of economic stabilization must also include enhancing job opportunities. This is a more daunting task, requiring more broad-scale planning. The economic problems of endangered language communities are in large part the problems of rural development in general, in which geographical remoteness, under-population and the sparseness of networks confer a competitive disadvantage on businesses and industries (see Chalmers and Danson 2006: 255). But creating jobs in a way that does not lead to cultural disruption adds another layer of challenge. Importation of outside industries poses the greatest risk. During the 1960s and 1970s, for example, the standard approach to addressing the economic lag of the Irish and Gaelic speaking regions of Ireland and Scotland respectively was the introduction of large-scale industrial projects. These undercut the language by requiring the importation of an outside workforce and consequent normalization of English in the workplace, and by focusing efforts on specific industrial sites while neglecting the surrounding rural areas (Chalmers and Danson 2006, McLeod 2002, Walsh 2006), without, ultimately, solving the economic problems of these regions. Economic schemes insufficiently sensitive to the special linguistic character of these areas continue. Walsh (2006: 273) cites the particularly egregious case of call-centres set up in the Irish *Gaeltachtaí* in 2004, whose employees spent the day making calls in English.

20.4.5   Minority languages as an economic resource

More recent trends in the general theory and practice of economic development have emphasized the cultivation of HUMAN CAPITAL (Chalmers and Danson 2006: 239). Prominent among the resources of minority-language communities are their languages, and attempts have been made to exploit these economically, including as a component of cultural tourism, in the production of literary, musical, theatrical and cinematic materials, in the generation of teaching materials and in residential language schools. Enterprises of this sort create local employment while at the same time increasing the value of the language in some ways, giving language-related employment to some native speakers, and increasing the profile of the language in the community. To continue the Celtic example, Chalmers and Danson (2006: 246), among many others, talk of the prospect for a 'Gaelic Economy' in Gaelic-speaking regions of Scotland, a sector of the economy based on local language and culture, as more appropriate to the needs and characteristics of the *Gàidhealtachd* than conventional enterprises, and a fertile basis for language regeneration. The critics of this concept, however, point out a number of potential problems with the treatment of minority languages and related cultural production as a sector of the economy, on a par with others (see, for example, McLeod 2002). Among the problems observed are the following:

1. commodifying the language in this way places emphasis on economic criteria for success, rather than linguistic ones. Language products like music and teaching materials are marketed to outside consumers often with little or no command of the language, as is cultural tourism, and many of these products consequently involve only token, symbolic uses of the language. This outward focus does little to strengthen the language in the community, especially since the language of the workplace in these industries is often the dominant language. McLeod (2002), for example, cites Gaelic television programme production as a notorious 'Potemkin Village' phenomenon, whose product is Gaelic, but whose working language is virtually exclusively English (see Moriarty, Chapter 22).

2. marketing to this class of consumers can in fact undercut the language by increasing the necessity of interacting in the language of the consumer. McLeod (2002), for example, claims that only those festivals in the Gaelic areas of Scotland which are conducted in English have proven commercially successful. Carnie (1996) observes that the establishment of Irish immersion schools in the *Gaeltachtaí* in Ireland, again intended to promote the language, has resulted in a seasonal influx of thousands of English speakers into these areas, and a shift in language use. I have observed similar effects at immersion schools in Wales and Scotland. The experience of the Celtic languages in cultural tourism has in general not been an entirely happy one. The problem there is perhaps compounded by the fact that the language of the tourists also happens to be the regionally dominant language. Grenoble and Whaley (1998: 13) and Crystal (2000: 133) mention a number of minority language areas in the Alpine countries, where the linguistic background of typical visitors is more diverse, which have benefited from cultural tourism. Even in the

Celtic case, it has been suggested that the problem has been undue linguistic deference on the part of Welsh and Gaelic speakers (John Norman MacLeod, cited in Hutchinson 2005: 207).

3. the commodification of cultural celebrations, ceremonies and symbols for purposes of cultural tourism risks distortion and loss of cultural authenticity (Bankston and Henry 2000) or folklorization (Paciotto 1996: 177).

4. in casting the language as simply another sector of the economy: this approach tends to isolate it from other aspects of daily life, thus further marginalizing it. Employment in this economic sector is restricted to a few centres of cultural and educational production, rather than being diffused throughout the whole area in which the language is used, and is highly dependent on public funding (McLeod 2002). Gardner *et al.* (2000: 329) report a similar result for Basque.

20.4.6 Normalization of minority languages

The aggregate experience has been that general intervention in the local economy through development of new industries and jobs may improve the situation of the local language by stemming out-migration, but can also pose a serious risk of introducing further destabilization, if it is not appropriate to the local linguistic and cultural circumstances. Efforts to market the local language and culture, while they can play an important role in building prestige and self-confidence, are not sufficient to meet the economic needs of the community, and can also pose their own risks to the language and culture by tending to marginalize and stereotype them. Neither the approach of importing new businesses or industries nor the approach of building new enterprises based on local linguistic and cultural wealth suffices to create an adequate economic basis for linguistic stabilization. McLeod (2002) and others maintain that that goal can be achieved only by way of NORMALIZATION of the minority language in all spheres of the local economy. Numerous initiatives, often non-governmental, have been deployed in different contexts to encourage bilingual workplace policies. These operate by persuading businesses that both they and the community stand to benefit from cultivation of the local language, and by providing resources to facilitate the creation and maintenance of such workplaces. Grin (1999: 181) reports on the case of the *Gaillimh le Gaeilge* ('Galway with Irish'), for example, in which business owners were convinced that Irish is an income-generating asset in the prevailing regulatory context, and that therefore businesses have a stake in strengthening its position and visibility. In Wales, *Menter a Busnes* ('Venture and Business') promotes entrepreneurship by Welsh speakers by means which include business management and vocational training programmes, as well as the promotion of cultural tourism (Williams 2000: 364–5). The *Mentrau Iaith* ('Language Ventures'), community-based organizations which promote increased use of Welsh in all domains of life, also include increased use of Welsh in the business sector among their goals. Beyond convincing businesses that the cost of voluntary adoption of bilingual policies may be offset by direct economic benefits, such initiatives also attempt to point out that the effects of their linguistic practices, positive or negative, are of sufficient importance to the life of the community that they should be taken into account in decision-making even if they do not result directly in profit ('internalizing externalities', as it is called in the economic literature). Normalization has been the central goal of official language policy in Catalonia, where it has been vigorously pursued, with some successes (Gardner *et al.* 2000). Since normalization efforts build on the underlying local economies and can be no stronger than these, they have proven more effective in partially urbanized Wales, for example, than in the more sparsely populated Gaelic regions of Scotland, where an institution originally created to further the managerial and entrepreneurial preparation of Gaelic native speakers has not generally succeeded as such, and now caters mostly to learners (Hutchinson 2005: 205).

Some critics claim that initiatives relying on the voluntary participation and goodwill of dominant-language speakers are not adequate to effect the normalization of minority languages, and accordingly advocate stronger forms of intervention by the government toward this goal, in the form of language laws, tax incentives or lending restrictions. McLeod notes that bilingual workplace policies take the form of legal requirements in some cases, e.g. Québec and Catalonia. The passage of measures of this type, too, is ultimately dependent on a dominant-language-speaking majority which is well-disposed toward the minority language, aware of the value of that language to regional or national identity, and sensitive to its peril. Thus, normalization initiatives typically include marketing components aimed at generating positive linguistic attitudes among speakers of the dominant language and persuading them of the merits of multilingual policies and practices, as well as increasing the self-confidence of speakers of the minority language (Wynne-Jones and Dafis 2000). Marketing campaigns have played a prominent role in the official Catalonian linguistic normalization programme as well.

Economic measures with language stabilization among their goals are most successful when coordinated with efforts on other fronts. A particularly interesting multipronged initiative with both economic and linguistics aspects is reported by Batibo (2008) in Western Botswana, which has successfully promoted economic activity based on indigenous knowledge, and left the local language, Naro, in a considerably strengthened position. The project, the Kuru Development Project, involved language planning (development of linguistic materials), teacher training, the organization of local decision-making bodies and efforts directed specifically toward the economic sphere, focusing on skill development in traditional crafts, the establishment of shops and training in income utilization methods. The project led to a substantial increase in per-capita income as well as slowing language shift.

20.5 Conclusion

The economic circumstances of speakers and language communities have important implications for the tasks of arresting and reversing language shift; however, the factors that lie behind these circumstances and the changes that can take place in them are complex and multifaceted. Various development strategies have been proposed to support minority and endangered languages, ranging from general economic and social development to specifically targeted initiatives. It is not fully clear so far what economic and development intervention measures can be best applied in minority- and endangered-language contexts to ensure the continued presence of these languages on the world stage.

21

Researcher training and capacity development in language documentation

Anthony Jukes

21.1 Introduction

With the emergence of the field of language documentation has come the development of accompanying proposals for 'best practice' (see the E-MELD School of Best Practice, for example), the realization that different sets of skills are required of prospective researchers, and massively raised expectations with regard to the quality (and quantity) of the data collected. Here quality relates not only to issues of the quality of the audio- or video-recordings themselves (see Nathan 2010a, Nathan, Chapter 13), but also the quality of the organization, management, analysis, presentation and archiving of the documentary corpus materials (see Good, Chapter 11, Conathan, Chapter 12). Likewise, there is a growing emphasis on linguists' responsibilities to communities they work with, on issues of maintenance and revitalization, and generally on the ethical and moral dimensions of work with endangered languages (Austin 2010b, Rice 2006, Dobrin and Berson, Chapter 10). Further, there has for some time been an 'emerging ideal in the field' that community members should have access to training to allow them to carry out endangered language documentation and development programmes themselves (Dobrin 2008: 302).

The emergence of these new expectations has uncovered a need for new types of training courses, as it is evident that the list of specialized skills needed for language documentation and support is often different from the skills commonly taught in most linguistics courses. It is also evident that the target audience for training courses in endangered language work is not at all a homogeneous group, but rather consists of people whose backgrounds, interests and intentions vary widely, making a one-size-fits-all approach to training untenable.

This chapter discusses the specific and general skills which are (or arguably should be) taught in language documentation training courses, attempts to identify the major types of likely target audience, and outlines the main approaches to training in language documentation up to the present day, from graduate courses to short workshops and summer schools. A caveat is in order: because of the rapidly changing nature of this developing field, this chapter can only attempt to be a brief history and a snapshot of the state of documentation training at the time of writing, and will likely be overtaken by events. Nevertheless, the chapter will end by looking to the future, with some observations and proposals based on experience and feedback from both trainers and trainees on various courses.

21.2 Skills needed for language documentation and conservation

In order to discuss researcher training it will first be necessary to identify the particular skills associated with language documentation and conservation (henceforth LDC), and to discuss where and how these differ from the types of skills a researcher is likely to acquire as part of general linguistic training.

21.2.1 Descriptive linguistic skills

On the assumption that LDC is largely going to be performed by linguists or involve teams that include linguists, those linguists must have a grounding in descriptive linguistics, and should have familiarity with linguistic typology and the structural diversity of the world's languages (Grenoble, Chapter 2). Even to proceed with basic transcription and annotation of a lesser known language requires skilled phonological and morphosyntactic analysis, including interactions between them (e.g. the influence of morphological and syntactic structures on tonal phonology in some Niger-Congo languages, or on nasalization in some Amazonian languages), and beyond that basic level, the more layers of grammatical and other linguistic analysis that a documentation contains, the more useful it will be to future users. One cannot overestimate the importance of well-rounded training in the various fields of linguistics, with data from a wide variety of languages, and analyses from a range of theoretical perspectives. Training that has been too narrowly situated within a particular theoretical orientation, or built around data drawn largely from English or another major language, will not adequately prepare a researcher for the goal of producing a multipurpose record of a language in the sense of Himmelmann (2006a).

21.2.2 Field methods and 'field skills'

LDC for the majority of researchers and teams will involve some type of fieldwork, and will therefore require familiarity with a set of skills relevant to the activity. Most universities with a linguistics programme offer a course (of one or two semesters' duration) entitled 'Field Methods' or something similar as part of a linguistics degree (although many do not); and there are several guides or handbooks which attempt to cover the methods of fieldwork to a greater or lesser degree (see for example Abbi 2001, Bowern 2008, Crowley 2007, Newman and Ratliff 2001a, Thieberger to appear, and Vaux, Cooper and Tucker 2007).

Field methods courses typically involve working in-class with a speaker of an 'exotic' or at least unfamiliar (to the students) language, and attempting to describe basic aspects of the grammar of the language through elicitation, or a limited amount of recording and analysis of narrative text. While this is in itself excellent training in linguistic analysis and problem solving, especially at an undergraduate level, of necessity the decontextualized, classroom-based nature of the course is far removed from the type of field experience a researcher is likely to undergo during actual postgraduate or professional research. From a purely phono-morphosyntactic perspective, few of the more complex patterns or puzzles of grammar are going to be solved (or even to have emerged) in such a short time. Beyond that, certainly there is little chance that complex semantic, sociolinguistic, pragmatic, psycholinguistic, or discourse/stylistic phenomena will have been considered. And last but by no means least, there will likely have been little real consideration of the intuitively understood but little-discussed area of 'field skills', as noted by Rehg (2007: 15) in his enumeration of the five areas in which he considers field linguists need training:

1. linguistic theory
2. fieldwork methods
3. methods of language conservation
4. area studies
5. field skills (a category that includes knowledge of ethics, health, hygiene and other capabilities that contribute to a fieldworker's well-being).

This final category of 'field skills' has some overlap with the issues relating to 'the human factor in fieldwork' as discussed by Newman (2009b): namely health, children, gender and sex, professional and personal ethics, and money.

A further, somewhat overlapping, set of concerns that field methods courses are likely to 'fail to deal pedagogically with' has been enumerated by Austin (2008b):

1. health and safety (both of the student and the group they work with);
2. dislocation and culture shock, equipment failure and living in unfamiliar conditions;
3. working outside the classroom, laboratory-like context with multiple speakers and dealing with the complexities of their lives

requiring (often delicate) negotiations about availability and competing demands on their time;

4. handling conversation and the apparently uncontrolled flood of input that comes from living and working closely with a group;

5. understanding and dealing with the expectations that individuals and communities might have about what the student is expected to 'give back' in compensation for time spent doing language work.

It could be added that successful fieldwork also relies to a large degree on good interpersonal skills, patience and resourcefulness, which can only be taught to a certain extent. But clearly, training in LDC needs to address the issues raised above. Thankfully, it does appear that linguistics as a discipline is beginning to take these matters seriously, as more and more linguists share both the good and bad experiences of fieldwork (see e.g. Macaulay 2004) and discuss the issues in professional fora (e.g. the workshop on non-linguistic aspects of fieldwork held at the 2009 Australian Linguistics Society conference)[1] and in training contexts (e.g. not only the documentation training courses discussed below, but other events such as the fieldwork workshops held at SOAS in May and December 2009).[2]

2.3 Documentation skills

In relation to skills more specific to LDC work, Austin (2007: 28) gives the following general list:

> Language documentation requires knowledge and application of a range of skills, including those traditionally associated with fieldwork and language description, as well as skills in the application of information, communications and media technologies (Munro 2005) and applied ethics. Increasingly also, documenters are expected to have knowledge and skills typically associated with areas of applied linguistics, such as orthography development, lexicography, translation, pedagogy and curriculum design, multimedia, language policy and needs assessment, and advocacy. The need for these skills arises from the desires and expectations of the language communities and the multidisciplinary orientations of the work.

Austin goes on (2007: 28–9), rather dauntingly, to list specific skills associated with LDC projects:

1. **Project conception, design and management** – familiarity with documentation theory, applied ethics, intellectual property rights and sociocultural issues, stakeholder communication;

2. **Grant application writing;**

3. **Media management** – recording techniques, field methods, data transfer, backup;

4. **Data and metadata management** – data and metadata represen-
    tation (XML, relational database models), transcription, linguistic
    analysis (phonetics, phonology, morphology, syntax, semantics) and
    annotation, use of linguistic software tools (Transcriber, Shoebox/
    Toolbox, ELAN, IMDI), data integrity and sustainability ... workflow
    design and management;
5. **Mobilization** – familiarity with applied linguistics concepts
    (orthography design, lexicography, curriculum development, policy
    formation, revitalization), publication skills, multimedia design and
    implementation;
6. **Team-based research** – skills sharing and transfer, capacity
    development;
7. **Reporting** – presentation, writing and communication skills.

Some of the skills are those associated with being a professional academic, grant application writing springs immediately to mind (see also
Bowern, Chapter 23), and hence some may not need to be taught to each
audience,[3] but others are more specialized and some are quite technical:
shooting and editing quality video are specialized professions in their own
right, and there are also particular software tools associated with linguistics and especially the field of LDC which are by no means simple to learn
to use.

Clearly no one person can have expert knowledge of all of these skills
and, even more clearly, they cannot all be taught comprehensively in
even a postgraduate programme running over several years, let alone at
a summer school, short course, or workshop. Thus, the above list must
be considered a wish list for an ideal researcher carrying out an ideal
project in an ideal world. In the real world, researchers must prioritize
and rank skills according to a multiplicity of factors, including the relative importance or universality of particular aspects of documentation,
the nature of specific projects, the needs and desires of particular communities, and the interests and aptitudes of individual researchers. No
training course can satisfy all these factors for every researcher, but the
examination of training courses in Section 21.5 will show which skills
have been prioritized by particular training institutions.

21.3 Target audiences

When discussing training it is necessary to determine who it actually is
that is being trained, who is in fact a 'language documenter'. They can
potentially come in a variety of types, but it can be useful to distinguish
at least the following two categories of potential audiences for documentation training:

1. new researchers with no previous background in either linguistics or
    language documentation. They are typically served in several ways,

such as postgraduate programmes (Section 21.4), summer schools, or short courses (see Section 21.5);

2. the ordinary working linguist (OWL).[4] These are usually researchers who already have a background as a linguist, are probably intending to do 'traditional' linguistic research on their target language, but are also concerned with the quality of their data and keen to maximize its potential use by other researchers and the language community itself. Some are highly trained, some are veterans but are not technologically literate, many have their own ideas of what a language documentation project should be. On the other hand some are young or new to the field, or may feel unequipped to offer their own ideas and would like to be given a blueprint to follow. There are several options for such researchers, including going back for postgraduate training (Section 21.4), topping up with summer schools or short courses (Section 21.5), or participating in specialized documentation courses offered through archives and generally supported by funding agencies primarily for recipients of research grants (such as DoBeS, ELDP, discussed in 21.5.1 below).

21.4   Postgraduate training programmes

This section discusses training programmes in LDC which lead to a recognized postgraduate degree. At present there are only two institutions offering dedicated postgraduate programmes in language documentation: SOAS in London and the University of Hawai'i at Mānoa.[5] The numbers of students are relatively small when one compares them to the numbers of students enrolled in more traditional linguistics programmes; however, it should be remembered that there are many linguistics departments in universities around the world which have strong traditions of field linguistics and have embraced to a greater or lesser extent the goals and methods of language documentation.

21.4.1   Postgraduate programmes at the
Endangered Languages Academic Programme, SOAS

Founded by a grant from Arcadia Trust (formerly the Lisbet Rausing Charitable Fund) in 2002, the Endangered Languages Academic Programme (ELAP) is the academic component[6] of the Hans Rausing Endangered Languages Project (HRELP), located within the Department of Linguistics at the School of Oriental and African Studies (SOAS) in London. The relevant programmes for this discussion are a one-year full-time Master of Arts in Language Documentation and Description (which can also be taken part-time over two or three years), and a three to four-year PhD in Field Linguistics.[7]

The MA in Language Documentation and Description is offered in two pathways: one is entitled Language Support and Revitalization and is intended for students without a background in linguistics; while the Field Linguistics pathway is intended for those with prior linguistic training. The course was split into two pathways after several years of teaching it as a single stream, partly because it transpired that few of the MA candidates had a background in linguistics, since it is 'usual in the UK for MA courses not to require previous knowledge of the content area' (Austin 2007: 38), and because many students were finding it difficult to reach the required level with some of the more technical and analytical subjects that make up the MA. That said, there are more commonalities than differences in the two pathways, as shall be seen.

Both pathways include two core subjects: *Issues in Language Documentation*, which covers both theoretical and practical concepts of documentation such as project design, ethics, the relationship between researchers and communities, and so forth; and *Applied Documentation and Description*, which covers topics such as orthography design, lexicography, language policy and other topics of applied linguistics. Additionally, there is a *Research Foundations* weekly seminar attended by students from both pathways (along with other MA students taking the non-specialist MA in Linguistics offered by the Department), which aims to enhance research skills and methodology as well as providing an opportunity for students to gain experience in preparing presentations and working in teams. Finally, there are optional courses offered each semester: these include courses on typology, syntax, phonology, areal studies and other areas of mainstream linguistic interest. Further courses of more specific endangered language content, such as language revitalization, are offered.

The differences between the two pathways are as follows: the Support and Revitalization pathway includes a two-semester mandatory introductory linguistics course (*Principles of Linguistic Analysis*) that is an introduction to traditional descriptive linguistics concepts, while the Field Linguistics pathway requires completion of a two-semester course on field methods and a one semester course on technological aspects of language documentation (ranging from recording skills to data modelling, corpus and workflow management, use of software tools and principles of multimedia publication).

In March 2009 the MA students were offered the opportunity to put their training into practice by carrying out fieldwork on one of the endangered languages of the British Isles, Dgèrnésiais (Guernésiais or Guernsey Norman French), with a two-week trip to the Channel Islands. This was reported to be a great success and it was repeated in 2010, with the expectation that it will become a regular part of the course training. Several other linguistics departments offer this kind of 'on-site' fieldwork training, including University of California, Berkeley (Andrew

Garrett, p.c.) and University of Arizona (Colleen Fitzgerald, p.c.), both of which take students to Indian Reservations for short fieldtrips.

SOAS also offers a PhD in Field Linguistics, which takes three–four years, with the MA in Language Documentation (or equivalent) being the usual prerequisite for entry into the PhD. The PhD programme is divided into two components: enrolment in an MPhil and then enrolment in the PhD proper. On successful completion of advanced level coursework and other requirements, MPhil students undertake an upgrade process to the PhD proper and in the second year can commence fieldwork, which is normally expected to last nine–twelve months. The third year (and commonly a fourth) are largely spent writing the dissertation, though it is also common for students to return to the field for several months to check analyses and fill gaps in the data. At the time of writing, six students had graduated from the PhD with a further fourteen at varying stages of completion.

In addition to the regular coursework, ELAP organizes additional training events intended primarily for PhD students and post-doctoral researchers; these often resemble shorter versions of the ELDP training courses described in Section 21.5.1, but there have also been specialized workshops such as an XML training day; and a workshop on audio-recording, digitization and archiving hosted by a professional audio-archivist.

21.4.2 Postgraduate programmes at Hawai'i

The Department of Linguistics at the University of Hawai'i at Mānoa has a history of descriptive and field linguistics concentrating on languages of the Pacific and Asia, and since 2003 has offered Language Documentation and Conservation (LDC) as one of the three streams of its Masters programme (the others are Linguistic Analysis and Language and Cognition). Relevant courses taught as part of the required syllabus include *Introduction to Documentary Linguistics*, *Methods of Language Documentation*, *Language Data Processing*, *Phonetic Fieldwork on Endangered Languages*, and *Methods of Language Conservation*, as well as courses on language planning, lexicography and grammar writing. There are about ten MA students at any given time.

Students who complete the MA in Language Documentation and Conservation are encouraged to apply to the PhD programme, where they are usually expected to continue documentation with extended fieldwork on the research language they selected for their MA.

The Department at Mānoa is also the home of the Language Documentation Training Centre (LDTC), an initiative which brings together volunteer postgraduate students in linguistics and speakers of under-documented languages (usually international students attending various courses at the university). Over the period of one semester the speakers receive training in basic linguistic concepts and techniques of language documentation, and work together with postgraduate student mentors to create websites presenting information about their chosen languages. At the time of writing the LDTC hosts websites in about fifty-eight languages from around the world,[8] some of which have little or no other information available elsewhere. As Rehg (2007:19–20) writes:

> It is difficult to overstate the impact that the LDTC has had on our department. It has provided a laboratory for our documentation students, it has resulted in a stirring sense of camaraderie among its participants, and it has been well-received, both on the campus and in the community. It is a project with goals that others can understand, perhaps especially in Hawai'i, where the indigenous language is highly endangered. The LDTC has also been given a substantial amount of publicity in newsletters, newspapers, and on the radio … Most recently, the LDTC has been invited to work with speakers of minority languages at one of the largest high schools in Honolulu. This activity will open up new opportunities for the center and allow our graduate students to become more directly involved with the community … Where feasible, I would urge other linguistics departments to consider establishing a comparable student-directed center. The payoffs can be substantial.

21.5 Training programmes, short courses and summer schools

This section will look at short courses and training programmes generally aimed at academic linguists but sometimes also including native speaker language activists. These include ELDP and DoBeS training courses, recurring summer schools such as InField and the 3L International Summer School on Language Documentation and Description, and a variety of events such as the DoBeS summer school in Frankfurt in 2004 and workshops on documentation held in Africa and Indonesia.

It is worth noting here that courses on language documentation (or at least fieldwork) have become more prominent in mainstream linguistics institutes. For example, the Linguistic Society of America Summer Institute in 2009 included a stream of seven courses on fieldwork and language documentation, including *Language Documentation for Cross-Linguistic Comparison*, *Language Documentation and Language Communities*, and *Data Management for Field Linguistics*.

21.5.1 Grantee training courses: DoBeS and ELDP

Two recurring streams of training courses are specifically intended for recipients of documentation project grants from ELDP or DoBeS.

Participants in these courses typically have prior training in linguistics as they are at least doctoral candidates, and more often post-doctoral or established researchers. The aim therefore is largely to improve technical and organizational skills needed for effective documentary work, and also to encourage debate about social, cultural and ethical aspects of documentation theory.

If we compare the two organizations' approach to training, it appears that DoBeS has much more emphasis on standards of uses of specified technological tools. Furthermore, the DoBeS courses are to a certain degree taught by the actual developers of commonly used language documentation software tools (such as ELAN; see also Good, Chapter 11) and those working for concrete standards of language documentation practice, while the ELDP courses reflect a more flexible (but more ambiguous) approach.

21.5.1.1   DoBeS training courses

The first training courses specifically for language documentation were those offered by the Volkswagen-funded programme Dokumentation Bedrohter Sprachen (Documentation of Endangered Languages, or DoBeS). DoBeS began running training courses for grantees in May 2002, and has been running courses roughly bi-annually since. They take place at the DoBeS home institution: the Max Planck Institute for Psycholinguistics in Nijmegen, the Netherlands. DoBeS also ran a summer school in Frankfurt in 2004, which is discussed in Section 21.5.7.

Unlike ELDP, DoBeS has not required that all grantees attend training courses, but rather they make the courses available for grantees and others if they wish to attend. They have also prepared a number of information sheets about such topics as video-editing and encoding, archiving, power and storage management in the field and so forth; these guides are freely available at the DoBeS website.[9]

Table 21.1 gives the programme for a recent DoBeS training course. It is obvious at a glance that the emphasis is on technical and technological aspects, and particularly on becoming familiar with the MPI's own software (ELAN, IMDI, LEXUS and LAMUS) and some other widely used software.

21.5.1.2   ELDP training courses

All recipients of grants from the Endangered Languages Documentation Programme (ELDP) are required by the terms of their grant to attend a training course in London which is run by staff of ELAP, ELAR and other specialists brought in specifically for particular topics. The first training course was run in 2004 and they have been offered once or twice a year since. The costs of grantees' travel and accommodation, as well as payment to external tutors are borne by ELDP. Non-grantees are not eligible to attend.

Table 21.1. *DOBES Training course June 2009*

Day 1	Day 2	Day 3	Day 4
Introduction to DOBES archiving	Power management, Storage management, A/V file formats, A/V compression	LEXUS introduction and practice	LAMUS archive management
Audio-recording, digital audio handling, tools and practice	Introduction to IMDI metadata and tools	ELAN introduction and practice	PRAAT and transcriber, introduction and practice
Video-recording, digital video handling	IMDI practice	ELAN practice	Access management system Workflow principles
Video tools and practice	Shoebox (Toolbox) introduction and practice	XML/Google Earth Unicode/Keyman	

Source: www.mpi.nl/DOBES/training_courses

The intention is for ELDP grantees to attend a training course quite early in their project. However because some time elapsed between the commencement of the earliest projects and when the first training courses were held, several of the earlier grantees did not attend a training course until their projects were well underway, or in some cases nearly complete. Needless to say this somewhat diminished the effectiveness of the training, but on the other hand meant that early cohorts of trainees included some who were quite experienced and had learnt through trial and error what types of things worked in the field and what did not.

The training offered has evolved over time to adapt to changing technologies and techniques and has also been sensitive to methodological and ethical issues that have arisen in the field. Table 21.2 shows a recent training-course timetable and subject list.

Trainee evaluation from ELDP training courses held over the years 2004–8 reveals increasing satisfaction with the training course. One reason is obviously that as the training staff became more experienced (and as they learned from previous evaluations), they became more adept at training and designed the course better. But another reason can also be surmised: as the field of language documentation matures, trainees have clearer expectations of what a course in language documentation should include.

21.5.2 InField

The Institute on Field Linguistics and Language Documentation (InField) is a six-week summer institute intended to be an ongoing biennial event, held at participating institutions in alternate years (the years in which

Table 21.2. *ELDP Grantee training course timetable, 27 August–2 September 2008. 90-minute sessions*

Day 1	Day 2	Day 3	Day 4	Day 5	Day 6
Welcome and introductions	Audio evaluation	Data management	Advice clinic	Videography and video practical	Field practical topics
Audio principles	ELAN		Linguistic elicitation		Multimedia / lexicography / advanced video / digitizing audio
Digital audio	Toolbox	XML	Corpus collection		Ethics and IP
Audio practical	Data practical – ELAN and Toolbox	Data practical – XML	Archiving	Video selection and editing	Wrap/ feedback

Source: www.hrelp.org/events/workshops/eldp2008_8/index.html

the Linguistic Society of America Summer Institute is not held). The first InField took place at the University of California, Santa Barbara in 2008 and the next is due to take place in 2010 at the University of Oregon.

InField targets two main audiences: linguists (both professional and postgraduate students), and community language activists. In fact, one of the explicit goals is to bring together language activists and linguists so that they can both benefit from shared training, with the aim of promoting a collaborative model of research and fruitful ways of working towards common goals. Another explicit goal is to enhance or refresh the fieldwork skills of working linguists, as: 'those who received their field training even 10–15 years ago could benefit from exposure to new tools and methods'.[10]

InField is divided into two main parts: two weeks of general workshops on a range of topics, followed by four weeks of intensive fieldwork training, the latter being intended mainly for postgraduate students in linguistics and expecting a certain level of prior linguistics training.

The general workshops at InField 2008 consisted of eighteen topics which were broadly divided into three main tracks: Track A intended largely for community language activists, Track B intended for postgraduate students in linguistics (those who would be going on to the four-week intensive field training), and Track C intended for OWLs (who would not be taking field training). The three tracks are shown in Table 21.3.

As can be seen, Tracks B and C were in fact largely identical, while Track A offered several different workshop topics.

Table 21.3. *The InField 2008 workshop tracks*

Track A	Track B	Track C
Steps in language documentation (4–5 hours)		
Models of language documentation and revitalization (10 hours)		
Audio recording (5–7 hours)		
Language activism (7 hours)	Data management and archiving (6 hours)	
Introduction to linguistics for language activists (10 hours)	Principles of database design (8 hours)	
Web and WIKIs for language documentation (7 hours)	Toolbox (6 hours)	
Language resources and the community (7 hours)	Life in the field (2 hours)	
Grant writing (5 hours)	Problematizing the field experience (6 hours)	
	Field phonetics (4 hours)	
	Intellectual property rights (3 hours)	
Other workshops as desired		

Source: www.linguistics.ucsb.edu/faculty/infield/tracks/index.html

Genetti and Siemens (2009) offer an evaluation of the first InField, reporting that the experience was extremely positive overall, but making the following observations based on participants' reports.

- There was an imbalance in the ratio of language activists to linguists as instructors, compared to the ratio as participants. Whilst language activists made up one third of the number of students (24/75), they were only 3 of the 27 instructors.
- Skill levels in the technical workshops were too mixed.
- There was dissatisfaction with having to choose between overlapping/clashing workshops.
- Many would have liked the workshops (and the programme in general) to have run for longer.

The first two of these issues are relatively easy to fix, by recruiting more language activists as instructors and by streaming the technical courses, and presumably will be taken on-board by the organizing committee for the next InField. The latter are perennial problems with this type of course; it is not possible to run a large number of different workshops without some running in parallel, and timetabling workshops of more than a few weeks, duration can discriminate against those who are not able to take long periods of time away from their jobs and families.

The four-week intensive field training which followed the InField workshops was split into three classes, each of which met for three hours each weekday for lectures and demonstrations, and further broken into pairs of students who would meet for two hours every other day with the speaker(s) for elicitation and recording sessions.

While the level of satisfaction was also high for this section of InField, Genetti and Siemens (2009) report that there were 'some feelings of disparity' based on the different approaches taken by each of the three groups. They recommend a more unified technological environment and note the importance of having multiple speakers available for each class. They also suggest 'insisting' that students take the relevant workshops during the two-week section thereby allowing the field training to commence at a higher level.

21.5.3   3L International Summer School on Language Documentation and Description

The 3L International Summer School on Language Documentation and Description is an annual two-week summer school organized by member institutions of the 3L consortium,[11] with the aim of introducing the concepts and practices of language documentation to future field linguists. The first was held in 2008 at the University of Lyon, the second was held at SOAS in London in 2009 and the third is scheduled for Leiden in 2010.

The 3L Summer School in 2009 attracted many more applications than there were places, showing that there is significant unmet demand for this type of training event. Ultimately places were offered to almost a hundred students rather than the original plan of fifty (the 2008 Summer School had similarly been increased to eighty-seven from a planned fifty).

The programme consisted of (Monday–Thursday) a set of plenary lectures and tutorial discussions offered to all students in the mornings, with elective courses held in the afternoons.

The plenary sessions covered the following topics (now published in Austin 2010a):

- Issues in language documentation
- Communities and ethics
- Data collection methods
- Documenting sign languages
- Digital language archiving
- Language documentation and linguistic theory
- Language policy
- Language documentation and typology.

The elective courses included such topics as: data and archiving, documenting sign languages, documenting special vocabulary, sociolinguistics of language endangerment and grammar writing, as well as courses of areal or typological interest. There were also practical workshops: one full-day workshop on video for documentation, and half-days on software tools, advanced audio, and applying for a research grant. A feature of the 3L Summer School is that at least some of the courses and tutorial sessions are run in French, as well as English, the main language of instruction.

21.5.4   Documentation workshops at Tokyo University of Foreign Studies

Starting in 2008 (and projected to run until 2012) the Institute for Languages and Cultures of Asia and Africa at Tokyo University of Foreign Studies has annually invited staff from ELAP and ELAR at SOAS to run 4-day or 5-day Language Documentation Workshops for postgraduate students and post-doctoral researchers from various Japanese universities. The workshops are a mix of practical topics such as audio-recording, data formats, software (Transcriber and Toolbox); and more theoretical topics such as ways to mobilize data for community or broader use, and intellectual property and ethics.[12] These workshops are attempting to fill a perceived gap in training for documentation and indeed fieldwork skills within linguistics courses in Japan, which have until recently tended to take a 'sink-or-swim' approach to fieldwork.

21.5.5   Volkswagen workshops in language documentation, Bali, Indonesia

In 2006 and 2007, at the instigation of Nikolaus Himmelmann and Margaret Florey, the Volkswagen Foundation (the funders of the DoBeS programme) provided funding to run courses in language documentation for Indonesian language professionals and community activists. The courses were taught in Bahasa Indonesia. They were planned as intensive, residential workshops, which were held over ten days in 2006 and six days in 2007 in Ubud, Bali. Airfares and accommodation for participants and some of the tutors were paid for by the Volkswagen Foundation, other tutors had funding from other sources or were able to attend without incurring a great deal of expense.[13]

There were twenty-five participants in the first workshop; these were selected by the eleven tutors, who were all linguists with research based in Indonesia. The main criteria for selection were: they should have a research interest in local languages, and they should be:

- early in their careers (and thus likely to use what training they received), or;
- in a position to teach language documentation techniques to others, or;
- a community-language worker (Florey and Himmelmann 2009).

Ultimately, it turned out that about half were postgraduate students; the others were a mix of university, institute or museum staff, and community activists. The majority came from eastern Indonesia, which is not altogether unexpected as there are more minority languages in the east of the country.

The workshop was scheduled as a mixture of lectures and longer tutorial sessions. The lecture topics were:

- Introduction to language documentation
- Recording technologies and techniques
- Speakers and speech communities
- Organizing metadata
- Capture of audio and video
- Basic orthography issues
- Using software for transcription
- Some principles for segmenting discourse
- Notes on dealing with conversation
- Notes on dealing with ritual language
- Preparing grant applications
- Toolbox
- Commenting on meaning
- Commenting on grammar

In the tutorial sessions the students (split into three groups, and often further split into pairs) practised recording with a variety of equipment, learnt the use of capture and editing software such as Audacity, and were introduced to ELAN and Toolbox (see Good, Chapter 11). They also split into six smaller groups to practise putting together a documentation project proposal of the sort that might be submitted to a funding body (see Bowern, Chapter 23), and presented their proposal to the group and the tutors for feedback.

The participants of the first workshop were invited to apply to attend the six-day follow-on workshop in 2007, on condition that they submit a detailed project proposal and a recording and transcription of at least 15 minutes of linguistic data. Sixteen fulfilled the conditions; however, only eleven were able to attend.

Lectures at the second workshop continued on from those of the first, with a few extra topics added by students' request. The lecture topics included:

- Documentation projects in Indonesia
- Using Edirol digital recorders
- A note on digital archives
- Transferring skills in language documentation
- Developing local language and culture centres
- Dictionary-making

In the tutorials the students worked individually on their own projects and their own data, using Audacity, ELAN, Toolbox (and the Multi-Dictionary Formatter), and preparing metadata, with one-on-one help from tutors when needed.

In each workshop an anonymous evaluation survey was distributed on the final day, and both workshops were evaluated very highly by the participants (they were also enjoyable, though exhausting, for the tutors). Furthermore, several of the students went on to share the knowledge they had acquired in a number of ways, including through coursework offered at a number of local universities such as Pattimura in Ambon and Udayana in Bali, and by organizing training courses held at the *Pusat Bahasa* (the national language institute). Some also went on to apply for language documentation funding; at the time of writing at least one had been successful.

However, as Florey and Himmelmann (2009) acknowledge, although the workshops can be considered a success, the model is not sustainable, as it relied on external funding and in large part the volunteering of time and expertise from Western researchers (not to mention that in most cases recording and computing equipment was supplied by the tutors themselves). Florey and Himmelmann (2009) conclude that the prospects of future language documentation in Indonesia would most likely best be served by instituting and supporting regional language centres, which could not only serve as local archives and repositories for recording and computing equipment, but also as local bases for training programmes.

21.5.6 Summer School on Documentary Linguistics in West Africa

In July 2008 Felix Ameka from the University of Leiden organized a ten-day training event at the University of Education, Winneba, Ghana, which was supported by a grant from ELDP. There were thirty participants, who came from Cameroon, Burkina Faso, Senegal, Togo, Benin, Sierra Leone, Cote d'Ivoire, Ghana and Nigeria. Tutors came from a variety of African and European institutions. The topics covered included:

- What is language documentation (including planning a language documentation project)
- Ethical and methodological issues in language documentation (including fieldwork)
- Techniques and methods of data collection
- Transcription and annotation and their tools (Transcriber, Praat, ELAN)
- Audio- and video-recording
- Principles of archiving and dissemination: metadata, media, file formats
- Ethnography in language documentation

- Lexicography and tools (Toolbox)
- Field semantics
- Field phonetics
- Grant application writing

A feature of this event was that sets of language documentation equipment (digital audio- and video-recorders, microphones and cables, and a laptop computer, all packed in a Peli case) were donated to representatives of each country which attended the summer school. The equipment was to be taken back to the home country and put to use in documenting local endangered languages. The general response to the summer school was that it was extremely useful, especially for attendees whose home institutions are notably lacking in infrastructure and skills of the type provided by the summer school. At least one participant has been subsequently accepted for a postgraduate programme in the UK. A follow-up summer school is planned for mid-2010, and plans are under way to run a similar programme in East Africa in the near future.

21.5.7   2004 International Summer School on language documentation: Methods and technology

This event, organized by DoBeS and supported by the Volkswagen Foundation, was the first summer school to take language documentation as its focus. It was held in September 2004 at the University of Frankfurt in Germany. The timetable for the event shows that a large amount of material was covered: there were nine days of instruction (with a two-day interdisciplinary conference in the middle), with each training day having four sessions comprising a lecture, a fieldwork tutorial, a lecture tutorial, and a seminar.[14]

The lectures covered such topics as cooperative fieldwork with communities, data handling, lexical knowledge, ethnography of language and archiving challenges. The fieldwork tutorials met in the same small groups every day to discuss basic and advanced fieldwork issues. The lecture tutorials typically had four sessions running in parallel, the topics ranging from the theoretical (documentation theory, ethical issues) to the technological (video recording and editing, metadata and annotation software). Most of the sessions were conducted in English, though the practical technological/software topics were also offered in German. Finally, the seminars ran in three parallel sessions and again offered a wide range of topics, including: using Praat for speech analysis, audio- / video-recording and editing, prosody and intonation, grammar writing, documenting gesture, and development of teaching materials.

Although there do not appear to be any plans to repeat the event, it is noteworthy as many of the names which appear repeatedly in the language-documentation literature began their careers in documentation training there, and many of the topics which have become staples of documentation training were likewise first offered there. It is also of course notable because the lectures of the summer school formed the basis for the resource book (Gippert *et al.* 2006) that is now widely used in language documentation courses.

21.5   Conclusions and recommendations

What follows is a set of preliminary conclusions and observations about training for language documentation, especially for endangered languages, based largely on evaluations from ELDP grantees, and my own observations as both a trainee and trainer at ELDP training courses, the DoBeS workshop in Indonesia, and the Tokyo training course (all described above):

1. streaming into interest groups – most courses need to be streamed, not just because attendees will have different skill levels, but also will likely fill different roles in a project. For example, not everyone in a project needs to know how to use ELAN, and not everyone needs to know everything about microphones;
2. focus on uses and potentials of tools rather than specific training – it is not entirely clear how useful it is to intensively teach the use of particular software tools such as ELAN or Toolbox to a general audience at a short course or even in a summer school. The reason is that some people are reasonably adept at learning how to use a software tool with minimal instruction and hands-on experience, whereas others find these things difficult and will probably never become effective users of these tools, relying on others to do this type of work. In this case it is probably enough to let such people know what the uses and limitations of software tools are (no, ELAN will not do your transcription for you; yes, if you do a time-aligned transcription in ELAN you will be able to search across an entire corpus of annotated recordings and bring up relevant examples to listen to/watch in context);
3. getting the computer software level right – training courses have sometimes included sessions in the use of advanced editing software such as Adobe Premiere (in my opinion, this is overkill for the rather simple types of editing likely to be needed by language documentation projects). What may be of more use is a simple introduction to the types of editing software available (including the possibilities of editing in camera) and a more general discussion of the goals of video in language documentation, e.g. when and how should video be recorded for inclusion in the documentary corpus? In what ways can video be used (e.g. to study articulation, record information on deixis and/or gesture, for the creation of learning materials, and so

on), and what are the consequences for framing, lighting, camera use etc? To what extent should researchers using video be concerned with the aesthetic or entertainment value of the video? Mastering the particular software suite chosen for video-editing should be the responsibility of the researchers themselves;

4. more time, longer courses – one notable point from all available evaluation of training courses is that in general students and attendees want longer courses. It is clear that a week (or less) is not long enough to cover the amount of material that needs to be taught, especially to novices starting out in language documentation, or OWLs starting from a relatively low technological skill base;

5. need for continuity and advanced training – it has become clear from the various workshops and summer schools that have been run internationally that there is a pressing need for follow-up training, and for progression through a series of stages in terms of acquisition of knowledge and skills. As Florey and Himmelmann (2009) note about the Indonesian workshops: 'most ... participants would need at least two further workshops of ten to fourteen days in order to achieve a skill level that would allow them to carry on independently and to transfer their skills to other interested members in their communities... Cycles of training workshops over an extended period of four to five years, however, are not possible under the present circumstances.' One problem with summer schools and workshops is a tendency to repeat introductory level courses, since they are the ones that attract most demand, and to not respond well to the needs of more experienced documenters who still need to improve their knowledge and skills. This is made more complex because the diversity of language documentation projects, contexts and researchers and communities (Dobrin and Berson, Chapter 10) means that the individual needs of trainees are typically extremely varied. The provision of one-on-one sessions where trainees can work intensively with trainers at more advanced tasks is one solution (as in the 2010 Tokyo training course where sessions on 'salvaging your data' were organized individually with the attendees); however, this tends to be very expensive in terms of time and money required;

6. training in training – another aspect to consider is that researchers may need themselves to train others. It is becoming increasingly common for a research project to collaborate with or employ community members in various roles, and these participants will need to be trained to carry out their tasks. For example, a research project on the documentation of Toratán which I led in North Sulawesi, Indonesia, employed four local people for data entry and analysis, including some who were semi-speakers of Toratán, at least one of whom became quite adept at interviewing and recording discourse with the remaining old fluent speakers. All these

participants needed basic training in recording techniques, transcription and ELAN software in order to input the data efficiently. A number of scholars have argued that this kind of skills transfer and capacity development should be seen as an ethical responsibility of researchers engaged in language documentation, and is to be expected (see Bowern, Chapter 23). Being able to run such training in a professional manner and hence being trained how to train is also an ethical requirement: if it is good enough for researchers to receive training from professionals in postgraduate courses, summer schools and workshops, then it is appropriate that members of documentation teams should be trained by someone in a position to do a professional job.

There has been a recent and exciting development in this area, which could have significant impacts on the goals, curricula, methods, evaluations and functions of language documentation training of all types, namely the proposal by Florey and Genetti (2009) to establish a Consortium on Training in Language Documentation and Conservation (CTLDC).[15] The proposal states that:

> the central aim of the CTLDC is to build a global resource for all those who are actively working to maintain linguistic diversity through fostering collaboration among people who are engaged in training in language documentation and conservation. The CTLDC will provide a critical network to foster communication and collaboration, and enhance the sharing of skills and resources.

The longer term goals of the CTLDC as stated in the proposal are to:

- construct a clearing house of materials accessible to LDC trainers and community members from across the globe;
- provide a forum for the sharing of curricula, teaching and assessment strategies, and methods;
- facilitate the explicit discussion of the goals and models currently being developed and implemented for training in language documentation and conservation (LDC);
- encourage partnerships between trainers of varied backgrounds and experiences;
- take into account a wide variety of perspectives and approaches by bringing together instructors from universities, communities, intensive institutes, school-based programmes, language centres and other initiatives;
- promote new collaborations, exchange ideas and support training efforts worldwide;
- identify successful practices for LDC education;
- establish ethical and other principles to guide practitioners in documentation, conservation and capacity-building activities;

- develop strategies to increase the range of funding opportunities to support LDC training at all levels;
- publicize LDC activities and events to raise greater awareness about the importance of linguistic diversity.

There are plans to hold an initial planning meeting of interested parties in 2010 and to seek funding to hold a larger full project meeting later. It will be interesting to see if and how CTLDC develops, and what results come from the discussions, networking and resource sharing that is planned. It will be especially interesting to find out what kinds of potential solutions emerge that respond to the six challenges identified about, as well as others that will no doubt will appear as more and more people and groups become involved in the documentation and revitalization of endangered languages and demand increased training of different types for a wide range of audiences.

Notes

1 blogs.usyd.edu.au/elac/2009/04/workshop_on_nonlinguistic_aspe. html
2 www.llas.ac.uk/events/3209, www.llas.ac.uk/events/3303
3 For example, the training courses for recipients of ELDP or DoBeS grants do not include sessions on writing grant applications (see Section 21.5.1).
4 The phrase appears to have been coined by John Lawler (www. linguistlist.org/issues/2/2-787.html).
5 Between 2004 and 2008, Monash University in Melbourne, Australia offered various courses under the rubric 'Studies in Language Endangerment': these included a Master of Linguistics in Language Endangerment Studies as well as a Postgraduate Diploma, a Graduate Certificate and a less formal Faculty Certificate largely intended for those without regular qualifications. However, with the departure of a key staff member in 2008, these courses are no longer being offered. On a more positive note, European International Masters in language documentation and description is being organized by the universities of the 3L Consortium (London (SOAS), Lyon, and Leiden). With SOAS as the London part of the consortium it seems likely that this Masters will draw heavily upon components of the ELAP MA described below.
6 The other components are the Endangered Languages Documentation Programme (ELDP), which grants funds for documentation projects; and the Endangered Languages Archive (ELAR).
7 Up-to-date information on these courses can be found at www.hrelp. org/courses/ma.
8 www.ling.hawaii.edu/~uhdoc/languages.html

 9 www.mpi.nl/corpus/a4guides

10 www.darkwing.uoregon.edu/~spike/Site/InField_2010.html

11 Consisting of the universities of Lyon, Leiden and London: specifically the Africa Latin America Endangered Languages (AALLED) programme of the Agence Nationale de la Recherche (ANR) of the University of Lyon, the Leiden University Centre of Linguistics, and the Hans Rausing Endangered Languages Project in the Department of Linguistics at the School of Oriental and African Studies (SOAS)

12 blogs.usyd.edu.au/elac/2008/02/taking_our_show_on_the_road_pe.html, blogs.usyd.edu.au/elac/2009/02/back_in_tokyo_peter_k_austin_1.html

13 For example some tutors were serendipitously conducting fieldwork at the time, or were *en route* to or from the field in Indonesia, and hence were able to attend.

14 www.titus.fkidg1.uni-frankfurt.de/curric/dobes/ssch6cir.htm

15 see www.rnld.org/node/106

22

New roles for endangered languages

22.1   Introduction

The majority of the world's endangered languages survive in societies and speech communities that are multilingual and often peripheral, where they fight for survival amongst 'bigger' languages. However, one of the consequences of globalization for so-called 'bigger' languages has been the lessening of their monopoly in domains such as media and pop-culture. Busch (2004) argues that as a result of the changes in global flows, linguistic diversity has become more visible, societies are more tolerant of linguistic creativity and there is evidence of the emergence of hybrid and mixed codes such as youth languages (see O'Shannessy, Chapter 5) and secret languages, which have been given market recognition through their use in radio and television programming (see Makoni et al. 2007). Endangered language revitalizers aim to develop new roles for endangered languages in contemporary society, to slow down or maybe even reverse the processes of language decline and death (see Hinton, Chapter 15). New media environments offer the possibility for evolution of new identities, which challenge the way in which speakers of endangered languages have understood themselves and been understood in majority-language media. However, it must be highlighted that the processes by which, and the extent to which, media and popular culture can positively affect perceptions, usage and viability of endangered languages is a complex one, and never more so than today.

The purposes of this chapter are therefore to address the potential benefits that the presence of endangered languages in media and popular culture domains can bring, with particular reference to the role of youth. This is followed by a discussion on new roles for endangered languages in the media, internet and popular culture domains, in which specific examples are highlighted. Finally, the chapter will foreground some of the new values and functions afforded to endangered languages.

22.2   New roles for endangered languages

While the presence of endangered languages in media and popular culture domains cannot secure the future of such languages, their role in
language maintenance and revitalization cannot be ignored (see also
Holton, Chapter 19). In UNESCO's framework for language revitalization
put forward by Brenzinger *et al.* 2003, the need to evaluate how endangered languages have responded to new media domains was highlighted.
The advantages of endangered language media and pop-culture presence
are many. First, such presence fulfils an important symbolic function
and challenges the traditional ideologies and associations of endangered
languages with labels such as 'outdated' and 'backward', concepts which
are given further attention in regards to prestige planning by Sallabank
(Chapter 14). Cormack and Hourigan (2007) argue that because endangered languages traditionally had little media exposure, it is particularly
significant that:

- some have a television presence, such as on the Taiwan Indigenous
  Television Network, Impraja Television in central Australia, or Maori
  Television in New Zealand;
- some are being used by successful hip-hop artists and rock musicians
  (such as OKI Ainu Dub Band in Japan, or Warumpi Band in Australia);
- text messaging is now in use in an increasing number of endangered
  languages, such as the widespread use of text messaging by speakers
  of indigenous Nigerian languages (McGill, p.c.).

Also the rise of newer media forms due to developments in digital
information, media and communications technologies (such as YouTube,
blogs, and social networking sites like Facebook, discussed by Holton,
Chapter 19) highlight the benefits that increased bilingualism and multilingualism in these domains can bring. The reality is that the majority
of the speakers of the world's endangered languages live in communities
where more than one language resides. Demonstrating that languages
can coexist in these media domains may serve to counteract language
shift patterns in the community.

Second, endangered language media and pop-culture can help to raise
the status of the relevant language, aid corpus planning through the dissemination of new terminology, and encourage language acquisition by
increasing language exposure in both the public and private domains.

A third significant advantage is the potential for increasing the socioeconomic status of the language, which typically is quite low amongst
endangered language speech communities. Mufwene (2001) and Harbert
(Chapter 20) argue that the survival of any language depends on its
ability to provide socioeconomic status to its users, which can be supported through the creation of fashionable domains of language use

and by converting linguistic skills into attractive job opportunities. The existence of media and a pop-culture in an endangered language does provide attractive job opportunities, particularly in the eyes of young people, the sector of the population that holds the key to language survival and maintenance.

Meek (2007) argued that the role of the youth in language maintenance has in many ways been under-estimated, and suggests that young people are the future of an endangered language, although it is often the case that adults are charged with attempts to revitalize it. If an endangered language is to carry any significance for the young and they are to maintain it and indeed pass it on to the next generation, it must be seen to be able to compete with the other language(s) that exist within the given community. There are many studies on endangered languages which demonstrate the importance of youth in the struggle to maintain and develop such languages, and the need for young people to be concerned about and engaged in keeping their endangered language strong. For example, Eisenlohr (2004: 35) argues:

> To reverse language shift, new avenues for publishing and circulating discourse must be linked to an ideological transformation among speakers, inducing them to re-establish routine use of language especially when interacting with children and adolescents.

Similarly Tulloch (2004), in her work on the Inuktitut language, identifies Inuit youth as playing a vital active role in the maintenance of their native tongue. Letsholo (2009), commenting on the situation of the endangered language Ikalanga of Botswana, argued that it or any other language can only survive if it is spoken by younger generations.

There is a need to move away from the association of endangered languages as old-fashioned, backward-looking, and a waste of time. When those involved in endangered language planning focus only on traditional domains for language revitalization, such as the educational system, and do not promote the use of such languages in domains that are often more relevant for young people, such as media, the process of language decline is more likely to continue. This has most certainly been the case in many European contexts such as Irish and Welsh, as well as for Māori as is discussed by Sallabank (Chapter 14). In each of these situations the educational system has benefited language maintenance in terms of increasing the number of potential speakers. However, by failing to provide a forum for the use of the language outside of these domains, these sociolinguistic contexts are typically marked by high levels of language attrition among young adults. Moriarty (2007) demonstrates how the availability of media in Irish is helping to overcome language revitalization obstacles. Media and pop-culture domains help to bridge the gap between language ability acquired in school or in the home and the potential to actually put it to use within the speech community.

For many young people ideas about what is cool and trendy come via the media, which on a global scale has been dominated by the English language. This is changing due to an ever-increasing presence of languages other than English in these domains, which in turn has consequences for how endangered languages are perceived and used by individuals. Television and music personalities show young people that they are willing to stand up and be counted as speakers of endangered languages in a very public way, thus sending a very strong message with regard to how a given language can and should be valued, and thereby conferring real-world status where endangered languages are seen as hip, trendy and cool.

It would, however, be naive to assume that the provision for endangered languages in media and pop-culture domains does not raise other language-revitalization issues. Often the unconventional manner in which endangered languages are used in media and popular culture is criticized by so-called 'language purists', who object to what they perceive as differences in pronunciation, grammar and vocabulary of younger speakers that diverge from more traditional norms (and complaining in terms of 'degradation' or 'corruption' of the language). Often the disparity between how elders within a given endangered language speech community and how young people envisage the future of the language leads to clashes between the two groups, with elders in communities expressing dismay at how the youth are using their language. When media outlets conform to prestige and standard varieties, young people may feel alienated from the language. For some Native American languages with a presence on radio and television, the decision to conform to the official standard made these media unattractive to younger audiences. Peterson (1997) found the Navajo radio station KTBS was serving to alienate younger Navajo speakers because of the tendency for DJs to tailor their language towards that of the older monolingual members of the Navajo speech community. But the inevitable fact is that languages change because the speech communities in which they may reside change; to enable any language to have a future it must keep up with these changes in order to develop, amongst other things, the vocabulary to express aspects of contemporary society. Perhaps for a language to have a real-world function for young people there need to be domain(s) in which they can make the language their own, and for these ideas to be explored through discussion of endangered languages in the broadcast, internet and pop-culture domains.

21.2.1 Endangered languages and the media

The relationship between endangered languages and media has been one of contention for many decades. Traditionally, the role of the media in language revitalization was not seen as a positive one, with scholars such as Cormack (2003: 1) arguing that: 'the media sector in its totality is more likely to interfere with mother-tongue transmission than support it.' Nevertheless, there is a strong feeling amongst some scholars that media in endangered languages are of paramount importance if the aims of any revitalization effort are to be realized (Riggins 1992, Cormack and Hourigan 2007, Kelly-Holmes *et al.* 2009). As Cormack (2007) states, media in endangered languages can be identified as contributing to language maintenance and preservation, visibility and domain expansion, while also fulfilling what can be regarded as a basic human right of equal access to public discourse, thus realizing an important symbolic function for speakers of endangered languages.

The benefits of having endangered language media were highlighted by Browne (1996: 59) who says that endangered language media help:

> to preserve and restore an indigenous language, to improve the self image of the minority and to change the negative impressions of the minority that are held by members of the majority culture.

In the context of Irish-language recovery, the introduction of the Irish-language television station TG4 has served as a catalyst for a new image of the language and for increased use of the language among younger generations. Irish has achieved a status of cool and trendy, a status that many cultural icons have tapped into, such as the comedian Des Bishop. This new status has not gone unnoticed by big companies, with brands such as Carlsberg and Tesco responding to this new status by using the Irish language in their advertising campaigns.

Endangered language media are of strategic importance in allowing all individuals access to cultural life. One of the difficulties for speakers of endangered languages is the lack of sufficient public arenas where they can come together and interact to feel part of a wider language-speaking community. Pietikäinen (2008), referring to the Sámi context, states that the rise in the availability of media in endangered languages creates a sense of belonging through television broadcasts, newspapers, on-line discussion forums and so on. Peterson (1997) argues with respect to the language situation in Botswana that one of the reasons why Setswana is used more frequently than Ikalanga is because of its presence on the media. Laughren (2000: 1) suggests that despite the fact that the number of Australian indigenous languages has decreased, those that remain have survived because they are represented in a variety of media. Endangered language media not only provide information; they also serve to empower the language. While print media offer numerous advantages, there are some disadvantages in contexts where the language lacks a writing system or a reading culture, which suggests that for some endangered languages the internet and broadcast media may prove to be more beneficial, Indeed, as argued by Lüpke (Chapter 16), there are some endangered language situations where it may not be best to encourage mother-tongue literacy. From this perspective television and radio are the most significant of the broadcast media as they provide information in a manner that is not disrupting to languages that have no writing system or those which have traditionally lacked a reading culture, while also often using the language in a more fun and entertaining way than print media do.

Bell (1991) suggests that the broadcast media are dominating presenters of language in society. In the early days of broadcast media, and in many contexts today, it was the dominant language and language varieties that benefited from most airtime, which had a negative impact on attitudes to endangered languages and language varieties. Language activists initially saw television as posing a significant threat to the future of such languages as they would be overshadowed by more dominant languages. Prior to the onset of broadcast media in endangered languages, radio and television were perceived to be aiding the decline of minority languages. Leitner (1996) points out that in the early 1970s researchers held the broadcast media responsible for influencing language shift in multilingual societies. Dorian (1981) suggested that such media were threatening the goals of language revitalization. The absence of minority languages from television served only to increase the association of such languages with the label 'backward' (O'Connell, 2003; Ó Laoire, 2000). And while it is most often the case that endangered languages do not receive the bulk of airtime, it can be argued that having even just limited space in this medium works to the advantage of an endangered language. The presence of endangered languages in the media thus fulfils an important symbolic function. The mass media are highly visible forums for endangered languages and today, as Cotter (2001: 144) suggests, the media are, in many contexts, used: 'on behalf of the obsolescing language to counteract its decline instead of functioning as a catalyst or a cause of obsolescence', even when broadcast time is limited. Media in endangered languages are also, according to Riggins (1992), a crucial tool in the preservation of ethnic identity. For example, indigenous animations in the Native American languages Cree and Cherokee draw on the tradition of creative storytelling, which enables young people to gain an understanding of their identity through the acquisition of both linguistic and cultural competencies.

The impact that the presence of minority languages on the media has on actual language practices is indirect and is often mediated through language attitudes. Baker (1992: 110) states: 'Television, records, cassettes, videos, satellite broadcasts, films, radio and computer software are often regarded as having an influence on the language attitudes of teenagers in particular.' A number of studies show television to be affecting language practices in minority-language situations. For example, O'Donnell (1996: 300) comments on the sociolinguistic impact of the production and consumption of Catalan telenovelas in the 1980s:

Though there is no reliable way of measuring the linguistic impact of productions such as these, there can be little doubt that they have been important elements in the process of normalization of Catalan, and there is some evidence of Castilian speakers learning Catalan in order to follow them better and to participate in the discussions they evoke.

Hourigan (2003: 34) claims that such channels provide 'an opportunity to create a new definition of social reality which conforms to the linguistic and cultural experience of these minorities'. As Amezaga (2000) points out, the presence of Basque in the public sphere due to the advent of the Basque-medium television station ETB-1 following regional autonomy helped to consolidate a sense of Basqueness amongst the population in the post-independence phase.

It was not long before campaigners recognized the potential of television as a promoter of the relevant language. Before initiatives were taken to create separate television channels in some European endangered languages, such as Scots Gaelic, Welsh and Irish, limited amounts of airtime on the relevant national broadcasters were allocated. Campaigns to obtain television channels for broadcasting in endangered languages are driven by what Thomas (1995: 5) describes as: 'the realisation that, in the modern world, television in your own language is a necessity for cultural and linguistic survival'. Hourigan (2003) also points out how television in an endangered language helps the community to compete with the dominant-language community. The existence of television channels broadcasting in an endangered language such as S4C (Welsh-language television) gives visibility to these languages and makes them available to anybody who may wish to tune in, and as a result such languages gain much greater associations with 'glamour, modernity and youth' (Hourigan, 2002: 8).

The existence of dedicated television channels in endangered languages requires the development of a variety of television programming styles. The dubbing of cartoons offers a less expensive option for children's programming than the in-house production of such programming does. Greymorning (2001) speaks of the delight of young members of the Native American Arapaho tribe being involved in the dubbing of *Bambi* into their own language. Similarly, the screening of sports with commentary in the endangered language offers such television channels a relatively cheap and attractive programming option. For example, the broadcasting of the Wimbledon tennis championships on the Irish-language television channel led to the development of new terminology to deal with tennis terms in the Irish language, which have been subsequently taken up by the Irish-language community.

The movie industry also provides much potential for endangered languages. The code-switching evidenced in movies such as *Mar Adentro*, for example, where there are examples of Castilian and Catalan code-switches, highlight the potential for majority and minority languages to coexist. The number of critically acclaimed documentaries on endangered languages has also increased in the last few years. Crystal (2004) highlights the significance of Serra and Sogues' documentary, *Ultima Palabra*, on the Lacandon, Popoluca and Mayo languages of Mexico in this respect.

As mentioned earlier, advances in endangered language broadcasting have also resulted in the use of such languages as a tool in marketing. The presence of endangered languages in the advertising domain adds to their value in what Bourdieu (1991) identifies as the linguistic market (see also Harbert, Chapter 20). Kelly-Holmes and Atkinson (2007: 36) argue: 'the appearance of a marginalized language in the familiar textual frame of an advertisement can also contribute positively towards its status and survival'.

However, despite the numerous advantages of broadcast and other media in endangered languages, they are often not considered a top priority for the promotion of minority languages because of the high costs involved compared to the small number of speakers. Indeed, various media available in endangered languages have, in economic terms, unrewarding audiences, and need subsidizing to survive. It is from this perspective that digital media can be seen as more advantageous. Digital media such as those found on the internet reduce some of the concerns relating to state financial support for television and other forms of audio-visual media.

22.2.2 Endangered languages and the internet

The relationship between endangered languages and digital media is not straightforward. On the one hand, developments in digital technology in their various guises give rise to many of the advantages previously mentioned with respect to broadcast media. There is an increase in the presence of minority languages in the public domain, increased associations of modernity, and so on. Digital media also offer endangered languages new opportunities for the production and consumption of media and provide speakers and learners new chances to learn and use an endangered language, given the ease with which words and sounds can be disseminated. Digital media also provide arenas for language archiving and language education that have the potential for wider dissemination and flexible access (see Nathan, Chapter 13). In addition, digital technologies are also powerful agents of promotion for majority languages. Perhaps the most significant of all digital platforms is the internet, the defining technology of globalization, which has fundamentally changed the relationship between language and society. Although the internet is often accredited with advancing the assumed power of English as a global lingua franca, in fact the internet, particularly with the spread of so-called Web 2.0 technologies (see Holton, Chapter 19), is also exerting an empowering effect on endangered languages, bringing new patterns of global flows for such language varieties. Thus the internet can be seen to be transforming the relationship between standard and colloquial languages which is leading to changes in the value and function ascribed to endangered languages. In recent years there has been a steady growth in the number of endangered language websites, blogs, web-forums, and chatrooms, and in the availability of interfaces for social networking sites. Facebook's homepage is now available in more than seventy languages including many minority languages e.g. Faroese, Galician. There are also a number of facebook groups who support indigenous languages. Of particular note is the Africa Languages group, which includes use of endangered languages such as Pehul and Diola-Fogny of Senegal. And if, as previously emphasized, young people are the key to endangered language survival, then the potential of the availability of digital media in endangered languages cannot be underestimated (Bucholtz, 2000). Emphasizing the significance of the internet for younger members of endangered language communities, Crystal (2007) states:

> The internet offers endangered languages a chance to have a public voice in a way that would not have been possible before. It doesn't matter how much activism you engage in on behalf of the language if you don't attract the teenagers, the parents of the next generation of children. And what turns teenagers on more than the internet these days? If you can get language out there, the youngsters are much more likely to think it is cool.

There are a myriad of factors that lead to language decline and language death (Grenoble, Chapter 2). Included within these are migration and reduction in membership of the speech community. The internet presents many opportunities to overcome these issues. For example, though email, voice-over-internet services such as Skype, chat, online forums and newsletters, and blogs (including micro-blogging on Twitter), diasporic communities can maintain cultural and linguistic links with their place of origin across physical and social spaces, thus aiding the maintenance of linguistic and cultural identities amongst people who otherwise would have little or no face-to-face contact.

Although digital media are widely and easily accessible, access to such technologies and/or the educational means to train individuals to use them are still proving problematic. These issues, especially in relation to internet penetration (but not mobile phones) are particularly felt in economically disadvantaged endangered language contexts such as in Africa. As Cunliffe and Herring (2005) note, in any discussion of the role of digital media in the revitalization of endangered languages one has to consider the problems associated with the so-called 'digital divide' and

to also be aware, as is highlighted by Holton (Chapter 19), that new technologies can run the risk of alienating older members of endangered
language speech communities. Danet and Herring (2003) highlight the
problems the World Wide Web creates for languages that are unwritten
or do not have a standardized orthography. Communities have had to
come together in an effort to make their orthographies web-friendly. As
Kelly-Holmes (2006) points out, one major development in recent years
which has enabled these increases in digital media in endangered languages has been the creation of the means of supporting different character sets through the development of Unicode (see Good, Chapter 11).

From a language-vitality perspective, a website wholly or partly in a
language may encourage people to use it, while also providing a new
domain for language learning. Kalish (2005) presents the results of a case
study of adoption of new media materials in learning the endangered
language Chiricahua, where the simultaneous presentation of sounds,
images and text was found to facilitate word acquisition, highlighting
the useful role of e-learning technology in the revitalization of minority
languages (see Holton, Chapter 19, for more examples). E-learning technologies have also greatly changed the production of endangered language textbooks. Rau and Yang (2008, 2009) in examining the case of
the endangered indigenous Taiwanese language Yami found that those
involved in teaching the language were very happy with the e-learning
material; they identified digital animation to be a particularly useful tool
in language revitalization. This is also the case with the Native American
languages Cree, Cherokee and Kwak'wala (Hearne 2009).

Gaming environments provide further opportunities to use endangered languages in the digital realm. Online multiplayer games are massively popular, with some games involving millions of players worldwide.
An array of specific literacy practices are associated with such games,
that utilize language to develop strong identities, thus providing endangered languages with another forum in which language immersion can
take place. Although some scholars have warned that the uptake of such
technology may be slow in some endangered language communities due
to the fact that it is often at odds with tradition, it may be argued that
young people are more likely to explore new technologies and reject older
forms. Using their own (or their parent's) language in domains such as
online gaming adds to their novelty and can support language acquisition. The use of endangered languages on gaming and social networking
sites has the potential to affect how speakers of endangered languages
perceive themselves, but also how they are perceived by members of the
majority language speech communities.

Mobile phone technologies provide another important modality for
endangered languages. In situations where computers are not widely
used for economic or other reasons, mobile phones provide a key alternative: Africa has the highest uptake of mobile phone technology in the

world. Text messaging allows for rapid and wide-reaching communication. Texting in the Kala Kawa Ya indigenous language of remote islands in the Torres Strait of Australia represents the most writing ever done in this language (Brady *et al.* 2008).

22.2.3 Endangered languages in pop-culture domains

The struggle to revitalize an endangered language can be bolstered by the fan base and iconicity created through the availability of music, movies and theatre in the particular language. A presence in pop-culture domains will impact positively on the language ideology maintained by its speakers, especially by younger people. Popular music fuses language to melodies and/or beats, and thus provides a memorable and enjoyable way to learn and practise languages.

Music is first and foremost a cultural product. The majority of the world's languages, including endangered languages, have their own musical traditions, with many of the songs telling of folklore and oral history. Mitchell (2003) highlights the importance of music as a tool in a strategy for the survival of local culture. In their work on the endangered language Iwaidja, Barwick *et al.* (2007) demonstrate the significance of bringing language and music together in a specific genre of love songs. However, endangered language communities are increasingly expanding their musical repertoires through the adoption and adaptation of new musical forms due to the global spread of music genres. Pietikäinen (2008) argues that popular music expressed through an endangered language is a nexus where traditional roles for endangered languages converge with more contemporary roles in a localized form of a global medium. Music genres such as pop, hip-hop and reggae can become more localized through the use of traditional instruments and local language(s), and allow for youth creativity and innovations. Popular music audiences have changed over recent decades and, as Bentahila and Davies (2002: 190) argue: 'seem more receptive to music using other languages'.[1]

From a sociolinguistic perspective, music in endangered languages serves a dual purpose. First, the presence of an endangered language in a number of popular music genres tells us something about the value of the language. Discussing music in Maori, Mitchell (2001: 30) argues:

> the incorporation of the Maori language into their music as part of a broader cultural and political project [served] to assert Maori sovereignty and ensure the survival of the language.

Second, music can fulfil an important pedagogical function, often providing teachers with a more relevant resource than formal language texts. As with audiovisual media, a major advantage of music is that different levels of literacy skills, or lack thereof, do not limit people from taking part in and enjoying the medium. The issue of language choice in popular music involves a wide range of linguistic phenomena, not least in the genre of hip-hop, rap and reggae, which has led to hip-hop becoming a distinct arena for sociolinguistic study (e.g. Alim *et al.* 2009).

From a sociocultural perspective, hip-hop, rap and reggae are important music genres for young people, providing a vehicle for them to voice their opinions and enabling them to use language in creative ways, with the aim of conveying powerful messages to the audience (e.g. an Inuit rap group known as Nuuk Posse criticize Danish language dominance in Greenland). Potter (1995) describes the language used in such domains as 'resistance vernaculars' which challenge standard languages and language varieties. Due to its universal appeal to youth cultures, hip-hop has spread to the world's furthest peripheries and as a result of this global spread, (Mitchell, 2001: 1–2) says:

> hip-hop and rap cannot be viewed simply as an expression of African-American culture; it has become a vehicle for global youth affiliations and a tool for reworking local identity all over the world.

In recent times there has been a steady increase in the number of hip-hop artists and, to a lesser extent, rap and reggae artists who perform in endangered languages (for example, Androutsopoulos 2007, Auzanneau, 2002, Ferrari 2005, Higgins 2007, Low *et al.* 2009, for discussions on rap in Tanzania, Gabon, Kenya, Germany and Montreal respectively). These genres of music often reflect the linguistic and cultural identity of the local community and can be identified as important tools for vernacular expression and the construction of identity (Pennycook 2007).

As has been well documented, (for example, Androutsopoulos 2007), rap and hip-hop outside the United States typically goes through a phase of linguistic emancipation. In endangered language hip-hop this happens when terminology is changed to better reflect the local community, but a more significant occurrence is when the language of the lyrics changes from English to the local language. An important example of how successful endangered language rap can be is evidenced by the Inari Sámi rapper Amoc, who is one of just 400 speakers of Inari Sámi (Pietikäinen, 2008). Amoc has a significant fan base and flattering media coverage of his success has benefitted the struggle to maintain the Inari Sámi language. The Liet Lavlut minority-language song contest in Europe is a further example of modern music in endangered languages.[2]

22.3   Conclusion

The dynamics of endangered language situations often include a mixed bag of cases in which one finds languages at different stages of the continuum from language decline to language revival. If a language is used in increasingly fewer domains it is a sign of lessening vitality. Gaining new domains through the presence of endangered languages in the media, the internet and popular culture may be indicative of a possible return to vitality. This in turn adds new value and function to such languages, allowing for the emergence of new codes and norms of use.

By highlighting the need to further embrace new technologies and new roles for endangered languages, this chapter has shown that when devising strategies for the revitalization of endangered languages it is important to promote the use of the language among young people. Arguably, lack of attention to young people's interests is one of the negative aspects of more traditional approaches to language revitalization and maintenance. While the role of the educational domain in assisting the acquisition of an endangered language cannot be overlooked, in order to meet the overall objective of language survival and maintenance it is also vitally important to make such languages relevant for younger members of the communities. The presence of endangered languages in media and popular culture domains, where young people are often involved, supports these languages by changing the ideology that surrounds them, which in turn can affect the ways in which they are used. In order to fully establish the role of these media in the future survival and maintenance of such languages, there is need for further research which examines how these new roles for endangered languages may change language practices, and how they can be incorporated into language planning, policy and revitalization initiatives.

Notes

1 The website www.lastfm.com (20 February, 2010) provides a repository where music in hundreds of languages can be listened to. Similarly, YouTube has music videos in a wide range of languages, including many endangered languages.
2 See www.liet.nl/en/internationaal (20 February, 2010).

23

Planning a language-documentation project

Claire Bowern

23.1 Introduction: Overarching concerns

Planning a language-documentation project can be a daunting task. After all, languages are very complex, and making a record of a language also involves thinking about much more than just the language itself.[1]

Project planning for language documentation is a little like house construction. In building a house, the technical aspects can be done more or less well; there are blueprints, plans and established procedures, there are people with specialist skills and things must be done in a certain order. The electrics and plumbing cannot be completed before the walls go up, for example. Furthermore, some people are professional builders while others work on their own houses for the fun of it, as enthusiastic and knowledgeable non-professionals. The same is true in documentation projects. Things work better with planning in language documentation, and with training the project participants get better. Also, just as all houses are different, all language-documentation projects are different (see Dobrin and Berson, Chapter 10).

There are three primary considerations in planning a project:

- what the community (and the linguist) want;
- what the linguist and community are capable of doing;
- what is feasible given the time and money available.

The success of a project also depends not only on the skill of participants, but also the enthusiasm, commitment and emotional investment of the project staff. In this chapter I lay out a general plan for structuring a documentation project, with examples from different geographical areas.[2]

Language documentation projects can be very varied, both in scope and outcomes. In order to limit this chapter and to provide some specific advice, I have made some assumptions about the most typical type of documentation project. First, I assume that a linguist will be involved, although I do not assume that they will necessarily be a university lecturer or professor. Second, I concentrate on projects where the language is endangered and where there are relatively few speakers, although most of the advice here is applicable to language documentation more generally (see Section 23.3.10 for some special notes for highly endangered languages). Third, I assume that the goal of the project (in the abstract) is a complete DOCUMENTATION of the language, and that the participants in the project are prepared for a medium to long-term commitment of at least a few years, although not all of this may take place in the field necessarily (this is not 'fly-in fly-out' documentation, nor a PhD dissertation with a few community materials, although that may be the origins of the project). I also assume that the project will have non-trivial community involvement. That is, I have nothing much to say about projects where the linguist does all the work and presents the community with the finished project at the end of it. This is because a lasting and comprehensive documentation project cannot succeed without the support of multiple people, especially community members. I have assumed that the linguist will not be a community member, since this is still the most common situation, but language documentation projects with linguistically trained community members are fortunately on the increase.[3]

I begin this chapter article with some principles of project planning and design. These are some of the most important considerations when beginning a documentation project. I then move on to discuss funding, including identifying sources of funding support and preparing an application (Sections 23.3 and 23.4). In Sections 5–7, I discuss the key stages of a project while it is in progress, possible future outcomes and foundations for further work.

23.2   Elements of a project

There are certain elements which are common to all documentation projects. Just as in building a modern house there are plumbers, electricians and bricklayers (and bricks and concrete) for all houses, so too in language documentation there are commonalities to many projects.

23.2.1   The people

Who will be involved and what will their roles be? What skills will they need? Perhaps some event triggered some interest in the community for language documentation. The first step is to find people who are interested in contributing to the documentation. The only prerequisites and qualifications are enthusiasm, and a willingness to learn new things (and even the second can be dispensed with on occasion). There are enough things to do in a documentation project that no one person has to have all the necessary skills to do documentation on their own. Jobs can be found for editors, coordinators, fundraisers and all sorts of other activities. Potential contributors might not know exactly how they can contribute initially. Furthermore, sometimes the most valuable contributors to documentation projects are people within the community who do not speak the language fluently, because they are more aware of what they do not know and can identify gaps in the documentation.

How you find the right people will depend on how big the language is and what existing community structures there are. It might be that the project starts with a group of friends who work well together, or with a group who met through cultural centres, as in the Kalaw Kawaw Ya documentation and revitalization project in Brisbane (Adidi, 2007). It might begin through a network of language activists, as in the case of a Kurdish documentation project in Turkey. It might be that a linguist starts working with speakers. In my experience as a linguist, I have never had any trouble in recruiting speakers of a language for a project; community members with an interest in the language have sought me out, and this was also the experience reported in Macaulay (2004).

There is more on the role of the linguist in such projects in Section 23.6 below.

23.2.2 Money and infrastructure

A project needs a certain amount of equipment, and money to pay for that equipment. In addition to the recording equipment, you will need somewhere to store the recordings and notes, money to pay people for their time, and some way to disseminate your results. There is more discussion of planning and finding funding in Section 23.4.

23.2.3 Tasks and outcomes

Documentations do not arise out of thin air: just planning to 'document a language' is not a detailed enough plan on its own unless you also consider the specifics of what language data will be collected, how it will be obtained, and what will be done with it once it has been acquired (see Woodbury (Chapter 9) and Good (Chapter 11) on the data of language documentation, Mosel (Chapter 17) on dictionary making, and Holton (Chapter 19) on language-learning tools using documentary materials). I discuss some relevant planning principles in Section 23.3.

23.2.4 Timelines, timeframes and workflows

The final foundation for a documentation project is a specification of the time in which various tasks need to be completed. Some tasks have a set order in which they must be done, while others can be ordered more freely. For example, transcriptions can not be completed before the audio/video material they are based on is recorded, but a storybook can be edited independently of when dictionary entries have examples added to them.

Project work is easier to organize if there is a WORKFLOW. A workflow is a specification of the project tasks that will be done, the order in which they need to be done and what day-to-day tasks have to be performed at each phase of the project, together with a statement about who will do what. There are some examples in Bowern (2008: 48), Wynne (2005) and Thieberger (2004). The amount of detail that needs to be developed for the workflow will depend in large part on the nature of the project; smaller projects may not need a very formal workflow document, and can rely on a set of agreed procedures to make sure that things are done at the proper time and that steps are not forgotten. Larger projects with more complex teams carrying out multiple tasks will need a more detailed workflow specification, and may even employ a staff member to develop and manage the workflow documentation (for further discussion see Good, Chapter 11 section 6.)

Knowing how long each stage of a documentation project will take is something that requires research and preparation, and advice from others who have had experience with the tasks and outcomes planned. Beginning researchers often underestimate the time required for various activities, including the time that needs to be allocated to training. For example, the time required for transcription can be of the order of 100-to-1 in relation to the elapsed time of recording, depending on a range of factors such as familiarity with the language being documented, adeptness with the relevant software and hardware, and the nature of the recordings. That is, 1 *minute* of audio/video can take up to 1.5 *hours* to transcribe; annotation (depending again on the nature and amount of the annotation) takes even longer. Some elements are unpredictable: everyone works at a different pace, and sometimes there are unforeseen delays; occasionally projects even proceed faster than expected. You can get an idea of how much time to allow for each stage of the project by talking to people who have done similar work.

23.3   Project management

Here is some general advice for getting started and continuing in a documentation project. These are points which have been brought up in informal discussions among colleagues, particularly with linguists working on documentation projects.

23.3.1 Modular and incremental project pieces

As mentioned above, it is very helpful to think of the documentation project as both MODULAR and INCREMENTAL. Modular planning implies that different parts of the project form separate pieces; incremental planning means that different parts of the project build on one another. My building analogy is appropriate here too: housing construction is incremental because certain parts of the building must be completed before others, but other parts are modular: fittings for rooms can be worked on in any order and independently of one another.

Modular and incremental planning is important for documentation projects, not only because some parts of the project are contingent on other parts (it is very difficult to produce a consistent book of texts before an orthography has been developed for the language), but for other reasons too. However, there are ways to build up the prerequisites for a documentation project while making that part of the documentation itself. For example, an alphabet book is a good way to test out a writing system.

There are some other reasons to think incrementally. Documentation projects can start with very high aims and then collapse because there is nothing to show for all the work that has been done before interest peters out. Starting with something small and building on it allows you to capitalize on initial enthusiasm and to realize that enthusiasm. For example, Mosel (Chapter 17) recommends that dictionary projects adopt a strategy of creating mini-dictionaries on particular topic areas that will both form stand-alone products and also build into an integrated set leading towards a more comprehensive dictionary.

23.3.2 Do not reinvent the wheel

Once you have a preliminary group of people[4] together, the next stage of the project involves finding out whether there are existing materials on the language, planning subparts of the project in more detail and applying for funding.

Research the existing material for your language. It is rare these days that there is not at least some material that has been collected on a language, but it may be difficult to identify and/or locate it. Research in libraries and archives will be needed, along with use of online search. Depending on where the language you wish to study is located, there may be specialist archives that it will be useful to visit, such as the University of California Berkeley language archives for California and other Native American languages, or the library and audiovisual archives of the Australian Institute of Aboriginal and Torres Strait Islander Studies, for example. Do not forget to search for documents written by missionaries, explorers and settlers as these may contain material on languages encountered, as well as descriptions of cultural and social background that will be helpful. There are increasing amounts of material that is available on the internet; search engines like Google and Bing, together with resources such as Google Scholar and Wikipedia are good places to start. The Open Language Archives Community (OLAC)[5] is a portal that has a searchable online catalogue of available digital material, and there are other collections such as the Aboriginal Languages of Australia Virtual Library[6] that have links to websites and digital resources (see Holton, Chapter 19, for other sources, especially for Alaskan languages). If you can find the name of a linguist, anthropologist or other researcher who has worked on the language or with the community, I encourage you to contact them and start a conversation about your plans and their experience and the outcomes of their research (and I encourage linguists and others to treat such requests for materials and advice seriously). Sometimes there is a local non-government organization (NGO) working in the community (on health, or human rights, or ecology) who can provide useful pointers and advice.

Talk to other people who have been involved in language documentation. There is an active web community of documentary linguists and language communities (examples are given on the companion website to Bowern (2008); see there for up-to-date information). Many documentation projects have their own web sites, some with sample data and discussion of workflows and project outcomes.

If possible, it is a good idea for all members of a documentation project team, including community-based participants, to attend a workshop or training course on language documentation. There are now a number of these held regularly in North America, the UK, elsewhere in Europe, in Japan and in Australia. You can also look at the contents on online archive catalogues for what others have done in documentary and descriptive projects. Have a look at other books, videos, DVDs and materials which were produced in language-documentation programmes. Learner's guides, language lessons, multimedia, dictionaries, oral history collections and flora and fauna books are all useful in forming an idea of what a project might be able to achieve.

23.3.3   Consultation and language politics

So far I have been proceeding as if the idea of language documentation is not controversial. In some communities it is very controversial. The very idea of writing down the language may not be something that everyone agrees with. The people who are working on the project may not have the universal support of the community (and the notion of 'community' itself is a complicated concept (see Spolsky, Chapter 8)). There may be doubt about which variety to document (and the selection of which variety to document brings with it complex social and political issues and choices – see Mosel, Chapter 17). There may be disagreements about where to house the project materials, and so forth. It is not possible to give any overall advice here because the social, cultural and political considerations within each community will differ considerably (see Dobrin and Berson, Chapter 10). It will be important, though by no means simple, to determine if individuals or groups in the community think that the language is valuable enough for them to spend a great deal of time thinking about the right way to document it, and getting involved in the necessary work. It is worth getting things right as early as possible, and continuing an ongoing dialogue with the various stakeholders about their roles and responsibilities. Sometimes there will be more than one possible direction to proceed, and documenters should keep an open mind and be flexible. Documentation projects which never get off the ground because the language-community members cannot agree on basic procedures let everyone down.[7]

23.3.4   Do not be scared of starting

The linguist in a documentation team can help with suggestions for where to begin. Where to begin will depend on how endangered the language is, how much material already exists, and what the skills of the participants are. If the language is highly endangered, it may be that getting as much language data as possible (by recording, transcribing and translating with native speakers) is your first priority. That is, if you wait until you have a well-defined writing system and a lot of funding, you may not have anything to document. In such a case, I recommend finding a linguist who has training in SALVAGE DOCUMENTATION, that is, working with the last elderly speakers of a language to gain as much information as possible, as quickly as possible, while dealing with difficult field conditions. They may be able to offer advice on how to proceed in the particular case. (Bowern 2008 gives some suggestions for working on a previously undescribed language.)

23.3.5   Take culture into account

A long-term documentation project will be shaped by the culture and society of the language speakers in many different ways. Some of these cultural considerations should be planned for from the very beginning. For example, if project participants cannot spend much time together because their work together would be not socially sanctioned (in Aboriginal Australia this could happen if they belonged to the wrong kinship groups or (sub)sections, for example), this is going to have a severe effect on project outcomes. More prosaically, a language-documentation project which expects rigid work hours in areas where clocks do not exist, or tend to be ignored, is bound to run into problems.

Other considerations concern the material collected. In many societies there are cultural restrictions on discussing certain topics in certain company; for example, talk about religious or ritual activities may be restricted to some audiences. If there is a plan to collect material of this type you will need some way of ensuring the integrity of the collection and appropriate access and usage restrictions (archives generally have well-worked-out systems for dealing with these (see Conathan, Chapter 12 section 5, and Nathan, Chapter 13) but the project needs to set up such a system for its own use). There may be cultural taboos on hearing the voices of people who have passed away. These taboos might be community-wide, or they might apply only to particular family members. In this case, you will need some way of making sure that the collection can still be accessed but certain materials can be restricted. Nothing could be worse than doing a fantastic and accessible documentation collection which is then not used because community members might be distressed by listening to certain material.

23.3.6 Manage the skills base appropriately

The appropriate use of technology is also something you should think about. There are many different types of audio-and video-recorders and computer software for data collection, organization and analysis. Functionality and ease of use of hardware and software differs, and it will be important to decide which the project wishes to employ and which it has the skills to use (or how these skills might be obtained). There is no point developing an expensive custom-made database if it will be so complex that most of the project team will not be able to use it. Be wary of solutions where only one person has the skills to keep the project running.

Conversely however, I also recommend against going for a 'lowest common denominator' solution, where project teams shy away from technology or assume that 'it is all too hard'. It might be very tempting not to use a database program at all, and to keep all files in text documents. Such a solution certainly avoids the need to master a more complex software program, but it introduces problems of its own. It is much easier to keep track of information in a database, so although deciding to use a word processor for text-based materials may save time in software learning at the beginning of the project, there is often an expensive trade-off later in the project. Good planning includes thinking about how to create and manage well-structured data that can be used for a range of purposes and be stored in non-proprietary well-documented formats (for more discussion see Good, Chapter 11).

Technophobia does not help anyone, but equally ignoring different skill levels and different degrees of comfort with hardware and software may damage the project. For someone who is coming to software programmes for the first time, the best thing to do may be to introduce the programmes one at a time and let the person get comfortable with each in turn, rather than introducing all parts and associated tools of the whole workflow at the beginning.

23.3.7 Think long term from the start

You need to take care of your documentation materials. There is no sense in documenting a language only to lose the materials created because there was no plan for preserving them. For information on this topic, see Conathan, Chapter 12, and Nathan, Chapter 13.

Materials also need to be organized while the project is ongoing. Making recordings using a digital recorder saves a great deal of time for transferring audio files to computers, making sound clips available, and so forth. In principle it also makes audio-files easier to share than those recorded on cassette tapes. A productive documentation project will very quickly gather many gigabytes of audio and video data, which will need to be stored, backed up, and archived. This is not an immense difficulty by any means, but it does require careful research and planning, including seeking advice on good practices (language archives can be particularly helpful with this). For example, if a documentation team wants to share audio-and video-files then using email to do so will usually not be a good plan because the files will be so large that most email systems will not be able to include them as an attachment. Sending flash cards, memory sticks, or portable hard drives by post may be better options, especially in countries where internet access is limited.

23.3.8 Keep a record of your plans and prioritize

Making plans is all very well but if no one can remember what the plans are they will not be much good. It is a good idea to keep a record of project ideas and plans. This can be divided into sections, including items you are already committed to and have funding for, day-to-day partial tasks within a larger project, items that you plan to do at some point with high probability, and 'wish list' items which may become feasible in the future but are either not high priority at present or cannot be done with current personnel or time/money constraints. A planning document like this is very valuable when developing grant applications, for assigning tasks if new people join the team or help becomes available, and is also useful for prioritizing work commitments.

At all stages of the documentation project there will be many possible things to do. The limitation will not be your ideas for the project but the time, money and skills available to do them. Therefore you will need to prioritize. Factors that come into consideration when prioritizing work include the following. Early in the project life cycle it is important to have a few activities that can be completed fairly quickly. This is important to maintain interest in the project and to show that you are serious about producing results. Priorities will also emerge from your INCREMENTAL PLANNING (that is, tasks which will serve as a general foundation for future work should generally be given a much higher priority early in the project than an activity which will not lead to other things). Tasks which the project team are more qualified for should be given higher priority: that is, you should prioritize work which you are more likely to do well.

23.3.9 Project roles and the role of the linguist

I recommend having a linguist involved with the documentation project, but it does not have to be all about the linguist. Language community members often report feeling a lack of control over the language documentation when a linguist takes charge. There might also be feelings of resentment that an outsider is involved; that outsider will come to know a great deal about the community, its people and its culture which might be quite incidental to the language. Community members often also report sometimes feeling that the linguist comes in, reifies the language, turns it into a commodity, and then takes it away (see Dobrin and Berson, Chapter 10). Such feelings may also arise if the linguist is a community member too.[8]

Linguists should recognize that these feelings may be present, and should do what they can to understand them and not to exacerbate them. Some strategies to respond to this are:

- community involvement in planning project outcomes and participation in activities;
- housing materials within the community;
- providing copies of documentation materials and outcomes;
- recognizing that language documentation, especially in highly endangered language communities, is not just about the language and its structures, but also has social, cultural and political dimensions.

Community members should recognize that the vast majority of linguists have good intentions but may give offence without realizing it, by the very fact that they are community outsiders and therefore do not always know the local social rules. Most linguists will be very happy to talk about concerns the community may have, but the community needs to make sure the linguist knows about the concerns. Documentation projects of this type require trust on both sides.

A frequent concern for linguists working on documentation projects is how the project will fit with their other work. Post-graduate students writing a PhD dissertation are in a very different position from tenured faculty members, and both are in a different position from a linguist employed full time by a tribe or community. An academic linguist may be working on more than one language at once; graduate students and tenure track faculty members have to produce academic publications in order to keep their jobs (or gain a first job). A great deal of language documentation is done by linguists who have funding to study particular language issues, or to write a grammar of a language, or to do a PhD. Post-graduate students in particular may be reluctant to become involved in a large-scale long-term documentation project. Junior faculty members and post-graduate students often feel that doing language documentation properly can hurt their prospects for a job or tenure.

There are some things that can be done to coordinate academic work with community-oriented projects in ways that do not sacrifice the usefulness of the community project or the rigour of the scientific work. The most important thing is to plan for the incorporation of multifunctional materials from the beginning of the project. For example, using a community-approved orthography for transcription of examples and texts will mean that materials will not have to be converted into another writing system for community use. Some data gathering tasks can be combined with community materials quite easily. Word lists for acoustic phonetic analysis can serve as the basis for talking dictionaries; with a little searching it is usually possible to get enough of the right types of word for the phonetic research using basic or common vocabulary, or words from a particular domain so that a thematic talking mini-dictionary can be produced. Another example is the use of a learner's guide template in preliminary grammatical elicitation. Hale (2001) describes how to target dictionary examples for preliminary grammatical elicitation (a similar idea lies behind the sentences in Bouquiaux and Thomas (1992)).

A further way to take some of the burdens off the linguist is to organize a truly collaborative project.[9] The linguist should not feel they have to do everything. Making the most of everyone's skills is important. For example, teachers might not know how to collect linguistic data, but they will have good ideas for how to adapt it for a lesson plan.

23.3.10 Special considerations for highly endangered languages
Planning to work on a highly endangered language (one with only a handful of fluent speakers, for example) requires thinking about project planning in a slightly different way. In previous sections I have described an incremental project development plan where the documentation is built up over some period. This may not be possible for a highly endangered language.

When the language is highly endangered, there can be certain temptations. One temptation is to record as much raw data as quickly as possible, on the assumption that it will always be possible to go back and analyse it later. This may be true, but only if you have the right type of data. To return to my housebuilding analogy, the danger is that the house may be built, but we forgot to add the internal doors in a hurry to erect as much of the external structure as possible.

It will be useful to determine the number of speakers and their fluency and language skills very early in the project (see Bradley, Chapter 4, on carrying out such surveys). For example, younger speakers may have considerable translation skills from the language into a lingua franca or major language, even if they themselves cannot tell stories or provide grammaticality judgements. Conversely, older speakers may be able to engage in fluent conversations with each other but be uninterested in translation or explication. In such a case, the project could make the most of the time available with the elderly fluent speakers by recording them and then working through the materials with the younger speakers in order to transcribe, translate and annotate them.

Producing rich documentation for highly endangered languages is possible, but to be successful it is important to work on the principle that complex materials can always be simplified later on, but simple materials cannot be complexified if the structures were never recorded. That is, I recommend against concentrating on easy beginner materials (like word lists, translations of simple sentences) to the exclusion of more complex materials (like folk stories or historical narratives).

23.4   Identification of funding support

It is advisable not wait for funding to become available before beginning work on aspects of the documentation project, if at all possible. Securing funding is easier once you have done the necessary background investigation and preparation, and created a research track record.

23.4.1   Doing without external funding

Language documentation projects can be carried out 'on the cheap' if necessary: in fact, some of the most inspiring language-documentation stories involve native speakers of endangered languages who began their own projects without external funding, without linguists with fancy audio-recorders or the latest software, and without publication subsidies. A great deal of documentation consists of people who sat down together when they had time and wrote down what they could think of. This is an important type of language documentation and should not be underestimated. Much can be achieved through the goodwill and dedication of language speakers with a paper and pencil.

However, just because it is possible to do things that way does not mean that it is preferable to work that way. Technology is not a substitute for enthusiasm, skill and training, but using it appropriately makes many things easier. The project will be much easier if there is access to a computer and some basic data management and analysis programmes. There are free software programmes for data organization and processing (Bowern 2008 and the website which accompanies the book mention some up-to-date examples). You might be able to get a small grant of a few hundred dollars to buy an audio-recorder and/or a video-camera and an external hard disk to backup the material. Do not underestimate what you can do on a shoestring.

Another approach would be to team up with someone who already has funding. For example, post-graduate students at some universities receive a certain amount of summer funding, and may be willing to work as a 'language-documentation intern' to help with a project. Advertising through the linguistics department at your local university would be a good way to locate relevant people. Culture programmes, local museums or non-government organizations may be able to help with infrastructure (such as access to a quiet recording location or meeting room, or safe storage of equipment and recordings).

While much can be accomplished using goodwill, donations and the spare time of participants, there are great advantages to professionalizing the documentation and applying for funding. There is a limit to how much can be done on goodwill alone. And large-scale documentation projects, if done properly, take a great deal of time. It is worth paying someone with the skills to manage it. My construction analogy is also appropriate here: while there are a few people who are able to build or renovate their own houses, the vast majority of people employ someone with special skills and training for at least part of the job.

23.4.2 Finding a funding agency

Obtaining funding for a language-documentation project involves doing research on funding agencies and finding someone who will give the project support. It is quite rare to find agencies who will fund 'documentation' in general; it is much more likely that you will have to apply for funding for a particular aspect of the project. This is a further argument for thinking in terms of incremental and modular planning. Finding funding is a two-way process: on the one hand, you will have ideas about what you would like to achieve, and therefore you can direct your search for funding agencies towards organizations which fund that type of project. Conversely, some projects are easier to find funds for than others. Sometimes grant agencies have priority areas, and they may change them for particular years; if you are flexible in what you wish to achieve at any given time, finding funding will be easier.

Different groups have access to different funding sources, so it is good to have more than one person involved. For example, in Australia there are community development grants, and sometimes schools can apply for them. Academics are usually ineligible to apply: the application has to come from an organization within the community. Linguists will probably have access to academic sources (like national funding agencies) but they may not have access to the other types of funding, and the community may not have access to academic funding.

Interdisciplinary research may also have an increased possibility for funding (e.g. flora and fauna identification through a fisheries project or ethnobotanical collaboration). Archives sometimes have funding available for visits from language speakers who need to work with their materials.

It is important to target appropriate institutions. Many grant applications fail not because they are bad projects, but simply because they are inappropriate for the agency they are submitted to. For example, the National Science Foundation (NSF) in the United States funds projects that have demonstrable intellectual merit as well as broader impacts beyond the principal investigator; they fund scientific projects. This means that they (and research organizations like them) do not fund work which does not have a research component. Therefore a project which involves only language revitalization or the creation of teaching materials is unlikely to succeed; independent of the merits of that application, it does not fall within the mandate of the agency. Other organizations, such as charitable funds, may concentrate on such 'applied' projects. Another important consideration is the size of the grant. Some organizations have limits of a few hundred or a few thousand dollars, while other organizations typically fund large projects (and some have minimum application amounts).

23.4.3 Other considerations

There are other things to consider when applying for funding beyond those which have already been mentioned. Grants are typically available for projects taking different amounts of time. Most smaller grants for endangered languages are for projects that must be completed within a year, whereas other grants can be for three or five years. It would be inappropriate to apply for a three-year grant and to propose only to do an alphabet book in that period. Related to the length of the grant is the amount of money. Many funding agencies have an explicit upper limit on the amount of money that can be applied for. Other grants have a lower limit; that is, a minimum amount of total funding.

Funding agencies differ widely in what are considered allowable expenses under the grant. Some grants are only for travel, others can be used to pay for other things. Some grants have citizenship requirements or particular administration requirements (that is, the grant may only be awarded to an individual, or to a company or organization). Applicants may need to do quite a bit of background reading and consultation to make sure that the grant they are thinking of applying for is appropriate. As a place to start, look at the funding sources for other endangered language projects and do some research into those funding organizations. (Funding sources are usually acknowledged in the academic products that arise from the funded project.)

Finally, you may need an organization or institution to administer the grant. For grants awarded to academics, the university will usually be the administering organization. A tribal council may be an appropriate body, or a Cultural (or Language) Centre. It is important to think about this as part of the planning process.

Applying for funding is a time-consuming and lengthy process. Expect to wait between six weeks and eight months from the grant submission deadline before you hear about the outcome of the application.

23.5 Preparing a funding application

While every application is different in the details, they have a lot in common. In the following sections I identify the most common components of language-documentation grant applications.[10]

23.5.1 Language background

First is the language background. The funding organization will want to know the number of speakers of the language (and the source of that information), the degree of endangerment, where the language is spoken, whether children are learning the language, and other information related to this. This may be part of the project description (or project statement), or it may be a separate section.

23.5.2 Project statement

Along with the budget (see 23.5.5), the project statement is the most important part of the application. Most applications will ask for a project statement, narrative or description which sets out in detail what the application is for. The statement should include not only a detailed description of the tasks to be carried out within the project, but also information about the personnel and their qualifications, background to the project (that is, why this project should be funded, what has been achieved to date by the project team and other relevant work). The instructions for the grant application will normally give information about what should be included. The statement should be written for an educated audience, but it cannot be assumed that the reviewers who decide whether or not to fund the project will necessarily be familiar with linguistics or language documentation, or with the particular language situation.

Project statements will have a required length. It may be stated as the maximum number of words or pages that can be submitted, but the most usual application requires around ten–twenty pages, unless the funding amount is very small. There will probably also be formatting guidelines. While it may be tempting to decrease font size or the margins in order to provide more information, this may cause the proposal to be rejected and it will not endear you to the reviewers who will usually be reading many statements in a short period of time. Project statements have a better chance of being favourably judged if the reviewer is able to find information easily. They should be explicit about the details of the project and organized into sections. Sometimes instead of a project narrative the grant application will consist of a series of questions which act as the equivalent of the sections of the narrative.

23.5.3   Project outcomes

In my experience, most grant applications fail either because they are too ambitious or because they are too vague. That is, either the applicant promises results which are unrealistic for the timeframe of the grant or the funding amount requested, or they are not specific enough about what they propose to do or how they propose to do it. There is a temptation to try to impress the grant organization and the reviewers by giving the impression that they will be getting a great deal by funding the project, but such applications merely create the impression that the applicant is not realistic and will not be able to follow through with the promises. A well-thought-out timeline with realistic achievement expectations is much more impressive than something that promises the world but probably will not deliver.

In addition to planning the outcomes of the project, appropriate consideration should be given to the dissemination of the project results. A language-documentation project cannot be said to have been successful if the results will simply gather dust in an archive without appropriate return of materials to the community in a form that will be useful and accessible.

23.5.4   Project summary/overview

In addition to the project statement, many grant organizations also require a summary of approximately one page. This is a non-technical summary of the most important parts of the project. It is used for preliminary project evaluation and screening and for refreshing the memory of the evaluators. It is an important part of the application and is worth spending some time over. It is often best written after the whole application has been completed.

23.5.5 Budgets

As part of the application process you will also need to write a budget and a budget justification. The budget sets out the total amount of money being asked for; it will be broken down into categories such as salaries, payments to language consultants, travel, equipment, consumables (pens, paper, batteries), report production and other similar items. The budget justification provides information about how you determined the amount requested (for instance, by providing quotes for airline travel or computer equipment) and explains what the money will be used for. For example, if you are asking for funds for five computers, you should explain briefly why you need five.

Constructing an appropriate budget is an art. Do not pad the budget with needless items, and do not ask for less than you need to be able to do the work (in the hope that the reviewers will like a 'low-cost' project). It is important to set priorities: if you are not funded for the full amount requested (and this is a common occurrence) how will it be possible to do the work in the project plan without being able to buy everything you asked for. In planning for the grant, it is useful to think of 'must have' items and parts of the budget which could be reduced if absolutely necessary. For example, a good quality microphone is a must-have item; the project cannot proceed if data cannot be properly recorded. Compensation for consultant time is also extremely important, but if you budget for 15 hours a week with consultants and then find that the budget must be cut back to 12 hours a week, that would usually not make the project impossible to complete.

In multiyear budgets, it is common to include provision for inflation. If the funds will be paid in a currency other than the one in which the project is working (for example, a grant from the US paid in US dollars for work in Central America), you may need to consider the possibility of currency fluctuations. There is more information about budgeting for linguistic projects in Bowern (2008: 173).

23.5.6 Other documentation

Funding applications often require curricula vitae or resumés for the main project participants. These documents and results of prior funding and track record can be kept up to date for insertion into applications as needed.

Grants submitted through a university usually require ethics clearance: either a statement that ethical review is not required or that the project application has been reviewed by the university Institutional Review Board or equivalent ethics body.

Grants often require supporting documentation. This could include statements from the organization which will administer the grant that they are willing to do so, sometimes statements from project participants that they are willing to participate or from an organization or group in the language community that they agree to the documentation project being carried out. Some grants require letters of reference or letters of support from people who are in a position to comment on the project application or the applicants. In other cases, such letters are not required. It is important to read the grant application guidelines and comply with them. Different funders have different requirements so be careful to provide the right information or the application may be rejected because it does not meet the requirements.

23.5.7　Summary

Writing a grant application takes a considerable amount of time and requires planning and coordination. It may also take quite a long time to hear back from the funding agency about the outcome of the grant application (success or failure). It may be practical to apply to several funding sources at once, although this requires careful planning because many grant organizations will not allow you to submit proposals for the same project to more than one place at the same time. This is an added argument in favour of modular planning, as you can submit different subprojects to different funding organizations which will give a greater chance of success in working on something.

23.6　Key stages of documentation projects

Documentation projects can be broken down into KEY STAGES, that is component parts of the project that occur in a given chronological order.

23.6.1　The initial planning stage

In the first stage of the project, time should be devoted explicitly to planning and prioritizing the work. This involves working out how to discover what has been collected on the language previously and who is available to work on the current project. In a documentation team, someone should be in charge and everyone should have a clear idea about what they are supposed to do. At this stage it is also important to develop an approximate timeline, at least for the short term and medium term. That is, work out in approximate terms what you would like to achieve in three months and what can be done in six months.

This is not to say that it is not possible to revisit and replan; in fact going back to the original planning documents and seeing how things have advanced, what needs revising and what can be added is an important part of the documentation itself.

Planning at this stage of the project does not only involve the linguistic aspects of getting ready to start work (such as the preparation of language elicitation materials). Much more time will be spent in planning things like how the collected data and analysis will be managed, finding somewhere to live in the field, applying for funding, and the many other tasks which do not involve linguistics but are necessary when beginning the project.

23.6.2   Pilot phase and initial documentation

The first stage of a documentation project itself should be considered a pilot for the main documentation. Once some data has been collected, it can be used to test the workflow and archiving plan. At this stage the team members are probably still getting to know each other, coming to grips with new hardware and software, and a new way of working. There will be aspects of the initial plan that will need to be altered, no matter how carefully the original planning was conducted.

23.6.3   The main project phases

The length of the pilot phase will depend on many factors, but once the project team is working well together, has received any necessary training, and any preliminary problems in the data gathering, analysis and management have been ironed out through testing (and possibly sending sample materials to an archive or other organization for checking and feedback – see Nathan, Chapter 13), the main part of the project can begin. For many researchers this phase will involve a field trip to the location where the language is spoken.

Within the main data gathering phase it may be possible to identify stages depending on the type of material collected, the interim outcomes, breaks in the work and transitions as new participants join the project and others leave. In my experience, the most common problem at this stage is gathering too much raw material too quickly. It is very easy to continue to make recordings and collect information without being certain of what has already been gathered. It is important to allow time for review and consolidation and not fall into the trap of believing that 'more data will solve the problem'.

23.6.4   Completion and evaluation

Wrapping up parts of the project also involves work which should be planned for. Funding agencies will have deadlines by which the funds in the grant must be spent. If you are unable to meet that deadline, it may be possible to apply for an extension in certain circumstances. You will need to prepare a final report for the funding agency which will set out what was achieved in the grant period, any problems, major findings and the outcomes. It may be necessary to provide the agency with copies of all materials produced in the project; however, not all agencies require or wish this. Also included in the final grant report will be a detailed statement of expenditure.

The preparation of the final report is an excellent opportunity to conduct your own evaluation of the project, although not all of the evaluation may need to be communicated to the grant agency. It is useful to think of what worked well in the grant, the unexpected hurdles and opportunities which came up, what you would do differently in future, which participants in the project were particularly good at certain tasks or were particularly enthusiastic or were particularly weak. These informal evaluations are very useful for planning future stages of projects, or developing new projects. They allow you to be more efficient and to work more effectively, to learn from errors and to capitalize on serendipitous discoveries.

23.7 Project outcomes

The term OUTCOMES refers to the tangible and intangible end products of the project. Project outcomes can be classified in several different ways. Project outcome issues have already been mentioned in conjunction with more general planning, but let us also consider outcomes explicitly.

23.7.1 Tangible and intangible outcomes

It is useful to think about the outcomes of the project in terms of the TANGIBLE outcomes and the INTANGIBLE ones. The tangible outcomes are the things that you can see, like the documentary corpus, archived collection, dictionaries and other similar items. Teaching programmes and teaching materials are also tangible outcomes. Intangible outcomes, on the other hand, are the more abstract results that may be just as valuable but are more difficult to describe. For example, there may be an increased value placed on the language within the community, it may have a higher profile in the local area, and this may translate into other positives (or negatives). The acquisition of skills by project members, such as younger speakers learning how to use computers or video-recorders, may increase their self-esteem and so can also be seen as intangible outcomes of the project. Do not mistake tangible outcomes for intangible ones. It is easy to spend a lot of time talking about the intangible benefits of programmes and documentation while under-planning for the tangible outcomes. On the other hand, projects that concentrate on how many gigabytes of data have been collected at the expense of creating intangible outcomes within the speech community are also unbalanced.

23.7.2 Evaluating the success of a project

How will you know if the project has succeeded? Success can be measured in many different ways, not only in terms of how many hours of recordings have been made and transcribed, or how many headwords are in the dictionary, but also how many people have been trained in different aspects of language work, the enthusiasm that has been generated for the language, the teachers drawn into language development and support, and other less tangible outcomes.

Successes may also be considered in terms of long-term and short-term outcomes. A short-term planned outcome might include the goal of recording a certain number of hours of recordings, while a longer term goal might be the transcription.

Discussing evaluations periodically among the project team is very useful on a long-term documentation project. The project team may have different expectations and may value various outcomes to a different extent: therefore what is perceived by some to be a successful project may have fallen short by the standards of others. These evaluations can be done formally or informally.

It is also a good idea to get feedback from people who have been using materials produced by the project. This again could be done formally, during a workshop or through a survey, or informally by chatting to community members.

Finally, revisit the planning documents periodically. Were the initial aims of the project achieved? If not, what prevented them from being achieved? Were they simply inappropriate given the personnel, project budget or time available? Did the course of the project itself cause aims to shift? For example, did the process of documentation open up new horizons and possibilities for the documentation team so that the original aims were superseded by more ambitious targets?

23.7.3 Foundations for future projects

If the principles of incremental design have been followed, in theory there is no end to a documentation project: each new subproject builds in a material way on what has gone before it, and each project opens up new ideas and lays the foundation for future work. The documentation can never be fully complete. It will always be possible to enrich or improve annotation of the corpus, for example, or to explore new analyses and theoretical proposals against the corpus materials. Even in cases when no native speakers remain, new work on a corpus can continue with new research results or the creation of new materials for community use by descendants of the speakers.

It is natural that interest, enthusiasm and energy will wax and wane over the lifetime of the documentation project. That is not something to be concerned about, as long as the documentation project is well set up and is itself documented so that it can be picked up and continued (such METADOCUMENTATION (that is documentation of the documentation project itself) will also be useful for an archive (see Conathan, Chapter 12), or another later researcher who wishes to understand how the original documentation project was carried out). This can even be a good thing; it is natural for the main participants in a project to get tired and taking a break can be beneficial for everyone.

Documentation projects may metamorphose into other things. They could become primarily teaching programmes, or language revitalization programmes. They might move from a documentation of the language to a greater focus on cultural materials, ceremony, social or cultural practices, or oral history. That is, they move from something in which the narratives and textual samples serve to illustrate the structure and function of the language to a project where those 'samples' are the main focus themselves (see Woodbury, Chapter 9).

23.8   Conclusions

Although planning is important, for all the reasons discussed above, occasionally projects can get bogged down in planning and endless arguments about details. Sometimes the most important thing is to go with one's instincts and one's heart. After all, language documentation and revitalization, particularly when it concerns highly endangered languages, is an emotional adventure for those involved in it. For most of the project team, it is not just a job. We have discussed the principles of project planning and design in some detail, but these principles are flexible: they should be a guide for documentation work, and not an end in itself. They are, to a certain extent, context specific and not everything will work in all projects.

Finally, aim high, have a reason for the decisions you take, keep the data and analysis safe, and do not give up: everything else is flexible.

Notes

1 I would like to thank David Costa, Daryl Baldwin and Susan Penfield for discussion of this topic, as well as the Aboriginal people in Northern

Australia who have shared their languages with me. My fieldwork on these languages has been funded by the National Science Foundation and the Australian Institute for Aboriginal and Torres Strait Islander Studies.

2 Language documentation is a 'record of the language' which can be used in various ways (see Woodbury, Chapter 9). Thus documentation and revitalization are not the same thing; nor are language documentation and language teaching, nor documentation and research on a single aspect of the language. I do not mean to imply that documentation can be (or should be) divorced from other language projects; on the contrary, as I argue in Bowern (2008: 10–12), documentation is most thorough and comprehensive when combined with analysis.

3 This article is addressed both to linguists working on documentation projects and to communities who want to work on a documentation of their own language. Thus the phrase 'your language' or 'the language' in this article means different things for different people: either the linguist's research language or the community's documentation language. While some take offence when linguists talk about 'my language' (Crowley, 2007: 175–6), I hope this will be excused as a device to include as many audiences as possible rather than as sanctioning the idea that a linguist 'owns' a language they have worked on.

4 I have not specified how many people should be in this group, in theory this might be a single person. For example, the Tsalagi (Cherokee) linguist Chief Sequoyah developed a writing system for his language around 1819 without a big project team. Individuals can achieve a great deal.

5 See www.olac.org

6 See www.dnathan.com/VL/austLang.htm

7 Work on Cornish-language revitalization was (until recently) stuck at this stage for many years because of difficulties in agreeing on which of the four competing writing systems should be used.

8 Communities wanting to start a documentation project should note that linguists are extremely useful in a project team. After all, they are trained in how to write down languages that they do not speak and to ask questions which will explore the structure and use of the language. They are trained in how to make a record that will be useful to communities now and in the future, they may have access to funding for projects or know how to apply for it, and often they know how to locate and analyse prior sources for the language. This is especially important if the language project is based mostly on old materials which require a great deal of interpretation, as Daryl Baldwin (p.c.) has pointed out.

9 I recognize that there will be cases where this is not possible.

10 This information was compiled during research for the chapter in
   Bowern (2008: 170–183) and has been derived from grant applica-
   tion information provided by the National Science Foundation, the
   Endangered Languages Documentation Programme, the Endangered
   Language Fund and other similar sources (see also Austin 2010a).

References

Abbi, Anvita 2001. *A Manual of Linguistic Fieldwork and Structures of Indian Languages.* Munich: Lincom Europa.

Aboriginal and Torres Strait Islander Library and Information Resources Network Protocols. 1995. www1.aiatsis.gov.au/atsilirn (15 January 2009).

Abrams, Daniel and Steven Strogatz 2003. Modelling the dynamics of language death. *Nature* **424**: 900.

Abu-Lughod, Lila 1991. Writing against culture. In Richard Fox (ed.), *Recapturing Anthropology: Working in the Present*, 137–62. Santa Fe, NM: School of American Research.

Adams, David Wallace 1995. *Education for Extinction: American Indians and the Boarding School Experience, 1875–1928.* Lawrence, KS: University Press of Kansas.

Adelaar, Willem F. H. 2007. Threatened languages in Hispanic South America. In Matthias Brenzinger (ed.), *Language Diversity Endangered* (Trends in Linguistics: Studies and Monographs 181), 9–28. Berlin: Mouton de Gruyter.

Adidi, L. 2007. Kalaw kawaw ya. In *Warra Wiltaniappendi: Strengthening Languages*, 10–11. Presented at the Proceedings of the Inaugural Indigenous Languages Conference (ILC), Adelaide: University of South Australia.

Ager, Dennis E. 2005. Prestige and image planning. *Current Issues in Language Planning* **6**: 1–43.

Agha, Asif 1994. Honorification. *Annual Review of Anthropology* **23**: 277–302.
  2007a. *Language and Social Relations.* Cambridge University Press.
  2007b. The object called 'language' and the subject of linguistics. *Journal of English Linguistics* **35**: 217–35.

Ahlers, Jocelyn C. and Suzanne Wertheim 2009. Introduction: reflecting on language and culture fieldwork in the early 21st century. *Language and Communication* **29**(3): 193–8.

Ahmad, M. 2008. What factors contribute to sign language endangerment? MA dissertation, School of Oriental and African Studies, London.

Aikhenvald, Alexandra Y. 1999. Areal diffusion and language contact in the Içana Vaupés basin, north-west Amazonia. In R. M. W. Dixon and Alexandra Y. Aikhenvald (eds.), *The Amazonian Languages*, 385–415. Cambridge University Press.

2000. *Classifiers: A Typology of Noun Categorization Devices*. Oxford University Press.

2003. Mechanisms of change in areal diffusion: new morphology and language contact. *Journal of Linguistics* **39**: 1–29.

2008. *The Manambu Language of East Sepik, Papua New Guinea*. Oxford University Press.

Aikio, Ante 2008. The Saami languages: history, present situation, and work on documentation. (Paper presented at University of Utah Linguistics Colloquium.)

Aikio, Marjut 1992. Are women innovators in the shift to a second language? A case study of Reindeer Sámi women and men. *International Journal of the Sociology of Language* **94**: 43–61.

al-Ali, Naji 2009. *A Child in Palestine*. London/New York: Verso.

Albright, Eric and John Hatton 2007. WeSay, a tool for engaging communities in dictionary building. In D. Victoria Rau and Margaret Florey (eds.), *Documenting and Revitalizing Austronesian Languages*, 189–201 (Language Documentation and Conservation Special Publication 1). Hawaii: University of Hawaii Press.

Alexandre, Pierre 1968. Some linguistic problems of nation-building in Negro Africa. In Joshua A. Fishman, Charles A. Ferguson and Jyotirinda Das Gupta (eds.), *Language Problems of Developing Nations*, 119–27. New York: John Wiley & Sons.

Alim, Samy H., Awad Ibrahim and Alastair Pennycook (eds.) 2009. *Global Linguistic Flows: Hip Hop Cultures, Youth Identities, and the Politics of Language*. London: Routledge.

Alvarez, Albert and Kenneth Hale 1970. Toward a manual of Papago grammar: some phonological terms, *International Journal of American Linguistics* **36**(2): 83–97.

Ameka, Felix K. 2006. Real descriptions: reflections on native speaker and non-native speaker descriptions of a language. In Felix K. Ameka, Alan Dench and Nicholas Evans (eds.), *Catching Language: The Standing Challenge of Grammar Writing* (Trends in Linguistics: Studies and Monographs 167), 69–112. Berlin: Mouton de Gruyter.

Ameka, Felix K., Alan Dench and Nicholas Evans (eds.) 2006. *Catching Language: The Standing Challenge of Grammar Writing* (Trends in Linguistics: Studies and Monographs 167). Berlin: Mouton de Gruyter.

Amery, Rob 1995. It's ours to keep and call our own: reclamation of the Nunga languages in the Adelaide region, South Australia. *International Journal of the Sociology of Language* **113**: 63–82.

2000 'Warrabarna Kaurna!' Reclaiming an Australian language, Multilingualism and Linguistic Diversity 1 Lisse, The Netherlands: Swets & Zeitlinger.

2001. Language planning and language revival. *Current Issues in Language Planning* **2**: 141–221.

2009. Phoenix or relic? documentation of languages with revitalization in Mind. *Language Documentation and Conservation* **3**(2): 138–48.

Amezaga, Josu 2000. Media and identity in the Basque Country. Paper presented at: First International Symposium on Basque Cultural Studies, 29 June – 2 July, 2000, Institute of Basque Studies, London Guildhall University.

Andersen, Roger W. 1982. Determining the linguistic attributes of language attrition. In Richard D. Lambert and Barbara F. Freed (eds.), *The Loss of Language Skills*, 83–118. Rowley, MA: Newbury House.

Anderson, Deborah 2003. Using the Unicode standard for linguistic data: preliminary guidelines, Proceedings of EMELD 2003: Workshop on Digitizing and Annotating Texts & Field Recordings. www.emeld. org/workshop/2003/anderson-paper.pdf (11 February 2010).

Androutsopoulos, Jannis 2007. Bilingualism in the mass media and on the internet. In Monica Heller (ed.), *Bilingualism: A Social Approach* (Palgrave Advances in Linguistics), 207–30. Palgrave MacMillan.

Annamalai, E. 2003. Reflections on a language policy for multilingualism. *Language Policy* **2**(2): 113–32.

Aoki, Haruo 2002. Writing a Nez Perce dictionary. In William Frawley, Kenneth C. Hill and Pamela Munro (eds.), *Making Dictionaries. Preserving Indigenous Languages of the Americas*, 285–98. Berkeley, CA: University of California Press.

Appadurai, Arjun 1996. *Modernity at Large: Cultural Dimensions of Globalization*. Minneapolis: University of Minnesota Press.

Arends, Jacques and Adrienne Bruyn 1994. Gradualist and developmental hypotheses. In Jacques Arends, Pieter Muysken and Norval Smith (eds.), *Pidgins and Creoles: An Introduction*, 111–20. Amsterdam: John Benjamins.

Arends, Jacques, Pieter Muysken and Norval Smith (eds.) 1994. *Pidgins and Creoles: An Introduction*. Amsterdam: John Benjamins.

Argenter, Joan A. and R. McKenna Brown (eds.) 2004. *On the Margins of Nations: Endangered Languages and Linguistic Rights: Proceedings of the Eighth FEL Conference, Barcelona (Catalonia), Spain 1–3 October 2004*. Bath: Foundation for Endangered Languages.

Arroyo de la Cuesta, Father Felipe. 1862. *Vocabulary or Phrase Book of the Mutsun Language of Alta California*. (Shea's Library of American Linguistics, Volume 8.) New York: Cramoisy. http://ia311216.us.archive. org/1/items/vocabularyorphra00arro/vocabularyorphra00arro.pdf (10 August 2010).

Artigal, Josep 1993. Catalan and Basque immersion programmes. In H. Baetens Beardsmore (ed.), *European Models of Bilingual Education*, 30–53. Clevedon: Multilingual Matters.

Asher, James J. 1982. *Learning another Language through Actions*. Los Gatos, CA: Sky Oaks Productions.

Ashmore, Richard D., Lee Jussim and David Wilder 2001. *Social Identity, Intergroup Conflict, and Conflict Reduction* (Rutgers Series on Self and Identity 3). Oxford University Press.

Atkins, B. T. Sue and Michael Rundell 2008. *The Oxford Guide to Practical Lexicography*. Oxford University Press.

Auer, Peter (ed.) 1998. *Code-switching in Conversation: Language, Interaction and Identity*. London: Routledge.

Auer, Peter 1999. From codeswitching via language mixing to fused lects: toward a dynamic typology of bilingual speech. *International Journal of Bilingualism* **3**(4): 309–32.

2000. A conversation analytic approach to code-switching and transfer. In Li Wei (ed.), *The Bilingualism Reader*, 166–87. London: Routledge.

Auld, Glenn 2007. Talking books for children's home use in a minority Indigenous Australian language context. *Australasian Journal of Educational Technology* **23**: 48–67.

Austin, Peter K. 2003. Introduction. In Peter K. Austin (ed.), *Language Documentation and Description*, vol. 1, 6–14. London: SOAS.

2006. Data and language documentation. In Jost Gippert, Nikolaus P. Himmelmann and Ulrike Mosel (eds.), *Essentials of Language Documentation* (Trends in Linguistics: Studies and Monographs 178), 87–112. Berlin: Mouton de Gruyter.

2008. Training for language documentation: Experiences at the School of Oriental and African Studies, *Language Documentation & Conservation* Special Publication No. 1: 25–41.

(ed.). 2009. *One Thousand Languages: Living, endangered, and lost*. London: Thames and Hudson and Berkeley, CA: University of California Press.

2010a. Communities, ethics and rights in language documentation. In Peter K. Austin (ed.), *Language Documentation and Description*, vol. 7, 34–54. London: SOAS.

2010b. Applying for a language documentation grant. In Peter K. Austin (ed.), *Language Documentation and Description*, vol. 7, 285–99. London: SOAS.

Austin, Peter K. and Lenore A. Grenoble 2007. Current trends in language documentation. In Peter K. Austin (ed.), *Language Documentation and Description*, vol. 4, 12–25. London: SOAS.

Auzanneau, Michelle 2002. Rap in Libreville, Gabon: an urban sociolinguistic space. In Alain-Philippe Durand (ed.), *Black, Blanc, Beur: Rap Music and Hip-hop Culture in the Francophone World*, 106–23. Lanham, MD: The Scarecrow Press.

Backus, Ad 2004. Convergence as a mechanism of language change. *Bilingualism: Language and Cognition* **7**(2): 179–81.

2005. Codeswitching and language change: one thing leads to another? *International Journal of Bilingualism* **9**(3–4): 307–40.

Baetens Beardsmore, Hugo 1993–1994. Language policy and planning in western European countries. *Annual Review of Applied Linguistics* **14**: 93–110.

Baker, Colin 1992. *Attitudes and Language* (Multilingual Matters 83). Clevedon: Multilingual Matters.

1999. *Encyclopaedia of Bilingualism and Bilingual Education*. Clevedon: Multilingual Matters.

2006. *Foundations of Bilingual Education and Bilingualism*, 4th edn. (Bilingual Education and Bilingualism 54). Clevedon: Multilingual Matters.

Bakker, Peter 1994. Michif, the Cree–French mixed language of the Métis buffalo hunters in Canada. In Peter Bakker and Maarten Mous (eds.), *Mixed Languages: 15 Case Studies in Language Intertwining* (Studies in Language and Language Use 13), 13–33. Amsterdam: IFOTT.

2003. Mixed languages as autonomous systems. In Yaron Matras and Peter Bakker (eds.), *The Mixed Language Debate*, 107–50. Berlin: Mouton de Gruyter.

Bakker, Peter and Pieter Muysken 1994. Mixed languages and language intertwining. In Jacques Arends, Pieter Muysken and Norval Smith (eds.), *Pidgins and Creoles: An Introduction*, 41–52. Amsterdam: John Benjamins.

Bakker, Peter and Robert A. Papen 2008. French influence on the native languages of Canada and adjacent USA. In Thomas Stolz, Dik Bakker and Rosa Salas Palomo (eds.), *Aspects of Language Contact: New Theoretical, Methodological and Empirical Findings with Special Focus on Romancisation processes* (Empirical Approaches to Language Typology 35), 239–86. Berlin: Mouton de Gruyter.

Baldauf, Richard B. 1993–1994. 'Unplanned' language policy and planning. *Annual Review of Applied Linguistics* **14**: 82–9.

2004. Micro language planning. In D. Atkinson, P. Bruthiaux, W. Grabe and V. Ramanathan (eds.), *Studies in Applied Linguistics: English for Academic Purposes, Discourse Analysis, and Language Policy and Planning (Essays in Honor of Robert B. Kaplan on the Occasion of his 75th Birthday)*. Clevedon: Multilingual Matters.

Baldwin, Daryl 2003. Miami language reclamation: from Ground Zero. A lecture presented by the Center for Writing and the Interdisciplinary Minor in Literacy and Rhetorical Studies. Speaker Series No. 24. University of Minnesota: Center for Writing.

Balluta, Andrew and Gladyz Evanoff 2005. *Dena'ina Qenaga Du'idnaghelnik*. Fairbanks and Anchorage: Alaska Native Language Center and Alaska Native Heritage Center. www.uaf.edu/anlc/dena%27ina.phrases/

Bamgbose, Ayo 2000. *Language and Exclusion: The Consequences of Language Policies in Africa*. London: LIT Verlag.

Bankston, Carl L. and Jacques Henry 2000. Spectacles of ethnicity: festivals and the commodification of ethnic culture among Louisiana Cajuns, *Sociological Spectrum* **20**: 377–407.

Bartholomew, Doris A. and Louise Schoenhals 1983. *Bilingual dictionaries for Indigenous Languages*. Hidalgo, Mexico: SIL.

Barwick, Linda, Allan Marett, Michael Walsh, Nicholas Reid and Lysheth Ford 2005. Communities of interest: issues in establishing a digital resource on Murrinh-patha song at Wadeye (Port Keats), NT. *Literary and Linguistic Computing* **20**: 383–97.

Barwick, Linda, Bruce Birch and Nicholas Evans 2007. Iwaidja Jurtbirrk songs: bringing language and music together. *Australian Aboriginal Studies* **2007**(2): 6–34.

Bashkow, Ira 2004. A neo-Boasian conception of cultural boundaries. *American Anthropologist* **106**(3): 443–58.

Basso, Keith H. 1996. *Wisdom Sits in Places: Landscape and Language among the Western Apache*. Albuquerque: University of New Mexico Press.

Batibo, Herman M. 2005. *Language Decline and Death in Africa: Causes, Consequences and Challenges* (Multilingual Matters 132). Clevedon: Multilingual Matters.

   2008. Poverty as a crucial factor in language maintenance and language death: case studies from Africa. In Wayne Harbert (ed.), *Language and Poverty*, 23–36. Clevedon: Multilingual Matters.

Bavin, Edith L. 1989. Some lexical and morphological changes in Warlpiri. In Nancy C. Dorian (ed.), *Investigating Obsolescence: Studies in Language Contraction and Death*, 267–86. Cambridge University Press.

BBC 2002. Cornish gains official recognition: BBC News. news.bbc.co.uk/1/hi/england/2410383.stm.

Bednar, Jenna, Aaron Bramson, Andrea, Jones-Rooy and Scott Page 2007. The emergence of cultural signatures and persistence of diversity: a model of conformity and consistency. Paper presented at the Midwest Political Science Association meeting, April 2006 and APSA September 2006.

Behar, Ruth 1996. *The Vulnerable Observer: Anthropology That Breaks Your Heart*. Boston: Beacon Press.

Bell, Allan 1991. *The Language of News Media* (Language in Society 17). Oxford: Blackwell Publishing.

Bell, John and Steven Bird 2000. A preliminary study of the structure of lexicon entries. Proceedings from the Workshop on Web-Based Language Documentation and Description. Philadelphia, PA, 12–15 December 2000. www.ldc.upenn.edu/exploration/expl2000/papers/bell/bell.html (12 February 2010).

Bender, Emily M., Dan Flickinger, Jeff Good and Ivan A. Sag 2004. Montage: leveraging advances in grammar engineering, linguistic ontologies, and mark-up for the documentation of underdescribed languages. Proceedings of the Workshop on First Steps for Language Documentation of Minority Languages: Computational Linguistic Tools for Morphology, Lexicon and Corpus Compilation, LREC 2004, Lisbon, Portugal.

Benham, Maenette Kape'ahiokalami Padeken and Joanne Elizabeth Cooper 1998. *Culture and Education Policy in Hawai'i: The Silencing of Native Voices.* Mahwah, NJ: Lawrence Erlbaum.

2000. *Indigenous Education Models: Our Mother's Voice.* Mahwah, NJ: Lawrence Erlbaum.

Bennett, Ruth 2003. Saving a language with computers, tape recorders, and radio. In Jon Reyhner, Octaviana Trujillo, Roberto Luis Carrasco and Louise Lockard (eds.), *Nurturing Native Languages*, 59–77. Flagstaff, AZ: Northern Arizona University, College of Education. jan.ucc.nau. edu/~jar/books.html.

Benson, Phil, Peter Grundy and Tove Skutnabb-Kangas 1998. Special issue on language rights. *Language Sciences* **20**: 1–112.

Bentahila, Abdelâli and Eirlys E. Davies 1995. Patterns of code-switching and patterns of language contact. *Lingua* **96**(2–3): 75–93.

2002. Language mixing in rai music: localisation or globalisation? *Language and Communication* **22**(2): 187–207.

Bercero, Rosa 2003. Normativisation, a priority for Aragonese. Paper presented to the Mercator International Conference on European Minority Languages and Research: Shaping an Agenda for the Global Age, Aberystwyth, 8–10 April.

Berez, Andrea L. 2007. Technology review: EUDICO Linguistic Annotator (ELAN), *Language Documentation and Conservation* **1**(2): 283–9.

Bergsland, Knut 1959. Aleut dialects of Atka and Attu, *Transactions of the American Philosophical Society*, New Series **49**(3): 1–128.

1994. *Aleut Dictionary / Unangam Tunudgusii: An Unabridged Lexicon of the Aleutian, Pribilof, and Commander Islands Aleut Language.* Fairbanks, AK: Alaska Native Language Center, University of Alaska Fairbanks.

1997. *Aleut Grammar / Unangam Tunuganaan Achixaasix (Alaska Native Language Center Research Paper 10).* Fairbanks, AK: Alaska Native Language Center, University of Alaska Fairbanks.

1998. *Ancient Aleut Personal Names / Kadaangim Asangin/Asangis: Materials from the Billings Expedition 1790–1792.* Fairbanks, AK: Alaska Native Language Center, University of Alaska Fairbanks.

Bergsland, Knut and Moses Dirks 1978. *Niiĝuĝim Tunugan Ilakuchangis / Introduction to Atkan Aleut Grammar and Lexicon.* Anchorage, AK: National Bilingual Materials Development Center, University of Alaska.

1981. *Atkan Aleut School Grammar.* Anchorage, AK: National Bilingual Materials Development Center, University of Alaska.

(eds.) 1990. *Unangam Ungiikangin kayux Tunusangin / Unangam Uniikangis ama Tunuzangis / Aleut Tales and Narratives: Collected 1909–1910 by Waldemar Jochelson.* Fairbanks, AK: Alaska Native Language Center, University of Alaska Fairbanks.

Berlin, Brent 1992. *Ethnobiological Classification.* Princeton University Press.

Berlin, Brent and Paul Kay 1969. *Basic Color Terms*. University of California Press.

Berman, Judith 1996. 'The culture as it appears to the Indian himself': Boas, George Hunt, and the Methods of Ethnography. In George W. Stocking, Jr. (ed.) *Volksgeist as Method and Ethic: Essays on Boasian Ethnography and the German Anthropological Tradition*, History of Anthropology vol. VIII, 215–56. Madison: University of Wisconsin Press.

Bert, Michel 2001. Rencontre de langues et francisation: l'exemple du Pilat (Loire), thèse de doctorat, Sciences du langage, Université Lumière Lyon2.

  2009. Typologie des locuteurs de langues menacées d'extinction: le cas du francoprovençal et de l'occitan dans la région du Pilat (France). In Claudine Fréchet (ed.), *Langues et cultures de France et d'ailleurs*, 25–38. Presses Universitaires de Lyon.

Bert, Michel, James Costa and Jean-Baptiste Martin 2009. *Francoprovençal – Occitan – Rhône-Alpes (FORA), état des lieux des langues régionales en Rhône-Alpes et propositions pour un politique linguistique régionale*, study carried out for Rhône-Alpes regional government. http://cr-ra.anti-search.net/cgi-bin/redirect?TYPE=URL&PARAMS=piemont&C=189&AGENT=user1&TARGET=http://www.rhonealpes.fr/include/viewFile.php?idtf=5067&path=b3%2FWEB_CHEMIN_5067_1255705111.pdf (8 October 2010).

Berthet, Ernest, Pierre Bonard, Guy Gauthier *et al.* 1982. *Langue dominante, langues dominées*. Paris: Edilig.

Bickel, Balthasar, Bernard Comrie and Martin Haspelmath 2004. *The Leipzig Glossing Rules: Conventions for Interlinear Morpheme-by-Morpheme Glosses*. Leipzig: Max Planck Institute for Evolutionary Anthropology. www.eva.mpg.de/lingua/files/morpheme.html (19 February 2010).

Bickerton, Derek 1984. The language bioprogram hypothesis. *Behavioral and Brain Sciences* **7**(2): 173–221.

Bielenberg, Brian 1999. Indigenous language codification: cultural effects. In Jon Reyhner, Gina Cantoni, Robert N. St. Clair and Evangeline Parsons Yazzie (eds.), *Revitalizing Indigenous Languages*, 103–12. Flagstaff, AZ: Northern Arizona University.

Bird, Steven 1999. Strategies for representing tone in African writing systems, *Written Language and Literacy* **2**: 1–44.

  2001. Orthography and identity in Cameroon. *Written Language and Literacy* **4**: 131–62.

  2009. Experiencing language death. Language Log, June 23. languagelog.ldc.upenn.edu/nll/?p=1528.

Bird, Steven and Gary F. Simons 2003. Seven dimensions of portability for language documentation and description. *Language* **79**(3): 557–82.

Blackwood, Robert J. 2008. *The State, the Activists and the Islanders: Language Policy on Corsica*. Dordrecht Netherlands: Springer.

Blanchard, Rosemary Ann, Charlie Perfilliea, Jennie DeGroat, Paul Platero and Shawn Secatero 2003. Borderlands of identity: revitalising language and cultural knowledge in a Navajo community living apart. In Leena Huss, Antoinette Camilleri Grima and Kendall King (eds.), *Transcending Multilingualism: Linguistic Revitalization in Education*, 192–223. Lisse Netherlands: Swets and Zeitlinger.

Blench, Roger 1998. The status of languages in central Nigeria. In Matthias Brenzinger (ed.), *Endangered Languages in Africa*, 187–205. Cologne: Rüdiger Köppe Verlag.

2007. Endangered languages in West Africa. In Matthias Brenzinger (ed.), *Language Diversity Endangered*, 140–62. Berlin: Mouton de Gruyter.

Blom, Jan-Petter and John J. Gumperz 1972. Social meaning in linguistic structure: code-switching in Norway. In John J. Gumperz and Dell Hymes (eds.), *Directions in Sociolinguistics: The Ethnography of Communication*, 407–34. New York: Holt, Rinehart and Winston.

Blommaert, Jan (ed.) 1999. *Language Ideological Debates*. Berlin: Mouton de Gruyter.

Blommaert, Jan 2001. The Asmara declaration as a sociolinguistic problem: reflections on scholarship and linguistic rights. *Journal of Sociolinguistics* **5**(1): 131–42.

2004. Writing as a problem: African grassroots writing, economies of literacy, and globalization. *Language in Society* **33**: 643–71.

2005. *Discourse: A Critical Introduction*. Cambridge University Press.

2009. Language, asylum, and the national order. *Current Anthropology* **50**(4): 415–41.

Blommaert, Jan and Jef Verschueren 1998. The role of language in European nationalist ideologies. In B. Schieffelin, K. Woolard and P. Kroskrity (eds.), *Language Ideologies: Practice and Theory*, 189–210. Oxford University Press.

Bloom, David E. and Gilles Grenier 1992. Economic perspectives on language: the relative value of bilingualism in Canada. In James Crawford (ed.), *Language Loyalties: A Source Book on the Official English Controversy*, 445–51 University of Chicago Press.

Bloomfield, Leonard 1926. A set of postulates for the science of language. *Language* **2**(3): 153–64.

1933. *Language*. Holt, Rinehart and Winston.

Boas, Franz 1911. Introduction. In Franz Boas (ed.) *Handbook of American Indian Languages* Part I (Smithsonian Institution Bureau of American Ethnology Bulletin 40), 1–83. Washington, DC: Government Printing Office.

1917. Introductory, *International Journal of American Linguistics* **1**(1): 1–8.

Boas, Franz and Ella Deloria 1941. *Dakota Grammar* (Memoirs of the National Academy of Sciences 23, Second Memoir). Washington, DC: Government Printing Office.

Bobaljik, Jonathan David 1998. Visions and realities: researcher–activist–indigenous collaborations in indigenous language maintenance. In Erich Kasten (ed.), *Bicultural Education in the North: Ways of Preserving and Enhancing Indigenous Peoples' Languages and Traditional Knowledge*, 13–28. Münster: Waxmann Verlag.

Boraas, Alan and Michael Christian no date. Kahtnuht'ana Qenaga: the Kenai People's Language.

Borneman, John and Abdellah Hammoudi 2009. *Being There: The Fieldwork Encounter and the Making of Truth*. Berkeley, CA: University of California Press.

Boroditsky, Lera 2001. Does language shape thought? English and Mandarin speakers' conceptions of time. *Cognitive Psychology* **43**(1): 1–22.

Boroditsky, Lera, Lauren Schmidt and Webb Phillips 2003. Sex, syntax, and semantics. In Dedre Gentner and Susan Goldin-Meadow (eds.), *Language in Mind: Advances in the Study of Language and Thought*. MIT Press.

Bouquiaux, Luc and Jacqueline M. Thomas (eds.) 1992. *Studying and Describing Unwritten Languages*. Dallas: Summer Institute of Linguistics.

Bourdieu, Pierre 1977a. *Outline of a Theory of Practice*. Cambridge University Press.

1977b. The economics of linguistic exchange, *Social Science Information* **16**: 645–68.

1990. *In Other Words: Essays Towards a Reflexive Sociology*. Cambridge: Polity Press.

1991. *Language and Symbolic Power*. Cambridge: Polity Press.

Bowern, Claire 2008. *Linguistic Fieldwork: A Practical Guide*. New York: Palgrave Macmillan.

Boynton, Jessica, Steven Moran, Anthony Aristar and Helen Aristar-Dry 2006. E-MELD and the School of Best Practice: an ongoing community effort. In Linda Barwick and Nicholas Thieberger (eds.), *Sustainable Data from Digital Fieldwork: From Creation to Archive and Back*. Sydney University Press. hdl.handle.net/2123/1296 (11 February 2010).

Bradin, Claire and Ennis Howard 1998. Streamlining HyperCard for CALL. Paper presented at Teachers of English to Speakers of Other Languages Conference, Seattle.

Bradley, David 1989. The disappearance of the Ugong in Thailand. In Nancy C. Dorian (ed.), *Investigating Obsolescence: Studies in Language Contraction and Death*, 33–40. Cambridge University Press.

2001a. Yi. In Joan Garry and Carl Rubino (eds.), *Facts about the World's Major Languages*, 826–9. Chester: H. W. Wilson.

2001b. Language policy for the Yi. In Stevan Harrell (ed.), *Perspectives on the Yi of Southwest China*, 195–214. Berkeley, CA: University of California Press.

Bradley, David (ed.) 2005b. *Heritage Maintenance for Endangered Languages in Yunnan, China* [in English and Chinese]. Bundoora: La Trobe University.

Bradley, David 2007a. Language endangerment in China and Southeast Asia. In Matthias Brenzinger (ed.), *Language Diversity Endangered*, 278–302. Berlin: Mouton de Gruyter.

2007b. East and south-east Asia. In Christopher J. Moseley (ed.), *Encyclopedia of the World's Endangered Languages*, 349–422. London: Routledge.

2007c. East and south-east Asia. In Ronald E. Asher and Christopher J. Moseley (eds.), *Atlas of the World's Languages*, 2nd edn, 157–208. London: Routledge.

2007d. Languages of mainland south-east Asia. In Osahito Miyaoka, Osamu Sakiyama and Michael E. Krauss (eds.), *The Vanishing Languages of the Pacific Rim*, 301–36. Oxford University Press.

2007e. What elicitation misses: dominant languages, dominant semantics. In Peter K. Austin (ed.), *Language Documentation and Description*, vol. 4, 136–44. London: SOAS.

2008. Birth-order terms in Lisu: inheritance and contact. *Anthropological Linguistics* **49**(1): 54–69.

2009. South-east Asia. In Christopher J. Moseley (ed.), *Atlas of the World's Languages in Danger of Disappearing*, 3rd edn. Paris: UNESCO.

Bradley, David and Maya Bradley (eds.) 2002. *Language Endangerment and Language Maintenance: An Active Approach*. London: Routledge.

Bradley, David, Maya Bradley and Li Yongxiang 1999. Language maintenance for endangered languages of southwestern China. In Nicholas Ostler (ed.), *Endangered Languages and Education. Proceedings of the Third FEL Conference*, 13–20. Bath: Foundation for Endangered Languages.

Brady, Fiona, Laura Dyson and Tina Aela 2008. Indigenous adoption of mobile phones and oral culture. In Fay Sudweeks, Herbert Hrachovech and Charles Ess (eds.), *Proceedings Cultural Attitudes Towards Communication and Technology*. Australia: Murdoch University Press.

Brenzinger, Matthias (ed.) 2007a. *Language Diversity Endangered* (Trends in Linguistics: Studies and Monographs 181). Berlin: Mouton de Gruyter.

Brenzinger, Matthias 2007b. Language endangerment in southern and eastern Africa. In Matthias Brenzinger (ed.), *Language Diversity Endangered* (Trends in Linguistics: Studies and Monographs 181), 179–204. Berlin: Mouton de Gruyter.

2008. Language diversity and poverty in Africa. in Wayne Harbert (ed.), *Language and Poverty*, 37–49. Clevedon: Multilingual Matters.

Brenzinger, Matthias, Arienne M. Dwyer, Tjeerd de Graaf, *et al.* 2003. *Language Vitality and Endangerment*. Paris: UNESCO. portal.unesco. org/culture/en/files/35646/12007687933Language_Vitality_and_

Endangerment.pdf/Language%2BVitality%2Band%2BEndangerment. pdf (10 January 2010).

Breton, Roland J.-L. 2003. Sub-Saharan Africa. In Jacques Maurais and Michael A. Morris (eds.), *Languages in a Globalising World*, 203–16. Cambridge University Press.

Brewer, M. B. 2001. Intergroup identification and intergroup conflict: when does ingroup love become outgroup hate? In Richard D. Ashmore, L. Jussim and D. Wilder (eds.), *Social Identity, Intergroup Conflict, and Conflict Reduction*, 17–41. Oxford University Press.

Briggs, Charles L. 1986. *Learning How to Ask: A Sociolinguistic Appraisal of the Role of the Interview in Social Science Research*. Cambridge University Press.

    2002. Linguistic Magic Bullets in the Making of a Modernist Anthropology, *American Anthropologist* **104**(2): 481–98.

Briggs, Charles and Richard Bauman 1999. 'The foundation of all future researches': Franz Boas, George Hunt, Native American texts, and the construction of modernity, *American Quarterly* **51**(3): 479–528.

Brock-Utne, Birgit 2005. Language-in-education practices in Africa with a special focus on Tanzania and South Africa: insights from research in practice. In Angel M.Y. Lin and Peter W. Martin (eds.), *Decolonisation, Globalisation: Language-in-Education Policy and Practice*, 173–93. Clevedon: Multilingual Matters.

Broeder, Daan, David Nathan, Sven Strömqvist and Remco van Veenendaal 2008. Building a Federation of Language Resource Repositories: the DAM-LR Project and its Continuation within CLARIN. In *Proceedings of the Sixth International Language Resources and Evaluation* (LREC 08, Marrakech, Morocco, 28–30 May). Online at www.lrec-conf.org/proceedings/lrec2008/summaries/370.html.

Brown, Roger and Eric Lenneberg 1954. A study in language and cognition. *Journal of Abnormal and Social Psychology* **49**: 454–62.

Browne, Donald R. 1996. *Electronic Media and Indigenous Peoples: A Voice of our Own?* Ames, IA: Iowa State University Press.

Brugman, Hennie, Daan Broeder and Gunter Senft 2003. Documentation of languages and archiving of language data at the Max Planck Institute for Psycholinguistics in Nijmegen, Paper presented at the Ringvorlesung 'Bedrohte Sprachen' Sprachenwert – Dokumentation – Revitalisierung. University of Bielefeld. www.mpi.nl/IMDI/documents/articles/BI-EL-PaperA2.pdf (12 February 2010).

Brumfit, Christopher 2006. A European perspective on language as liminality. In Clare Mar-Molinero and Patrick Stevenson (eds.), *Language Ideologies, Policies and Practices: Language and the Future of Europe*, 28–43. Basingstoke: Palgrave Macmillan.

Brumman, Cristoph 1999. Writing for culture: why a successful concept should not be discarded. *Current Anthropology* **40**(S): 1–27.

Bucholtz, Mary 2000. Language and youth culture. *American Speech* **75**(3): 280–3.

  2001. The whiteness of nerds: superstandard English and racial markedness. *Journal of Linguistic Anthropology* **11**(1): 84–100.

Bullock, Barbara E. and Chip Gerfen 2004. Frenchville French: a case study in phonological attrition. *International Journal of Bilingualism* **8**(3): 303–20.

Burling, Robbins 1964. Cognition and componential analysis: God's truth or hocus-pocus? *American Anthropologist* **66**: 20–8.

Burnaby, Barbara 1996. Aboriginal language maintenance, development, and enhancement: a review of the literature. In Gina Cantoni (ed.), *Stabilizing Indigenous Languages*, 22–40. Northern Arizona University.

Burnaby, Barbara and Jon Reyhner (eds.) 2002. *Indigenous Languages across the Community*. Flagstaff, AZ: Northern Arizona University, College of Education. jan.ucc.nau.edu/~jar/books.html (26 January 2010).

Burridge, Kate 2002. Changes within Pennsylvania German grammar as enactments of Anabaptist world view In Nick Enfield (ed.), *Ethnosyntax*, 207–30. Oxford University Press.

Busch, Brigitta 2004. *Sprachen im Disput: Medien und Öffentlichkeit in multilingualen Gesellschaften* (Drava Diskurs 1). Klagenfurt: Drava.

Buszard-Welcher, Laura 2001. Can the web help save my language? In Leanne Hinton and Ken Hale (eds.), *The Green Book of Language Revitalization in Practice*, 331–45. San Diego, CA: Academic Press.

Bybee, Joan and Paul Hopper 2001. *Frequency and the Emergence of Linguistic Structure*. John Benjamins.

Cabau, Béatrice 2009. The irresistible rise and hegemony of a linguistic fortress: English teaching in Sweden. *International Multilingual Research Journal* **3**(2): 134–52.

Caldas, Stephen J. 2006. *Raising Bilingual-Biliterate Children in Monolingual Cultures*. Clevedon: Multilingual Matters.

  2008. Changing bilingual self-perceptions from early adolescence to early adulthood: empirical evidence from a mixed-methods case study. *Applied Linguistics* **29**(2): 290–311.

Caldas, Stephen J. and Suzanne Caron-Caldas 2000. The influence of family, school, and community on bilingual preference: results from a Louisiana/Quebec case study. *Applied Psycholinguistics* **21**(3): 365–81.

Calvet, Louis-Jean 1987. *La guerre des langues: et les politiques linguistiques*. Paris: Payot.

  1998. *Language Wars and Linguistic Politics* (Michel Petheram, Trans.). Oxford University Press.

  2006. *Towards an Ecology of World Languages*. Cambridge: Polity Press.

Cameron, Deborah 1995. *Verbal Hygiene*. Didcot, Oxon: Routledge.

  1998. Problems of empowerment in linguistic research. *Cahiers de l'ILSL* **10**: 23–38.

2007. Language endangerment and verbal hygiene: history, morality and politics. In Alexandre Duchêne and Monica Heller (eds.), *Discourses of Endangerment: Ideology and Interest in the Defence of Languages*, 268–85. London: Continuum.

Cameron, Deborah, Elizabeth Frazer, Penelope Harvey, M. B. H. Rampton and Kay Richardson 1992. *Researching Language: Issues of Power and Method*. London: Routledge.

1993a. The relations between researcher and researched: ethics, advocacy and empowerment. In D. Graddol, J. Maybin and B. Stierer (eds.), *Researching Language and Literacy in Social Context*, 18–25. Clevedon: The Open University/Multilingual Matters.

1993b. Ethics, advocacy and empowerment: issues of method in researching language. *Language and Communication* **13**(2): 81–94.

Campbell, Lyle 1973. On glottalic consonants. *International Journal of American Linguistics* **39**: 44–6.

1993. On proposed universals of grammatical borrowing. In Henk Aertsen and Robert J. Jeffers (eds.), *Historical Linguistics 1989: 9th International Conference on Historical Linguistics* (Current Issues in Linguistic Theory 106), 91–109. Amsterdam: Benjamins.

In preparation. La gramática Nivaclé (Chulupí).

Campbell, Lyle and Verónica Grondona 2007. Internal reconstruction in Chulupí (Nivaclé), *Diachronica* **24**: 1–29.

Campbell, Lyle and Martha C. Muntzel 1989. The structural consequences of language death. In Nancy C. Dorian (ed.), *Investigating Obsolescence: Studies in Language Contraction and Death*, 181–96. Cambridge University Press.

Canagarajah, A. Suresh 2005. *Reclaiming the Local in Language Policy and Practice*. Mahwah, NJ: Lawrence Erlbaum.

Cantoni, Gina (ed.) 1996. *Stabilizing Indigenous Languages*. Flagstaff, AZ: Northern Arizona University, College of Education. jan.ucc.nau.edu/~jar/books.html (26 January 2010).

Carnie, Andrew 1996. Modern Irish: a case study in language revival failure, *MIT Working Papers in Linguistics* **28**: 99–114.

Carroll, John B. 1956. *Language, Thought and Reality: Selected Writings of Benjamin Lee Whorf*. Cambridge, MA: MIT Press.

Casals, Neus Torbisco 2006. *Group Rights as Human Rights: A Liberal Approach to Multiculturalism*. Springer.

Castells, M. 2004. *The Power of Identity*, vol. II: *The Information Age: Economy, Society, and Culture*. Oxford: Blackwell.

Cenoz, Jasone 2008. The status of Basque in the Basque Country. In Monica Barni and Guus Extra (eds.), *Mapping Linguistic Diversity in Multicultural Contexts*, 93–113. Berlin: Mouton de Gruyter.

Cerrón-Palomino, Rodolfo 1997. Pasado y presente del quechua. *Yachay Wasi* **4**: 49–64.

Chalmers, Douglas and Mike Danson 2006. Language and economic development – complementary or antagonistic? In Wilson McLeod (ed.), *Revitalizing Gaelic in Scotland*, 239–56. Edinburgh: Dunedin Academic Press.

Charity, Anne H. 2008. Linguists as agents for social change. *Language and Linguistics Compass* **2**(5): 923–39.

Chaudenson, Robert and Salikoko S. Mufwene 2001. *Creolization of Language and Culture*. London: Routledge.

Childs, Tucker and Taziff Koroma 2008. Problematizing the field experience. Lectures presented at the Institute on Field Linguistics and Language Documentation, 23 June – 3 July University of California, Santa Barbara.

Chomsky, Noam 1982. *Language and the Study of Mind*. Tokyo: Sansyusya Publishing.

Christen, Kimberly 2008. Archival Challenges and digital solutions in Aboriginal Australia. *SAA Archeological Recorder* **8**(2): 21–4.

2009. Access and accountability: the ecology of information sharing in the digital age. *Anthropology News* **50**(4): 4–5.

Clifford, James 1988. *The Predicament of Culture: Twentieth Century Ethnography, Literature and Art*. Cambridge, MA: Harvard University Press.

Clifford, James and George E. Marcus (eds.) 1986. *Writing Culture: The Poetics and Politics of Ethnography*. Berkeley, CA: University of California Press.

Clyne, Michael G. 1980. Triggering and language processing. *Canadian Journal of Psychology/Revue canadienne de psychologie* **34**(4): 400–6.

2003. *Dynamics of Language Contact: English and Immigrant Languages* (Cambridge Approaches to Language Contact). Cambridge University Press.

COACADI (Coordinadora Cakchiquel de Desarrollo Integral) 1985. *El Idioma: Centro de Nuestro Cultura*. B'okob', Departamento de Investigaciones Culturales.

Coates, Jennifer (ed.) 1998. *Language and Gender: A Reader*. Oxford: Blackwell.

COBUILD 1987. *Collins Cobuild English Language Dictionary*. London: Harper Collins Publishers.

Cohen, Daniel J. and Roy Rosenzweig 2006. *Digital History: A Guide to Gathering, Preserving and Presenting the Past on the Web*. Philadelphia, PA: University of Pennsylvania Press.

Cole, Douglas 1983. 'The value of a person lies in his Herzensbildung': F. Boas' Baffin Island Letter-Diary, 1883–1884. In George W. Stocking, Jr. (ed.), *Observers Observed: Essays on Ethnographic Fieldwork*, 13–52. Madison, WI: University of Wisconsin Press.

Collier, Virginia P. and Wayne P. Thomas 2004. The astounding effectiveness of dual language education for all. *NABE [National Association for Bilingual Education] Journal of Research and Practice* **2**(1): 1–20.

Collins, Wesley M. 2005. Codeswitching avoidance as a strategy for Mam (Maya) linguistic revitalization. *International Journal of American Linguistics* **71**(3): 239–76.

Coluzzi, Paolo 2005. Language planning for the smallest language minority in Italy: the Cimbrians of Veneto and Trentino-Alto Adige, *Language Problems and Language Planning* **29**: 247–69.

Comajoan, Llorenç 2009. Language revitalisation in a globalised world: lessons learned from Catalan [Revitalizació lingüística en un món globalitzat: Lliçons apreses a partir del cas català.]. In M. Carme Junyent (ed.), *Transferences: The Expression of Extra-linguistic Processes in the World's Languages* [Transferències: La manifestació dels processos extralingüístics en les llengües del món], 269–99. Vic: Eumo Editorial.

Commission of the European Communities 2004. *Recommendation of the European Commission on Turkey's Progress towards Accession, 18*. Brussels: Commission of the European Communities.

Cook Eung Do 1989. Is phonology going haywire in dying languages? Phonological variations in Chipewyan and Sarcee, *Language in Society* **18**: 235–55.

Cooper, Robert L. 1989. *Language Planning and Social Change*. Cambridge University Press.

Cormack, Mike 2003. Developing minority language media studies. *First Mercator International Symposium on Minority Languages and Research*. www.aber.ac.uk/cgi-bin/user/merwww/index.pl?rm=content; content=20;lang=1 (26 February 2010).

2007. Introduction. In Mike Cormack and Niamh Cormack (eds.), *Minority Language Media: Concepts, Critiques and Case Studies*, 1–16. Clevedon: Multilingual Matters.

Coronel-Molina, Serafín M. 2005. Lenguas originarias cruzando el puente de la brecha digital: Nuevas formas de revitalización del quechua y del aimara. In Serafín M. Coronel-Molina and Linda Grabner (eds.), *Lenguas e identidades en los Andes: Perspectivas ideológicas y culturales*, 31–82. Quito: Ediciones Abya Yala.

Costa, David 2003. *The Miami Illinois Language*. University of Nebraska Press.

Cotter, Colleen 2001. Continuity and vitality: expanding domains through Irish-language radio. In Leanne Hinton and Ken Hale (eds.), *The Green Book of Language Revitalisation in Practice*, 301–11. San Diego, CA: Academic Press.

Coulmas, Florian 2003. *Writing Systems. An Introduction to their Linguistic Analysis*. Cambridge University Press.

Counceller, April and Amy Steffian 2003. *Sharing Words*. Kodiak, AK: Alutiiq Museum and Archaeological Repository.

Coward, David and Charles E. Grimes 2000. *Making Dictionaries: A Guide to Lexicography and the Multi-Dictionary Formatter*. Waxhaw, NC: SIL International. www.sil.org/computing/shoebox/MDF_2000.pdf.

Cox, Christopher and Andrea Berez 2009. CuPED (Customizable Presentation of ELAN Documents). Paper presented at the 1st International Conference on Language Documentation and Conservation. Honolulu, March 12–14. hdl.handle.net/10125/4969

Craig, Colette G. 1992a. Miss Nora, rescuer of the Rama language: a story of power and empowerment. In Kira Hall, Mary Bucholtz and Birch Moonwomon (eds.), *Locating Power: Second Berkeley Women and Language Conference* 1: 80–8. Berkeley, CA: Berkeley Women and Language Group.

  1992b. A constitutional response to language endangerment: the case of Nicaragua, *Language* **68**: 17–24.

  1993. Fieldwork on endangered languages: a forward look at ethical issues. In Andre Crochetière, Jean-Claude Boulanger and Conrad Ouellon (eds.), *Proceedings of the XVth International Congress of Linguists* 1, 33–42. Saint Foy, Canada: Les Presses de l'Université Laval.

Crawford, James 1992. *Hold your Tongue: Bilingualism and the Politics of English Only*. Flag Staff, AZ: Addison-Wesley.

  1996. Seven hypotheses on language loss: causes and cures. In Gina Cantoni (ed.), *Stabilizing Indigenous Languages*, 51–68. Northern Arizona University.

  2000. *At War with Diversity: US Language Policy in an Age of Anxiety*. Clevedon, Avon: Multilingual Matters Ltd.

Crowley, Terry 2007. *Field Linguistics: A Beginner's Guide*. Oxford University Press.

Cruse, D. Alan 1986. *Lexical Semantics*. Cambridge University Press.

  2000. *Meaning in Language: An Introduction to Semantics and Pragmatics*. Oxford University Press.

Cruz, Hilaria 2009. Chatino oratory in San Juan Quiahije. PhD qualifying paper, University of Texas at Austin.

Crystal, David 2000. *Language Death*. Cambridge University Press.

  2003. *English as a Global Language* 2nd edn. Cambridge University Press.

  2004. *Creating a World of Languages*. In FIPLV (International Federation of Language Teacher Associations), World News 61, December, 22–35. (Contribution to Linguapax conference on Diversity, Sustainability and Peace, Barcelona, 20–23 May, 2004)

  2006. *Language and the Internet* (2nd edn). Cambridge University Press.

  2007. Interview by Robin Turner, published in the *Western Mail* on 21 June. www.walesonline.co.uk/news/wales-news/tm_headline=welsh-joins-navajo-and-breton-as-the-coolest-languages-on-the-internet&method=full&objectid=19330469&siteid=50082-name_page.html.

Csató, Éva Á. and David Nathan. 2007. Multiliteracy, past and present in the Karaim communities. In Peter K. Austin (ed.) *Language Documentation and Description*, vol. 4, 207–30. London: SOAS.

Cummins, Jim 1979. Linguistic interdependence and the educational development of bilingual children. *Review of Educational Research* **49**: 221–51.

1991. Interdependence of first- and second-language proficiency in bilingual children. In Ellen Bialystok (ed.), *Language Processing in Bilingual Children*, Cambridge University Press.

Cummins, Jim and Merrill Swain 1986. *Bilingualism in Education: Aspects of Theory, Research, and Practice*. London: Longman.

Cunliffe, Daniel and Susan C. Herring 2005. Introduction to minority languages, multimedia and the web. *New Review of Hypermedia and Multimedia* 11(2): 131–37.

Czaykowska-Higgins, Ewa 2009. Research models, community engagement, and linguistic fieldwork: reflections on working with Canadian indigenous communities. *Language Documentation and Conservation* **3**(1): 15–50.

D'Andrade, Roy 1995. *The Development of Cognitive Anthropology*. Cambridge University Press.

Daftary, Farmiah 2000. *Insular Autonomy: A Framework for Conflict Settlement? A Comparative Study of Corsica and the Aaland Islands*. Flensburg: European Centre for Minority Issues.

Dalby, Andrew 2002. *Language in Danger*. London: Penguin.

Danet, Brenda and Susan C. Herring (eds.) 2003. The multilingual internet. Special issue of the *Journal of Computer Mediated Communication* **9**(1). jcmc.indiana.edu/vol9/issue1/intro.html.

Darnell, Regna 2001. *Invisible Genealogies: A History of Americanist Anthropology*. Lincoln: University of Nebraska Press.

Daubenmier, Judith M. 2008. *The Meskwaki and Anthropologists: Action Anthropology Reconsidered*. Lincoln: University of Nebraska Press.

Dauenhauer, Nora Marks and Richard Dauenhauer 1998. Technical, emotional, and ideological issues in reversing language shift: examples from Southeast Alaska. In Lenore A. Grenoble and Lindsay J. Whaley (eds.), *Endangered Languages: Current Issues and Future Prospects*, 57–98. Cambridge University Press.

Dawkins, Richard 1976. *The Selfish Gene*. Oxford University Press.

Debenport, Erin 2010. The potential complexity of 'universal ownership': cultural property, textual circulation, and linguistic fieldwork. *Language and Communication* **30**: 204–10.

de Swaan, Abram 1998. A political sociology of the world language system (1): the dynamics of language spread. *Language Problems and Language Planning*, **22**(1), 63–78.

2001. *Words of the World: The Global Language System*. Cambridge: Blackwell.

DeFrancis, John 1984. Digraphia. *Word* **35**: 59–66.

Dench, Alan 1987. Kinship and collective activity in the Ngayarda languages of Australia. *Language in Society* **16**: 321–9.

Dennett, Daniel 1991. *Consciousness explained*. Penguin Press.

Derbyshire, Desmond C. 1979. *Hixkaryana*. (Lingua Descriptive Studies, 1.) Amsterdam: North-Holland.

Derbyshire, Desmond and Geoffrey Pullum 1986. Introduction. Desmond Derbyshire and Geoffrey Pullum (eds.), *Handbook of Amazonian Languages*, vol. I, 1–28. Berlin: Mouton de Gruyter.

Describing Archives: A Content Standard. 2007. Chicago: Society of American Archivists.

Desveaux, David 2008. Total immersion plus. *Mac-talla Gaelic Supplement No. 7. Shunpiking Magazine* 50, Summer. www.electricscotland.com/gaelic/finlay/finlay1.htm (2 July 2009).

Diamond, Jared M. 1991. Interview techniques in ethnobiology. In Andrew M. Pawley (ed.), *Man and a Half: Essays in Pacific Anthropology and Ethnobiology in Honour of Ralph Bullmer*, 83–6. Auckland: The Polynesian Society.

Dimmendaal, Gerrit J. 1989. On language death in eastern Africa. In Nancy C. Dorian (ed.), *Investigating Obsolescence: Studies in Language Contraction and Death*, 13–32. Cambridge University Press.

Dimmendaal, Gerrit J. and F. K. Erhard Voeltz 2007. Africa. In Christopher J. Moseley (ed.), *Encyclopedia of the World's Endangered Languages*, 579–634. London: Routledge.

Diringer, David and Reinhold Regensburger 1968. *The Alphabet: A Key to the History of Mankind*. London,: Hutchinson.

Dixon, R. M. W. 1972. *The Dyirbal Language of North Queensland* (Cambridge Studies in Linguistics 9). Cambridge University Press.

  1994. *Ergativity*. (Cambridge Studies in Linguistics, 69.) Cambridge University Press.

  2007. Field linguistics: a minor manual. *Sprachtypologie und Universalienforchung* **60.1**: 12–31.

Dixon, R. M. W. (ed.) 1976. *Grammatical Categories in Australian Languages (Linguistic Series 22)*. Canberra: Australian Institute of Aboriginal Studies.

Dobel, Christian, Gil Diesendruck and Jens Bölte 2007. How writing system and age influence spatial representations of actions: a developmental, cross-linguistic study. *Psychological Science* **18**: 487–91.

Dobrin, Lise M. 2008. From linguistic elicitation to eliciting the linguist: lessons in community empowerment from Melanesia, *Language* **84**(2): 300–24.

Dobrin, Lise M., Peter K. Austin and David Nathan 2009. Dying to be counted: the commodification of endangered languages in documentary linguistics. In Peter K. Austin (ed.), *Language Documentation and Description*, vol. 6, 37–52. London: SOAS.

Dobrin, Lise M. and Jeff Good 2009. Practical language development: whose mission? *Language* **85**(3): 619–29.

Dobrin, Lise M. and Daniel Pitti 2009. The Arapesh grammar and digital language Archive. www.arapesh.org.

Doig River First Nation 2007. Dane Wajich: Dane-zaa stories and songs. Available online at www.virtualmuseum.ca/Exhibitions/Danewajichv (13 August 2010).

Dorian, Nancy C. 1977. The problem of the semi-speaker in language death. In *International Journal of the Sociology of Language*, **12**: 23–32.

1978. The dying dialect and the role of the schools: East Sutherland Gaelic and Pennsylvania Dutch. In J. E. Alatis (ed.), *International Dimensions of Bilingual Education*. Washington, DC: Georgetown University Press.

1980. Maintenance and loss of same-meaning structures in language death. *Word* **31**: 39–45.

1981. *Language Death: The Life Cycle of a Scottish Gaelic Dialect*. Philadelphia, PA: University of Pennsylvania Press.

1982. Defining the speech community to include its working margins. In Suzanne Romaine (ed.), *Sociolinguistic Variation in Speech Communities*, 25–33. London: Edward Arnold.

1987. The value of maintenance efforts which are unlikely to succeed. *International Journal of the Sociology of Language* **68**: 57–67.

1993. A response to Ladefoged's other view of endangered languages. *Language* **69**: 575–9.

1994. Purism vs. compromise in language revitalization and language revival. *Language in Society* **23**(4): 479–94.

1998. Western language ideologies and small-language prospects. In Lenore A. Grenoble and Lindsay J. Whaley (eds.), *Endangered Languages: Language Loss and Community Response*, 3–21. Cambridge University Press.

1999. Linguistic and ethnographic fieldwork. In Joshua Fishman (ed.), *Handbook of Language and Ethnic Identity*, 25–41. Oxford University Press.

2009. Age and speaker skills in receding languages. *International Journal of the Sociology of Language* **200**: 11–25.

Dressler, Wolfgang U. 1981. Language shift and language death: a Protean challenge for the linguist. *Folia Linguistica* **15**: 5–28.

Dryer, Matthew S. 2006. Descriptive theories, explanatory theories, and basic linguistic theory. In Felix K. Ameka, Alan Dench and Nicholas Evans (eds.), *Catching Language: The Standing Challenge of Grammar Writing* (Trends in Linguistics: Studies and Monographs 167), 207–34. Berlin: Mouton de Gruyter.

Duchêne, Alexandre and Monica Heller 2007. *Discourses of Endangerment: Ideology and Interest in the Defence of Languages*. Advances in Sociolinguistics. London: Continuum.

Duffy, Jonathan 2002. Back from the dead: UK's new language: BBC News Online, news.bbc.co.uk/1/hi/uk/2206191.stm 6 November 2009.

Dumestre, Gérard (ed.) 1994. *Stratégies communicatives au Mali: langues régionales, bambara, français*. Paris: Didier Erudition.

Dumestre, Gérard. 1997. De l'école au Mali. *Nordic Journal of African Studies* **6**: 31–52.

Dumézil, George 1965. *Documents anatoliens sur les langues et les traditions du Caucase, III: Nouvelles études oubykhs*. Paris: Librairie Maisonneuve.

Duranti, Alessandro 1981. *The Samoan fono: A Sociolinguistic Study*. Pacific Linguistics Monographs, Series B, vol. 80. Australian National University.

   1993. Intentions, self, and responsibility: an essay in Samoan ethnopragmatics. In Jane Hill and Judith Irvine (eds.), *Responsibility and Evidence in Oral Discourse*, 24–47. Cambridge University Press.

   1994. *From Grammar to Politics: Linguistic Anthropology in a Western Samoan Village*. University of California Press.

   1997. *Linguistic Anthropology*. Cambridge University Press.

   2003. Language as culture in U.S. anthropology: three paradigms. *Current Anthropology*, **44**(3): 323–47.

Durham, William 1991. *Coevolution: Genes, Culture, and Human Diversity*. Stanford University Press.

Durkheim, Emile 1912. *Les formes élémentaires de la vie religieuse*. Paris: Felix Alcan.

   1947 [1893]. *The Division of Labor in Society*. New York: Free Press.

Dwyer, Arienne M. 2006. Ethics and practicalities of cooperative fieldwork and analysis. In Jost Gippert, Nikolaus P. Himmelmann and Ulrike Mosel (eds.), *Essentials of Language Documentation* (Trends in Linguistics: Studies and Monographs 178), 31–66. Berlin: Mouton de Gruyter.

Eades, Diana 1979. Gumbaynggir. In R. M. W. Dixon and B. J. Blake (eds.), *Handbook of Australian Languages* Vol I, 242–361. Canberra: Australian National University Press.

Eckert, Penelope 1980. Diglossia: Separate and unequal. *Linguistics* **18**: 1053–64.

   2000. *Linguistic Variation as Social Practice: The Linguistic Construction of Identity in Belten High* (Language in Society 27). Oxford: Blackwell.

Edelsky, Carole, Sarah Hudelson, Barbara Flores, Florence Barkin, Bess Altwerger and Kristina Jilbert 1983. Semilingualism and language deficit. *Applied Linguistics* **4**: 1–22.

Edwards, John R. (ed.) 1984. *Linguistic Minorities, Policy and Pluralism*. London: Academic Press.

Edwards, John R. 2007a. Review of *Saving Languages: An Introduction to Language Revitalization* by Lenore Grenoble and Lindsay Whaley, *Canadian Journal of Applied Linguistics* **10**(1): 99–120.

   2007b. Back from the brink: the revival of endangered languages. In Marlis Hellinger and Anne Pauwels (eds.), *Handbook of Language and Communication: Diversity and Change*, 241–69. Berlin: Mouton de Gruyter.

Edwards, Viv and Lynda Pritchard Newcombe 2005a. Language transmission in the family in Wales: an example of innovative language planning. *Language Problems and Language Planning* **29**.135–50.

2005b. When school is not enough: new initiatives in intergenerational language transmission in Wales. *International Journal of Bilingual Education and Bilingualism* **8**: 298–312.

Eira, Christina and Tonya N. Stebbins 2008. Authenticities and lineages: revisiting concepts of continuity and change in language. *International Journal of the Sociology of Language* **189**: 1–30.

Eisenlohr, Patrick 2004. Language revitalisation and new technologies: cultures of electronic mediation and refiguring of communities. *Annual Review of Anthropology* **33**(1): 21–45.

Ellis, P. B. 1974. *The Cornish Language and its Literature*. London: Routledge and Kegan Paul.

Elwert, Georg 2001. Societal literacy: writing culture and development. In David R. Olson and Nancy Torrance (eds.), *The Making of Literate Societies*, 54–67. Malden MA/Oxford: Blackwell.

Elyachar, Julia 2006. Best practices: research, finance, and NGOs in Cairo. *American Ethnologist* **33**(3): 413–26.

Enfield, Nick 2002a. *Ethnosyntax: Explorations in Grammar and Culture*. Oxford University Press.

2002b. Ethnosyntax: introduction. In Nick Enfield (ed.), *Ethnosyntax: Explorations in Grammar and Culture*, 3–30. Oxford University Press.

2007. Review of *Ethnopragmatics: Understanding discourse in cultural context* ed. Cliff Goddard. *Intercultural Pragmatics* **4**(3): 419–33.

Enfield, Nick and Tanya Stivers 2007. *Person Reference in Interaction: Linguistic, Cultural, and Social Perspectives*. Cambridge University Press.

England, Nora C. 1998. Mayan efforts towards language preservation. In Lenore Grenoble and Lindsey Whaley (eds.), *Endangered Languages: Current Issues and Future Prospects*, 99–116. Cambridge University Press.

2003. Mayan language revival and revitalization politics: linguists and linguistic ideologies. *American Anthropologist* **105**(4): 733–43.

Epps, Patience 2005. Areal diffusion and the development of evidentiality: evidence from Hup. *Studies in Language* **29**: 617–50.

Epps, Patience and Herb Ladley 2009. Syntax, souls, or speakers? On SIL and community language development. *Language* **85**(3): 640–6.

Erickson, Frederick 2004. *Talk and Social Theory*. Cambridge: Polity Press.

Errington, Joseph 2001. Colonial linguistics, *Annual Review of Anthropology* **30**: 19–39.

2003. Getting language rights: the rhetorics of language endangerment and loss. *American Anthropologist* **105**(4): 723–32.

Evans, Nicholas 2001. The last speaker is dead – long live the last speaker! In Paul Newman and Martha Ratliff (eds.), *Linguistic Fieldwork*, 250–81. Cambridge University Press.

2003. Context, culture, and structuration in the languages of Australia. *Annual Review of Anthropology* **32**: 13–40.

2008. Review of *Essentials of Language Documentation*, *Language Documentation and Conservation* **2**(2): 340–50. nflrc.hawaii.edu/ldc/ (19 February 2010).

Evans, Nicholas and Stephen Levinson 2009. The myth of language universals: language diversity and its importance for cognitive science. *Behavioral and Brain Sciences*, **32**(5): 429–48.

Evans, Nick and Hans-Jürgen Sasse 2007. Searching for meaning in the Library of Babel: field semantics and problems of digital archiving, in Peter K. Austin (ed.), *Language Documentation and Description*, vol. 6, 58–99. London: SOAS.

Evas, Jeremy 2000. Declining density: a danger for language? In Colin Williams (ed.), *Language Revitalization: Policy and Planning in Wales*, 292–310. Cardiff: University of Wales Press.

Everett, Daniel L. 1984. Sociophonetic restrictions on subphonemic elements in Pirahã. *Proceedings of the X International Congress of Phonetic Sciences*, A. Cohen and M. P. R. van den Broecke (eds.), 606–10. Dordrecht: Foris.

Fabian, Johannes 2002[1983]. *Time and the Other: How Anthropology Makes Its Object*, 2nd edn. New York: Columbia University Press.

2008. *Ethnography as Commentary: Writing from the Virtual Archive*. Durham: Duke University Press.

Fang, Meili and David Nathan 2009. Language documentation and pedagogy for endangered languages: a mutual revitalisation. In P. K. Austin (ed.), *Language Documentation and Description* vol. 6. London: SOAS.

Fennell, Desmond 1981. Can a shrinking minority be saved? Lessons from the Irish experience. In E. Haugen, J. D. McClure and D. Thompson (eds.), *Minority Languages Today: A Selection from the Papers Read at the First Conference on Minority Languages at Glasgow University 8–3 September 1980*, 32–9. Edinburgh University Press.

Ferguson, Charles A. 1959. Diglossia. *Word* **15**: 325–40.

Ferrari, Aurelia 2005. Interférence entre swahili et sheng dans l'enseignement à Nairobi. Paper presented at AILA (Association Internationale de Linguistique Appliquée) conference, Madison, Wisconsin.

Ferrer, Rachel Casesnoves 2004. Transmission, education and integration in projections of language shift in Valencia. *Language Policy* **3**: 107–31.

Fettes, M. 1997. Language planning and education. In Ruth Wodak and David Corson (eds.), *Language Policy and Critical Issues in Education* 13–22. Dordrecht: Kluwer Academic.

Fill, Alwin, and Peter Mühlhäusler (eds.) 2001. *The Ecolinguistics Reader*. London: Continuum.

Finlayson, Rosalie 1984. The changing nature of isihlonipho sabafazi, *African Studies* **43**(2): 137–46.

Fishman, Joshua A. 1967. Bilingualism with and without diglossia: diglossia with and without bilingualism, *Journal of Social Issues* **23**(2): 29–38.

1972. Domains and the relationship between micro- and macrosociolinguistics. In John J. Gumperz and Dell Hymes (eds.), *Directions in Sociolinguistics*, 435–53. New York: Holt Rinehart and Winston.

1989. *Language and Ethnicity in Minority Sociolinguistic Perspective.* Clevedon: Multilingual Matters.

1991. *Reversing Language Shift: Theoretical and Empirical Foundations of Assistance to Threatened Languages* (Multilingual Matters 76). Clevedon: Multilingual Matters.

1995. On the limits of ethnolinguistic democracy. In Tove Skuttnab-Kangas and Robert Phillipson (eds.), *Linguistic Human Rights. Overcoming Linguistic Discrimination*, 49–62. Berlin: Mouton de Gruyter.

1996. Maintaining languages: what works and what doesn't. In Gina Cantoni (ed.), *Stabilizing Indigenous Languages*, 165–75. Flagstaff, AZ: Northern Arizona University.

1997. *In Praise of the Beloved Language: A Comparative View of Positive Ethnolinguistic Consciousness.* Berlin: Mouton de Gruyter.

1999. Concluding remarks. In J. Fishman (ed.), *Handbook of Language and Ethnic Identity*, pp. 444–54. Oxford University Press.

2001b. Why is it so hard to save a threatened language? In Joshua Fishman (ed.), *Can threatened languages be saved?*, 1–22. Clevedon: Multilingual Matters.

2001c. If threatened languages can be saved, then can dead languages be revived? *Current Issues in Language Planning* **2**(2): 222–30.

2002. Diglossia and societal multilingualism: Dimensions of similarity and difference. *International Journal of the Sociology of Language* **157**: 93–100.

2006. *Do Not Leave Your Language Alone.* Mahwah, NJ: Lawrence Erlbaum.

Fishman, Joshua A. (ed.) 1974. *Advances in Language Planning.* The Hague: Mouton.

2001a. *Can Threatened Languages be Saved? Reversing Language Shift, Revisited: A 21st Century Perspective.* Clevedon: Multilingual Matters.

Florey, Margaret 2008. Language activism and the 'new linguistics': expanding opportunities for documenting endangered languages in Indonesia. In P. Austin (ed.), *Language Documentation and Description*, 5: 121–35. London: SOAS.

Florey, Margaret and Carol Genetti 2009. Consortium on training in language documentation and conservation. www.rnld.org/node/106 (20 February 2010).

Florey, Margaret and Nikolaus Himmelmann 2009. New directions in field linguistics: training strategies for language documentation in

Indonesia. In Margaret Florey (ed.), *Endangered Languages of Austronesia*, 121–40. Oxford University Press.

2010. New directions in field linguistics: training strategies for language documentation in Indonesia, in Margaret Florey (ed.) *Endangered Languages of Austronesia* 121–40. Oxford University Press.

Foley, William A. 1997. *Anthropological Linguistics.*Wiley-Blackwell.

2005. Personhood and linguistic identity, purism and variation. In Peter K. Austin (ed.), *Language Documentation and Description* vol. III, 157–80. London: SOAS.

Fox, Naomi P. 2005. Language contact on Walpole Island. MA Essay. Wayne State University.

Francis, Norbert and Jon Reyhner 2002. *Language and Literacy Teaching for Indigenous Education: A Bilingual Approach.* Clevedon: Multilingual Matters.

Frawley, William, Kenneth C. Hill and Pamela Munro (eds.) 2002. *Making Dictionaries. Preserving Indigenous Languages of the Americas.* Berkeley, CA: University of California Press.

Freeland, Jane and Donna Patrick (eds.) 2004. *Language Rights and Language Survival. Encounters.* Manchester: St Jerome Publishing.

Fulu, Mose 1997. *O le mafuaala o upu o taumafa. O le tusi faamatala upu o le gagana Samoa.* Apia, Samoa: Ministry of Youth, Sports and Culture.

Gainey, Jerry W. and Theraphan L. Thongkum 1977a. *Language Map of Thailand 1977.* Bangkok: Indigenous Languages of Thailand Research Project.

1977b. *Language Map of Thailand Handbook.* Bangkok: Indigenous Languages of Thailand Research Project.

Gal, Susan 1978. Peasant men can't get wives: language change and sex roles in a bilingual community. *Language in Society* 7: 1–16.

1979. *Language Shift: Social Determinants of Linguistic Change in Bilingual Austria.* New York: Academic Press.

1988. The political economy of code choice. In Monica Heller (ed.), *Codeswitching: Anthropological and Sociolinguistic Perspectives* (Contributions to the Sociology of Language 48), 245–64. Berlin: Mouton de Gruyter.

1989. Lexical innovation and loss: the use and value of restricted Hungarian. In Nancy C. Dorian (ed.), *Investigating Obsolescence: Studies in Language Contraction and Death*, 313–31. Cambridge University Press.

García, María Elena 2004. Rethinking bilingual education in Peru: inter-cultural politics, state policy, and indigenous rights. *International Journal of Bilingual Education and Bilingualism* 7(5): 348–67.

2005. *Making Indigenous Citizens: Identities, Education, and Mulicultural Development in Peru.* Stanford University Press.

Gardner, Nicholas, Maite Puigdevall Serralvo and Colin H. Williams 2000. Language revitalization in comparative context: Ireland, the Basque Country and Catalonia. In Colin Williams (ed.), *Language*

Revitalization: Policy and Planning in Wales, 311–61. Cardiff: University of Wales Press.

Gardner, Stelómethet Ethel B. 2005. Designing an e-master–apprentice pedagogy research for critically endangered languages. Ms.

Garrett, Andrew 2004. Structure, context, and community in language documentation: the new look of linguistic methodology [Workshop held by the Department of Linguistics, University of California, Berkeley, 19 November 2005].

Garrett, Paul B. 2006. Contact languages as 'endangered' languages: what is there to lose? *Journal of Pidgin and Creole Languages* **21**(1): 175–90.

Garrett, Peter, Nikolas Coupland and Angie Williams 2003. *Investigating Language Attitudes: Social Meanings of Dialect, Ethnicity and Performance.* Cardiff: University of Wales Press.

Gearing, Fred, Robert McC. Netting and Lisa R. Peattie (eds.) 1960. *Documentary History of the Fox Project.* Chicago: University of Chicago Department of Anthropology.

Geertz, Clifford 1973. *The Interpretation of Cultures: Selected Essays.* Basic Books.

Genetti, Carol and Rebekka Siemens 2009. InField 2008: Evaluations, recommendations, impacts. Paper presented at 1st International Conference on Language Documentation and Conservation (ICLDC). University of Hawai'i, Manoa.

Gentner, Dedre and Susan Goldin-Meadow 2003. *Language in Mind: Advances in the Study of Language and Thought.* Cambridge MA: MIT Press.

Gibson, Joel 2007. Indigenous school plan criticised. *Sydney Morning Herald*, 26 May. www.smh.com.au/news/national/indigenous-school-plan-cri ticised/2007/05/25/1179601669092.html.

Giddens, Anthony 1979. *Central Problems in Social Theory: Action, Structure and Contradiction in Social Analysis.* Macmillan.
    1984. *The Constitution of Society: Outline of the Theory of Structuration.* Cambridge: Polity Press.

Giles, Howard and Nikolas Coupland 1991. *Language: Contexts and Consequences* (Mapping Social Psychology). Milton Keynes: Open University Press.

Giles, Howard, Richard Y. Bourhis and Donald M. Taylor 1977. Towards a theory of language in ethnic group relations. In Howard Giles (ed.), *Language, Ethnicity and Intergroup Relations* (European Monographs in Social Psychology 13), 307–48. London: Academic Press.

Giles, Howard, Nikolas Coupland and Justine Coupland 1991. Accommodation theory: Communication, context, and conse-quence. In Howard Giles, Justine Coupland and Nikolas Coupland (eds.), *Contexts of Accommodation: Developments in Applied Sociolinguistics* (Studies in Emotion and Social Interaction), 1–68. Cambridge University Press.

Gill, Saran Kaur 2005. Language policy in Malaysia: reversing direction. *Language Policy*, **4**(3): 241–60.

Ginsburg, Faye and Fred Myers 2006. A History of Aboriginal futures. *Critique of Anthropology* **26**: 27–45.

Gippert, Jost 2006. Linguistic documentation and the encoding of textual materials. In Jost Gippert, Nikolaus P. Himmelmann and Ulrike Mosel (eds.), *Essentials of Language Documentation* (Trends in Linguistics: Studies and Monographs 178), 337–61. Berlin: Mouton de Gruyter.

Gippert, Jost, Nikolaus P. Himmelmann and Ulrike Mosel (eds.) 2006. *Essentials of Language Documentation* (Trends in Linguistics: Studies and Monographs 178). Berlin: Walter de Gruyter.

Goddard, Cliff 2001. Lexico-semantic universals. *Linguistic Typology* **5**: 1–65.

2002. Ethnosyntax, ethnopragmatics, sign-functions, and culture. In Nick Enfield (ed.), *Ethnosyntax*, 52–73. Oxford University Press.

2006a. *Ethnopragmatics: Understanding Discourse in Cultural Context*. Berlin: Mouton de Gruyter.

2006b. Ethnopragmatics: a new paradigm. In Cliff Goddard (ed.), *Ethnopragmatics*, 1–29. Berlin: Mouton de Gruyter.

2007. A response to N. J. Enfield's review of *Ethnopragmatics* (Goddard, ed. 2006). Intercultural Pragmatics 4(4): 531–8.

Goddard, Ives 1994. *Leonard Bloomfield's Fox Lexicon*. Winnipeg: Algonquian and Iroquoian Linguistics.

Golla, Victor K. 2001. What does it mean for a language to survive? Some thoughts on the (not-so-simple) future of small languages. In Osamu Sakiyama (ed.), *Lectures on Endangered Languages: 2 – From the Kyoto Conference 2000 – (ELPR Publication Series C002)*, 171–7. Tokyo: ELPR.

González, Roseann Dueñas, with Melis Ildikó 2001. *Language Ideologies: Critical Perspectives on the Official English Movement*, vol. I: Education and the Social Implications of Official Language. Urbana, IL: National Council of Teachers of English. Mahwah, NJ: Lawrence Erlbaum Associates.

Good, Jeff 2002. A gentle introduction to metadata. Open Language Archives Community. www.language-archives.org/documents/gentle-intro.html (12 February 2010).

Goodenough, Ward 1956. Componental analysis and the study of meaning. *Language* 32: 195–216.

1957. Cultural anthropology and linguistics. In Paul Garvin (ed.), *Report on the Seventh Annual Georgetown Roundtable Meeting in Linguistics and Language Study*, 167–73. Georgetown University Monograph Series on Language and Linguistics 9. Georgetown University, Washington D. C.

1970. *Description and Comparison in Cultural Anthropology*. Chicago: Aldine.

Goodwin, Charles and John Heritage 1990. Conversational Analysis. *Annual Review of Anthropology*, **19**: 283–307.

Gordon, Raymond G. (ed.) 2005. *Ethnologue. Languages of the world*. 15th edn. Dallas: SIL International. www.ethnologue.com/15/show_country.asp?name=CN.

Graham, Laura R. 2002. How should an Indian speak? Amazonian Indians and the symbolic politics of language in the global public sphere. In Kay B. Warren and Jean E. Jackson (eds.), *Indigenous Movements, Self-Representation, and the State in Latin America*, 181–228. Austin: University of Texas Press.

Greenberg, Joseph H. 1966 [1963]. Some universals of grammar with particular reference to the order of meaningful elements. In Joseph H. Greenberg (ed.), *Universals of Language*, 2nd edn., 73–113. Cambridge, MA: MIT Press.

1978. *Universals of Human Language*. Stanford University Press.

Greenberg, Robert D. 2004. *Language and Identity in the Balkans: Serbo-Croatian and Its Disintegration*. Oxford University Press.

Grenoble, Lenore A. 2000. Morphosyntactic change: the impact of Russian on Evenki. In Dicky G. Gilbers, John Nerbonne and Jos Schaeken (eds.), *Languages in Contact* (Studies in Slavic and General Linguistics 28), 105–20. Amsterdam: Rodopi.

2009a. 'Conflicting ideologies and beliefs in the field'. Paper presented at ELAP Workshop on Beliefs and Ideology on Endangered Languages, SOAS, London, 27th February 2009.

2009b. Linguistic cages and the limits of linguists. In Jon Reyhner and Louise Lockard (eds.), *Indigenous Language Revitalization: Encouragement, Guidance and Lessons Learned*, 61–9. Flagstaff, AZ: Northern Arizona University, College of Education. jan.ucc.nau.edu/~jar/books.html (26 January 2010).

Grenoble, Lenore A. and Lindsay J. Whaley 1998. Toward a typology of language endangerment. In Lenore Grenoble and Lindsay Whaley (eds.), *Endangered Languages: Current Issues and Future Prospects*, 22–54. Cambridge University Press.

2005. Review of *Language Endangerment and Language Maintenance*, ed. by David Bradley and Maya Bradley, and *Language Death and Language Maintenance*, ed. by Mark Janse and Sijmen Tol. *Language* **81**(4): 965–74.

2006. *Saving Languages: An Introduction to Language Revitalization*. Cambridge University Press.

Grenoble, Lenore, Keren Rice and Norvin Richards 2008. The role of the linguist in language maintenance and revitalization: documentation, training and materials development. In Wayne Harbert (ed.), *Language and Poverty*, 183–201. Clevedon: Multilingual Matters.

Greymorning, Stephen 2001. Reflections on the Arapaho language project or, when Bambi spoke Arapaho and other tales of Arapaho language revitalization efforts. In Leanne Hinton and Ken Hale (eds.), *The Green Book of Language Revitalization in Practice*, 287–97. San Diego, CA: Academic Press.

Grierson, George Abraham 1903–1928. *Linguistic Survey of India*. Calcutta, India: Office of the Superintendent of Government Printing.

Grillo, Ralph 1989. *Dominant Languages: Language and Hierarchy in Britain and France*. Cambridge University Press.

Grimes, Barbara F. (ed.) 1992. *Ethnologue. Languages of the World*. 12th edn. Dallas: SIL International.

Grimes, Barbara F. and Joseph E. Grimes (eds.) 2000. *Ethnologue: Languages of the World*. 14th edn. Dallas, TX: SIL International.

Grimes, Joseph E. 2002. Lexical functions as a heuristic for Huichol. In William Frawley, Kenneth C. Hill and Pamela Munro (eds.), *Making Dictionaries. Preserving Indigenous Languages of the Americas*, 70–85. Berkeley: University of California Press.

Grin, François 1989. The economic approach to minority languages. In D. Gorter, J. F. Hoekstra, L. G. Jansma and J. Ytsma (eds.), *Fourth International Conference on Minority Languages*, 31–48. Clevedon: Multilingual Matters.

　1992. Towards a threshold theory of minority language survival. *Kyklos* **45**: 69–97.

　1994. Combining immigrant and autochthonous language rights: a territorial approach to multilingualism. In T. Skutnabb-Kangas, R. Phillipson and M. Rannut (eds.), *Linguistic Human Rights: Overcoming Linguistic Discrimination*, 31–48. Berlin: Mouton de Gruyter.

　1999. Market forces, language spread and linguistic diversity. In Miklós Kontra, Robert Phillipson, Tove Skutnabb-Kangas and Tibor Várady (eds.), *Language: A Right and a Resource. Approaching Linguistic Human Rights*, 169–86. Budapest: Central European Press.

　2007. Economics and language policy. In Marlis Hellinger and Anne Pauwels (eds.), *Handbook of Language and Communication: Diversity and Change*, 271–97. Berlin: Mouton de Gruyter.

Grinevald, Colette 1997. Language contact and language degeneration. In Florian Coulmas (ed.), *The Handbook of Sociolinguistics*, 257–70. Oxford: Blackwell.

　2001. Encounters at the brink: Linguistic fieldwork among speakers of endangered languages. In Osamu Sakiyama and Fubito Endo (eds.), *Lectures on Endangered Languages 2: From Kyoto Conference 2000* (Endangered Languages of the Pacific Rim Series C002), 285–313. Kyoto: Endangered Languages of the Pacific Rim.

　2002. Linguistique et langues mayas du Guatemala. In J. Landaburu (ed.), *MésoAmérique, Caraïbes, Amazonie. Faits de Langues*, 17–25.

2003. Speakers and documentation of endangered languages. In Peter K. Austin (ed.), *Language Documentation and Description*, vol. 1, 52–72. London: SOAS.

2005. Why Rama and not Rama Cay Creole? In Peter K. Austin (ed.), *Language Documentation and Description*, Vol. III, 196–224. London: SOAS.

2007. Encounters at the brink: linguistic fieldwork among speakers of endangered languages. In O. Miyaoka, O. Sakiyama and M. Krauss (eds.), *The Vanishing Languages of the Pacific Rim*, 36–76. Oxford University Press.

Grivelet, Stéphane 2001. Introduction. *International Journal for the Society of Language* 150: 1–10.

Grosjean, François 2008. *Studying Bilinguals* (Oxford Linguistics). Oxford University Press.

Grounds, Richard A. 2007. Documentation or implementation, *Cultural Survival Quarterly* **31**(2). www.culturalsurvival.org/publications/cultural-survival-quarterly/richard-grounds/documentation-or-implementation (19 February 2010).

Guérin, Valérie and Sébatien Lacrampe 2007. Review of LexiquePro. *Language Documentation and Conservation* **1**: 293–300.

Gumperz, John J. 1962. Types of linguistic communities, *Anthropological Linguistics* **4**(1): 28–40.

1964. Linguistic and social interaction in two communities. *American Anthropologist* **66**(6): 137–53.

1968. The speech community. In David L. Sills (ed.), *International Encyclopedia of the Social Sciences* Vol. IX, 381–6. New York: The Macmillan Company.

1982. *Discourse Strategies* (Studies in Interactional Sociolinguistics 1). Cambridge University Press.

Gumperz, John J. and Robert Wilson 1971. Convergence and creolization: a case from the Indo-Aryan/Dravidian border in India. In Dell Hymes (ed.), *Pidginization and Creolization of Languages*, 151–67. Cambridge University Press.

Gupta, Akhil, and James Ferguson (eds.) 1997. *Anthropological Locations: Boundaries and Grounds of a Field Science*. Berkeley: University of California Press.

Haarmann, Harald 1984. Sprachplanung und Prestigeplanung [Language Planning and Prestige Planning]. *Europa Ethnica* **41**: 81–9.

1990. Language planning in the light of a general theory of language: a methodological framework. *International Journal of the Sociology of Language* **86**: 103–26.

1999. History. In Joshua Fishman (ed.), *Handbook of Language and Ethnic Identity*, 60–76. Oxford University Press.

Haig, Geoffrey 2001. Linguistic diffusion in present-day East Anatolia: from top to bottom. In Alexandra Y. Aikhenvald and R. M. W. Dixon (eds.), *Areal Diffusion and Genetic Inheritance: Problems in Comparative Linguistics* (Oxford Linguistics), 195–224. Oxford University Press.

Hale, Kenneth 1965. On the use of informants in field-work. *Canadian Journal of Linguistics* **10**(2,3): 108–19.

1966. Kinship reflections in syntax: Some Australian languages. *Word* **22**: 318–24.

1971. A note on a Walbiri tradition of antonymy. In Danny D. Steinberg and Leon A. Jacobovits (eds.), *Semantics: An Interdisciplinary Reader in Philosophy, Linguistics and Psychology*, 472–82. Cambridge University Press.

1975. Gaps in grammar and culture. In M. Dale Kinkade, Kenneth L. Hale and Oswald Werner (eds.), *Linguistics and Anthropology: In Honor of C. F. Voegelin*, 295–315. Lisse: The Peter de Ridder Press.

1983. Warlpiri and the grammar of non-configurational languages, *Natural Language and Linguistic Theory* **1**(1): 5–47.

1992. Language endangerment and the human value of linguistic diversity, *Language* **68**(1): 35–42.

1998. On endangered languages and the importance of linguistic diversity. In Lenore Grenoble and Lindsay J. Whaley (eds.), *Endangered Languages*, 192–216. Cambridge University Press.

2001. Ulwa (Southern Sumu): the beginnings of a language research project. In Paul Newman and Martha Ratliff (eds.), *Linguistic Fieldwork*, 76–101. Cambridge University Press.

Hale, Ken, Michael Krauss, Lucille J. Watahomigie, *et al.* 1992. Endangered languages. *Language* **68**(1): 1–42.

Hanks, William F. 1987. Discourse genres in a theory of practice. *American Ethnologist*, **14**(4): 668–92.

1996. Language and communicative practices. *Westview Press*.

2009. Fieldwork on deixis. *Journal of Pragmatics* **41**: 10–24.

Hargus, Sharon 2007. Design issues in Athabaskan dictionaries. Paper presented at Athabascan/Dene Languages Conference, Cold Lake, Alberta.

Harlow, Ray 2007. *Māori: A Linguistic Introduction*. Cambridge University Press.

Harlow, Stephen and David Bradley 1994. East and south east Asia. In Ronald E. Asher and Christopher J. Moseley (eds.), *Atlas of the World's Languages*, 1st edn., 157–92. London: Routledge.

Harrington, John P. 1907–1959. Papers. Smithsonian Institution National Anthropological Archives.

Harris, John W. 1991. Kriol – the creation of a new language. In Suzanne Romaine (ed.), *Language in Australia*, 195–203. Cambridge University Press.

1993. Losing and gaining a language: the story of Kriol in the Northern Territory. In Michael Walsh and Colin Wallop (eds.), *Language and Culture in Aboriginal Australia*, 145–54. Canberra: Aboriginal Studies Press.

Harris, Judith Rich 1998. *The Nurture Assumption: Why Children Turn out the Way they Do*. New York: Free Press.

Harris, Marvin 1999. *Theories of Culture in Postmodern Times*. Lanham, MD: Altamira Press.

Harrison, K. David 2005. Ethnographically informed language documentation. In Peter K. Austin (ed.), *Language Documentation and Description*, vol. 3, 22–41. London: SOAS.

   2007. *When Languages Die: The Extinction of the World's Languages and the Erosion of Human Knowledge*. Oxford University Press.

Harshav, Benjamin 1993. *Language in Time of Revolution*. Berkeley: University of California Press.

Haspelmath, Martin, Matthew S. Dryer, David Gil, and Bernard Comrie 2005. *The World Atlas of Language Structures*. Oxford University Press.

Haude, Katharina 2006. *A Grammar of Movima*. Zetten, NL: Manta.

Haugen, Einar 1950. The analysis of linguistic borrowing. *Language* **26**(2): 210–31.

   1966. *Language Conflict and Language Planning: The Case of Modern Norwegian*. Cambridge, MA: Harvard University Press.

   1971. The ecology of language. *The Linguistic Reporter, Supplement* **25**: 19–26.

   1972. *The Ecology of Language: Essays by Einar Haugen*. Stanford University Press.

Haviland, John B. 2005. Directional precision in Zinacantec deictic gestures: (cognitive) preconditions of talk about space. *Intellectica* 2005 (2–3): 25–54.

   2006. Documenting lexical knowledge. In Jost Gippert, Nikolaus Himmelmann and Ulrike Mosel (eds.), *Essentials of Language Documentation*, 129–62. Berlin: Mouton de Gruyter.

Hayden, Corinne P. 2003. *When Nature Goes Public: The Making and Unmaking of Bioprospecting in Mexico*. Princeton University Press.

Hearne, Joanne. 2009. Indigenous animation: educational programming, narrative interventions and children's culture. In Pamela Wilson and Michelle Stewart (eds.), *Global Indigenous Media: Cultures, Poetics and Politics*, 91–108. London: Duke University Press.

Heath, Jeffrey 1978. *Linguistic Diffusion in Arnhem Land* (Research and Regional Studies 13). Canberra: Australian Institute of Aboriginal Studies.

   1984. Language contact and language change. *Annual Review of Anthropology* **13**: 367–84.

   1985. Discourse in the field: clause structure in Ngandi. In Johanna Nichols and Anthony C. Woodbury (eds.), *Grammar Inside and Outside the Clause: Some Approaches to Theory from the Field*, 89–110. Cambridge University Press.

Heine, Bernd and Tania Kuteva 2008. Constraints on contact-induced linguistic change. *Journal of Language Contact* (Thema) **2**: 57–90.

Heinrich, Patrick 2004. Language planning and language ideology in the Ryukyu Islands. *Language Policy* **3**: 153–79.

Heller, Monica 2003. Globalization, the new economy, and the commodification of language and identity. *Journal of Sociolinguistics* **7**(4): 473–92.

Heller-Roazen, Daniel 2005. *Echolalias*. New York: Zone Books.

Henderson, John and David Nash (eds.) 2002. *Language in Native Title*. Canberra: Aboriginal Studies Press.

Higgins, Christina 2007. Battling HIV Bongo Flava: advocating for Tanzanian youth. Paper presented at the 6th International Symposium on Bilingualism, Hamburg.

Hill, Jane. H. 1978. Language death, language contact, and language evolution. In W. C. McCormack and S. A. Wurm (eds.), *Approaches to Language: Anthropological Issues*, 45–78. The Hague: Mouton.

1983. Language death in Uto-Aztecan. *International Journal of American Linguistics*. **49**(3): 258–76.

2001. What is lost when names are forgotten. In G. Sanga and G. Ortalli (eds.), *Nature Knowledge: Ethnoscience, Cognition, and Utility*, 161–84. Oxford: Berghahn Books.

2002. 'Expert rhetorics' in advocacy for endangered languages: who is listening, and what do they hear? *Journal of Linguistic Anthropology* **12**(2): 119–33.

2006. The ethnography of language and language documentation. In Jost Gippert, Nikolaus P. Himmelmann and Ulrike Mosel (eds.), *Essentials of Language Documentation* (Trends in Linguistics: Studies and Monographs 178), 113–28. Berlin: Mouton de Gruyter.

Hill, Jane H. and Kenneth C. Hill 1986. *Speaking Mexicano: Dynamics of Syncretic Language in Central Mexico*. Tucson, AZ: University of Arizona Press.

Hill, Kenneth C. 2002. On publishing the *Hopi* dictionary. In William Frawley, Kenneth C. Hill and Pamela Munro (eds.), *Making Dictionaries. Preserving Indigenous Languages of the Americas*, 299–311, Berkeley: University of California Press.

Hill, Richard and Stephen May 2010. Exploring biliteracy in Māori-medium education: an ethnographic perspective. In Teresa L. McCarty (ed.), *Ethnography and Language Policy*, New York: Routledge.

Himmelmann, Nikolaus P. 1998. Documentary and descriptive linguistics. *Linguistics* **36**(1): 161–95.

2002. Documentary and descriptive linguistics (full version). In Osamu Sakiyama and Fubito Endo (eds.), *Lectures on Endangered Languages 5*. Kyoto: Endangered Languages of the Pacific Rim.

2006a. Language documentation: what is it and what is it good for? In Jost Gippert, Nikolaus P. Himmelmann and Ulrike Mosel (eds.), *Essentials of Language Documentation* (Trends in Linguistics: Studies and Monographs 178), 1–30. Berlin: Mouton de Gruyter.

2006b. The challenges of segmenting spoken language. In Jost Gippert, Nikolaus P. Himmelmann and Ulrike Mosel (eds.), *Essentials of Language Documentation* (Trends in Linguistics: Studies and Monographs 178), 253–74. Berlin: Mouton de Gruyter.

2008. Reproduction and preservation of linguistic knowledge: linguistics' response to language endangerment. *Annual Review of Anthropology* 37: 337–50.

Hinton, Leanne 1994a. Ashes, ashes: John Peabody Harrington – then and now. In Leanne Hinton, *Flutes of Fire: Essays on California Indian Languages*, 195–210. Berkeley, CA: Heyday Press.

1994b. *Flutes of Fire*. Berkeley, CA: Heyday Books.

1998. Language loss and revitalization in California: overview. *International Journal of the Sociology of Language* **132:** 83–93.

2001a. Audio-video documentation. In Leanne Hinton and Ken Hale (eds.), *The Green Book of Language Revitalization in Practice*, 265–71. San Diego, CA: Academic Press.

2001b. The master–apprentice language learning program. In Leanne Hinton and Ken Hale (eds.), *The Green Book of Language Revitalization in Practice*, 217–26. San Diego, CA: Academic Press.

2001c. Sleeping languages. Can they be awakened? In Leanne Hinton and Ken Hale (eds.), *The Green Book of Language Revitalization in Practice*, 413–17. San Diego, CA: Academic Press.

2001d. The use of linguistics archives in language revitalization: the Native California language restoration workshop. In Leanne Hinton and Ken Hale (eds.), *The Green Book of Language Revitalization in Practice*, 419–24. San Diego, CA: Academic Press.

2002. Commentary: internal and external language advocacy. *Journal of Linguistic Anthropology* **12**(2): 150–6.

2004. The death and rebirth of Native American languages. In J. A. Argenters and R. McKenna Brown (eds.), *Endangered Languages and Linguistic Rights. On the Margin on Nations*, Proceedings of the Eighth FEL Conference, Barcelona, 19–24.

2008a. Language revitalization. In Garrick Bailey (ed.), Indians In Contemporary Society. Vol. II, *Handbook of North American Indians*, Vol. II *Indians in Contemporary Society*, 31–54. Washington, DC: Smithsonian Institution.

2008b. Orthography wars. ms.

Hinton, Leanne and Ken Hale (eds.) 2001. *The Green Book of Language Revitalization in Practice*. San Diego, CA: Academic Press.

Hinton, Leanne and William Weigel. 2002. A dictionary for whom? Tensions between academic and nonacademic functions of bilingual dictionaries. In William Frawley, Kenneth C. Hill and Pamela Munro (eds.), *Making Dictionaries. Preserving Indigenous Languages of the Americas*, 155–70. Berkeley: University of California Press.

Hinton, Leanne, Matt Vera, and Nancy Steele. 2002. *How to Keep your Language Alive: A Commonsense Approach to One-on-one Language Learning.* Berkeley, CA: Heyday Books.

Hirvonen, Vuokko 2008. 'Out on the fells, I feel like a Sámi': Is there linguistic and cultural equality in the Sámi school? In Nancy H. Hornberger (ed.), *Can Schools Save Indigenous Languages? Policy and Practice on Four Continents,* 15–41. New York: Palgrave Macmillan.

Hoffman, Katherine E. 2003. Emigration, gender and the burden of language preservation. In J. Blythe and R. McKenna Brown (eds.) *Maintaining the Links: Language Identity and the Land: Proceedings of the Foundation for Endangered Languages 7th conference,* 93–100. Bath: Foundation for Endangered Languages.

Hoijer, Harry 1933. Tonkawa: an Indian language of Texas. *Handbook of American Indian Languages,* vol. III, ed. by Franz Boas, i–x, 1–148. New York: Columbia University Press.

1946. Tonkawa. In Harry Hoijer (eds.) *Linguistic Structures of Native America,* 289–311. (Viking Fund Publications in Anthropology, 6.) New York: The Viking Fund.

Holdstock, Marshall and Jean Holdstock 1992. *Introduction to Conversational Beaver.* Charlie Lake, BC: Summer Institute of Linguistics.

Holm, John 1988. *Pidgins and Creoles I: Theory and Structure.* Cambridge University Press.

1989. *Pidgins and Creoles II: Reference Survey.* Cambridge University Press.

Holton, Gary, Andrea Berez and Sadie Williams. 2007. Building the Dena'ina language archive. In L. E. Dyson, M. Hendriks and S. Grant (eds.), *Information Technology and Indigenous Peoples,* 205–9. Hershey, Pennsylvania: Idea Group.

Hornberger, Nancy H. 1987. Literacy, language maintenance, and linguistic human rights: three telling tales. *International Journal of the Sociology of Language* **127**: 87–103.

2003. *Continua of Biliteracy: An Ecological Framework for Educational Policy.* Clevedon: Multilingual Matters.

2006. Frameworks and models in language policy and planning. In T. Ricento (ed.) *An Introduction to Language Policy: Theory and Method,* 24–41. Oxford: Blackwell.

Hornberger, Nancy H. (ed.) 1996. *Indigenous Literacies in the Americas: Language Planning from the Bottom Up.* Berlin: Mouton.

2008. *Can Schools Save Indigenous Languages? Policy and Practice on Four Continents.* Basingstoke: Palgrave Macmillan.

Hornberger, Nancy H. and Serafin M. Coronel-Molina 2004. Quechua language shift, maintenance, and revitalization in the Andes: the case for language planning. *International Journal of the Sociology of Language* **167**: 9–67.

Hornberger, Nancy H. and Kendall King 1996. Language revitalization in the Andes: can the schools reverse language shift? *Journal of Multilingual and Multicultural Development* **17**: 427–41.

2001. Reversing Quechua language shift in South America. In Joshua A. Fishman (ed.), *Can Threatened Languages be Saved?* 166–94. Clevedon, Multilingual Matters.

Hornberger, Nancy H. and Luis Enrique López 1998. Policy, possibility and paradox: indigenous multilingualism and education in Peru and Bolivia. In J. Cenoz and F. Genesee (eds.), *Beyond Bilingualism: Multilingualism and Multilingual Education*, pp. 206–42. Clevedon, Somerset: Multilingual Matters.

Hornsby, Michael 2008. The incongruence of the Breton linguistic landscape for young speakers of Breton, *Journal of Multilingual and Multicultural Development* **29**(2): 127–38.

Hourigan, Niamh 2002. New social movement theory and minority language media campaigns. In Toloy Miller (ed.) *Television: A Critical Reader*, 227–48. New York: Routledge.

2003. *Escaping the Global Village: Media, Language and Protest.* Lanham MD: Lexington Books.

Humboldt, Wilhelm von 1988[1836]. *On language: on the diversity of human language constructions and its influence on the mental development of the human species.* Cambridge University Press.

Humery-Dieng, Marie-Eve 2001. Le paradis, le mariage et la terre: des langues de l'écrit en milieu fuutanke (arabe, français et pulaar). *Cahier d'études africaines* **163–164**: 565–694.

2010. Multilinguisme et plurigraphie dans le Fuuta sénégalais: quelques outils d'analyse. In Friederike Lüpke and Mary Chambers (eds.), *Multilingualism and Language Contact in West Africa. Journal of Language Contact*, 205–27.

Hunn, Eugene 1982. The utilitarian factor in folk biological classification. *American Anthropologist* **84**(4): 830–47.

Hurston, Zora Neale 1935. *Mules and Men.* Philadelphia, PA: J. B. Lippincott.

Huson, Daniel H. 1998. SplitsTree: a program for analyzing and visualizing evolutionary data. *Bioinformatics* **14**(10): 68–73.

Hutchinson, Roger 2005. *A Waxing Moon: the Modern Gaelic Revival.* Edinburgh: Scottish Arts Council.

Hymes, Dell 1964. Introduction: towards ethnographies of speaking. *American Anthropologist* **66**(6): 1–34.

1967. Models of the interaction of language and social setting. *Journal of Social Issues* **23**(2): 8–38.

1972. Models of the interaction of language and social life. In John J. Gumperz and Dell Hymes (eds.), *Directions in Sociolinguistics: The Ethnography of Communication*, 35–71. New York: Holt, Rinehart and Winston.

1974a. *Foundations in Sociolinguistics: An Ethnographic Approach.* Philadelphia, PA: University of Pennsylvania Press.

1974b. Ways of speaking. In R. Bauman and J. Sherzer, *Explorations in the Ethnography of Speaking.* Cambridge University Press.

1977. *Foundations in Sociolinguistics.* London: Tavistock.

1981[1975]. Breakthrough into performance. collected in Dell Hymes (ed.), *'In Vain I Tried to Tell You': Essays in Native American Ethnopoetics,* 79–141. Reprint edition, with an new preface by the author. Lincoln: University of Nebraska Press.

1986. Models of the interaction of language and social life. In Dell Hymes and John J. Gumperz (eds.), *Directions in Sociolinguistics: The Ethnography of Communication.* Oxford: Blackwell.

IASA (International Association of Sound and Audiovisual Archives) 2005. The safeguarding of the audio heritage: ethics, principles and preservation strategy. Technical Committee, Standards, Recommended Practices and Strategies (IASA-TC 03). Version 3, December 2005. Online at www.iasa-web.org/downloads/publications/tc03_english.pdf.

INALI 2008. Catálogo de las lenguas indígenas nacionales: Variantes lingüísticas de México con sus autodenominaciones y referencias geoestadísticas: Secretaria de Educación Pública, Mexico.

Irvine, Judith T. 2001. 'Style' as distinctiveness: the culture and ideology of linguistic differentiation. In Penelope Eckert and John R. Rickford (eds.), *Style and Sociolinguistic Variation,* 21–43. Cambridge University Press.

Irvine, Judith T. and Susan Gal 2000. Language ideology and linguistic differentiation. In Paul V. Kroskrity (ed.), *Regimes of Language: Ideologies, Polities, and Identities* (School of American Research Advanced Seminar Series), 35–83. Oxford: James Currey.

Jacobs, Kaia'titahkhe Annette 1998. A chronology of Mohawk language instruction at Kahnawà:ke. In Lenore A. Grenoble and Lindsay J. Whaley (eds.), *Endangered languages: Language Loss and Community Response,* 117–23. Cambridge University Press.

Jaffe, Alexandra 2003. La polynomie dans une école bilingue corse: bilan et défis. *Marges linguistiques* (10): 1–19.

2008. Language ecologies and the meaning of diversity: Corsican bilingual education and the concept of 'polynomie'. In Nancy Hornberger (ed.), *Encyclopaedia of Language and Education.* vol. IX, 225–36. New York: Springer.

Jake, Janice L. and Carol Myers-Scotton 1997. Relating interlanguage to codeswitching: the composite matrix language. In Elizabeth Hughes, Mary Hughes and Annabel Greenhill (eds.), *21st Annual Boston University Conference on Language Development (BUCLD 21)* 319–30, Someville, MA: Cascadilla Press.

2003. The out-of-sight in codeswitching and related contact phenomena. In Lorenza Mondada and Simona P. Doehler (eds.), *Plurilinguisme,*

Mehrsprachigkeit, & Plurlilingualism, 221–33. Tübingen & Basel: A. Francke.

Jakobson, Roman 1968. Poetry of grammar and grammar of poetry. *Lingua* **21**: 597–609.

1971. Shifters, verbal categories and the Russian verb. In Roman Jakobson (ed.), *Word and Language*, 131–47. The Hague: Mouton.

1978[1942]. *Six Lectures on Sound and Meaning*. Cambridge, MA: MIT Press.

Jansma, Lammert Gosse 2000. Migration and language maintenance: Frisian cultural organizations outside Friesland. In Peter Wynne Thomas and Jayne Mathias (eds.), *Developing Minority Languages: Proceedings of the Fifth International Conference on Minority Languages*, 55–71. Cardiff: Gomer Press.

Jernudd, Björn, and Jiří V. Neustupný 1987. Language planning: for whom? In L. LaForge (ed.), *Proceedings of the international colloquium on Language Planning* 69–84. Québec, Canada: Presses de l'Université Laval.

Jocks, Christopher 1998. Living words and cartoon translations: Longhouse texts and the limitations of English. In Lenore A. Grenoble and Lindsay J. Whaley, (eds.), *Endangered Languages: Current Issues and Future Prospects*, 217–33. Cambridge University Press.

Johanson, Lars 2002. *Structural Factors in Turkic Language Contacts*. Richmond: Curzon.

Johns, Alana, and Irene Mazurkewich 2001. The role of the university in the training of native language teachers: Labrador. In Leanne Hinton and Ken Hale (eds.), *The Green Book of Language Revitalization in Practice* 355–66. New York: Academic Press.

Johnson, Heidi 2004. Language documentation and archiving, or how to build a better corpus. In Peter K. Austin (ed.), *Language Documentation and Description*, Vol. II, 140–53. London: SOAS.

Jones, Robert Owen 1993. The sociolinguistics of Welsh. In Martin Ball (ed.), *The Celtic Languages*, 536–605. London: Routledge.

Joseph, John Earl 1987. *Eloquence and Power: The Rise of Language Standards and Standard Languages*. Oxford: Blackwell.

2004. *Language and Identity: National, Ethnic, Religious*. Houndsmills, Basingstoke: Palgrave MacMillan.

Junyent, M. Carme 1999. El català: Una llengua en perill d'extinció? *Revista d'Igualada* **1**: 27–38.

Kaldor, Susan and Ian G. Malcolm 1991. Aboriginal English: an overview. In Suzanne Romaine (ed.), *Language in Australia*, 67–83. Cambridge University Press.

Kalish, M. 2005. Immersion multimedia for adult Chiricahua language learners. *New Review of Hypermedia and Multimedia* **11**(2): 181–203.

Kaplan, Robert B. and Richard B. Baldauf 1997. *Language Planning: From Practice to Theory*. Clevedon: Multilingual Matters.

2003. *Language and Language-in-Education Planning in the Pacific Basin.* Dordrecht: Kluwer.

Kapono, Eric 1995. Hawaiian language revitalisation and immersion education. *International Journal of the Sociology of Language* **112**: 121–35.

Karetu, Timoti S. 1994. Maori language rights in New Zealand. In T. Skutnabb-Kangas, R. Phillipson and M. Rannut (eds.), *Linguistic Human Rights: Overcoming Linguistic Discrimination*, 208–18. Berlin: Mouton de Gruyter.

Kari, James and Andrea Berez 2005. *Dach' Dena'inaq' Qeyegh Nuqelnixch': They tell about this in Dena'ina.* Anchorage: Alaska Native Heritage Center.

Kari, James and Gary Holton 2005. Dena'ina field recordings: Kenai Dialect. Fairbanks and Anchorage: Alaska Native Language Center and Alaska Native Heritage Center.

Karlström, Anna 2002. Spiritual materiality: heritage preservation in a Buddhist world? *Journal of Social Archaeology* **5**: 338–55.

Kaufman, Terrence, John Justeson and Roberto Zavala Maldonado 2001. *Project for the Documentation of the Languages of Mesoamerica (PDLMA).* Albany, NY: State University of New York. www.albany.edu/pdlma/ (25 January 2010).

Kay, Paul and Chad McDaniel 1978. The linguistic significance of the meanings of basic color terms. *Language* **54**(3): 610–46.

Keating, Elizabeth 1998. *Power Sharing: Language, Rank, Gender, and Social Space in Pohnpei, Micronesia.* Oxford University Press.

2001. The ethnography of communication. In P. Atkinson, A. Coffey, S. Delamont, J. Lofland, and L. Lofland, *Handbook of Ethnography*, 285–301. London: Sage Publications.

Keenan, Elinor Ochs 1976. The universality of conversational postulates. *Language in Society* **5**(1): 67–80.

Kelly-Holmes, Helen 2006. Multilingualism and commercial language practices on the internet. *Journal of Sociolinguistics* **10**(4): 507–19.

Kelly-Holmes, Helen and David Atkinson 2007. Minority language advertising: a profile of two Irish-language newspapers, *Journal of Multilingual and Multicultural Development* **28**(1): 34–50.

Kelly-Holmes, Helen, Máiréad Moriarty and Sari Pietikäinen 2009. Convergence and divergence in Basque, Irish and Sámi media language policing. *Language Policy* **8**(3): 227–42.

Kenner, Charmian 2003. Biliteracy benefits. *Literacy Today* **37**. www.literacytrust.org.uk/Pubs/kenner.html (1 March 2010).

Kerr, A. F. G. 1927. Two Lawa vocabularies. *Journal of the Siam Society* **21**(1): 53–63.

Keskitalo, Isak 1981. The status of the Sámi language. In E. Haugen, J. D. McClure and D. Thompson (eds.), *Minority Languages Today: A Selection from the Papers Read at the First Conference on Minority Languages at Glasgow University 8–13 September 1980*, 152–62. Edinburgh University Press.

Kibrik, Alexander E. 1977. *The Methodology of Field Linguistics*. The Hague, Paris: Mouton.

King, Jeanette 2000. Te Kōhanga Reo: Māori language revitalization. In Leanne Hinton and Ken Hale (eds.), *The Green Book of Language Revitalization in Practice*, 119–28. San Diego, CA: Academic Press.

King, Kendall A. 2001. *Language Revitalization Processes and Prospects: Quichua in the Ecuadorian Andes*. Clevedon: Multilingual Matters.

Kipp, Darrell 2000. Encouragement, guidance, insights, and lessons learned for Native language activists developing their own tribal language programs. Piegan Institute.

Kirshenblatt-Gimblett, Barbara 2006. World heritage and cultural economics. In Ivan Karp, Corinne A. Kratz, Lynn Szwaja and Tomás Ybarra-Frausto (eds.), *Museum Frictions: Public Cultures/Global Transformations*, 161–202. Durham: Duke University Press.

Kloss, Heinz 1968. Notes concerning a language-nation typology. In Joshua A. Fishman, Charles A. Ferguson and J. Das Gupta (eds.) *Language problems of developing nations*, 69–85. New York: Wiley.

Kloss, Heinz and Albert Verdoodt 1969. *Research Possibilities on Group Bilingualism: A Report*. Quebec: C.I.R.B.

Koepke, Wulf 1990. Johann Gottfried Herder: language, history, and the Enlightenment. Camden House.

Kontra, Miklos, Robert Phillipson, Tove Skutnabb-Kangas and Tibor Várady (eds.), 1999. *Language: A Right and a Resource: Approaches to Linguistic Human Rights*. Budapest: Central European University Press.

Korpela, Jukka n.d. *A Tutorial on Character Code Issues*. www.cs.tut.fi/~jkorpela/chars.html (15 June 2009).

Kramsch, Claire, and Anne Whiteside 2008. Language ecology in multilingual settings: towards a theory of symbolic competence. *Applied Linguistics* **29**(4): 655–71.

Krashen, Stephen 1997. Bilingualism and bilingual education: good for English, good for the bilingual, good for society, *American Language Review* **1**(2): 12–32.

Krashen, Stephen and Grace McField 2005. What works? Reviewing the latest evidence on bilingual education. *Language Learner* **1**(2): 7–10, 34.

Krauss, Michael E. 1980. *Alaska Native languages: Past, Present, and Future* (Alaska Native Language Center Research Papers 4). Fairbanks, AK: Alaska Native Language Center, University of Alaska Fairbanks.

   1992. The world's languages in crisis, *Language* **68**(1): 4–10.

   1997. The indigenous languages of the North: a report on their present state. In Hiroshi Shoji and Juha Janhunen (eds.), *Northern Minority Languages: Problems of Survival* (Senri Ethnological Studies 44), 1–34. Osaka: National Museum of Ethnology.

1998. The condition of Native North American languages: the need for realistic assessment and action. *International Journal of the Sociology of Language* **132**: 9–21.

2007. Classification and terminology for degrees of language endangerment. In Matthias Brenzinger (ed.), *Language Diversity Endangered* (Trends in Linguistics: Studies and Monographs 181), 1–8. Berlin: Mouton de Gruyter.

Kroeber, Theodora 1961. *Ishi in Two Worlds: A Biography of the Last Wild Indian in North America*. Berkeley: University of California Press.

Kroskrity, Paul V. 1978. Aspects of syntactic and semantic variation within the Arizona Tewa speech community. *Anthropological Linguistics* **20**(6): 235–57.

2000. *Regimes of Language: Ideologies, Polities, and Identities*. Oxford: James Currey.

2009. Language renewal as sites of language ideological struggle: the need for ideological clarification. In Jon Reyhner and Louise Lockard (eds.), *Indigenous Language Revitalization: Encouragement, Guidance, and Lessons Learned*, 71–83. Flagstaff, AZ: Northern Arizona University.

Kroskrity, Paul and Jennifer Reynolds 2001. On using multimedia in language renewal: observations on making the CD-ROM Taitaduhaan. In Leanne Hinton and Ken Hale (eds.), *The Green Book of Language Revitalization in Practice*, 317–29. San Diego: Academic Press.

Kroskrity, Paul, Rosalie Bethel and Jennifer Reynolds 2002. *Taitaduhaan: Western Mono Ways of Speaking*. Norman: University of Oklahoma Press.

Kutscher, Silvia 2008. The language of the Laz in Turkey: contact-induced change or gradual language loss? *Turkic Languages* **12**(1): 82–102.

Kutscher, Silvia and Nuran Sevim Genç 1998. *Ardeşeni na isinapinenpe – Ardeşen narrates: A Collection of Laz Spoken Texts with Glosses and Translations into English, German and Turkish* (Languages of the World/ Text Collections 14). Munich: Lincom Europa.

Kymlicka, Will and Alan Patten (eds.) 2003. *Language Rights and Political Theory*. Oxford University Press.

Labov, William 1966. *The Social Stratification of English in New York City*. Washington, DC: Center for Applied Linguistics.

1972. On the mechanism of sociolinguistic change. In *Sociolinguistic Patterns*, 160–182. University of Pennsylvania Press.

2008. Unendangered dialects, endangered people. In Kendall A. King, Natalie Schilling-Estes, Lyn Fogle, Jackie Lou Lia and Barbara Soukup (eds.), *Sustaining Linguistic Diversity: Endangered and Minority Languages and Language Varieties* (Georgetown University Round Table on Languages and Linguistics) 219–38. Washington DC: Georgetown University Press.

Ladefoged, Peter 1992. Another view of endangered languages. *Language* **68**(4): 809–11.

Ladefoged, Peter and Daniel Everett 1996. The status of phonetic rarities. *Language* **72**: 794–800.

Ladefoged, Peter and Ian Maddieson 1996. *The Sounds of the World's Languages*. Oxford: Blackwell.

Lakoff, George 1987. *Women, Fire, and Dangerous Things*. University of Chicago Press.

Langacker, Ronald 1987. *Foundations of Cognitive Grammar* vol. I: *Theoretical Prerequisites*. Stanford University Press.

   2002. A study in unified diversity: English and Mixtec locatives. In Nick Enfield (ed.), *Ethnosyntax*, 138–61. Oxford University Press.

Lanza, Elizabeth and Bente Ailin Svendsen 2007. Tell me who your friends are and I might be able to tell you what language(s) you speak: social network analysis, multilingualism, and identity. *International Journal of Bilingualism* **11**: 275–300.

Lastra, Yolanda 2001. Otomí language shift and some recent efforts to reverse it. in Joshua Fishman (ed.), *Can Threatened Languages Be Saved?* 142–65. Clevedon: Multilingual Matters.

Latour, Bruno 2005. *Reassembling the Social: An Introduction to Actor-Network Theory*. Oxford University Press.

Laughren, Mary 2000. Australian Aboriginal languages: their contemporary status and functions. *The Handbook of Australian Languages* vol V, 1–32. Oxford University Press.

LDOCE 2005. *Longman Dictionary of Contemporary English*. 4th edn. Harlow: Pearson Education.

Le Page, Robert B. and Andrée Tabouret-Keller 1985. *Acts of Identity: Creole-based Approaches to Language and Ethnicity*. Cambridge University Press.

Leach, Edmund 1974. *Lévi-Strauss*. Second edition. London: Fontana.

Lee, Dorothy 1944. Categories of the generic and particular in Wintu. *American Anthropologist* **46**: 362–9.

Lee, Jennifer R. 1987. *Tiwi Today: A Study of Language Change in a Contact Situation* (Pacific Linguistics C96). Canberra: Australian National University.

Lee, Tiffany 2007. If they want Navajo to be learned, then they should require it in all schools: Navajo teenagers' experiences, choices, and demands regarding Navajo language. *Wicazo SA Review* **22**(1): 7–33.

Lee, Tiffany and D. McLaughlin 2001. Reversing Navajo language shift, revisited. In Joshua A. Fishman (ed.), *Can Threatened Languages be Saved? Reversing Language Shift, Revisited: A 21st Century Perspective* (Multilingual Matters 116), 23–43. Clevedon: Multilingual Matters.

Lefebvre, Claire 1998. *Creole Genesis and the Acquisition of Grammar: The Case of Haitian Creole* (Cambridge Studies in Linguistics 88). Cambridge University Press.

2008. Relabelling: a major process in language contact, *Journal of Language Contact* (Thema) **2**: 91–111.

Lehmann, Christian 2001. Language documentation: a program. In Walter Bisang (ed.), *Aspects of Typology and Universals* (Studia Typologica 1), 83–97. Berlin: Akademie Verlag.

Leitner, G. 1996. The sociolinguistics of communication media. In Florian Coulmas (ed.), *The Handbook of Sociolinguistics*, 187–204. Cambridge: Blackwell Publishing.

Leonard, Wesley 2007. Miami language reclamation in the home: a case study. University of California: Berkeley Ph. D. dissertation.

Leonard, Wesley Y. and Scott M. Shoemaker Forthcoming. 'I heart this camp'. Participant perspectives within the story of Miami youth camps. In Karl S. Hele and Regna Darnell (eds.), Proceedings of the 40th annual Algonquian Conference. London: The University of Western Ontario.

Lepsius, Carl R. 1863. *Standard Alphabet for Reducing Unwritten and Foreign Graphic Systems to a Uniform Orthography in European Letters*. London: Williams & Norgate.

Letsholo, Rose 2009. Language maintenance or shift? Attitudes of Bakalanga youth towards their mother tongue. *International Journal of Bilingual Education and Bilingualism* 12(5): 581–95.

Levenshtein, Vladimir 1966. Binary codes capable of correcting deletions, insertions and reversals. *Soviet Physics Doklady* **10**: 707–10.

Levinson, Paul 1999. *Digital McLuhan*. London: Routledge.

Levinson, Stephen C. 1983. *Pragmatics* (Cambridge Textbooks in Linguistics). Cambridge University Press.

2000. Yeli Dnye and the theory of basic color terms. *Journal of Linguistic Anthropology* **10**(1): 3–55.

Levinson, Stephen and Sergio Meira 2003. 'Natural concepts' in the spatial topological domain – adpositional meanings in cross-linguistic perspective. *Language* **79**(3): 485–516.

Lévi-Strauss, Claude 1958. *Anthropologie structurale*. Paris: Plon.

Lewis, M. Paul (ed.) 2009. *Ethnologue: Languages of the World*. 16th edn. Dallas, TX: SIL International. www.ethnologue.com (8 January 2010).

Liberman, Mark 2006. The problems of scale in language documentation. Talk. Texas Linguistics Society X Conference: Computational Linguistics for Less-Studied Languages, University of Texas at Austin. Available at uts.cc.utexas.edu/~tls/2006tls/abstracts/pdfs/liberman.pdf (abstract only).

Lieb, Hans-Heinrich and Sebastian Drude 2000. Advanced glossing: a language documentation format [DOBES internal Working Paper]. www.mpi.nl/DOBES/documents/Advanced-Glossing1.pdf (19 January 2010).

Lindblom, Björn, and Ian Maddieson 1988. Phonetic universals in consonant systems. In Larry Hyman and Charles Li (eds.), *Language,*

Speech, and Mind: Studies in Honour of Victoria A. Fromkin, 62–78. London: Routledge.

Lindgren, Anna-Riitta 1984. What can we do when a language is dying? *Journal of Multilingual and Multicultural Development* **5**: 293–300.

Lindstrom, Lamont 2009. Grammars of the South Pacific. *Reviews in Anthropology* **38**(1): 88–109.

Linguistic Society of America 1994. The need for the documentation of linguistic diversity. lsadc.org/info/lsa-res-diverse.cfm.

2005. Statement on Digital Repositories. www.lsadc.org/info/pdf_files/bulletin/June-08-Bulletin.pdf

Littlebear, Richard 1996. Preface. In Gina Cantoni (ed.), *Stabilizing indigenous Languages*, xiii–xv. Flagstaff: Northern Arizona University Center for Excellence in Education.

López, Luis Enrique and Inge Sichra (online). Intercultural bilingual education among indigenous peoples in Latin America, 1–14. La Paz: PROEIB-Andes. fundacion.proeibandes.org/bvirtual/docs/indigenous_bilingual_education.pdf (25 October 2009).

Lösch, Hellmut 2000. *Die französichen Varietäten auf den Kanalinseln in Vergangeneit, Gegenwart und Zukunft*. Vienna: Edition Praesens.

Loukotka, Čestemír 1968. *Classification of South American Indian Languages* (Reference Series 7). Los Angeles: University of California, Latin American Center.

Lounsbury, Floyd 1956. A semantic analysis of Pawnee kinship usage. *Language* **39**: 170–210.

Low, Bronwen, Mela Sarkar and Lise Winer 2009. 'Ch'us mon proper Bescherelle': challenges from the hip-hop nation to the Quebec nation, Journal of Sociolinguistics **13**(1): 59–82.

Lucy, John A. 1992. *Language Diversity and Thought: A Reformulation of the Linguistic Relativity Hypothesis* (Studies in the Social and Cultural Foundations of Language 12). Cambridge University Press.

1993. *Reflexive Language: Reported Speech and Metapragmatics*. Cambridge University Press.

1997. The linguistics of 'color'. In C. L. Hardin and Luisa Maffi (eds.), *Color categories in thought and language*, 320–46. New York: Cambridge University Press.

Lüpke, Friederike 2004. Language planning in West Africa – who writes the script? *Language Documentation and Description* **2**: 90–107.

2005. A grammar of Jalonke argument structure. PhD thesis. Radboud Universiteit Nijmegen.

Lüpke, Friederike, Erhard F. K. Voeltz and Adama Camara 2000. Jalonke. Syllabaire en langue jalonke. Nijmegen: Max Planck Institute for Psycholinguistics.

Maass, Anne, and Aurore Russo 2003. Directional bias in the mental representation of spatial events: nature or culture? *Psychological Science* **14**: 296–301.

MacAlpine, Donna Miller, Alice Taff, Sharon Hargus, *et al.* 2007. Deg xinag aɫixi ni'elyoy: deg xinag Learners' Dictionary.

Macaulay, Monica 2004. Training linguistics students for the realities of fieldwork. *Anthropological Linguistics* **46**(2): 194–209.

Mackey, William F. 1989. Determining the status and function of languages in multinational societies. In Ulrich Ammon (ed.), *Status and Function of Languages and Language Varieties*, 3–20. Berlin: Walter de Gruyter.

    2001 [1980]. The ecology of language shift. In Alwin Fill and Peter Mühlhäusler (eds), *The Ecolinguistics Reader*, 67–74. London: Continuum.

MacKinnon, Kenneth 2000. Occupational class, age, and gender in the Gaelic speech community from census data. In Peter Wynn Thomas and Jayne Mathias (eds.), *Developing Minority Languages: Proceedings of the Fifth International Conference on Minority Languages*, 72–98. Cardiff: Gomer Press.

Maddieson, Ian 1984. *Patterns of Sounds.* Cambridge University Press.

    2001. Phonetic fieldwork. In Paul Newman and Martha Ratliff (eds.), *Linguistic Fieldwork*, 211–29. Cambridge University Press.

Maffi, Luisa 2003. The 'business' of language endangerment: saving languages or helping people keep them alive? In H. Tonkin and T. G. Reagan (eds.), *Language in the Twenty-first Century: Selected Papers of the Millennial Conferences of the Center for Research and Documentation on World Language Problems*, 67–86. Amsterdam: John Benjamins.

Maffi, Luisa (ed.) 2001. *On Biocultural Diversity: Linking Language, Knowledge and the Environment.* London: Smithsonian Institution Press.

Magga, Ole Henrik and Tove Skutnabb-Kangas 2003. Life or death for languages and human beings: experiences from Saamiland. In Leena Huss, Antoinette C. Grima and Kendall A. King (eds.), *Transcending Monolingualism: Linguistic Revitalization in Education*, 35–52. Lisse: Swets and Zeitlinger.

Mahapatra, B. P. 1989. The problems in learning minority languages with special reference to tribal languages. *International Journal of the Sociology of Language* **75**: 73–8.

Makoni, Sinfree and Alastair Pennycook (eds.) 2006. *Disinventing and Reconstituting Languages.* Clevedon: Multilingual Matters.

Makoni, Sinfree, Jamina Brutt-Griffler and Pedzisai Mashiri 2007. The use of 'indigenous' and urban vernaculars in Zimbabwe. *Language in Society* **36**(1): 25–49.

Malinowski, Bronislaw 1935. *Coral Gardens and their Magic: A Study of the Methods of Tilling the Soil and of Agricultural Rites in the Trobriand Islands.* New York: American Book Company.

    1939. The group and the individual in functional analysis. *American Journal of Sociology* **44**: 938–44.

Mandelbaum, David G. 1949. *Selected Writings of Edward Sapir.* Berkeley, CA: University of California Press.

Marcellesi, Jean-Baptiste 1984. La définition des langues en domaine romane: les enseignements à tirer de la situation corse. Paper presented at the Actes du XVIIème Congrès International de Linguistique et de Philologie Romanes, 29 August – 3 September 1983, Aix en Provence: Université de Provence.

1989. Corse et théorie sociolinguistique: reflets croisés. In G. Ravis-Giordani (ed.), *L'île miroir.* Ajaccio: La Marge.

Marcus, George E. and Michael M. J. Fischer, (eds.) 1986. *Anthropology as Cultural Critique: An Experimental Moment in the Human Sciences.* University of Chicago Press.

Mar-Molinero, Clare and Patrick Stevenson (eds.) 2006. *Language Ideologies, Policies and Practices: Language and the Future of Europe* (Language and Globalization. Basingstoke: Palgrave Macmillan.

Marti, Felix, Paul Ortega, Andoni Barena, *et al.* 2005. *Words and Worlds: World Languages Review.* Clevedon: Multilingual Matters.

Matharu, Kabir 2009. Using indigenous Australian drama to break cultural barriers in healthcare relationships. *Medical Humanities* 35: 47–53.

Matras, Yaron 1998. Utterance modifiers and universals of grammatical borrowing, *Linguistics* **36**(2): 281–331.

2000a. Fusion and the cognitive basis for bilingual discourse markers, *International Journal of Bilingualism* **4**(4): 505–28.

2000b. Mixed languages: A functional–communicative approach, *Bilingualism: Language and Cognition* **3**(2): 79–99.

Matras, Yaron and Peter Bakker 2003. The study of mixed languages,. In Yaron Matras and Peter Bakker (eds.), *The Mixed Language Debate*, 1–20. Berlin: Mouton de Gruyter.

Matras, Yaron, and Peter Bakker (eds.) 2003. *The Mixed Language Debate: Theoretical and Empirical Advances.* Berlin: Mouton de Gruyter.

Matras, Yaron, Hazel Gardner, Charlotte Jones and Veronica Schulman 2007. Angloromani: a different kind of language? *Anthropological Linguistics* **49**(2): 142–84.

Maurais, Jacques and Michael A. Morris (eds.) 2003. *Languages in a Globalising World.* Cambridge University Press.

May, Stephen 2003. Rearticulating the case for minority language rights. *Current Issues in Language Planning* **4**: 95–125.

2004. Rethinking linguistic human rights: answering questions of identity, essentialism and mobility. In J. Freeland and D. Patrick (eds.), *Language Rights and Language Survival*, 35–54. Manchester: St Jerome.

2005. Introduction. Bilingual/immersion education in Aotearoa/New Zealand: Setting the context. *International Journal of Bilingual Education and Bilingualism* **8**(5): 365–76.

May, Stephen and Sheila Aikman 2003. Indigenous education: address-ing current issues and developments. *Comparative Education* **39**(2): 139–45.

May, Stephen and Richard Hill 2005. Māori-medium education: current issues and challenges. *International Journal of Bilingual Education and Bilingualism* **8**(5): 377–403.

2008. Māori-Medium education: current issues and challenges. In Nancy H. Hornberger (ed.), *Can Schools Save Indigenous Languages? Policy and Practice on Four Continents*, 66–98. Basingstoke: Palgrave Macmillan.

McCarty, Teresa L. 1998. Schooling, resistance, and American Indian lan-guages. *International Journal of the Sociology of Language* **132**: 27–41.

2002. *A Place to be Navajo*. Mahwah, NJ: Lawrence Erlbaum.

2010. *Language Planning and Policy in Native America – History, Theory, Praxis*. Clevedon, Somerset: Multilingual Matters.

McCarty, Teresa and Ofelia Zepeda 1999. Amerindians. In Joshua Fishman (ed.), *Handbook of Language and Ethnic Identity*, 197–210. Oxford University Press.

McCarty, Teresa L., Mary Eunice Romero-Little, Larisa Warhol and Ofelia Zepeda 2009. Indigenous youth as language policy makers. *Journal of Language, Identity, and Education* **8**(4): 1–16.

McConvell, Patrick 2008. Mixed languages as outcomes of code-switch-ing: recent examples from Australia and their implications, *Journal of Language Contact* (Thema) **2**: 187–212.

McConvell, Patrick and Felicity Meakins 2005. Gurindji Kriol: a mixed language emerges from code-switching, *Australian Journal of Linguistics* **25**(1): 9–30.

McDonald, Maryon 1989. *We are not French! Language, Culture and Identity in Brittany*. London: Routledge.

McGill, Stuart, and Israel Wade 2008. Writing system questionnaire and proposal for the Cicipu language. ms., School of Oriental and African Studies and Theological College of Northern Nigeria.

McGroarty, Mary 1992. The societal context of bilingual education. *Edu-cational Researcher*, 21(2), Special Issue on Bilingual Education 7–9+24

McKay, Graham R. 2007. Language maintenance, shift – and planning. In Gerhard Leitner and Ian G. Malcom (eds.), *The Habitat of Australia's Aboriginal Languages: Past, Present and Future*, 101–30. Berlin: Mouton de Gruyter.

McLaughlin, Fiona, and Thierno Seydou Sall 2001. The give and take of fieldwork: noun classes and other concerns in Fatick, Senegal. In Paul Newman and Martha Ratliff (eds.), *Linguistic Fieldwork*, 189–210. Cambridge University Press.

McLeod, Wilson 2002. Language planning as regional development? The growth of the Gaelic economy. *Scottish Affairs* **32**: 51–72. www.arts. ed.ac.uk/celtic/papers/gaeliceconomy.html (4 January 2009).

McWhorter, John H. 1998. Identifying the creole prototype: vindicating a typological class, *Language* **74**(4): 788–818.

2005. *Defining Creole*. Oxford University Press.

Meakins, Felicity and Carmel O'Shannessy 2010. Ordering arguments about: word order and discourse motivations in the development and use of the ergative marker in two Australian mixed languages *Lingua*. 120(7): 1607–1886.

Meek, Barbra A. 2007. Respecting the language of elders: ideological shift and linguistic discontinuity in a Northern Athapascan community *Journal of Linguistic Anthropology* **17**(1): 23–43.

Meir, Irit, Wendy Sandler, Carol Padden and Mark Aronoff in press. Emerging sign languages. In M. Marschark and P. Spencer (eds.), *Oxford Handbook of Deaf Studies, Language, and Education*, vol. II. Oxford University Press.

Mesthrie, Raj (ed.) 2002. *Language in South Africa*. Cambridge University Press.

Meyer, Lois M. and Fernando Soberanes Bojórquez 2009. *El Nido de Lengua. Orientación para sus Guías*. Oaxaca: Movimiento Pedagógico.

Michael, Lev to appear. Evidential practice and event responsibility in Nanti society (Kampan, Arawak, Peruvian Amazonia). *Journal of Pragmatics*.

Milner, George B. 1966. *Samoan Dictionary*. Oxford University Press.

Milroy, James and Lesley Milroy 1999. *Authority in Language: Investigating Language Prescription and Standardisation*. London: Routledge.

Milroy, Lesley 1980. *Languages and Social Networks*. Oxford: Basil Blackwell.

2002. Social networks. In J. K. Chambers, Peter Trudgill and N. Schilling-Estes (eds.), *The Handbook of Language Variation and Change*, 549–72. Oxford: Blackwell.

Mitchell, Tony 2001. *Global Noise: Rap and Hip-Hop outside the USA*. Middletown: Wesleyan University Press.

2003. Doin' damage in my native language: the use of 'resistance vernaculars' in hip-hop in France, Italy and Aotearoa/New Zealand. In Harris M. Berger and Michael T. Carroll (eds.), *Global Pop,Local Language*, 3–18. Jackson: Mississippi University Press.

Mithun, Marianne 1989. The incipient obsolescence of polysynthesis: Cayuga in Ontario and Oklahoma. In Nancy C. Dorian (ed.), *Investigating Obsolescence: Studies in Language Contraction and Death*, 243–58. Cambridge University Press.

2001. Who shapes the record: the speaker and the linguist. In Paul Newman and Martha Ratliff (eds.), *Linguistic Fieldwork*, 34–54. Cambridge University Press.

Moore, Robert E. 1988. Lexicalization and lexical loss in Wasco-Wishram language obsolescence. *International Journal of American Linguistics* **54**(4): 453–68.

2006. Disappearing, Inc.: glimpsing the sublime in the politics of access to endangered languages. *Language and Communication* **26**(3–4): 296–315.

Moore, Robert E., Sari Pietikäinen and Jan Blommaert n.d. Counting the losses: numbers as the language of language endangerment. [Under review for Sociolinguistic Studies.]

Moriarty, Máiréad 2007. Minority language television as a mechanism of language policy. A comparative study of the Irish and Basque socio-linguistic contexts. PhD dissertation, University of Limerick.

Morphy, Howard 2006. The practice of an expert: anthropology in native title. *Anthropological Forum* **16**: 135–51.

Mosel, La'i Ulrike and Mose Fulu 1997. *O le fale*. Apia, Western Samoa: Ministry of Youth, Sports and Culture. Apia.

Mosel, Ulrike 2006. Sketch grammar. In Jost Gippert, Nikolaus P. Himmelmann and Ulrike Mosel (eds.), *Essentials of Language Documentation* (Trends in Linguistics: Studies and Monographs 178), 301–9. Berlin: Mouton de Gruyter.

Moseley, Christopher J. (ed.) 2007. *Encyclopedia of Endangered Languages*. London: Routledge.

2009. *UNESCO Atlas of the World's Languages in Danger of Disappearing*: UNESCO/Routledge. Online edn at www.unesco.org/culture/ich/index.php?pg=00206.

Mougeon, Raymond and Edouard Beniak 1989. Language contraction and linguistic change: the case of Welland French. In N. Dorian (ed.), *Investigating Obsolescence*, 287–312. Cambridge University Press.

Mous, Maarten 2003. *The Making of a Mixed Language: The case of Ma'a/Mbugu* (Creole Language Library 26). Amsterdam: John Benjamins.

Muehlbach, Andrea 2001. 'Making place' at the United Nations: Indigenous cultural politics at the U.N. Working Group on Indigenous Populations. *Cultural Anthropology* **16**(3): 415–48.

Muehlmann, Shaylih 2005. Conservation and contestation: in the cross-fire over 'diversity'. Proceedings of the Twelfth Annual symposium about Language and Society – Austin, Texas Linguistic Forum 48: 139–47.

2008. 'Spread your ass cheeks': and other things that should not be said in indigenous languages. *American Ethnologist* **35**: 34–48.

Mufwene, Salikoko S. 2001. *The Ecology of Language Evolution* (Cambridge Approaches to Language Contact). Cambridge University Press.

2004. Language birth and death. *Annual Review of Anthropology* **33**: 201–22.

2008. *Language Evolution: Contact, Competition and Change*. London: Continuum.

Mühlhäusler, Peter 1986. *Pidgin and Creole Linguistics* (Language in Society 11). Oxford: Blackwell.

1990. 'Reducing' Pacific languages to writing. In John Joseph and Taylor Talbot (eds.), *Ideologies of Language*, 189–205. London: Routledge.

1996. *Linguistic Ecology: Language Change and Linguistic Imperialism in the Pacific Region* (The Politics of Language). London: Routledge.

2000. Language planning and language ecology, *Current Issues in Language Planning* **1**(3): 306–67.

2002. Why one cannot preserve languages (but can preserve language ecologies). In David Bradley and Maya Bradley (eds.), *Language Endangerment and Language Maintenance*, 34–9. London: RoutledgeCurzon.

2003. Language endangerment and language revival. *Journal of Sociolinguistics* **7**: 232–45.

Munro, Robert 2005. The digital skills of language documentation. In Peter K. Austin (ed.) *Language Documentation and Description*, Vol III. 141–56. London: SOAS.

Muysken, Pieter 1981. Halfway between Quechua and Spanish: the case for relexification. In Arnold Highfield and Albert Valdman (eds.), *Historicity and Variation in Creole Studies*, 52–78. Ann Arbor, MI: Karoma.

1994. Media lengua. In Peter Bakker and Maarten Mous (eds.), *Mixed Languages: 15 Case Studies in Language Intertwining* (Studies in Language and Language Use 13), 201–5. Amsterdam: IFOTT.

1995. Code-switching and grammatical theory. In Lesley Milroy and Pieter Muysken (eds.), *One Speaker, Two Languages: Cross-disciplinary Perspectives on Code-switching*, 177–98. Cambridge University Press.

1997. Code-switching processes: alternation, insertion, congruent lexicalization. In Martin Pütz (ed.), *Language Choices: Conditions, Constraints, and Consequences* (Impact: Studies in Language and Society 1), 361–80. Amsterdam: John Benjamins.

2000. *Bilingual Speech: A Typology of Code-mixing*. Cambridge University Press.

2007. Mixed codes. In Peter Auer and Li Wei (eds.), *Handbook of Multilingualism and Multilingual Communication* (Handbooks of Applied Linguistics 5), 315–40. Berlin: Mouton de Gruyter.

Muysken, Pieter and Norval Smith (eds.) 1986. *Substrata versus Universals in Creole Genesis* (Creole Language Library 1). Amsterdam: John Benjamins.

Myers-Scotton, Carol 1988. Codeswitching as indexical of social negotiations. In Monica Heller (ed.), *Codeswitching: Anthropological and Sociolinguistic Perspectives* (Contributions to the Sociology of Language 48), 151–86. Berlin: Mouton de Gruyter.

1993. *Duelling Languages: Grammatical Structure in Codeswitching*. Oxford University Press.

2002a. *Contact Linguistics: Bilingual Encounters and Grammatical Outcomes* (Oxford Linguistics). Oxford University Press.

2002b. Frequency and intentionality in (un)marked choices in codeswitching: 'This is a 24-hour country', *International Journal of Bilingualism* **6**(2): 205–19.

2003. What lies beneath: split (mixed) languages as contact phenomena. In Yaron Matras and Peter Bakker (eds.), *The Mixed Language Debate*, 73–106. Berlin: Mouton de Gruyter.

2006. *Multiple Voices: An Introduction to Bilingualism.* Oxford: Blackwell.

Myers-Scotton, Carol and Janice L. Jake 2000. Four types of morpheme: evidence from aphasia, code switching, and second-language acquisition. *Linguistics* **38**(6): 1053–100.

NANA 2007. *Iñupiaq (Coastal): Level 1.* Kotzebue, Alaska: NANA Regional Corporation.

Nathan, David 2000. The spoken Karaim CD: sound, text, lexicon and active morphology for language learning multimedia. In Asli Goksel and Celia Kerslake (eds.) *Studies on Turkish and Turkic Languages.* 405–13 Wiesbaden: Harrassowitz.

2004. Developing multimedia documentation. In Peter K. Austin (ed.), *Language Documentation and Description*, Vol. 2, 154–68. London: SOAS.

2006a. Proficient, permanent, or pertinent: aiming for sustainability. In Linda Barwick and Tom Honeyman (eds.), *Sustainable Data from Digital Sources: From Creation to Archive and Back*, 57–68. Sydney University Press.

2006b. Thick interfaces: mobilizing language documentation with multimedia. In Jost Gippert, Nikolaus P. Himmelmann and Ulrike Mosel (eds.), *Essentials of Language Documentation* (Trends in Linguistics: Studies and Monographs 178), 363–79. Berlin: Mouton de Gruyter.

2010a. Sound and unsound practices in documentary linguistics: towards an epistemology for audio. In Peter K. Austin (ed.), *Language Documentation and Description*, Vol. 7, 172–208. London: SOAS.

2010b. Language documentation and archiving: from disk space to MySpace. In Peter K. Austin (ed.), *Language Documentation and Description*, Vol. 7, 262–284. London: SOAS.

2010c. Archives 2.0 for endangered languages: from disk space to MySpace. In *International Journal of Humanities and Arts Computing*, 4 (Special issue).

Nathan, David and Peter K. Austin 2004. Reconceiving metadata: language documentation through thick and thin. In Peter K. Austin (ed.), *Language Documentation and Description*, Vol. 2, 179–87. London: SOAS.

Native Hawaiian Education Council 2002. *Nā Honua Mauli Ola – Hawai'i Guidelines for Culturally Healthy and Responsive Learning Environments.* Hilo and Honolulu, HI: Native Hawaiian Education Council and Ka Haka 'Ula O Keÿelikōlani, University of Hawai'i at Hilo. www.olelo.hawaii.edu/olelo/nhmo.php (29 October 2009).

Nekvapil, Jiří 2006. From language planning to language management. *Sociolinguistica* **20**: 92–104.

Nettle, Daniel and Suzanne Romaine 2000. *Vanishing Voices: The Extinction of the World's Languages.* Oxford University Press.

Neustupný, Jiří V. and Jiří Nekvapil 2003. Language management in the Czech republic. *Current Issues in Language Planning,* **4**(3–4): 181–366.

New Zealand Ministry of Education (1999). *Ngā Kete Kōrero Framework: Teacher Handbook. A Framework for Organising Junior Māori Reading Texts.* Wellington, NZ: Ministry of Education.

Newman, Paul 2003. The endangered languages issue as a hopeless cause. In Mark Janse and Sijmen Tol (eds.), *Language Death and Language Maintenance,* 1–13. Amsterdam: John Benjamins.

2007. Copyright essentials for linguists. *Language Documentation and Conservation,* **1**(1): 28–43.

2009a. Linguistic fieldwork as a scientific enterprise. Paper presented at the First International Conference on Language Documentation and Conservation, University of Hawai'i. Honolulu, Hawai'i, March 2009.

2009b. Fieldwork and field methods in linguistics. *Language Documentation and Conservation* **3**(1): 113–125.

Newman, Paul and Martha Ratliff (eds.) 2001a. *Linguistic Fieldwork.* Cambridge University Press.

Newman, Paul and Martha Ratliff 2001b. Introduction. In Paul Newman and Martha Ratliff (eds.), *Linguistic Fieldwork,* 1–14. Cambridge University Press.

Nichols, Johanna 1992. *Linguistic Diversity in Space and Time.* University of Chicago Press.

Niezen, Ronald 2003. *The Origins of Indigenism: Human Rights and the Politics of Identity.* Berkeley: University of California Press.

Nonaka, Angela 2004. Sign languages – The forgotten endangered languages: lessons on the importance of remembering. *Language in Society* **33**(5): 737–67.

Nordhoff, Sebastian 2008. Electronic reference grammars for typology: challenges and solutions. *Language Documentation and Conservation* **2**(2): 296–324.

Nordlinger, Rachel and Luisa Sadler 2004. Nominal tense in cross-linguistic perspective. *Language* **80**: 776–806.

Nunan, David 1991. *Language Teaching Methodology: A Textbook for Teachers.* Hemel Hemstead: Prentice Hall.

1999. *Second Language Teaching and Learning.* Boston, MA: Heinle and Heinle.

Ó Laoire, Muiris 1995. An historical perspective on the revival of Irish outside the Gaeltacht, 1880–1930, with reference to the revitalization of Hebrew. *Current Issues in Language and Society,* 2(3): 223–35.

2000. Learning Irish for participation in the Irish language speech community outside the Gaeltacht. *Journal of Celtic Language Learning* **5**: 20–33.

Ó Riagáin, Pádraig 2004. Does achieving the status of an official language make a difference in the long-term viability of a previously dominated minority language? Paper presented to the Linguapax Congress 2004: Dialogue on Language Diversity, Sustainability and Peace, Barcelona, 2004.

O'Connell, Eithne 2003. *Minority Language Dubbing for Children: Screen Translation from German to Irish.* Bern: Peter Lang.

O'Donnell, Hugh 1996. From a Manichean universe to the kitchen sink: the telenovela in the Iberian Peninsula. *International Journal of Iberian Studies* **9**(1): 7–18.

O'Meara, Carolyn and Jeff Good 2010. Ethical issues in legacy language resources. *Language and Communication* **30**(3): 162–70.

O'Shannessy, Carmel 2005. Light Warlpiri – a new language. *Australian Journal of Linguistics* **25**(1): 31–57.

2007. Ignorance-based policy from Australia's Indigenous Affairs Minister. Transient Languages and Cultures [blog], May 25. blogs.usyd.edu.au/elac/2007/05/how_can_the_indigenous_affairs.html

OAIS 2002. Consultative Committee for Space Data Systems (CCSDS). CCSDS 650.0-B-1. Reference Model for an Open Archival Information System (OAIS). Blue Book. Issue 1. (January). public.ccsds.org/publications/archive/650x0b1.pdf (19 April 2008).

OALD 2000. Oxford Advanced Learner's Dictionary. Oxford University Press.

Ochs, Elinor 1988. *Culture and language development: language acquisition and language socialization in a Samoan village.* Cambridge University Press.

Ochs, Elinor and Bambi Schieffelin 1979. *Developmental Pragmatics.* New York: Academic Press.

Odlin, Terence 1991. Irish English idioms and language transfer, *English World-Wide* **12**(2): 175–93.

1997. Bilingualism and substrate influence: a look at clefts and reflexives In Jeffrey Kallen (ed.), *Focus on Ireland* (Varieties of English around the World G21), 35–50. Amsterdam: John Benjamins.

Okrand, Marc 1977. *Mutsun Grammar.* Berkeley, CA: University of California.

Omoniyi, Tope and Goodith White (eds.) 2006. *The Sociolinguistics of Identity.* London: Continuum.

Ostler, Nicholas 1998. *Endangered Languages: What Role for the Specialist?* Proceedings of the Second Foundation for Endangered Languages conference, Edinburgh. Bath: Foundation for Endangered Languages.

Paciotto, Carla 1996. The Tarahumara of Mexico. In Gina Cantoni (ed.), *Stabilizing Indigenous Languages*, 174–81. Northern Arizona University.

Palmer, Alexis and Katrin Erk 2007. IGT-XML: an XML format for interlinearized glossed texts, *Proceedings of the Linguistic Annotation Workshop (LAW)*, 176–83. www.aclweb.org/anthology/W/W07/W07-1528.pdf (12 February 2010).

Palmer, Gary 1996. *Towards a Theory of Cultural Linguistics*. Austin, TX: University of Texas Press.

Pandit, Prabodh B. 1975. The linguistic survey of India – perspectives on language use. In Sirarpi Ohannessian, Charles A. Ferguson and Edgar C. Polom (eds.), *Language Surveys in Developing Nations* (pp. 71–85). Arlington, VA: Center for Applied Linguistics.

Parker, Gary J. 1963. La clasificación genética de los dialectos Quechuas. *Revista del Museo Nacional* **32**: 241–52.

  1969–1971. Comparative Quechua phonology and grammar, I–IV. Working Papers in Linguistics. University of Hawaii, Department of Linguistics.

Patrick, Donna 2004. The politics of language rights in the eastern Canadian Arctic. In J. Freeland and D. Patrick (eds.), *Language Rights and Language Survival*, 171–90. Manchester: St Jerome.

Patrick, Peter L. 2002. The speech community. In J. K. Chambers, Peter Trudgill and Natalie Schilling-Estes (eds.), *Handbook of Language Variation and Change*, 573–97. Oxford: Blackwell.

Paulston, Christina Bratt 1987. Catalan and Occitan: Comparative test cases for a theory of language maintenance and shift. *International Journal of the Sociology of Language* **63**: 31–62.

  1994. *Linguistic Minorities in Multilingual Settings: Implications for Language Policies*. Amsterdam: John Benjamins Publishing Company.

Pawley, Andrew K. 1992. Grammarian's lexicon, lexicographer's lexicon: worlds apart. In Jan Svartvik (ed.), *Words KVHAA Konferenser* 36: 189–211. Stockholm: Kungl. Vitterhets Historie och Antikvitets Akademien.

  1993. A language which defies description by ordinary means. In William A. Foley (ed.), *The Role of Theory in Language Description*, 87–129. Berlin: Mouton de Gruyter.

  2009. On the treatment of animal and plant names in bilingual dictionaries: lessons from Oceania, 11th International Conference on Austronesian Linguistics, Aussois, 22–25 June.

Pawu-Kurlpurlurnu, Wanta Jampijinpa, Miles Holmes and Alan Box 2008. *Ngurrakurlu: A Way of Working with Warlpiri People*. Alice Springs: Desert Knowledge Cooperative Research Centre.

Payne, Thomas E. and David J. Weber (eds.) 2007. *Perspectives on Grammar Writing* (Benjamins Current Topics 11). Amsterdam: John Benjamins.

Pearce-Moses, Richard 2005. *A Glossary of Archival and Records Terminology.* Chicago: Society of American Archivists.

Pease Pretty-On-Top, Janine n.d. Native American language immersion: innovative Native education for children and families. Native American College Fund.

Pecos, Regis and Rebecca Blum-Martinez 2001. The key to cultural survival: language planning and revitalization in the Pueblo de Cochiti. In Kenneth Hale and Leanne Hinton (eds.), *The Green Book of Language Revitalization in Practice*, 75–82. San Diego: Academic Press.

Pelkey, Jamin 2008. The Phula languages in synchronic and diachronic perspective. PhD thesis, La Trobe University.

Pennycook, Alastair 2006. Postmodernism in language policy. In T. Ricento (ed.), *An Introduction to Language Policy: Theory and Method*, 60–76. Oxford: Blackwell.

2007. *Global Englishes and Transcultural Flows.* London: Routledge.

Peterson, Leighton 1997. Tuning in to Navajo: the role of radio in native language maintenance. In Jon Reyhner (ed.), *Teaching Indigenous Languages*, 214–21. Flagstaff: Northern Arizona University.

Pfaff, Carol W. 1982. Constraints on language mixing: intrasentential code-switching and borrowing in Spanish/English. In Jon Amastae and Lucía Elías-Olivares (eds.), *Spanish in the United States: Sociolinguistic Aspects*, 264–97. Cambridge University Press.

Philips, John Edward 2000. *Spurious Arabic. Hausa and Colonial Nigeria.* Madison WI: University of Wisconsin-Madison.

Philips, Susan U., Susan Steele and Christine Tanz 1987. *Language, Gender and Sex in Comparative Perspective.* Cambridge University Press.

Phillipson, Robert and Tove Skutnabb-Kangas 1995a. Language rights in postcolonial Africa. In Robert Phillipson, Mart Rannut and Tove Skutnabb-Kangas (eds.), *Linguistic Human Rights: Overcoming Linguistic Discrimination*, 335–46. Berlin: Mouton de Gruyter.

1995b. Linguistic rights and wrongs. *Applied Linguistics* **16**: 483–504.

Phillipson, Robert, Mart Rannut and Tove Skutnabb-Kangas (eds.) 1995. *Linguistic Human Rights.* Berlin: Mouton de Gruyter.

Piaget, Jean 1952. *The Origins of Intelligence in Children.* New York: Norton.

Pietikäinen, Sari 2008. Language vitality and cultural hybridization. *Journal of Multicultural Discourses* **3**(1): 22–35.

2008. Sami in the media: questions of language vitality and cultural hybridisation. *Journal of Multicultural Discourses* **3**(1): 22–35.

Pike, Kenneth Lee 1947. *Phonemics: A Technique for Reducing Languages to Writing.* Ann Arbor: University of Michigan Press.

Pittman, Richard S. (ed.) 1969. *Ethnologue: Languages of the World.* Dallas, Texas: Summer Institute of Linguistics.

Platero, Paul R. 2001. Navajo Head Start language study. In Leanne Hinton and Ken Hale (eds.), *The Green Book of Language Revitalization in Practice*, 87–97. San Diego, CA: Academic Press.

Poedjosoedarmo, Gloria 2006. The effect of Bahasa Indonesia as a lingua franca on the Javanese system of speech levels and their functions, *International Journal of the Sociology of Language* **177**: 111–21.

Pooley, Tim 1998. Picard and regional French as symbols of identity in the Nord. In D. Marley, M. A. Hintze and G. Parker (eds.) *Linguistic Identities and Policies in France and the French-speaking World*, 43–55. London: Centre for Information on Language Teaching and Research.

2003. La différenciation hommes-femmes dans la pratique des langues régionales de France. *Language et Société* **106**: 9–31.

Poplack, Shana 1980. Sometimes I'll start a sentence in Spanish y termino en Español: toward a typology of code-switching, *Linguistics* **18**(7–8): 581–618.

Poplack, Shana and Marjory Meechan 1995. Patterns of language mixture: nominal structure in Wolof-French and Fongbe-French bilingual discourse. In Lesley Milroy and Pieter Muysken (eds.), *One Speaker, Two Languages: Cross-disciplinary Perspectives on Code-switching*, 199–232. Cambridge University Press.

Posey, Darrell A. 2004. *Indigenous Knowledge and Ethics: A Darrell Posey Reader.* Kristina Plenderleith (ed.). New York: Routledge.

Potter, Russell 1995. *Spectacular Vernaculars*. New York: Syracuse University Press.

Prah, Kweshi K. 2001. Language, literacy, the production and reproduction of knowledge, and the challenge of African development. In David R. Olson and Nancy Torrance (eds.), *The Making of Literate Societies*, 123–41. Malden MA/Oxford: Blackwell.

Premsrirat, Suwilai, and Sakol Panyim 2000. *Ethnolinguistic Maps of Thailand* [in Thai]. Bangkok: Office of the National Cultural Commission, Ministry of Culture.

Protocols for Native American Materials. 2007. www2.nau.edu/libnap-p/protocols.html (15 January 2009).

Pujolar i Cos, Joan 2000. The effect of migration on patterns of language use in Catalonia. In Peter Wynn Thomas and Jayne Mathias (eds.), *Developing Minority Languages: Proceedings of the Fifth International Conference on Minority Languages*, 115–29. Cardiff: Gomer Press.

Pütz, Martin 1996. *Discrimination through Language in Africa? Perspectives on the Namibian Experience*. Berlin: Mouton de Gruyter.

Queixalos, Francisco and Odile Renault-Lescure (eds.) 2000. *As Línguas amazônicas hoje; The Amazonian Languages Today*. IRD, ISA, MPEG Instituto socioambiental, Sao Paolo.

Radcliffe-Brown, Alfred R. 1935. On the concept of function in social science. *American Anthropologist* **37**(3): 394–402.

1940. On social structure. *The Journal of the Royal Anthropological Institute of Great Britain and Ireland* **70**(1): 1–12.

Ramanathan, Vaidehi 2005. Rethinking language planning and policy from the ground up: refashioning institutional realities and human lives. *Current Issues in Language Planning* **6**: 89–101.

Rappa, Antonio L. and Lionel Wee 2006. *Language Policy and Modernity in Southeast Asia: Malaysia, the Philippines, Singapore, and Thailand*. New York: Springer.

Rassool, Naz 2007. *Global Issues in Language, Education and Development*. Clevedon: Multilingual Matters.

Rau, Cath 2005. Literacy acquisition, assessment and achievement of year two students in total immersion in Māori programmes. *International Journal of Bilingual Education and Bilingualism* **8**(5): 404–32.

Rau, Victoria and Meng Chien Yang 2008. e-Learning in endangered language documentation and revitalisation. Paper presented at the International Conference on Austronesian Endangered Language Documentation, Providence University, Taiwan.

  2009. Digital transmission of language and culture. In Margaret Florey (ed.), *Endangered Languages of Austronesia*, 207–24. Oxford University Press.

Regier, Terry, Kay Paul, Gilbert Aubrey and Ivry Richard 2010. Language and thought: which side are you on anyway? In Barbara Malt and Phillip Wolff (eds.), *Words and the Mind: How Words Capture Human Experience*. New York: Oxford University Press.

Rehg, Kenneth L. 2007. The language documentation and conservation initiative at the University of Hawai'i at Mānoa. *Language Documentation and Conservation* Special Publication No. 1. 13–24.

  2009. FINE Grammars for Small Languages. Paper presented at the International Symposium on Theoretical and Methodological Issues in Language Description and Grammar Writing, Research Institute for Languages and Cultures of Asia and Africa (ILCAA), Tokyo University of Foreign Studies. Tokyo, Japan, December 2009.

Reyhner, Jon (ed.) 1997. *Teaching Indigenous Languages*. Flagstaff, AZ: Northern Arizona University, College of Education. jan.ucc.nau.edu/~jar/books.html (26 January 2010).

Reyhner, Jon and Louise Lockard (eds.) 2009. *Indigenous Language Revitalization: Encouragement, Guidance and Lessons Learned*. Flagstaff, AZ: Northern Arizona University, College of Education. jan.ucc.nau.edu/~jar/books.html (26 January 2010).

Reyhner, Jon, Gina Cantoni, Robert N. St. Clair and Yazzie Evangeline Parsons (eds.) 1999. *Revitalizing Indigenous Languages*. Flagstaff, AZ: Northern Arizona University, College of Education. jan.ucc.nau.edu/~jar/books.html (26 January 2010).

Reyhner, Jon, Joseph Martin, Louise Lockard and Gilbert W. Sakiestewa (eds.) 2000. *Learn in Beauty: Indigenous Education for a New Century*. Flagstaff, AZ: Northern Arizona University, College of Education. jan.ucc.nau.edu/~jar/books.html (26 January 2010).

Reyhner, Jon, Octaviana Trujillo, Roberto Luis Carrasco and Louise Lockard (eds.) 2003. *Nurturing Native Languages*. Flagstaff, AZ: Northern Arizona University, College of Education. jan.ucc.nau.edu/~jar/books.html (26 January 2010).

Reynolds, Jennifer F. 2009. Shaming the shift generation: intersecting ideologies of family and linguistic revitalization in Guatemala. In Paul V. Kroskrity and Margaret C. Field (eds.), *Native American Language Ideologies: Beliefs, Practices, and Struggles in Indian Country*, 213–37. Tucson: University of Arizona Press.

Rhodes, Richard A., Lenore A. Grenoble, Anna Berge and Paula Radetzky 2006. Adequacy of documentation: a preliminary report to the CELP [Committee on Endangered Languages and their Preservation, Linguistic Society of America]. ms. Washington, DC: Linguistic Society of America.

Rice, Keren 2006. Ethical issues in linguistic fieldwork: an overview, *Journal of Academic Ethics* **4**: 123–55.

  2007. Review of David Harrison, *When Languages Die: The Extinction of the World's Languages and the Erosion of Human Knowledge. Language Documentation and Conservation* **1**(2): 317–21.

  2009. Must there be two solitudes? Language activists and linguists working together. In Jon Reyhner and Louise Lockard (eds.), *Indigenous Language Revitalization: Encouragement, Guidance and Lessons Learned*, 37–59. Flagstaff, AZ: Northern Arizona University, College of Education. jan.ucc.nau.edu/~jar/books.html (26 January 2010).

Rice, Keren and Leslie Saxon 2002. Issues of standardisation and community in aboriginal lexicography. In William Frawley, Kenneth C. Hill and Pamela Munro (eds.), *Making Dictionaries. Preserving Indigenous Languages of the Americas*, 125–54. Berkeley: University of California Press.

Ricento, Thomas (ed.) 2006. *An Introduction to Language Policy*. Oxford: Blackwell.

Riggins, Steve H. 1992. *Ethnic Minority Media: An International Perspective*. London: Sage Publications.

Rigsby, Bruce and Peter Sutton 1980. Speech communities in Aboriginal Australia. *Anthropological Forum* **5**(1): 8–23.

Rinehart, Melissa A. 2007. Miami Indian Language Shift and Recovery. Unpublished Ph.D. dissertation, Department of Anthropology, Michigan State University, Lansing, MI.

Robinson, Clinton D. W. 1996. *Language Use in Rural Development: An African Perspective*. Berlin: Mouton de Gruyter.

Rodriguez, Clara 1991. *Puerto Ricans: Born in the USA*. Boulder, CO: Westview Press.

Rogers, Chris 2008. Xinkan vowel harmony. Unpublished manuscript.

Rogers, Chris, Naomi Palosaari, Lyle Campbell and Terrence Kaufman. In preparation. Xinkan comparative dictionary and grammar.

Romaine, Suzanne 2002a. Can stable diglossia help to preserve endangered languages? *International Journal of the Sociology of Language* **157**: 135–40.

  2002b. The impact of language policy on endangered languages. *International Journal on Multicultural Societies* **4**: 194–212.

2006a. Planning for the survival of linguistic diversity. *Language Policy* **5**: 441–473.

2006b. The bilingual and multilingual community. In Tej K. Bhatia and William C. Ritchie (eds.), *The Handbook of Bilingualism*, 385–405. Malden MA: Blackwell.

2008. Linguistic diversity, sustainability, and the future of the past. In K. King, N. Schilling-Estes, L. Fogle, and J. Lou (eds.) *Sustaining Linguistic Diversity: Endangered and Minority Languages and Language Varieties*. Washington, DC: Georgetown University Press.

2009. Biodiversity, linguistic diversity and poverty: some global patterns and missing links. In Wayne Harbert *et al.* (eds.), *Language and Poverty*, 127–46. Clevedon: Multilingual Matters.

Rosaldo, Michelle 1982. The things we do with words: Ilongot speech acts and speech act theory in philosophy. *Language in Society* **11**(2): 203–37.

Rosaldo, Renato 1993. *Culture and Truth: The Remaking of Social Analysis.* London: Routledge.

Rosch, Eleanor 1975. Cognitive representations of semantic categories. *Journal of Experimental Psychology* **104**(3): 192–233.

Rosen, Nicole and Heather Souter 2009. Language revitalization in a multilingual community: the case of Michif. Presentation at the First International Conference on Language Documentation and Conservation, 12–14 March. University of Hawai'i, Hilo, Hawai'i.

Rubin, J. and B. H. Jernudd (eds.) 1971. *Can Language be Planned?* Honolulu: East–West Center.

Ruíz, R. 1984. Orientations in language planning. *NABE Journal* **8**: 15–34. Reprinted in Sandra Lee McKay and Sau-Ling Cynthia Wong (eds.) 1988. *Language Diversity: Problem or Resource?* New York: Newbury House.

Rules for Archival Description. 2008. Ottawa: Bureau of Canadian Archivists. www.cdncouncilarchives.ca/RAD/RADComplete_July2008.pdf (15 January 2009).

Rumsey, Alan 1990. Word, meaning, and linguistic ideology. *American Anthropologist*, **92**(2): 346–61.

Sacks, Harvey, Emmanuel Schegloff and Gail Jefferson 1974. A simplest systematics for the organization of turn-taking for conversation. *Language* **50**(4): 696–735.

Sakel, Jeanette 2007. Language contact between Spanish and Mosetén: a study of grammatical integration, *International Journal of Bilingualism* **11**(1): 25–53.

Sallabank, Julia 2002. Writing in an unwritten language: the case of Guernsey French. *Reading Working Papers in Linguistics* 6: 217–44.

2005. Prestige from the bottom up: a review of language planning in Guernsey. *Current Issues in Language Planning* **6**(1): 44–63.

2006. Prospects for linguistic diversity in Europe and beyond: views from a small island. In C. Leung and J. Jenkins (eds.), *Reconfiguring*

Europe: The Contribution of Applied Linguistics, 42–63. London: Equinox.

(forthcoming) Endangered language maintenance and revitalisation: the role of social networks. Submitted to *Anthropological Linguistics*.

Samarin, William J. 1967. *Field Linguistics: A Guide to Linguistic Field Work.* New York: Holt, Rinehart and Winston.

Samuels, David 2006. Bible translation and medicine man talk: missionaries, indexicality, and the 'language expert' on the San Carlos Apache Reservation. *Language in Society* **35**: 529–57.

Sandefur, John R. 1979. *An Australian Creole in the Northern Terrritory: A Description of Ngukurr-Bamyili Dialects I* (SIL-AAIB B3). Darwin: Summer Institute of Linguistics, Australian Aborigines and Islanders Branch.

Sansom, Basil 2007. Yulara and future expert reports in native title cases, *Anthropological Forum* **17**(1): 71–92.

Sapir, Edward 1916. *Time Perspective in Aboriginal American Culture: A Study in Method.* Geological Survey Memoir 90 (13), Anthropological Series. Ottawa: Government Printing Bureau.

1964[1931]. Conceptual categories in primitive languages. In Dell Hymes (ed.), *Language and Culture in Culture and Society: A Reader in Linguistics and Anthropology.* New York: Harper and Row.

Saussure, Ferdinand de 1931. *Cours de linguistique générale.* Paris: Payot.

Saville-Troike, Muriel 1982. *The Ethnography of Communication: An Introduction* (Language in Society). Wiley-Blackwell.

Schieffelin, Bambi 1986. Teasing and shaming Kaluli children's interactions. In B. Schieffelin and E. Ochs (eds.), *Language Socialization across Cultures*, 165–81. Cambridge University Press.

Schieffelin, Bambi and Elinor Ochs 1986. *Language Socialization across Cultures.* Cambridge University Press.

Schieffelin, Bambi, Kathryn Woolard and Paul Kroskrity 1998. *Language Ideologies: Practice and Theory.* Oxford University Press.

Schiffman, Harold F. 1996. *Linguistic Culture and Language Policy.* London: Routledge.

Schmidt, Annette 1985a. The fate of ergativity in dying Dyirbal. *Language* **61**(2): 378–96.

1985b. *Young People's Dyirbal: An Example of Language Death from Australia* (Cambridge Studies in Linguistics). Cambridge University Press.

Schneider, David 1968. *American Kinship: A Cultural Account.* University of Chicago Press.

Schroeter, Ronald and Nicholas Thieberger 2006. EOPAS, the EthnoER online representation of interlinear text. In Linda Barwick and Nicholas Thieberger (eds.), *Sustainable Data from Digital Fieldwork*, 99–124. Sydney University Press.

Schultze-Berndt, Eva 2006. Linguistic annotation. In Jost Gippert, Nikolaus P. Himmelmann and Ulrike Mosel (eds.), *Essentials of Language*

Documentation (Trends in Linguistics: Studies and Monographs 178), 213–51. Berlin: Mouton de Gruyter.

Schwartz, Marcia L., Ruth Saovana Spriggs, Ulrike Mosel, Ruth Siimaa Rigamu, Jeremiah Vaabero, and Naphtaly Maion 2007. The Teop lexical database. www.mpi.nl/dobes/projects/teop

Sealey, Alison and Bob Carter 2004. *Applied Linguistics as Social Science*. London: Continuum.

Seifart, Frank 2006. Orthography development. In Jost Gippert, Nikolaus Himmelmann and Ulrike Mosel (eds.), *Essentials of Language Documentation*, 275–99. Berlin: Mouton de Gruyter.

Shearer, Walter and Sun Hongkai 2002. *Speakers of the Non-Han Languages and Dialects of China*. Lewiston, Queenston and Lampeter: The Edwin Mellen Press.

Sherzer, Joel 1983. *Kuna Ways of Speaking: An Ethnographic Perspective*. Austin, TX: University of Texas Press.

1987. A discourse-centered approach to language and culture. *American Anthropologist*, New Series **89**(2): 295–309.

Shohamy, Elana 2006. *Language Policy: Hidden Agendas and New Approaches*. Abingdon: Routledge New York: Routledge.

Siegel, Jeff 2000. Substrate influence in Hawai'i Creole English, *Language in Society* **29**(2): 197–236.

2003. Substrate influence in creoles and the role of transfer in second language acquisition, *Studies in Second Language Acquisition* **25**(2): 185–209.

Siewierska, Anna 1988. *Word order rules*. New York: Croon Helm.

Silva-Corvalán, Carmen 2008. The limits of convergence in language contact. *Journal of Language Contact* (Thema) **2**: 213–24.

Silverstein, Michael 1976. Shifters, linguistic categories, and cultural description. In Keith Basso and Henry Selby (eds.), *Meaning in Anthropology*, 11–55. Albuquerque: University of New Mexico.

1979. Language structure and language ideology. In Paul Clyne, William Hanks and Carol Hofbauer (eds.), *The Elements: A Parasession on Linguistic Units and Levels*, 193–247. Chicago Linguistic Society.

1987. The three faces of 'function': preliminaries to a psychology of language. In M. Hickman (ed.), *Social and Functional Approaches to Language and Thought*, 17–38. Chicago: Academic Press.

1996. Monoglot 'standard' in America: standardization and metaphors of linguistic hegemony. In Donald Brenneis and Ronald K. S. Macaulay (eds.), *The Matrix of Language: Contemporary Linguistic Anthropology*, 284–306. Boulder: Westview.

1998a. Contemporary transformations of local linguistic communities. *Annual Review of Anthropology* **27**: 401–26.

1998b. The uses and utility of ideology: a commentary. In Bambi B. Schieffelin, Kathryn A. Woolard and Paul V. Kroskrity (eds.), *Language Ideologies: Practice and Theory*, 123–45. Oxford University Press.

2003. Indexical order and the dialectics of sociolinguistic life. *Language and Communication* **23**(3–4): 193–229.

Simons, Gary F., Kenneth S. Olson and Paul S. Frank 2007. Ngbugu digital wordlist: a test case for best practices in archiving and presenting language documentation. *Linguistic Discovery* **5**(1): 28–39.

Simons, Gary and Steven Bird (eds.) 2008. *OLAC Metadata*. Open Language Archives Community. www.language-archives.org/OLAC/metadata.html (12 February 2010).

Simpson, Jane 2006. Sovereignty over languages and land. Transient languages and cultures [blog], November 25. blogs.usyd.edu.au/elac/2006/11/sovereignty_over_languages_and_1.html (15 July 2009)

Sims, Christine 1998. Community-based efforts to preserve Native languages: a descriptive study of the Karuk Tribe of northern California. *International Journal of the Sociology of Language* 132: 95–113.

Skeet, Rachel M. 2000. Remarks on language revival and survival: a case study of Jersey Norman French. Unpublished MA dissertation, University of Newcastle upon Tyne.

Skutnabb-Kangas, Tove 2000. *Linguistic Genocide in Education – or Worldwide Diversity and Human Rights?* Mahwah, NJ: Lawrence Erlbaum.

2002. Language key to life on Earth. *Language Magazine*, 22–4.

Skutnabb-Kangas, Tove, and Robert Phillipson 1995. Linguistic human rights, past and present. In Tove Skuttnab-Kangas and Robert Phillipson (eds.), *Linguistic Human Rights. Overcoming Linguistic Discrimination*, 71–110. Berlin: Mouton de Gruyter.

Skutnabb-Kangas, Tove, Robert Phillipson and Mart Rannut (eds.) 1995. *Linguistic Human Rights*. Berlin: Mouton de Gruyter.

Slate, Clay 1993. Finding a place for Navajo. *Tribal College Journal* **4**(4): 10–14.

Slimane, Mourad Ben 2008. Appropriating new technology for minority language revitalization: The Welsh case. PhD dissertation, Frei Universität Berlin.

So'o, Ainslie and La'i Ulrike Mosel 2000. Utugagana. O le tusi fa'amatala 'upu fa'apitoa mo tamaiti a'oga o le Tausaga 7 & 8 o Samoa. Apia, Samoa: Department of Education.

Spears, Arthur K. and Donald Winford (eds.) 1997. *The Structure and Status of Pidgins and Creoles: Including Selected Papers from the Meetings of the Society for Pidgin and Creole Linguistics* (Creole Language Library 19). Amsterdam: John Benjamins.

Speck, Frank G. 1918. Penobscot transformer tales. *International Journal of American Linguistics* **1**(3): 187–244.

Spence, Nichol C. W. 1993. *A Brief History of Jèrriais*. Jersey: Le Don Balleine.

Sperber, Dan 1996. *Explaining Culture: A Naturalistic Approach*. Blackwell.

Spolsky, Bernard 1989. Maori bilingual education and language revitalization. *Journal of Multilingual and Multicultural Development* **9**(6): 1–18.

2003. Reassessing Māori regeneration. *Language in Society* **32**(4): 553–78.

2004. *Language Policy.* Cambridge University Press.

2005. Maori lost and regained. In Allan Bell, Ray Harlow and Donna Starks (eds.), *Languages of New Zealand*, 67–85. Wellington: Victoria University Press.

2009a. *Language Management.* Cambridge University Press.

2009b. Religious language management. In Li Wei and Vivian Cook (eds.), *Contemporary Applied Linguistics*, vol. II *Linguistics for the Real World*, 65–82. London: Continuum.

Srivastava, R. N. 1988. Societal bilingualism and bilingual education: a study of the Indian situation. In Christina Bratt Paulston (ed.), *International Handbook of Bilingualism and Bilingual Education*, 247–74. New York: Greenwood Press.

Stewart, William 1968. A sociolinguistic typology for describing national multilingualism. In Joshua A. Fishman (ed.), *Readings in the Sociology of Language*, 531–45. The Hague: Mouton.

Stiles, Dawn B. 1997. Four successful indigenous language programs. In Jon Reyhner (ed.), *Teaching Indigenous Languages*, 148–262. Flagstaff, AZ: Northern Arizona University. jan.ucc.nau.edu/~jar/TIL_21.html, accessed 25 February 2010.

Stocking, George W. 1968. *Race, Culture, and Evolution: Essays in the Historiography of Anthropology.* New York: Free Press.

Sunder, Madhavi 2007. The invention of traditional knowledge. *Law and Contemporary Problems* **70**(2): 97–124.

Suslak, Daniel F. 2009. The sociolinguistic problem of generations. *Language and Communication* **29**(3): 199–209.

Sutherland, William J. 2003. Parallel extinction risk and global distribution of languages and species. *Nature* **423**: 276–9.

Sutton, Peter 2003. *Native Title in Australia: An Ethnographic Perspective.* Cambridge University Press.

Svelmoe, William L. 2009. 'We do not want to masquerade as linguists': a short history of SIL and the academy. *Language* **85**(3): 629–35.

Svensén, Bo 1993. *Practical Lexicography.* Oxford University Press.

Swadesh, Morris 1934. The phonetics of Chitimacha. *Language* **10**: 345–62.

1946. Chitimacha. In Cornelius Osgood (ed.), *Linguistic Structures of Native America*, Viking Fund Publications in Anthropology, no.6., 312–36. New York: Viking Fund.

Taff, Alice 1997. Learning ancestral languages by telephone. In Jon Reyhner (ed.), *Teaching Indigenous Languages*, 40–5. Flagstaff, AZ: Northern Arizona University.

2004. Aleut conversation corpus. Hans Rausing Endangered Languages Documentation Project Individual Postgraduate Fellowship. www.hrelp.org/grants/projects/index.php?lang=4 (9 August 2010).

Tauli, Valter 1968. *Introduction to a Theory of Language Planning*. University of Uppsala.

Tax, Sol 1952. Action anthropology. *América Indígena* **12**: 103–6.

Terraza, Jimena 2008. Gramática del wichí: fonología y morfología. PhD dissertation, Université du Québec à Montréal.

Terrill, Angela 2002. Why make books for people who don't read? A perspective on documentation of an endangered language from the Solomon Islands. *International Journal of the Sociology of Language* **155–156**: 205–19.

Terrill, Angela and Michael Dunn 2003. Orthography design in the Solomon Islands. *Written Language and Literacy* **6**: 177–92.

Thieberger, Nicholas 2002. Extinction in whose terms? Which parts of a language constitute a target for language maintenance programmes? In David Bradley and Maya Bradley (eds.), *Language Endangerment and Language Maintenance*, 310–28. London: Curzon.

2004. Documentation in practice: developing a linked media corpus of South Efate. In Peter K. Austin (ed.), *Language Documentation and Description*, Vol II, 169–78. London: SOAS.

2006. *A Grammar of South Efate: An Oceanic Language of Vanuatu*. Honolulu: University of Hawai'i Press.

Thieberger, Nicholas (ed.) To appear. *The Oxford Handbook of Linguistic Fieldwork*. Oxford University Press.

Thiers, Ghjacumu 1986. Epilinguisme, elaboration linguistique et volonté populaire, trois supports de l'individuation sociolinguistique corse. *Langages* **21**: 65–74.

Thiers, Jacques 1999. Langue Corse, standardisation et polynomie. *Revista de Llengua i Dret* **32**: 127–36.

Thomas, Ned 1994. Cymry Cymraeg fel Lleiafrif Ieithyddol Tirogaethol yn yr Undeb Ewropeaidd / Welsh-speakers as a territorial linguistic minority in the European Union. In Rhian Williams, Hywel Williams and Elaine Davies (eds.), *Gwaith Cymdeithasol a'r Iaith Gymraeg / Social Work and the Welsh Language*, 155–72. Cardiff: University of Wales Press.

1995. *The Mercator Media Forum*. Forward. Aberystwyth: Mercator Media Forum.

Thomason, Sarah G. 1997. A typology of contact languages. In Arthur K. Spears and Donald Winford (eds.), *The Structure and Status of Pidgins and Creoles: Including Selected Papers from the Meetings of the Society for Pidgin and Creole Linguistics* (Creole Language Library 19), 71–88. Amsterdam: John Benjamins.

2001. *Language Contact: An Introduction*. Edinburgh University Press.

2003. Social factors and linguistic processes in the emergence of stable mixed languages. In Yaron Matras and Peter Bakker (eds.), *The Mixed Language Debate*, 21–39. Berlin: Mouton de Gruyter.

2008. Social and linguistic factors as predictors of contact-induced change. *Journal of Language Contact* (Thema) **2**: 42–56.

Thomason, Sarah G. and Terrence Kaufman 1988. *Language Contact, Creolization, and Genetic Linguistics*. Berkeley, CA: University of California Press.

Toba Sueyoshi, Ingrid Toba and Novel Kishor Rai 2002. *UNESCO Language Survey Report: Nepal*. Kathmandu: UNESCO.

2005. *Diversity and Endangerment of Languages in Nepal* (Kathmandu Series of Monographs and Working Papers 7). Kathmandu: UNESCO.

Toelken, Barre 1998. The Yellowman tapes, 1966–1997. *The Journal of American Folklore* **111**(442): 381–91.

Tollefson, James W. 1991. *Planning Language, Planning Inequality: Language Policy in the Community*. London: Longman.

Tomei, Joseph 1995. The practice of preservation: views from linguists working with language renewal. A report on a session of the 1993 meeting of the American Anthropological Association. *International Journal of the Sociology of Language* **115**: 173–82.

Tonhauser, Judith 2007. Nominal tense? The meaning of Guaraní nominal temporal markers. *Language* **83**: 831–69.

Tonkin, Humphrey 2003. The search for a global linguistic strategy. In Jacques Maurais and Michael A. Morris (eds.), *Languages in a Globalising World*, 319–33. Cambridge University Press.

Torero, Alfredo 1964. Los dialectos quechuas. *Anales Científicos de la Universidad Agraria* **2**: 446–78.

1974. *El quechua y la historia social andina*. Lima, Peru: University Ricardo Palma.

Triebel, Armin 2001. The roles of literacy practices in the activities and instutions of developed and developing countries. In David R. Olson and Nancy Torrance (eds.), *The Making of Literate Societies*, 19–53. Malden MA: Blackwell.

Trilsbeek, Paul and Peter Wittenburg 2006. Archiving Challenges. In Jost Gippert, Nikolaus P. Himmelmann and Ulrike Mosel (eds.), *Essentials of Language Documentation*, 311–35. Berlin: Mouton de Gruyter.

Trubetzkoy, Nikolai S. 1928. Proposition 16, *1st International Congress of Linguists*, 17–18. Leiden: A. W. Sijthoff.

Trudell, Barbara 2006. Language development and social uses of literacy: a study of literacy practices in Cameroonian minority language communities. *The International Journal of Bilingual Education and Bilingualism* **9**: 625–42.

Trudgill, Peter 1986. *Dialects in Contact* (Language in Society 10). Oxford: Blackwell.

1992. Ausbau sociolinguistics and the perception of language status in contemporary Europe. *International Journal of Applied Linguistics* **2**: 167–77.

Tsunoda, Tasaku 2005. *Language Endangerment and Language Revitalization* (Trends in Linguistics: Studies and Monographs 148). Berlin: Mouton de Gruyter.

Tulloch, Shelly 2004. Inuktitut and Inuit youth: language attitudes as a basis for language planning. PhD Dissertation, Université Laval.

Turner, Victor 1967. *The Forest of Symbols: Aspects of Ndembu Ritual*. Cornell University Press.

Tylor, Edward 1871[1958]. *Primitive Culture*. New York: Harper and Row.

UNESCO. 2003a. Recommendations for Action Plans, 4. www.unesco.org/culture/ich/doc/src/00117-EN.pdf, (1 October 2009).

2003b. Intangible cultural heritage. portal.unesco.org/culture/en/ev.php-URL_ID=34325andURL_DO=DO_TOPICandURL_SECTION=201.html, (1 October 2009).

(2010) Survey: Linguistic vitality and diversity www.eva.mpg.de/lingua/tools-at-lingboard/pdf/Unesco_Vitality_Diversity_%20Questionnaire1.pdf, (2 March 2010).

UNESCO Ad Hoc Expert Group on Endangered Languages 2003. Language Vitality and Endangerment. portal.unesco.org/culture/en/files/35646/12007687933Language_Vitality_and_Endangerment.pdf/Language%2BVitality%2Band%2BEndangerment.pdf (4 January 2009).

UNESCO Intangible Cultural Heritage. 2008. Linguistic vitality and diversity survey. www.unesco.org/culture/ich/index.php?pg144 (15 January 2009).

Declaration on the Rights of Indigenous Peoples. www.un.org/esa/socdev/unpfii/en/declaration.html (3 March 2010).

Urla, Jacqueline 1988. Ethnic protest and social planning: a look at Basque language revival. *Cultural Anthropology* **3**(4): 379–94.

Urtéaga, Eguzki 2005. La langue basque au début du XXIe siècle [The Basque language in the early 21st century]. *Marges Linguistiques* **10**: 175–89.

Vaillancourt, François 2008. Language and poverty: measurement, determinants and policy responses. In Wayne Harbert (ed.), *Language and Poverty*, 147–60. Clevedon: Multilingual Matters.

Van Coetsem, Frans 2000. *A General and Unified Theory of the Transmission Process in Language Contact* (Monographien zur Sprachwissenschaft 19). Heidelberg: Winter.

Vanni, Robert J. 2002. Deeds of gift: caressing the hand that feeds. In Tomas Lipinski (ed.), *Libraries, Museums and Archives: Legal Issues and Ethical Challenges in the New Information Era*, 1–29. Lanham, Maryland: Scarecrow Press.

Vaux, Bert, Justin Cooper and Emily Tucker 2007. *Introduction into Linguistic Field Methods*. München/Newcastle: Lincom Europa. Eugene, OR: Wipf & Stock Publishers.

Venezky, Richard L. 2004. In search of the perfect orthography. *Written Language and Literacy* **7**: 139–63.

Villa, Daniel J. 2002. Integrating technology into minority language preservation and teaching efforts: an inside job. *Language Learning and Technology* **6**: 92–101.

Voegelin, Carl F. and Florence M. Voegelin 1977. *Classification and Index of the World's Languages*. New York: Elsevier.

Voegelin, Carl F., Florence M. Voegelin and Noel W. Schutz, Jr. 1967. The language situation in Arizona as part of the Southwest culture area. In Dell H. Hymes and William E. Bittle (eds.), *Studies in Southwestern Ethnolinguistics: Meaning and History in the Languages of the American Southwest*, 403–51. The Hague: Mouton.

Vogt, Hans 1963. *Dictionnaire de la langue oubykh*. Oslo: Universitetsforlaget.

Vydrine, Valentin 1998. Sur l'écriture mandingue et mande en caractères arabes (mandinka, bambara, soussou, mogofin). *Mandenkan* **33**: 1–87.

1999. *Manding–English Dictionary*. St. Petersburg: Dimitry Bulanin Publishing House.

Vygotsky, Lev 1962. *Thought and Language*. MIT Press.

1978. *Mind in Society: The Development of Higher Psychological Processes*. Harvard University Press.

Walker, Roland 1993. Language shift in Europe and Irian Jaya, Indonesia: toward the heart of the matter. In Kees de Bot (ed.), *Case Studies in Minority Languages: AILA Review* **10**: 71–87.

Wallace, Anthony and John Atkins 1960. The meaning of kinship terms. *American Anthropologist* **62**: 58–80.

Walsh, John 2006. Language and socio-economic development: experiences from the Scottish Gàidhealtachd and the Irish Gaeltacht. In Wilson McLeod (ed.), *Revitalizing Gaelic in Scotland*, 257–78. Edinburgh: Dunedin Academic Press.

Walter, Stephen L. 2008. The language of instruction issue: framing an empirical perspective. In Bernard Spolsky and Francis M. Hult (eds.), *Handbook of Educational Linguistics*, 129–46. Malden MA: Blackwell.

Ward, Monica and Josef van Genabith 2003. CALL for endangered languages: Challenges and rewards. *Computer Assisted Language Learning* **16**: 233–58.

Warner, Natasha, Lynnika Butler and Quirina Luna-Costillas 2006. Making a dictionary for community use in language revitalization: the case of Mutsun. *International Journal of Lexicography* **19**: 257–85.

Warner, Natasha, Quirina Luna and Lynnika Butler 2007. Ethics and revitalization of dormant languages: the Mutsun language. *Language Documentation and Conservation* **1**: 58–76.

Warner, Natasha, Quirina Luna, Lynnika Butler, and Heather Van Volkinburg 2009. Revitalization in a scattered language community: problems and methods from the perspective of Mutsun language revitalization. *International Journal of the Sociology of Language* **198**: 135–48.

Warner Sam L. No'Eau 1999. The right, responsibility, and authority of indigenous peoples to speak and make decisions for themselves in language and cultural revitalization. *Anthropology and Education Quarterly* **30**(1): 68–93.

2001. The movement to revitalize Hawaiian language and culture. In Leanne Hinton and Ken Hale (eds.), *The Green Book of Language Revitalization in Practice*, 133–44. San Diego: Academic Press.

Watahomigie, Lucille J. and Teresa L. McCarty 1994. Bilingual/bicultural education at Peach Springs. a Hualapai way of schooling. *Peabody Journal of Education* **69**(2): 26–42.

Watson, Seosamh 1989. Scottish and Irish Gaelic: the giant's bedfellow. In Nancy C. Dorian (ed.), *Investigating Obsolescence: Studies in Language Contraction and Language Death*, 41–59. New York: Cambridge University Press.

Webster, Donald and Wilfried Zibell 1970. *Iñupiat Eskimo Dictionary*. Fairbanks: Summer Institute of Linguistics.

Wee, Lionel 2005. Intra-language discrimination and linguistic human rights: the case of Singlish. *Applied Linguistics* **26:** 48–69.

Weinreich, Uriel 1953. *Languages in Contact: Findings and Problems* (Publications of the Linguistic Circle of New York 1). New York: Linguistic Circle of New York.

West, Paige 2006. *Conservation is our Government Now: The Politics of Ecology in Papua New Guinea*. Durham: Duke University Press.

Whalen, Douglas H. 2003. How the study of endangered languages will revolutionize linguistics. In Piet van Sterkenburg (ed.), *Linguistics Today*, 321–42. Amsterdam: John Benjamins.

Whiteside, Anne 2006. 'We are the explorers': transnational Yucatec Maya-speakers negotiating multilingual California. Unpublished PhD, University of California, Berkeley.

Whorf, Benjamin 1956. *Language, Thought, and Reality: Selected Writings of Benjamin Lee Whorf*. MIT Press.

Wierzbicka, Anna 1979. Ethnosyntax and the philosophy of grammar. *Studies in Language* **3**: 313–83.

1985. Different cultures, different languages, different speech acts: Polish vs. English. *Journal of Pragmatics* **9**(2/3): 145–78.

1991. *Cross-cultural Pragmatics*. Berlin: Mouton de Gruyter.

1992. *Semantics, Culture, and Cognition*. Oxford University Press.

1997. *Understanding Cultures through their Key Words: English, Russian, Polish, German, and Japanese*. Oxford University Press.

Wilkins, David P. 1992. Linguistic research under Aboriginal control: a personal account of field work in central Australia, *Australian Journal of Linguistics* **12**(1): 171–200.

Williams, Colin 1990. The Anglicization of Wales. In Nikolas Coupland (ed.), *English in Wales: Diversity, Conflict and Change*, 19–47. Clevedon: Multilingual Matters.

2000. Conclusion: economic development and political responsibility. In Colin Williams (ed.), *Language Revitalization: Policy and Planning in Wales*, 362–79 Cardiff: University of Wales Press.

Williams, Glyn 1992. *Sociolinguistics: A Sociological Critique*. London: Routledge.

1996. Language planning as discourse. In Rajendra Singh (ed.) *Towards a Critical Sociolinguistics*, 281–304. Amsterdam: John Benjamins.

Williams, Hywel 1994. Gwaith Cymdeithasol a'r Iaith Gymraeg/ Social Work and the Welsh Language. In Rhian Williams, Hywel Williams and Elaine Davies (eds.), *Gwaith Cymedeithasol a'r Iaith Gymraeg/ Social Work and the Welsh Language*, 173–96, Cardiff: University of Wales Press.

Williams, Raymond 1973. *The Country and the City*. Oxford University Press.

Williams, Sadie 2005. Dena'ina alphabet. Ms.

Williamson, Robert C. 1991. *Minority Languages and Bilingualism: Case Studies in Maintenance and Shift*. Norwood, NJ: Ablex.

Wilson, William H. 1999. The sociopolitical context of establishing Hawaiian-medium education. In S. May (ed.), *Indigenous Community-Based Education*, 95–108. Clevedon: Multilingual Matters.

Wilson, William H. and Kauanoe Kamanā 2001. 'Mai loko mai o ka 'I''ini: proceeding from a dream': the "Aha Pūnana Leo connection in Hawaiian language revitalization. In Leanne Hinton and Ken Hale (eds.), *The Green Book of Language Revitalization in Practice*, 147–76. San Diego, CA: Academic Press.

2006. 'For the interest of the Hawaiians themselves': reclaiming the benefits of Hawaiian-medium education. *Hūlili: Multidisciplinary Research on Hawaiian Well-Being* **3**(1); 153–81.

Wilson, William H. and Keiki Kawai'ae'a 2007. I kuku; I lālā: 'Let there be sources; let there be branches': teacher education in the College of Hawaiian Language. *Journal of American Indian Education* **46**(3): 37–53.

Wilson, William H., K. Kamanā and N. Rawlins 2006. Nāwahī Hawaiian Laboratory School. *Journal of American Indian Education* **45**(2): 42–4.

Winford, Donald 2003. *An Introduction to Contact Linguistics* (Language in Society 33). Oxford: Blackwell.

Wolfram, Walt 2000. Endangered dialects and social commitment. In Joy Peyton, Peg Griffin, Walt Wolfram, and Ralph W. Fasold (eds.), *Language in Action: New Studies of Language in Society*, 19–39. Cresshill: Hampton Press.

Wood, Alan n.d. Unicode. www.alanwood.net/unicode/. (30 June 2009).

Wood, Karenne 2009. The language ghost: linguistic heritage and collective identity among Monacan Indians of Central Virginia. Dissertation Proposal, Department of Anthropology, University of Virginia.

Woodbury, Anthony C. 1993. A defense of the proposition, 'When a language dies, a culture dies', *Texas Linguistic Forum* **33**: 101–29.

1998. Documenting rhetorical, aesthetic, and expressive loss in language shift. In Lenore A. Grenoble and Lindsay J. Whaley (eds.), *Endangered Languages: Language Loss and Community Response*, 234–58. Cambridge University Press.

2003. Defining documentary linguistics. In Peter K. Austin (ed.), *Language Documentation and Description*, vol. 1, 35–51. London: SOAS.

2005. Ancestral languages and (imagined) creolization. In Peter K. Austin (ed.), *Language Documentation and Description*, vol. 3, 252–62. London: SOAS.

2007. On thick translation in language documentation. In Peter K. Austin (ed.), *Language Documentation and Description*, vol. 4, 120–35. London: SOAS.

2010. Building projects around community members: the story of the Chatino language documentation project. Archiving ethically: mediating the demands of communities and institutional sponsors when producing language documentation. Annual Meeting of the Linguistic Society of America, Baltimore, Maryland. www.lsadc.org/info/pdf_files/2010Handbook.pdf (24 February 2010).

Woodbury, Anthony C. and Nora C. England 2004. Training speakers of indigenous languages of Latin America at a US university. In Peter K. Austin (ed.), *Language Documentation and Description*, vol. 2, 122–39. London: SOAS.

Woodbury, Hanni 2003. *Onondaga–English/English–Onondaga Dictionary*. University of Toronto Press.

Woolard, Kathryn 1998. Language ideology as a field of inquiry. In Bambi Schieffelin, Kathryn Woolard and Paul Kroskrity (eds.) *Language Ideologies: Practice and Theory*, 3–47. Oxford University Press.

Wright, Sue 2004. *Language Policy and Language Planning: Nationalism and Globalisation*. Basingstoke: Palgrave Macmillan.

2007. The right to speak one's own language: reflections on theory and practice. *Language Policy* 6:203–24, DOI 10.1007/s10993–007–9050–y.

Wurm, Stephen A. 1998. Methods of language maintenance and revival, with selected cases of language endangerment in the world. In Kazuto Matsumura (ed.). *Studies in Endangered Languages: Papers from the International Symposium on Endangered Languages, Tokyo, November 18–20*, 191–211. Tokyo: Hituzi Syobo.

Wurm, Stephen A. (ed.) 1996. *Atlas of the World's Languages in Danger of Disappearing*. 1st edn. Canberra: Pacific Linguistics.

2001. *Atlas of the World's Languages in Danger of Disappearing*. 2nd edn. Paris: UNESCO.

Wurm, Stephen A., Benjamin K. T'sou and David Bradley (eds.) 1987. *Language Atlas of China*. Hong Kong: Longman.

Wyman, Lyland C. (ed.) 1957. *Beautyway: A Navaho Ceremonial*. New York: Pantheon Books.

Wynne, Martin 2005. Developing linguistic corpora: a guide to good practice. ahds.ac.uk/creating/guides/linguistic-corpora/index.htm

Wynne-Jones, Allan and Llinos Dafis 2000. Why should the devil have all the good tunes? Marketing: a valuable discipline in language planning. In Peter Wynne Thomas and Jayne Mathias (eds.), *Developing Minority Languages: The Proceedings of the Fifth International Conference on Minority Languages*, 163–73. Cardiff: University of Wales.

Yakel, Elizabeth, Seth Shaw and Polly Reynolds 2007. Creating the next generation of archival finding aids. *D-Lib Magazine* **13**(5/6).

Yamane, Linda 2000. New life for a lost language. In Leanne Hinton and Ken Hale (eds.), *The Green Book of Language Revitalization in Practice*, 429–32. San Diego, CA: Academic Press.

Yang, Cathryn Forthcoming a. *A Survey of Nisu Dialects* (SIL Linguistic Surveys). Dallas: SIL International.

Forthcoming b. Dialect survey of the Lalo of Yunnan. PhD thesis, La Trobe University.

Yukon Native Language Centre 1996. *Dákeyi: Southern Tutchone Place Names*. Whitehorse, Yukon: Yukon Native Language Centre.

2006. YNLC Fonts and Keyboards. www.ynlc.ca/languages/font/ (11 October 2010).

Zima, Petr 1974. Digraphia: the case of Hausa. *Linguistics* **124**: 57–70.

Zuckermann, Ghil'ad 2006. A new vision for Israeli Hebrew: theoretical and practical implications of analyzing Israel's main language as a semi-engineered Semito-European hybrid language. *Journal of Modern Jewish Studies* **5**(1): 57–71.

Zwilling, Carolin 2004. Minority protection and language policy in the Czech Republic. *Noves SL Revista de Sociolinguistica* (Autumn). www6.gencat.net/llengcat/noves/hm04tardor/zwilling1_3.htm (6 November 2009).

Index of language names

Index

teacher education, 296, 302, 303, 361, 362, 421
teacher training. *See* teacher education
technophobia, 466
tense, 90, 107, 129, 341
tense-aspect, 108, 127
terminal speaker, 48, 49, 50, 51, 57
text, 75, 122, 163, 165, 168, 169, 178, 182, 183,
    213, 217, 257, 258, 345, 372, 376, 392, 425,
    455, 466. *See also* plain text
  interlinear, 389. *See* interlinear glossed text
  messaging, 328, 329, 393, 447, 456
  morphologically analysed.
    See morphologically analysed text
thematic approach, 337, 350.
    See also dictionary
thematic dictionary, 341. *See also* dictionary
Toolbox, 183, 221, 232, 268, 338, 344, 346,
    384, 427, 437
total immersion plus. *See* immersion
Total Physical Response, 300
traditional knowledge, 199. *See also* indigenous
    knowledge
traditional speaker, 49
training, 20, 172, 176, 304, 426, 427, 441, 442,
    443, 464
  community members, 15, 145, 177, 205, 208,
    308, 309, 350, 439
  for revitalization, 303, 309
  language researchers, 16, 63, 164, 183, 263,
    423, 424, 431
  teachers. *See* teacher education
transcription, 160, 168, 174, 178, 179, 183, 215,
    216, 248, 257, 261, 263, 313, 321, 380, 389,
    424, 438, 462, 469. *See also* annotation;
    interlinear; phonetic
  phonemic, 331
  time-aligned, 239, 380
  tool, 389, 438, 441
transfer. *See* transference
  digital, 258. *See* digital
  intergenerational. *See* intergenerational
    transmission
  of rights. *See* rights; intellectual property
transference, 80, 82, 87, 88, 89, 90, 114
transformation
  of data, 217. *See also* mobilization
transitional bilingual education. *See* education
transitional bilingualism. *See* bilingualism
translation, 9, 137, 159, 160, 163, 178, 179, 183,
    184, 218, 252, 295, 338, 344, 345, 346, 347,
    377, 384, 387, 392, 394, 470
  Bible, 152, 206, 323
  free, 166
  interlinear. *See* interlinear
tuyu, 71
typological similarity, 88
typology, 100. *See also* language typology;
    typology of speakers
  of documentation, 179
  of economic circumstances of endangered
    languages, 405, 406
  of language situations, 405
typology of speakers, 46, 47, 49, 52, 60

under-generalization, 113, 114
under-specification, 313, 332
UNESCO, 3, 4, 7, 14, 36, 37, 38, 59, 62, 66, 76,
    199, 200, 282, 283, 320, 413, 447
Unicode, 224, 258, 263, 268, 328, 328, 334,
    372, 379
unique speech sounds, 101
universals. *See* language universals
unstable bilingualism. *See* bilingualism
urbanization, 33, 35, 56, 407
usefulness, 11, 92, 150, 271

variation, 18, 31, 75, 92, 111, 112, 144, 145,
    180, 317, 321, 341
velar
  consonant, 111
  nasal, 333
  stop, 101
verbal art, 116, 162, 163, 168, 181, 376
verbal repertoire, 126
vernacular, 141, 142, 143, 160, 180, 192, 193,
    195, 198, 199, 279, 312, 313, 329, 457
video, 12, 171, 214, 222, 243, 244, 261, 268,
    269, 351, 358, 380, 393, 427, 432, 437, 441,
    451. *See also* recordings
virtual language communities, 371, 390
vitality, 3, 38, 39, 40, 41, 42, 43, 44, 46, 48,
    51, 52, 59, 60, 76, 142, 195, 282, 286, 301,
    368, 455
  assessing level of endangerment, 43, 44, 48,
    55, 191, 195, 413
  at risk language, 40
vitality scale, 42
vowel harmony, 103, 244

ways of speaking, 127, 147, 167, 179.
    See also typology of speakers
web portal, 383, 387, 388, 390. *See also* internet
web-based, 378. *See also* internet
  catalogue system, 271
  language courses, 393. *See also* computer-
    assisted language learning
  multimedia, 387. *See also* multimedia
  resources, 13
  technology, 393
word list, 219, 225, 238, 253, 338, 342, 343,
    345, 375, 469
word order, 90, 91, 105, 106, 115
  basic, 106
  free, 90
  universals, 106
workflow, 232, 351, 427, 461, 477
workshop, 304, 351, 352
  Breath of Life, 172
writing system, i, 279, 296, 297, 307, 313, 322,
    326, 335, 371, 450, 463, 465, 469

XML, 225, 226, 244, 260, 386, 427

Yinka Dené Language Institute, 310
young fluent speakers, 49, 50
Yukon Native Language Center, 310
yuyan, 70

CPSIA information can be obtained
at www.ICGtesting.com
Printed in the USA
LVHW021729220119
604822LV00009B/183/P